A THOUSAND MILES UP THE NILE

WHEN a trip into the middle of Africa is still something of an adventure, it is astonishing to think that over a century ago a lady of solid Victorian upbringing decided, on perhaps no more than a whim, to embark on an extraordinary journey 1,000 miles up the Nile—in a wooden dahabeeyah.

Amelia Edwards embarked on this voyage full of unrestrained enthusiasm for Egypt and a compulsive interest in all its archaeological treasures. The Egypt she saw was little changed since Pharonic times; the people living lives regulated by the seasons, unaltered for thousands of years, the pyramids and temples unrestored and for the most part unexplored. She describes in graphic detail the splendours of the Great Pyramid, the wonders of Karnak and the Valley of the Kings at Thebes, for she visits most of the great antiquities of Ancient Egypt.

Her account of this voyage is written with an artist's eye for local colour and is crammed with lively anecdotes imbuing the journey with a spirit of adventure. This is the first time that the book has been re-issued since the nineteenth century and it is introduced by Quentin Crewe, who has himself just returned from a similar voyage up the Nile.

The cover shows "Philae on the Nile" by Edward Lear.

GREAT ROCK-CUT TEMPLE, ABOU SIMBEL, NUBIA.

A THOUSAND MILES UP THE NILE

AMELIA B. EDWARDS

Introduction by Quentin Crewe

CENTURY

LONDON MELBOURNE AUCKLAND JOHANNESBURG

First published in 1877 by Longmans

© Century Hutchinson 1982
© Introduction Quentin Crewe 1982

This edition first published in 1982, reprinted in 1983, 1984, 1985, 1986
by Century, an imprint of Century Hutchinson Ltd, Brookmount House,
62–65 Chandos Place, London WC2N 4NW

Century Hutchinson Australia (Pty) Ltd,
PO Box 496, 16–22 Church Street, Hawthorn, Melbourne, Victoria 3122

Century Hutchinson New Zealand Limited,
PO Box 40–086, 32–34 View Road, Glenfield, Auckland 10

Century Hutchinson South Africa (Pty) Ltd,
PO Box 337, Berglvei 2012, South Africa

ISBN 0 7126 0037 X (cased)
      0 7126 0038 8 (paper)

Printed in Great Britain by Richard Clay (The Chaucer Press) Ltd,
Bungay, Suffolk

PREFACE

TO THE SECOND EDITION

FIRST published in 1877, this book has been out of print for several years. I have therefore very gladly revised it for a new and cheaper edition. In so revising it, I have corrected some of the historical notes by the light of later discoveries ; but I have left the narrative untouched. Of the political changes which have come over the land of Egypt since that narrative was written, I have taken no note ; and because I in no sense offer myself as a guide to others, I say nothing of the altered conditions under which most Nile travellers now perform the trip. All these things will be more satisfactorily, and more practically, learned from the pages of Baedeker and Murray.

AMELIA B. EDWARDS.

WESTBURY-ON-TRYM,
October 1888.

PREFACE TO THE FIRST EDITION.

" Un voyage en Égypte, c'est une partie d'ânes et une promenade en bateau entremêlées de ruines."—AMPÈRE.

AMPÈRE has put Egypt in an epigram. "A donkey-ride and a boating-trip interspersed with ruins" does, in fact, sum up in a single line the whole experience of the Nile traveller. Àpropos of these three things—the donkeys, the boat, and the ruins—it may be said that a good English saddle and a comfortable dahabeeyah add very considerably to the pleasure of the journey ; and that the more one knows about the past history of the country, the more one enjoys the ruins.

Of the comparative merits of wooden boats, iron boats, and steamers, I am not qualified to speak. We, however, saw one iron dahabeeyah aground upon a sandbank, where, as we afterwards learned, it remained for three weeks. We also saw the wrecks of three steamers between Cairo and the First Cataract. It certainly seemed to us that the old-fashioned wooden dahabeeyah—flat-bottomed, drawing little water, light in hand, and easily poled off when stuck—was the one vessel best constructed for the navigation of the Nile. Other considerations, as time and cost, are, of course, involved in this question. The choice between dahabeeyah and steamer is like the choice between travelling with post-horses and travelling by rail. The one is expensive, leisurely, delightful ; the other is cheap, swift, and comparatively comfortless.   Those who are content to snatch but a glimpse of the Nile will doubtless prefer the steamer.   I may add that the whole cost of the Philæ—food, dragoman's wages, boat - hire, cataract, everything included except wine—was about £10 per day.

With regard to temperature, we found it cool—even cold, sometimes—in December and January ; mild in February ; very warm in March and April.   The climate of Nubia is simply perfect.   It never rains ; and once past the limit of the tropic, there is no morning or evening chill upon the air.   Yet even in Nubia, and especially along the forty miles which divide Abou Simbel from Wady Halfeh, it is cold when the wind blows strongly from the north.[1]

Touching the title of this book, it may be objected that the distance from the port of Alexandria to the Second Cataract falls short of a thousand miles.   It is, in fact, calculated at $964\frac{1}{2}$ miles.   But from the Rock of Abusîr, five miles above Wady Halfeh, the traveller looks over an extent of country far exceeding the thirty or thirty-five miles necessary to make up the full tale of a thousand.   We distinctly saw from this point the summits of mountains which lie about 145 miles to the southward of Wady Halfeh, and which look down upon the Third Cataract.

Perhaps I ought to say something in answer to the repeated inquiries of those who looked for the publication of this volume a year ago.   I can, however, only reply that the Writer, instead of giving one year, has given two years to the work.   To write

---

[1] For the benefit of any who desire more exact information, I may add that a table of average temperatures, carefully registered day by day and week by week, is to be found at the end of Mr. H. Villiers Stuart's ' *Nile Gleanings*.'   [Note to Second Edition.]

rapidly about Egypt is impossible. The subject grows with the book, and with the knowledge one acquires by the way. It is, moreover, a subject beset with such obstacles as must impede even the swiftest pen ; and to that swiftest pen I lay no claim. Moreover, the writer who seeks to be accurate, has frequently to go for his facts, if not actually to original sources (which would be the texts themselves), at all events to translations and commentaries locked up in costly folios, or dispersed far and wide among the pages of scientific journals and the transactions of learned societies. A date, a name, a passing reference, may cost hours of seeking. To revise so large a number of illustrations, and to design tailpieces from jottings taken here and there in that pocket sketch-book which is the sketcher's constant companion, has also consumed no small amount of time. This by way of apology.

More pleasant is it to remember labour lightened than to consider time spent ; and I have yet to thank the friends who have spared no pains to help this book on its way. To S. Birch, Esq., LL.D., etc. etc., so justly styled "the Parent in this country of a sound school of Egyptian philology," who besides translating the hieratic and hieroglyphic inscriptions contained in Chapter xviii., has also, with infinite kindness, seen the whole of that chapter through the press ; to Reginald Stuart Poole, Esq. ; to Professor R. Owen, C.B., etc. etc. ; to Sir G. W. Cox, I desire to offer my hearty and grateful acknowledgments. It is surely not least among the glories of learning, that those who adorn it most and work hardest should ever be readiest to share the stores of their knowledge.

I am anxious also to express my cordial thanks to Mr. G. Pearson, under whose superintendence the whole of the illustrations have been engraved. To say that his patience and courtesy have been inexhaustible, and that he has spared neither time nor cost in the preparation of the blocks, is but a dry statement of facts, and conveys no idea of the kind of labour involved. Where engravings of this kind are executed, not from drawings made at first-hand upon the wood, but from water-colour drawings which have not only to be reduced in size, but to be, as it were, translated into black and white, the difficulty of the work is largely increased. In order to meet this difficulty and to ensure accuracy, Mr. Pearson has not only called in the services of accomplished draughtsmen, but in many instances has even photographed the subjects direct upon the wood. Of the engraver's work—which speaks for itself—I will only say that I do not know in what way it could be bettered. It seems to me that some of these blocks may stand for examples of the farthest point to which the art of engraving upon wood has yet been carried.

The principal illustrations have all been drawn upon the wood by Mr. Percival Skelton ; and no one so fully as myself can appreciate how much the subjects owe to the delicacy of his pencil, and to the artistic feelings with which he has interpreted the original drawings.

Of the fascination of Egyptian travel, of the charm of the Nile, of the unexpected and surpassing beauty of the desert, of the ruins which are the wonder of the world, I have said enough elsewhere. I must, however, add that I brought home with me an impression that things and people are much less changed in Egypt than we of the present day are wont to suppose. I believe that the physique and life of the modern Fellâh is almost identical with the physique and life of that ancient Egyptian labourer whom we know so well in the wall-paintings of the tombs. Square in the shoulders, slight but strong in the limbs, full-lipped, brown-skinned, we see him wearing the same loin-cloth, plying the same shâdûf, ploughing with the same plough, preparing the same food in the same way, and eating it with his fingers from the same bowl, as did his forefathers of six thousand years ago.

The household life and social ways of even the provincial gentry are little changed. Water is poured on one's hands before going to dinner from just such a ewer and into just such a basin as we see pictured in the festival-scenes at Thebes. Though the lotus-blossom is missing, a bouquet is still given to each guest when he takes his place at table. The head of the sheep killed for the banquet is still given to the poor. Those who are helped to meat or drink touch the head and breast in acknowledgment, as of old. The musicians still sit at the lower end of the hall ; the singers yet clap their hands in time to their own voices ; the dancing-girls still dance, and the buffoon in his high cap still performs his uncouth antics, for the entertainment of the guests. Water is brought to table in jars of the same shape manufactured at the same town, as in the days of Cheops and Chephren ; and the mouths of the bottles are filled in precisely the same way with fresh leaves and flowers. The cucumber stuffed with minced-meat was a favourite dish in those times of old ; and I can testify to its excellence in 1874. Little boys in Nubia yet wear the side-lock that graced the head of Rameses in his youth ; and little girls may be seen in a garment closely resembling the girdle worn by young princesses of the time of Thothmes the First. A Sheykh still walks with a long staff; a Nubian belle still plaits her tresses in scores of little tails ; and the pleasure-boat of the modern Governor or Mudîr, as well as the dahabeeyah hired by the European traveller, reproduces in all essential features the painted galleys represented in the tombs of the kings.

In these and in a hundred other instances, all of which came under my personal observation and have their place in the following pages, it seemed to me that any obscurity which yet hangs over the problem of life and thought in ancient Egypt originates most probably with ourselves. Our own habits of life and thought are so complex that they shut us off from the simplicity of that early world. So it was with the problem of hieroglyphic writing. The thing was so obvious that no one could find it out. As long as the world persisted in believing that every hieroglyph was an abstruse symbol, and every hieroglyphic inscription a profound philosophical rebus, the mystery of Egyptian literature remained insoluble. Then at last came Champollion's famous letter to Dacier, showing that the hieroglyphic signs were mainly alphabetic and syllabic, and that the language they spelt was only Coptic after all.

If there were not thousands who still conceive that the sun and moon were created, and are kept going, for no other purpose than to lighten the darkness of our little planet ; if only the other day a grave gentleman had not written a perfectly serious essay to show that the world is a flat plain, one would scarcely believe that there could still be people who doubt that ancient Egyptian is now read and translated as fluently as ancient Greek. Yet an Englishman whom I met in Egypt—an Englishman who had long been resident in Cairo, and who was well acquainted with the great Egyptologists who are attached to the service of the Khedive— assured me of his profound disbelief in the discovery of Champollion. " In my opinion," said he, " not one of these gentlemen can read a line of hieroglyphics."

As I then knew nothing of Egyptian, I could say nothing to controvert this speech.   Since that time, however, and while writing this book, I have been led on step by step to the study of hieroglyphic writing ; and I now know that Egyptian can be read, for the simple reason that I find myself able to read an Egyptian sentence.

My testimony may not be of much value ; but I give it for the little that it is worth.

The study of Egyptian literature has advanced of late years with rapid strides.   Papyri are found less frequently than they were some thirty or forty years ago ; but the translation of those contained in the museums of Europe goes on now more diligently than at any former time.   Religious books, variants of the Ritual, moral essays, maxims, private letters, hymns, epic poems, historical chronicles, accounts, deeds of sale, medical, magical, and astronomical treatises, geographical records, travels, and even romances and tales, are brought to light, photographed, facsimiled in chromo-lithography, printed in hieroglyphic type, and translated in forms suited both to the learned and to the general reader.

Not all this literature is written, however, on papyrus. The greater proportion of it is carved in stone.   Some is painted on wood, written on linen, leather, potsherds, and other substances.   So the old mystery of Egypt, which was her literature, has vanished.   The key to the hieroglyphs is the master-key that opens every door.   Each year that now passes over our heads sees some old problem solved.   Each day brings some long-buried truth to light.

Some thirteen years ago,[1] a distinguished American artist

---

[1] These dates, it is to be remembered, refer to the year 1877, when the first edition of this book was published.   [Note to Second Edition.]

painted a very beautiful picture called *The Secret of the Sphinx.* In its widest sense, the Secret of the Sphinx would mean, I suppose, the whole uninterpreted and undiscovered past of Egypt. In its narrower sense, the Secret of the Sphinx was, till quite lately, the hidden significance of the human-headed lion which is one of the typical subjects of Egyptian Art.

Thirteen years is a short time to look back upon ; yet great things have been done in Egypt, and in Egyptology, since then. Edfu, with its extraordinary wealth of inscriptions, has been laid bare. The whole contents of the Boulak Museum have been recovered from the darkness of the tombs. The very mystery of the Sphinx has been disclosed ; and even within the last eighteen months, M. Chabas announces that he has discovered the date of the pyramid of Mycerinus ; so for the first time establishing the chronology of ancient Egypt upon an ascertained foundation. Thus the work goes on ; students in their libraries, excavators under Egyptian skies, toiling along different paths towards a common goal. The picture means more to-day than it meant thirteen years ago—means more, even, than the artist intended. The Sphinx has no secret now, save for the ignorant.

In the picture, we see a brown, half-naked, toil-worn Fellâh laying his ear to the stone lips of a colossal Sphinx, buried to the neck in sand. Some instinct of the old Egyptian blood tells him that the creature is God-like. He is conscious of a great mystery lying far back in the past. He has, perhaps, a dim, confused notion that the Big Head knows it all, whatever it may be. He has never heard of the morning-song of Memnon ; but he fancies, somehow, that those closed lips might speak if questioned. Fellâh and Sphinx are alone together in the desert. It is night, and the stars are shining.

Has he chosen the right hour? What does he seek to know? What does he hope to hear?

Mr. Vedder has permitted me to enrich this book with an engraving from his picture. It tells its own tale ; or rather it tells as much of its own tale as the artist chooses.

Each must interpret for himself
The Secret of The Sphinx.

AMELIA B. EDWARDS.

WESTBURY-ON-TRYM,
GLOUCESTERSHIRE,
Dec. 1877.

CONTENTS

APPENDIX.

LIST OF ILLUSTRATIONS.

HIERATIC INSCRIPTION,

N. WALL OF SPEOS.

Translated by S. Birch, Esq., L.L.D., &c., &c.

. . . . thy son having . . . . . . thou hast conquered the worlds at once Ammon Ra-Harmachis, † the God at the first time,* who gives life, health, and a time of many praises to the groom . . . . . . of the Khen,** son of the Royal son of Cush, †† Opener of the road, Maker of transport boats, Giver of instructions to his Lord . . . . Amenshaa . . . . . .

---

† *i.e.* Ammon Ra, the Sun God, in conjunction or identification with Har-em-aχu, of Horus-on-the-Horizon, another Solar deity.

* The primæval God.

** Inner place, or Sanctuary.

†† Ethiopia.

INTRODUCTION

EVER since Herodotus ventured up the Nile in the middle of the fifth century B.C. this most intriguing of the world's rivers has exerted a fascination on Europeans.

The mystery of its source was not finally solved until Stanley returned from his journey down the Lualaba and the Congo in 1877.

In the nineteenth century the romantic movement was much excited by monuments of Egypt, concerned as they are so largely with death. Napoleon had recognised Egypt as a vital link for trade with the East and had invaded the country in 1789.

Despite all this, Amelia B. Edwards, one of the most engaging chroniclers of the Nile, arrived in Cairo in November 1873 almost by chance. She came to get away from the rain in Europe, where she had been travelling with a friend. She stayed to become a leading Egyptologist.

Amelia was one of those intrepid Victorian spinsters who is a delight to read about but who, one fears, might have been a considerable trial to know. That, at least, is the first impression created by this book; but in time, as one reads and re-reads her, she becomes a real, if mildly formidable, friend. Her great concern for people, her understanding of strange cultures, her wry detachment from her own countrymen gradually make her more and more sympathetic.

From an extremely early age it was plain that she had exceptional talent. Her father was an army officer who had fought with Wellington in the Peninsula War. Her mother was descended from the Walpole family. The combination seemed to give her both courage and an artistic flair. At the age of seven, Amelia had a poem published in a weekly journal. By the time she was sixteen she could have chosen to be an opera singer, an artist or a writer. Eventually she settled on journalism and writing.

Between 1855 and 1880 she wrote eight novels, albeit of no great distinction, and contributed to a wide variety of newspapers and magazines. She also edited popular books on history and art.

Yet it was not until she was forty-two that she was to have the adventure that gave her a mission in life and gave us the happy memorial of her in the form of *A Thousand Miles up the Nile*.

To us it is surprising that two ladies could, in 1873, undertake a journey up the Nile in a flat-bottomed, wooden boat. After all, Livingstone had only died in May of that year, Gordon was not to arrive for three months for his first journey to Khartoum. The Suez Canal had only been open four years. Cleopatra's Needle had not yet been pinched by the British.

It is true that Thomas Cook had already started steamer trips up the river (Amelia said their boats were often stuck on sandbanks) but it was still a great adventure.

Amelia Edwards' account of this adventure is superb, because she informs it with a vividness of phrase which often jolts her reader with pleasure, with an erudition which almost alarms and with a passion for detail which makes it an invaluable historical document.

Only a born writer could conjure up such a phrase as: "Greeks in absurdly stiff white tunics, like walking penwipers . . .". Only Amelia could worry or know about the quality of the cheap tobacco for which her crew was so grateful when she gave out some as a bonus. "This abominable mixture sells in the bazaars at sixpence the pound, the plant from which it is gathered being raised from inferior seed in a soil chemically unsuitable, because wholly devoid of potash." No other writer has told me about a donkey with "close-shaven legs and hindquarters . . . painted in blue and white zig-zags picked out with bands of pale yellow".

Naturally, the largest part of this book is devoted to the

ruins and monuments of Ancient Egypt. Amelia measures, sketches, describes, lists every conceivable detail. She gets quite cross with a young honeymoon couple who actually go so far as to skip some temples altogether; whereas Amelia will ride a donkey for three hours in temperatures of more than 100°F in order to re-visit a temple.

Amelia is, however, quite human enough to worry lest life has changed so much that she may have missed the best. Indeed she devotes almost two pages of her preface to explaining how little Egypt has changed since the time of the Pharaohs. She also gets in quite a few digs at the modern tourist in his Thomas Cook steamer—the very steamers perhaps which Kitchener was to commandeer some twenty-five years later to sail to Khartoum to avenge the murder of Gordon.

For us today the same worry must exist. How one envies Amelia wandering round the ruins of Karnak almost by herself, while we must mingle with coachloads of tourists.

How extraordinary and exciting it seems to us that someone in Amelia's party should have discovered an unknown tomb at Abou Simbel. In another way it was extraordinary that she should have set her crew to cleaning one of the colossal figures of Rameses II at Abou Simbel. It had been "disfigured by the plaster left on it when the great cast was taken by Mr Hay more than half a century before". Merrily they scrubbed away, staining with coffee any lingering pale patches.

Against all that, we have so much that Amelia never saw. The exquisite solar boat, excavated from a trough near the Great Pyramid—arguably the most beautiful boat in the world. Kom Ombo, which intrigued Amelia, was not excavated until 1893 and to some extent justifies her hopes. Esneh has been uncovered, although not to such great advantage.

Curiously enough, for Amelia's taste, which was most scholarly, we have the advantage: while for laymen the more romantic, wilder ruins must have had greater appeal.

For my part, while I am grateful to Amelia for her abundant archaelogical information, I am even more so for those small illuminations of human nature which enliven her pages. I love her self-mockery, wondering at the sorry figure she and her companion cut "with our hideous palm-leaf hats, green veils and white umbrellas". I admire her interest in the lives of her crew of twenty, whose names she knew within days and whose welfare troubled her always. I like her understanding of Egyptian customs, her account of dinners with every mouthful recorded, of a Coptic service with every detail observed. I enjoy immensely her account of a first camel ride which no-one has ever surpassed and her sangfroid when a baby is shot by one of her party . . but you will read it.

Amelia went on, after her journey, to become an authority on Egyptology. She founded the Egypt Exploration Fund and campaigned for the preservation of monuments. She died in 1892, leaving her library to University College, London, together with some money to found the first chair of Egyptology in England. And she left for us one of the great classics in the history of the Nile.

Quentin Crewe 1982

CHAPTER I.

CAIRO AND THE GREAT PYRAMID.

IT is the traveller's lot to dine at many table-d'hôtes in the course of many wanderings ; but it seldom befalls him to make one of a more miscellaneous gathering than that which overfills the great dining-room at Shepheard's Hotel in Cairo during the beginning and height of the regular Egyptian season. Here assemble daily some two to three hundred persons of all ranks, nationalities, and pursuits ; half of whom are Anglo-Indians homeward or outward bound, European residents, or visitors established in Cairo for the winter. The other half, it may be taken for granted, are going up the Nile. So composite and incongruous is this body of Nile-goers, young and old, well-dressed and ill-dressed, learned and unlearned, that the new-comer's first impulse is to inquire from what motives so many persons of dissimilar tastes and training can be led to embark upon an expedition which is, to say the least of it, very tedious, very costly, and of an altogether exceptional interest.

His curiosity, however, is soon gratified. Before two days are over, he knows everybody's name and everybody's business ; distinguishes at first sight between a Cook's tourist and an independent traveller ; and has discovered that nine-tenths of those whom he is likely to meet up the river are English or American. The rest will be mostly German, with a sprinkling of Belgian and French. So far *en bloc ;* but the details are more heterogeneous still. Here are invalids in search of health ; artists in search of subjects ; sportsmen keen upon crocodiles ; statesmen out for a holiday ; special correspondents alert for gossip; collectors on the scent of papyri and mummies; men of science with only scientific ends in view; and the usual surplus of idlers who travel for the mere love of travel, or the satisfaction of a purposeless curiosity.

Now in a place like Shepheard's, where every fresh arrival has the honour of contributing, for at least a few minutes, to the general entertainment, the first appearance of L. and the Writer, tired, dusty, and considerably sunburnt, may well have given rise to some of the comments in usual circulation at those crowded tables. People asked each other, most likely, where these two wandering Englishwomen had come from; why they had not dressed for dinner; what brought them to Egypt; and if they also were going up the Nile—to which questions it would have been easy to give satisfactory answers.

We came from Alexandria, having had a rough passage from Brindisi followed by forty-eight hours of quarantine. We had not dressed for dinner because, having driven on from the station in advance of dragoman and luggage, we were but just in time to take seats with the rest. We intended, of course, to go up the Nile; and had any one ventured to inquire in so many words what brought us to Egypt, we should have replied :—" Stress of weather."

For in simple truth we had drifted hither by accident, with no excuse of health, or business, or any serious object whatever; and had just taken refuge in Egypt as one might turn aside into the Burlington Arcade or the Passage des Panoramas —to get out of the rain.

And with good reason. Having left home early in September for a few weeks' sketching in central France, we had been pursued by the wettest of wet weather. Washed out of the hill-country, we fared no better in the plains. At Nismes, it poured for a month without stopping. Debating at last whether it were better to take our wet umbrellas back at once to England, or push on farther still in search of sunshine, the talk fell upon Algiers—Malta—Cairo; and Cairo carried it. Never was distant expedition entered upon with less premeditation. The thing was no sooner decided than we were gone. Nice, Genoa, Bologna, Ancona flitted by, as in a dream; and Bedreddin Hassan when he awoke at the gates of

Damascus was scarcely more surprised than the writer of these pages, when she found herself on board the *Simla*, and steaming out of the port of Brindisi.

Here, then, without definite plans, outfit, or any kind of Oriental experience, behold us arrived in Cairo on the 29th of November 1873, literally, and most prosaically, in search of fine weather.

But what had memory to do with rains on land, or storms at sea, or the impatient hours of quarantine, or anything dismal or disagreeable, when one awoke at sunrise to see those grey-green palms outside the window solemnly bowing their plumed heads towards each other, against a rose-coloured dawn ? It was dark last night, and I had no idea that my room overlooked an enchanted garden, far-reaching and solitary, peopled with stately giants beneath whose tufted crowns hung rich clusters of maroon and amber dates. It was a still, warm morning. Grave grey and black crows flew heavily from tree to tree, or perched, cawing meditatively, upon the topmost branches. Yonder, between the pillared stems, rose the minaret of a very distant mosque ; and here where the garden was bounded by a high wall and a windowless house, I saw a veiled lady walking on the terraced roof in the midst of a cloud of pigeons. Nothing could be more simple than the scene and its accessories ; nothing, at the same time, more Eastern, strange, and unreal.

But in order thoroughly to enjoy an overwhelming, ineffaceable first impression of Oriental out-of-doors life, one should begin in Cairo with a day in the native bazaars ; neither buying, nor sketching, nor seeking information, but just taking in scene after scene, with its manifold combinations of light and shade, colour, costume, and architectural detail. Every shop-front, every street corner, every turbaned group is a ready-made picture. The old Turk who sets up his cake-stall in the recess of a sculptured doorway ; the donkey-boy with his gaily caparisoned ass, waiting for customers ; the beggar asleep on the steps of the mosque ; the veiled woman filling her water jar at the public fountain—they all look as if they had been put there expressly to be painted.

Nor is the background less picturesque than the figures.

The houses are high and narrow. The upper stories project ;
and from these again jut windows of delicate turned lattice-
work in old brown wood, like big bird-cages. The street is
roofed in overhead with long rafters and pieces of matting,

CAIRO DONKEY.

through which a dusty sunbeam straggles here and there, casting patches of light upon the moving crowd. The unpaved
thoroughfare—a mere narrow lane, full of ruts and watered
profusely twice or thrice a day—is lined with little wooden
shop-fronts, like open cabinets full of shelves, where the
merchants sit cross-legged in the midst of their goods, looking
out at the passers-by and smoking in silence. Meanwhile, the
crowd ebbs and flows unceasingly—a noisy, changing, restless,
parti-coloured tide, half European, half Oriental, on foot, on
horseback, and in carriages. Here are Syrian dragomans in
baggy trousers and braided jackets ; barefooted Egyptian
fellaheen in ragged blue shirts and felt skull-caps ; Greeks in

absurdly stiff white tunics, like walking penwipers; Persians
with high mitre-like caps of dark woven stuff; swarthy Bedouins
in flowing garments, creamy-white with chocolate stripes a foot
wide, and head-shawl of the same bound about the brow with
a fillet of twisted camel's hair; Englishmen in palm-leaf hats
and knickerbockers, dangling their long legs across almost
invisible donkeys; native women of the poorer class, in black
veils that leave only the eyes uncovered, and long trailing
garments of dark blue and black striped cotton; dervishes in
patchwork coats, their matted hair streaming from under
fantastic head-dresses; blue-black Abyssinians with incredibly
slender, bowed legs, like attenuated ebony balustrades;
Armenian priests, looking exactly like Portia as the Doctor, in
long black gowns and high square caps; majestic ghosts of
Algerine Arabs, all in white; mounted Janissaries with jingling
sabres and gold-embroidered jackets; merchants, beggars,
soldiers, boatmen, labourers, workmen, in every variety of
costume, and of every shade of complexion from fair to dark,
from tawny to copper-colour, from deepest bronze to bluest
black.

Now a water-carrier goes by, bending under the weight of
his newly-replenished goatskin, the legs of which being tied up,
the neck fitted with a brass cock, and the hair left on, looks
horribly bloated and life-like. Now comes a sweetmeat-vendor
with a tray of that gummy compound known to English
children as " Lumps of Delight "; and now an Egyptian lady
on a large grey donkey led by a servant with a showy sabre
at his side. The lady wears a rose-coloured silk dress and
white veil, besides a black silk outer garment, which, being
cloak, hood, and veil all in one, fills out with the wind as she
rides, like a balloon. She sits astride; her naked feet, in their
violet velvet slippers, just resting on the stirrups. She takes
care to display a plump brown arm laden with massive gold
bracelets, and, to judge by the way in which she uses a pair of
liquid black eyes, would not be sorry to let her face be seen
also. Nor is the steed less well dressed than his mistress.
His close-shaven legs and hindquarters are painted in blue
and white zigzags picked out with bands of pale yellow; his
high-pommelled saddle is resplendent with velvet and em-

broidery; and his headgear is all tags, tassels, and fringes. Such a donkey as this is worth from sixty to a hundred pounds sterling.   Next passes an open barouche full of laughing Englishwomen; or a grave provincial sheykh all in black, riding a handsome bay Arab, *demi-sang;* or an Egyptian gentleman in European dress and Turkish fez, driven by an English groom in an English phaeton.   Before him, wand in hand, bare-legged, eager-eyed, in Greek skull-cap and gorgeous gold-embroidered waistcoat and fluttering white tunic, flies a native Saïs, or running footman.   No person of position drives in Cairo without one or two of these attendants.   The Saïs (strong, light, and beautiful, like John of Bologna's Mercury) are said to die young.   The pace kills them.   Next passes a lemonade-seller, with his tin jar in one hand, and his decanter and brass cups in the other; or an itinerant slipper-vendor with a bunch of red and yellow morocco shoes dangling at the end of a long pole; or a London-built miniature brougham containing two ladies in transparent Turkish veils, preceded by a Nubian outrider in semi-military livery; or, perhaps, a train of camels, ill-tempered and supercilious, craning their scrannel necks above the crowd, and laden with canvas bales scrawled over with Arabic addresses.

But the Egyptian, Arab, and Turkish merchants, whether mingling in the general tide or sitting on their counters, are the most picturesque personages in all this busy scene.   They wear ample turbans, for the most part white; long vests of striped Syrian silk reaching to the feet; and an outer robe of braided cloth or cashmere.   The vest is confined round the waist by a rich sash; and the outer robe, or *gibbeh,* is generally of some beautiful degraded colour, such as maize, mulberry, olive, peach, sea-green, salmon-pink, sienna-brown, and the like.   That these stately beings should vulgarly buy and sell, instead of reposing all their lives on luxurious divans and being waited upon by beautiful Circassians, seems altogether contrary to the eternal fitness of things.   Here, for instance, is a Grand Vizier in a gorgeous white and amber satin vest, who condescends to retail pipe-bowls,—dull red clay pipe-bowls of all sizes and prices.   He sells nothing else, and has not only a pile of them on the counter, but a binful at the back of his

TUNIS MARKET, CAIRO.

shop. They are made at Siout in Upper Egypt, and may be bought at the Algerine shops in London almost as cheaply as in Cairo. Another majestic Pasha deals in brass and copper vessels, drinking-cups, basins, ewers, trays, incense-burners, chafing-dishes, and the like; some of which are exquisitely engraved with Arabesque patterns or sentences from the poets. A third sells silks from the looms of Lebanon, and gold and silver tissues from Damascus. Others, again, sell old arms, old porcelain, old embroideries, second-hand prayer-carpets, and quaint little stools and cabinets of ebony inlaid with mother-of-pearl. Here, too, the tobacco-merchant sits behind a huge cake of Latakia as big as his own body; and the sponge-merchant smokes his long chibouk in a bower of sponges.

Most amusing of all, however, are those bazaars in which each trade occupies its separate quarter. You pass through an old stone gateway or down a narrow turning, and find yourself amid a colony of saddlers stitching, hammering, punching, riveting. You walk up one alley and down another, between shop-fronts hung round with tasselled head-gear and hump-backed saddles of all qualities and colours. Here are ladies' saddles, military saddles, donkey-saddles, and saddles for great officers of state; saddles covered with red leather, with crimson and violet velvet, with maroon, and grey, and purple cloth; saddles embroidered with gold and silver, studded with brass-headed nails, or trimmed with braid.

Another turn or two, and you are in the slipper bazaar, walking down avenues of red and yellow morocco slippers; the former of home manufacture, the latter from Tunis. Here are slippers with pointed toes, turned-up toes, and toes as round and flat as horse-shoes; walking slippers with thick soles, and soft yellow slippers to be worn as inside socks, which have no soles at all. These absurd little scarlet bluchers with tassels are for little boys; the brown morocco shoes are for grooms; the velvet slippers embroidered with gold and beads and seed-pearls are for wealthy hareems, and are sold at prices varying from five shillings to five pounds the pair.

The carpet bazaar is of considerable extent, and consists of a network of alleys and counter-alleys opening off to the right of the Muski, which is the Regent Street of Cairo. The houses in most of these alleys are rich in antique lattice-windows and Saracenic doorways. One little square is tapestried all round with Persian and Syrian rugs, Damascus saddle-bags, and Turkish prayer-carpets. The merchants sit and smoke in the midst of their goods ; and up in one corner an old

CARPET BAZAAR, CAIRO.

"Kahwagee," or coffee-seller, plies his humble trade. He has set up his little stove and hanging-shelf beside the doorway of a dilapidated Khan, the walls of which are faced with Arabesque panellings in old carved stone. It is one of the most pictur-esque "bits" in Cairo. The striped carpets of Tunis ; the dim grey and blue, or grey and red fabrics of Algiers ; the shaggy rugs of Laodicea and Smyrna ; the rich blues and greens and subdued reds of Turkey ; and the wonderfully varied, harmonious patterns of Persia, have each their local habitation in the neighbouring alleys.   One is never tired of traversing these half-lighted avenues all aglow with gorgeous colour and peopled with figures that come and go like the actors in some Christmas piece of Oriental pageantry.

In the Khan Khaleel, the place of the gold and silver smiths' bazaar, there is found, on the contrary, scarcely any display of goods for sale.   The alleys are so narrow in this part that two persons can with difficulty walk in them abreast ; and the shops, tinier than ever, are mere cupboards with about three feet of frontage.   The back of each cupboard is fitted with tiers of little drawers and pigeon-holes, and in front is a kind of matted stone step, called a mastabah, which serves for seat and counter.   The customer sits on the edge of the mastabah ; the merchant squats, cross-legged, inside.   In this position he can, without rising, take out drawer after drawer ; and thus the space between the two becomes piled with gold and silver ornaments.   These differ from each other only in the metal, the patterns being identical ; and they are sold by weight, with a due margin for profit.   In dealing with strangers who do not understand the Egyptian system of weights, silver articles are commonly weighed against rupees or five-franc pieces, and gold articles against napoleons or sovereigns.   The ornaments made in Cairo consist chiefly of chains and earrings, anklets, bangles, necklaces strung with coins or tusk-shaped pendants, amulet-cases of filigree or repoussé work, and penannular bracelets of rude execution, but rich and ancient designs.   As for the merchants, their civility and patience are inexhaustible. One may turn over their whole stock, try on all their bracelets, go away again and again without buying, and yet be always welcomed and dismissed with smiles.   L. and the Writer spent many an hour practising Arabic in the Khan Khaleel, without, it is to be feared, a corresponding degree of benefit to the merchants.

There are many other special bazaars in Cairo, as the Sweetmeat Bazaar ; the Hardware Bazaar ; the Tobacco Bazaar ; the Sword-mounters' and Coppersmiths' Bazaars ; the Moorish

Bazaar, where fez caps, burnouses, and Barbary goods are sold ; and some extensive bazaars for the sale of English and French muslins, and Manchester cotton goods ; but these last are, for the most part, of inferior interest. Among certain fabrics manufactured in England expressly for the Eastern market, we observed a most hideous printed muslin representing small black devils capering over a yellow ground, and we learned that it was much in favour for children's dresses.

But the bazaars, however picturesque, are far from being the only sights of Cairo. There are mosques in plenty ; grand old Saracenic gates ; ancient Coptic churches ; the museum of Egyptian antiquities ; and, within driving distance, the tombs of the Caliphs, Heliopolis, the Pyramids, and the Sphinx. To remember in what order the present travellers saw these things would now be impossible ; for they lived in a dream, and were at first too bewildered to catalogue their impressions very methodically. Some places they were for the present obliged to dismiss with only a passing glance ; others had to be wholly deferred till their return to Cairo.

In the meanwhile, our first business was to look at dahabeeyahs ; and the looking at dahabeeyahs compelled us constantly to turn our steps and our thoughts in the direction of Boulak—a desolate place by the river, where some two or three hundred Nile-boats lay moored for hire. Now, most persons know something of the miseries of house-hunting ; but only those who have experienced them know how much keener are the miseries of dahabeeyah-hunting. It is more bewildering and more fatiguing, and is beset by its own special and peculiar difficulties. The boats, in the first place, are all built on the same plan, which is not the case with houses ; and except as they run bigger or smaller, cleaner or dirtier, are as like each other as twin oysters. The same may be said of their captains, with the same differences ; for to a person who has been only a few days in Egypt, one black or copper-coloured man is exactly like every other black or copper-coloured man. Then each Reïs, or captain, displays the certificates given to him by former travellers ; and these certificates, being apparently in active circulation, have a mysterious way of turning up again and again on board different boats and in the hands of different claimants.   Nor is this all.   Dahabeeyahs are given to changing their places, which houses do not do ; so that the boat which lay yesterday alongside the eastern bank may be over at the western bank to-day, or hidden in the midst of a dozen others half a mile lower down the river.   All this is very perplexing ; yet it is as nothing compared with the state of confusion one gets into when attempting to weigh the advantages or disadvantages of boats with six cabins and boats with eight ; boats provided with canteen, and boats without ; boats that can pass the cataract, and boats that can't ; boats that are only twice as dear as they ought to be, and boats with that defect five or six times multiplied.   Their names, again— Ghazal, Sarawa, Fostat, Dongola,—unlike any names one has ever heard before, afford as yet no kind of help to the memory. Neither do the names of their captains ; for they are all Mohammeds or Hassans.   Neither do their prices ; for they vary from day to day, according to the state of the market as shown by the returns of arrivals at the principal hotels.

Add to all this the fact that no Reïs speaks anything but Arabic, and that every word of inquiry or negotiation has to be filtered, more or less inaccurately, through a dragoman, and then perhaps those who have not yet tried this variety of the pleasures of the chase may be able to form some notion of the weary, hopeless, puzzling work which lies before the dahabeeyah hunter in Cairo.

Thus it came to pass that, for the first ten days or so, some three or four hours had to be devoted every morning to the business of the boats ; at the end of which time we were no nearer a conclusion than at first.   The small boats were too small for either comfort or safety, especially in what Nile-travellers call "a big wind."   The medium-sized boats (which lie under the suspicion of being used in summer for · the transport of cargo) were for the most part of doubtful cleanliness. The largest boats, which alone seemed unexceptionable, contained from eight to ten cabins, besides two saloons, and were obviously too large for a party consisting of only L., the Writer, and a maid.   And all were exorbitantly dear. Encompassed by these manifold difficulties ; listening now to this and now to that person's opinion ; deliberating, haggling, comparing, hesitating, we vibrated daily between Boulak and Cairo, and led a miserable life. Meanwhile, however, we met some former acquaintances ; made some new ones ; and when not too tired or down-hearted, saw what we could of the sights of Cairo—which helped a little to soften the asperities of our lot.

One of our first excursions was, of course, to the Pyramids, which lie within an hour and a half's easy drive from the hotel door. We started immediately after an early luncheon, followed an excellent road all the way, and were back in time for dinner at half-past six. But it must be understood that we did not go to *see* the Pyramids. We went only to look at them. Later on (having meanwhile been up the Nile and back, and gone through months of training), we came again, not only with due leisure, but also with some practical understanding of the manifold phases through which the arts and architecture of Egypt had passed since those far-off days of Cheops and Chephren. Then, only, we can be said to have seen the Pyramids ; and till we arrive at that stage of our pilgrimage, it will be well to defer everything like a detailed account of them or their surroundings. Of this first brief visit, enough therefore a brief record.

The first glimpse that most travellers now get of the Pyramids is from the window of the railway carriage as they come from Alexandria ; and it is not impressive. It does not take one's breath away, for instance, like a first sight of the Alps from the high level of the Neufchâtel line, or the outline of the Acropolis at Athens as one first recognises it from the sea. The well-known triangular forms look small and shadowy, and are too familiar to be in any way startling. And the same, I think, is true of every distant view of them,—that is, of every view which is too distant to afford the means of scaling them against other objects. It is only in approaching them, and observing how they grow with every foot of the road, that one begins to feel they are not so familiar after all.

But when at last the edge of the desert is reached, and the long sand-slope climbed, and the rocky platform gained, and the Great Pyramid in all its unexpected bulk and majesty towers close above one's head, the effect is as sudden as it is

overwhelming.   It shuts out the sky and the horizon.   It shuts
out all the other Pyramids.   It shuts out everything but the
sense of awe and wonder.

Now, too, one discovers that it was with the forms of the
Pyramids, and only their forms, that one had been acquainted
all these years past.   Of their surface, their colour, their
relative position, their number (to say nothing of their size),
one had hitherto entertained no kind of definite idea.   The
most careful study of plans and measurements, the clearest
photographs, the most elaborate descriptions, had done little or
nothing, after all, to make one know the place beforehand.
This undulating table-land of sand and rock, pitted with open
graves and cumbered with mounds of shapeless masonry, is
wholly unlike the desert of our dreams.   The Pyramids of
Cheops and Chephren are bigger than we had expected ;
the Pyramid of Mycerinus is smaller.   Here, too, are nine
Pyramids, instead of three.   They are all entered in the plans
and mentioned in the guide-books ; but, somehow, one is un-
prepared to find them there, and cannot help looking upon
them as intruders.   These six extra Pyramids are small and
greatly dilapidated.   One, indeed, is little more than a big
cairn.

Even the Great Pyramid puzzles us with an unexpected
sense of unlikeness.   We all know, and have known from
childhood, that it was stripped of its outer blocks some five
hundred years ago to build Arab mosques and palaces ; but
the rugged, rock-like aspect of that giant staircase takes us by
surprise, nevertheless.   Nor does it look like a partial ruin,
either.   It looks as if it had been left unfinished, and as if the
workmen might be coming back to-morrow morning.

The colour again is a surprise.   Few persons can be
aware beforehand of the rich tawny hue that Egyptian limestone assumes after ages of exposure to the blaze of an Egyptian
sky.   Seen in certain lights, the Pyramids look like piles of
massy gold.

Having but one hour and forty minutes to spend on the
spot, we resolutely refused on this first occasion to be shown
anything, or told anything, or to be taken anywhere,—except,
indeed, for a few minutes to the brink of the sand-hollow in

which the Sphinx lies couchant. We wished to give our whole attention, and all the short time at our disposal, to the Great Pyramid only. To gain some impression of the outer aspect and size of this enormous structure,—to steady our minds to something like an understanding of its age,—was enough, and more than enough, for so brief a visit.

For it is no easy task to realise, however imperfectly, the duration of six or seven thousand years ; and the Great Pyramid, which is supposed to have been some four thousand two hundred and odd years old at the time of the birth of Christ, is now in its seventh millennary. Standing there close against the base of it ; touching it ; measuring her own height against one of its lowest blocks ; looking up all the stages of that vast, receding, rugged wall, which leads upward like an Alpine buttress and seems almost to touch the sky, the Writer suddenly became aware that these remote dates had never presented themselves to her mind until this moment as any-thing but abstract numerals. Now, for the first time, they resolved themselves into something concrete, definite, real. They were no longer figures, but years with their changes of season, their high and low Niles, their seed-times and harvests. The consciousness of that moment will never, perhaps, quite wear away. It was as if one had been snatched up for an instant to some vast height overlooking the plains of Time, and had seen the centuries mapped out beneath one's feet.

To appreciate the size of the Great Pyramid is less difficult than to apprehend its age. No one who has walked the length of one side, climbed to the top, and learned the dimensions from Murray, can fail to form a tolerably clear idea of its mere bulk. The measurements given by Sir Gardner Wilkinson are as follows :—length of each side, 732 feet ; perpendicular height, 480 feet 9 inches ; area 535,824 square feet.[1] That is to say, it stands 115 feet 9 inches higher than the cross on the top of St. Paul's, and about 20 feet lower than Box Hill in Surrey ; and if transported bodily to London, it would a little

---

[1] Since the first edition of this book was issued, the publication of Mr. W. M. Flinders Petrie's standard work, entitled *The Pyramids and Temples of Gizeh,* has for the first time placed a thoroughly accurate and scientific description of the Great Pyramid at the disposal of students. Calculating

more than cover the whole area of Lincoln's Inn Fields. These are sufficiently matter-of-fact statements, and sufficiently intelligible ; but, like most calculations of the kind, they diminish rather than do justice to the dignity of the subject.

More impressive by far than the weightiest array of figures or the most striking comparisons, was the shadow cast by the Great Pyramid as the sun went down. That mighty Shadow, sharp and distinct, stretched across the stony platform of the desert and over full three-quarters of a mile of the green plain below. It divided the sunlight where it fell, just as its great original divided the sunlight in the upper air ; and it darkened the space it covered, like an eclipse. It was not without a thrill of something approaching to awe that one remembered how this self-same Shadow had gone on registering, not only the height of the most stupendous gnomon ever set up by human hands, but the slow passage, day by day, of more than sixty centuries of the world's history.

It was still lengthening over the landscape as we went down the long sand-slope and regained the carriage. Some six or eight Arabs in fluttering white garments ran on ahead to bid us a last good-bye. That we should have driven over from Cairo only to sit quietly down and look at the Great Pyramid had filled them with unfeigned astonishment. With

from the rock-cut sockets at the four corners, and from the true level of the pavement, Mr. Petrie finds that the square of the original base of the structure, in inches, is of these dimensions :—

	Length.	Difference from Mean.	Azimuth.	Difference from Mean.
N	9069·4	+ ·6	− 3′ 20″	+ 23″
E	9067·7	− 1·1	− 3′ 57″	− 14″
S	9069·5	+ ·7	− 3′ 41″	+ 2″
W	9068·6	− ·2	− 3′ 54″	− 11″
Mean	9068·8	·65	− 3′ 43″	12″

For the height, Mr. Petrie, after duly weighing all data, such as the thickness of the three casing-stones yet *in situ*, and the presumed thickness of those which formerly faced the upper courses of the masonry, gives from his observations of the mean angle of the Pyramid, a height from base to apex of 5776·0 ± 7·0 inches. See *The Pyramids and Temples of Gizeh*, chap. vi. pp. 37 to 43. [Note to the Second Edition].

such energy and despatch as the modern traveller uses, we might have been to the top, and seen the temple of the Sphinx, and done two or three of the principal tombs in the time.

"You come again!" said they. "Good Arab show you everything. You see nothing this time!"

So, promising to return ere long, we drove away; well content, nevertheless, with the way in which our time had been spent.

The Pyramid Bedouins have been plentifully abused by travellers and guide-books, but we found no reason to complain of them now or afterwards. They neither crowded round us, nor followed us, nor importuned us in any way. They are naturally vivacious and very talkative; yet the gentle fellows were dumb as mutes when they found we wished for silence. And they were satisfied with a very moderate bakhshîsh at parting.

As a fitting sequel to this excursion, we went, I think next day, to see the mosque of Sultan Hassan, which is one of those mediæval structures said to have been built with the casing-stones of the Great Pyramid.

CHAPTER II.

THE mosque of Sultan Hassan, confessedly the most beautiful in Cairo, is also perhaps the most beautiful in the Moslem world. It was built at just that happy moment when Arabian art in Egypt, having ceased merely to appropriate or imitate, had at length evolved an original architectural style out of the heterogeneous elements of Roman and early Christian edifices. The mosques of a few centuries earlier (as, for instance, that of Tulûn, which marks the first departure from the old Byzantine model) consisted of little more than a courtyard with colonnades leading to a hall supported on a forest of pillars. A little more than a century later, and the national style had already experienced the beginnings of that prolonged eclipse which finally resulted in the bastard Neo-Byzantine Renaissance represented by the mosque of Mehemet Ali. But the mosque of Sultan Hassan, built ninety-seven years before the taking of Constantinople, may justly be regarded as the highest point reached by Saracenic art in Egypt after it had used up the Greek and Roman material of Memphis, and before its new-born originality became modified by influences from beyond the Bosphorus. Its pre-eminence is due neither to the greatness of its dimensions nor to the splendour of its materials. It is neither so large as the great mosque at Damascus, nor so rich in costly marbles as Saint Sophia in Constantinople ; but in design, proportion, and a certain lofty grace impossible to describe, it surpasses these, and every other mosque, whether original or adapted, with which the writer is acquainted.

The whole structure is purely national. Every line and curve in it, and every inch of detail, is in the best style of the best period of the Arabian school. And above all, it was designed expressly for its present purpose. The two famous mosques of Damascus and Constantinople having, on the contrary, been Christian churches, betray evidences of adaptation. In Saint Sophia, the space once occupied by the figure of the Redeemer may be distinctly traced in the mosaic-work of the apse, filled in with gold tesseræ of later date ; while the magnificent gates of the great mosque at Damascus are decorated, among other Christian emblems, with the sacramental chalice. But the mosque of Sultan Hassan, built by En Nasîr Hassan in the high and palmy days of the Memlook rule, is marred by no discrepancies. For a mosque it was designed, and a mosque it remains. Too soon it will be only a beautiful ruin.

A number of small streets having lately been demolished in this quarter, the approach to the mosque lies across a desolate open space littered with débris, but destined to be laid out as a public square. With this desirable end in view, some half dozen workmen were lazily loading as many camels with rubble, which is the Arab way of carting rubbish. If they persevere, and the Minister of Public Works continues to pay their wages with due punctuality, the ground will perhaps get cleared in eight or ten years' time.

Driving up with some difficulty to the foot of the great steps, which were crowded with idlers smoking and sleeping, we observed a long and apparently fast-widening fissure reaching nearly from top to bottom of the main wall of the building, close against the minaret. It looked like just such a rent as might be caused by a shock of earthquake, and, being still new to the East, we wondered the Government had not set to work to mend it. We had yet to learn that nothing is ever mended in Cairo. Here, as in Constantinople, new ·buildings spring up apace, but the old, no matter how venerable, are allowed to moulder away, inch by inch, till nothing remains but a heap of ruins.

Going up the steps and through a lofty hall, up some more steps and along a gloomy corridor, we came to the great court, before entering which, however, we had to take off our boots

and put on slippers brought for the purpose.   The first sight
of this court is an architectural surprise.   It is like nothing
one has seen before, and its beauty equals its novelty.
Imagine an immense marble quadrangle, open to the sky and
enclosed within lofty walls, with, at each side, a vast recess
framed in by a single arch.   The quadrangle is more than 100
feet square, and the walls are more than 100 feet high.   Each
recess forms a spacious hall for rest and prayer, and all are
matted ; but that at the eastern end is wider and considerably
deeper than the other three, and the noble arch that encloses it
like the proscenium of a splendid stage, measures, according to
Fergusson, 69 feet 5 inches in the span.   It looks much
larger.   This principal hall, the floor of which is raised one
step at the upper end, measures 90 feet in depth and 90 in
height.   The dais is covered with prayer-rugs, and contains
the holy niche and the pulpit of the preacher.   We observed
that those who came up here came only to pray.   Having
prayed, they either went away or turned aside into one of the
other recesses to rest.   There was a charming fountain in the
court, with a dome-roof as light and fragile-looking as a big
bubble, at which each worshipper performed his ablutions on
coming in.   This done, he left his slippers on the matting and
trod the carpeted dais barefoot.

This was the first time we had seen Moslems at prayer,
and we could not but be impressed by their profound and
unaffected devotion.   Some lay prostrate, their foreheads
touching the ground ; others were kneeling ; others bowing in
the prescribed attitudes of prayer.   So absorbed were they,
that not even our unhallowed presence seemed to disturb them.
We did not then know that the pious Moslem is as devout out
of the mosque as in it ; or that it is his habit to pray when
the appointed hours come round, no matter where he may be,
or how occupied.   We soon became so familiar, however, with
this obvious trait of Mohammedan life, that it seemed quite a
matter of course that the camel-driver should dismount and
lay his forehead in the dust by the roadside ; or the merchant
spread his prayer-carpet on the narrow mastabah of his little
shop in the public bazaar ; or the boatman prostrate himself
with his face to the east, as the sun went down behind the
hills of the Libyan desert.

While we were admiring the spring of the roof and the intricate Arabesque decorations of the pulpit, a custode came up with a big key and invited us to visit the tomb of the founder. So we followed him into an enormous vaulted hall a hundred feet square, in the centre of which stood a plain, railed-off tomb, with an empty iron-bound coffer at the foot. We afterwards learned that for five hundred years—that is to say, ever since the death and burial of Sultan Hassan—this coffer had contained a fine copy of the Korân, traditionally said to have been written by Sultan Hassan's own hand ; but that the Khedive, who is collecting choice and antique Arabic MSS., had only the other day sent an order for its removal.

Nothing can be bolder or more elegant than the propor- tions of this noble sepulchral hall, the walls of which are covered with tracery in low relief incrusted with discs and tesseræ of turquoise-coloured porcelain ; while high up, in order to lead off the vaulting of the roof, the corners are rounded by means of recessed clusters of exquisite Arabesque woodwork, like pendent stalactites. But the tesseræ are fast falling out, and most of their places are vacant ; and the beautiful woodwork hangs in fragments, tattered and cob- webbed, like time-worn banners which the first touch of a brush would bring down.

Going back again from the tomb to the courtyard, we everywhere observed· traces of the same dilapidation. The fountain, once a miracle of Saracenic ornament, was fast going to destruction. The rich marbles of its basement were cracked and discoloured, its stuccoed cupola was flaking off piecemeal, its enamels were dropping out, its lace-like wood tracery shredding away by inches.

Presently a tiny brown and golden bird perched with pretty confidence on the brink of the basin, and having splashed, and drunk, and preened its feathers like a true believer at his ablutions, flew up to the top of the cupola and sang deliciously. All else was profoundly still. Large spaces of light and shadow divided the quadrangle. The sky showed overhead as a square opening of burning solid blue ; while here and there, reclining, praying, or quietly occupied, a number of turbaned figures were picturesquely scattered over the matted floors of the open halls around. Yonder sat a tailor cross-legged, making a waistcoat ; near him, stretched on his face at full length, sprawled a basket-maker with his half-woven basket and bundle of rushes beside him ; and here, close against the main entrance, lay a blind man and his dog ; the master asleep, the dog keeping watch. It was, as I have said, our first mosque, and I well remember the surprise with which we saw that tailor sewing on his buttons, and the sleepers lying about in the shade. We did not then know that a Mohammedan mosque is as much a place of rest and refuge as of prayer ; or that the houseless Arab may take shelter there by night or day as freely as the birds may build their nests in the cornice, or as the blind man's dog may share the cool shade with his sleeping master.

From the mosque of this Memlook sovereign it is but a few minutes' uphill drive to the mosque of Mehemet Ali, by whose orders the last of that royal race were massacred just sixty-four years ago.[1] This mosque, built within the precincts of the citadel on a spur of the Mokattam Hills overlooking the city, is the most conspicuous object in Cairo. Its attenuated minarets and clustered domes show from every point of view for miles around, and remain longer in sight, as one leaves, or returns to, Cairo, than any other landmark. It is a spacious, costly, gaudy, commonplace building, with nothing really beautiful about it, except the great marble courtyard and fountain. The inside, which is entirely built of Oriental alabaster, is carpeted with magnificent Turkey carpets and hung with innumerable cut-glass chandeliers, so that it looks like a huge vulgar drawing-room from which the furniture has been cleared out for dancing.

The view from the outer platform is, however, magnificent. We saw it on a hazy day, and could not therefore distinguish the point of the Delta, which ought to have been visible on the north ; but we could plainly see as far southward as the Pyramids of Sakkârah, and trace the windings of the Nile for many miles across the plain. The Pyramids of Ghîzeh, on their daïs of desert rock about twelve miles off, looked, as they

[1] Now, seventy-seven years ago ; the first Edition of this book having been published thirteen years ago. [Note to Second Edition.]

always do look from a distance, small and unimpressive ; but the great alluvial valley dotted over with mud villages and intersected by canals and tracts of palm forest ; the shining river specked with sails ; and the wonderful city, all flat roofs, cupolas, and minarets, spread out like an intricate model at one's feet, were full of interest and absorbed our whole attention. Looking down upon it from this elevation, it is as easy to believe that Cairo contains four hundred mosques, as it is to stand on the brow of the Pincio and believe in the three hundred and sixty-five churches of modern Rome.

As we came away, they showed us the place in which the Memlook nobles, four hundred and seventy [1] in number, were shot down like mad dogs in a trap, that fatal first of March A.D. 1811. We saw the upper gate which was shut behind them as they came out from the presence of the Pasha, and the lower gate which was shut before them to prevent their egress. The walls of the narrow roadway in which the slaughter was done are said to be pitted with bullet-marks ; but we would not look for them.

I have already said that I do not very distinctly remember the order of our sight-seeing in Cairo, for the reason that we saw some places before we went up the river, some after we came back, and some (as for instance the Museum at Boulak) both before and after, and indeed as often as possible. But I am at least quite certain that we witnessed a performance of howling dervishes, and the departure of the caravan for Mecca, before starting.

Of all the things that people do by way of pleasure, the pursuit of a procession is surely one of the most wearisome. They generally go a long way to see it ; they wait a weary time ; it is always late ; and when at length it does come, it is over in a few minutes. The present pageant fulfilled all these conditions in a superlative degree. We breakfasted uncomfortably early, started soon after half-past seven, and had taken up

---

[1] One only is said to have escaped—a certain Emín Bey, who leaped his horse over a gap in the wall, alighted safely in the piazza below, and galloped away into the desert. The place of this famous leap continued to be shown for many years, but there are no gaps in the wall now, the citadel being the only place in Cairo which is kept in thorough repair.

our position outside the Báb en-Nasr, on the way to the desert, by half-past eight.   Here we sat for nearly three hours, exposed to clouds of dust and a burning sun, with nothing to do but to watch the crowd and wait patiently.   All Shepheard's Hotel was there, and every stranger in Cairo ; and we all had smart open carriages drawn by miserable screws and driven by bare-legged Arabs.   These Arabs, by the way, are excellent whips, and the screws get along wonderfully ; but it seems odd at first, and not a little humiliating, to be whirled along behind a coachman whose only livery consists of a rag of dirty white turban, a scant tunic just reaching to his knees, and the top-boots with which Nature has provided him.

Here, outside the walls, the crowd increased momentarily. The place was like a fair with provision-stalls, swings, story-tellers, serpent-charmers, cake-sellers, sweetmeat-sellers, sellers of sherbet, water, lemonade, sugared nuts, fresh dates, hard-boiled eggs, oranges, and sliced water-melon.   Veiled women carrying little bronze Cupids of children astride upon the right shoulder, swarthy Egyptians, coal-black Abyssinians, Arabs and Nubians of every shade from golden-brown to chocolate, fellahs, dervishes, donkey-boys, street urchins, and beggars with every imaginable deformity, came and went ; squeezed themselves in and out among the carriages ; lined the road on each side of the great towered gateway ; swarmed on the top of every wall ; and filled the air with laughter, a Babel of dialects, and those odours of Araby that are inseparable from an Eastern crowd. A harmless, unsavoury, good-humoured, inoffensive throng, one glance at which was enough to put to flight all one's precon-ceived notions about Oriental gravity of demeanour !   For the truth is that gravity is by no means an Oriental characteristic. Take a Mohammedan at his devotions, and he is a model of religious abstraction ; bargain with him for a carpet, and he is as impenetrable as a judge ; but see him in his hours of relaxa-tion, or on the occasion of a public holiday, and he is as gar-rulous and full of laughter as a big child.   Like a child, too, he loves noise and movement for the mere sake of noise and movement, and looks upon swings and fireworks as the height of human felicity.   Now swings and fireworks are Arabic for bread and circuses, and our pleb's passion for them is insatiable.

He not only indulges in them upon every occasion of public rejoicing, but calls in their aid to celebrate the most solemn festivals of his religion. It so happened that we afterwards came in the way of several Mohammedan festivals both in Egypt and Syria, and we invariably found the swings at work all day and the fireworks going off every evening.

To-day, the swings outside the Báb en-Nasr were never idle. Here were creaking Russian swings hung with little painted chariots for the children ; and plain rope swings, some of them as high as Haman's gallows, for the men. For my own part, I know no sight much more comic and incongruous than the serene enjoyment with which a bearded, turbaned, middle-aged Egyptian squats upon his heels on the tiny wooden seat of one of these enormous swings, and, holding on to the side-ropes for dear life, goes careering up forty feet high into the air at every turn.

At a little before midday, when the heat and glare were becoming intolerable, the swings suddenly ceased going, the crowd surged in the direction of the gate, and a distant drumming announced the approach of the procession. First came a string of baggage-camels laden with tent-furniture ; then some two hundred pilgrims on foot, chanting passages from the Korân ; then a regiment of Egyptian infantry, the men in a coarse white linen uniform consisting of coat, baggy trousers and gaiters, with cross-belts and cartouche-boxes of plain black leather, and the red fez, or tarboosh, on the head. Next after these came more pilgrims, followed by a body of dervishes carrying green banners embroidered with Arabic sentences in white and yellow ; then a native cavalry regiment headed by a general and four colonels in magnificent gold embroidery and preceded by an excellent military band ; then another band and a second regiment of infantry ; then more colonels, followed by a regiment of lancers mounted on capital grey horses and carrying lances topped with small red and green pennants. After these had gone by there was a long stoppage, and then, with endless breaks and interruptions, came a straggling irregular crowd of pilgrims, chiefly of the fellah class, beating small darabukkehs, or native drums. Those about us estimated their number at two thousand. And now, their guttural chorus

audible long before they arrived in sight, came the howling
dervishes—a ragged, wild-looking, ruffianly set, rolling their
heads from side to side, and keeping up a hoarse incessant cry
of "Allàh! Allàh! Allàh!"   Of these there may have been a
couple of hundred.   The sheykhs of the principal orders of
dervishes came next in order, superbly dressed in robes of
brilliant colours embroidered with gold, and mounted on magnificent Arabs.   Finest of all, in a green turban and scarlet
mantle, rode the Sheykh of the Hasaneyn, who is a descendant
of the Prophet ; but the most important, the Sheykh el Bekree,
who is a sort of Egyptian Archbishop of Canterbury and head
of all the dervishes, came last, riding a white Arab with gold-
embroidered housings.   He was a placid-looking old man, and
wore a violet robe and an enormous red and green turban.

This very reverend personage was closely followed by the
chief of the carpet-makers' guild—a handsome man sitting
sidewise on a camel.

Then happened another break in the procession—an eager
pause—a gathering murmur.   And then, riding a gaunt
dromedary at a rapid trot, his fat sides shaking, and his head
rolling in a stupid drunken way at every step, appeared a
bloated, half-naked Silenus, with long fuzzy black locks and a
triple chin, and no other clothing than a pair of short white
drawers and red slippers.   A shiver of delight ran through the
crowd at sight of this holy man—the famous Sheykh of the
Camel (Sheykh el-Gemel), the "great, good Priest"—the idol
of the people.   We afterwards learned that this was his
twentieth pilgrimage, and that he was supposed to fast, roll his
head, and wear nothing but this pair of loose drawers, all the
way to and from Mecca.

But the crowning excitement was yet to come, and the
rapture with which the crowd had greeted the Sheykh el-Gemel
was as nothing compared with their ecstasy when the Mahmal,
preceded by another group of mounted officers and borne by a
gigantic camel, was seen coming through the gateway.   The
women held up their children ; the men swarmed up the
scaffoldings of the swings and behind the carriages.   They
screamed ; they shouted ; they waved handkerchiefs and turbans ; they were beside themselves with excitement.   Mean-

while the camel, as if conscious of the dignity of his position and the splendour of his trappings, came on slowly and ponderously with his nose in the air, and passed close before our horses' heads. We could not possibly have had a better view of the Mahmal; which is nothing but a sort of cage, or pagoda, of gilded tracery very richly decorated. In the days of the Memlooks, the Mahmal represented the litter of the Sultan, and went empty, like a royal carriage at a public funeral;[1] but we were told that it now carried the tribute-carpet sent annually by the carpet-makers of Cairo to the tomb of the Prophet.

This closed the procession. As the camel passed, the crowd surged in, and everything like order was at an end. The carriages all made at once for the Gate, so meeting the full tide of the outpouring crowd and causing unimaginable confusion. Some stuck in the sand half-way—our own among the number; and all got into an inextricable block in the narrow part just inside the gate. Hereupon the drivers abused each other, and the crowd got impatient, and some Europeans got pelted.

Coming back, we met two or three more regiments. The men, both horse and foot, seemed fair average specimens, and creditably disciplined. They rode better than they marched, which was to be expected. The uniform is the same for cavalry and infantry throughout the service; the only difference being that the former wear short black riding boots, and the latter, Zouave gaiters of white linen. They are officered up to

---

[1] "It is related that the Sultan Ez-Zahir Beybars, King of Egypt, was the first who sent a Mahmal with the caravan of pilgrims to Mecca, in the year of the Flight 670 (A.D. 1272) or 675; but this custom, it is generally said, had its origin a few years before his accession to the throne. Sheger-ed-Durr, a beautiful Turkish female slave, who became the favourite wife of the Sultan Es-Sáleh Negm-ed-Deen, and on the death of his son (with whom terminated the dynasty of the house of the Eiyoob) caused herself to be acknowledged as Queen of Egypt, performed the pilgrimage in a magnificent 'hódag,' or covered litter, borne by a camel; and for several successive years her empty 'hódag' was sent with the caravan, merely for the sake of state. Hence, succeeding princes of Egypt sent with each year's caravan of pilgrims a kind of 'hódag' (which received the name of Mahmal) as an emblem of royalty."—*The Modern Egyptians*, by E. W. Lane, chap. xxiv. London, 1860.

a certain point by Egyptians; but the commanding officers and the staff (among whom are enough colonels and generals to form an ordinary regiment) are chiefly Europeans and Americans.

It had seemed, while the procession was passing, that the proportion of pilgrims was absurdly small when compared with the display of military; but this, which is called the departure of the caravan, is in truth only the procession of the sacred carpet from Cairo to the camp outside the walls; and the troops are present merely as part of the pageant. The true departure takes place two days later. The pilgrims then muster in great numbers; but the soldiery is reduced to a small escort. It was said that seven thousand souls went out this year from Cairo and its neighbourhood.

The procession took place on Thursday the 21st day of the Mohammedan month of Showwál, which was our 11th of December. The next day, Friday, being the Mohammedan Sabbath, we went to the Convent of the Howling Dervishes, which lies beyond the walls in a quiet nook between the river-side and the part known as Old Cairo.

We arrived a little after two, and passing through a court-yard shaded by a great sycamore, were ushered into a large, square, whitewashed hall with a dome-roof and a neatly-matted floor. The place in its arrangements resembled none of the mosques that we had yet seen. There was, indeed, nothing to arrange—no pulpit, no holy niche, no lamps, no prayer-carpets; nothing but a row of cane-bottomed chairs at one end, some of which were already occupied by certain of our fellow-guests at Shepheard's Hotel. A party of some forty or fifty wild-looking dervishes were squatting in a circle at the opposite side of the hall, their outer kuftâns and queer pyramidal hats lying in a heap close by.

Being accommodated with chairs among the other spectators, we waited for whatever might happen. More dervishes and more English dropped in from time to time. The new dervishes took off their caps and sat down among the rest, laughing and talking together at their ease. The English sat in a row, shy, uncomfortable, and silent; wondering whether they ought to behave as if they were in church, and mortally ashamed of their feet. For we had all been obliged to take off or cover our boots before going in, and those who had forgotten to bring slippers had their feet tied up in pocket-handkerchiefs.

A long time went by thus. At last, when the number of dervishes had increased to about seventy, and every one was tired of waiting, eight musicians came in—two trumpets, two lutes, a cocoa-nut fiddle, a tambourine, and two drums. Then the dervishes, some of whom were old and white-haired and some mere boys, formed themselves into a great circle, shoulder to shoulder; the band struck up a plaintive, discordant air; and a grave middle-aged man, placing himself in the centre of the ring, and inclining his head at each repetition, began to recite the name of Allàh.

Softly at first, and one by one, the dervishes took up the chant :—" Allàh ! Allàh ! Allàh !" Their heads and their voices rose and fell in unison. The dome above gave back a hollow echo. There was something strange and solemn in the ceremony.

Presently, however, the trumpets brayed louder—the voices grew hoarser—the heads bowed lower—the name of Allàh rang out faster and faster, fiercer and fiercer. The leader, himself cool and collected, began sensibly accelerating the time of the chorus ; and it became evident that the performers were possessed by a growing frenzy. Soon the whole circle was madly rocking to and fro ; the voices rose to a hoarse scream ; and only the trumpets were audible above the din. Now and then a dervish would spring up convulsively some three or four feet above the heads of the others; but for the most part they stood rooted firmly to one spot—now bowing their heads almost to their feet—now flinging themselves so violently back, that we, standing behind, could see their faces foreshortened upside down ; and this with such incredible rapidity, that their long hair had scarcely time either to rise or fall, but remained as if suspended in mid-air. Still the frenzy mounted ; still the pace quickened. Some shrieked—some groaned—some, unable to support themselves any longer, were held up in their places by the bystanders. All were mad for the time being. Our own heads seemed to be going round at last ; and more than one of the ladies present looked longingly towards the door. It was, in truth, a horrible sight, and needed only darkness and torchlight to be quite diabolical.

At length, just as the fury was at its height and the very building seemed to be rocking to and fro above our heads, one poor wretch staggered out of the circle and fell writhing and shrieking close against our feet. At the same moment, the leader clapped his hands ; the performers, panting and exhausted, dropped into a sitting posture ; and the first zikr, as it is called, came abruptly to an end. Some few, however, could not stop immediately, but kept on swaying and muttering to themselves ; while the one in the fit, having ceased to shriek, lay out stiff and straight, apparently in a state of coma.

There was a murmur of relief and a simultaneous rising among the spectators. It was announced that another zikr, with a reinforcement of fresh dervishes, would soon begin ; but the Europeans had had enough of it, and few remained for the second performance.

Going out, we paused beside the poor fellow on the floor, and asked if nothing could be done for him.

" He is struck by Mohammed," said gravely an Egyptian official who was standing by.

At that moment, the leader came over, knelt down beside him, touched him lightly on the head and breast, and whispered something in his ear. The man was then quite rigid, and white as death. We waited, however, and after a few more minutes saw him struggle back into a dazed, half-conscious state, when he was helped to his feet and led away by his friends.

The courtyard as we came out was full of dervishes sitting on cane benches in the shade, and sipping coffee. The green leaves rustled overhead, with glimpses of intensely blue sky between ; and brilliant patches of sunshine flickered down upon groups of wild-looking, half-savage figures in parti-coloured garments. It was one of those ready-made subjects that the sketcher passes by with a sigh, but which live in his memory for ever.

From hence, being within a few minutes' drive of Old Cairo. we went on as far as the Mosque of 'Amr—an unin-

teresting ruin standing alone among the rubbish-mounds of the
first Mohammedan capital of Egypt. It is constructed on the
plan of a single quadrangle 225 feet square, surrounded by a
covered colonnade one range of pillars in depth on the west
(which is the side of the entrance) ; four on the north ; three
on the south ; and six on the east, which is the place of prayer,
and contains three holy niches and the pulpit. The columns,
245 in number, have been brought from earlier Roman and
Byzantine buildings. They are of various marbles and have
all kinds of capitals. Some being originally too short, have
been stilted on disproportionately high bases ; and in one
instance the necessary height has been obtained by adding a
second capital on the top of the first. We observed one
column of that rare black and white speckled marble of which
there is a specimen in the pulpit of St. Mark's in Venice ; and
one of the holy niches contains some fragments of Byzantine
mosaics. But the whole building seems to have been put
together in a barbarous way, and would appear to owe its
present state of dilapidation more to bad workmanship than to
time. Many of the pillars, especially on the western side, are
fallen and broken ; the octagonal fountain in the centre is a
roofless ruin ; and the little minaret at the S.E. corner is no
longer safe.

Apart, however, from its poverty of design and detail, the
Mosque of 'Amr is interesting as a point of departure in the
history of Saracenic architecture. It was built by 'Amr Ebn
el-'As, the Arab conqueror of Egypt, in the twenty-first year
of the Hegira (A.D. 642), just ten years after the death of
Mohammed ; and it is the earliest Saracenic edifice in Egypt.
We were glad, therefore, to have seen it for this reason, if for
no other. But it is a barren, dreary place ; and the glare
reflected from all sides of the quadrangle was so intense that
we were thankful to get away again into the narrow streets
beside the river.

Here we presently fell in with a wedding procession consisting of a crowd of men, a band, and some three or four hired
carriages full of veiled women, one of whom was pointed out
as the bride. The bridegroom walked in the midst of the men,
who seemed to be teasing him, drumming round him, and

opposing his progress ; while high above the laughter, the shouting, the jingle of tambourines and the thrumming of darabukkehs, was heard the shrill squeal of some instrument that sounded exactly like a bagpipe.

It was a brilliant afternoon, and we ended our day's work, I remember, with a drive on the Shubra road and a glance at the gardens of the Khedive's summer palace. The Shubra road is the Champs Elysées of Cairo, and is thronged every day from four to half-past six. Here little sheds of roadside cafés alternate with smart modern villas ; ragged fellâheen on jaded donkeys trot side by side with elegant attachés on high-stepping Arabs ; while tourists in hired carriages, Jew bankers in unexceptionable phaetons, veiled hareems in London-built broughams, Italian shopkeepers in preposterously fashionable toilettes, grave sheykhs on magnificent Cairo asses, officers in frogged and braided frocks, and English girls in tall hats and close-fitting habits followed by the inevitable little solemn-looking English groom, pass and repass, precede and follow each other, in one changing, restless, heterogeneous stream, the like of which is to be seen in no other capital in the world. The sons of the Khedive drive here daily, always in separate carriages and preceded by four Saïses and four guards. They are of all ages and sizes, from the Hereditary Prince, a pale, gentlemanly-looking young man of four or five and twenty, down to one tiny, imperious atom of about six, who is dressed like a little man, and is constantly leaning out of his carriage-window and shrilly abusing his coachman.[1]

Apart, however, from those who frequent it, the Shubra road is a really fine drive, broad, level, raised some six or eight feet above the cultivated plain, closely planted on both sides with acacias and sycamore fig-trees, and reaching straight away for four miles out of Cairo, counting from the railway terminus to the Summer Palace. The carriage-way is about as wide as the road across Hyde Park which connects Bays-water with Kensington ; and towards the Shubra end, it runs close beside the Nile. Many of the scyamores are of great size and quite patriarchal girth. Their branches meet overhead

---

[1] The Hereditary Prince, it need scarcely be said, is the present Khedive, Tewfik Pasha. [Note to Second Edition.]

nearly all the way, weaving a delicious shade and making a cool green tunnel of the long perspective.

We did not stay long in the Khedive's gardens, for it was already getting late when we reached the gates ; but we went far enough to see that they were tolerably well kept, not over formal, and laid out with a view to masses of foliage, shady paths, and spaces of turf inlaid with flower-beds, after the style of the famous Sarntheim and Moser gardens at Botzen in the Tyrol. Here are Sont trees (*Acacia Nilotica*) of unusual size, powdered all over with little feathery tufts of yellow blossom ; orange and lemon-trees in abundance ; heaps of little green limes ; bananas bearing heavy pendent bunches of ripe fruit ; winding thickets of pomegranates, oleanders, and salvias ; and great beds, and banks, and trellised walks of roses. Among these, however, I observed none of the rarer varieties. As for the Pointsettia, it grows in Egypt to a height of twenty feet, and bears blossoms of such size and colour as we in England can form no idea of. We saw large trees of it both here and at Alexandria that seemed as if bending beneath a mantle of crimson stars, some of which cannot have measured less than twenty-two inches in diameter.

A large Italian fountain in a rococo style is the great sight of the place. We caught a glimpse of it through the trees, and surprised the gardener who was showing us over by declining to inspect it more nearly. He could not understand why we preferred to give our time to the shrubs and flower-beds.

Driving back presently towards Cairo with a big handful of roses apiece, we saw the sun going down in an aureole of fleecy pink and golden clouds, the Nile flowing by like a stream of liquid light, and a little fleet of sailing boats going up to Boulak before a puff of north wind that had sprung up as the sun neared the horizon. That puff of north wind, those gliding sails, had a keen interest for us now, and touched us nearly ; because—I have delayed this momentous revelation till the last moment—because we were to start to-morrow !

And this is why I have been able, in the midst of so much that was new and bewildering, to remember quite circumstantially the dates, and all the events connected with these last two days. They were to be our last two days in Cairo ;

and to-morrow morning, Saturday the 13th of December, we were to go on board a certain dahabeeyah now lying off the iron bridge at Boulak, therein to begin that strange aquatic life to which we had been looking forward with so many hopes and fears, and towards which we had been steering through so many preliminary difficulties.

But the difficulties were all over now, and everything was settled ; though not in the way we had at first intended. For, in place of a small boat, we had secured one of the largest on the river ; and instead of going alone, we had decided to throw in our lot with that of three other travellers. One of these three was already known to the Writer. The other two, friends of the first, were on their way out from Europe, and were not expected in Cairo for another week. We knew nothing of them but their names.

Meanwhile L. and the Writer, assuming sole possession of the dahabeeyah, were about to start ten days in advance ; it being their intention to push on as far as Rhoda (the ultimate point then reached by the Nile railway), and there to await the arrival of the rest of the party. Now Rhoda (more correctly Roda) is just one hundred and eighty miles south of Cairo ; and we calculated upon seeing the Sakkârah pyramids, the Turra quarries, the tombs of Beni Hassan, and the famous grotto of the Colossus on the Sledge, before our fellow-travellers should be due.

"It depends on the wind, you know," said our dragoman, with a lugubrious smile.

We knew that it depended on the wind ; but what then ? In Egypt, the wind is supposed always to blow from the north at this time of the year, and we had ten good days at our disposal. The observation was clearly irrelevant.

CHAPTER III.

CAIRO TO BEDRESHAYN.

A RAPID raid into some of the nearest shops, for things
remembered at the last moment—a breathless gathering up of
innumerable parcels—a few hurried farewells on the steps of
the hotel—and away we rattle as fast as a pair of rawboned
greys can carry us. For this morning every moment is of
value. We are already late; we expect visitors to luncheon
on board at midday; and we are to weigh anchor at two P.M.
Hence our anxiety to reach Boulak before the bridge is opened,
that we may drive across to the western bank against which
our dahabeeyah lies moored. Hence also our mortification
when we arrive just in time to see the bridge swing apart, and
the first tall mast glide through.

Presently, however, when those on the look-out have
observed our signals of distress, a smart-looking sandal, or
jolly-boat, decked with gay rugs and cushions, manned by five
smiling Arabs, and flying a bright little new Union Jack, comes
swiftly threading her way in and out among the lumbering
barges now crowding through the bridge. In a few more
minutes, we are afloat. For this is our sandal, and these are
five of our crew; and of the three dahabeeyahs moored over
yonder in the shade of the palms, the biggest by far, and the
trimmest, is our own dear, memorable 'Philæ.'

Close behind the Philæ lies the 'Bagstones,'—a neat little
dahabeeyah in the occupation of two English ladies who
chanced to cross with us in the 'Simla' from Brindisi, and of
whom we have seen so much ever since that we regard them

by this time as quite old friends in a strange land.   I will call
them the M. B.'s.   The other boat, lying off a few yards ahead,
carries the tricolor, and is chartered by a party of French
gentlemen.   All three are to sail to-day.

And now we are on board, and have shaken hands with
the captain, and are as busy as bees; for there are cabins to
put in order, flowers to arrange, and a hundred little things to
be seen to before the guests arrive.   It is wonderful, however,
what a few books and roses, an open piano, and a sketch or
two, will do.   In a few minutes the comfortless hired look has
vanished, and long enough before the first comers are announced,
the Philæ wears an aspect as cosy and home-like as if she had
been occupied for a month.

As for the luncheon, it certainly surprised the givers of the
entertainment quite as much as it must have surprised their
guests.   Being, no doubt, a pre-arranged display of professional
pride on the part of dragoman and cook, it was more like an
excessive Christmas dinner than a modest midday meal.   We
sat through it unflinchingly, however, for about an hour and
three quarters, when a startling discharge of firearms sent us all
running upon deck, and created a wholesome diversion in our
favour.   It was the French boat signalling her departure,
shaking out her big sail, and going off triumphantly.

I fear that we of the Bagstones and Philæ—being mere
mortals and Englishwomen—could not help feeling just a
little spiteful when we found the tricolor had started first; but
then it was a consolation to know that the Frenchmen were
going only to Assuân.   Such is the *esprit du Nil.*   The
people in dahabeeyahs despise Cook's tourists; those who are
bound for the Second Cataract look down with lofty compassion
upon those whose ambition extends only to the First; and
travellers who engage their boat by the month hold their heads
a trifle higher than those who contract for the trip.   We, who
were going as far as we liked and for as long as we liked,
could afford to be magnanimous.   So we forgave the Frenchmen, went down again to the saloon, and had coffee and music.

It was nearly three o'clock when our Cairo visitors wished
us 'bon voyage' and good-bye.   Then the M. B.'s, who, with
their nephew, had been of the party, went back to their own

boat ; and both captains prepared to sail at a given signal. For the M. B.'s had entered into a solemn convention to start with us, moor with us, and keep with us, if practicable, all the way up the river. It is pleasant now to remember that this sociable compact, instead of falling through as such compacts are wont to do, was quite literally carried out as far as Aboo Simbel ; that is to say, during a period of seven weeks' hard going, and for a distance of upwards of eight hundred miles.

At last all is ready. The awning that has all day roofed in the upper deck is taken down ; the captain stands at the head of the steps ; the steersman is at the helm ; the dragoman has loaded his musket. Is the Bagstones ready? We wave a handkerchief of inquiry—the signal is answered— the mooring ropes are loosened—the sailors pole the boat off from the bank—bang go the guns, six from the Philæ, and six from the Bagstones, and away we go, our huge sail filling as it takes the wind !

Happy are the Nile travellers who start thus with a fair breeze on a brilliant afternoon. The good boat cleaves her way swiftly and steadily. Water-side palaces and gardens glide by, and are left behind. The domes and minarets of Cairo drop quickly out of sight. The mosque of the citadel, and the ruined fort that looks down upon it from the mountain ridge above, diminish in the distance. The Pyramids stand up sharp and clear.

We sit on the high upper deck, which is furnished with lounge-chairs, tables and foreign rugs, like a drawing-room in the open air, and enjoy the prospect at our ease. The valley is wide here and the banks are flat, showing a steep verge of crumbling alluvial mud next the river. Long belts of palm groves, tracts of young corn only an inch or two above the surface, and clusters of mud huts relieved now and then by a little whitewashed cupola or a stumpy minaret, succeed each other on both sides of the river, while the horizon is bounded to right and left by long ranges of yellow limestone mountains, in the folds of which sleep inexpressibly tender shadows of pale violet and blue.

Thus the miles glide away, and by and by we approach Turra—a large, new-looking mud village, and the first of any

extent that we have yet seen.   Some of the houses are whitewashed ; a few have glass windows, and many seem to be
unfinished.   A space of white, stony, glaring plain separates
the village from the quarried mountains beyond, the flanks of
which show all gashed and hewn away.   One great cliff seems
to have been cut sheer off for a distance of perhaps half a mile.
Where the cuttings are fresh, the limestone comes out dazzling
white, and the long slopes of débris heaped against the foot of
the cliffs glisten like snow-drifts in the sun.   Yet the outer
surface of the mountains is orange-tawny, like the Pyramids.
As for the piles of rough-hewn blocks that lie ranged along the
bank ready for transport, they look like salt rather than stone.
Here lies moored a whole fleet of cargo boats, laden and
lading ; and along the tramway that extends from the river-
side to the quarries, we see long trains of mule-carts coming
and going.

For all the 'new buildings in Cairo, the Khedive's palaces,
the public offices, the smart modern villas, the glaring new
streets, the theatres, and foot-pavements, and cafés, all come
from these mountains—just as the Pyramids did, more than
six thousand years ago.   There are hieroglyphed tablets and
sculptured grottoes to be seen in the most ancient part of the
quarries, if one were inclined to stop for them at this early
stage of the journey ; and Champollion tells of two magnificent
outlines done in red ink upon the living rock by some master-
hand of Pharaonic times, the cutting of which was never even
begun.   A substantial new barrack and an esplanade planted
with sycamore figs bring the straggling village to an end.

And now, as the afternoon wanes, we draw near to a dense,
wide-spreading forest of stately date-palms on the western
bank, knowing that beyond them, though unseen, lie the
mounds of Memphis and all the wonders of Sakkârah.   Then
the sun goes down behind the Libyan hills ; and the palms
stand out black and bronzed against a golden sky ; and the
Pyramids, left far behind, look grey and ghostly in the
distance.

Presently, when it is quite dusk and the stars are out, we
moor for the night at Bedreshayn, which is the nearest point
for visiting Sakkârah.   There is a railway station here, and

also a considerable village, both lying back about half a mile from the river ; and the distance from Cairo, which is reckoned at fifteen miles by the line, is probably about eighteen by water.

Such was our first day on the Nile. And perhaps, before going farther on our way, I ought to describe the Philæ, and introduce Reïs Hassan and his crew.

A dahabeeyah, at the first glance, is more like a civic or an Oxford University barge, than anything in the shape of a boat with which we in England are familiar. It is shallow and flat-bottomed, and is adapted for either sailing or rowing. It carries two masts ; a big one near the prow, and a smaller one at the stern. The cabins are on deck, and occupy the after-part of the vessel ; and the roof of the cabins forms the raised deck, or open-air drawing-room already mentioned. This upper deck is reached from the lower deck by two little flights of steps, and is the exclusive territory of the passengers. The lower deck is the territory of the crew. A dahabeeyah is, in fact, not very unlike the Noah's Ark of our childhood, with this difference—the habitable part, instead of occupying the middle of the vessel, is all at one end, top-heavy and many-windowed ; while the fore-deck is not more than six feet above the level of the water. The hold, however, is under the lower deck, and so counterbalances the weight at the other end. Not to multiply comparisons unnecessarily, I may say that a large dahabeeyah reminds one of old pictures of the Bucentaur ; especially when the men are at their oars.

The kitchen—which is a mere shed like a Dutch oven in shape, and contains only a charcoal stove and a row of stew-pans—stands between the big mast and the prow, removed as far as possible from the passengers' cabins. In this position the cook is protected from a favourable wind by his shed ; but in the case of a contrary wind he is screened by an awning. How, under even the most favourable circumstances, these men can serve up the elaborate dinners which are the pride of a Nile cook's heart, is sufficiently wonderful ; but how they achieve the same results when wind-storms and sand-storms are blowing, and every breath is laden with the fine grit of the desert, is little short of miraculous.

Thus far, all dahabeeyahs are alike. The cabin arrangements differ, however, according to the size of the boat; and it must be remembered that in describing the Philæ, I describe a dahabeeyah of the largest build—her total length from stem to stern being just one hundred feet, and the width of her upper deck at the broadest part little short of twenty.

Our floor being on a somewhat lower level than the men's deck, we went down three steps to the entrance door, on each side of which was an external cupboard, one serving as a store-room and the other as a pantry. This door led into a passage out of which opened four sleeping-cabins, two on each side. These cabins measured about eight feet in length by four and a half in width, and contained a bed, a chair, a fixed washing-stand, a looking-glass against the wall, a shelf, a row of hooks, and under each bed two large drawers for clothes. At the end of this little passage another door opened into the dining saloon —a spacious, cheerful room, some twenty-three or twenty-four feet long, situate in the widest part of the boat, and lighted by four windows on each side and a skylight. The panelled walls and ceiling were painted in white picked out with gold; a cushioned divan covered with a smart woollen reps ran along each side; and a gay Brussels carpet adorned the floor. The dining-table stood in the centre of the room; and there was ample space for a piano, two little bookcases, and several chairs. The window-curtains and portières were of the same reps as the divan, the prevailing colours being scarlet and orange. Add a couple of mirrors in gilt frames; a vase of flowers on the table (for we were rarely without flowers of some sort, even in Nubia, where our daily bouquet had to be made with a few bean blossoms and castor-oil berries); plenty of books; the gentlemen's guns and sticks in one corner; and the hats of all the party hanging in the spaces between the windows; and it will be easy to realise the homely, habitable look of our general sitting-room.

Another door and passage opening from the upper end of the saloon led to three more sleeping-rooms, two of which were single and one double; a bath-room; a tiny back staircase leading to the upper deck; and the stern cabin saloon. This last, following the form of the stern, was semicircular, lighted by eight windows, and surrounded by a divan. Under this, as under the saloon divans, there ran a row of deep drawers, which, being fairly divided, held our clothes, wine, and books. The entire length of the dahabeeyah being exactly one hundred feet, I take the cabin part to have occupied about fifty-six or fifty-seven feet (that is to say, about six or seven feet over the exact half), and the lower deck to have measured the remaining forty-three feet. But these dimensions, being given from memory, are approximate.

For the crew there was no sleeping accommodation whatever, unless they chose to creep into the hold among the luggage and packing-cases. But this they never did. They just rolled themselves up at night, heads and all, in rough brown blankets, and lay about the lower deck like dogs.

The Reïs, or captain, the steersman, and twelve sailors, the dragoman, head cook, assistant cook, two waiters, and the boy who cooked for the crew, completed our equipment. Reïs Hassan—short, stern-looking, authoritative—was a Cairo Arab. The dragoman, Elias Talhamy, was a Syrian of Beyrout. The two waiters, Michael and Habîb, and the head cook (a wizened old *cordon bleu* named Hassan Bedawee) were also Syrians. The steersman and five of the sailors were from Thebes; four belonged to a place near Philæ; one came from a village opposite Kom Ombo ; one from Cairo, and two were Nubians from Assuân. They were of all shades, from yellowish bronze to a hue not far removed from black ; and though, at the first mention of it, nothing more incongruous can well be imagined than a sailor in petticoats and a turban, yet these men in their loose blue gowns, bare feet, and white muslin turbans, looked not only picturesque, but dressed exactly as they should be. They were for the most part fine young men, slender but powerful, square in the shoulders, like the ancient Egyptian statues, with the same slight legs and long flat feet. More docile, active, good-tempered, friendly fellows never pulled an oar. Simple and trustful as children, frugal as anchorites, they worked cheerfully from sunrise to sunset, sometimes towing the dahabeeyah on a rope all day long, like barge-horses ; sometimes punting for hours, which is the hardest work of all ; yet always singing at their task, always smiling when spoken to, and made as happy as princes with a handful of coarse Egyptian tobacco, or a bundle of fresh sugar-canes bought for a few pence by the river-side. We soon came to know them all by name—Mehemet Ali, Salame, Khalîfeh, Riskali, Hassan, Mûsa, and so on ; and as none of us ever went on shore without one or two of them to act as guards and attendants, and as the poor fellows were constantly getting bruised hands or feet, and coming to the upper deck to be doctored, a feeling of genuine friendliness was speedily established between us.

The ordinary pay of a Nile sailor is two pounds a month, with an additional allowance of about three and sixpence a month for flour. Bread is their staple food, and they make it themselves at certain places along the river where there are large public ovens for the purpose. This bread, which is cut up in slices and dried in the sun, is as brown as gingerbread and as hard as biscuit. They eat it soaked in hot water, flavoured with oil, pepper, and salt, and stirred in with boiled lentils till the whole becomes of the colour, flavour, and consistence of thick pea-soup. Except on grand occasions, such as Christmas Day or the anniversary of the Flight of the Prophet, when the passengers treat them to a sheep, this mess of bread and lentils, with a little coffee twice a day, and now and then a handful of dates, constitutes their only food throughout the journey.

The Nile season is the Nile sailors' harvest-time. When the warm weather sets in and the travellers migrate with the swallows, these poor fellows disperse in all directions ; some to seek a living as porters in Cairo ; others to their homes in Middle and Upper Egypt where, for about fourpence a day, they take hire as labourers, or work at Shâdûf irrigation till the Nile again overspreads the land. The Shâdûf work is hard, and a man has to keep on for nine hours out of every twenty-four ; but he prefers it, for the most part, to employment in the government sugar-factories, where the wages average at about the same rate, but are paid in bread, which, being doled out by unscrupulous inferiors, is too often of light weight and bad quality. The sailors who succeed in getting a berth on board a cargo-boat for the summer are the most fortunate.

Our captain, pilot, and crew were all Mohammedans. The

cook and his assistant were Syrian Mohammedans. The dragoman and waiters were Christians of the Syrian Latin church. Only one out of the fifteen natives could write or read ; and that one was a sailor named Egendi, who acted as a sort of second mate. He used sometimes to write letters for the others, holding a scrap of tumbled paper across the palm of his left hand, and scrawling rude Arabic characters with a reed-pen of his own making. This Egendi, though perhaps the least interesting of the crew, was a man of many accomplishments—an excellent comic actor, a bit of a shoe-maker, and a first-rate barber. More than once, when we happened to be stationed far from any village, he shaved his messmates all round, and turned them out with heads as smooth as billiard balls.

There are, of course, good and bad Mohammedans as there are good and bad churchmen of every denomination ; and we had both sorts on board. Some of the men were very devout, never failing to perform their ablutions and say their prayers at sunrise and sunset. Others never dreamed of doing so. Some would not touch wine—had never tasted it in their lives, and would have suffered any extremity rather than break the law of their Prophet. Others had a nice taste in clarets, and a delicate appreciation of the respective merits of rum or whisky punch. It is, however, only fair to add that we never gave them these things except on special occasions, as on Christmas Day, or when they had been wading in the river, or in some other way undergoing extra fatigue in our service. Nor do I believe there was a man on board who would have spent a para of his scanty earnings on any drink stronger than coffee. Coffee and tobacco are, indeed, the only luxuries in which the Egyptian peasant indulges ; and our poor fellows were never more grateful than when we distributed among them a few pounds of cheap native tobacco. This abominable mixture sells in the bazaars at sixpence the pound, the plant from which it is gathered being raised from inferior seed in a soil chemically unsuitable, because wholly devoid of potash.

Also it is systematically spoiled in the growing. Instead of being nipped off when green and dried in the shade, the leaves are allowed to wither on the stalk before they are gathered. The result is a kind of rank hay without strength or flavour, which is smoked by only the very poorest class, and carefully avoided by all who can afford to buy Turkish or Syrian tobacco.

Twice a day, after their midday and evening meals, our sailors were wont to sit in a circle and solemnly smoke a certain big pipe of the kind known as a hubble-bubble. This hubble-bubble (which was of most primitive make and consisted of a cocoa-nut and two sugar-canes) was common property; and, being filled by the captain, went round from hand to hand, from mouth to mouth, while it lasted.

They smoked cigarettes at other times, and seldom went on shore without a tobacco-pouch and a tiny book of cigarette-papers. Fancy a bare-legged Arab making cigarettes! No Frenchman, however, could twist them up more deftly, or smoke them with a better grace.

A Nile sailor's service expires with the season, so that he is generally a landsman for about half the year; but the captain's appointment is permanent. He is expected to live in Cairo, and is responsible for his dahabeeyah during the summer months, while it lies up at Boulak. Reïs Hassan had a wife and a comfortable little home on the outskirts of Old Cairo, and was looked upon as a well-to-do personage among his fellows. He received four pounds a month all the year round from the owner of the Philæ—a magnificent broad-shouldered Arab of about six foot nine, with a delightful smile, the manners of a gentleman, and the rapacity of a Shylock.

Our men treated us to a concert that first night, as we lay moored under the bank near Bedreshayn. Being told that it was customary to provide musical instruments, we had given them leave to buy a tar and darabukkeh before starting. The tar, or tambourine, was pretty enough, being made of rosewood inlaid with mother-of-pearl; but a more barbarous affair than the darabukkeh was surely never constructed. This primitive drum is about a foot and a half in length, funnel-shaped, moulded of sun-dried clay like the kullehs, and covered over at the top with strained parchment. It is held under the left arm and played like a tom-tom with the fingers of the right hand; and it weighs about four pounds. We would willingly have added a double pipe or a cocoa-nut fiddle [1] to the strength of the band, but none of our men could play them. The tar and darabukkeh, however, answered the purpose well enough, and were perhaps better suited to their strange singing than more tuneful instruments.

We had just finished dinner when they began. First came a prolonged wail that swelled, and sank, and swelled again, and at last died away. This was the principal singer leading off with the keynote. The next followed suit on the third of the key; and finally all united in one long, shrill descending

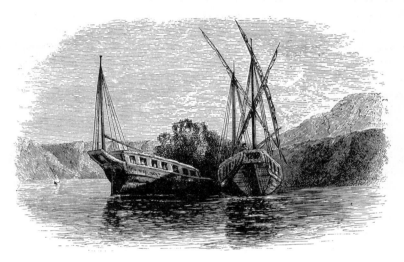

NATIVE CANGIAS.

cry, like a yawn, or a howl, or a combination of both. This, twice repeated, preluded their performance and worked them up, apparently, to the necessary pitch of musical enthusiasm. The primo tenore then led off in a quavering roulade, at the end of which he slid into a melancholy chant to which the rest sang chorus. At the close of each verse they yawned and howled again; while the singer, carried away by his emotions, broke out every now and then into a repetition of the same amazing and utterly indescribable vocal wriggle with which he

[1] Arabic—*Kemengeh.*

had begun.   Whenever he did this, the rest held their breath
in respectful admiration, and uttered an approving " Ah !"—
which is here the customary expression of applause.

We thought their music horrible that first night, I remember;
though we ended, as I believe most travellers do, by liking it.
We, however, paid them the compliment of going upon deck
and listening to their performance.   As a night-scene, nothing
could be more picturesque than this group of turbaned Arabs
sitting in a circle, cross-legged, with a lantern in the midst.
The singer quavered ; the musicians thrummed ; the rest softly
clapped their hands to time, and waited their turn to chime in
with the chorus.   Meanwhile the lantern lit up their swarthy
faces and their glittering teeth.   The great mast towered up
into the darkness.   The river gleamed below.   The stars shone
overhead.   We felt we were indeed strangers in a strange land.

CHAPTER IV.

SAKKÂRAH AND MEMPHIS.

HAVING arrived at Bedreshayn after dark and there moored for the night, we were roused early next morning by the furious squabbling and chattering of some fifty or sixty men and boys who, with a score or two of little rough-coated, depressed-look-ing donkeys, were assembled on the high bank above. Seen thus against the sky, their tattered garments fluttering in the wind, their brown arms and legs in frantic movement, they looked like a troop of mad monkeys let loose. Every moment the uproar grew shriller. Every moment more men, more boys, more donkeys, appeared upon the scene. It was as if some new Cadmus had been sowing boys and donkeys broad-cast, and they had all come up at once for our benefit.

Then it appeared that Talhamy, knowing how eight donkeys would be wanted for our united forces, had sent up to the village for twenty-five, intending, with perhaps more wisdom than justice, to select the best and dismiss the others. The result was overwhelming. Misled by the magnitude of the order and concluding that Cook's party had arrived, every man, boy, and donkey in Bedreshayn and the neighbouring village of Mîtrahîneh had turned out in hot haste and rushed down to the river ; so that by the time breakfast was over there were steeds enough in readiness for all the English in Cairo. I pass over the tumult that ensued when our party at last mounted the eight likeliest beasts and rode away, leaving the indignant multitude to disperse at leisure.

And now our way lies over a dusty flat, across the railway

line, past the long straggling village, and through the famous
plantations known as the Palms of Memphis.   There is a
crowd of patient-looking fellaheen at the little whitewashed
station, waiting for the train, and the usual rabble of clamorous
water, bread, and fruit-sellers.   Bedreshayn, though a collection of mere mud hovels, looks pretty, nestling in the midst of
stately date-palms.   Square pigeon-towers, embedded round the
top with layers of wide-mouthed pots and stuck with rows of
leafless acacia-boughs like ragged banner-poles, stand up at
intervals among the huts.   The pigeons go in and out of the
pots, or sit preening their feathers on the branches.   The dogs
dash out and bark madly at us, as we go by.   The little brown
children pursue us with cries of " Bakhshîsh!"   The potter,
laying out rows of soft, grey, freshly-moulded clay bowls and
kullehs[1] to bake in the sun, stops open-mouthed, and stares as
if he had never seen a European till this moment.   His young
wife snatches up her baby and pulls her veil more closely over
her face, fearing the evil eye.

   The village being left behind, we ride on through one long
palm grove after another ; now skirting the borders of a large
sheet of tranquil back-water ; now catching a glimpse of the
far-off pyramids of Ghîzeh, now passing between the huge
irregular mounds of crumbled clay which mark the site of
Memphis.   Next beyond these we come out upon a high embanked road some twenty feet above the plain, which here
spreads out like a wide lake and spends its last dark-brown
alluvial wave against the yellow rocks which define the edge of
the desert.   High on this barren plateau, seen for the first time
in one unbroken panoramic line, there stands a solemn company
of pyramids ; those of Sakkârah straight before us, those of
Dahshûr to the left, those of Abusir to the right, and the great
Pyramids of Ghîzeh always in the remotest distance.

   It might be thought there would be some monotony in such
a scene, and but little beauty.   On the contrary, however, there
is beauty of a most subtle and exquisite kind—transcendent
beauty of colour, and atmosphere, and sentiment ; and no

---

[1] The goolah, or kulleh, is a porous water-jar of sun-dried Nile mud.
These jars are made of all sizes and in a variety of remarkably graceful
forms, and cost from about one farthing to twopence apiece.

monotony either in the landscape or in the forms of the pyramids. One of these which we are now approaching is built in a succession of platforms gradually decreasing towards the top. Another down yonder at Dahshûr curves outward at the angles, half dome, half pyramid, like the roof of the Palais de Justice in Paris. No two are of precisely the same size, or built at precisely the same angle ; and each cluster differs somehow in the grouping.

Then again the colouring !—colouring not to be matched with any pigments yet invented. The Libyan rocks, like rusty gold—the paler hue of the driven sand-slopes—the warm maize of the nearer Pyramids which, seen from this distance, takes a tender tint of rose, like the red bloom on an apricot—the delicate tone of these objects against the sky—the infinite gradation of that sky, soft and pearly towards the horizon, blue and burning towards the zenith—the opalescent shadows, pale blue, and violet, and greenish-grey, that nestle in the hollows of the rock and the curves of the sand-drifts—all this is beautiful in a way impossible to describe, and alas ! impossible to copy. Nor does the lake-like plain with its palm-groves and corn-flats form too tame a foreground. It is exactly what is wanted to relieve that glowing distance.

And now, as we follow the zigzags of the road, the new pyramids grow gradually larger ; the sun mounts higher ; the heat increases. We meet a train of camels, buffaloes, shaggy brown sheep, men, women, and children of all ages. The camels are laden with bedding, rugs, mats, and crates of poultry, and carry, besides, two women with babies and one very old man. The younger men drive the tired beasts. The rest follow behind. The dust rises after them in a cloud. It is evidently the migration of a family of three, if not four generations. One cannot help being struck by the patriarchal simplicity of the incident. Just thus, with flocks and herds and all his clan, went Abraham into the land of Canaan close upon four thousand years ago ; and one at least of these Sakkârah pyramids was even then the oldest building in the world.

It is a touching and picturesque procession—much more picturesque than ours, and much more numerous ; notwithstanding that our united forces, including donkey-boys, porters, and

miscellaneous hangers-on, number nearer thirty than twenty
persons.   For there are the M. B.s and their nephew, and L.
and the Writer, and L.'s maid, and Talhamy, all on donkeys ;
and then there are the owners of the donkeys, also on
donkeys ; and then every donkey has a boy ; and every boy has
a donkey ; and every donkey-boy's donkey has an inferior boy
in attendance.   Our style of dress, too, however convenient, is
not exactly in harmony with the surrounding scenery ; and one
cannot but feel, as these draped and dusty pilgrims pass us on
the road, that we cut a sorry figure with our hideous palm-leaf
hats, green veils, and white umbrellas.

But the most amazing and incongruous personage in our
whole procession is unquestionably George.   Now George is
an English north-country groom whom the M. B.s have brought
out from the wilds of Lancashire, partly because he is a good
shot and may be useful to " Master Alfred " after birds and
crocodiles ; and partly from a well-founded belief in his general
abilities.   And George, who is a fellow of infinite jest and
infinite resource, takes to Eastern life as a duckling to the water.
He picks up Arabic as if it were his mother tongue.   He skins
birds like a practised taxidermist.   He can even wash and iron
on occasion.   He is, in short, groom, footman, housemaid,
laundry-maid, stroke oar, gamekeeper, and general factotum
all in one.   And besides all this, he is gifted with a comic
gravity of countenance that no surprises and no disasters can
upset for a moment.   To see this worthy anachronism canter-
ing along in his groom's coat and gaiters, livery-buttons, spotted
neckcloth, tall hat, and all the rest of it ; his long legs dangling
within an inch of the ground on either side of the most diminu-
tive of donkeys ; his double-barrelled fowling-piece under his
arm, and that imperturbable look in his face, one would have
sworn that he and Egypt were friends of old, and that he had
been brought up on pyramids from his earliest childhood.

It is a long and shelterless ride from the palms to the
desert ; but we come to the end of it at last, mounting just
such another sand-slope as that which leads up from the Ghîzeh
road to the foot of the Great Pyramid.   The edge of the
plateau here rises abruptly from the plain in one long range of
low perpendicular cliffs pierced with dark mouths of rock-cut

sepulchres, while the sand-slope by which we are climbing pours down through a breach in the rock, as an Alpine snow-drift flows through a mountain gap from the ice-level above.

And now, having dismounted through compassion for our unfortunate little donkeys, the first thing we observe is the curious mixture of débris underfoot. At Ghîzeh one treads only sand and pebbles ; but here at Sakkârah the whole plateau is thickly strewn with scraps of broken pottery, lime-stone, marble, and alabaster ; flakes of green and blue glaze ; bleached bones ; shreds of yellow linen ; and lumps of some odd-looking dark brown substance, like dried-up sponge. Presently some one picks up a little noseless head of one of the common blue-ware funereal statuettes, and immediately we all fall to work, grubbing for treasure—a pure waste of precious time ; for though the sand is full of débris, it has been sifted so often and so carefully by the Arabs that it no longer contains anything worth looking for. Meanwhile, one finds a fragment of iridescent glass—another, a morsel of shattered vase—a third, an opaque bead of some kind of yellow paste. And then, with a shock which the present writer, at all events, will not soon forget, we suddenly discover that these scattered bones are human—that those linen shreds are shreds of cerement cloths—that yonder odd-looking brown lumps are rent fragments of what once was living flesh ! And now for the first time we realise that every inch of this ground on which we are standing, and all these hillocks and hollows and pits in the sand, are violated graves.

" Ce n'est que le premier pas que coûte." We soon became quite hardened to such sights, and learned to rummage among dusty sepulchres with no more compunction than would have befitted a gang of professional body-snatchers. These are experiences upon which one looks back afterwards with wonder, and something like remorse ; but so infectious is the universal callousness, and so overmastering is the passion for relic-hunt-ing, that I do not doubt we should again do the same things under the same circumstances. Most Egyptian travellers, if questioned, would have to make a similar confession. Shocked at first, they denounce with horror the whole system of sepulchral excavation, legal as well as predatory ; acquiring,

however, a taste for scarabs and funerary statuettes, they soon
begin to buy with eagerness the spoils of the dead ; finally,
they forget all their former scruples, and ask no better fortune
than to discover and confiscate a tomb for themselves.

Notwithstanding that I had first seen the Pyramids of
Ghîzeh, the size of the Sakkârah group—especially of the
Pyramid in platforms—took me by surprise. They are all
smaller than the Pyramids of Khufu and Khafra, and would no
doubt look sufficiently insignificant if seen with them in close
juxtaposition ; but taken by themselves they are quite vast
enough for grandeur. As for the Pyramid in platforms (which
is the largest at Sakkârah, and next largest to the Pyramid of
Khafra) its position is so fine, its architectural style so exceptional, its age so immense, that one altogether loses sight of
these questions of relative magnitude. If Egyptologists are
right in ascribing the royal title hieroglyphed on the inner door
of this pyramid to Ouenephes, the fourth king of the First
Dynasty, then it is the most ancient building in the world. It
had been standing from five to seven hundred years when King
Khufu began his Great Pyramid at Ghîzeh. It was over two
thousand years old when Abraham was born. It is now about
six thousand eight hundred years old according to Manetho
and Mariette, or about four thousand eight hundred according
to the computation of Bunsen. One's imagination recoils upon
the brink of such a gulf of time.

The door of this pyramid was carried off, with other
precious spoils, by Lepsius, and is now in the museum at
Berlin. The evidence that identifies the inscription is tolerably
direct. According to Manetho, an Egyptian historian who
wrote in Greek and lived in the reign of Ptolemy Philadelphus,
King Ouenephes built for himself a pyramid at a place called
Kokhome. Now a tablet discovered in the Serapeum by
Mariette gives the name of Ka-kem to the necropolis of
Sakkârah ; and as the pyramid in stages is not only the largest
on this platform, but is also the only one in which a royal
cartouche has been found, the conclusion seems obvious.

When a building has already stood for five or six thousand
years in a climate where mosses and lichens, and all those
natural signs of age to which we are accustomed in Europe

are unknown, it is not to be supposed that a few centuries more or less can tell upon its outward appearance ; yet to my thinking the pyramid of Ouenephes looks older than those of Ghîzeh.   If this be only fancy, it gives one, at all events, the impression of belonging structurally to a ruder architectural period.   The idea of a monument composed of diminishing platforms is in its nature more primitive than that of a smooth four-sided pyramid.   We remarked that the masonry on one side—I think on the side facing eastwards—was in a much more perfect condition than on either of the others.

Wilkinson describes the interior as "a hollow dome supported here and there by wooden rafters," and states that the sepulchral chamber was lined with blue porcelain tiles.[1]   We would have liked to go inside, but this is no longer possible, the entrance being blocked by a recent fall of masonry.

Making up now for lost time, we rode on as far as the house built in 1850 for Mariette's accommodation during the excavation of the Serapeum—a labour which extended over a period of more than four years.

The Serapeum, it need hardly be said, is the famous and long-lost sepulchral temple of the sacred bulls.   These bulls (honoured by the Egyptians as successive incarnations of Osiris) inhabited the temple of Apis at Memphis while they lived ; and, being mummied after death, were buried in catacombs prepared for them in the desert.   In 1850, Mariette, travelling in the interests of the French Government, discovered both the temple and the catacombs, being, according to his own narrative, indebted for the clue to a certain passage in Strabo, which describes the Temple of Serapis as being situate in a district where the sand was so drifted by the wind that the approach to it was in danger of being overwhelmed ; while the sphinxes on either side of the great avenue were already more or less buried, some having only their heads above the surface.   "If Strabo had not written this passage," says Mariette, "it is probable that the Serapeum would still be lost under the sands

---

[1] Some of these tiles are to be seen in the Egyptian department of the British Museum.   They are not blue, but of a bluish green.   For a view of the sepulchral chamber, see Maspero's *Archéologie Egyptienne*, Fig. 230, p. 256.   [Note to the Second Edition.]

of the necropolis of Sakkârah.   One day, however (in 1850), being attracted to Sakkârah by my Egyptological studies, I perceived the head of a sphinx showing above the surface.   It evidently occupied its original position.   Close by lay a libation-table on which was engraved a hieroglyphic inscription to Apis-Osiris.   Then that passage in Strabo came to my memory, and I knew that beneath my feet lay the avenue leading to the long and vainly sought Serapeum.   Without saying a word to any one, I got some workmen together and we began excavating.   The beginning was difficult ; but soon the lions, the peacocks, the Greek statues of the Dromos, the inscribed tablets of the Temple of Nectanebo [1] rose up from the sands.   Thus was the Serapeum discovered."

The house—a slight, one-storied building on a space of rocky platform—looks down upon a sandy hollow which now presents much the same appearance that it must have presented when Mariette was first reminded of the fortunate passage in Strabo.   One or two heads of sphinxes peep up here and there in a ghastly way above the sand, and mark the line of the great avenue.   The upper half of a boy riding on a peacock, apparently of rude execution, is also visible.   The rest is already as completely overwhelmed as if it had never been uncovered. One can scarcely believe that only twenty years ago, the whole place was entirely cleared at so vast an expenditure of time and labour.   The work, as I have already mentioned, took four years to complete.   This avenue alone was six hundred feet in length and bordered by an army of sphinxes, one hundred and forty-one of which were found *in situ*.   As the excavation neared the end of the avenue, the causeway, which followed a gradual descent between massive walls, lay seventy feet below the surface.   The labour was immense, and the difficulties were innumerable.   The ground had to be contested inch by inch. " In certain places," says Mariette, " the sand was fluid, so to speak, and baffled us like water continually driven back and seeking to regain its level." [2]

[1] Nectanebo I and Nectanebo II were the last native Pharaohs of ancient Egypt, and flourished between B.C. 378 and B.C. 340. An earlier temple must have preceded the Serapeum built by Nectanebo I.

[2] For an excellent and exact account of the Serapeum and the monu-

　　If, however, the toil was great, so also was the reward.　A main avenue terminated by a semicircular platform, around which stood statues of famous Greek philosophers and poets ; a second avenue at right angles to the first ; the remains of the great Temple of the Serapeum ; three smaller temples ; and three distinct groups of Apis catacombs, were brought to light.　A descending passage opening from a chamber in the great Temple led to the catacombs—vast labyrinths of vaults and passages hewn out of the solid rock on which the Temples were built.　These three groups of excavations represent three epochs of Egyptian history.　The first and most ancient series consists of isolated vaults dating from the XVIIIth to the XXIInd dynasty ; that is to say, from about B.C. 1703 to B.C. 980.　The second group, which dates from the reign of Sheshonk I (XXIInd dynasty, B.C. 980) to that of Tirhakah, the last king of the XXVth dynasty, is more systematically planned, and consists of one long tunnel bordered on each side by a row of funereal chambers.　The third belongs to the Greek period, beginning with Psammetichus I (XXVIth dynasty, B.C. 665) and ending with the latest Ptolemies.　Of these, the first are again choked with sand ; the second are considered unsafe ; and the third only is accessible to travellers.

　　After a short but toilsome walk, and some delay outside a prison-like door at the bottom of a steep descent, we were admitted by the guardian—a gaunt old Arab with a lantern in his hand.　It was not an inviting looking place within. The outer daylight fell upon a rough step or two, beyond which all was dark.　We went in.　A hot, heavy atmosphere met us on the threshold ; the door fell to with a dull clang, the echoes of which went wandering away as if into the central recesses of the earth ; the Arab chattered and gesticulated.　He was telling us that we were now in the great vestibule, and that it measured ever so many feet in this and that direction ; but we could see nothing—neither the vaulted roof overhead, nor the walls on any side, nor even the ground beneath our feet.　It was like the darkness of infinite space.

　　A lighted candle was then given to each person, and the

ments there discovered, see M. Arthur Rhoné's *L'Égypte en Petites Journées,* of which a new edition is now in the press.　[Note to Second Edition.]

Arab led the way.   He went dreadfully fast, and it seemed at
every step as if one were on the brink of some frightful chasm.
Gradually, however, our eyes became accustomed to the gloom,
and we found that we had passed out of the vestibule into the
first great corridor.   All was vague, mysterious, shadowy.   A
dim perspective loomed out of the darkness.   The lights
twinkled and flitted, like wandering sparks of stars.   The Arab
held his lantern to the walls here and there, and showed us
some votive tablets inscribed with records of pious visits paid
by devout Egyptians to the sacred tombs.   Of these they
found five hundred when the catacombs were first opened ;
but Mariette sent nearly all to the Louvre.

A few steps farther, and we came to the tombs—a succession of great vaulted chambers hewn out at irregular distances
along both sides of the central corridor, and sunk some six or
eight feet below the surface.   In the middle of each chamber
stood an enormous sarcophagus of polished granite.   The Arab,
flitting on ahead like a black ghost, paused a moment before
each cavernous opening, flashed the light of his lantern on the
sarcophagus, and sped away again, leaving us to follow as we
could.

So we went on, going every moment deeper into the solid
rock, and farther from the open air and the sunshine.   Thinking
it would be cold underground, we had brought warm wraps in
plenty ; but the heat, on the contrary, was intense, and the
atmosphere stifling.   We had not calculated on the dryness of
the place, nor had we remembered that ordinary mines and
tunnels are cold because they are damp.   But here for incalculable ages—for thousands of years probably before the Nile
had even cut its path through the rocks of Silsilis—a cloudless
African sun had been pouring its daily floods of light and heat
upon the dewless desert overhead.   The place might well be
unendurable.   It was like a great oven stored with the slowly
accumulated heat of cycles so remote, and so many, that the
earliest periods of Egyptian history seem, when compared with
them, to belong to yesterday.

Having gone on thus for a distance of nearly two hundred
yards, we came to a chamber containing the first hieroglyphed
sarcophagus we had yet seen ; all the rest being polished, but

plain. Here the Arab paused ; and finding access provided by means of a flight of wooden steps, we went down into the chamber, walked round the sarcophagus, peeped inside by the help of a ladder, and examined the hieroglyphs with which it is covered. Enormous as they look from above, one can form no idea of the bulk of these huge monolithic masses except from the level on which they stand. This sarcophagus, which dates from the reign of Amasis, of the XXVIth dynasty, measured fourteen feet in length by eleven in height, and consisted of a single block of highly-wrought black granite. Four persons might sit in it round a small card-table, and play a rubber comfortably.

From this point the corridor branches off for another two hundred yards or so, leading always to more chambers and more sarcophagi, of which last there are altogether twenty-four. Three only are inscribed ; none measure less than from thirteen to fourteen feet in length ; and all are empty. The lids in every instance have been pushed back a little way, and some are fractured ; but the spoilers have been unable wholly to remove them. According to Mariette, the place was pillaged by the early Christians, who, besides carrying off whatever they could find in the way of gold and jewels, seem to have destroyed the mummies of the bulls, and razed the great Temple nearly to the ground. Fortunately, however, they either overlooked, or left as worthless, some hundreds of exquisite bronzes and the five hundred votive tablets before mentioned, which, as they record not only the name and rank of the visitor, but also, with few exceptions, the name and year of the reigning Pharaoh, afford invaluable historical data, and are likely to do more than any previously discovered documents towards clearing up disputed points of Egyptian chronology.

It is a curious fact that one out of the three inscribed sarcophagi should bear the oval of Cambyses—that Cambyses of whom it is related that, having desired the priests of Memphis to bring before him the God Apis, he drew his dagger in a transport of rage and contempt, and stabbed the animal in the thigh. According to Plutarch, he slew the beast and cast out its body to the dogs ; according to Herodotus, " Apis lay some time pining in the temple, but at last died of his wound, and the priests buried him secretly ;" but according to one of these precious Serapeum tablets, the wounded bull did not die till the fourth year of the reign of Darius. So wonderfully does modern discovery correct and illustrate tradition.

And now comes the sequel to this ancient story in the shape of an anecdote related by M. About, who tells how Mariette, being recalled suddenly to Paris some months after the opening of the Serapeum, found himself without the means of carrying away all his newly-excavated antiquities, and so buried fourteen cases in the desert, there to await his return. One of these cases contained an Apis mummy which had escaped discovery by the early Christians ; and this mummy was that of the identical Apis stabbed by Cambyses. That the creature had actually survived his wound was proved by the condition of one of the thigh-bones, which showed unmistakable signs of both injury and healing.

Nor does the story end here. Mariette being gone, and having taken with him all that was most portable among his treasures, there came to Memphis one whom M. About indicates as "a young and august stranger" travelling in Egypt for his pleasure. The Arabs, tempted perhaps by a princely bakh- shîsh, revealed the secret of the hidden cases ; whereupon the Archduke swept off the whole fourteen, despatched them to Alexandria, and immediately shipped them for Trieste.[1] "Quant au coupable," says M. About, who professes to have had the story direct from Mariette, "il a fini si tragiquement dans un autre hemisphère que, tout bien pesé, je renonce à publier son nom." But through so transparent a disguise it is not difficult to identify the unfortunate hero of this curious anecdote.

The sarcophagus in which the Apis was found remains in the vaults of the Serapeum ; but we did not see it. Having come more than two hundred yards already, and being by this time wellnigh suffocated, we did not care to put two hundred yards more between ourselves and the light of day. So we turned back at the half distance—having, however, first burned a pan of magnesian powder, which flared up wildly for a few

---

[1] These objects, known as "The Miramar Collection," and catalogued by Professor Reinisch, are now removed to Vienna. [Note to Second Edition.]

seconds ; lit the huge gallery and all its cavernous recesses and the wondering faces of the Arabs ; and then went out with a plunge, leaving the darkness denser than before.

From hence, across a farther space of sand, we went in all the blaze of noon to the tomb of one Ti, a priest and commoner of the Fifth Dynasty, who married with a lady named Nefer-hotep-s, the granddaughter of a Pharaoh, and here built himself a magnificent tomb in the desert.

Of the façade of this tomb, which must originally have looked like a little temple, only two large pillars remain. Next comes a square courtyard surrounded by a roofless colonnade, from one corner of which a covered passage leads to two chambers. In the centre of the courtyard yawns an open pit some twenty-five feet in depth, with a shattered sarcophagus just visible in the gloom of the vault below. All here is limestone—walls, pillars, pavements, even the excavated débris with which the pit had been filled in when the vault was closed for ever. The quality of this limestone is close and fine like marble, and so white that, although the walls and columns of the courtyard are covered with sculptures of most exquisite execution and of the greatest interest, the reflected light is so intolerable, that we find it impossible to examine them with the interest they deserve. In the passage, however, where there is shade, and in the large chamber, where it is so dark that we can see only by the help of lighted candles, we find a succession of bas-reliefs so numerous and so closely packed that it would take half a day to see them properly. Ranged in horizontal parallel lines about a foot and a half in depth, these extraordinary pictures, row above row, cover every inch of wall-space from floor to ceiling. The relief is singularly low. I should doubt if it anywhere exceeds a quarter of an inch. The surface, which is covered with a thin film of very fine cement, has a quality and polish like ivory. The figures measure an average height of about twelve inches, and all are coloured.

Here, as in an open book, we have the biography of Ti. His whole life, his pleasures, his business, his domestic relations, are brought before us with just that faithful simplicity which makes the charm of Montaigne and Pepys. A child might read the pictured chronicles which illuminate these walls, and take as keen a pleasure in them as the wisest of archæologists.

Ti was a wealthy man, and his wealth was of the agricultural sort. He owned flocks and herds and vassals in plenty. He kept many kinds of birds and beasts—geese, ducks, pigeons, cranes, oxen, goats, asses, antelopes, and gazelles. He was fond of fishing and fowling, and used sometimes to go after crocodiles and hippopotamuses, which came down as low as Memphis in his time. He was a kind husband too, and a good father, and loved to share his pleasures with his family. Here we see him sitting in state with his wife and children, while professional singers and dancers perform before them. Yonder they walk out together and look on while the farm-servants are at work, and watch the coming in of the boats that bring home the produce of Ti's more distant lands. Here the geese are being driven home ; the cows are crossing a ford ; the oxen are ploughing ; the sower is scattering his seed ; the reaper plies his sickle ; the oxen tread the grain ; the corn is stored in the granary. There are evidently no independent tradesfolk in these early days of the world. Ti has his own artificers on his own estate, and all his goods and chattels are home-made. Here the carpenters are fashioning new furniture for the house ; the shipwrights are busy on new boats ; the potters mould pots ; the metal-workers smelt ingots of red gold. It is plain to see that Ti lived like a king within his own boundaries. He makes an imposing figure, too, in all these scenes, and, being represented about eight times as large as his servants, sits and stands a giant among pigmies. His wife (we must not forget that she was of the blood royal) is as big as himself ; and the children are depicted about half the size of their parents. Curiously enough, Egyptian art never outgrew this early naïveté. The great man remained a big man to the last days of the Ptolemies, and the fellah was always a dwarf.[1]

[1] A more exhaustive study of the funerary texts has of late revolutionised our interpretation of these, and similar sepulchral tableaux. The scenes they represent are not, as was supposed when this book was first written, mere episodes in the daily life of the deceased ; but are links in the elaborate story of his burial and his ghostly existence after death. The corn

Apart from these and one or two other mannerisms, nothing can be more natural than the drawing, or more spirited than the action, of all these men and animals. The most difficult and transitory movements are expressed with masterly certitude. The donkey kicks up his heels and brays —the crocodile plunges—the wild duck rises on the wing ; and the fleeting action is caught in each instance with a truthfulness that no Landseer could distance. The forms, which have none of the conventional stiffness of later Egyptian work, are modelled roundly and boldly, yet finished with exquisite precision and delicacy. The colouring, however, is purely decorative ; and being laid on in single tints, with no attempt at gradation or shading, conceals rather than enhances the beauty of the sculptures. These, indeed, are best seen where the colour is entirely rubbed off. The tints are yet quite brilliant in parts of the larger chamber ; but in the passage and courtyard, which have been excavated only a few years and are with difficulty kept clear from day to day, there is not a vestige of colour left. This is the work of the sand—that patient labourer whose office it is not only to preserve but to destroy. The sand secretes and preserves the work of the sculptor, but it effaces the work of the painter. In sheltered places where it accumulates passively like a snow-drift, it brings away only the surface-detail, leaving the under colours rubbed and dim. But nothing, as I had occasion constantly to remark in the course of the journey, removes colour so effectually as sand which is exposed to the shifting action of the wind.

This tomb, as we have seen, consists of a portico, a courtyard, two chambers, and a sepulchral vault ; but it also contains a secret passage of the kind known as a "serdab." These "serdabs," which are constructed in the thickness of the walls and have no entrances, seem to be peculiar to tombs of the Ancient Empire (*i.e.* the period of the Pyramid Kings) ; and

is sown, reaped, and gathered in order that it may be ground and made into funerary cakes ; the oxen, goats, gazelles, geese, and other live stock are destined for sacrificial offerings ; the pots, and furniture, and household goods are for burying with the mummy in his tomb ; and it is his "Ka," or ghostly double, that takes part in these various scenes, and not the living man. [Note to Second Edition.]

they contain statues of the deceased of all sizes, in wood, limestone, and granite. Twenty statues of Ti were here found immured in the serdab of his tomb, all broken save one—a spirited figure in limestone, standing about seven feet high,

and now in the museum at Boulak. This statue represents a fine young man in a white tunic, and is evidently a portrait. The features are regular ; the expression is good-natured ; the whole tournure of the head is more Greek than Egyptian. The flesh is painted of a yellowish brick tint, and the figure stands in the usual hieratic attitude, with the left leg advanced, the hands clenched, and the arms straightened close to the sides. One seems to know Ti so well after seeing the wonderful pictures in his tomb, that this charming statue interests one like the portrait of a familiar friend.[1]

HEAD OF TI.

How pleasant it was, after being suffocated in the Serapeum and broiled in the tomb of Ti, to return to Mariette's deserted house, and eat our luncheon on the cool stone terrace that looks northward over the desert ! Some wooden tables and benches are hospitably left here for the accommodation of travellers, and fresh water in ice-cold kullehs is provided by the old Arab guardian. The yards and offices at the back are full of broken statues and fragments of inscriptions in red and black granite. Two sphinxes from the famous avenue adorn the terrace, and look down upon their half-buried companions in the sand-hollow below. The yellow desert, barren and undulating, with a line of purple peaks on the horizon, reaches away into the far distance. To the right, under a jutting ridge of rocky plateau not two hundred yards from the house, yawns an open-mouthed black-looking cavern shored up with heavy beams and approached by a slope of débris. This is

---

[1] These statues were not mere portrait-statues ; but were designed as bodily habitations for the incorporeal ghost, or "*Ka*," which it was supposed needed a body, food, and drink, and must perish everlastingly if not duly supplied with these necessaries. Hence the whole system of burying food-offerings, furniture, stuffs, etc., in ancient Egyptian sepulchres. [Note to Second Edition.]

the forced entrance to the earlier vaults of the Serapeum, in one of which was found a mummy described by Mariette as that of an Apis, but pronounced by Brugsch to be the body of Prince Kha-em-uas, governor of Memphis and the favourite son of Rameses the Great.

This remarkable mummy, which looked as much like a bull as a man, was found covered with jewels and gold chains and precious amulets engraved with the name of Kha-em-uas, and had on its face a golden mask ; all which treasures are now to be seen in the Louvre. If it was the mummy of an Apis, then the jewels with which it was adorned were probably the offering of the prince at that time ruling in Memphis. If, on the contrary, it was the mummy of a man, then, in order to be buried in a place of peculiar sanctity, he probably usurped one of the vaults prepared for the god. The question is a curious one, and remains unsolved to this day ; but it could no doubt be settled at a glance by Professor Owen.[1]

Far more startling, however, than the discovery of either Apis or jewels, was the sight beheld by Mariette on first entering that long-closed sepulchral chamber. The mine being sprung and the opening cleared, he went in alone ; and there, on the thin layer of sand that covered the floor, he found the footprints of the workmen who, 3700 years [2] before, had laid that shapeless mummy in its tomb and closed the doors upon it, as they believed, for ever.

And now—for the afternoon is already waning fast—the donkeys are brought round, and we are told that it is time to move on. We have the site of Memphis and the famous prostrate colossus yet to see, and the long road lies all before us. So back we ride across the desolate sands ; and with a last, long, wistful glance at the pyramid in platforms, go down from the territory of the dead into the land of the living.

There is a wonderful fascination about this pyramid. One is never weary of looking at it—of repeating to one's self that it is indeed the oldest building on the face of the whole earth.

---

[1] The actual tomb of Prince Kha-em-uas has been found at Memphis by M. Maspero, within the last three or four years. [Note to Second Edition.]

[2] The date is Mariette's.

The king who erected it came to the throne, according to Manetho, about eighty years after the death of Mena, the founder of the Egyptian monarchy.   All we have of him is his pyramid ; all we know of him is his name.   And these belong, as it were, to the infancy of the human race.   In dealing with Egyptian dates, one is apt to think lightly of periods that count only by centuries ; but it is a habit of mind which leads to error, and it should be combated.   The present writer found it useful to be constantly comparing relative chronological eras ; as, for instance, in realising the immense antiquity of the Sakkârah pyramid, it is some help to remember that from the time when it was built by King Ouenephes to the time when King Khufu erected the great Pyramid of Ghîzeh, there probably lies a space of years equivalent to that which, in the history of England, extends from the date of the Conquest to the accession of George the Second.[1]   And yet Khufu himself—the Cheops of the Greek historians—is but a shadowy figure hovering upon the threshold of Egyptian history.

And now the desert is left behind, and we are nearing the palms that lead to Memphis.   We have of course been dipping into Herodotus—every one takes Herodotus up the Nile—and our heads are full of the ancient glories of this famous city. We know that Mena turned the course of the river in order to build it on this very spot, and that all the most illustrious Pharaohs adorned it with temples, palaces, pylons, and precious sculptures.   We had read of the great Temple of Ptah that Rameses the Great enriched with colossi of himself ; and of the sanctuary where Apis lived in state, taking his exercise in a pillared courtyard where every column was a statue ; and of the artificial lake, and the sacred groves, and the obelisks, and all the wonders of a city which even in its later days was one of the most populous in Egypt.

[1] There was no worship of Apis in the days of King Ouenephes, nor, indeed, until the reign of Kaiechos, more than one hundred and twenty years after his time.   But at some subsequent period of the Ancient Empire, his pyramid was appropriated by the priests of Memphis for the mummies of the Sacred Bulls.   This, of course, was done before any of the known Apis-catacombs were excavated.   There are doubtless many more of these catacombs yet undiscovered, nothing prior to the XVIIIth Dynasty having yet been found.

Thinking over these things by the way, we agree that it is well to have left Memphis till the last. We shall appreciate it the better for having first seen that other city on the edge of the desert to which, for nearly six thousand years, all Memphis was quietly migrating, generation after generation. We know now how poor folk laboured, and how great gentlemen amused themselves, in those early days when there were hundreds of country gentlemen like Ti, with town-houses at Memphis and villas by the Nile. From the Serapeum, too, buried and ruined as it is, one cannot but come away with a profound impression of the splendour and power of a religion which could command for its myths such faith, such homage, and such public works.

And now we are once more in the midst of the palm-woods, threading our way among the same mounds that we passed in the morning. Presently those in front strike away from the beaten road across a grassy flat to the right ; and the next moment we are all gathered round the brink of a muddy pool in the midst of which lies a shapeless block of blackened and corroded limestone. This, it seems, is the famous prostrate colossus of Rameses the Great, which belongs to the British nation, but which the British Government is too economical to remove.[1] So here it lies, face downward ; drowned once a year by the Nile ; visible only when the pools left by the inundation have evaporated, and all the muddy hollows are dried up. It is one of two which stood at the entrance to the great Temple of Ptah ; and by those who have gone down into the hollow and seen it from below in the dry season, it is reported of as a noble and very beautiful specimen of one of the best periods of Egyptian art.

Where, however, is the companion colossus ? Where is the Temple itself ? Where are the pylons, the obelisks, the avenues of sphinxes ? Where, in short, is Memphis ?

The dragoman shrugs his shoulders and points to the barren mounds among the palms.

They look like gigantic dust-heaps, and stand from thirty to forty feet above the plain. Nothing grows upon them, save

---

[1] This colossus is now raised upon a brick pedestal. [Note to Second Edition.]

here and there a tuft of stunted palm ; and their substance seems to consist chiefly of crumbled brick, broken potsherds, and fragments of limestone.   Some few traces of brick foundations and an occasional block or two of shaped stone are to be seen in places low down against the foot of one or two of the mounds ; but one looks in vain for any sign which might indicate the outline of a boundary wall, or the position of a great public building.

And is this all ?

No—not quite all.   There are some mud-huts yonder, in among the trees ; and in front of one of these we find a number of sculptured fragments—battered sphinxes, torsos without legs, sitting figures without heads—in green, black, and red granite.   Ranged in an irregular semicircle on the sward, they seem to sit in forlorn conclave, half solemn, half ludicrous, with the goats browsing round, and the little Arab children hiding behind them.

Near this, in another pool, lies another red granite colossus —not the fellow to that which we saw first, but a smaller one —also face downwards.

And this is all that remains of Memphis, eldest of cities—a few huge rubbish-heaps, a dozen or so of broken statues, and a name !   One looks round, and tries in vain to realise the lost splendours of the place.   Where is the Memphis that King Mena came from Thinis to found—the Memphis of Ouenephes, and Khufu, and Khafra, and all the early kings who built their pyramid-tombs in the adjacent desert ?   Where is the Memphis of Herodotus, of Strabo, of 'Abd-el-Latîf ?   Where are those stately ruins which, even in the middle ages, extended over a space estimated at " half a day's journey in every direction " ?   One can hardly believe that a great city ever flourished on this spot, or understand how it should have been effaced so utterly.   Yet here it stood—here where the grass is green, and the palms are growing, and the Arabs build their hovels on the verge of the inundation.   The great colossus marks the site of the main entrance to the Temple of Ptah.   It lies where it fell, and no man has moved it.   That tranquil sheet of palm-fringed back-water, beyond which we see the village of Mitrâhîneh and catch a distant glimpse of the pyramids of

Ghizeh, occupies the basin of a vast artificial lake excavated by Mena. The very name of Memphis survives in the dialect of the fellah, who calls the place of the mounds Tell Monf[1]— just as Sakkârah fossilises the name of Sokari, one of the special denominations of the Memphite Osiris.

No capital in the world dates so far back as this, or kept its place in history so long. Founded four thousand years before our era, it beheld the rise and fall of thirty-one dynasties ; it survived the rule of the Persian, the Greek, and the Roman ; it was, even in its decadence, second only to Alexandria in population and extent ; and it continued to be inhabited up to the time of the Arab invasion. It then became the quarry from which Fostât' (Old Cairo) was built ; and as the new city rose on the eastern bank, the people of Memphis quickly abandoned their ancient capital to desolation and decay.

Still a vast field of ruins remained. 'Abd-el-Latîf, writing at the commencement of the thirteenth century, speaks with enthusiasm of the colossal statues and lions, the enormous pedestals, the archways formed of only three stones, the bas-reliefs and other wonders that were yet to be seen upon the spot. Marco Polo, if his wandering tastes had led him to the Nile, might have found some of the palaces and temples of Memphis still standing ; and Sandys, who in A.D. 1610 went at least as far south of Cairo as Kafr el Iyat, says that " up the River for twenty miles space there was nothing but ruines." Since then, however, the very " ruines " have vanished ; the palms have had time to grow ; and modern Cairo has doubtless absorbed all the building material that remained from the middle ages.

Memphis is a place to read about, and think about, and remember ; but it is a disappointing place to see. To miss it, however, would be to miss the first link in the whole chain of monumental history which unites the Egypt of antiquity with the world of to-day. Those melancholy mounds and that heron-haunted lake must be seen, if only that they may take their due place in the picture-gallery of one's memory.

---

[1] *Tell:* Arabic for Mound. Many of these mounds preserve the ancient names of the cities they entomb ; as Tell Basta (Bubastis) ; Kóm Ombo (Ombos) ; etc. etc. *Tell* and *Kóm* are synonymous terms.

It had been a long day's work, but it came to an end at last ; and as we trotted our donkeys back towards the river, a gorgeous sunset was crimsoning the palms and pigeon-towers of Bedreshayn. Everything seemed now to be at rest. A buffalo, contemplatively chewing the cud, lay close against the path and looked at us without moving. The children and pigeons were gone to bed. The pots had baked in the sun and been taken in long since. A tiny column of smoke went up here and there from amid the clustered huts ; but there was scarcely a moving creature to be seen. Presently we passed a tall, beautiful fellah woman standing grandly by the wayside, with her veil thrown back and falling in long folds to her feet. She smiled, put out her hand, and murmured " Bakhshîsh !" Her fingers were covered with rings, and her arms with silver bracelets. She begged because to beg is honourable, and customary, and a matter of inveterate habit ; but she evidently neither expected nor needed the bakhshîsh she condescended to ask for.

A few moments more and the sunset has faded, the village is left behind, the last half-mile of plain is trotted over. And now—hungry, thirsty, dusty, worn out with new knowledge,. new impressions, new ideas—we are once more at home and at rest.

MITRÂHÎNEH.

CHAPTER V.

BEDRESHAYN TO MINIEH.

IT is the rule of the Nile to hurry up the river as fast as
possible, leaving the ruins to be seen as the boat comes back
with the current ; but this, like many another canon, is by no
means of universal application. The traveller who starts late
in the season has, indeed, no other course open to him. He
must press on with speed to the end of his journey, if he would
get back again at low Nile without being irretrievably stuck on
a sand-bank till the next inundation floats him off again. But
for those who desire not only to see the monuments, but to
follow, however superficially, the course of Egyptian history as
it is handed down through Egyptian art, it is above all things
necessary to start early and to see many things by the way.

For the history of ancient Egypt goes against the stream.
The earliest monuments lie between Cairo and Siout, while the
latest temples to the old gods are chiefly found in Nubia.
Those travellers, therefore, who hurry blindly forward with or
without a wind, now sailing, now tracking, now punting, passing
this place by night, and that by day, and never resting till they
have gained the farthest point of their journey, begin at the
wrong end and see all their sights in precisely inverse order.
Memphis and Sakkârah and the tombs of Beni Hassan should
undoubtedly be visited on the way up. So should El Kâb
and Tell el Amarna, and the oldest parts of Karnak and Luxor.
It is not necessary to delay long at any of these places. They
may be seen cursorily on the way up, and be more carefully
studied on the way down ; but they should be seen as they

come, no matter at what trifling cost of present delay, and
despite any amount of ignorant opposition. For in this way
only is it possible to trace the progression and retrogression of
the arts from the pyramid-builders to the Cæsars ; or to understand at the time, and on the spot, in what order that vast
and august procession of dynasties swept across the stage of
history.

For ourselves, as will presently be seen, it happened that we
could carry only a part of this programme into effect ; but that
part, happily, was the most important. We never ceased to
congratulate ourselves on having made acquaintance with the
Pyramids of Ghîzeh and Sakkârah before seeing the tombs of
the kings at Thebes ; and I feel that it is impossible to over-
estimate the advantage of studying the sculptures of the tomb
of Ti before one's taste is brought into contact with the debased
style of Denderah and Esneh. We began the Great Book, in
short, as it always should be begun—at its first page ; thereby
acquiring just that necessary insight without which many an
after-chapter must have lost more than half its interest.

If I seem to insist upon this point, it is because things contrary to custom need a certain amount of insistance, and are
sure to be met by opposition. No dragoman, for example,
could be made to understand the importance of historical
sequence in a matter of this kind ; especially in the case of a
contract trip. To him, Khufu, Rameses, and the Ptolemies are
one. As for the monuments, they are all ancient Egyptian,
and one is just as odd and unintelligible as another. He cannot quite understand why travellers come so far and spend so
much money to look at them ; but he sets it down to a habit
of harmless curiosity—by which he profits.

The truth is, however, that the mere sight-seeing of the Nile
demands some little reading and organising, if only to be
enjoyed. We cannot all be profoundly learned ; but we can
at least do our best to understand what we see—to get rid of
obstacles—to put the right thing in the right place. For the
land of Egypt is, as I have said, a Great Book—not very easy
reading, perhaps, under any circumstances ; but at all events
quite difficult enough already without the added puzzlement of
being read backwards.

And now our next point along the river, as well as our next
link in the chain of early monuments, was Beni Hassan, with its
famous rock-cut tombs of the XIIth dynasty; and Beni
Hassan was still more than a hundred and forty-five miles distant. We ought to have gone on again directly—to have
weighed anchor and made a few miles that very evening on
returning to the boats; but we insisted on a second day in the
same place. This, too, with the favourable wind still blowing.
It was against all rule and precedent. The captain shook his
head, the dragoman remonstrated, in vain.

"You will come to learn the value of a wind, when you
have been longer on the Nile," said the latter, with that air of
melancholy resignation which he always assumed when not
allowed to have his own way. He was an indolent good-
tempered man, spoke English fairly well, and was perfectly
manageable; but that air of resignation came to be aggravating
in time.

The M. B.'s being of the same mind, however, we had our
second day, and spent it at Memphis. We ought to have
crossed over to Turra, and have seen the great quarries from
which the casing-stones of the Pyramids came, and all the finer
limestone with which the temples and palaces of Memphis
were built. But the whole mountain-side seemed as if glowing
at a white heat on the opposite side of the river, and we said
we would put off Turra till our return. So we went our own
way; and Alfred shot pigeons; and the Writer sketched
Mitrâhîneh, and the palms, and the sacred lake of Mena; and
the rest grubbed among the mounds for treasure, finding many
curious fragments of glass and pottery, and part of an engraved
bronze Apis; and we had a green, tranquil, lovely day, barren
of incident, but very pleasant to remember.

The good wind continued to blow all that night; but fell
at sunrise, precisely when we were about to start. The river
now stretched away before us, smooth as glass, and there was
nothing for it, said Reïs Hassan, but tracking. We had heard
of tracking often enough since coming to Egypt, but without
having any definite idea of the process. Coming on deck,
however, before breakfast, we found nine of our poor fellows
harnessed to a rope like barge-horses, towing the huge boat

against the current.   Seven of the M. B.'s crew, similarly
harnessed, followed at a few yards' distance.   The two ropes
met and crossed and dipped into the water together.   Already
our last night's mooring-place was out of sight, and the
Pyramid of Ouenephes stood up amid its lesser brethren on
the edge of the desert, as if bidding us good-bye.   But the
sight of the trackers jarred, somehow, with the placid beauty
of the picture.   We got used to it, as one gets used to everything, in time ; but it looked like slaves' work, and shocked our
English notions disagreeably.

That morning, still tracking, we pass the Pyramids of
Dahshûr.   A dilapidated brick pyramid standing in the midst
of them looks like an aiguille of black rock thrusting itself up
through the limestone bed of the desert.   Palms line the bank
and intercept the view ; but we catch flitting glimpses here and
there, looking out especially for that dome-like pyramid which
we observed the other day from Sakkârah.   Seen in the full
sunlight, it looks larger and whiter, and more than ever like
the roof of the old Palais de Justice far away in Paris.

Thus the morning passes.   We sit on deck writing letters ;
reading ; watching the sunny river-side pictures that glide by
at a foot's pace and are so long in sight.   Palm-groves, sandbanks, patches of fuzzy-headed dura[1] and fields of some yellow-
flowering herb, succeed each other.   A boy plods along the
bank, leading a camel.   They go slowly ; but they soon leave
us behind.   A native boat meets us, floating down side-wise
with the current.   A girl comes to the water's edge with a
great empty jar on her head, and waits to fill it till the trackers
have gone by.   The pigeon-towers of a mud-village peep above
a clump of lebbek trees, a quarter of a mile inland.   Here a
solitary brown man, with only a felt skull-cap on his head and
a slip of scanty tunic fastened about his loins, works a shâdûf,[2]

---

[1] *Sorghum vulgare.*

[2] The Shâdûf has been so well described by the Rev. F. B. Zincke,
that I cannot do better than quote him verbatim :—" Mechanically, the
Shadoof is an application of the lever.   In no machine which the wit of
man, aided by the accumulation of science, has since invented, is the
result produced so great in proportion to the degree of power employed.
The level of the Shadoof is a long stout pole poised on a prop.   The pole
is at right angles to the river.   A large lump of clay from the spot is

stooping and rising, stooping and rising, with the regularity of
a pendulum. It is the same machine which we shall see by
and by depicted in the tombs at Thebes ; and the man is so

THE SHÂDÛF.

evidently an ancient Egyptian, that we find ourselves wondering how he escaped being mummified four or five thousand
years ago.

appended to the inland end. To the river end is suspended a goat-skin
bucket. This is the whole apparatus. The man who is working it stands
on the edge of the river. Before him is a hole full of water fed from the
passing stream. When working the machine, he takes hold of the cord by
which the empty bucket is suspended, and bending down, by the mere
weight of his shoulders dips it in the water. His effort to rise gives the
bucket full of water an upward cant, which, with the aid of the equipoising
lump of clay at the other end of the pole, lifts it to a trough into which, as
it tilts on one side, it empties its contents. What he has done has raised

By and by, a little breeze springs up. The men drop the rope and jump on board—the big sail is set—the breeze freshens—and away we go again, as merrily as the day we left Cairo. Towards sunset we see a strange object, like a giant obelisk broken off half-way, standing up on the western bank against an orange-gold sky. This is the Pyramid of Meydûm, commonly called the False Pyramid. It looks quite near the bank ; but this is an effect of powerful light and shadow, for it lies back at least four miles from the river. That night, having sailed on till past nine o'clock, we moor about a mile from Beni Suêf, and learn with some surprise that a man must be despatched to the governor of the town for guards. Not that anything ever happened to anybody at Beni Suêf, says Talhamy ; but that the place is supposed not to have a first-rate reputation. If we have guards, we at all events make the governor responsible for our safety and the safety of our possessions. So the guards are sent for ; and being posted on the bank, snore loudly all night long, just outside our windows.

Meanwhile the wind shifts round to the south, and next morning it blows full in our faces. The men, however, track up to Beni Suêf to a point where the buildings come down to the water's edge and the towing-path ceases ; and there we lay-to for awhile among a fleet of filthy native boats, close to the landing-place.

The approach to Beni Suêf is rather pretty. The Khedive has an Italian-looking villa here, which peeps up white and dazzling from the midst of a thickly-wooded park. The town lies back a little from the river. A few coffee-houses and a kind of promenade face the landing-place ; and a mosque built to the verge of the bank stands out picturesquely against the bend of the river.

And now it is our object to turn that corner, so as to get into a better position for starting when the wind drops. The

the water six or seven feet above the level of the river. But if the river has subsided twelve or fourteen feet, it will require another Shadoof to be worked in the trough into which the water of the first has been brought. If the river has sunk still more, a third will be required before it can be lifted to the top of the bank, so as to enable it to flow off to the fields that require irrigation."—*Egypt of the Pharaohs and the Khedive,* p. 445 *et seq.*

current here runs deep and strong, so that we have both wind and water dead against us. Half our men clamber round the corner like cats, carrying the rope with them ; the rest keep the dahabeeyah off the bank with punting poles. The rope strains—a pole breaks—we struggle forward a few feet, and can get no farther. Then the men rest awhile ; try again ; and are again defeated. So the fight goes on. The promenade and the windows of the mosque become gradually crowded with lookers-on. Some three or four cloaked and bearded men have chairs brought, and sit gravely smoking their chibouques on the bank above, enjoying the entertainment. Meanwhile the water-carriers come and go, filling their goat-skins at the landing-place ; donkeys and camels are brought down to drink ; girls in dark blue gowns and coarse black veils come with huge water-jars laid sidewise upon their heads, and, having filled and replaced them upright, walk away with stately steps, as if each ponderous vessel were a crown.

So the day passes. Driven back again and again, but still resolute, our sailors, by dint of sheer doggedness, get us round the bad corner at last. The Bagstones follows suit a little later ; and we both moor about a quarter of a mile above the town. Then follows a night of adventures. Again our guards sleep profoundly ; but the bad characters of Beni Suêf are very wide awake. One gentleman, actuated no doubt by the friendliest motives, pays a midnight visit to the Bagstones ; but being detected, chased, and fired at, escapes by jumping overboard. Our turn comes about two hours later, when the Writer, happening to be awake, hears a man swim softly round the Philæ. To strike a light and frighten everybody into sudden activity is the work of a moment. The whole boat is instantly in an uproar. Lanterns are lighted on deck ; a patrol of sailors is set ; Talhamy loads his gun ; and the thief slips away in the dark, like a fish.

The guards, of course, slept sweetly through it all. Honest fellows ! They were paid a shilling a night to do it, and they had nothing on their minds.

Having lodged a formal complaint next morning against the inhabitants of the town, we received a visit from a sallow personage clad in a long black robe and a voluminous white turban.　This was the Chief of the Guards.　He smoked a great many pipes ; drank numerous cups of coffee ; listened to all we had to say ; looked wise ; and finally suggested that the number of our guards should be doubled.

I ventured to object that if they slept unanimously, forty would not be of much more use than four.　Whereupon he rose, drew himself to his full height, touched his beard, and said with a magnificent melodramatic air :—" If they sleep, they shall be bastinadoed till they die !"

And now our good luck seemed to have deserted us.　For three days and nights the adverse wind continued to blow with such force that the men could not even track against it. Moored under that dreary bank, we saw our ten days' start melting away, and could only make the best of our misfortunes. Happily the long island close by, and the banks on both sides of the river, were populous with sand-grouse ; so Alfred went out daily with his faithful George and his unerring gun, and brought home game in abundance, while we took long walks, sketched boats and camels, and chaffered with native women for silver torques and bracelets.　These torques (in Arabic *Tôk*) are tubular but massive, penannular, about as thick as one's little finger, and finished with a hook at one end and a twisted loop at the other.　The girls would sometimes put their veils aside and make a show of bargaining ; but more frequently, after standing for a moment with great wondering black velvety eyes staring shyly into ours, they would take fright like a troop of startled deer, and vanish with shrill cries, half of laughter, half of terror.

At Beni Suêf we encountered our first sand-storm.　It came down the river about noon, showing like a yellow fog on the horizon, and rolling rapidly before the wind.　It tore the river into angry waves, and blotted out the landscape as it came.　The distant hills disappeared first ; then the palms beyond the island ; then the boats close by.　Another second, and the air was full of sand.　The whole surface of the plain seemed in motion.　The banks rippled.　The yellow dust poured down through every rift and cleft in hundreds of tiny cataracts.　But it was a sight not to be looked upon with impunity.　Hair, eyes, mouth, ears, were instantly filled, and we were driven to take refuge in the saloon. Here, although every window and door had been shut before the storm came, the sand found its way in clouds. Books, papers, carpets, were covered with it ; and it settled again as fast as it was cleared away. This lasted just one hour, and was followed by a burst of heavy rain ; after which the sky cleared and we had a lovely afternoon. From this time forth, we saw no more rain in Egypt.

At length, on the morning of the fourth day after our first appearance at Beni Suêf and the seventh since leaving Cairo, the wind veered round again to the north, and we once more got under way. It was delightful to see the big sail again towering up overhead, and to hear the swish of the water under the cabin windows ; but we were still one hundred and nine miles from Rhoda, and we knew that nothing but an extraordinary run of luck could possibly get us there by the twenty-third of the month, with time to see Beni Hassan on the way. Meanwhile, however, we make fair progress, mooring at sunset when the wind falls, about three miles north of Bibbeh. Next day, by help of the same light breeze which again springs up a little after dawn, we go at a good pace between flat banks fringed here and there with palms, and studded with villages more or less picturesque. There is not much to see, and yet one never wants for amusement. Now we pass an island of sand-bank covered with snow-white paddy-birds, which rise tumultuously at our approach. Next comes Bibbeh perched high along the edge of the precipitous bank, its odd-looking Coptic Convent roofed all over with little mud domes, like a cluster of earth-bubbles. By and by we pass a deserted sugar-factory, with shattered windows and a huge, gaunt, blackened chimney, worthy of Birmingham or Sheffield. And now we catch a glimpse of the railway, and hear the last scream of a departing engine. At night, we moor within sight of the factory chimneys and hydraulic tubes of Magagha, and next day get on nearly to Golosanèh, which is the last station-town before Minieh.

It is now only too clear that we must give up all thought of pushing on to Beni Hassan before the rest of the party shall come on board. We have reached the evening of our ninth day ;

we are still forty-eight miles from Rhoda ; and another adverse
wind might again delay us indefinitely on the way.   All risks
taken into account, we decide to put off our meeting till the
twenty-fourth, and transfer the appointment to Minieh ; thus
giving ourselves time to track all the way in case of need.   So
an Arabic telegram is concocted, and our fleetest runner starts
off with it to Golosanèh before the office closes for the night.

The breeze, however, does not fail, but comes back next
morning with the dawn.   Having passed Golosanèh, we come
to a wide reach in the river, at which point we are honoured
by a visit from a Moslem Santon of peculiar sanctity, named

"HOLY SHEYKH COTTON."

"Holy Sheykh Cotton."   Now
Holy Sheykh Cotton, who is a
well-fed, healthy-looking young
man of about thirty, makes his
first appearance swimming, with
his garments twisted into a huge
turban on the top of his head, and
only his chin above water.   Having made his toilet in the small
boat, he presents himself on deck,
and receives an enthusiastic welcome.   Reïs Hassan hugs him—
the pilot kisses him—the sailors
come up one by one, bringing little
tributes of tobacco and piastres
which he accepts with the air of a

Pope receiving Peter's Pence.   All dripping as he is, and smiling
like an affable Triton, he next proceeds to touch the tiller,
the ropes, and the ends of the yards, "in order," says Talhamy,
"to make them holy ;" and then, with some kind of final
charm or muttered incantation, he plunges into the river
again, and swims off to repeat the same performance on board
the Bagstones.

From this moment the prosperity of our voyage is assured.
The captain goes about with a smile on his stern face, and the
crew look as happy as if we had given them a guinea.   For
nothing can go wrong with a dahabeeyah that has been "made
holy" by Holy Sheykh Cotton.   We are certain now to have

favourable winds—to pass the Cataract without accident—to come back in health and safety, as we set out. But what, it may be asked, has Holy Sheykh Cotton done to make his blessing so efficacious ? He gets money in plenty ; he fasts no oftener than other Mohammedans ; he has two wives ; he never does a stroke of work ; and he looks the picture of sleek prosperity. Yet he is a saint of the first water ; and when he dies, miracles will be performed at his tomb, and his eldest son will succeed him in the business.

We had the pleasure of becoming acquainted with a good many saints in the course of our Eastern travels ; but I do not know that we ever found they had done anything to merit the position. One very horrible old man named Sheykh Saleem has, it is true, been sitting on a dirt heap near Farshût, unclothed, unwashed, unshaven, for the last half-century or more, never even lifting his hand to his mouth to feed himself ; but Sheykh Cotton had gone to no such pious lengths, and was not even dirty.

We are by this time drawing towards a range of yellow cliffs that have long been visible on the horizon, and which figure in the maps as Gebel et Tâyr. The Arabian desert has been closing up on the eastern bank for some time past, and now rolls on in undulating drifts to the water's edge. Yellow boulders crop out here and there above the mounded sand, which looks as if it might cover many a forgotten temple. Presently the clay bank is gone, and a low barrier of limestone rock, black and shiny next the water-line, has taken its place. And now, a long way ahead, where the river bends and the level cliffs lead on into the far distance, a little brown speck is pointed out as the Convent of the Pulley. Perched on the brink of the precipice, it looks no bigger than an ant-heap. We had heard much of the fine view to be seen from the platform on which this Convent is built, and it had originally entered into our programme as a place to be visited on the way. But Minieh has to be gained now at all costs ; so this project has to be abandoned with a sigh.

And now the rocky barrier rises higher, quarried here and there in dazzling gaps of snow-white cuttings. And now the Convent shows clearer ; and the cliffs become loftier ; and the bend in the river is reached ; and a long perspective of flat-topped precipice stretches away into the dim distance.

It is a day of saints and swimmers. As the dahabeeyah approaches, a brown poll is seen bobbing up and down in the water a few hundred yards ahead. Then one, two, three bronze figures dash down a steep ravine below the Convent walls, and plunge into the river—a shrill chorus of voices, growing momentarily more audible, is borne upon the wind—and in a few minutes the boat is beset by a shoal of mendicant monks vociferating with all their might "*Ana Christian ya Hawadji !— Ana Christian ya Hawadji !*" (I am a Christian, oh traveller!) As these are only Coptic monks and not Moslem santons, the sailors, half in rough play, half in earnest, drive them off with punting poles ; and only one shivering, streaming object, wrapped in a borrowed blanket, is allowed to come on board. He is a fine shapely man, aged about forty, with splendid eyes and teeth, a well-formed head, a skin the colour of a copper beech-leaf, and a face expressive of such ignorance, timidity, and half-savage watchfulness as makes one's heart ache.

And this is a Copt ; a descendant of the true Egyptian stock ; one of those whose remote ancestors exchanged the worship of the old gods for Christianity under the rule of Theodosius some fifteen hundred years ago, and whose blood is supposed to be purer of Mohammedan intermixture than any in Egypt. Remembering these things, it is impossible to look at him without a feeling of profound interest. It may be only fancy, yet I think I see in him a different type to that of the Arab—a something, however slight, which recalls the sculptured figures in the tomb of Ti.

But while we are thinking about his magnificent pedigree, our poor Copt's teeth are chattering piteously. So we give him a shilling or two for the sake of all that he represents in the history of the world ; and with these, and the donation of an empty bottle, he swims away contented, crying again and again :—"*Ketther-kháyrak Sittát ! Ketther-kháyrak keteer !*" (Thank you, ladies ! thank you much !")

And now the Convent with its clustered domes is passed and left behind. The rock here is of the same rich tawny hue as at Turra, and the horizontal strata of which it is composed have evidently been deposited by water. That the Nile must at some remote time have flowed here at an immensely higher level seems also probable ; for the whole face of the range is honeycombed and water-worn for miles in succession. Seeing how these fantastic forms—arched, and clustered, and pendent —resemble the recessed ornamentation of Saracenic buildings, I could not help wondering whether some early Arab architect might not once upon a time have taken a hint from some such rocks as these.

Thus the day wanes, and the level cliffs keep with us all the way—now breaking into little lateral valleys and *culs-de-sac* in which nestle clusters of tiny huts and green patches of lupin ; now plunging sheer down into the river ; now receding inland and leaving space for a belt of cultivated soil and a fringe of feathery palms. By and by comes the sunset, when every cast shadow in the recesses of the cliffs turns to pure violet ; and the face of the rock glows with a ruddier gold ; and the palms on the western bank stand up in solid bronze against a crimson horizon. Then the sun dips, and instantly the whole range of cliffs turns to a dead, greenish grey, while the sky above and behind them is as suddenly suffused with pink. When this effect has lasted for something like eight minutes, a vast arch of deep blue shade, about as large in diameter as a rainbow, creeps slowly up the eastern horizon, and remains distinctly visible as long as the pink flush against which it is defined yet lingers in the sky. Finally the flush fades out ; the blue becomes uniform ; the stars begin to show ; and only a broad glow in the west marks which way the sun went down. About a quarter of an hour later comes the after-glow, when for a few minutes the sky is filled with a soft, magical light, and the twilight gloom lies warm upon the landscape. When this goes, it is night ; but still one long beam of light streams up in the track of the sun, and remains visible for more than two hours after the darkness has closed in.

Such is the sunset we see this evening as we approach Minieh ; and such is the sunset we are destined to see with scarcely a shade of difference at the same hour and under precisely the same conditions for many a month to come. It is very beautiful, very tranquil, full of wonderful light and most subtle gradations of tone, and attended by certain phenomena of which I shall have more to say presently ; but it lacks the variety and gorgeousness of our northern skies. Nor, given the dry atmosphere of Egypt, can it be otherwise. Those who go up the Nile expecting, as I did, to see magnificent Turneresque pageants of purple, and flame-colour, and gold, will be disappointed as I was. For your Turneresque pageant cannot be achieved without such accessories of cloud and vapour as in Nubia are wholly unknown, and in Egypt are of the rarest occurrence. Once, and only once, in the course of an unusually protracted sojourn on the river, had we the good fortune to witness a grand display of the kind ; and then we had been nearly three months in the dahabeeyah.

Meanwhile, however, we never weary of these stainless skies, but find in them, evening after evening, fresh depths of beauty and repose. As for that strange transfer of colour from the mountains to the sky, we had repeatedly observed it while travelling in the Dolomites the year before, and had always found it take place, as now, at the moment of the sun's first disappearance. But what of this mighty after-shadow, climbing half the heavens and bringing night with it ? Can it be the rising Shadow of the World projected on the one horizon as the sun sinks on the other ? I leave the problem for wiser travellers to solve. We had not science enough amongst us to account for it.

That same evening, just as the twilight came on, we saw another wonder—the new moon on the first night of her first quarter ; a perfect orb, dusky, distinct, and outlined all round with a thread of light no thicker than a hair. Nothing could be more brilliant than this tiny rim of flashing silver ; while every detail of the softly-glowing globe within its compass was clearly visible. Tycho with its vast crater showed like a volcano on a raised map ; and near the edge of the moon's surface, where the light and shadow met, keen sparkles of mountain-summits catching the light and relieved against the dusk, were to be seen by the naked eye. Two or three evenings later, however, when the silver ring was changed to a broad crescent, the unilluminated part was as it were extinguished, and could no longer be discerned even by help of a glass.

The wind having failed as usual at sunset, the crew set to

work with a will and punted the rest of the way, so bringing us to Minieh about nine that night. Next morning we found ourselves moored close under the Khedive's summer palace— so close that one could have tossed a pebble against the lattice windows of his Highness's hareem. A fat gate-keeper sat outside in the sun, smoking his morning chibouque and gossiping with the passers-by. A narrow promenade scantily planted with sycamore figs ran between the palace and the river. A steamer or two, and a crowd of native boats, lay moored under the bank ; and yonder, at the farther end of the promenade, a minaret and a cluster of whitewashed houses showed which way one must turn in going to the town.

It chanced to be market-day ; so we saw Minieh under its best aspect, than which nothing could well be more squalid, dreary, and depressing. It was like a town dropped unexpectedly into the midst of a ploughed field ; the streets being mere trodden lanes of mud dust, and the houses a succession of windowless mud prisons with their backs to the thoroughfare. The Bazaar, which consists of two or three lanes a little wider than the rest, is roofed over here and there with rotting palm-rafters and bits of tattered matting ; while the market is held in a space of waste ground outside the town. The former, with its little cupboard-like shops in which the merchants sit cross-legged like shabby old idols in shabby old shrines—the ill-furnished shelves—the familiar Manchester goods—the gaudy native stuffs—the old red saddles and faded rugs hanging up for sale—the smart Greek stores where Bass's ale, claret, curaçoa, Cyprus, Vermouth, cheese, pickles, sardines, Worcester sauce, blacking, biscuits, preserved meats, candles, cigars, matches, sugar, salt, stationery, fireworks, jams, and patent medicines can all be bought at one fell swoop—the native cook's shop exhaling savoury perfumes of Kebabs and lentil soup, and presided over by an Abyssinian Soyer blacker than the blackest historical personage ever was painted—the surging, elbowing, clamorous crowd—the donkeys, the camels, the street-cries, the chatter, the dust, the flies, the fleas, and the dogs, all put us in mind of the poorer quarters of Cairo. In the market, it is even worse. Here are hundreds of country folk sitting on the ground behind their baskets of fruits and

vegetables. Some have eggs, butter, and buffalo-cream for
sale, while others sell sugar-canes, limes, cabbages, tobacco,
barley, dried lentils, split beans, maize, wheat, and dura. The
women go to and fro with bouquets of live poultry. The
chickens scream ; the sellers rave ; the buyers bargain at the
tops of their voices ; the dust flies in clouds ; the sun pours
down floods of light and heat ; you can scarcely hear yourself
speak ; and the crowd is as dense as that other crowd which
at this very moment, on this very Christmas Eve, is circulating
among the alleys of Leadenhall Market.

The things were very cheap. A hundred eggs cost about
fourteen-pence in English money ; chickens sold for fivepence
each ; pigeons from twopence to twopence-halfpenny ; and
fine live geese for two shillings a head. The turkeys, however, which were large and excellent, were priced as high as
three-and-sixpence ; being about half as much as one pays in
Middle and Upper Egypt for a lamb. A good sheep may be
bought for sixteen shillings or a pound. The M. B.'s, who had
no dragoman and did their own marketing, were very busy
here, laying in stores of fresh provision, bargaining fluently in
Arabic, and escorted by a bodyguard of sailors.

A solitary dôm palm, the northernmost of its race and the
first specimen one meets with on the Nile, grows in a garden
adjoining this market-place : but we could scarcely see it for
the blinding dust. Now, a dôm palm is just the sort of tree
that De Wint should have painted—odd, angular, with long
forked stems, each of which terminates in a shock-headed
crown of stiff finger-like fronds shading heavy clusters of big
shiny nuts about the size of Jerusalem artichokes. It is, I
suppose, the only nut in the world of which one throws away
the kernel and eats the shell ; but the kernel is as hard as
marble, while the shell is fibrous, and tastes like stale gingerbread. The dôm palm must bifurcate, for bifurcation is the
law of its being ; but I could never discover whether there was
any fixed limit to the number of stems into which it might
subdivide. At the same time, I do not remember to have
seen any with less than two heads or more than six.

Coming back through the town, we were accosted by a
withered one-eyed hag like a re-animated mummy, who

offered to tell our fortunes. Before her lay a dirty rag of handkerchief full of shells, pebbles, and chips of broken glass and pottery. Squatting toad-like under a sunny bit of wall, the lower part of her face closely veiled, her skinny arms covered with blue and green glass bracelets and her fingers with misshapen silver rings, she hung over these treasures; shook, mixed, and interrogated them with all the fervour of divination; and delivered a string of the prophecies usually forthcoming on these occasions.

"You have a friend far away, and your friend is thinking of you. There is good fortune in store for you; and money coming to you; and pleasant news on the way. You will soon receive letters in which there will be something to vex you, but more to make you glad. Within thirty days you will unexpectedly meet one whom you dearly love," etc. etc. etc.

It was just the old familiar story retold in Arabic, without even such variations as might have been expected from the lips of an old fellâha born and bred in a provincial town of Middle Egypt.

It may be that ophthalmia especially prevailed in this part of the country, or that being brought unexpectedly into the midst of a large crowd, one observed the people more narrowly, but I certainly never saw so many one-eyed human beings as that morning at Minieh. There must have been present in the streets and market-place from ten to twelve thousand natives of all ages, and I believe it is no exaggeration to say that at least every twentieth person, down to little toddling children of three and four years of age, was blind of an eye. Not being a particularly well-favoured race, this defect added the last touch of repulsiveness to faces already sullen, ignorant, and unfriendly. A more unprepossessing population I would never wish to see—the men half stealthy, half insolent; the women bold and fierce; the children filthy, sickly, stunted, and stolid. Nothing in provincial Egypt is so painful to witness as the neglected condition of very young children. Those belonging to even the better class are for the most part shabbily clothed and of more than doubtful cleanliness; while the off-spring of the very poor are simply encrusted with dirt and sores, and swarming with vermin. It is at first hard to believe

that the parents of these unfortunate babies err, not from
cruelty, but through sheer ignorance and superstition. Yet so
it is ; and the time when these people can be brought to com-
prehend the most elementary principles of sanitary reform is
yet far distant. To wash young children is injurious to health ;
therefore the mothers suffer them to fall into a state of personal
uncleanliness which is alone enough to engender disease. To
brush away the flies that beset their eyes is impious ; hence
ophthalmia and various kinds of blindness. I have seen infants
lying in their mothers' arms with six or eight flies in each
eye. I have seen the little helpless hands put down reprov-
ingly, if they approached the seat of annoyance. I have seen
children of four and five years old with the surface of one or
both eyes eaten away ; and others with a large fleshy lump
growing out where the pupil had been destroyed. Taking
these things into account, the wonder is, after all, not that
three children should die in Egypt out of every five—not that
each twentieth person in certain districts should be blind, or
partially blind ; but that so many as forty per cent of the
whole infant population should actually live to grow up, and
that ninety-five per cent should enjoy the blessing of sight.
For my own part, I had not been many weeks on the Nile
before I began systematically to avoid going about the native
towns whenever it was practicable to do so. That I may so
have lost an opportunity of now and then seeing more of the
street-life of the people is very probable ; but such outside
glimpses are of little real value, and I at all events escaped the
sight of much poverty, sickness, and squalor. The condition
of the inhabitants is not worse, perhaps, in an Egyptian Beled[1]
than in many an Irish village ; but the condition of the children
is so distressing that one would willingly go any number of
miles out of the way rather than witness their suffering, without
the power to alleviate it.[2]

If the population in and about Minieh are personally

[1] *Beled*—village.

[2] Miss Whately, whose evidence on this subject is peculiarly valuable,
states that the majority of native children die off at, or under, two years of
age (*Among the Huts*, p. 29) ; while M. About, who enjoyed unusual
opportunies of inquiring into facts connected with the population and
resources of the country, says that the nation loses three children out of

unattractive, their appearance at all events matches their reputation, which is as bad as that of their neighbours. Of the
manners and customs of Beni Suêf we had already some experience ; while public opinion charges Minieh, Rhoda, and
most of the towns and villages north of Siût, with the like
marauding propensities. As for the villages at the foot of Beni
Hassan, they have been mere dens of thieves for many generations ; and though razed to the ground some years ago by way
of punishment, are now rebuilt, and in as bad odour as ever.
It is necessary, therefore, in all this part of the river, not only
to hire guards at night, but, when the boat is moored, to keep a
sharp look-out against thieves by day. In Upper Egypt it is very
different. There the natives are good-looking, good-natured,
gentle, and kindly ; and though clever enough at manufacturing
and selling modern antiquities, are not otherwise dishonest.

That same evening—(it was Christmas Eve)—nearly two
hours earlier than their train was supposed to be due, the rest
of our party arrived at Minieh.

every five.   " L'ignorance publique, l'oubli des premiers éléments d'hygiène,
la mauvaise alimentation, l'absence presque totale des soins médicaux,
tarissent la nation dans sa source.   Un peuple qui perd régulièrement
trios enfants sur cinq ne saurait croître sans miracle."—*Le Fellah*, p. 165.

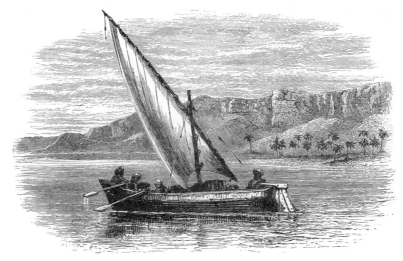

MARKET BOAT MINIEH.

CHAPTER VI.

MINIEH TO SIÛT.

IT is Christmas Day. The M. B.'s are coming to dinner ; the cooks are up to their eyes in entrées ; the crew are treated to a sheep in honour of the occasion ; the new-comers are unpacking ; and we are all gradually settling down into our respective places. Now, the new-comers consist of four persons :——a Painter, a Happy Couple, and a maid. The Painter has already been up the Nile three times, and brings a fund of experience into the council. He knows all about sandbanks, and winds, and mooring-places ; is acquainted with most of the native governors and consuls along the river ; and is great on the subject of what to eat, drink, and avoid. The stern-cabin is given to him for a studio, and contains frames, canvases, drawing-paper, and easels enough to start a provincial school of art. He is going to paint a big picture at Aboo-Simbel. The Happy Couple, it is unnecessary to say, are on their wedding tour. In point of fact, they have not yet been married a month. The bridegroom is what the world chooses to call an idle man ; that is to say, he has scholarship, delicate health, and leisure. The bride, for convenience, shall be called the Little Lady. Of people who are struggling through that helpless phase of human life called the honeymoon, it is not fair to say more than that they are both young enough to make the situation interesting.

Meanwhile the deck must be cleared of the new luggage that has come on board, and the day passes in a confusion of unpacking, arranging, and putting away. Such running to

and fro as there is down below ; such turning-out of boxes and
knocking-up of temporary shelves ; such talking, and laughing,
and hammering !   Nor is the bustle confined to downstairs.
Talhamy and the waiters are just as busy above, adorning the
upper deck with palm-branches and hanging the boat all round
with rows of coloured lanterns.   One can hardly believe, however, that it is Christmas Day—that there are fires blazing at
home in every room ; that the church-field, perhaps, is white
with snow ; and that the familiar bells are ringing merrily
across the frosty air.   Here at midday it is already too hot on
deck without the awning, and when we moor towards sunset
near a riverside village in a grove of palms, the cooler air of
evening is delicious.

There is novelty in even such a commonplace matter as
dining out, on the Nile.   You go and return in your felucca,
as if it were a carriage ; and your entertainers summon you by
firing a dinner-gun, instead of sounding a gong.   Wise people
who respect the feelings of their cooks fire a dressing-gun as
well ; for watches soon differ in a hopeless way for want of
the church-clock to set them by, and it is always possible that
host and guest may be an hour or two apart in their reckoning.

The customary guns having therefore been fired, and the
party assembled, we sat down to one of cook Bedawee's prodigious banquets.   Not, however, till the plum-pudding, blazing
demoniacally, appeared upon the scene, did any of us succeed
in believing that it was really Christmas Day.

Nothing could be prettier or gayer than the spectacle that
awaited us when we rose from table.   A hundred and fifty
coloured lanterns outlined the boat from end to end, sparkled
up the masts, and cast broken reflections in the moving
current.   The upper-deck, hung with flags and partly closed
in with awnings, looked like a bower of palms.   The stars and
the crescent moon shone overhead.   Dim outlines of trees and
headlands, and a vague perspective of gleaming river, were
visible in the distance ; while a light gleamed now and then
in the direction of the village, or a dusky figure flitted along
the bank.

Meanwhile, there was a sound of revelry by night ; for our
sailors had invited the Bagstones' crew to unlimited coffee and

tobacco, and had quite a large party on the lower deck. They drummed, they sang, they danced, they dressed up, improvised a comic scene, and kept their audience in a roar. Reïs Hassan did the honours. George, Talhamy, and the maids sat apart at the second table and sipped their coffee genteelly. We looked on and applauded. At ten o'clock a pan of magnesium powder was burned, and our Fantasia ended with a blaze of light, like a pantomime.

In Egypt, by the way, any entertainment which is enlivened by music, dancing, or fireworks is called a Fantasia.

And now, sometimes sailing, sometimes tracking, sometimes punting, we go on day by day, making what speed we can. Things do not, of course, always fall out exactly as one would have them. The wind too often fails when we most need it, and gets up when there is something to be seen on shore. Thus, after a whole morning of tracking, we reach Beni Hassan at the moment when a good breeze has suddenly filled our sails for the first time in forty-eight hours ; and so, yielding to counsels which we afterwards deplored, we pass on with many a longing look at the terraced doorways pierced along the cliffs. At Rhoda, in the same way, we touch for only a few minutes to post and inquire for letters, and put off till our return the inland excursion to Dayr el Nakhl, where is to be seen the famous painting of the Colossus on the Sledge. But sights deferred are fated sometimes to remain unseen, as we found by and by to our exceeding loss and regret.

Meanwhile, the skies are always cloudless, the days warm, the evenings exquisite. We of course live very much in the open air. When there is no wind, we land and take long walks by the river-side. When on board, we sketch, write letters, read Champollion, Bunsen, and Sir Gardner Wilkinson ; and work hard at Egyptian dynasties. The sparrows and water-wagtails perch familiarly on the awnings and hop about the deck ; the cocks and hens chatter, the geese cackle, the turkeys gobble in their coops close by ; and our sacrificial sheep, leading a solitary life in the felucca, comes baaing in the rear. Sometimes we have as many as a hundred chickens on board (to say nothing of pigeons and rabbits) and two or even three sheep in the felucca. The poultry yard is railed off, however, at the extreme end of the stern, so that the creatures are well away from the drawing-room ; and when we moor at a suitable place, they are let out for a few hours to peck about the banks and enjoy their liberty. L. and the Little Lady feed these hapless prisoners with breakfast-scraps every morning, to the profound amusement of the steersman, who, unable to conceive any other motive, imagines they are fatting them for table.

Such is our Noah's Ark life, pleasant, peaceful, and patriarchal. Even on days when there is little to see and nothing to do, it is never dull. Trifling incidents which have for us the excitement of novelty are continually occurring. Other dahabeeyahs, their flags and occupants, are a constant source of interest. Meeting at mooring-places for the night, we now and then exchange visits. Passing each other by day, we dip ensigns, fire salutes, and punctiliously observe the laws of maritime etiquette. Sometimes a Cook's Excursion-steamer hurries by, crowded with tourists ; or a government tug towing three or four great barges closely packed with wretched-looking, half-naked fellâheen bound for forced labour on some new railway or canal. Occasionally we pass a dahabeeyah sticking fast upon a sandbank ; and sometimes we stick on one ourselves. Then the men fly to their punting poles, or jump into the river like water-dogs, and, grunting in melancholy cadence, shove the boat off with their shoulders.

The birds, too, are new, and we are always looking out for them. Perhaps we see a top-heavy pelican balancing his huge yellow bill over the edge of the stream, and fishing for his dinner—or a flight of wild geese trailing across the sky towards sunset—or a select society of vultures perched all in a row upon a ledge of rock, and solemn as the bench of bishops. Then there are the herons who stand on one leg and doze in the sun ; the strutting hoopoes with their legendary top-knots ; the blue and green bee-eaters hovering over the uncut dura. The pied kingfisher, black and white like a magpie, sits fearlessly under the bank and never stirs, though the tow-rope swings close above his head and the dahabeeyah glides within a few feet of the shore. The paddy-birds whiten the sandbanks by hundreds, and rise in a cloud at our approach. The sacred hawk, circling overhead, utters the same sweet, piercing, melancholy note that the Pharaohs listened to of old.

The scenery is for the most part of the ordinary Nile pattern ; and for many a mile we see the same things over and over again :—the level bank shelving down steeply to the river ; the strip of cultivated soil, green with maize or tawny with dura ; the frequent mud-village and palm-grove ; the deserted sugar-factory with its ungainly chimney and shattered windows ; the water-wheel slowly revolving with its necklace of pots ; the shâdûf worked by two brown athletes ; the file of

GEBEL ABUFAYDA.

laden camels ; the desert, all sand-hills and sand-plains, with its background of mountains ; the long reach, and the gleaming sail ahead. Sometimes, however, as at Kom Ahmar, we skirt the ancient brick mounds of some forgotten city, with fragments of arched foundations, and even of walls and door-ways, reaching down to the water's edge ; or, sailing close under ranges of huge perpendicular cliffs, as at Gebel Abufayda, startle the cormorants from their haunts, and peer as we pass into the dim recesses of many a rock-cut tomb excavated just above the level of the inundation.

This Gebel Abufayda has a bad name for sudden winds ; especially at the beginning and end of the range, where the

Nile bends abruptly and the valley opens out at right angles to the river. It is fine to see Reïs Hassan, as we approach one of the worst of these bad bits—a point where two steep ravines divided by a bold headland command the passage like a pair of grim cannon, and rake it with blasts from the North-Eastern desert. Here the current, flowing deep and strong, is met by the wind and runs high in crested waves. Our little captain, kicking off his shoes, himself springs up the rigging and there stands silent and watchful. The sailors, ready to shift our mainsail at the word of command, cling some to the shoghool [1] and some to the end of the yard ; the boat tears on before the wind ; the great bluff looms up darker and nearer. Then comes a breathless moment. Then a sharp, sudden word from the little man in the main rigging ; a yell and a whoop from the sailors ; a slow, heavy lurch of the flapping sail ; and the corner is turned in safety.

The cliffs here are very fine ; much loftier and less uniform than at Gebel et Tayr ; rent into strange forms, as of sphinxes, cheesewrings, towers, and bastions ; honeycombed with long ranges of rock-cut tombs ; and undermined by water-washed caverns in which lurk a few lingering crocodiles. If at Gebel et Tayr the rock is worn into semblances of Arabesque ornamentation, here it looks as if inscribed all over with mysterious records in characters not unlike the Hebrew. Records they are, too, of prehistoric days—chronicles of his own deeds carved by the great God Nile himself, the Hapimu of ancient time—but the language in which they are written has never been spoken by man.

As for the rock-cut tombs of Gebel Abufayda, they must number many hundreds. For nearly twelve miles, the range runs parallel to the river, and throughout that distance the face of the cliffs is pierced with innumerable doorways. Some are small and square, twenty or thirty together, like rows of port-holes. Others are isolated. Some are cut so high up that they must have been approached from above ; others again come close upon the level of the river. Some of the doorways are faced to represent jambs and architraves ; some, excavated laterally, appear to consist of a series of chambers, and are lit

[1] Arabic—*shoghool :* a rope by which the mainsail is regulated.

from without by small windows cut in the rock. One is approached by a flight of rough steps leading up from the water's edge ; and another, hewn high in the face of the cliff, just within the mouth of a little ravine, shows a simple but imposing façade supported by four detached pillars. No modern travellers seem to visit these tombs ; while those of the old school, as Wilkinson, Champollion, etc., dismiss them with a few observations. Yet, with the single exception of the mountains behind Thebes, there is not, I believe, any one spot in Egypt which contains such a multitude of sepulchral excavations. Many look, indeed, as if they might belong to the same interesting and early epoch as those of Beni Hassan.

I may here mention that about half-way, or rather less than half-way, along the whole length of the range, I observed two large hieroglyphed stelæ incised upon the face of a projecting mass of boldly-rounded cliff at a height of perhaps a hundred and fifty feet above the river. These stelæ, apparently royal ovals, and sculptured as usual side by side, may have measured from twelve to fifteen feet in height ; but in the absence of any near object by which to scale them, I could form but a rough guess as to their actual dimensions. The boat was just then going so fast, that to sketch or take notes of the hieroglyphs was impossible. Before I could adjust my glass they were already in the rear ; and by the time I had called the rest of the party together, they were no longer distinguishable.

Coming back several months later, I looked for them again, but without success ; for the intense midday sun was then pouring full upon the rocks, to the absolute obliteration of everything like shallow detail. While watching vainly, however, for the stelæ, I was compensated by the unexpected sight of a colossal bas-relief high up on the northward face of a cliff standing, so to say, at the corner of one of those little recesses or *culs-de-sac* which here and there break the uniformity of the range. The sculptural relief of this large subject was apparently very low ; but, owing to the angle at which it met the light, one figure, which could not have measured less than eighteen or twenty feet in height, was distinctly visible. I immediately drew L.'s attention to the spot ; and she not only discerned the figure without the help of a glass, but believed like myself that she could see traces of a second.

As neither the stelæ nor the bas-relief would seem to have been observed by previous travellers, I may add for the guidance of others that the round and tower-like rock upon which the former are sculptured lies about a mile to the south-ward of the Sheykh's tomb and palm-tree (a strikingly pictur-esque bit which no one can fail to notice), and a little beyond some very large excavations near the water's edge ; while the bas-relief is to be found at a short distance below the Coptic convent and cemetery.

Having for nearly twelve miles skirted the base of Gebel Abufayda—by far the finest panoramic stretch of rock scenery on this side of the second cataract—the Nile takes an abrupt bend to the eastward, and thence flows through many miles of cultivated flat. On coming to this sudden elbow, the wind which had hitherto been carrying us along at a pace but little inferior to that of a steamer, now struck us full on the beam, and drove the boat to shore with such violence that all the steersman could do was just to run the Philæ's nose into the bank, and steer clear of some ten or twelve native cangias that had been driven in before us. The Bagstones rushed in next ; and presently a large iron-built dahabeeyah, having come gallantly along under the cliffs with all sail set, was seen to make a vain struggle at the fatal corner, and then plunge head-long at the bank, like King Agib's ship upon the Loadstone Mountain.

Imprisoned here all the afternoon, we exchanged visits of condolence with our neighbours in misfortune ; had our ears nearly cut to pieces by the driving sand ; and failed signally in the endeavour to take a walk on shore. Still the fury of the storm went on increasing. The wind howled ; the river raced in turbid waves ; the sand drove in clouds ; and the face of the sky was darkened as if by a London fog. Meanwhile, one boat after another was hurled to shore, and before night-fall we numbered a fleet of some twenty odd craft, native and foreign.

It took the united strength of both crews all next day to warp the Philæ and Bagstones across the river by means of a rope and an anchor ; an expedient that deserves special mention, not for its amazing novelty or ingenuity, but because our men declared it to be impracticable. Their fathers, they said, had never done it. Their fathers' fathers had never done it. Therefore it was impossible. Being impossible, why should they attempt it ?

They did attempt it, however, and, much to their astonishment, they succeeded.

It was, I think, towards the afternoon of this second day, when strolling by the margin of the river, that we first made the acquaintance of that renowned insect, the Egyptian beetle. He was a very fine specimen of his race, nearly half an inch long in the back, as black and shiny as a scarab cut in jet, and busily engaged in the preparation of a large rissole of mud, which he presently began laboriously propelling up the bank. We stood and watched him for some time, half in admiration, half in pity. His rissole was at least four times bigger than himself, and to roll it up that steep incline to a point beyond the level of next summer's inundation was a labour of Hercules for so small a creature. One longed to play the part of the *Deus ex machina,* and carry it up the bank for him ; but that would have been a dénouement beyond his power of appreciation.

We all know the old story of how this beetle lays its eggs by the river's brink ; encloses them in a ball of moist clay ; rolls the ball to a safe place on the edge of the desert ; buries it in the sand ; and when his time comes, dies content, having provided for the safety of his successors. Hence his mythic fame ; hence all the quaint symbolism that by degrees attached itself to his little person, and ended by investing him with a special sacredness which has often been mistaken for actual worship. Standing by thus, watching the movements of the creature, its untiring energy, its extraordinary muscular strength, its business-like devotion to the matter in hand, one sees how subtle a lesson the old Egyptian moralists had presented to them for contemplation, and with how fine a combination of wisdom and poetry they regarded this little black scarab not only as an emblem of the creative and preserving power, but perhaps also of the immortality of the soul. As a type, no insect has ever had so much greatness thrust upon him. He became a hieroglyph, and stood for a word signifying both To Be and To Transform. His portrait was multiplied a million-fold ; sculptured over the portals of temples ; fitted to the shoulders of a God ; engraved on gems ; moulded in pottery ; painted on sarcophagi and the walls of tombs ; worn by the living and buried with the dead.

Every traveller on the Nile brings away a handful of the smaller scarabs, genuine or otherwise. Some may not particu-larly care to possess them ; yet none can help buying them, if only because other people do so, or to get rid of a troublesome dealer, or to give to friends at home. I doubt, however, if even the most enthusiastic scarab-fanciers really feel in all its force the symbolism attaching to these little gems, or appreciate the exquisite naturalness of their execution, till they have seen the living beetle at its work.

In Nubia, where the strip of cultivable land is generally but a few feet in breadth, the scarab's task is comparatively light, and the breed multiplies freely. But in Egypt he has often a wide plain to traverse with his burden, and is therefore scarce in proportion to the difficulty with which he maintains the struggle for existence. The scarab race in Egypt would seem indeed to have diminished very considerably since the days of the Pharaohs, and the time is not perhaps far distant when the naturalist will look in vain for specimens on this side of the first cataract. As far as my own experience goes, I can only say that I saw scores of these beetles during the Nubian part of the journey ; but that to the best of my recollection this was the only occasion upon which I observed one in Egypt.

The Nile makes four or five more great bends between Gebel Abufayda and Siût ; passing Manfalût by the way, which town lies some distance back from the shore. All things taken into consideration—the fitful wind that came and went con-tinually ; the tremendous zigzags of the river ; the dead calm which befell us when only eight miles from Siût ; and the long day of tracking that followed, with the town in sight the whole way—we thought ourselves fortunate to get in by the evening of the third day after the storm. These last eight miles are, however, for open, placid beauty, as lovely in their way as any-

thing north of Thebes. The valley is here very wide and
fertile ; the town, with its multitudinous minarets, appears first
on one side and then on the other, according to the windings
of the river ; the distant pinky mountains look almost as transparent as the air or the sunshine ; while the banks unfold an
endless succession of charming little subjects, every one of
which looks as if it asked to be sketched as we pass.   A
shâdûf and a clump of palms—a triad of shaggy black buffaloes,
up to their shoulders in the river, and dozing as they stand—a
wide-spreading sycamore fig, in the shade of which lie a man
and camel asleep—a fallen palm uprooted by the last inunda-

RIVER-SIDE TOMBS NEAR SIÛT.

tion, with its fibrous roots yet clinging to the bank and its
crest in the water—a group of sheykhs' tombs with glistening
white cupolas relieved against a background of dark foliage—
an old disused water-wheel lying up sidewise against the bank
like a huge teetotum, and garlanded with wild tendrils of a
gourd—such are a few out of many bits by the way, which, if
they offer nothing very new, at all events present the old
material under fresh aspects, and in combination with a distance
of such ethereal light and shade, and such opalescent tenderness
of tone, that it looks more like an air-drawn mirage than a
piece of the world we live in.
      Like a mirage, too, that fairy town of Siût seemed always
to hover at the same unattainable distance, and after hours of

SIÛT.

tracking to be no nearer than at first. Sometimes, indeed, following the long reaches of the river, we appeared to be leaving it behind ; and although, as I have said, we had eight miles of hard work to get to it, I doubt whether it was ever more than three miles distant as the bird flies. It was late in the afternoon, however, when we turned the last corner ; and the sun was already setting when the boat reached the village of Hamra, which is the mooring-place for Siût—Siût itself, with clustered cupolas and arrowy minarets, lying back in the plain, at the foot of a great mountain pierced with tombs.

Now, it was in the bond that our crew were to be allowed twenty-four hours for making and baking bread at Siût, Esneh, and Assuân. No sooner, therefore, was the dahabeeyah moored than Reïs Hassan and the steersman started away at full speed on two little donkeys, to buy flour ; while Mehemet Ali, one of our most active and intelligent sailors, rushed off to hire the oven. For here, as at Esneh and Assuân, there are large flour-stores and public bakehouses for the use of sailors on the river, who make and bake their bread in large lots ; cut it into slices ; dry it in the sun ; and preserve it in the form of rusks for months together. Thus prepared, it takes the place of ship-biscuit ; and it is so far superior to ship-biscuit that it neither moulds nor breeds the maggot, but remains good and wholesome to the last crumb.

Siût, frequently written Asyoot, is the capital of Middle Egypt, and has the best bàzaars of any town up the Nile. Its red and black pottery is famous throughout the country ; and its pipe-bowls (supposed to be the best in the East), being largely exported to Cairo, find their way not only to all parts of the Levant, but to every Algerine and Japanese shop in London and Paris. No lover of peasant pottery will yet have forgotten the Egyptian stalls in the Ceramic Gallery of the International Exhibition of 1871. All those quaint red vases and lustrous black tazzas, all those exquisite little coffee services, those crocodile paper-weights, those barrel-shaped and bird-shaped bottles, came from Siût. There is a whole street of such pottery here in the town. Your dahabeeyah is scarcely made fast before a dealer comes on board and ranges his brittle wares along the deck. Others display their goods upon the bank. But the best things are only to be had in the bazaars ; and not even in Cairo is it possible to find Siût ware so choice in colour, form, and design as that which the two or three best dealers bring out, wrapped in soft paper, when a European customer appears in the market.

Besides the street of pottery, there is a street of red shoes ; another of native and foreign stuffs ; and the usual run of saddlers' shops, kebab-stalls, and Greek stores for the sale of everything in heaven or earth from third-rate cognac to patent wax vestas. The houses are of plastered mud or sun-dried bricks, as at Minieh. The thoroughfares are dusty, narrow, unpaved and crowded, as at Minieh. The people are one-eyed, dirty, and unfragrant, as at Minieh. The children's eyes are full of flies and their heads are covered with sores, as at Minieh. In short, it is Minieh over again on a larger scale ; differing only in respect of its inhabitants, who, instead of being sullen, thievish, and unfriendly, are too familiar to be pleasant, and the most unappeasable beggars out of Ireland. So our mirage turns to sordid reality, and Siût, which from afar off looked like the capital of Dreamland, resolves itself into a big mud town as ugly and ordinary as its fellows. Even the minarets, so elegant from a distance, betray for the most part but rough masonry and clumsy ornamentation when closely looked into.

A lofty embanked road planted with fine sycamore-figs leads from Hamra to Siût ; and another embanked road leads from Siût to the mountain of tombs. Of the ancient Egyptian city no vestige remains, the modern town being built upon the mounds of the earlier settlement ; but the City of the Dead— so much of it, at least, as was excavated in the living rock— survives, as at Memphis, to commemorate the departed splendour of the place.

We took donkeys next day to the edge of the desert, and went up to the sepulchres on foot. The mountain, which looked a delicate salmon pink when seen from afar, now showed bleached and arid and streaked with ochreous yellow. Layer above layer, in beds of strongly marked stratification, it towered over-head ; tier above tier, the tombs yawned, open-mouthed, along the face of the precipice. I picked up a fragment of the rock, and found it light, porous, and full of little cells, like pumice.

The slopes were strewn with such stones, as well as with fragments of mummy, shreds of mummy-cloth, and human bones all whitening and withering in the sun.

The first tomb we came to was the so-called Stabl Antar —a magnificent but cruelly mutilated excavation, consisting of a grand entrance, a vaulted corridor, a great hall, two side-chambers, and a sanctuary. The ceiling of the corridor, now smoke-blackened and defaced, has been richly decorated with intricate patterns in light green, white, and buff, upon a ground of dark bluish-green stucco. The wall to the right on entering is covered with a long hieroglyphic inscription. In the sanctuary, vague traces of seated figures, male and female, with lotus blossoms in their hands, are dimly visible. Two colossal warriors incised in outline upon the levelled rock—the one very perfect, the other hacked almost out of recognition—stand on each side of the huge portal. A circular hole in the threshold marks the spot where the great door once worked upon its pivot ; and a deep pit, now partially filled in with rubbish, leads from the centre of the hall to some long-rifled vault deep down in the heart of the mountain. Wilful destruction has been at work on every side. The wall-sculptures are chipped and defaced—the massive pillars that once supported the superincumbent rock have been quarried away—the interior is heaped high with débris. Enough is left, however, to attest the antique stateliness of the tomb ; and the hieroglyphic inscription remains almost intact to tell its age and history.

This inscription (erroneously entered in Murray's Guide as uncopied, but interpreted by Brugsch, who published extracts from it as far back as 1862) shows the excavation to have been made for one Hepoukefa, or Haptefa, nomarch of the Lycopolite Nome, and Chief Priest of the jackal god of Siût.[1] It is also famous among scientific students for certain passages which contain important information regarding the intercalary

[1] The known inscriptions in the tomb of Haptefa have recently been recopied, and another long inscription, not previously transcribed, has been copied and translated, by Mr. F. Llewellyn Griffith, acting for the Egypt Exploration Fund. Mr. Griffith has for the first time fixed the date of this famous tomb, which was made during the reign of Usertesen I, of the XIIth dynasty. [Note to Second Edition.]

days of the Egyptian kalendar.[1] We observed that the full-length figures on the jambs of the doorway appeared to have been incised, filled in with stucco, and then coloured. The stucco had for the most part fallen out, though enough remained to show the style of the work.[2]

From this tomb to the next we crept by way of a passage, tunnelled in the mountain, and emerged into a spacious, quadrangular grotto, even more dilapidated than the first. It had been originally supported by square pillars left standing in the substance of the rock ; but, like the pillars in the tomb of Hepoukefa, they had been hewn away in the middle and looked like stalactite columns in process of formation. For the rest, two half-filled pits, a broken sarcophagus, and a few painted hieroglyphs upon a space of stuccoed wall, were all that remained.

One would have liked to see the sepulchre in which Ampère, the brilliant and eager disciple of Champollion, deciphered the ancient name of Siût ; but since he does not specify the cartouche by which it could be identified, one might wander about the mountain for a week without being able to find it. Having first described the Stabl Antar, he says :—" In another grotto I found twice over the name of the city written in hieroglyphic characters, *Çi-ou-t*. This name forms part of an inscription which also contains an ancient royal cartouche ; so proving that the present name of the city dates back to Pharaonic times." [3]

Here, then, we trace a double process of preservation. This town, which in the ancient Egyptian was written Ssout, became Lycopolis under the Greeks ; continued to be called Lycopolis throughout the period of Roman rule in Egypt ; reverted to its old historic name under the Copts of the middle ages, who wrote it Siôout ; and survives in the Asyoot of the

---

[1] See *Recueil des Monuments Egyptiens*, Brugsch. Part I. Planche xi. Published 1862.

[2] Some famous tombs of very early date, enriched with the same kind of inlaid decoration, are to be seen at Meydûm, near the base of the Meydûm Pyramid.

[3] *Voyage en Egypte et en Nubie*, by J. J. Ampère. The cartouche may perhaps be that of *Rakameri*, mentioned by Brugsch : *Histoire d Egypte*, chap. vi., first edition.

Arab fellâh.　Nor is this by any means a solitary instance. Khemmis in the same way became Panopolis, reverted to the Coptic Chmin, and to this day as Ekhmîm perpetuates the legend of its first foundation.　As with these fragments of the old tongue, so with the race.　Subdued again and again by invading hordes ; intermixed for centuries together with Phœnician, Persian, Greek, Roman, and Arab blood, it fuses these heterogeneous elements in one common mould, reverts persistently to the early type, and remains Egyptian to the last.　So strange is the tyranny of natural forces.　The sun and soil of Egypt demand one special breed of men, and will tolerate no other.　Foreign residents cannot rear children in the country.　In the Isthmus of Suez, which is considered the healthiest part of Egypt, an alien population of twenty thousand persons failed in the course of ten years to rear one infant born upon the soil.　Children of an alien father and an Egyptian mother will die off in the same way in early infancy, unless brought up in the simple native fashion.　And it is affirmed of the descendants of mixed marriages, that after the third generation the foreign blood seems to be eliminated, while the traits of the race are restored in their original purity.

These are but a few instances of the startling conservatism of Egypt,—a conservatism which interested me particularly, and to which I shall frequently have occasion to return.

Each Nome, or province, of ancient Egypt had its sacred animal ; and Siût was called Lycopolis by the Greeks [1] because the wolf (now almost extinct in the land) was there held in the same kind of reverence as the cat at Bubastis, the crocodile at Ombos, and the lion at Leontopolis.　Mummy-wolves are, or used to be, found in the smaller tombs about the mountain, as well as mummy-jackals ; Anubis, the jackal-headed god, being the presiding deity of the district.　A mummied jackal from this place, curiously wrapped in striped bandages, is to be seen in the First Egyptian Room at the British Museum.

But the view from the mountain above Siût is finer than its tombs and more ancient than its mummies.　Seen from within the great doorway of the second grotto, it looks like a

---

[1] The Greeks translated the sacred names of Egyptian places ; the Copts adopted the civil names.

framed picture. For the foreground, we have a dazzling slope of limestone débris; in the middle distance, a wide plain clothed with the delicious tender green of very young corn; farther away yet, the cupolas and minarets of Siût rising from the midst of a belt of palm-groves; beyond these again, the molten gold of the great river glittering away, coil after coil, into the far distance; and all along the horizon, the everlasting boundary of the desert. Large pools of placid water left by the last inundation lie here and there, like lakes amid the green. A group of brown men are wading yonder with their nets. A funeral comes along the embanked road—the bier carried at a rapid pace on men's shoulders, and covered with a red shawl; the women taking up handfuls of dust and scattering it upon their heads as they walk. We can see the dust flying, and hear their shrill wail borne upon the breathless air. The cemetery towards which they are going lies round to the left, at the foot of the mountain—a wilderness of little white cupolas, with here and there a tree. Broad spaces of shade sleep under the spreading sycamores by the road-side; a hawk circles overhead; and Siût, bathed in the splendour of the morning sun, looks as fairy-like as ever.

Lepsius is reported to have said that the view from this hill-side was the finest in Egypt. But Egypt is a long country, and questions of precedence are delicate matters to deal with. It is, however, a very beautiful view; though most travellers who know the scenery about Thebes and the approach to Assûan would hesitate, I should fancy, to give the preference to a landscape from which the nearer mountains are excluded by the position of the spectator.

The tombs here, as in many other parts of Egypt, are said to have been largely appropriated by early Christian anchorites during the reigns of the later Roman emperors; and to these recluses may perhaps be ascribed the legend that makes Lycopolis the abode of Joseph and Mary during the years of their sojourn in Egypt. It is, of course, but a legend, and wholly improbable. If the Holy Family ever journeyed into Egypt at all, which certain Biblical critics now hold to be doubtful, they probably rested from their wanderings at some town not very far from the eastern border—as Tanis, or Pithom, or

Bubastis.   Siût would, at all events, lie at least 250 miles to the southward of any point to which they might reasonably be supposed to have penetrated.

Still, one would like to believe a story that laid the scene of Our Lord's childhood in the midst of this beautiful and glowing Egyptian pastoral.   With what a profound and touching interest it would invest the place!   With what different eyes we should look down upon a landscape which must have been dear and familiar to Him in all its details, and which, from the nature of the ground, must have remained almost unchanged from His day to ours!   The mountain with its tombs, the green corn-flats, the Nile and the desert, looked then as they look now.   It is only the Moslem minarets that are new.   It is only the pylons and sanctuaries of the ancient worship that have passed away.

CHAPTER VII.

SIÛT TO DENDERAH.

WE started from Siût with a couple of tons of new brown bread on board, which, being cut into slices and laid to dry in the sun, was speedily converted into rusks and stored away in two huge lockers on the upper deck. The sparrows and water-wagtails had a good time while the drying went on ; but no one seemed to grudge the toll they levied.

We often had a " big wind " now ; though it seldom began to blow before ten or eleven A.M., and generally fell at sunset. Now and then, when it chanced to keep up, and the river was known to be free from shallows, we went on sailing through the night ; but this seldom happened, and when it did happen, it made sleep impossible—so that nothing but the certainty of doing a great many miles between bedtime and breakfast could induce us to put up with it.

We had now been long enough afloat to find out that we had almost always one man on the sick list, and were there-fore habitually short of a hand for the navigation of the boat. There never were such fellows for knocking themselves to pieces as our sailors. They were always bruising their feet, wounding their hands, getting sunstrokes, and whitlows, and sprains, and disabling themselves in some way. L., with her little medicine chest and her roll of lint and bandages, soon had a small but steady practice, and might have been seen about the lower deck most mornings after breakfast, repairing these damaged Alis and Hassans. It was well for them that we carried "an experienced surgeon," for they were entirely

helpless and despondent when hurt, and ignorant of the com-
monest remedies.   Nor is this helplessness confined to natives
of the sailor and fellâh class.   The provincial proprietors and
officials are to the full as ignorant, not only of the uses of such
simple things as poultices or wet compresses, but of the most
elementary laws of health.   Doctors there are none south of
Cairo ; and such is the general mistrust of State medicine, that
when, as in the case of any widely-spread epidemic, a medical
officer is sent up the river by order of the Government, half the
people are said to conceal their sick, while the other half reject
the remedies prescribed for them.   Their trust in the skill
of the passing European is, on the other hand, unbounded.
Appeals for advice and medicine were constantly being made
to us by both rich and poor ; and there was something very
pathetic in the simple faith with which they accepted any little
help we were able to give them.   Meanwhile L.'s medical
reputation, being confirmed by a few simple cures, rose high
among the crew.   They called her the Hakîm Sitt (the Doctor-
Lady) ; obeyed her directions and swallowed her medicines as
reverently as if she were the College of Surgeons personified ;
and showed their gratitude in all kinds of pretty, child-like
ways—singing her favourite Arab song as they ran beside her
donkey—searching for sculptured fragments whenever there
were ruins to be visited—and constantly bringing her little
gifts of pebbles and wild flowers.

Above Siût, the picturesqueness of the river is confined for
the most part to the eastern bank.   We have almost always a
near range of mountains on the Arabian side, and a more distant chain on the Libyan horizon.   Gebel Sheykh el Raáineh
succeeds to Gebel Abufayda, and is followed in close succession
by the cliffs of Gow, of Gebel Sheykh el Hereedee, of Gebel
Ayserat and Gebel Tûkh—all alike rigid in strongly-marked
beds of level limestone strata ; flat-topped and even, like lines of
giant ramparts ; and more or less pierced with orifices which we
know to be tombs, but which look like loopholes from a distance.

Flying before the wind with both sails set, we see the rapid
panorama unfold itself day after day, mile after mile, hour after
hour.   Villages, palm-groves, rock-cut sepulchres, flit past and
are left behind.   To-day we enter the region of the dôm palm.

To-morrow we pass the map-drawn limit of the crocodile. The cliffs advance, recede, open away into desolate-looking valleys, and show faint traces of paths leading to excavated tombs on distant heights. The headland that looked shadowy in the distance a couple of hours ago, is reached and passed. The cargo-boat on which we have been gaining all the morning is outstripped and dwindling in the rear. Now we pass a bold bluff sheltering a sheykh's tomb and a solitary dôm palm— now an ancient quarry from which the stone has been cut out in smooth masses, leaving great halls, and corridors, and stages in the mountain side. At Gow,[1] the scene of an insurrection headed by a crazy dervish some ten years ago, we see, in place of a large and populous village, only a tract of fertile corn-ground, a few ruined huts, and a group of decapitated palms. We are now skirting Gebel Sheykh el Hereedee ; here bordered by a rich margin of cultivated flat ; yonder leaving space for scarce a strip of roadway between the precipice and the river. Then comes Raáineh, a large village of square mud towers, lofty and battlemented, with string-courses of pots for the pigeons—and later on, Girgeh, once the capital town of Middle Egypt, where we put in for half an hour to post and inquire for letters. Here the Nile is fast eating away the bank and carrying the town by storm. A ruined mosque with pointed arches, roofless cloisters, and a leaning column that must surely have come to the ground by this time, stands just above the landing-place. A hundred years ago, it lay a quarter of a mile

---

[1] According to the account given in her letters by Lady Duff Gordon, this dervish, who had acquired a reputation for unusual sanctity by repeating the name of Allah 3000 times every night for three years, believed that he had by these means rendered himself invulnerable ; and so, proclaiming himself the appointed Slayer of Antichrist, he stirred up a revolt among the villages bordering Gebel Sheykh Hereedee, instigated an attack on an English dahabeeyah, and brought down upon himself and all that country-side the swift and summary vengeance of the Government. Steamers with troops commanded by Fadl Pasha were despatched up the river ; rebels were shot ; villages sacked ; crops and cattle confiscated. The women and children of the place were then distributed among the neighbouring hamlets ; and Gow, which was as large a village as Luxor, ceased to exist. The dervish's fate remained uncertain. He was shot, according to some ; and by others it was said that he had escaped into the desert under the protection of a tribe of Bedouins.

from the river ; ten years ago it was yet perfect ; after a few
more inundations it will be swept away.   Till that time comes,
however, it helps to make Girgeh one of the most picturesque
towns in Egypt.

At Farshût we see the sugar-works in active operation—
smoke pouring from the tall chimneys ; steam issuing from the
traps in the basement ; cargo-boats unlading fresh sugar-cane
against the bank ; heavily-burdened Arabs transporting it to
the factory ; bullock-trucks laden with cane-leaf for firing.   A
little higher up, at Sahîl Bajûra on the opposite side of the
river, we find the bank strewn for full a quarter of a mile with
sugar-cane *en masse.*   Hundreds of camels are either arriving
laden with it, or going back for more—dozens of cargo-boats
are drawn up to receive it—swarms of brown fellâheen are stack-
ing it on board for unshipment again at Farshût.   The camels
snort and growl ; the men shout ; the overseers, in blue-fringed
robes and white turbans, stalk to and fro, and keep the work
going.   The mountains here recede so far as to be almost out
of sight, and a plain rich in sugar-cane and date-palms widens
out between them and the river.

And now the banks are lovely with an unwonted wealth of
verdure.   The young corn clothes the plain like a carpet,
while the yellow-tasselled mimosa, the feathery tamarisk, the
dôm and date palm, and the spreading sycamore-fig, border
the towing-path like garden trees beside a garden walk.

Farther on still, when all this greenery is left behind and
the banks have again become flat and bare, we see to our
exceeding surprise what seems to be a very large grizzled ape
perched on the top of a dust-heap on the western bank.   The
creature is evidently quite tame, and sits on its haunches in
just that chilly, melancholy posture that the chimpanzee is
wont to assume in his cage at the Zoological Gardens.   Some
six or eight Arabs, one of whom has dismounted from his camel
for the purpose, are standing round and staring at him, much
as the British public stands and stares at the specimen in the
Regent's Park.   Meanwhile a strange excitement breaks out
among our crew.   They crowd to the side ; they shout ; they
gesticulate ; the captain salaams ; the steersman waves his
hand ; all eyes are turned towards the shore.

GIRGEH.

"Do you see Sheykh Selîm?" cries Talhamy breathlessly, rushing up from below. "There he is! Look at him! That is Sheykh Selîm!"

And so we find out that it is not a monkey but a man— and not only a man, but a saint. Holiest of the holy, dirtiest of the dirty, white-pated, white-bearded, withered, bent, and knotted up, is the renowned Sheykh Selîm—he who, naked and unwashed, has sat on that same spot every day through summer heat and winter cold for the last fifty years; never providing himself with food or water; never even lifting his hand to his mouth; depending on charity not only for his food but for his feeding! He is not nice to look at, even by this dim light, and at this distance; but the sailors think him quite beautiful, and call aloud to him for his blessing as we go by.

"It is not by our own will that we sail past, O father!" they cry. "Fain would we kiss thy hand; but the wind blows and the mérkeb (boat) goes, and we have no power to stay!"

But Sheykh Selîm neither lifts his head nor shows any sign of hearing, and in a few minutes the mound on which he sits is left behind in the gloaming.

At How, where the new town is partly built on the mounds of the old (Diospolis Parva), we next morning saw the natives transporting small boat-loads of ancient brick-rubbish to the opposite side of the river, for the purpose of manuring those fields from which the early durra crop had just been gathered in. Thus, curiously enough, the mud left by some inundation of two or three thousand years ago comes at last to the use from which it was then diverted, and is found to be more fertilising than the new deposit. At Kasr es Sayd, a little farther on, we came to one of the well-known "bad bits"—a place where the bed of the river is full of sunken rocks, and sailing is impossible. Here the men were half the day punting the dahabeeyah over the dangerous part, while we grubbed among the mounds of what was once the ancient city of Chenoboscion. These remains, which cover a large superficial area and consist entirely of crude brick foundations, are very interesting, and in good preservation. We traced the ground-plans of several houses; followed the passages by which they were separated; and observed many small arches which seemed built on too small a scale for doors or windows, but for which it was difficult to account in any other way. Brambles and weeds were growing in these deserted enclosures ; while rubbish-heaps, excavated pits, and piles of broken pottery divided the ruins and made the work of exploration difficult. We looked in vain for the dilapidated quay and sculptured blocks mentioned in Wilkinson's *General View of Egypt ;* but if the foundation stones of the new sugar-factory close against the mooring-place could speak, they would no doubt explain the mystery. We saw nothing, indeed, to show that Chenoboscion had contained any stone structures whatever, save the broken shaft of one small granite column.

KASR ES SYAD.

The village of Kasr es Syad consists of a cluster of mud huts and a sugar factory ; but the factory was idle that day, and the village seemed half deserted. The view here is particularly fine. About a couple of miles to the southward, the mountains, in magnificent procession, come down again at right angles to the river, and thence reach away in long ranges of precipitous headlands. The plain, terminating abruptly against the foot of this gigantic barrier, opens back eastward to the remotest horizon——an undulating sea of glistening sand, bordered by a chaotic middle distance of mounded ruins. Nearest of all, a narrow foreground of cultivated soil, green with young crops and watered by frequent shâdûfs, extends along the river-side to the foot of the mountains. A sheykh's tomb shaded by a single dôm palm is conspicuous on the bank ;

while far away, planted amid the solitary sands, we see a large
Coptic convent with many cupolas ; a cemetery full of Christian
graves ; and a little oasis of date palms indicating the presence
of a spring.

The chief interest of this scene, however, centres in the
ruins ; and these—looked upon from a little distance, blackened,
desolate, half-buried, obscured every now and then, when the
wind swept over them, by swirling clouds of dust—reminded
us of the villages, we had seen not two years before, half-over-
whelmed and yet smoking, in the midst of a lava-torrent below
Vesuvius.

We now had the full moon again, making night more
beautiful than day. Sitting on deck for hours after the sun
had gone down, when the boat glided gently on with half-filled
sail and the force of the wind was spent, we used to wonder if
in all the world there was another climate in which the effect
of moonlight was so magical. To say that every object far or
near was visible as distinctly as by day, yet more tenderly, is
to say nothing. It was not only form that was defined ; it
was not only light and shadow that were vivid—it was colour
that was present. Colour neither deadened nor changed ; but
softened, glowing, spiritualised. The amber sheen of the sand-
island in the middle of the river, the sober green of the palm-
grove, the Little Lady's turquoise-coloured hood, were clear to
the sight and relatively true in tone. The oranges showed
through the bars of the crate like nuggets of pure gold. L.'s
crimson shawl glowed with a warmer dye than it ever wore by
day. The mountains were flushed as if in the light of sunset.
Of all the natural phenomena that we beheld in the course of
the journey, I remember none that surprised us more than this.
We could scarcely believe at first that it was not some effect
of afterglow, or some miraculous aurora of the East. But the
sun had nothing to do with that flush upon the mountains.
The glow was in the stone, and the moonlight but revealed the
local colour.

For some days before they came in sight, we had been
eagerly looking for the Theban hills ; and now, after a night
of rapid sailing, we woke one morning to find the sun rising
on the wrong side of the boat, the favourable wind dead against

us, and a picturesque chain of broken peaks upon our starboard bow. By these signs we knew that we must have come to the great bend in the river between How and Keneh, and that these new mountains, so much more varied in form than those of Middle Egypt, must be the mountains behind Denderah. They seemed to lie upon the eastern bank, but that was an illusion which the map disproved, and which lasted only till the great corner was fairly turned. To turn that corner, however, in the teeth of wind and current, was no easy task, and cost us two long days of hard tracking.

At a point about ten miles below Denderah, we saw some thousands of fellâheen at work amid clouds of sand upon the embankments of a new canal. They swarmed over the mounds like ants, and the continuous murmur of their voices came to us across the river like the humming of innumerable bees. Others, following the path along the bank, were pouring towards the spot in an unbroken stream. The Nile must here be nearly half a mile in breadth ; but the engineers in European dress, and the overseers with long sticks in their hands, were plainly distinguishable by the help of a glass. The tents in which these officials were camping out during the progress of the work gleamed white among the palms by the river-side. Such scenes must have been common enough in the old days when a conquering Pharaoh, returning from Libya or the land of Kush, set his captives to raise a dyke, or excavate a lake, or quarry a mountain. The Israelites building the massive walls of Pithom and Rameses with bricks of their own making, must have presented exactly such a spectacle.

That we were witnessing a case of forced labour, could not be doubted. Those thousands yonder had most certainly been drafted off in gangs from hundreds of distant villages, and were but little better off, for the time being, than the captives of the ancient Empire. In all cases of forced labour under the present *régime*, however, it seems that the labourer is paid, though very insufficiently, for his unwilling toil ; and that his captivity only lasts so long as the work for which he has been pressed remains in progress. In some cases the term of service is limited to three or four months, at the end of which time the men are supposed to be returned in barges towed by Govern-

ment steam-tugs.   It too often happens, nevertheless, that the
poor souls are left to get back how they can ; and thus many
a husband and father either perishes by the way, or is driven
to take service in some village far from home.   Meanwhile his
wife and children, being scantily supported by the Sheykh el
Beled, fall into a condition of semi-serfdom ; and his little
patch of ground, left untilled through seed-time and harvest,
passes after the next inundation into the hands of a stranger.

But there is another side to this question of forced labour.
Water must be had in Egypt, no matter at what cost.   If the
land is not sufficiently irrigated, the crops fail and the nation
starves.   Now, the frequent construction of canals has from
immemorial time been reckoned among the first duties of an
Egyptian ruler ; but it is a duty which cannot be performed
without the willing or unwilling co-operation of several thousand
workmen.   Those who are best acquainted with the character
and temper of the fellâh maintain the hopelessness of looking
to him for voluntary labour of this description.   Frugal, patient,
easily contented as he is, no promise of wages, however high,
would tempt him from his native village.   What to him are the
needs of a district six or seven hundred miles away ?   His own
shâdûf is enough for his own patch, and so long as he can raise
his three little crops a year, neither he nor his family will starve.
How, then, are these necessary public works to be carried out,
unless by means of the *corvée ?*   M. About has put an ingenious summary of this " other-side " argument into the mouth of
his ideal fellâh.   " It is not the Emperor," says Ahmed to the
Frenchman, " who causes the rain to descend upon your lands ;
it is the west wind—and the benefit thus conferred upon you
exacts no penalty of manual labour.   But in Egypt, where the
rain from heaven falls scarcely three times in the year, it is the
prince who supplies its place to us by distributing the waters
of the Nile.   This can only be done by the work of men's
hands ; and it is therefore to the interest of all that the hands
of all should be at his disposal."

We regarded it, I think, as an especial piece of good fortune,
when we found ourselves becalmed next day within three or
four miles of Denderah.   Abydos comes first in order according
to the map ; but then the Temples lie seven or eight miles

DENDERAH.

from the river, and as we happened just thereabouts to be making some ten miles an hour, we put off the excursion till our return.   Here, however, the ruins lay comparatively near at hand, and in such a position that we could approach them from below and rejoin our dahabeeyah a few miles higher up the river.   So, leaving Reïs Hassan to track against the current, we landed at the first convenient point, and finding neither donkeys nor guides at hand, took an escort of three or four sailors, and set off on foot.

The way was long, the day was hot, and we had only the map to go by.   Having climbed the steep bank and skirted an extensive palm-grove, we found ourselves in a country without paths or roads of any kind.   The soil, squared off as usual like a gigantic chess-board, was traversed by hundreds of tiny water-channels, between which we had to steer our course as best we could.   Presently the last belt of palms was passed— the plain, green with young corn and level as a lake, widened out to the foot of the mountains—and the Temple, islanded in that sea of rippling emerald, rose up before us upon its platform of blackened mounds.

It was still full two miles away ; but it looked enormous— showing from this distance as a massive, low-browed, sharply-defined mass of dead-white masonry.   The walls sloped in slightly towards the top ; and the façade appeared to be supported on eight square piers, with a large doorway in the centre. If sculptured ornament, or cornice, or pictured legend enriched those walls, we were too far off to distinguish them.   All looked strangely naked and solemn—more like a tomb than a temple.

Nor was the surrounding scene less deathlike in its solitude. Not a tree, not a hut, not a living form broke the green monotony of the plain.   Behind the Temple, but divided from it by a farther space of mounded ruins, rose the mountains— pinky, aerial, with sheeny sand-drifts heaped in the hollows of their bare buttresses, and spaces of soft blue shadow in their misty chasms.   Where the range receded, a long vista of glittering desert opened to the Libyan horizon.

Then as we drew nearer, coming by and by to a raised causeway which apparently connected the mounds with some point down by the river, the details of the Temple gradually emerged into distinctness. We could now see the curve and under-shadow of the cornice; and a small object in front of the façade which looked at first sight like a monolithic altar, resolved itself into a massive gateway of the kind known as a single pylon. Nearer still, among some low outlying mounds, we came upon fragments of sculptured capitals and mutilated statues half-buried in rank grass—upon a series of stagnant nitre-tanks and deserted workshops—upon the telegraph-poles and wires which here come striding along the edge of the desert and vanish southward with messages for Nubia and the Soudan.

Egypt is the land of nitre. It is found wherever a crude-brick mound is disturbed or an antique stone structure demolished. The Nile mud is strongly impregnated with it; and in Nubia we used to find it lying in thick talc-like flakes upon the surface of rocks far above the present level of the inundation. These tanks at Denderah had been sunk, we were told, when the great Temple was excavated by Abbas Pasha more than twenty years ago. The nitre then found was utilised out of hand; washed and crystallised in the tanks; and converted into gunpowder in the adjacent workshops. The telegraph wires are more recent intruders, and the work of the Khedive; but one longed to put them out of sight, to pull down the gunpowder sheds, and to fill up the tanks with débris. For what had the arts of modern warfare or the wonders of modern science to do with Hathor, the Lady of Beauty and the Western Shades, the Nurse of Horus, the Egyptian Aphrodite, to whom yonder mountain of wrought stone and all these wastes were sacred?

We were by this time near enough to see that the square piers of the façade were neither square nor piers, but huge round columns with human-headed capitals; and that the walls, instead of being plain and tomb-like, were covered with an infinite multitude of sculptured figures. The pylon—rich with inscriptions and bas-reliefs, but disfigured by myriads of tiny wasps' nests, like clustered mud-bubbles—now towered high above our heads, and led to a walled avenue cut direct through the mounds, and sloping downwards to the main entrance of the Temple.

Not, however, till we stood immediately under those
ponderous columns, looking down upon the paved floor below
and up to the huge cornice that projected overhead like the
crest of an impending wave, did we realise the immense proportions of the building.   Lofty as it looked from a distance,
we now found that it was only the interior that had been
excavated, and that not more than two-thirds of its actual
height were visible above the mounds.   The level of the
avenue was, indeed, at its lowest part full twenty feet above
that of the first great hall ; and we had still a steep temporary
staircase to go down before reaching the original pavement.

The effect of the portico as one stands at the top of this
staircase is one of overwhelming majesty.   Its breadth, its
height, the massiveness of its parts, exceed in grandeur all
that one has been anticipating throughout the long two miles
of approach.   The immense girth of the columns, the huge
screens which connect them, the ponderous cornice jutting
overhead, confuse the imagination, and in the absence of given
measurements [1] appear, perhaps, even more enormous than they
are.   Looking up to the architrave, we see a kind of Egyptian
Panathenaic procession of carven priests and warriors, some with
standards and some with musical instruments.   The winged
globe, depicted upon a gigantic scale in the curve of the cornice,
seems to hover above the central doorway.   Hieroglyphs,
emblems, strange forms of Kings and Gods, cover every foot of
wall-space, frieze, and pillar.   Nor does this wealth of surface-
sculpture tend in any way to diminish the general effect of size.
It would seem, on the contrary, as if complex decoration were
in this instance the natural complement to simplicity of form.
Every group, every inscription, appears to be necessary and in its
place ; an essential part of the building it helps to adorn.   Most
of these details are as perfect as on the day when the last workman went his way, and the architect saw his design completed.
Time has neither marred the surface of the stone nor blunted

[1] Sir G. Wilkinson states the total length of the Temple to be 93
paces, or 220 feet ; and the width of the portico 50 paces.   Murray
gives no measurements ; neither does Mariette Bey in his delightful little
" Itineraire " ; neither does Fergusson, nor Champollion, nor any other
writer to whose works I have had access.

the work of the chisel. Such injury as they have sustained is from the hand of man ; and in no country has the hand of man achieved more and destroyed more than in Egypt. The Persians overthrew the masterpieces of the Pharaohs ; the Copts mutilated the temples of the Ptolemies and Cæsars ; the Arabs stripped the pyramids and carried Memphis away piecemeal. Here at Denderah we have an example of Græco-Egyptian work and early Christian fanaticism. Begun by Ptolemy XI,[1] and bearing upon its latest ovals the name and style of Nero, the present building was still comparatively new when, in A.D. 379, the ancient religion was abolished by the edict of Theodosius. It was then the most gorgeous as well as the most recent of all those larger temples built during the prosperous foreign rule of the last seven hundred years. It stood, surrounded by groves of palm and acacia, within the precincts of a vast enclosure, the walls of which, 1000 feet in length, 35 feet in height, and 15 feet thick, are still traceable. A dromos, now buried under twenty feet of débris, led from

---

[1] The names of Augustus, Caligula, Tiberius, Domitian, Claudius, and Nero are found in the royal ovals ; the oldest being those of Ptolemy XI, the founder of the present edifice, which was, however, rebuilt upon the site of a succession of older buildings, of which the most ancient dated back as far as the reign of Khufu, the builder of the Great Pyramid. This fact, and the still more interesting fact that the oldest structure of all was believed to belong to the inconceivably remote period of the *Horshesu*, or "followers of Horus" (*i.e.* the petty chiefs, or princes, who ruled in Egypt before the foundation of the first monarchy), is recorded in the following remarkable inscription discovered by Mariette in one of the crypts constructed in the thickness of the walls of the present temple. The first text relates to certain festivals to be celebrated in honour of Hathor, and states that all the ordained ceremonies had been performed by King Thothmes III (XVIIIth dynasty) "in memory of his mother, Hathor of Denderah. And they found the great fundamental rules of Denderah in ancient writing, written on goatskin in the time of the Followers of Horus. This was found in the inside of a brick wall during the reign of King Pepi (VIth dynasty)." In the same crypt, another and a more brief inscription runs thus :— "Great fundamental rule of Denderah. Restorations done by Thothmes III, according to what was found in ancient writing of the time of King Khufu." Hereupon Mariette remarks—"The temple of Denderah is not, then, one of the most modern in Egypt, except in so far as it was constructed by one of the later Lagidæ. Its origin is literally lost in the night of time." See *Dendérah, Description Générale*, chap. i. pp. 55, 56.

the pylon to the portico. The pylon is there still, a partial ruin ; but the Temple, with its roof, its staircases, and its secret treasure-crypts, is in all essential respects as perfect as on the day when its splendour was given over to the spoilers.

CLEOPATRA.

One can easily imagine how these spoilers sacked and ravaged all before them ; how they desecrated the sacred places, and cast down the statues of the Goddess, and divided the treasures of the sanctuary. They did not, it is true, commit such wholesale destruction as the Persian invaders of nine hundred years before ; but they were merciless iconoclasts, and hacked away the face of every figure within easy reach both inside and outside the building.

Among those which escaped, however, is the famous external bas-relief of Cleopatra on the back of the Temple. This curious sculpture is now banked up with rubbish for its better preservation, and can no longer be seen by travellers. It was, however, admirably photographed some years ago by Signor Beati ; which photograph is faithfully reproduced in the annexed engraving. Cleopatra is here represented with a headdress combining the attributes of three goddesses ; namely the Vulture of Maut (the head of which is modelled in a masterly way), the horned disc of Hathor, and the throne' of Isis. The falling mass below the headdress is intended to represent hair dressed according to the Egyptian fashion, in an infinite number of small plaits, each finished off with an ornamental tag. The women of Egypt and Nubia wear their hair so to this day, and unplait it, I am sorry to say, not oftener than once in every eight or ten weeks. The Nubian girls fasten each separate tail with a lump of Nile mud daubed over with yellow ochre ; but Queen Cleopatra's silken tresses were probably tipped with gilded wax or gum.

It is difficult to know where decorative sculpture ends and portraiture begins in a work of this epoch. We cannot even be certain that a portrait was intended ; though the introduction of the royal oval in which the name of Cleopatra (Klaupatra) is spelt with its vowel sounds in full, would seem to point that way. If it is a portrait, then large allowance must be made for conventional treatment. The fleshiness of the features and the intolerable simper are common to every head of the Ptolemaic period. The ear, too, is pattern work, and the drawing of the figure is ludicrous. Mannerism apart, however, the face wants for neither individuality nor beauty. Cover the mouth, and you have an almost faultless profile. The chin and throat are also quite lovely ; while the whole face, suggestive of cruelty, subtlety, and voluptuousness, carries with it an indefinable impression not only of portraiture, but of likeness.

It is not without something like a shock that one first sees the unsightly havoc wrought upon the Hathor-headed columns of the façade at Denderah. The massive folds of the head-gear are there ; the ears, erect and pointed like those of a heifer, are there ; but of the benignant face of the Goddess not a feature remains. Ampère, describing these columns in one of his earliest letters from Egypt, speaks of them as being still "brilliant with colours that time had had no power to efface." Time, however, must have been unusually busy during the thirty years that have gone by since then ; for though we presently found several instances of painted bas-reliefs in the small inner chambers, I do not remember to have observed any remains of colour (save here and there a faint trace of yellow ochre) on the external decorations.

Without, all was sunshine and splendour ; within, all was silence and mystery.   A heavy, death-like smell, as of long-imprisoned gases, met us on the threshold.   By the half-light that strayed in through the portico, we could see vague outlines of a forest of giant columns rising out of the gloom below and vanishing into the gloom above.   Beyond these again appeared shadowy vistas of successive halls leading away into depths of inpenetrable darkness.   It required no great courage to go down those stairs and explore those depths with a party of fellow-travellers ; but it would have been a gruesome place to venture into alone.

Seen from within, the portico shows as a vast hall, fifty feet in height and supported on twenty-four Hathor-headed columns. Six of these, being engaged in the screen, form part of the façade, and are the same upon which we have been looking from without.   By degrees, as our eyes become used to the twilight, we see here and there a capital which still preserves the vague likeness of a gigantic female face ; while, dimly visible on every wall, pillar, and doorway, a multitude of fantastic forms — hawk-headed, ibis-headed, cow-headed, mitred, plumed, holding aloft strange emblems, seated on thrones, performing mysterious rites—seem to emerge from their places, like things of life.   Looking up to the ceiling, now smoke-blackened and defaced, we discover elaborate paintings of scarabæi, winged globes, and zodiacal emblems divided by borders of intricate Greek patterns, the prevailing colours of which are verditer and chocolate.   Bands of hieroglyphic inscriptions, of royal ovals, of Hathor heads, of mitred hawks, of lion-headed chimeras, of divinities and kings in bas-relief, cover the shafts of the great columns from top to bottom ; and even here, every accessible human face, however small, has been laboriously mutilated.

Bewildered at first sight of these profuse and mysterious decorations, we wander round and round ; going on from the first hall to the second, from the second to the third ; and plunging into deeper darkness at every step.   We have been reading about these gods and emblems for weeks past—we have studied the plan of the Temple beforehand ; yet now that we are actually here, our book knowledge goes for nothing, and we feel as hopelessly ignorant as if we had been suddenly landed in a new world. Not till we have got over this first feeling of confusion—not till, resting awhile on the base of one of the columns, we again open out the plan of the building, do we begin to realise the purport of the sculptures by which we are surrounded.

The ceremonial of Egyptian worship was essentially processional. Herein we have the central idea of every Temple, and the key to its construction. It was bound to contain store-chambers in which were kept vestments, instruments, divine emblems, and the like ; laboratories for the preparation of perfumes and unguents ; treasuries for the safe custody of holy vessels and precious offerings ; chambers for the reception and purification of tribute in kind ; halls for the assembling and marshalling of priests and functionaries ; and, for processional purposes, corridors, staircases, courtyards, cloisters, and vast enclosures planted with avenues of trees and surrounded by walls which hedged in with inviolable secrecy the solemn rites of the priesthood.

In this plan, it will be seen, there is no provision made for anything in the form of public worship ; but then an Egyptian Temple was not a place for public worship. It was a treasure-house, a sacristy, a royal oratory, a place of preparation, of consecration, of sacerdotal privacy. There, in costly shrines, dwelt the divine images. There they were robed and unrobed ; perfumed with incense ; visited and worshipped by the King. On certain great days of the kalendar, as on the occasion of the festival of the new year, or the panegyries of the local gods, these images were brought out, paraded along the corridors of the temple, carried round the roof, and borne with waving of banners, and chanting of hymns, and burning of incense, through the sacred groves of the enclosure. Probably none were admitted to these ceremonies save persons of royal or priestly birth. To the rest of the community, all that took place within those massy walls was enveloped in mystery. It may be questioned, indeed, whether the great mass of the people had any kind of personal religion. They may not have been rigidly excluded from the temple-precincts, but they seem to have been allowed no participation in the worship of the Gods. If now and then, on high festival days, they beheld the sacred bark of the deity carried in procession round the temenos, or caught a glimpse of moving figures and glittering ensigns in the pillared dusk of the Hypostyle Hall, it was all they ever beheld of the solemn services of their church.

The Temple of Denderah consists of a portico ; a hall of entrance ; a hall of assembly ; a third hall, which may be called the hall of the sacred boats ; one small ground floor chapel ; and upwards of twenty side chambers of various sizes, most of which are totally dark. Each one of these halls and chambers bears the sculptured record of its use. Hundreds of tableaux in bas-relief, thousands of elaborate hieroglyphic inscriptions, cover every foot of available space on wall and ceiling and soffit, on doorway and column, and on the lining-slabs of passages and staircases. These precious texts contain, amid much that is mystical and tedious, an extraordinary wealth of indirect history. Here we find programmes of ceremonial observances ; numberless legends of the Gods ; chronologies of Kings with their various titles ; registers of weights and measures ; catalogues of offerings ; recipes for the preparation of oils and essences ; records of repairs and restorations done to the Temple ; geographical lists of cities and provinces ; inventories of treasure, and the like. The hall of assembly contains a kalendar of festivals, and sets forth with studied precision the rites to be performed on each recurring anniversary. On the ceiling of the portico we find an astronomical zodiac ; on the walls of a small temple on the roof, the whole history of the resurrection of Osiris, together with the order of prayer for the twelve hours of the night, and a kalendar of the festivals of Osiris in all the principal cities of Upper and Lower Egypt. Seventy years ago, these inscriptions were the puzzle and despair of the learned ; but since modern science has plucked out the heart of its mystery, the whole Temple lies before us as an open volume filled to overflowing with strange and quaint and heterogeneous matter—a Talmud in sculptured stone.[1]

---

[1] See Mariette's *Denderah*, which contains the whole of these multitudinous inscriptions in 166 plates ; also a selection of some of the most interesting in Brugsch and Dümichen's *Recueil de Monuments Egyptiens* and *Geographische Inschriften*, 1862-3-5-6.

Given such help as Mariette's handbook affords, one can trace out most of these curious things, and identify the uses of every hall and chamber throughout the building. The King, in his double character of Pharaoh and high priest, is the hero of every sculptured scene. Wearing sometimes the truncated crown of Lower Egypt, sometimes the helmet-crown of Upper Egypt, and sometimes the pschent, which is a combination of both, he figures in every tableau and heads every procession. Beginning with the sculptures of the portico, we see him arrive, preceded by his five royal standards. He wears his long robe ; his sandals are on his feet ; he carries his staff in his hand. Two goddesses receive him at the door and conduct him into the presence of Thoth, the ibis-headed, and Horus, the hawk-headed, who pour upon him a double stream of the waters of life. Thus purified, he is crowned by the Goddesses of Upper and Lower Egypt, and by them consigned to the local deities of Thebes and Heliopolis, who usher him into the supreme presence of Hathor. He then presents various offerings and recites certain prayers ; whereupon the goddess promises him length of days, everlasting renown, and other good things. We next see him, always with the same smile and always in the same attitude, doing homage to Osiris, to Horus and other divinities. He presents them with flowers, wine, bread, incense ; while they in return promise him life, joy, abundant harvests, victory, and the love of his people. These pretty speeches— chefs d'œuvre of diplomatic style and models of elegant flattery —are repeated over and over again in scores of hieroglyphic groups. Mariette, however, sees in them something more than the language of the court grafted upon the language of the hierarchy ; he detects the language of the schools, and discovers in the utterances here ascribed to the King and the Gods a reflection of that contemporary worship of the Beautiful, the Good, and the True, which characterised the teaching of the Alexandrian Museum.[1]

---

[1] Hathor (or more correctly Hat-hor, *i.e.* the abode of Horus), is not merely the Aphrodite of ancient Egypt : she is the pupil of the eye of the Sun : she is the goddess of that beneficent planet whose rising heralds the waters of the inundation ; she represents the eternal youth of nature, and is the direct personification of the Beautiful. She is also Goddess of Truth.

Passing on from the portico to the Hall of Assembly, we
enter a region of still dimmer twilight, beyond which all is
dark.   In the side-chambers, where the heat is intense and the
atmosphere stifling, we can see only by the help of lighted
candles.   These rooms are about twenty feet in length ; separate, like prison cells ; and perfectly dark.   The sculptures
which cover their walls are, however, as numerous as those in
the outer halls, and indicate in each instance the purpose for
which the room was designed.   Thus in the laboratories we
find bas-reliefs of flasks and vases, and figures carrying
perfume-bottles of the familiar aryballos form ; in the tribute-
chambers, offerings of lotus-lilies, wheat sheaves, maize, grapes,
and pomegranates ; in the oratories of Isis, Amen, and Sekhet,
representations of these divinities enthroned, and receiving the
homage of the King ; while in the treasury, both King and
Queen appear laden with precious gifts of caskets, necklaces,
pectoral ornaments, sistrums, and the like.   It would seem that
the image-breakers had no time to spare for these dark cells ;
for here the faces and figures are unmutilated, and in some
places even the original colouring remains in excellent preservation.   The complexion of the goddesses, for instance, is
painted of a light buff ; the King's skin is dark-red ; that of
Amen, blue.   Isis wears a rich robe of the well-known Indian
pine-pattern ; Sekhet figures in a many-coloured garment
curiously diapered ; Amen is clad in red and green chain
armour.   The skirts of the goddesses are inconceivably scant ;
but they are rich in jewellery, and their headdresses, necklaces,
and bracelets are full of minute and interesting detail.   In one

" I offer the Truth to thee, O Goddess of Denderah !" says the King, in
one of the inscriptions of the sanctuary of the Sistrum ; " for truth is thy
work, and thou thyself art Truth."   Lastly, her emblem is the Sistrum,
and the sound of the Sistrum, according to Plutarch, was supposed to
terrify and expel Typhon (the evil principle) ; just as in mediæval times
the ringing of church-bells was supposed to scare Beelzebub and his crew.
From this point of view, the Sistrum becomes typical of the triumph of
Good over Evil.   Mariette, in his analysis of the decorations and inscriptions of this temple, points out how the builders were influenced by the
prevailing philosophy of the age, and how they veiled the Platonism of
Alexandria beneath the symbolism of the ancient religion.   The Hat-hor
of Denderah was in fact worshipped in a sense unknown to the Egyptians
of pre-Ptolemaic times.

of the four oratories dedicated to Sekhet, the King is depicted in the act of offering a pectoral ornament of so rich and elegant a design that, had there been time and daylight to spare, the Writer would fain have copied it.

In the centre room at the extreme end of the Temple, exactly opposite the main entrance, lies the oratory of Hathor. This dark chamber, into which no ray of daylight has ever penetrated, contains the sacred niche, the Holy of Holies, in which was kept the great Golden Sistrum of the Goddess. The King alone was privileged to take out that mysterious emblem. Having done so, he enclosed it in a costly shrine, covered it with a thick veil, and placed it in one of the sacred boats of which we find elaborate representations sculptured on the walls of the hall in which they were kept. These boats, which were constructed of cedar-wood, gold, and silver, were intended to be hoisted on wrought poles, and so carried in procession on the shoulders of the priests. The niche is still there—a mere hole in the wall, some three feet square and about eight feet from the ground.

Thus, candle in hand, we make the circuit of these outer chambers. In each doorway, besides the place cut out for the bolt, we find a circular hole drilled above and a quadrant-shaped hollow below, where once upon a time the pivot of the door turned in its socket. The paved floors, torn up by treasure-seekers, are full of treacherous holes and blocks of broken stone. The ceilings are very lofty. In the corridors a dim twilight reigns ; but all is pitch-dark beyond these gloomy thresholds. Hurrying along by the light of a few flaring candles, one cannot but feel oppressed by the strangeness and awfulness of the place. We speak with bated breath, and even our chattering Arabs for once are silent. The very air tastes as if it had been imprisoned here for centuries.

Finally, we take the staircase on the northern side of the Temple, in order to go up to the roof. Nothing that we have yet seen surprises and delights us so much, I think, as this staircase.

We have hitherto been tracing in their order all the preparations for a great religious ceremony. We have seen the King enter the Temple ; undergo the symbolical purification ;

receive the twofold crown ; and say his prayers to each divinity in turn. We have followed him into the laboratories, the oratories, and the holy of holies. All that he has yet done, however, is preliminary. The procession is yet to come, and here we have it. Here, sculptured on the walls of this dark staircase, the crowning ceremony of Egyptian worship is brought before our eyes in all its details. Here, one by one, we have the standard-bearers, the hierophants with the offerings, the priests, the whole long, wonderful procession, with the King marching at its head. Fresh and uninjured as if they had but just left the hand of the sculptor, these figures—each in his habit as he lived, each with his foot upon the step—mount with us as we mount, and go beside us all the way. Their attitudes are so natural, their forms so roundly cut, that one could almost fancy them in motion as the lights flicker by. Surely there must be some one weird night in the year when they step out from their places, and take up the next verse of their chanted hymn, and, to the sound of instruments long mute and songs long silent, pace the moonlit roof in ghostly order !

The sun is already down and the crimson light has faded, when at length we emerge upon that vast terrace. The roofing-stones are gigantic. Striding to and fro over some of the biggest, our Idle Man finds several that measure seven paces in length by four in breadth. In yonder distant corner, like a little stone lodge in a vast courtyard, stands a small temple supported on Hathor-headed columns ; while at the eastern end, forming a second and loftier stage, rises the roof of the portico.

Meanwhile, the afterglow is fading. The mountains are yet clothed in an atmosphere of tender half-light ; but mysterious shadows are fast creeping over the plain, and the mounds of the ancient city lie at our feet, confused and tumbled, like the waves of a dark sea. How high it is here—how lonely— how silent ! Hark that thin plaintive cry ! It is the wail of a night-wandering jackal. See how dark it is yonder, in the direction of the river ! Quick, quick ! We have lingered too long. We must be gone at once ; for we are already benighted.

We ought to have gone down by way of the opposite staircase (which is lined with sculptures of the descending procession) and out through the Temple ; but there is no time to do anything but scramble down by a breach in the wall at a point where the mounds yet lie heaped against the south side of the building.   And now the dusk steals on so rapidly that before we reach the bottom we can hardly see where to tread.   The huge side-wall of the portico seems to tower above us to the very heavens.   We catch a glimpse of two colossal figures, one lion-headed and the other headless, sitting outside with their backs to the Temple.   Then, making with all speed for the

SHEYKH SELIM.

open plain, we clamber over scattered blocks and among shapeless mounds.   Presently night overtakes us.,   The mountains disappear ; the Temple is blotted out ; and we have only the faint starlight to guide us.   We stumble on, however, keeping all close together ; firing a gun every now and then, in the hope of being heard by those in the boats ; and as thoroughly and undeniably lost as the Babes in the Wood.

At last, just as some are beginning to knock up and all to despair, Talhamy fires his last cartridge.   An answering shot replies from near by ; a wandering light appears in the distance ; and presently a whole bevy of dancing lanterns and friendly brown faces comes gleaming out from among a plantation of sugar-canes, to welcome and guide us home.   Dear, sturdy, faithful little Reïs Hassan, honest Khalîfeh, laughing Salame, gentle Mehemet Ali, and Mûsa " black but comely "—they were all there.   What a shaking of hands there was—what a gleaming of white teeth—what a shower of mutually unintelligible congratulations !   For my own part, I may say with truth that I was never much more rejoiced at a meeting in my life.

CHAPTER VIII.

THEBES AND KARNAK.

COMING on deck the third morning after leaving Denderah, we found the dahabeeyah decorated with palm-branches, our sailors in their holiday turbans, and Reïs Hassan *en grande tenue ;* that is to say in shoes and stockings, which he only wore on very great occasions.

"Nehârak-saʿïd—good morning—Luxor!" said he, all in one breath.

It was a hot, hazy morning, with dim ghosts of mountains glowing through the mist, and a warm wind blowing.

We ran to the side ; looked out eagerly ; but could see nothing. Still the Captain smiled and nodded ; and the sailors ran hither and thither, sweeping and garnishing ; and Egendi, to whom his worst enemy could not have imputed the charge of bashfulness, said "Luxor—kharûf [1]—all right!" every time he came near us.

We had read and dreamed so much about Thebes, and it had always seemed so far away, that but for this delicate allusion to the promised sheep, we could hardly have believed we were really drawing nigh unto those famous shores. About ten, however, the mist was lifted away like a curtain, and we saw to the left a rich plain studded with palm-groves ; to the right a broad margin of cultivated lands bounded by a bold range of limestone mountains ; and on the farthest horizon another range, all grey and shadowy.

"Karnak—Gournah—Luxor!" says Reïs Hassan triumph-

[1] *Arabic,* "kharûf," pronounced "haroof"—*English,* sheep.

antly, pointing in every direction at once.   Talhamy tries to show us Medinet Habu and the Memnonium.   The Painter vows he can see the heads of the sitting Colossi and the entrance to the Valley of the Tombs of the Kings.

We, meanwhile, stare bewildered, incredulous ; seeing none of these things ; finding it difficult, indeed, to believe that any one else sees them.   The river widens away before us ; the flats are green on either side ; the mountains are pierced with terraces of rock-cut tombs ; while far away inland, apparently on the verge of the desert, we see here a clump of sycamores— yonder a dark hillock—midway between both a confused heap of something that may be either fallen rock or fallen masonry ; but nothing that looks like a Temple, nothing to indicate that we are already within recognisable distance of the grandest ruins in the world.

Presently, however, as the boat goes on, a massive, window-less structure which looks (Heaven preserve us !) just like a brand-new fort or prison, towers up above the palm-groves to the left.   This, we are told, is one of the propylons of Karnak ; while a few whitewashed huts and a little crowd of masts now coming into sight a mile or so higher up, mark the position of Luxor.   Then up capers Egendi with his never-failing " Luxor —kharûf—all right !" to fetch down the tar and darabukkeh. The captain claps his hands.   A circle is formed on the lower deck.   The men, all smiles, strike up their liveliest chorus, and so, with barbaric music and well-filled sails, and flags flying, and green boughs waving overhead, we make our triumphal entry into Luxor.

The top of another pylon ; the slender peak of an obelisk ; a colonnade of giant pillars half-buried in the soil ; the white houses of the English, American, and Prussian Consuls, each with its flagstaff and ensign ; a steep slope of sandy shore ; a background of mud walls and pigeon-towers ; a foreground of native boats and gaily-painted dahabeeyahs lying at anchor— such, as we sweep by, is our first panoramic view of this famous village.   A group of turbaned officials sitting in the shade of an arched doorway rise and salute us as we pass.   The as-sembled dahabeeyahs dozing with folded sails, like sea-birds asleep, are roused to spasmodic activity.   Flags are lowered ;

guns are fired ; all Luxor is startled from its midday siesta. Then, before the smoke has had time to clear off, up comes the Bagstones in gallant form ; whereupon the dahabeeyahs blaze away again as before.

COLONNADE OF HOREMHEB,
FROM A PHOTOGRAPH BY BRUGSCH-BEY.

And now there is a rush of donkeys and donkey-boys, beggars, guides, and antiquity-dealers, to the shore—the children screaming for backshîsh ; the dealers exhibiting strings of imitation scarabs ; the donkey-boys vociferating the names and praises of their beasts ; all alike regarding us as their lawful prey.

"Hi, lady ! Yankee-Doodle donkey; try Yankee-Doodle !" cries one.

"Far-away Moses ! " yells another. "Good donkey—fast donkey—best donkey in Luxor !"

"This Prince of Wales's donkey !" shouts a third, hauling forward a decrepit little weak-kneed, moth-eaten looking animal, about as good to ride upon as a towel-horse. "First-rate donkey ! splendid donkey ! God save the Queen ! Hurrah !"

But neither donkeys nor scarabs are of any importance in

our eyes just now, compared with the letters we hope to find
awaiting us on shore.   No sooner, therefore, are the boats
made fast than we are all off, some to the British Consulate
and some to the Poste Restante, from both of which we return
rich and happy.

Meanwhile we proposed to spend only twenty-four hours
in Luxor.   We were to ride round Karnak this first afternoon ;
to cross to Medinet Habu and the Ramesseum [1] to-morrow
morning ; and to sail again as soon after midday as possible.
We hope thus to get a general idea of the topography of
Thebes, and to carry away a superficial impression of the architectural style of the Pharaohs.   It would be but a glimpse ;
yet that glimpse was essential.   For Thebes represents the
great central period of Egyptian art.   The earlier styles lead
up to that point ; the later depart from it ; and neither the
earlier nor the later are intelligible without it.   At the same
time, however, travellers bound for the Second Cataract do
well to put off everything like a detailed study of Thebes till
the time of coming back.   For the present, a rapid survey of
the three principal groups of ruins is enough.   It supplies the
necessary link.   It helps one to a right understanding of Edfu,
of Philæ, of Abu Simbel.   In a word, it enables one to put
things in their right places ; and this, after all, is a mental
process which every traveller must perform for himself.

Thebes, I need scarcely say, was built like London on
both sides of the river.   Its original extent must have been
very great ; but its public buildings, its quays, its thousands
of private dwellings, are gone and have left few traces.   The
secular city, which was built of crude brick, is represented by
a few insignificant mounds ; while of the sacred edifices, five
large groups of limestone ruins—three on the western bank
and two on the eastern, together with the remains of several
small temples and a vast multitude of tombs—are all that
remain in permanent evidence of its ancient splendour.   Luxor

---

[1] This famous building is supposed by some to be identical both with
the Memnonium of Strabo and the Tomb of Osymandias as described by
Diodorus Siculus.   Champollion, however, following the sense of the
hieroglyphed legends, in which it is styled " The House of Rameses " (the
Second), has given to it the more appropriate name of the Ramesseum.

is a modern Arab village occupying the site of one of the oldest of these five ruins. It stands on the eastern bank, close against the river, about two miles south of Karnak and nearly opposite the famous sitting Colossi of the Western plain. On the opposite bank lie Gournah, the Ramesseum, and Medinet Habu. A glance at the map will do more than pages of explanation to show the relative position of these ruins. The Temple of Gournah, it will be seen, is almost *vis-à-vis* of Karnak. The Ramesseum faces about half-way between Karnak and Luxor. Medinet Habu is placed farther to the south than any building on the eastern side of the river. Behind these three western groups, reaching far and wide along the edge of the Libyan range, lies the great Theban Necropolis ; while farther back still, in the radiating valleys on the other side of the mountains, are found the Tombs of the Kings. The distance between Karnak and Luxor is a little less than two miles ; while from Medinet Habu to the Temple of Gournah may be roughly guessed at something under four. We have here, therefore, some indication of the extent, though not of the limits, of the ancient city.

Luxor is a large village inhabited by a mixed population of Copts and Arabs, and doing a smart trade in antiquities. The temple has here formed the nucleus of the village, the older part of which has grown up in and about the ruins. The grand entrance faces north, looking down towards Karnak. The twin towers of the great propylon, dilapidated as they are, stripped of their cornices, encumbered with débris, are magnificent still. In front of them, one on each side of the central gateway, sit two helmeted colossi, battered, and featureless, and buried to the chin, like two of the Proud in the doleful Fifth Circle. A few yards in front of these again stands a solitary obelisk, also half-buried. The colossi are of black granite ; the obelisk is of red, highly polished, and covered on all four sides with superb hieroglyphs in three vertical columns. These hieroglyphs are engraved with the precision of the finest gem. They are cut to a depth of about two inches in the outer columns, and five inches in the central column of the inscription. The true height of this wonderful monolith is over seventy feet, between thirty and forty of which are hidden

under the accumulated soil of many centuries. Its companion obelisk, already scaling away by imperceptible degrees under the skyey influences of an alien climate, looks down with melancholy indifference upon the petty revolutions and counter-revolutions of the Place de la Concorde. On a line with the two black colossi, but some fifty feet or so farther to the west, rises a third and somewhat smaller head of chert or limestone, the fellow to which is doubtless hidden among the huts that encroach half-way across the face of the eastern tower. The whole outer surface of these towers is covered with elaborate sculptures of gods and men, horses and chariots, the pageantry of triumph and the carnage of war. The King in his chariot draws his terrible bow, or slays his enemies on foot, or sits enthroned, receiving the homage of his court. Whole regiments armed with lance and shield march across the scene. The foe flies in disorder. The King, attended by his fan-bearers, returns in state, and the priests burn incense before him.

This king is Rameses the Second, called Sesostris and Osymandias by ancient writers, and best known to history as Rameses the Great. His actual names and titles as they stand upon the monuments are Ra-user-ma Sotp-en-Ra Ra-messu Mer-Amen ; that is to say, " Ra strong in Truth, Approved of Ra, Son of Ra, Beloved of Amen."

The battle-scenes here represented relate to that memorable campaign against the Kheta which forms the subject of the famous Third Sallier Papyrus,[1] and is commemorated upon the walls of almost every temple built by this monarch. Separated from his army and surrounded by the enemy, the King, attended only by his chariot-driver, is said to have six times charged the foe—to have hewn them down with his sword of might— to have trampled them like straw beneath his horse's feet—to have dispersed them single-handed, like a god. Two thousand five hundred chariots were there, and he overthrew them ; one hundred thousand warriors, and he scattered them. Those that he slew not with his hand, he chased unto the water's

---

[1] Translated into French by the late Vicomte de Rougé under the title of *Le Poëme de Pentaour*, 1856 ; into English by Mr. Goodwin, 1858 ; and again by Professor Lushington in 1874. See *Records of the Past*, vol. ii.

edge, causing them to leap to destruction as leaps the crocodile. Such was the immortal feat of Rameses, and such the chronicle written by the Royal Scribe, Pentaur.

Setting aside the strain of Homeric exaggeration which runs through this narrative, there can be no doubt that it records some brilliant deed of arms actually performed by the King within sight, though not within reach, of his army ; and the hieroglyphic texts interpersed among these tableaux state that the events depicted took place on the fifth day of the month Epiphi, in the fifth year of his reign. By this we must understand the fifth year of his sole reign, which would be five years after the death of his father, Seti I, with whom he had, from an early age, been associated on the throne. He was a man in the prime of life at the time of this famous engagement, which was fought under the walls of Kadesh on the Orontes ; and the bas-relief sculptures show him to have been accompanied by several of his sons, who, though evidently very young, are represented in their war-chariots fully armed and taking part in the battle.[1]

The mutilated colossi are portrait statues of the conqueror. The obelisk, in the pompous style of Egyptian dedications, proclaims that "The Lord of the World, Guardian-Sun of Truth, approved of Ra, has built this edifice in honour of his Father Amen-Ra, and has erected to him these two great obelisks of stone in face of the house of Rameses in the City of Ammon."

So stately was the approach made by Rameses the Great to the temple founded about a hundred and fifty years before his time by Amenhotep III. He also built the courtyard upon which this pylon opened, joining it to the older part of the building in such wise that the original first court became now the second court, while next in order came the portico, the hall of assembly, and the sanctuary. By and by, when the long line of

---

[1] According to the great inscription of Abydos translated by Professor Maspero, Rameses II would seem to have been in some sense King from his birth, as if the throne of Egypt came to him through his mother, and as if his father, Seti I, had reigned for him during his infancy as King-Regent. Some inscriptions, indeed, show him to have received homage even *before* his birth.

Rameses had passed away, other and later kings put their hands to the work. The names of Shabaka (Sabaco), of Ptolemy Philopater, and of Alexander the Younger, appear among the later inscriptions ; while those of Amenhotep IV (Khu-en-Aten), Horemheb, and Seti, the father of Rameses the Great, are found in the earlier parts of the building. It was in this way that an Egyptian temple grew from age to age, owing a colonnade to this king and a pylon to that, till it came in time to represent the styles of many periods. Hence, too, that frequent irregularity of plan, which, unless it could be ascribed to the caprices of successive builders, would form so unaccountable a feature in Egyptian architecture. In the present instance, the pylon and courtyard of Rameses II are set at an angle of five degrees to the courtyard and sanctuary of Amenhotep III. This has evidently been done to bring the Temple of Luxor into a line with the Temple of Karnak, in order that the two might be connected by means of that stupendous avenue of sphinxes, the scattered remains of which yet strew the course of the ancient roadway.

As I have already said, these half-buried pylons, this solitary obelisk, those giant heads rising in ghastly resurrection before the gates of the Temple, were magnificent still. But it was as the magnificence of a splendid prologue to a poem of which only garbled fragments remain. Beyond that entrance lay a smoky, filthy, intricate labyrinth of lanes and passages. Mud hovels, mud pigeon-towers, mud yards, and a mud mosque, clustered like wasps' nests in and about the ruins. Architraves sculptured with royal titles supported the roofs of squalid cabins. Stately capitals peeped out from the midst of sheds in which buffaloes, camels, donkeys, dogs, and human-beings were seen herding together in unsavoury fellowship. Cocks crew, hens cackled, pigeons cooed, turkeys gobbled, children swarmed, women were baking and gossiping, and all the sordid routine of Arab life was going on, amid winding alleys that masked the colonnades and defaced the inscriptions of the Pharaohs. To trace the plan of this part of the building was then impossible.

All communication being cut off between the courts and the portico, we had to go round outside and through a door at

the farther end of the Temple, in order to reach the sanctuary
and the adjoining chambers.   The Arab who kept the key
provided an inch or two of candle.   For it was very dark in
there ; the roof being still perfect, with a large, rambling,
modern house built on the top of it—so that if this part of the
Temple was ever partially lighted, as at Denderah and elsewhere, by small wedge-like openings in the roof, even those
faint gleams were excluded.

The sanctuary, which was rebuilt in the reign of Alexander
Ægus ; some small side chambers ; and a large hall, which was
perhaps the hall of assembly, were all that remained under
cover of the original roofing-stones.   Some half-buried and broken
columns on the side next the river showed, however, that this
end was formerly surrounded by a colonnade.   The sanctuary
—an oblong granite chamber with its own separate roof—
stands enclosed in a larger hall, like a box within a box, and
is covered inside and outside with bas-reliefs.   These sculptures
(among which I observed a kneeling figure of the king,
offering a kneeling image to Amen Ra) are executed in the
mediocre style of the Ptolemies.   That is to say, the forms are
more natural but less refined than those of the Pharaonic
period.   The limbs are fleshy, the joints large, the features
insignificant.   Of actual portraiture one cannot detect a trace ;
while every face wears the same objectionable smirk which
disfigures the Cleopatra of Denderah.

In the large hall, which I have called the Hall of Assembly,
one is carried back to the time of the founder.   Between
Amenhotep III and Alexander Ægus there lies a great gulf
of 1200 years ; and their styles are as widely separated
as their reigns.   The merest novice could not possibly
mistake the one for the other.   Nothing is, of course, more
common than to find Egyptian and Græco-Egyptian work side
by side in the same temple ; but nowhere are the distinctive
characteristics of each brought into stronger contrast than in
these dark chambers of Luxor.   In the sculptures that line the
hall of Amenhotep we find the pure lines, the severe and
slender forms, the characteristic heads, of a period when the
art, having as yet neither gained nor lost by foreign influences,
was entirely Egyptian.   The subjects relate chiefly to the

infancy of the King ; but it is difficult to see anything properly by the light of a candle tied to the end of a stick ; and here, where the bas-relief is so low and the walls are so high, it is almost impossible to distinguish the details of the upper tableaux.

I could make out, however, that Amen, Maut, and their son Khonsu, the three personages of the Theban triad, are the presiding deities of these scenes ; and that they are in some way identified with the fortunes of Thothmes IV, his queen, and their son Amenhotep III. Amenhotep is born, apparently, under the especial protection of Maut, the Divine Mother ; brought up with the youthful god Khonsu ; and received by Amen as the brother and equal of his own divine son. I think it was in this hall that I observed a singular group representing Amen and Maut in an attitude symbolical perhaps of troth-plight, or marriage. They sit face to face, the goddess holding in her right hand the left hand of the god, while in her left hand she supports his right elbow. Their thrones, meanwhile, rest on the heads, and their feet are upheld on the hands of two female genii. It is significant that Rameses III and one of the ladies of his so-called hareem are depicted in the same attitude in one of the famous domestic subjects sculptured on the upper storeys of the Pavilion at Medinet Habu.

We saw this interesting Temple much too cursorily ; yet we gave more time to it than the majority of those who year after year anchor for days together close under its majestic columns. If the whole building could be transported bodily to some point between Memphis and Siût where the river is bare of ruins, it would be enthusiastically visited. Here it is eclipsed by the wonders of Karnak and the western bank, and is undeservedly neglected. Those parts of the original building which yet remain are, indeed, peculiarly precious ; for Amen-hotep, or Amunoph, the Third, was one of the great builder-kings of Egypt, and we have here one of the few extant specimens of his architectural work.[1]

[1] The ruins of the Great Temple of Luxor have undergone a complete transformation since the above description was written ; Professor Maspero, during the two last years of his official rule as successor to the late Mariette-Pasha, having done for this magnificent relic of Pharaonic times what his predecessor did for the more recent Temple of Edfoo. The diffi-culties of carrying out this great undertaking were so great as to appear at

The Coptic quarter of Luxor lies north of the great pylon, and partly skirts the river.   It is cleaner, wider, more airy than that of the Arabs.   The Prussian Consul is a Copt ; the polite postmaster is a Copt ; and in a modest lodging built half beside and half over the Coptic church, lives the Coptic Bishop.   The postmaster (an ungainly youth in a European suit so many sizes too small that his arms and legs appeared to be sprouting out at the ends of his garments) was profuse in his offers of service.   He undertook to forward letters to us at Assûan, Korosko, and Wady Halfah, where post-offices had lately been established.   And he kept his promise, I am bound to say, with perfect punctuality ;—always adding some queer little complimentary message on the outer wrapper, such as

first sight almost insurmountable.   The fellaheen refused at first to sell their houses ; Mustapha Aga asked the exorbitant price of £3000 for his Consular residence, built as it was between the columns of Horemheb facing the river ; and for no pecuniary consideration whatever was it possible to purchase the right of pulling down the mosque in the first great courtyard of the Temple.   After twelve months of negotiation, the fellaheen were at last bought out on fair terms, each proprietor receiving a stated price for his dwelling and a piece of land elsewhere, upon which to build another.   Some thirty families were thus got rid of, about eight or ten only refusing to leave at any price.   The work of demolition was begun in 1885.   In 1886, the few families yet lingering in the ruins followed the example of the rest ; and in the course of that season the Temple was cleared from end to end, only the little native mosque being left standing within the precincts, and Mustapha Aga's house on the side next the landing-place.   Professor Maspero's resignation followed in 1887, since when the work has been carried on by his successor, M. Grébaut, with the result that in place of a crowded, sordid, unintelligible labyrinth of mud-huts, yards, stables, alleys, and dung-heaps, a noble Temple, second only to that of Karnak for grandeur of design and beauty of proportion, now marshals its avenues of columns and uplifts its sculptured architraves along the crest of the ridge which here rises high above the eastern bank of the Nile.   Some of those columns, now that they are cleared down to the level of the original pavement, measure 57 feet in the shaft ; and in the great courtyard built by Rameses II, which measures 190 feet by 170, a series of beautiful colossal statues of that Pharaoh in highly polished red granite have been discovered, some yet standing *in situ*, having been built into the walls of mud structures and imbedded (for who shall say how many centuries ?) in a sepulchre of ignoble clay.   Last of all, Mustapha Aga, the kindly and popular old British Consul, whose hospitality will long be remembered by English travellers, died about twelve months since, and the house in which he entertained so many English visitors, and upon which he set so high a value, is even now in course of demolition.

" I hope you well my compliments ;" or " Wishes you good news pleasant voyage." As a specimen of his literary style I copied the following notice, of which it was evident that he was justly proud :—

" NOTICE : On the commandation. We have ordered the post stations in lower Egypt from Assiut to Cartoom. Belonging to the Post Kedevy Egyptian in a good order. Now to pay for letters in lower Egypt is as in upper Egypt twice. Means that the letters which goes from here far than Asiut ; must pay for it two piastres per ten grs. Also that which goes far than Cartoom. The letters which goes between Asiut and Cartoom ; must pay only one piastre per ten grs. This and that is, to buy stamps from the Post and put it upon the letter. Also if somebody wishes to send letters insuranced, must two piastres more for any letter. There is orderation in the Post to receive the letters which goes to Europe, America and Asia, as England France, Italy Germany, Syria, Constantinople etc. Also to send newspapers patterns and other things. Luxor the 1st January 1874. *L'Ispettore*, M. ADDA."

This young man begged for a little stationery and a pen-knife at parting. We had, of course, much pleasure in presenting him with such a modest testimonial. We afterwards learned that he levied the same little tribute on every dahabeeyah that came up the river ; so I conclude that he must by this time have quite an interesting collection of small cutlery.

From the point where the railroad ends, the Egyptian and Nubian mails are carried by runners stationed at distances of four miles all along the route. Each man runs his four miles, and at the end thereof finds the next man ready to snatch up his bag and start off at full speed immediately. The next man transfers it in like manner to the next ; and so it goes by day and night without a break, till it reaches the first railway station. Each runner is supposed to do his four miles in half-an-hour, and the mail which goes out every morning from Luxor reaches Cairo in six days. Considering that Cairo was 450 miles away, that 268 miles of this distance had to be done on foot, and that the trains went only once a day, we thought this a very creditable speed.

In the afternoon we took donkeys, and rode out to Karnak. Our way lay through the bazaar, which was the poorest we had yet seen. It consisted of only a few open sheds, in one of which, seated on a mud-built divan, cross-legged and turban-less like a row of tumbler mandarins, we saw five of our sailors under the hands of the Luxor barber. He had just lathered all five heads, and was complacently surveying the effect of his work, much as an artistic cook might survey a dish of particularly successful méringues à la crême. The méringues looked very sheepish when we laughed and passed by.

Next came the straggling suburb where the dancing girls most do congregate. These damsels, in gaudy garments of emerald green, bright rose, and flaming yellow, were squatting outside their cabins or lounging unveiled about the thresholds of two or three dismal dens of cafés in the market-place. They showed their teeth, and laughed familiarly in our faces. Their eyebrows were painted to meet on the bridge of the nose ; their eyes were blackened round with kohl ; their cheeks were extravagantly rouged ; their hair was gummed, and greased, and festooned upon their foreheads, and plaited all over in innumerable tails. Never before had we seen anything in female form so hideous. One of these houris was black ; and she looked quite beautiful in her blackness, compared with the painting and plastering of her companions.

We now left the village behind, and rode out across a wide plain, barren and hillocky in some parts ; overgrown in others with coarse halfeh grass ; and dotted here and there with clumps of palms. The Nile lay low and out of sight, so that the valley seemed to stretch away uninterruptedly to the mountains on both sides. Now leaving to the left a Sheykh's tomb, topped by a little cupola and shaded by a group of tamarisks ; now following the bed of a dry watercourse ; now skirting shapeless mounds that indicated the site of ruins un-explored, the road, uneven but direct, led straight to Karnak. At every rise in the ground we saw the huge propylons towering higher above the palms. Once, but for only a few moments, there came into sight a confused and wide-spread mass of ruins, as extensive, apparently, as the ruins of a large town. Then our way dipped into a sandy groove bordered by mud-walls and plantations of dwarf-palms. All at once this groove widened, became a stately avenue guarded by a double file of shattered sphinxes, and led towards a lofty pylon standing up alone against the sky.

Close beside this grand gateway, as if growing there on purpose, rose a thicket of sycamores and palms ; while beyond it were seen the twin pylons of a Temple. The sphinxes were colossal, and measured about ten feet in length. One or two were ram-headed. Of the rest—some forty or fifty in number —all were headless, some split asunder, some overturned, others so mutilated that they looked like torrent-worn boulders. This avenue once reached from Luxor to Karnak. Taking into account the distance (which is just two miles from Temple to Temple) and the short intervals at which the sphinxes are placed, there cannot originally have been fewer than five hundred of them ; that is to say two hundred and fifty on each side of the road.

Dismounting for a few minutes, we went into the Temple ; glanced round the open courtyard with its colonnade of pillars ; peeped hurriedly into some ruinous side-chambers ; and then rode on. Our books told us that we had seen the small Temple of Rameses the Third. It would have been called large anywhere but at Karnak.

I seem to remember the rest as if it had all happened in a dream. Leaving the small Temple, we turned towards the river, skirted the mud-walls of the native village, and approached the Great Temple by way of its main entrance. Here we entered upon what had once been another great avenue of sphinxes, ram-headed, couchant on plinths deep cut with hieroglyphic legends, and leading up from some grand landing-place beside the Nile.

And now the towers that we had first seen as we sailed by in the morning rose straight before us, magnificent in ruin, glittering to the sun, and relieved in creamy light against blue depths of sky. One was nearly perfect ; the other, shattered as if by the shock of an earthquake, was still so lofty that an Arab clambering from block to block midway of its vast height looked no bigger than a squirrel.

On the threshold of this tremendous portal we again dis-

mounted.   Shapeless crude-brick mounds, marking the limits
of the ancient wall of circuit, reached far away on either side.
An immense perspective of pillars and pylons leading up to
a very distant obelisk opened out before us.   We went in, the
great walls towering up like cliffs above our heads, and entered
the First Court.   Here, in the midst of a large quadrangle
open to the sky stands a solitary column, the last of a central
avenue of twelve, some of which, disjointed by the shock, lie
just as they fell, like skeletons of vertebrate monsters left
stranded by the Flood.

Crossing this Court in the glowing sunlight, we came to a
mighty doorway between two more propylons—the doorway
splendid with coloured bas-reliefs ; the propylons mere cataracts
of fallen blocks piled up to right and left in grand confusion.
The cornice of the doorway is gone.   Only a jutting fragment
of the lintel stone remains.   That stone, when perfect, measured
forty feet and ten inches across.   The doorway must have
been full a hundred feet in height.

We went on.   Leaving to the right a mutilated colossus
engraven on arm and breast with the cartouche of Rameses II,
we crossed the shade upon the threshold, and passed into the
famous Hypostyle Hall of Seti the First.

It is a place that has been much written about and often
painted ; but of which no writing and no art can convey more
than a dwarfed and pallid impression.   To describe it, in the
sense of building up a recognisable image by means of words,
is impossible.   The scale is too vast ; the effect too tremendous ;
the sense of one's own dumbness, and littleness, and incapacity,
too complete and crushing.   It is a place that strikes you into
silence ; that empties you, as it were, not only of words but of
ideas.   Nor is this a first effect only.   Later in the year, when
we came back down the river and moored close by, and spent
long days among the ruins, I found I never had a word to say
in the Great Hall.   Others might measure the girth of those
tremendous columns ; others might climb hither and thither,
and find out points of view, and test the accuracy of Wilkinson
and Mariette ; but I could only look, and be silent.

Yet to look is something, if one can but succeed in remembering ; and the Great Hall of Karnak is photographed in

some dark corner of my brain for as long as I have memory.
I shut my eyes, and see it as if I were there—not all at once,
as in a picture ; but bit by bit, as the eye takes note of large
objects and travels over an extended field of vision.   I stand
once more among those mighty columns, which radiate into

HYPOSTYLE HALL, KARNAK.

avenues from whatever point one takes them.   I see them
swathed in coiled shadows and broad bands of light.   I see
them sculptured and painted with shapes of Gods and Kings,
with blazonings of royal names, with sacrificial altars, and forms
of sacred beasts, and emblems of wisdom and truth.   The
shafts of these columns are enormous.   I stand at the foot of

one—or of what seems to be the foot; for the original pavement lies buried seven feet below. Six men standing with
extended arms, finger-tip to finger-tip, could barely span it
round. It casts a shadow twelve feet in breadth—such a
shadow as might be cast by a tower. The capital that juts
out so high above my head looks as if it might have been
placed there to support the heavens. It is carved in the
semblance of a full-blown lotus, and glows with undying colours
—colours that are still fresh, though laid on by hands that have
been dust these three thousand years and more. It would take
not six men, but a dozen to measure round the curved lip of
that stupendous lily.

Such are the twelve central columns. The rest (one
hundred and twenty-two in number) are gigantic too; but
smaller. Of the roof they once supported, only the beams
remain. Those beams are stones—huge monoliths[1] carved
and painted, bridging the space from pillar to pillar, and
patterning the trodden soil with bands of shadow.

Looking up and down the central avenue, we see at the
one end a flame-like obelisk; at the other, a solitary palm
against a background of glowing mountain. To right, to left,
showing transversely through long files of columns, we catch
glimpses of colossal bas-reliefs lining the roofless walls in every
direction. The King, as usual, figures in every group, and
performs the customary acts of worship. The Gods receive
and approve him. Half in light, half in shadow, these slender,
fantastic forms stand out sharp, and clear, and colourless;
each figure some eighteen or twenty feet in height. They
could scarcely have looked more weird when the great roof

---

[1] The size of these stones not being given in any of our books, I paced
the length of one of the shadows, and (allowing for so much more at each
end as would be needed to reach to the centres of the two capitals on
which it rested) found the block above must measure at least 25 feet in
length. The measurements of the Great Hall are, in plain figures, 170
feet in length by 329 in breadth. It contains 134 columns, of which the
central twelve stand 62 feet high in the shaft (or about 70 with the plinth
and abacus), and measure 34 feet 6 inches in circumference. The smaller
columns stand 42 feet 5 inches in the shaft, and measure 28 feet in circumference. All are buried to a depth of between six or seven feet in the
alluvial deposits of between three and four thousand annual inundations.

was in its place and perpetual twilight reigned. But it is difficult to imagine the roof on, and the sky shut out. It all looks right as it is ; and one feels, somehow, that such columns should have nothing between them and the infinite blue depths of heaven.

The great central avenue was, however, sufficiently lighted by means of a double row of clerestory windows, some of which are yet standing. Certain writers have suggested that they may have been glazed ; but this seems improbable for two reasons. Firstly, because one or two of these huge window-frames yet contain the solid stone gratings which in the present instance seem to have done duty for a translucent material : and, secondly, because we have no evidence to show that the early Egyptians, though familiar since the days of Cheops with the use of the blow-pipe, ever made glass in sheets, or introduced it in this way into their buildings.

How often has it been written, and how often must it be repeated, that the Great Hall at Karnak is the noblest architectural work ever designed and executed by human hands ? One writer tells us that it covers four times the area occupied by the Cathedral of Nôtre Dame in Paris. Another measures it against St. Peter's. All admit their inability to describe it ; yet all attempt the description. To convey a concrete image of the place to one who has not seen it, is, however, as I have already said, impossible. If it could be likened to this place or that, the task would not be so difficult ; but there is, in truth, no building in the wide world to compare with it. The Pyramids are more stupendous. The Colosseum covers more ground. The Parthenon is more beautiful. Yet in nobility of conception, in vastness of detail, in majesty of the highest order, the Hall of Pillars exceeds them every one. This doorway, these columns, are the wonder of the world. How was that lintel-stone raised ? How were these capitals lifted ? Entering among those mighty pillars, says a recent observer, " you feel that you have shrunk to the dimensions and feebleness of a fly." But I think you feel more than that. You are stupefied by the thought of the mighty men who made them. You say to yourself :—" There were indeed giants in those days."

It may be that the traveller who finds himself for the first

time in the midst of a grove of *Wellingtonia gigantea* feels
something of the same overwhelming sense of awe and wonder ;
but the great trees, though they have taken three thousand
years to grow, lack the pathos and the mystery that comes of
human labour. They do not strike their roots through six
thousand years of history. They have not been watered with
the blood and tears of millions.[1] Their leaves know no sounds
less musical than the singing of birds, or the moaning of the
night-wind as it sweeps over the highlands of Calaveros. But
every breath that wanders down the painted aisles of Karnak
seems to echo back the sighs of those who perished in the
quarry, at the oar, and under the chariot-wheels of the
conqueror.

The Hypostyle Hall, though built by Seti, the father
of Rameses II, is supposed by some Egyptologists to have
been planned, if not begun, by that same Amenhotep III who
founded the Temple of Luxor and set up the famous Colossi
of the Plain. However this may be, the cartouches so lavishly
sculptured on pillar and architrave contain no names but those
of Seti, who undoubtedly executed the work *en bloc*, and of
Rameses, who completed it.

And now, would it not be strange if we knew the name
and history of the architect who superintended the building of
this wondrous Hall, and planned the huge doorway by which
it was entered, and the mighty pylons which lie shattered on
either side ? Would it not be interesting to look upon his
portrait, and see what manner of man he was ? Well, the
Egyptian room in the Glyptothek Museum at Munich contains
a statue found some seventy years ago at Thebes, which almost
certainly represents that man, and is inscribed with his history.
His name was Bak-en-Khonsu (servant of Khonsu). He sits
upon the ground, bearded and robed, in an attitude of meditation. That he was a man of unusual ability is shown by the
inscriptions engraved upon the back of the statue. These
inscriptions record his promotion step by step to the highest
grade of the hierarchy. Having attained the dignity of High
Priest and First Prophet of Amen during the reign of Seti the

---

[1] It has been calculated that every stone of these huge Pharaonic
temples cost at least one human life.

First, he became Chief Architect of the Thebaid under Rameses II, and received a royal commission to superintend the embellishment of the Temples. When Rameses II " erected a monument to his Divine Father Amen Ra," the building thereof was executed under the direction of Bak-en-Khonsu. Here the inscription, as translated by M. Deveria, goes on to say that " he made the sacred edifice in the upper gate of the Abode of Amen.[1] He erected obelisks of granite. He made golden flagstaffs. He added very, very great colonnades."

M. Deveria suggests that the Temple of Gournah may here be indicated ; but to this it might be objected that Gournah is situated in the lower and not the upper part of Thebes ; that at Gournah there are no great colonnades and no obelisks ; and that, moreover, for some reason at present unknown to us, the erection of obelisks seems to have been almost wholly confined to the eastern bank of the Nile. It is, however, possible that the works here enumerated may not all have been executed for one and the same Temple. The " sacred edifice in the upper gate of the Abode of Amen " might be the Temple of Luxor, which Rameses did in fact adorn with the only obelisks we know to be his in Thebes ; the monument erected by him to his Divine Father Amen (evidently a new structure) would scarcely be any other than the Ramesseum ; while the " very, very great colonnades," which are expressly specified as additions, would seem as if they could only belong to the Hypostyle Hall of Karnak. The question is at all events interesting ; and it is pleasant to believe that in the Munich statue we have not only a portrait of one who at Karnak played the part of Michael Angelo to some foregone and forgotten Bramante, but who was also the Ictinus of the Ramesseum. For the Ramesseum is the Parthenon of Thebes.

The sun was sinking and the shadows were lengthening when, having made the round of the principal ruins, we at length mounted our donkeys and turned towards Luxor. To describe all that we saw after leaving the Great Hall would fill

---

[1] *i.e. Per Amen*, or *Pa-Amen ;*—one of the ancient names of Thebes, which was the city especially dedicated to Amen. Also *Apt*, or *Abot*, or *Apetou*, by some ascribed to an Indo-Germanic root signifying Abode. Another name for Thebes, and probably the one most in use, was *Uas*.

a chapter. Huge obelisks of shining granite—some yet erect, some shattered and prostrate ; vast lengths of sculptured walls covered with wondrous battle subjects, sacerdotal processions, and elaborate chronicles of the deeds of Kings ; ruined court-yards surrounded by files of headless statues ; a sanctuary built all of polished granite, and engraven like a gem ; a second Hall of Pillars dating back to the early days of Thothmes the Third ; labyrinths of roofless chambers ; mutilated colossi, shattered pylons, fallen columns, unintelligible foundations and hieroglyphic inscriptions without end, were glanced at, passed by, and succeeded by fresh wonders. I dare not say how many small outlying temples we saw in the course of that rapid survey. In one place we came upon an undulating tract of coarse halfeh grass, in the midst of which, battered, defaced, forlorn, sat a weird company of green granite Sphinxes and lioness-headed Basts. In another, we saw a magnificent colossal hawk upright on his pedestal in the midst of a bergfall of ruins. More avenues of Sphinxes, more pylons, more colossi were passed before the road we took in returning brought us round to that by which we had come. By the time we reached the Sheykh's tomb, it was nearly dusk. We rode back across the plain, silent and bewildered. Have I not said that it was like a dream ?

CHAPTER IX.

THEBES TO ASSÛAN.

HURRYING close upon the serenest of Egyptian sunsets came a night of storms. The wind got up about ten. By midnight the river was racing in great waves, and our dahabeeyah rolling at her moorings like a ship at sea. The sand, driving in furious gusts from the Lybian desert, dashed like hail against our cabin windows. Every moment we were either bumping against the bank, or being rammed by our own felucca. At length, a little before dawn, a huge slice of the bank gave way, thundering like an avalanche upon our decks ; whereupon Reïs Hassan, being alarmed for the safety of the boat, hauled us up to a little sheltered nook a few hundred yards higher. Taking it altogether, we had not had such a lively night since leaving Benisouef.

The look-out next morning was dismal—the river running high in yeasty waves ; the boats all huddled together under the shore ; the western bank hidden in clouds of sand. To get under way was impossible, for the wind was dead against us ; and to go anywhere by land was equally out of the question. Karnak in a sand-storm would have been grand to see ; but one would have needed a diving helmet to preserve eyes and ears from destruction.

Towards afternoon, the fury of the wind so far subsided that we were able to cross the river and ride to Medinet Habu and the Ramesseum. As we achieved only a passing glimpse of these wonderful ruins, I will for the present say nothing about them. We came to know them so well hereafter that no mere first impression would be worth record.

A light but fitful breeze helped us on next day as far as Erment, the Ptolemaic Hermonthis, once the site of a goodly temple, now of an important sugar-factory. Here we moored for the night, and after dinner received a visit of ceremony from the Bey—a tall, slender, sharp-featured, bright-eyed man in European dress, remarkably dignified and well-bred—who came attended by his secretary, Kawass, and pipe-bearer. Now the Bey of Erment is a great personage in these parts. He is governor of the town as well as superintendent of the sugar-factory ; holds a military command ; has his palace and gardens close by, and his private steamer on the river ; and is, like most high officials in Egypt, a Turk of distinction. The secretary, who was the Bey's younger brother, wore a brown Inverness cape over a long white petticoat, and left his slippers at the saloon door. He sat all the time with his toes curiously doubled under, so that his feet looked like clenched fists in stockings. Both gentlemen wore tarbooshes, and carried visiting canes. The visiting cane, by the way, plays a conspicuous part in modern Egyptian life. It measures about two and a half feet in length, is tipped at both ends with gold or silver, and is supposed to add the last touch of elegance to the bearer.

We entertained our guests with coffee and lemonade, and, as well as we could, with conversation. The Bey, who spoke only Turkish and Arabic, gave a flourishing account of the sugar-works, and despatched his pipe-bearer for a bundle of fresh canes and some specimens of raw and candied sugars. He said he had an English foreman and several English work-men, and that for the English as a nation he had the highest admiration and regard ; but that the Arabs "had no heads." To our inquiries about the ruins, his replies were sufficiently discouraging. Of the large Temple every vestige had long since disappeared ; while of the smaller one only a few columns and part of the walls were yet standing. They lay out beyond the town and a long way from the river. There was very little to see. It was all "sagheer" (small) ; "moosh-taïb" (bad) ; not worth the trouble of the walk. As for "anteekahs," they were rarely found here, and when found were of slight value.

A scarab which he wore in a ring was then passed round and admired. It fell to our Little Lady's turn to examine it last, and restore it to the owner. But the owner, with a bow and a deprecating gesture, would have none of it. The ring was a toy—a nothing—the lady's—his no longer. She was obliged to accept it, however unwillingly. To decline would have been to offend. But it was the way in which the thing was done that made the charm of this little incident. The grace, the readiness, the courtesy, the lofty indifference of it, were alike admirable. Macready in his best days could have done it with as princely an air ; but even he would probably have missed something of the Oriental reticence of the Bey of Erment.

He then invited us to go over the sugar-factory (which we declined on account of the lateness of the hour), and presently took his leave. About ten minutes after, came a whole posse of presents—three large bouquets of roses for the Sittàt (ladies), two scarabei, a small funereal statuette in the rare green porcelain, and a live turkey. We in return sent a complicated English knife with all sorts of blades, and some pots of English jam.

The wind rose next morning with the sun, and by break-fast-time we had left Erment far behind. All that day the good breeze served us well. The river was alive with cargo-boats. The Philæ put on her best speed. The little Bagstones kept up gallantly. And the Fostat, a large iron dahabeeyah full of English gentlemen, kept us close company all the after-noon. We were all alike bound for Esneh, which is a large trading town, and lies twenty-six miles south of Erment.

Now, at Esneh the men were to bake again. Great, there-fore, was Reïs Hassan's anxiety to get in first, secure the oven, and buy the flour before dusk. The Reïs of the Fostat and he of the Bagstones were equally anxious, and for the same reasons. Our men, meanwhile, were wild with excitement, watching every manœuvre of the other boats ; hanging on to the shoghool like a swarm of bees ; and obeying the word of command with unwonted alacrity. As we neared the goal, the race grew hotter. The honour of the boats was at stake, and the bread question was for the moment forgotten. Finally all three dahabeeyahs ran in abreast, and moored side by side in front of a row of little open cafés just outside the town.

Esneh (of which the old Egyptian civil name was Sni, and the Roman name Latopolis) stands high upon the mounds of the ancient city. It is a large place—as large, apparently, as Minieh, and like Minieh, it is the capital of a province. Here dragomans lay in provision of limes, charcoal, flour, and live stock, for the Nubian journey; and crews bake for the last time before their return to Egypt. For in Nubia food is scarce, and prices are high, and there are no public ovens.

It was about five o'clock on a market-day when we reached Esneh, and the market was not yet over. Going up through the usual labyrinth of windowless mud-alleys where the old men crouched, smoking, under every bit of sunny wall, and the children swarmed like flies, and the cry for backshîsh buzzed incessantly about our ears, we came to an open space in the upper part of the town, and found ourselves all at once in the midst of the market. Here were peasant folk selling farm-produce; stall-keepers displaying combs, looking-glasses, gaudy printed handkerchiefs and cheap bracelets of bone and coloured glass; camels lying at ease and snarling at every passer-by; patient donkeys; ownerless dogs; veiled women; blue and black robed men; and all the common sights and sounds of a native market. Here, too, we found Reïs Hassan bargaining for flour; Talhamy haggling with a charcoal-dealer; and the M. B.'s buying turkeys and geese for themselves and a huge store of tobacco for their crew. Most welcome sight of all, however, was a dingy chemist's shop about the size of a sentry-box, over the door of which was suspended an Arabic inscription; while inside, robed all in black, sat a lean and grizzled Arab, from whom we bought a big bottle of rose water to make eye-lotion for L.'s ophthalmic patients.

Meanwhile there was a Temple to be seen at Esneh; and this Temple, as we had been told, was to be found close against the market-place. We looked round in vain, however, for any sign of pylon or portico. The chemist said it was "kureiyib," which means "near by." A camel-driver pointed to a dilapidated wooden gateway in a recess between two neighbouring houses. A small boy volunteered to lead the way. We were greatly puzzled. We had expected to see the Temple towering above the surrounding houses, as at Luxor, and could by no means understand how any large building to which that gateway might give access, should not be visible from without.

The boy, however, ran and thumped upon the gate, and shouted "Abbas! Abbas!" Mehemet Ali, who was doing escort, added some thundering blows with his staff, and a little crowd gathered, but no Abbas came.

The bystanders, as usual, were liberal with their advice ; recommending the boy to climb over, and the sailor to knock louder, and suggesting that Abbas the absent might possibly be found in a certain neighbouring café. At length I somewhat impatiently expressed my opinion that there was " Mafeesh Birbeh " (no Temple at all) ; whereupon a dozen voices were raised to assure me that the Birbeh was no myth—that it was " kebîr " (big)—that it was " kwy-ees " (beautiful)—and that all the " Ingleez " came to see it.

In the midst of the clamour, however, and just as we are about to turn away in despair, the gate creaks open ; the gentlemen of the Fostat troop out in puggeries and knickerbockers ; and we are at last admitted.

This is what we see—a little yard surrounded by mudwalls ; at the farther end of the yard a dilapidated doorway ; beyond the doorway, a strange-looking, stupendous mass of yellow limestone masonry, long, and low, and level, and enormously massive. A few steps farther, and this proves to be the curved cornice of a mighty Temple—a Temple neither ruined nor defaced, but buried to the chin in the accumulated rubbish of a score of centuries. This part is evidently the portico. We stand close under a row of huge capitals. The columns that support them are buried beneath our feet. The ponderous cornice juts out above our heads. From the level on which we stand to the top of that cornice may measure about twenty-five feet. A high mud-wall runs parallel to the whole width of the façade, leaving a passage of about twelve feet in breadth between the two. A low mud-parapet and a hand-rail reach from capital to capital. All beyond is vague, cavernous, mysterious—a great shadowy gulf, in the midst of which dim ghosts of many columns are darkly visible. From an opening between two of the capitals, a flight of brick steps

leads down into a vast hall so far below the surface of the
outer world, so gloomy, so awful, that it might be the portico
of Hades.

Going down these steps we come to the original level of
the Temple.   We tread the ancient pavement.   We look up
to the massive ceiling, recessed, and sculptured, and painted,
like the ceiling at Denderah.   We could almost believe, indeed,
that we are again standing in the portico of. Denderah.   The
number of columns is the same.   The arrangement of the
intercolumnar screen is the same.   The general effect and the
main features of the plan are the same.   In some respects,
however, Esneh is even more striking.   The columns, though
less massive than those of Denderah, are more elegant, and
look loftier.   Their shafts are covered with figures of gods,
and emblems, and lines of hieroglyphed inscription, all cut in
low relief.   Their capitals, in place of the huge draped Hathor-
heads of Denderah, are studied from natural forms—from the
lotus-lily, the papyrus-blossom, the plumy date-palm.   The
wall-sculpture, however, is inferior to that at Denderah, and
immeasurably inferior to the wall-sculpture at Karnak.   The
figures are of the meanest Ptolemaic type, and all of one size.
The inscriptions, instead of being grouped wherever there
happened to be space, and so producing the richest form of
wall-decoration ever devised by man, are disposed in symmetrical columns, the effect of which, when compared with the florid
style of Karnak, is as the methodical neatness of an engrossed
deed to the splendid freedom of an illuminated manuscript.

The steps occupy the place of the great doorway.   The
jambs and part of the cornice, the intercolumnar screen, the
shafts of the columns under whose capitals we came in, are
all there, half-projecting from, and half-imbedded in the solid
mound beyond.   The light, however, comes in from so high
up, and through so narrow a space, that one's eyes need to
become accustomed to the darkness before any of these details
can be distinguished.   Then, by degrees, forms of deities
familiar and unfamiliar emerge from the gloom.

The Temple is dedicated to Knum or Kneph, the Soul
of the World, whom we now see for the first time.   He is
ram-headed, and holds in his hand the "ankh," or emblem of

TEMPLE OF ESNEH.

life.[1]   Another new acquaintance is Bes,[2] the grotesque god of mirth and jollity.

Two singular little erections, built in between the columns to right and left of the steps, next attract our attention.   They are like stone sentry-boxes.   Each is in itself complete, with roof, sculptured cornice, doorway, and, if I remember rightly, a small square window in the side.   The inscriptions upon two similar structures in the portico at Edfû show that the right-hand closet contained the sacred books belonging to the Temple, while in the closet to the left of the main entrance the King underwent the ceremony of purification.   It may therefore be taken for granted that these at Esneh were erected for the same purposes.

And now we look round for the next Hall—and look in vain.   The doorway which should lead to it is walled up.   The portico was excavated by Mohammed Ali in 1842 ; not in any spirit of antiquarian zeal, but in order to provide a safe underground magazine for gunpowder.   Up to that time, as may be seen by one of the illustrations to Wilkinson's *Thebes and General View of Egypt*, the interior was choked to within a few feet of the capitals of the columns, and used as a cotton-store.   Of the rest of the building, nothing is known ; nothing

---

1 Knum was one of the primordial Gods of the Egyptian cosmogony ; the divine potter ; he who fashioned man from the clay, and breathed into him the breath of life.   He is sometimes represented in the act of fashioning the first man, or that mysterious egg from which not only man but the universe proceeded, by means of the ordinary potter's wheel.   Sometimes also he is depicted in his boat, moving upon the face of the waters at the dawn of creation.   About the time of the XXth dynasty Knum became identified with Ra.   He also was identified with Amen, and was worshipped in the Great Oasis in the Greek period as Amen-Knum.   He is likewise known as "The Soul of the Gods," and in this character, as well as in his Solar character, he is represented with the head of a ram, or in the form of a ram.   Another of his titles is "The Maker of Gods and Men."   Knum was also one of the Gods of the Cataract, and chief of the Triad worshipped at Elephantiné.   An inscription at Philæ styles him "Maker of all that is, Creator of all beings, First existent, the Father of Fathers, the Mother of Mothers."

2 *Bes.*   "La culte de Bes parait être une importation Asiatique. Quelquefois le dieu est armé d'une épée qu'il brandit au-dessus de sa tête ; dans ce rôle, il semble le dieu des combats.   Plus souvent c'est le dieu de la danse, de la musique, des plaisirs."—*Mariette Bey.*

is visible. It is as large, probably, as Denderah or Edfû, and in as perfect preservation. So, at least, says local tradition ; but not even local tradition can point out to what extent it underlies the foundations of the modern houses that swarm above its roof. An inscription first observed by Champollion states that the sanctuary was built by Thothmes III. Is that antique sanctuary still there ? Has the Temple grown step by step under the hands of successive Kings, as at Luxor ? Or has it been re-edified *ab ovo,* as at Denderah ? These are "puzzling questions," only to be resolved by the demolition of a quarter of the town. Meanwhile, what treasures of sculptured history, what pictured chambers, what buried bronzes and statues may here await the pick of the excavator !

All next day, while the men were baking, the Writer sat in a corner of the outer passage, and sketched the portico of the Temple. The sun rose upon the one horizon and set upon the other before that drawing was finished ; yet for scarcely more than one hour did it light up the front of the Temple. At about half-past nine A.M. it first caught the stone fillet at the angle. Then, one by one, each massy capital became outlined with a thin streak of gold. As this streak widened, the cornice took fire, and presently the whole stood out in light against the sky. Slowly then, but quite perceptibly, the sun travelled across the narrow space overhead ; the shadows became vertical ; the light changed sides ; and by ten o'clock there was shade for the remainder of the day. Towards noon, however, the sun being then at its highest and the air transfused with light, the inner columns, swallowed up till now in darkness, became illumined with a wonderful reflected light, and glowed from out the gloom like pillars of fire.

Never to go on shore without an escort is one of the rules of Nile life, and Salame has by this time become my exclusive property. He is a native of Assûan, young, active, intelligent, full of fun, hot-tempered withal, and as thorough a gentleman as I have ever had the pleasure of knowing. For a sample of his good breeding, take this day at Esneh—a day which he might have idled away in the bazaars and cafés, and which it must have been dull work to spend cooped up between a mud-wall and an outlandish Birbeh, built by the Djinns who reigned before Adam. Yet Salame betrays no discontent. Curled up in a shady corner, he watches me like a dog ; is ready with an umbrella as soon as the sun comes round ; and replenishes a water-bottle or holds a colour-box as deftly as though he had been to the manner born. At one o'clock arrives my luncheon, enshrined in a pagoda of plates. Being too busy to leave off work, however, I put the pagoda aside, and despatch Salame to the market, to buy himself some dinner ; for which purpose, wishing to do the thing handsomely, I present him with the magnificent sum of two silver piastres, or about fivepence English. With this he contrives to purchase three or four cakes of flabby native bread, a black-looking rissole of chopped meat and vegetables, and about a pint of dried dates.

Knowing this to be a better dinner than my friend gets every day, knowing also that our sailors habitually eat at noon, I am surprised to see him leave these dainties untasted. In vain I say " Bismillah " (in the name of God) ; pressing him to eat in vocabulary phrases eked out with expressive pantomime. He laughs, shakes his head, and, asking permission to smoke a cigarette, protests he is not hungry. Thus three more hours go by. Accustomed to long fasting and absorbed in my sketch, I forget all about the pagoda ; and it is past four o'clock when I at length set to work to repair tissue at the briefest possible cost of time and daylight. And now the faithful Salame falls to with an energy that causes the cakes, the rissole, the dates, to vanish as if by magic. Of what remains from my luncheon he also disposes in a trice. Never, unless in a pantomime, have I seen mortal man display so prodigious an appetite.

I made Talhamy scold him, by and by, for this piece of voluntary starvation.

" By my Prophet !" said he, " am I a pig or a dog, that I should eat when the Sitt was fasting ? "

It was at Esneh, by the way, that that hitherto undiscovered curiosity, an ancient Egyptian coin, was offered to me for sale. The finder was digging for nitre, and turned it up at an immense depth below the mounds on the outskirts of the town. He volunteered to show the precise spot, and told his artless tale with childlike simplicity. Unfortunately, however, for the authenticity of this remarkable relic, it bore, together with the familiar profile of George IV, a superscription of its modest value, which was precisely one farthing. On another occasion, when we were making our long stay at Luxor, a coloured glass button of honest Birmingham make was brought to the boat by a fellâh who swore that he had himself found it upon a mummy in the Tombs of the Queens at Kûrnet Murraee. The same man came to my tent one day when I was sketching, bringing with him a string of more than doubtful scarabs—all veritable " anteekahs," of course, and all backed up with undeniable pedigrees.

"La, la (no, no),—bring me no more anteekahs," I said, gravely. "They are old and worn out, and cost much money. Have you no imitation scarabs, new and serviceable, that one might wear without the fear of breaking them?"

"These are imitations, O Sitt!" was the ready answer.

"But you told me a moment ago they were genuine anteekahs."

"That was because I thought the Sitt wanted to buy anteekahs," he said, quite shamelessly.

"See now," I said, "if you are capable of selling me new things for old, how can I be sure that you would not sell me old things for new?"

To this he replied by declaring that he had made the scarabs himself. Then, fearing I should not believe him, he pulled a scrap of coarse paper from his bosom, borrowed one of my pencils, and drew an asp, an ibis, and some other common hieroglyphic forms, with tolerable dexterity.

"Now you believe?" he asked, triumphantly.

"I see that you can make birds and snakes," I replied ; "but that neither proves that you can cut scarabs, nor that these scarabs are new."

"Nay, Sitt," he protested, "I made them with these hands. I made them but the other day. By Allah! they cannot be newer."

Here Talhamy interposed.

"In that case," he said, "they are too new, and will crack before a month is over. The Sitt would do better to buy some that are well seasoned."

Our honest Fellâh touched his brow and breast.

"Now in strict truth, O Dragoman !" he said, with an air of the most engaging candour, "these scarabs were made at the time of the inundation. They are new ; but not too new. They are thoroughly seasoned. If they crack, you shall denounce me to the governor, and I will eat stick for them !"

Now it has always seemed to me that the most curious feature in this little scene was the extraordinary simplicity of the Arab. With all his cunning, with all his disposition to cheat, he suffered himself to be turned inside-out as unsuspiciously as a baby. It never occurred to him that his untruthfulness was being put to the test, or that he was committing himself more and more deeply with every word he uttered. The fact is, however, that the Fellâh is half a savage. Notwithstanding his mendacity—(and it must be owned that he is the most brilliant liar under heaven)—he remains a singularly transparent piece of humanity, easily amused, easily deceived, easily angered, easily pacified. He steals a little, cheats a little, lies a great deal ; but on the other hand he is patient, hospitable, affectionate, trustful. He suspects no malice, and bears none. He commits no great crimes. He is incapable of revenge. In short, his good points outnumber his bad ones ; and what man or nation need hope for a much better character ?

To generalise in this way may seem like presumption on the part of a passing stranger ; yet it is more excusable as regards Egypt than it would be of any other equally accessible country. In Europe, and indeed in most parts of the East, one sees too little of the people to be able to form an opinion about them ; but it is not so on the Nile. Cut off from hotels, from railways, from Europeanised cities, you are brought into continual intercourse with natives. The sick who come to you for medicines, the country gentlemen and government officials who visit you on board your boat and entertain you on shore, your guides, your donkey-boys, the very dealers who live by cheating you, furnish endless studies of character, and teach you more of Egyptian life than all the books of Nile-travel that ever were written.

Then your crew, part Arab, part Nubian, are a little world in themselves. One man was born a slave, and will carry the dealer's brand-marks to his grave. Another has two children in Miss Whateley's school at Cairo. A third is just married, and has left his young wife sick at home. She may be dead by the time he gets back, and he will hear no news of her meanwhile. So with them all. Each has his simple story— a story in which the local oppressor, the dreaded conscription, and the still more dreaded *corvée*, form the leading incidents. The poor fellows are ready enough to pour out their hopes, their wrongs, their sorrows. Through sympathy with these, one comes to know the men ; and through the men, the nation. For the life of the Beled repeats itself with but little variation wherever the Nile flows and the Khedive rules. The characters are the same ; the incidents are the same. It is only the *mise en scène* which varies.

And thus it comes to pass that the mere traveller who spends but half-a-year on the Nile may, if he takes an interest in Egypt and the Egyptians, learn more of both in that short time than would be possible in a country less singularly narrowed in all ways—politically, socially, geographically.

And this reminds me that the traveller on the Nile really sees the whole land of Egypt. Going from point to point in other countries, one follows a thin line of road, railway, or river, leaving wide tracts unexplored on either side ; but there are few places in Middle or Upper Egypt, and none at all in Nubia, where one may not, from any moderate height, survey the entire face of the country from desert to desert. It is well to do this frequently. It helps one, as nothing else can help one, to an understanding of the wonderful mountain waste through which the Nile has been scooping its way for uncounted cycles. And it enables one to realise what a mere slip of alluvial deposit is this famous land which is " the gift of the river."

A dull grey morning, a faint and fitful breeze, carried us slowly on our way from Esneh to Edfû. The new bread—a heavy boat-load when brought on board—lay in a huge heap at the end of the upper deck. It took four men one whole day to cut it up. Their incessant gabble drove us nearly distracted.

" Uskût, Khaleefeh ! Uskût, Ali !" (Silence, Khaleefeh ! Silence, Ali !) Talhamy would say from time to time. " You

are not on your own deck. The Howadji can neither read
nor write for the clatter of your tongues."

And then, for about a minute and a half, they would be
quiet.

But you could as easily keep a monkey from chattering as
an Arab. Our men talked incessantly; and their talk was
always about money. Listen to them when we might, such
words as "Khámsa gurûsh" (five piastres), "nûs riyâl"
(half-a-dollar), "ethneen shilling" (two shillings), were perpetually coming to the surface. We never could understand how
it was that money, which played so small a part in their lives,
should play so large a part in their conversation.

It was about midday when we passed El Kab, the ancient
Eileithyias. A rocky valley narrowing inland; a Sheykh's
tomb on the mountain-ridge above; a few clumps of date-
palms; some remains of what looked like a long crude-brick
wall running at right angles to the river; and an isolated mass
of hollowed limestone rock left standing apparently in the
midst of an exhausted quarry, were all we saw of El Kab as
the dahabeeyah glided by.

And now, as the languid afternoon wears on, the propylons
of Edfû loom out of the misty distance. We have been
looking for them long enough before they come into sight—
calculating every mile of the way; every minute of the daylight. The breeze, such as it was, has dropped now. The
river stretches away before us, smooth and oily as a pond.
Nine of the men are tracking. Will they pull us to Edfû in
time to see the Temple before nightfall?

Reïs Hassan looks doubtful; but takes refuge as usual
in "Inshallah!" (God willing). Talhamy talks of landing a
sailor to run forward and order donkeys. Meanwhile the Philæ
creeps lazily on; the sun declines unseen behind a filmy veil;
and those two shadowy towers, rising higher and ever higher
on the horizon, look grey, and ghostly, and far distant still.

Suddenly the trackers stop, look back, shout to those on
board, and begin drawing the boat to shore. Reïs Hassan
points joyously to a white streak breaking across the smooth
surface of the river about half-a-mile behind. The Fostât's
sailors are already swarming aloft—the Bagstones' trackers are

making for home—our own men are preparing to fling in the rope and jump on board as the Philæ nears the bank.

For the capricious wind, that always springs up when we don't want it, is coming!

And now the Fostât, being hindmost, flings out her big sail and catches the first puff; the Bagstones' turn comes next; the Philæ shakes her wings free, and shoots ahead; and in fewer minutes than it takes to tell, we are all three scudding along before a glorious breeze.

The great towers that showed so far away half-an-hour ago are now close at hand. There are palm-woods about their feet, and clustered huts, from the midst of which they tower up against the murky sky magnificently. Soon they are passed and left behind, and the grey twilight takes them, and we see them no more. Then night comes on, cold and starless; yet not too dark for going as fast as wind and canvas will carry us.

And now, with that irrepressible instinct of rivalry that flesh—especially flesh on the Nile—is heir to, we quickly turn our good going into a trial of speed. It is no longer a mere business-like devotion to the matter in hand. It is a contest for glory. It is the Philæ against the Fostât, and the Bagstones against both. In plain English, it is a race. The two leading dahabeeyahs are pretty equally matched. The Philæ is larger than the Fostât; but the Fostât has a bigger mainsail. On the other hand, the Fostât is an iron boat; whereas the Philæ, being wooden-built, is easier to pole off a sandbank, and lighter in hand. The Bagstones carries a capital mainsail, and can go as fast as either upon occasion. Meanwhile, the race is one of perpetually varying fortunes. Now the Fostât shoots ahead; now the Philæ. We pass and re-pass; take the wind out of one another's sails; economise every curve; hoist every stitch of canvas; and, having identified ourselves with our boats, are as eager to win as if a great prize depended on it. Under these circumstances, to dine is difficult—to go to bed super-fluous—to sleep impossible. As to mooring for the night, it is not to be thought of for a moment. Having begun the contest, we can no more help going than the wind can help blowing; and our crew are as keen about winning as ourselves.

As night advances, the wind continues to rise, and our

excitement with it.   Still the boats chase each other along the
dark river, scattering spray from their bows and flinging out
broad foam-tracks behind them.   Their cabin-windows, all
alight within, cast flickering flames upon the waves below.   The
coloured lanterns at their mast-heads, orange, purple, and
crimson, burn through the dusk like jewels.   Presently the
mist blows off ; the sky clears ; the stars come out ; the wind
howls ; the casements rattle ; the tiller scroops ; the sailors
shout, and race, and bang the ropes about overhead ; while we,
sitting up in our narrow berths, spend half the night watching
from our respective windows.

In this way some hours go by.   Then, about three in the
morning, with a shock, a recoil, a yell, and a scuffle, we all
three rush headlong upon a sandbank !   The men fly to the
rigging, and furl the flapping sail.   Some seize punting poles.
Others, looking like full-grown imps of darkness, leap overboard
and set their shoulders to the work.   A strophe and antistrophe
of grunts are kept up between those on deck and those in the
water.   Finally, after some ten minutes' frantic struggle, the
Philæ slips off, leaving the other two aground in the middle of
the river.

Towards morning, the noisy night having worn itself away,
we all fall asleep—only to be roused again by Talhamy's voice
at seven, proclaiming aloud that the Bagstones and Fostât are
once more close upon our heels ; that Silsilis and Kom Ombo
are passed and left behind ; that we have already put forty-six
miles between ourselves and Edfû ; and that the good wind
is still blowing.

We are now within fifteen miles of Assûan.   The Nile is
narrow here, and the character of the scenery has quite changed.
Our view is bounded on the Arabian side by a near range of
black granitic mountains ; while on the Libyan side lies a
chain of lofty sand-hills, each curiously capped by a crown of
dark boulders.   On both banks the river is thickly fringed
with palms.

Meanwhile the race goes on.   Last night it was sport ;
to-day it is earnest.   Last night we raced for glory ; to-day
we race for a stake.

"A guinée for Reïs Hassan, if we get first to Assûan!"

Reïs Hassan's eyes glisten. No need to call up the dragoman to interpret between us. The look, the tone, are as intelligible to him as the choicest Arabic ; and the magical word 'guinée' stands for a sovereign now, as it stood for one pound one in the days of Nelson and Abercrombie. He touches his head and breast ; casts a backward glance at the pursuing dahabeeyahs, a forward glance in the direction of Assûan ; kicks off his shoes ; ties a handkerchief about his waist ; and stations himself at the top of the steps leading to the upper deck. By the light in his eye and the set look about his mouth, Reïs Hassan means winning.

Now to be first in Assûan means to be first on the governor's list, and first up the Cataract. And as the passage of the Cataract is some two or three days' work, this little question of priority is by no means unimportant. Not for five times the promised 'guinée' would we have the Fostât slip in first, and so be kept waiting our turn on the wrong side of the frontier.

And now, as the sun rises higher, so the race waxes hotter. At breakfast time, we were fifteen miles from Assûan. Now the fifteen miles have gone down to ten ; and when we reach yonder headland, they will have dwindled to seven. It is plain to see, however, that as the distance decreases between ourselves and Assûan, so also it decreases between ourselves and the Fostât. Reïs Hassan knows it. I see him measuring the space by his eye. I see the frown settling on his brow. He is calculating how much the Fostât gains in every quarter of an hour, and how many quarters we are yet distant from the goal. For no Arab sailor counts by miles. He counts by time, and by the reaches in the river ; and these may be taken at a rough average of three miles each. When, therefore, our captain, in reply to an oft-repeated question, says we have yet two bends to make, we know that we are about six miles from our destination.

Six miles—and the Fostât creeping closer every minute ! Just now we were all talking eagerly ; but as the end draws near, even the sailors are silent. Reïs Hassan stands motionless at his post, on the look-out for shallows. The words "Shamàl—Yemîn" (left—right), delivered in a short, sharp tone, are the only sounds he utters. The steersman, all eye and ear, obeys him like his hand. The sailors squat in their places, quiet and alert as cats.

And now it is no longer six miles but five—no longer five, but four. The Fostât, thanks to her bigger sail, has well-nigh overtaken us; and the Bagstones is not more than a hundred yards behind the Fostât. On we go, however, past palm-woods of nobler growth than any we have yet seen; past forlorn homeward-bound dahabeeyahs lying-to against the wind; past native boats, and river-side huts, and clouds of driving sand; till the corner is turned, and the last reach gained, and the minarets of Assûan are seen as through a shifting fog in the distance. The ruined tower crowning yonder promontory stands over against the town; and those black specks midway in the bed of the river are the first outlying rocks of the Cataract. The channel there is hemmed in between reefs and sandbanks, and to steer it is difficult in even the calmest weather. Still our canvas strains to the wind, and the Philæ rushes on full-tilt, like a racer at the hurdles.

Every eye now is turned upon Reïs Hassan; and Reïs Hassan stands rigid, like a man of stone. The rocks are close ahead—so close that we can see the breakers pouring over them, and the swirling eddies between. Our way lies through an opening between the boulders. Beyond that opening, the channel turns off sharply to the left. It is a point at which everything will depend on the shifting of a sail. If done too soon, we miss the mark; if too late, we strike upon the rocks.

Suddenly our Captain flings up his hand, takes the stairs at a bound, and flies to the prow. The sailors spring to their feet, gathering some round the shoghool, and some round the end of the yard. The Fostât is up beside us. The moment for winning or losing is come.

And now, for a couple of breathless seconds, the two dahabeeyahs plunge onward side by side, making for that narrow passage which is only wide enough for one. Then the iron boat, shaving the sandbank to get a wider berth, shifts her sail first, and shifts it clumsily, breaking or letting go her shoghool. We see the sail flap, and the rope fly, and all hands rushing to retrieve it.

In that moment Reïs Hassan gives the word. The Philæ
bounds forward—takes the channel from under the very bows
of the Fostât—changes her sail without a hitch—and dips
right away down the deep water, leaving her rival hard and
fast among the shallows.

The rest of the way is short and open. In less than five
minutes we have taken in our sail, paid Reïs Hassan his well-
earned guinée, and found a snug corner to moor in. And so
ends our memorable race of nearly sixty-eight miles from
Edfû to Assûan.

NATIVE BOAT, ASSÛAN.

CHAPTER X.

ASSÛAN AND ELEPHANTINE.

THE green island of Elephantine, which is about a mile in length, lies opposite Assûan and divides the Nile in two channels. The Libyan and Arabian deserts—smooth amber sand-slopes on the one hand ; rugged granite cliffs on the other—come down to the brink on either side. On the Libyan shore a Sheykh's tomb, on the Arabian shore a bold fragment of Moorish architecture with ruined arches open to the sky, crown two opposing heights, and keep watch over the gate of the Cataract. Just under the Moorish ruin, and separated from the river by a slip of sandy beach, lies Assûan.

A few scattered houses, a line of blank wall, the top of a minaret, the dark mouths of one or two gloomy alleys, are all that one sees of the town from the mooring-place below. The black boulders close against the shore, some of which are superbly hieroglyphed, glisten in the sun like polished jet.[1] The beach is crowded with bales of goods ; with camels laden and unladen ; with turbaned figures coming and going ; with damaged cargo-boats lying up high and dry, and half heeled over, in the sun. Others, moored close together, are taking in or discharging cargo. A little apart from these lie some

---

[1] "At the Cataracts of the great rivers Orinoco, Nile, and Congo, the syenitic rocks are coated by a black substance, appearing as if they had been polished with plumbago. The layer is of extreme thinness ; and on analysis by Berzelius it was found to consist of the oxides of manganese and iron. . . . The origin, however, of these coatings of metallic oxides, which seem as if cemented to the rocks, is not understood ; and no reason, I believe, can be assigned for their thickness remaining the same."— *Journal of Researches*, by Charles Darwin, chap. i. p. 12, ed. 1845.

three or four dahabeeyahs flying English, American, and Belgian flags. Another has cast anchor over the way at Elephantine. Small row-boats cross and recross, meanwhile, from shore to shore ; dogs bark ; camels snort and snarl ; donkeys bray ; and clamorous curiosity-dealers scream, chatter, hold their goods at arm's length, battle and implore to come on board, and are only kept off the landing plank by means of two big sticks in the hands of two stalwart sailors.

The things offered for sale at Assûan are altogether new and strange. Here are no scarabæi, no funerary statuettes, no bronze or porcelain gods, no relics of a past civilisation ; but, on the contrary, such objects as speak only of a rude and barbarous present—ostrich eggs and feathers, silver trinkets of rough Nubian workmanship, spears, bows, arrows, bucklers of rhinoceros-hide, ivory bracelets cut solid from the tusk, porcu-pine quills, baskets of stained and plaited reeds, gold nose-rings, and the like. One old woman has a Nubian lady's dressing-case for sale—an uncouth, Fetish-like object with a cushion for its body, and a top-knot of black feathers. The cushion con-tains two Kohl-bottles, a bodkin, and a bone comb.

But the noisiest dealer of the lot is an impish boy blessed with the blackest skin and the shrillest voice ever brought together in one human being. His simple costume consists of a tattered shirt and a white cotton skull-cap ; his stock-in-trade, of a greasy leather fringe tied to the end of a stick. Flying from window to window of the saloon on the side next the shore, scrambling up the bows of a neighbouring cargo-boat so as to attack us in the rear, thrusting his stick and fringe in our faces whichever way we turn, and pursuing us with eager cries of "Madame Nubia! Madame Nubia!" he skips, and screams, and grins like an ubiquitous goblin, and throws every competitor into the shade.

Having seen a similar fringe in the collection of a friend at home, I at once recognised in "Madame Nubia" one of those curious girdles which, with the addition of a necklace and a few bracelets, form the entire wardrobe of little girls south of the Cataract. They vary in size according to the age of the wearer ; the largest being about twelve inches in depth and twenty-five in length. A few are ornamented with beads and small shells ; but these are *parures de luxe.* The ordinary article is cheaply and unpretentiously trimmed with castor-oil. That is to say, the girdle when new is well soaked in the oil, which softens and darkens the leather, besides adding a perfume dear to native nostrils.

For to the Nubian, who grows his own plants and bruises his own berries, this odour is delicious. He reckons castor-oil among his greatest luxuries. He eats it as we eat butter. His wives saturate their plaited locks in it. His little girls perfume their fringes with it. His boys anoint their bodies with it. His home, his breath, his garments, his food, are redolent of it. It pervades the very air in which he lives and has his being. Happy the European traveller who, while his lines are cast in Nubia, can train his degenerate nose to delight in the aroma of castor-oil !

The march of civilisation is driving these fringes out of fashion on the frontier. At Assûan, they are chiefly in demand among English and American visitors. Most people purchase a " Madame Nubia " for the entertainment of friends at home. L., who is given to vanities in the way of dress, bought one so steeped in fragrance that it scented the Philæ for the rest of the voyage, and retains its odour to this day.

Almost before the mooring-rope was made fast, our Painter, arrayed in a gorgeous keffîyeh [1] and armed with the indispensable visiting-cane, had sprung ashore and hastened to call upon the Governor. A couple of hours later the Governor (having promised to send at once for the Sheykh of the Cataract and to forward our going by all means in his power) returned the visit. He brought with him the Mudîr [2] and Kadi [3] of Assûan, each attended by his pipe-bearer.

We received our guests with due ceremony in the saloon. The great men placed themselves on one of the side-divans, and the Painter opened the conversation by offering them champagne, claret, port, sherry, curaçoa, brandy, whisky, and Angostura bitters. Talhamy interpreted.

The Governor laughed. He was a tall young man, grace-

---

[1] *Keffîyeh :* A square head-shawl, made of silk or woollen. European travellers wear them as puggarees.

[2] *Mudîr :* Chief Magistrate.　　　[3] *Kadi :* Judge.

ful, lively, good-looking, and black as a crow. The Kadi and Mudîr, both elderly Arabs, yellow, wrinkled, and precise, looked shocked at the mere mention of these unholy liquors. Somebody then proposed lemonade.

The Governor turned briskly towards the speaker.

" Gazzoso ? " he said interrogatively.

To which Talhamy replied : " Aïwah (Yes), Gazzoso."

Aerated lemonade and cigars were then brought. The Governor watched the process of uncorking with a face of profound interest, and drank with the undisguised greediness of a schoolboy. Even the Kadi and Mudîr relaxed somewhat of the gravity of their demeanour. To men whose habitual drink consists of lime-water and sugar, bottled lemonade represents champagne mousseux of the choicest brand.

Then began the usual attempts at conversation ; and only those who have tried small-talk by proxy know how hard it is to supply topics, suppress yawns, and keep up an animated expression of countenance, while the civilities on both sides are being interpreted by a dragoman.

We began, of course, with the temperature ; for in Egypt, where it never rains and the sun is always shining, the thermometer takes the place of the weather as a useful platitude. Knowing that Assûan enjoys the hottest reputation of any town on the surface of the globe, we were agreeably surprised to find it no warmer than England in September. The Governor accounted for this by saying that he had never known so cold a winter. We then asked the usual questions about the crops, the height of the river, and so forth ; to all of which he replied with the ease and *bonhomie* of a man of the world. Nubia, he said, was healthy—the date-harvest had been abundant—the corn promised well—the Soudan was quiet and prosperous. Referring to the new postal arrangements, he congratulated us on being able to receive and post letters at the Second Cataract. He also remarked that the telegraphic wires were now in working order as far as Khartûm. We then asked how soon he expected the railway to reach Assûan ; to which he replied—" In two years, at latest."

At length our little stock of topics came to an end, and the entertainment flagged.

"What shall I say next?" asked the dragoman.

"Tell him we particularly wish to see the slave-market."

The smile vanished from the Governor's face. The Mudîr set down a glass of fizzing lemonade, untasted. The Kadi all but dropped his cigar. If a shell had burst in the saloon, their consternation could scarcely have been greater.

The Governor, looking very grave, was the first to speak.

"He says there is no slave-trade in Egypt, and no slave-market in Assûan," interpreted Talhamy.

Now we had been told in Cairo, on excellent authority, that slaves were still bought and sold here, though less publicly than of old ; and that of all the sights a traveller might see in Egypt, this was the most curious and pathetic.

"No slave-market!" we repeated incredulously.

The Governor, the Kadi, and the Mudîr shook their heads, and lifted up their voices, and said all together, like a trio of Mandarins in a comic opera :—

"Là, là, là! Mafeesh bazaar—mafeesh bazaar!" (No, no, no! No bazaar—no bazaar!)

We endeavoured to explain that in making this inquiry we desired neither the gratification of an idle curiosity, nor the furtherance of any political views. Our only object was sketching. Understanding, therefore, that a private bazaar still existed in Assûan . . . .

This was too much for the judicial susceptibilities of the Kadi. He would not let Talhamy finish.

"There is nothing of the kind," he interrupted, puckering his face into an expression of such virtuous horror as might become a reformed New Zealander on the subject of cannibalism. "It is unlawful—unlawful."

An awkward silence followed. We felt we had committed an enormous blunder, and were disconcerted accordingly.

The Governor saw, and with the best grace in the world took pity upon, our embarrassment. He rose, opened the piano, and asked for some music ; whereupon the Little Lady played the liveliest thing she could remember, which happened to be a waltz by Verdi.

The Governor, meanwhile, sat beside the piano, smiling and attentive. With all his politeness, however, he seemed to be looking for something—to be not altogether satisfied. There was even a shade of disappointment in the tone of his " Kettherkhayrik ketîr," when the waltz finally exploded in a shower of arpeggios. What could it be? Was it that he wished for a song? Or would a pathetic air have pleased him better?

Not a bit of it. He was looking for what his quick eye presently detected—namely some printed music, which he seized triumphantly and placed before the player. What he wanted was " music played from a book."

Being asked whether he preferred a lively or a plaintive melody, he replied that " he did not care, so long as it was *difficult.*"

Now it chanced that he had pitched upon a volume of Wagner ; so the Little Lady took him at his word, and gave him a dose of " Tannhaüser." Strange to say, he was delighted. He showed his teeth ; he rolled his eyes ; he uttered the long-drawn " Ah !" which in Egypt signifies applause. The more crabbed, the more far-fetched, the more unintelligible the movement, the better, apparently, he liked it.

I never think of Assûan but I remember that curious scene —our Little Lady at the piano ; the black Governor grinning in ecstasies close by ; the Kadi in his magnificent shawl-turban ; the Mudîr half asleep ; the air thick with tobacco-smoke ; and above all—dominant, tyrannous, overpowering— the crash and clang, the involved harmonies, and the multitudinous combinations of Tannhaüser.

The linked sweetness of an Oriental visit is generally drawn out to a length that sorely tries the patience and politeness of European hosts. A native gentleman, if he has any business to attend to, gets through his work before noon, and has nothing to do but smoke, chat, and doze away the remainder of the day. For time, which hangs heavily on his hands, he has absolutely no value. His main object in life is to consume it, if possible, less tediously. He pays a visit, therefore, with the deliberate intention of staying as long as possible. Our guests on the present occasion remained the best part of two hours ; and the Governor, who talked of going to England shortly, asked for all our names and addresses, that he might come and see us at home.

Leaving the cabin, he paused to look at our roses, which stood near the door.   We told him they had been given to us by the Bey of Erment.

"Do they grow at Erment?" he asked, examining them with great curiosity.   "How beautiful! Why will they not grow in Nubia?"

We suggested that the climate was probably too hot for them.

He stooped, inhaling their perfume.   He looked puzzled.

"They are very sweet," he said.   "Are they roses?"

The question gave us a kind of shock.   We could hardly believe we had reached a land where roses were unknown. Yet the Governor, who had smoked a rose-water narghilé, and drunk rose-sherbet, and eaten conserve of roses all his days, recognised them by their perfume only.   He had never been out of Assûan in his life ; not even as far as Erment.   And he had never seen a rose in bloom.

We had hoped to begin the passage of the Cataract on the morning of the day following our arrival at the frontier ; but some other dahabeeyah, it seemed, was in the act of fighting its way up to Philæ ; and till that boat was through, neither the Sheykh nor his men would be ready for us.   At eight o'clock in the morning of the next day but one, however, they promised to take us in hand.   We were to pay £12 English for the double journey ; that is to say, £9 down, and the remaining £3 on our return to Assûan.

Such was the treaty concluded between ourselves and the Sheykh of the Cataract at a solemn conclave over which the Governor, assisted by the Kadi and Mudîr, presided.

Having a clear day to spend at Assûan, we of course gave part thereof to Elephantine, which in the inscriptions is called Abu, or the Ivory Island.   There may perhaps have been a depôt, or "treasure-city," here for the precious things of the Upper Nile country ; the gold of Nubia and the elephant-tusks of Kush.

It is a very beautiful island—rugged and lofty to the south ; low and fertile to the north ; with an exquisitely varied coast-line full of wooded creeks and miniature beaches, in which one might expect at any moment to meet Robinson

Crusoe with his goat-skin umbrella, or man Friday bending under a load of faggots. They are all Fridays here, however ; for Elephantine, being the first Nubian outpost, is peopled by Nubians only. It contains two Nubian villages, and the mounds of a very ancient city which was the capital of all Egypt under the Pharaohs of the VIth Dynasty, between three and four thousand years before Christ. Two temples, one of which dated from the reign of Amenhotep III, were yet standing here some seventy years ago. They were seen by Belzoni in 1815, and had just been destroyed to build a palace and barracks when Champollion went up in 1829. A ruined gateway of the Ptolemaic period and a forlorn-looking sitting statue of Menephtah, the supposed Pharaoh of the Exodus, alone remain to identify the sites on which they stood.

Thick palm-groves and carefully-tilled patches of castor-oil and cotton plants, lentils, and durra, make green the heart of the island. The western shore is wooded to the water's edge. One may walk here in the shade at hottest noon, listening to the murmur of the Cataract and seeking for wild flowers —which, however, would seem to blossom nowhere save in the sweet Arabic name of Gezîret-el-Zahr, the Island of Flowers.

Upon the high ground at the southern extremity of the island, among rubbish heaps, and bleached bones, and human skulls, and the sloughed skins of snakes, and piles of parti-coloured potsherds, we picked up several bits of inscribed terra-cotta—evidently fragments of broken vases. The writing was very faint, and in part obliterated. We could see that the characters were Greek ; but not even our Idle Man was equal to making out a word of the sense. Believing them to be mere disconnected scraps to which it would be impossible to find the corresponding pieces—taking it for granted, also, that they were of comparatively modern date—we brought away some three or four as souvenirs of the place, and thought no more about them.

We little dreamed that Dr. Birch, in his cheerless official room at the British Museum so many thousand miles away, was at this very time occupied in deciphering a collection of similar fragments, nearly all of which had been brought from

this same spot.[1]   Of the curious interest attaching to these
illegible scrawls, of the importance they were shortly to acquire
in the eyes of the learned, of the possible value of any chance
additions to their number we knew, and could know, nothing.
Six months later, we lamented our ignorance and our lost
opportunities.

For the Egyptians, it seems, used potsherds instead of
papyrus for short memoranda ; and each of these fragments
which we had picked up contained a record complete in itself.
I fear we should have laughed if any one had suggested that
they might be tax-gatherer's receipts.   Yet that is just what
they were—receipts for government dues collected on the
frontier during the period of Roman rule in Egypt.   They
were written in Greek, because the Romans deputed Greek

---

[1] The results of Dr. Birch's labours were given to the public in his
" Guide to the First and Second Egyptian Rooms," published by order of
the Trustees of the British Museum in May 1874.   Of the contents of
case 99 in the Second Room, he says : " The use of potsherds for documents received a great extension at the time of the Roman Empire, when
receipts for the taxes were given on these fragments by the collectors of
revenue at Elephantine or Syene, on the frontier of Egypt.   These receipts
commenced in the reign of Vespasian, A.D. 77, and are found as late as
M. Aurelius and L. Verus, A.D. 165.   It appears from them that the
capitation and trades tax, which was 16 drachms in A.D. 77, rose to 20 in
A.D. 165, having steadily increased.   The dues were paid in instalments
called *merismoi,* at three periods of the year.   The taxes were farmed out
to publicans, *misthotai,* who appear from their names to have been Greeks.
At Elephantine the taxes were received by tax-gatherers, *prakteres,* who
seem to have been appointed as early as the Ptolemies.   Their clerks were
Egyptians, and they had a chest and treasure, *phylax.*"   See p. 109, *as
above ;* also Birch's *History of Ancient Pottery,* chap. i. p. 45.

These barren memoranda are not the only literary curiosities found at
Elephantine.   Among the Egyptian MSS. of the Louvre may be seen
some fragments of the XVIIIth Book of the *Iliad,* discovered in a tomb
upon the island.   How they came to be buried there no one knows.   A
lover of poetry would like to think, however, that some Greek or Roman
officer, dying at his post upon this distant station, desired, perhaps, to
have his Homer laid with him in his grave.

NOTE TO SECOND EDITION.—Other fragments of the *Iliad* have been
found from time to time in various parts of Egypt ; some (now in the
Louvre) being scrawled, like the above-mentioned tax-receipts, on mere
potsherds.   The finest specimen ever found in Egypt or elsewhere, and
the earliest, has however been discovered this year, 1888, by Mr. Flinders
Petrie in the grave of a woman at Hawara, in the Fayûm.

scribes to perform the duties of this unpopular office ; but the Greek is so corrupt and the penmanship so clownish that only a few eminent scholars can read them.

Not all the inscribed fragments found at Elephantine, however, are tax-receipts, or written in bad Greek. The British Museum contains several in the demotic, or current script of the people, and a few in the more learned hieratic or priestly hand. The former have not yet been translated. They are probably business memoranda and short private letters of Egyptians of the same period.

But how came these fragile documents to be preserved, when the city in which their writers lived, and the temples in which they worshipped, have disappeared and left scarce a trace behind ? Who cast them down among the potsherds on this barren hillside ? Are we to suppose that some kind of Public Record - Office once occupied the site, and that the receipts here stored were duplicates of those given to the payers ? Or is it not even more probable that this place was the Monte Testaccio of the ancient city, to which all broken pottery, written as well as unwritten, found its way sooner or later ?

With the exception of a fine fragment of Roman quay nearly opposite Assûan, the ruined gateway of Alexander and the battered statue of Menephtah are the only objects of archæological interest in the island. But the charm of Elephantine is the everlasting charm of natural beauty—of rocks, of palm-woods, of quiet waters.

The streets of Assûan are just like the streets of every other mud town on the Nile. The bazaars reproduce the bazaars of Minieh and Siût. The environs are noisy with cafés and dancing girls, like the environs of Esneh and Luxor. Into the mosque, where some kind of service was going on, we peeped without entering. It looked cool, and clean, and spacious ; the floor being covered with fine matting, and some scores of ostrich-eggs depending from the ceiling. In the bazaars we bought baskets and mats of Nubian manufacture, woven with the same reeds, dyed with the same colours, shaped after the same models, as those found in the tombs at Thebes. A certain oval basket with a vaulted cover, of which specimens are preserved in the British Museum, seems still to be the pattern most in demand at Assûan. The basket-makers have neither changed their fashion nor the buyers their taste since the days of Rameses the Great.

Here also, at a little cupboard of a shop near the Shoe Bazaar, we were tempted to spend a few pounds in ostrich feathers, which are conveyed to Assûan by traders from the Soudan. The merchant brought out a feather at a time, and seemed in no haste to sell. We also affected indifference. The haggling on both sides was tremendous. The bystanders, as usual, were profoundly interested, and commented on every word that passed. At last we carried away an armful of splendid plumes, most of which measured from two and a half to three feet in length. Some were pure white, others white tipped with brown. They had been neither cleaned nor curled, but were just as they came from the hands of the ostrich-hunters.

By far the most amusing sight in Assûan was the traders' camp down near the landing-place. Here were Abyssinians like slender-legged baboons; wild-looking Bishariyah and Ababdeh Arabs with flashing eyes and flowing hair; sturdy Nubians the colour of a Barbedienne bronze; and natives of all tribes and shades, from Kordofân and Sennâr, the deserts of Bahuda and the banks of the Blue and White Niles. Some were returning from Cairo; others were on their way thither. Some, having disembarked their merchandise at Mahatta (a village on the other side of the Cataract), had come across the desert to re-embark it at Assûan. Others had just disembarked theirs at Assûan, in order to re-embark it at Mahatta. Meanwhile, they were living *sub Jove;* each entrenched in his own little redoubt of piled-up bales and packing-cases, like a spider in the centre of his web; each provided with his kettle and coffee-pot, and an old rug to sleep and pray upon. One sulky old Turk had fixed up a roof of matting, and furnished his den with a *Kafas,* or palm-wood couch; but he was a self-indulgent exception to the rule.

Some smiled, some scowled, when we passed through the camp. One offered us coffee. Another, more obliging than the rest, displayed the contents of his packages. Great bundles of lion and leopard skins, bales of cotton, sacks of henna-leaves, elephant-tusks swathed in canvas and matting, strewed the sandy bank. Of gum-arabic alone there must have been several hundred bales ; each bale sewn up in a raw hide and tied with thongs of hippopotamus leather. Towards dusk, when the camp-fires were alight and the evening meal was in course of preparation, the scene became wonderfully picturesque. Lights gleamed ; shadows deepened ; strange figures stalked to and fro, or squatted in groups amid their merchandise. Some were baking flat cakes ; others stirring soup, or roasting coffee. A hole scooped in the sand, a couple of stones to support the kettle, and a handful of dry sticks, served for kitchen-range and fuel. Meanwhile all the dogs in Assûan prowled round the camp, and a jargon of barbaric tongues came and went with the breeze that followed the sunset.

I must not forget to add that among this motley crowd we saw two brothers, natives of Khartûm. We met them first in the town, and afterwards in the camp. They wore voluminous white turbans, and flowing robes of some kind of creamy cashmere cloth. Their small proud heads and delicate aristocratic features were modelled on the purest Florentine type ; their eyes were long and liquid ; their complexions, free from any taint of Abyssinian blue or Nubian bronze, were intensely, lustrously, magnificently black. We agreed that we had never seen two such handsome men. They were like young and beautiful Dantes carved in ebony ; Dantes unembittered by the world, unsicklied by the pale cast of thought, and glowing with the life of the warm South.

Having explored Elephantine and ransacked the bazaars, our party dispersed in various directions. Some gave the remainder of the day to letter-writing. The Painter, bent on sketching, started off in search of a jackal-haunted ruin up a wild ravine on the Libyan side of the river. The Writer and the Idle Man boldly mounted camels and rode out into the Arabian desert.

Now the camel-riding that is done at Assûan is of the most commonplace description, and bears to genuine desert travelling about the same relation that half-an-hour on the Mer de Glace bears to the passage of the Mortaretsch glacier or the ascent of Monte Rosa. The short cut from Assûan to Philæ, or at least the ride to the granite quarries, forms part of every dragoman's programme, and figures as the crowning achievement of every Cook's tourist. The Arabs themselves perform these little journeys much more pleasantly and expeditiously on donkeys. They take good care, in fact, never to scale the summit of a camel if they can help it. But for the impressionable traveller, the Assûan camel is *de rigueur.* In his interests are those snarling quadrupeds be-tasselled and be-rugged, taken from their regular work, and paraded up and down the landing-place. To transport cargoes disembarked above and below the Cataract is their vocation. Taken from this honest calling to perform in an absurd little drama got up especially for the entertainment of tourists, it is no wonder if the beasts are more than commonly ill-tempered. They know the whole proceeding to be essentially cockney, and they resent it accordingly.

The ride, nevertheless, has its advantages; not the least being that it enables one to realise the kind of work involved in any of the regular desert expeditions. At all events, it entitles one to claim acquaintance with the ship of the desert, and (bearing in mind the probable inferiority of the specimen) to form an *ex pede* judgment of his qualifications.

The camel has his virtues—so much at least must be admitted; but they do not lie upon the surface. My Buffon tells me, for instance, that he carries a fresh-water cistern in his stomach; which is meritorious. But the cistern ameliorates neither his gait nor his temper—which are abominable. Irreproachable as a beast of burden, he is open to many objections as a steed. It is unpleasant, in the first place, to ride an animal which not only objects to being ridden, but cherishes a strong personal antipathy to his rider. Such, however, is his amiable peculiarity. You know that he hates you, from the moment you first walk round him, wondering where and how to begin the ascent of his hump. He does not, in fact, hesitate to tell you so in the roundest terms. He swears freely while you are taking your seat; snarls if you but move in the saddle; and stares you angrily in the face, if you attempt to turn his head in any direction save that which he himself prefers. Should you persevere, he tries to bite your feet. If biting your feet does not answer, he lies down.

Now the lying-down and getting-up of a camel are performances designed for the express purpose of inflicting grievous bodily harm upon his rider. Thrown twice forward and twice backward, punched in his "wind" and damaged in his spine, the luckless novice receives four distinct shocks, each more violent and unexpected than the last. For this "execrable hunchback" is fearfully and wonderfully made. He has a superfluous joint somewhere in his legs, and uses it to revenge himself upon mankind.

His paces, however, are more complicated than his joints and more trying than his temper. He has four :—a short walk, like the rolling of a small boat in a chopping sea ; a long walk which dislocates every bone in your body ; a trot that reduces you to imbecility ; and a gallop that is sudden death. One tries in vain to imagine a crime for which the *peine forte et dure* of sixteen hours on camel-back would not be a full and sufficient expiation. It is a punishment to which one would not willingly be the means of condemning any human being—not even a reviewer.

They had been down on the bank for hire all day long— brown camels and white camels, shaggy camels and smooth camels ; all with gay worsted tassels on their heads, and rugs flung over their high wooden saddles, by way of housings. The gentlemen of the Fostât had ridden away hours ago, cross-legged and serene; and we had witnessed their demeanour with mingled admiration and envy. Now, modestly conscious of our own daring, we prepared to do likewise. It was a solemn moment when, having chosen our beasts, we prepared to encounter the unknown perils of the desert. What wonder if the Happy Couple exchanged an affecting farewell at parting ?

We mounted and rode away; two imps of darkness follow-ing at the heels of our camels, and Salame performing the part of bodyguard. Thus attended, we found ourselves pitched, swung, and rolled along at a pace that carried us rapidly up the slope, past a suburb full of cafés and grinning dancing girls, and out into the desert. Our way for the first half-mile or so lay among tombs. A great Mohammedan necropolis, part ancient, part modern, lies behind Assûan, and covers more ground than the town itself. Some scores of tiny mosques, each topped by its little cupola, and all more or less dilapidated, stand here amid a wilderness of scattered tombstones. Some are isolated ; some grouped picturesquely together. Each covers, or is supposed to cover, the grave of a Moslem Santon ; but some are mere commemorative chapels dedicated to saints and martyrs elsewhere buried. Of simple head-stones defaced, shattered, overturned, propped back to back on cairns of loose stones, or piled in broken and dishonoured heaps, there must be many hundreds. They are for the most part rounded at the top like ancient Egyptian stelæ, and bear elaborately-carved inscriptions, some of which are in the Cufic character, and more than a thousand years old. Seen when the sun is bending westward and the shadows are lengthening, there is something curiously melancholy and picturesque about this City of the Dead in the dead desert.

Leaving the tombs, we now strike off towards the left, bound for the obelisk in the quarry, which is the stock sight of the place. The horizon beyond Assûan is bounded on all sides by rocky heights, bold and picturesque in form, yet scarcely lofty enough to deserve the name of mountains. The sandy bottom under our camel's feet is strewn with small pebbles, and tolerably firm. Clustered rocks of black and red granite profusely inscribed with hieroglyphed records crop up here and there, and serve as landmarks just where landmarks are needed. For nothing would be easier than to miss one's way among these tawny slopes, and to go wandering off, like lost Israelites, into the desert.

Winding in and out among undulating hillocks and tracts of rolled boulders, we come at last to a little group of cliffs, at the foot of which our camels halt unbidden. Here we dismount, climb a short slope, and find the huge monolith at our feet.

Being cut horizontally, it lies half buried in drifted sand, with nothing to show that it is not wholly disengaged and ready for transport. Our books tell us, however, that the under-cutting has never been done, and that it is yet one with the granite bottom on which it seems to lie. Both ends are hidden ; but one can pace some sixty feet of its yet visible surface. That surface bears the tool-marks of the workmen. A slanting groove pitted with wedge-holes indicates where it was intended to taper towards the top. Another shows where it was to be reduced at the side. Had it been finished, this would have been the largest obelisk in the world. The great obelisk of Queen Hatshepsu at Karnak, which, as its inscriptions record, came also from Assûan, stands ninety-two feet high, and measures eight feet square at the base ;[1] but this which lies sleeping in the desert would have stood ninety-five feet in the shaft, and have measured over eleven feet square at the base. We can never know now why it was left here, nor guess with what royal name it should have been inscribed. Had the king said in his heart that he would set up a mightier obelisk than was ever yet seen by eyes of men, and did he die before the block could be extracted from the quarry ? Or were the quarrymen driven from the desert, and the Pharaoh from his throne, by the hungry hordes of Ethiopia, or Syria, or the islands beyond the sea ? The great stone may be older than Rameses the Great, or as modern as the last of the Romans ; but to give it a date, or to divine its history, is impossible. Egyptology, which has solved the enigma of the Sphinx, is powerless here. The obelisk of the quarry holds its secret safe, and holds it for ever.

Ancient Egyptian quarrying is seen under its most striking aspect among extensive limestone or sandstone ranges, as at Turra and Silsilis ; but the process by which the stone was extracted can nowhere be more distinctly traced than at Assûan. In some respects, indeed, the quarries here, though on a smaller scale than those lower down the river, are even more interesting. Nothing surprises one at Silsilis, for instance, more than the economy with which the sandstone has been cut from the heart of the mountain ; but at Assûan, as the material

---

[1] These are the measurements given in Murray's Handbook. The new English translation of Mariette's *Itinéraire de la Haute Egypte* gives the obelisk of Hatshepsu 108 feet 10 inches in height. See *The Monuments of Upper Egypt*, translated by Alphonse Mariette : London, 1877.

was more precious, so does the economy seem to have been still greater. At Silsilis, the yellow cliffs have been sliced as neatly as the cheeses in a cheesemonger's window. Smooth, upright walls alone mark the place where the work has been done ; and the amount of débris is altogether insignificant. But at Assûan, when extracting granite for sculptural purposes, they attacked the form of the object required, and cut it out roughly to shape. The great obelisk is but one of many cases in point. In the same group of rocks, or one very closely adjoining, we saw a rough-hewn column, erect and three-parts detached, as well as the semi-cylindrical hollow from which its fellow had been taken. One curious recess from which a quadrant - shaped mass had been cut away puzzled us immensely. In other places the blocks appeared to have been coffer-shaped. We sought in vain, however, for the broken sarcophagus mentioned in Murray.

But the drifted sands, we may be sure, hide more precious things than these. Inscriptions are probably as abundant here as in the breccia of Hamamat. The great obelisk must have had a fellow, if we only knew where to look for it. The obelisks of Queen Hatshepsu, and the sarcophagi of many famous kings, might possibly be traced to their beds in these quarries. So might the casing stones of the Pyramid of Menkara, the massive slabs of the Temple of the Sphinx, and the walls of the sanctuary of Philip Aridæus at Karnak. Above all, the syenite Colossus of the Ramesseum and the monster Colossus of Tanis,[1] which was the largest detached statue in the world, must each have left its mighty matrix among the rocks close by. But these, like the song of the sirens or the alias of Achilles, though "not beyond all conjecture," are among the things that will never now be discovered.

As regards the process of quarrying at Assûan, it seems that rectangular granite blocks were split off here, as the softer limestone and sandstone elsewhere, by means of wooden wedges. These were fitted to holes already cut for their

[1] For an account of the discovery of this enormous statue and the measurements of its various parts, see *Tanis*, Part I, by W. M. Flinders Petrie, chap. ii. pp. 22 *et seq.* published by the Egypt Exploration Fund, 1885. [Note to Second Edition.]

reception ; and, being saturated with water, split the hard rock by mere force of expansion. Every quarried mass hereabouts is marked with rows of these wedge-holes.

Passing by the way a tiny oasis where there were camels, and a well, and an idle water-wheel, and a patch of emerald-green barley, we next rode back nearly to the outskirts of Assûan, where, in a dismal hollow on the verge of the desert, may be seen a small, half-buried temple of Ptolemaic times. Traces of colour are still visible on the winged globe under the cornice, and on some mutilated bas-reliefs at either side of the principal entrance. Seeing that the interior was choked with rubbish, we made no attempt to go inside ; but rode away again without dismounting.

And now, there being still an hour of daylight, we signified our intention of making for the top of the nearest hill, in order to see the sun set. This, clearly, was an unheard-of innovation. The camel-boys stared, shook their heads, protested there was "mafeesh sikkeh " (no road), and evidently regarded us as lunatics. The camels planted their splay feet obstinately in the sand, tried to turn back, and, when obliged to yield to the force of circumstances, abused us all the way. Arrived at the top, we found ourselves looking down upon the island of Elephantine, with the Nile, the town, and the dahabeeyahs at our feet. A prolongation of the ridge on which we were standing led, however, to another height crowned by a ruined tomb ; and seemed to promise a view of the Cataract. Seeing us prepare to go on, the camel-boys broke into a *furore* of remonstrance, which, but for Salame's big stick, would have ended in downright mutiny. Still we pushed forward, and, still dissatisfied, insisted on attacking a third summit. The boys now trudged on in sullen despair. The sun was sinking ; the way was steep and difficult ; the night would soon come on. If the Howadji chose to break their necks, it concerned nobody but themselves ; but if the camels broke theirs, who was to pay for them ?

Such—expressed half in broken Arabic, half in gestures— were the sentiments of our youthful Nubians. Nor were the camels themselves less emphatic. They grinned ; they sniffed ; they snorted ; they snarled ; they disputed every foot of the

way. As for mine (a gawky, supercilious beast with a blood-
shot eye and a battered Roman nose), I never heard any dumb
animal make use of so much bad language in my life.
The last hill was very steep and stony ; but the view from
the top was magnificent. We had now gained the highest
point of the ridge which divides the valley of the Nile from
the Arabian desert. The Cataract, widening away reach after
reach and studded with innumerable rocky islets, looked more
like a lake than a river. Of the Libyan desert we could see
nothing beyond the opposite sand-slopes, gold-rimmed against
the sunset. The Arabian desert, a boundless waste edged by
a serrated line of purple peaks, extended eastward to the
remotest horizon. We looked down upon it as on a raised
map. The Moslem tombs, some five hundred feet below,
showed like toys. To the right, in a wide valley opening away
southwards, we recognised that ancient bed of the Nile which
serves for the great highway between Egypt and Nubia. At
the end of the vista, some very distant palms against a rocky
background pointed the way to Philæ.

Meanwhile the sun was fast sinking—the lights were crimsoning—the shadows were lengthening. All was silent ; all
was solitary. We listened, but could scarcely hear the murmur
of the rapids. We looked in vain for the quarry of the obelisk.
It was but one group of rocks among scores of others, and to
distinguish it at this distance was impossible.

Presently, a group of three or four black figures, mounted
on little grey asses, came winding in and out among the tombs,
and took the road to Philæ. To us they were moving specks ;
but our lynx-eyed camel-boys at once recognised the " Sheykh
el Shellàl " (Sheykh of the Cataract) and his retinue. More
dahabeeyahs had come in ; and the worthy man, having spent
the day in Assûan visiting, palavering, bargaining, was now
going home to Mahatta for the night. We watched the retreat-
ing riders for some minutes, till twilight stole up the ancient
channel like a flood, and drowned them in warm shadows.

The afterglow had faded off the heights when we at length
crossed the last ridge, descended the last hill-side, and regained
the level from which we had started. Here once more we met
the Fostât party. They had ridden to Philæ and back by the

desert, and were apparently all the worse for wear. Seeing us, they urged their camels to a trot, and tried to look as if they liked it. The Idle Man and the Writer wreathed their countenances in ghastly smiles, and did likewise. Not for worlds would they have admitted that they found the pace difficult. Such is the moral influence of the camel. He acts as a tonic ; he promotes the Spartan virtues ; and if not himself heroic, is at least the cause of heroism in others.

It was nearly dark when we reached Assûan. The cafés were all alight and astir. There were smoking and coffee-drinking going on outside ; there were sounds of music and laughter within. A large private house on the opposite side of the road was being decorated, as if for some festive occasion. Flags were flying from the roof, and two men were busy putting up a gaily-painted inscription over the doorway. Asking, as was natural, if there was a marriage or a fantasia afoot, it was not a little startling to be told that these were signs of mourning, and that the master of the house had died during the interval that elapsed between our riding out and riding back again.

In Egypt, where the worship of ancestry and the preservation of the body were once among the most sacred duties of the living, they now make short work with their dead. He was to be buried, they said, to-morrow morning, three hours after sunrise.

CAMEL AT ASSÛAN.

CHAPTER XI.

THE CATARACT AND THE DESERT.

AT Assûan, one bids good-bye to Egypt and enters Nubia through the gates of the Cataract—which is, in truth, no cataract, but a succession of rapids extending over two-thirds of the distance between Elephantine and Philæ. The Nile—diverted from its original course by some unrecorded catastrophe, the nature of which has given rise to much scientific conjecture—here spreads itself over a rocky basin bounded by sand-slopes on the one side, and by granite cliffs on the other. Studded with numberless islets, divided into numberless channels, foaming over sunken rocks, eddying among water-worn boulders, now shallow, now deep, now loitering, now hurrying, here sleeping in the ribbed hollow of a tiny sand-drift, there circling above the vortex of a hidden whirlpool, the river, whether looked upon from the deck of the dahabeeyah or the heights along the shore, is seen everywhere to be fighting its way through a labyrinth, the paths of which have never yet been mapped or sounded.

Those paths are everywhere difficult and everywhere dangerous; and to that labyrinth the Shellalee, or Cataract-Arab, alone possesses the key. At the time of the inundation, when all but the highest rocks are under water, and navigation is as easy here as elsewhere, the Shellalee's occupation is gone. But as the floods subside and travellers begin to reappear, his work commences. To haul dahabeeyahs up those treacherous rapids by sheer stress of rope and muscle; to steer skilfully down again through channels bristling with rocks and boiling with foam, becomes now, for some five months of the year, his principal industry. It is hard work ; but he gets well paid for it, and his profits are always on the increase. From forty to fifty dahabeeyahs are annually taken up between November and March ; and every year brings a larger influx of travellers. Meanwhile, accidents rarely happen ; prices tend continually upwards ; and the Cataract Arabs make a little fortune by their singular monopoly.[1]

The scenery of the First Cataract is like nothing else in the world—except the scenery of the Second. It is altogether new, and strange, and beautiful. It is incomprehensible that travellers should have written of it in general with so little admiration. They seem to have been impressed by the wildness of the waters, by the quaint forms of the rocks, by the desolation and grandeur of the landscape as a whole ; but scarcely at all by its beauty—which is paramount.

The Nile here widens to a lake. Of the islands, which it would hardly be an exaggeration to describe as some hundreds in number, no two are alike. Some are piled up like the rocks at the Land's End in Cornwall, block upon block, column upon column, tower upon tower, as if reared by the hand of man. Some are green with grass ; some golden with slopes of drifted sand ; some planted with rows of blossoming lupins, purple and white. Others again are mere cairns of loose blocks, with here and there a perilously balanced top-boulder. On one, a singular upright monolith, like a menhir, stands conspicuous, as if placed there to commemorate a date, or to point the way to Philæ. Another mass rises out of the water squared and buttressed, in the likeness of a fort. A third, humped and shining like the wet body of some amphibious beast, lifts what seems to be a horned head above the surface of the rapids. All these blocks and boulders and fantastic rocks are granite ; some red, some purple, some black. Their forms are rounded by the friction of ages. Those nearest the

---

[1] The increase of steamer traffic has considerably altered the conditions of Nile travelling since this was written, and fewer dahabeeyahs are consequently employed. By those who can afford it, and who really desire to get the utmost pleasure, instruction, and interest from the trip, the dahabeeyah will, however, always be preferred. [Note to Second Edition.]

brink reflect the sky like mirrors of burnished steel. Royal ovals and hieroglyphed inscriptions, fresh as of yesterday's cutting, start out here and there from those glittering surfaces with startling distinctness. A few of the larger islands are crowned with clumps of palms ; and one, the loveliest of any, is completely embowered in gum-trees and acacias, dôm and date palms, and feathery tamarisks, all festooned together under a hanging canopy of yellow-blossomed creepers.

On a brilliant Sunday morning, with a favourable wind, we entered on this fairy archipelago. Sailing steadily against the current, we glided away from Assûan, left Elephantine behind, and found ourselves at once in the midst of the islands. From this moment every turn of the tiller disclosed a fresh point of view, and we sat on deck, spectators of a moving panorama. The diversity of subjects was endless. The combinations of form and colour, of light and shadow, of foreground and distance, were continually changing. A boat or a few figures alone were wanting to complete the picturesqueness of the scene ; but in all those channels, and among all those islands, we saw no sign of any living creature.

Meanwhile the Sheykh of the Cataract—a flat-faced, fishy-eyed old Nubian, with his head tied up in a dingy yellow silk handkerchief—sat apart in solitary grandeur at the stern, smoking a long chibouque. Behind him squatted some five or six dusky strangers ; and a new steersman, black as a negro, had charge of the helm. This new steersman was our pilot for Nubia. From Assûan to Wady Halfeh, and back again to Assûan, he alone was now held responsible for the safety of the dahabeeyah and all on board.

At length a general stir among the crew warned us of the near neighbourhood of the first rapid. Straight ahead, as if ranged along the dyke of a weir, a chain of small islets barred the way ; while the current, divided into three or four headlong torrents, came rushing down the slope, and reunited at the bottom in one tumultuous race.

That we should ever get the Philæ up that hill of moving water seemed at first sight impossible. Still our steersman held on his course, making for the widest channel. Still the Sheykh smoked imperturbably. Presently, without removing

the pipe from his mouth, he delivered the one word—" Roóhh !"
(Forward !)

Instantly, evoked by his nod, the rocks swarmed with
natives. Hidden till now in all sorts of unseen corners, they
sprang out shouting, gesticulating, laden with coils of rope,
leaping into the thick of the rapids, splashing like water-dogs,
bobbing like corks, and making as much show of energy as
if they were going to haul us up Niagara. The thing was
evidently a *coup de théatre,* like the apparition of Clan Alpine's
warriors in the Donna del Lago—with backshîsh in the
background.

The scene that followed was curious enough. Two ropes
were carried from the dahabeeyah to the nearest island, and
there made fast to the rocks. Two ropes from the island were
also brought on board the dahabeeyah. A double file of men
on deck, and another double file on shore, then ranged themselves along the ropes ; the Sheykh gave the signal ; and, to
a wild chanting accompaniment and a movement like a
barbaric Sir Roger de Coverley dance, a system of double
hauling began, by means of which the huge boat slowly and
steadily ascended. We may have been a quarter of an hour
going up the incline ; though it seemed much longer. Meanwhile, as they warmed to their work, the men chanted louder
and pulled harder, till the boat went in at last with a rush,
and swung over into a pool of comparatively smooth water.

Having moored here for an hour's rest, we next repeated
the performance against a still stronger current a little higher
up. This time, however, a rope broke. Down went the
haulers, like a row of cards suddenly tipped over—round
swung the Philæ, receiving the whole rush of the current on
her beam ! Luckily for us, the other rope held fast against
the strain. Had it also broken, we must have been wrecked
then and there ignominiously.

Our Nubian auxiliaries struck work after this. Fate, they
said, was adverse ; so they went home, leaving us moored for
the night in the pool at the top of the first rapid. The Sheykh
promised, however, that his people should begin work next
morning at dawn, and get us through before sunset. Next
morning came, however, and not a man appeared upon the

scene.   At about mid-day they began dropping in, a few at a time ; hung about in a languid, lazy way for a couple of hours or so ; moved us into a better position for attacking the next rapid ; and then melted away mysteriously by twos and threes among the rocks, and were no more seen.

We now felt that our time and money were being recklessly squandered, and we resolved to bear it no longer.   Our Painter therefore undertook to remonstrate with the Sheykh, and to convince him of the error of his ways.   The Sheykh listened ; smoked ; shook his head ; replied that in the Cataract, as elsewhere, there were lucky and unlucky days, days when men felt inclined to work, and days when they felt disinclined. To-day, as it happened, they felt disinclined.   Being reminded that it was unreasonable to keep us three days going up five miles of river, and that there was a governor at Assûan to whom we should appeal to-morrow unless the work went on in earnest, he smiled, shrugged his shoulders, and muttered something about " destiny."

Now the Painter, being of a practical turn, had compiled for himself a little vocabulary of choice Arabic maledictions, which he carried in his note-book for reference when needed. Having no faith in its possible usefulness, we were amused by the industry with which he was constantly adding to this collection.   We looked upon it, in fact, as a harmless pleasantry —just as we looked upon his pocket-revolver, which was never loaded ; or his brand-new fowling-piece, which he was never known to fire.

But the Sheykh of the Cataract had gone too far.   The fatuity of that smile would have exasperated the meekest of men ; and our Painter was not the meekest of men.   So he whipped out his pocket-book, ran his finger down the line, and delivered an appropriate quotation.   His accent may not have been faultless ; but there could be no mistake as to the energy of his style or the vigour of his language.   The effect of both was instantaneous. The Sheykh sprang to his feet as if he had been shot—turned pale with rage under his black skin—vowed the Philæ might stay where she was till doomsday, for aught that he or his men would do to help her a foot farther—bounded into his own ricketty sandal and rowed away, leaving us to our fate.

We stood aghast. It was all over with us. We should never see Abou Simbel now—never write our names on the Rock of Aboosîr, nor slake our thirst at the waters of the Second Cataract. What was to be done? Must the Sheykh be defied, or propitiated? Should we appeal to the Governor, or should we immolate the Painter? The majority were for immolating the Painter.

We went to bed that night, despairing ; but lo! next morning at sunrise appeared the Sheykh of the Cataract, all smiles, all activity, with no end of ropes and a force of two hundred men. We were his dearest friends now. The Painter was his brother. He had called out the ban and arrière ban of the Cataract in our service. There was nothing, in short, that he would not do to oblige us.

The dragoman vowed that he had never seen Nubians work as those Nubians worked that day. They fell to like giants, tugging away from morn till dewy eve, and never giving over till they brought us round the last corner, and up the last rapid. The sun had set, the afterglow had faded, the twilight was closing in, when our dahabeeyah slipped at last into level water, and the two hundred, with a parting shout, dispersed to their several villages.

We were never known to make light of the Painter's repertory of select abuse after this. If that note-book of his had been the drowned book of Prospero, or the magical Papyrus of Thoth fished up anew from the bottom of the Nile, we could not have regarded it with a respect more nearly bordering upon awe.

Though there exists no boundary line to mark where Egypt ends and Nubia begins, the nationality of the races dwelling on either side of that invisible barrier is as sharply defined as though an ocean divided them. Among the Shellalee, or Cataract villagers, one comes suddenly into the midst of a people that have apparently nothing in common with the population of Egypt. They belong to a lower ethnological type, and they speak a language derived from purely African sources. Contrasting with our Arab sailors the sulky-looking, half-naked, muscular savages who thronged about the Philæ during her passage up the Cataract, one could not but perceive that they are to this day as distinct and inferior a people as when their Egyptian conquerors, massing together in one contemptuous epithet all nations south of the frontier, were wont to speak of them as " the vile race of Kush." Time has done little to change them since those early days. Some Arabic words have crept into their vocabulary. Some modern luxuries—as tobacco, coffee, soap, and gunpowder— have come to be included in the brief catalogue of their daily wants. But in most other respects they are living to this day as they lived in the time of the Pharaohs; cultivating lentils and durra, brewing barley beer, plaiting mats and baskets of stained reeds, tracing rude patterns upon bowls of gourd-rind, flinging the javelin, hurling the boomerang, fashioning bucklers of crocodile-skin and bracelets of ivory, and supplying Egypt with henna. The dexterity with which, sitting as if in a wager boat, they balance themselves on a palm-log, and paddle to and fro about the river, is really surprising. This barbaric substitute for a boat is probably more ancient than the pyramids.

Having witnessed the passage of the first few rapids, we were glad to escape from the dahabeeyah, and spend our time sketching here and there on the borders of the desert, and among the villages and islands round about. In all Egypt and Nubia there is no scenery richer in picturesque bits than the scenery of the Cataract. An artist might pass a winter there, and not exhaust the pictorial wealth of those five miles which divide Assûan ˙from Philæ. Of tortuous creeks shut in by rocks fantastically piled—of sand-slopes golden to the water's edge—of placid pools low-lying in the midst of lupin-fields and tracts of tender barley—of creeking Sakkiehs, half hidden among palms and dropping water as they turn—of mud dwellings, here clustered together in hollows, there perched separately on heights among the rocks, and perpetuating to this day the form and slope of Egyptian pylons—of rude boats drawn up in sheltered coves, or going to pieces high and dry upon the sands—of water-washed boulders of crimson, and black, and purple granite, on which the wild fowl cluster at mid-day and the fisher spreads his nets to dry at sunset —of camels, and caravans, and camps on shore—of cargo-boats and cangias on the river—of wild figures of half-naked athletes

—of dusky women decked with barbaric ornaments, unveiled, swift-gliding, trailing long robes of deepest gentian blue—of ancient crones, and little naked children like live bronzes—of these, and a hundred other subjects, in infinite variety and combination, there is literally no end. It is all so picturesque, indeed, so biblical, so poetical, that one is almost in danger of forgetting that the places are something more than beautiful backgrounds, and that the people are not merely appropriate figures placed there for the delight of sketchers, but are made of living flesh and blood, and moved by hopes, and fears, and sorrows, like our own.

Mahatta—green with sycamores and tufted palms ; nestled in the hollow of a little bay ; half-islanded in the rear by an arm of backwater, curved and glittering like the blade of a Turkish

SOUDAN TRADERS AT MAHATTA.

scimetar—is by far the most beautifully situated village on the Nile. It is the residence of the principal Sheykh, and, if one may say so, is the capital of the Cataract. The houses lie some way back from the river. The bay is thronged with native boats of all sizes and colours. Men and camels, women and children, donkeys, dogs, merchandise, and temporary huts put together with poles and matting, crowd the sandy shore. It is Assûan over again ; but on a larger scale. The shipping is tenfold more numerous. The traders' camp is in itself a village. The beach is half a mile in length, and a quarter of a mile in the slope down to the river. Mahatta is, in fact,

the twin port to Assûan.   It lies, not precisely at the other
extremity of the great valley between Assûan and Philæ, but
at the nearest accessible point above the Cataract.   It is here
that the Soudan traders disembark their goods for re-embarka-
tion at Assûan.   Such ricketty, barbaric-looking craft as these
Nubian cangias we had not yet seen on the river.   They
looked as old and obsolete as the Ark.   Some had curious
carved verandahs outside the cabin - entrance.   Others were
tilted up at the stern like Chinese junks.   Most of them had
been slavers in the palmy days of Defterdar Bey ; plying then
as now between Wady Halfeh and Mahatta ; discharging their
human cargoes at this point for re-shipment at Assûan ; and
rarely passing the Cataract, even at the time of inundation.
If their wicked old timbers could have spoken, they might
have told us many a black and bloody tale.

Going up through the village and the palm-gardens, and
turning off in a north-easterly direction towards the desert, one
presently comes out about midway of that valley to which I
have made allusion more than once already.   No one, however unskilled in physical geography, could look from end to
end of that huge furrow and not see that it was once a river-
bed.   We know not for how many tens of thousands, or
hundreds of thousands, of years the Nile may have held on its
course within those original bounds..   Neither can we tell when
it deserted them.   It is, however, quite certain that the river
flowed that way within historic times ; that is to say, in the
days of Amenemhat III (*circa* B.C. 2800).   So much is held to
be proven by certain inscriptions [1] which record the maximum

---

[1] " The most important discovery which we have made here, and which
I shall only mention briefly, is a series of short rock-inscriptions, which
mark the highest rises of the Nile during a series of years under the
government of Amenemhat III and of his immediate successors. . . .
They prove that the river, above four thousand years ago, rose more than
twenty-four feet higher than now, and thereby must have produced totally
different conditions in the inundation and in the whole surface of the
ground, both above and below this spot."—Lepsius's *Letters from Egypt*,
etc., Letter xxvi.

" The highest rise of the Nile in each year at Semneh was registered by
a mark indicating the year of the king's reign, cut in the granite, either on
one of the blocks forming the foundation of the fortress, or on the cliff,
and particularly on the east or right bank, as best adapted for the purpose.

height of the inundation at Semneh during various years of that king's reign. The Nile then rose in Ethiopia to a level some 27 feet in excess of the highest point to which it is ever known to attain at the present day. I am not aware what relation the height of this ancient bed bears to the levels recorded at Semneh, or to those now annually self-registered upon the furrowed banks of Philæ; but one sees at a glance, without aid of measurements or hydrographic science, that if the river were to come down again next summer in a mighty "bore," the crest of which rose 27 feet above the highest ground now fertilised by the annual overflow, it would at once refill its long-deserted bed, and convert Assûan into an island.

Granted, then, that the Nile flowed through the desert in the time of Amenemhat III, there must at some later period have come a day when it suddenly ran dry. This catastrophe is supposed to have taken place about the time of the expulsion of the Hyksos (*circa* B.C. 1703), when a great disruption of the rocky barrier at Silsilis is thought to have taken place; so draining Nubia, which till now had played the part of a vast reservoir, and dispersing the pent-up floods over the plains of Southern Egypt. It would, however, be a mistake to conclude that the Nile was by this catastrophe turned aside in order to be precipitated in the direction of the Cataract. One arm of the river must always have taken the present lower and deeper course; while the other must of necessity have run low— perhaps very nearly dry—as the inundation subsided every spring.

Of these markings eighteen still remain, thirteen of them having been made in the reign of Mœris (Amenemhat III) and five in the time of his next two successors. . . . We have here presented to us the remarkable facts that the highest of the records now legible, viz. that of the thirtieth year of the reign of Amenemhat, according to exact measurements which I made, is 8.17 metres (26 feet 8 inches) higher than the highest level to which the Nile rises in years of the greatest floods; and, further, that the lowest mark, which is on the east bank and indicated the fifteenth year of the same king, is still 4.14 metres (13 feet 6½ inches); and the single mark on the west bank indicating the ninth year, is 2.77 metres (9 feet) above the highest level."—Lepsius's *Letter to Professor Ehrenberg.* See Appendix to the above.

There remains no monumental record of this event; but the facts speak for themselves. The great channel is there. The old Nile-mud is there—buried for the most part in sand, but still visible on many a rocky shelf and plateau between Assûan and Philæ. There are even places where the surface of the mass is seen to be scooped out, as if by the sudden rush of the departing waters. Since that time, the tides of war and commerce have flowed in their place. Every conquering Thothmes and Rameses bound for the land of Kush, led his armies that way. Sabacon, at the head of his Ethiopian hordes, took that short cut to the throne of all the Pharaohs. The French under Desaix, pursuing the Memlooks after the battle of the Pyramids, swept down that pass to Philæ. Meanwhile the whole trade of the Soudan, however interrupted at times by the ebb and flow of war, has also set that way. We never crossed those five miles of desert without encountering a train or two of baggage-camels laden either with European goods for the far South, or with Oriental treasures for the North.

I shall not soon forget an Abyssinian caravan which we met one day just coming out from Mahatta. It consisted of seventy camels laden with elephant tusks. The tusks, which were about fourteen feet in length, were packed in half-dozens and sewn up in buffalo hides. Each camel was slung with two loads, one at either side of the hump. There must have been about eight hundred and forty tusks in all. Beside each shambling beast strode a bare-footed Nubian. Following these, on the back of a gigantic camel, came a hunting leopard in a wooden cage, and a wild cat in a basket. Last of all marched a coal-black Abyssinian nearly seven feet in height, magnificently shawled and turbaned, with a huge scimetar dangling by his side, and in his belt a pair of enormous inlaid seventeenth-century pistols, such as would have become the holsters of Prince Rupert. This elaborate warrior represented the guard of the caravan. The hunting leopard and the wild cat were for Prince Hassan, the third son of the Viceroy. The ivory was for exportation. Anything more picturesque than this procession, with the dust driving before it in clouds, and the children following it out of the village, it would be difficult to conceive.   One longed for Gerôme to paint it on the spot.

The rocks on either side of the ancient river-bed are profusely hieroglyphed.   These inscriptions, together with others found in the adjacent quarries, range over a period of between three and four thousand years, beginning with the early reigns of the Ancient Empire, and ending with the Ptolemies and Cæsars.   Some are mere autographs.   Others run to a considerable length.   Many are headed with figures of gods and worshippers.   These, however, are for the most part mere graffiti, ill drawn and carelessly sculptured.   The records they illustrate are chiefly votive.   The passer-by adores the gods of the Cataract ; implores their protection ; registers his name, and states the object of his journey.   The votaries are of various ranks, periods, and nationalities ; but the formula in most instances is pretty much the same.   Now it is a citizen of Thebes performing the pilgrimage to Philæ ; or a general at the head of his troops returning from a foray in Ethiopia ; or a tributary Prince doing homage to Rameses the Great, and associating his suzerain with the divinities of the place.   Occasionally we come upon a royal cartouche and a pompous catalogue of titles, setting forth how the Pharaoh himself, the Golden Hawk, the Son of Ra, the Mighty, the Invincible, the Godlike, passed that way.

It is curious to see how royalty, so many thousand years ago, set the fashion in names, just as it does to this day. Nine-tenths of the ancient travellers who left their signatures upon these rocks were called Rameses or Thothmes or Usertasen.   Others, still more ambitious, took the names of gods. Ampère, who hunted diligently for inscriptions both here and among the islands, found the autographs of no end of merely mortal Amens and Hathors.[1]

Our three days' detention in the Cataract was followed by

[1] For copies and translations of a large number of the graffiti of Assûan, see Lepsius's *Denkmäler ;* also, for the most recent and the fullest collection of the rock-cut inscriptions of Assûan and its neighbourhood, including the hitherto uncopied inscriptions of the Saba Rigaleh Valley, of Elephantine, of the rocks above Silsileh, etc. etc., see Mr. W. M. Flinders Petrie's latest volume, entitled *A Season's Work in Egypt, 1887,* published by Field and Tuer, 1888.   [Note to Second Edition.]

a fourth of glassy calm.   There being no breath of air to fill our sails and no footing for the trackers, we could now get along only by dint of hard punting ; so that it was past midday before the Philæ lay moored at last in the shadow of the holy island to which she owed her name.

PHARAOH'S BED, PHILÆ.

CHAPTER XII.

PHILÆ.

HAVING been for so many days within easy reach of Philæ, it is not to be supposed that we were content till now with only an occasional glimpse of its towers in the distance. On the contrary, we had found our way thither towards the close of almost every day's excursion. We had approached it by land from the desert; by water in the felucca; from Mahatta by way of the path between the cliffs and the river. When I add that we moored here for a night and the best part of two days on our way up the river, and again for a week when we came down, it will be seen that we had time to learn the lovely island by heart.

The approach by water is quite the most beautiful. Seen from the level of a small boat, the island, with its palms, its colonnades, its pylons, seems to rise out of the river like a mirage. Piled rocks frame it in on either side, and purple mountains close up the distance. As the boat glides nearer between glistening boulders, those sculptured towers rise higher and ever higher against the sky. They show no sign of ruin or of age. All looks solid, stately, perfect. One forgets for the moment that anything is changed. If a sound of antique chanting were to be borne along the quiet air—if a procession of white-robed priests bearing aloft the veiled ark of the God, were to come sweeping round between the palms and the pylons—we should not think it strange.

Most travellers land at the end nearest the Cataract; so coming upon the principal temple from behind, and seeing it in reverse order. We, however, bid our Arabs row round to the·southern end, where was once a stately landing-place with steps down to the river. We skirt the steep banks, and pass close under the beautiful little roofless Temple commonly known as Pharaoh's Bed — that Temple which has been so often painted, so often photographed, that every stone of it, and the platform on which it stands, and the tufted palms that cluster round about it, have been since childhood as familiar to our mind's eye as the Sphinx or the Pyramids. It is larger, but not one jot less beautiful than we had expected. And it is exactly like the photographs. Still, one is conscious of perceiving a shade of difference too ,subtle for analysis ; like the difference between a familiar face and the reflection of it in a looking-glass. Anyhow, one feels that the real Pharaoh's Bed will henceforth displace the photographs in that obscure mental pigeon-hole where till now one has been wont to store the well-known image ; and that even the photographs have undergone some kind of change.

And now the corner is rounded ; and the river widens away southwards between mountains and palm-groves ; and the prow touches the débris of a ruined quay. The bank is steep here. We climb ; and a wonderful scene opens before our eyes. We are standing at the lower end of a courtyard leading up to the propylons of the great Temple. The courtyard is irregular in shape, and enclosed on either side by covered colonnades. The colonnades are of unequal lengths and set at different angles. One is simply a covered walk ; the other opens upon a row of small chambers, like a monastic cloister opening upon a row of cells. The roofing-stones of these colonnades are in part displaced, while here and there a pillar or a capital is missing ; but the twin towers of the propylon, standing out in sharp unbroken lines against the sky and covered with colossal sculptures, are as perfect, or very nearly as perfect, as in the days of the Ptolemies who built them.

The broad area between the colonnades is honeycombed with crude-brick foundations ; vestiges of a Coptic village of early Christian time. Among these we thread our way to the foot of the principal propylon, the entire width of which is

GRAND COLONNADE, PHILÆ.

1 20 feet. The towers measure 60 feet from base to parapet. These dimensions are insignificant for Egypt ; yet the propylon, which would look small at Luxor or Karnak, does not look small at Philæ. The key-note here is not magnitude, but beauty. The island is small—that is to say it covers an area about equal to the summit of the Acropolis at Athens ; and the scale of the buildings has been determined by the size of the island. As at Athens, the ground is occupied by one principal Temple of moderate size, and several subordinate Chapels. Perfect grace, exquisite proportion, most varied and capricious grouping, here take the place of massiveness ; so lending to Egyptian forms an irregularity of treatment that is almost Gothic, and a lightness that is almost Greek.

And now we catch glimpses of an inner court, of a second propylon, of a pillared portico beyond ; while, looking up to the colossal bas-reliefs above our heads, we see the usual mystic forms of kings and deities, crowned, enthroned, worshipping and worshipped. These sculptures, which at first sight looked no less perfect than the towers, prove to be as laboriously mutilated as those of Denderah. The hawk-head of Horus and the cow-head of Hathor have here and there escaped destruction ; but the human-faced deities are literally " sans eyes, sans nose, sans ears, sans everything."

We enter the inner court—an irregular quadrangle en-closed on the east by an open colonnade, on the west by a chapel fronted with Hathor-headed columns, and on the north and south sides by the second and first propylons. In this quadrangle a cloistral silence reigns. The blue sky burns above—the shadows sleep below—a tender twilight lies about our feet. Inside the chapel there sleeps perpetual gloom. It was built by Ptolemy Euergetes II, and is one of that order to which Champollion gave the name of Mammisi. It is a most curious place, dedicated to Hathor and commemorative of the nurture of Horus. On the blackened walls within, dimly visible by the faint light which struggles through screen and doorway, we see Isis, the wife and sister of Osiris, giving birth to Horus. On the screen panels outside we trace the story of his infancy, education, and growth. As a babe at the breast, he is nursed in the lap of Hathor, the divine foster-mother. As a young child, he stands at his mother's knee and listens to the playing of a female harpist (we saw a bare-footed boy the other day in Cairo thrumming upon a harp of just the same shape, and with precisely as many strings) ; as a youth, he sows grain in honour of Isis, and offers a jewelled collar to Hathor. This Isis, with her long aquiline nose, thin lips, and haughty aspect, looks like one of the complimentary portraits so often introduced among the temple sculptures of Egypt. It may represent one of the two Cleopatras wedded to Ptolemy Physcon.

Two greyhounds with collars round their necks are sculptured on the outer wall of another small chapel adjoining. These also look like portraits. Perhaps they were the favourite dogs of some high priest of Philæ.

Close against the greyhounds and upon the same wall-space, is engraven that famous copy of the inscription of the Rosetta Stone first observed here by Lepsius in A.D. 1843. It neither stands so high nor looks so illegible as Ampère (with all the jealousy of a Champollionist and a Frenchman) is at such pains to make out. One would have said that it was in a state of more than ordinarily good preservation.

As a reproduction of the Rosetta decree, however, the Philæ version is incomplete. The Rosetta text, after setting forth with official pomposity the victories and munificence of the King, Ptolemy V, the Ever-living, the Avenger of Egypt, concludes by ordaining that the record thereof shall be engraven in hieroglyphic, demotic, and Greek characters, and set up in all temples of the first, second, and third class throughout the Empire. Broken and battered as it is, the precious black basalt [1] of the British Museum fulfils these conditions. The

[1] Mariette, at the end of his *Aperçu de l'histoire d'Egypte*, gives the following succinct account of the Rosetta Stone, and the discovery of Champollion :—

"Découverte, il y a 65 ans environ, par des soldats français qui creusaient un retranchement près d'une redoute située à Rosette, la pierre qui porte ce nom a joué le plus grand rôle dans l'archéologie égyptienne. Sur la face principale sont gravées *trois* inscriptions. Les deux premières sont en langue égyptienne et écrites dans les deux écritures qui avaient cours à cette époque. L'une est en écriture hiéroglyphique réservée aux prêtres : elle ne compte plus que 14 lignes tronquées par la brisure de

three writings are there. But at Philæ, though the original
hieroglyphic and demotic texts are reproduced almost verbatim,
the priceless Greek transcript is wanting. It is provided for,
as upon the Rosetta Stone, in the preamble. Space has been
left for it at the bottom of the tablet. We even fancied we
could here and there distinguish traces of red ink where the
lines should come. But not one word of it has ever been cut
into the surface of the stone.

la pierre. L'autre est en une écriture cursive appliquée principalement
aux usages du peuple et comprise par lui : celle-ci offre 32 lignes de
texte. Enfin, la troisième inscription de la stèle est en langue grecque
et comprend. 54 lignes. C'est dans cette dernière partie que réside l'intérêt
du monument trouvé à Rosette. Il résulte, en effet, de l'interprétation
du texte grec de la stèle que ce texte n'est qu'une version de l'original
transcrit plus haut dans les deux écritures égyptiennes. La Pierre de
Rosette nous donne donc, dans une langue parfaitement connue (le grec)
la traduction d'un texte conçu dans une autre langue encore ignorée au
moment où la stèle a été découverte. Qui ne voit l'utilité de cette mention ?
Remonter du connu à l'inconnu n'est pas une opération en dehors des
moyens d'une critique prudente, et déjà l'on devine que si la Pierre de
Rosette a acquis dans la science la célébrité dont elle jouit aujourd'hui,
c'est qu'elle a fourni la vraie clef de cette mystérieuse écriture dont l'Égypte
a si longtemps gardé le secret. Il ne faudrait pas croire cependant que le
déchiffrement des hiéroglyphes au moyen de la Pierre de Rosette ait été
obtenu du premier coup et sans tâtonnements. Bien au contraire, les
savants s'y essayèrent sans succès pendant 20 ans. Enfin, Champollion
parut. Jusqu'à lui, on avait cru que chacune des lettres qui composent
l'écriture hiéroglyphique etait un *symbole ;* c'est à dire, que dans une seule
de ces lettres était exprimée une *idée* complète. Le mérite de Champollion
été de prouver qu'au contraire l'écriture égyptienne contient des signes qui
expriment véritablement des *sons.* En d'autres termes qu'elle est *Alpha-
bétique.* Il remarqua, par exemple, que partout où dans le texte grec de
Rosette se trouve le nom propre *Ptolémée,* on rencontre à l'endroit cor-
respondant du texte égyptien un certain nombre de signes enfermés dans
un encadrement elliptique. Il en conclut : 1°, que les noms des rois
étaient dans le systeme hiéroglyphique signalés à l'attention par une sorte
d'écusson qu'il appela *cartouche :* 2°, que les signes contenus dans cet
écusson devaient être lettre pour lettre le nom de Ptolémée. Déjà donc
en supposant les voyelles omises, Champollion était en possession de cinq
lettres—P, T, L, M, S. D'un autre côté, Champollion savait, d'après une
seconde inscription grecque gravée sur une obélisque de Philæ, que sur cet
obélisque un cartouche hiéroglyphique qu'on y voit devait être celui de
Cléopâtre. Si sa première lecture était juste, le P, le L, et le T, de
Ptolémée devaient se retrouver dans le second nom propre ; mais en même
temps ce second nom propre fournissait un K et un R nouveaux. Enfin,

Taken by itself, there is nothing strange in this omission ; but taken in connection with a precisely similar omission in another inscription a few yards distant, it becomes something more than a coincidence. This second inscription is cut upon the face of a block of living rock which forms part of the foundation of the easternmost tower of the second propylon. Having enumerated certain grants of land made to the Temple by the VIth and

appliqué à d'autres cartouches, l'alphabet encore très imparfait révélé à Champollion par les noms de Cléopâtre et de Ptolémée le mit en possession d'à peu près toutes les autres consonnes. Comme *prononciation* des signes, Champollion n'avait donc pas à hésiter, et dès le jour où cette constatation eut lieu, il put certifier qu'il était en possession de l'alphabet égyptien. Mais restait la langue ; car prononcer des mots n'est rien si l'on ne sait pas ce que ces mots veulent dire. Ici le génie de Champollion se donna libre cours. Il s'aperçut en effet que son alphabet tiré des noms propres et appliqué aux mots de la langue donnait tout simplement du *Copte.* Or, le Copte à son tour est une langue qui, sans être aussi explorée que le grec, n'en était pas moins depuis longtemps accessible. Cette fois le voile était donc complétement levé. La langue égyptienne n'est que du Copte écrit en hiéroglyphes ; ou, pour parler plus exactement, le Copte n'est que la langue des anciens Pharaons, écrite, comme nous l'avons dit plus haut, en lettres grecques. Le reste se devine. D'indices en indices, Champollion procéda véritablement du connu à l'inconnu, et bientôt l'illustre fondateur de l'égyptologie put poser les fondements de cette belle science qui a pour objet l'interprétation des hiéroglyphes. Tel est la Pierre de Rosette."— *Aperçu de l'histoire d'Egypte :* Mariette Bey, p. 189 *et seq.* : 1872.

In order to have done with this subject, it may be as well to mention that another trilingual tablet was found by Mariette while conducting his excavations at Sân (Tanis) in 1865. It dates from the ninth year of Ptolemy Euergetes, and the text ordains the deification of Berenice, a daughter of the king, then just dead (B.C. 254). This stone, preserved in the museum at Boulak, is known as the Stone of Sân, or the Decree of Canopus. Had the Rosetta Stone never been discovered, we may fairly conclude that the Canopic Decree would have furnished some later Champollion with the necessary key to hieroglyphic literature, and that the great discovery would only have been deferred till the present time.

NOTE TO SECOND EDITION.—A third copy of the Decree of Canopus, the text engraved in hieroglyphs only, was found at Tell Nebireh in 1885, and conveyed to the Boulak Museum. The discoverer of this tablet, however, missed a much greater discovery, reserved, as it happened, for Mr. W. M. F. Petrie, who came to the spot a month or two later, and found that the mounds of Tell Nebireh entombed the remains of the famous and long-lost Greek city of Naukratis. See *Naukratis*, Part I, by W. M. F. Petrie, published by the Egypt Exploration Fund, 1886.

VIIth Ptolemies, it concludes, like the first, by decreeing that
this record of the royal bounty shall be engraven in the hieroglyphic, demotic, and Greek : that is to say, in the ancient
sacred writing of the priests, the ordinary script of the people,
and the language of the Court. But here again the sculptor
has left his work unfinished. Here again the inscription breaks
off at the end of the demotic, leaving a blank space for the
third transcript. This second omission suggests intentional
neglect ; and the motive for such neglect would not be far to
seek. The tongue of the dominant race is likely enough to
have been unpopular among the old noble and sacerdotal
families ; and it may well be that the priesthood of Philæ,
secure in their distant, solitary isle, could with impunity evade
a clause which their brethren of the Delta were obliged to
obey.

It does not follow that the Greek rule was equally unpopular.
We have reason to believe quite otherwise. The conqueror
of the Persian invader was in truth the deliverer of Egypt.
Alexander restored peace to the country, and the Ptolemies
identified themselves with the interests of the people. A
dynasty which not only lightened the burdens of the poor but
respected the privileges of the rich ; which honoured the priesthood, endowed the Temples, and compelled the Tigris to
restore the spoils of the Nile, could scarcely fail to win the
suffrages of all classes. The priests of Philæ might despise
the language of Homer while honouring the descendants of
Philip of Macedon. They could naturalise the King. They
could disguise his name in hieroglyphic spelling. They could
depict him in the traditional dress of the Pharaohs. They
could crown him with the double crown, and represent him in
the act of worshipping the gods of his adopted country. But
they could neither naturalise nor disguise his language. Spoken
or written, it was an alien thing. Carven in high places, it
stood for a badge of servitude. What could a conservative
hierarchy do but abhor, and, when possible, ignore it ?

There are other sculptures in this quadrangle which one
would like to linger over ; as, for instance, the capitals of the
eastern colonnade, no two of which are alike, and the
grotesque bas-reliefs of the frieze of the Mammisi. Of these,

a quasi-heraldic group, representing the sacred hawk sitting in the centre of a fan-shaped persea tree between two supporters, is one of the most curious ; the supporters being on the one side a maniacal lion, and on the other a Typhonian hippopotamus, each grasping a pair of shears.

Passing now through the doorway of the second propylon, we find ourselves facing the portico—the famous painted portico of which we had seen so many sketches that we fancied we knew it already. That second-hand knowledge goes for nothing, however, in presence of the reality ; and we are as much taken by surprise as if we were the first travellers to set foot within these enchanted precincts.

For here is a place in which time seems to have stood as still as in that immortal palace where everything went to sleep for a hundred years. The bas-reliefs on the walls, the intricate paintings on the ceilings, the colours upon the capitals, are incredibly fresh and perfect. These exquisite capitals have long been the wonder and delight of travellers in Egypt. They are all studied from natural forms—from the lotus in bud and blossom, the papyrus, and the palm. Conventionalised with consummate skill, they are at the same time so justly proportioned to the height and girth of the columns as to give an air of wonderful lightness to the whole structure. But above all, it is with the colour—colour conceived in the tender and pathetic minor of Watteau and Lancret and Greuze—that one is most fascinated. Of those delicate half-tones, the facsimile in the "Grammar of Ornament" conveys not the remotest idea. Every tint is softened, intermixed, degraded. The pinks are coralline ; the greens are tempered with verditer ; the blues are of a greenish turquoise, like the western half of an autumnal evening sky.

Later on, when we returned to Philæ from the Second Cataract, the Writer devoted the best part of three days to making a careful study of a corner of this portico ; patiently matching those subtle variations of tint, and endeavouring to master the secret of their combination.[1]

---

[1] The famous capitals are not the only specimens of admirable colouring in Philæ. Among the battered bas-reliefs of the great colonnade at the south end of the island, there yet remain some isolated patches of

The annexed woodcut can do no more than reproduce the forms. Architecturally, this court is unlike any we have yet seen, being quite small, and open to the sky in the centre, like the atrium of a Roman house. The light thus admitted glows overhead, lies in a square patch on the ground below, and is reflected upon the pictured recesses of the ceiling. At the upper end, where the pillars stand two deep, there was originally an intercolumnar screen. The rough sides of the columns show where the connecting blocks have been torn away. The pavement, too, has been pulled up by treasure-seekers, and the ground is strewn with broken slabs and fragments of shattered cornice.

These are the only signs of ruin—signs traced not by the finger of Time, but by the hand of the spoiler. So fresh, so fair is all the rest, that we are fain to cheat ourselves for a moment into the belief that what we see is work not marred, but arrested. Those columns, depend on it, are yet unfinished. That pavement is about to be relaid. It would not surprise us to find the masons here to-morrow morning, or the sculptor, with mallet and chisel, carrying on that band of lotus buds and bees. Far more difficult is it to believe that they all struck work for ever some two-and-twenty centuries ago.

Here and there, where the foundations have been disturbed, one sees that the columns are constructed of sculptured blocks, the fragments of some earlier Temple ; while, at a height of about six feet from the ground, a Greek cross cut deep into the side of the shaft stamps upon each pillar the seal of Christian worship.

uninjured and very lovely ornament. See, more particularly, the mosaic pattern upon the throne of a divinity just over the second doorway in the western wall ; and the designs upon a series of other thrones a little farther along towards the north, all most delicately drawn in uniform compartments, picked out in the three primary colours, and laid on in flat tints of wonderful purity and delicacy. Among these a lotus between two buds, an exquisite little sphinx on a pale red ground, and a series of sacred hawks, white upon red, alternating with white upon blue, all most exquisitely conventionalised, may be cited as examples of absolutely perfect treatment and design in polychrome decoration. A more instructive and delightful task than the copying of these precious fragments can hardly be commended to students and sketchers on the Nile.

PAINTED COLUMNS, PORTICO OF LARGE TEMPLE, PHILÆ.

For the Copts who choked the colonnades and courtyards with their hovels seized also on the Temples. Some they pulled down for building material ; others they appropriated. We can never know how much they destroyed ; but two large convents on the eastern bank a little higher up the river, and a small basilica at the north end of the island, would seem to have been built with the magnificent masonry of the southern

EARLY CHRISTIAN SHRINE, PHILÆ.

quay, as well as with blocks taken from a structure which once occupied the south-eastern corner of the great colonnade. As for this beautiful painted portico, they turned it into a chapel. A little rough-hewn niche in the east wall, and an overturned credence-table fashioned from a single block of limestone, mark the site of the chancel. The Arabs, taking this last for a gravestone, have pulled it up, according to their usual practice, in search of treasure buried with the dead. On the front of the credence-table,[1] and over the niche which some unskilled but pious hand has decorated with rude Byzantine carvings, the Greek cross is again conspicuous. The religious history of Philæ is so curious that it is a pity it should not find an historian. It shared with Abydos and some other places the reputation of being the burial-place of Osiris. It was called "the Holy Island." Its very soil was sacred. None might land upon its shores, or even approach them too nearly, without permission. To obtain that permission and perform the pilgrimage to the tomb of the God, was to the pious Egyptian what the Mecca pilgrimage is to the pious Mussulman of to-day. The most solemn oath to which he could give utterance was " By Him who sleeps in Philæ."

When and how the island first came to be regarded as the resting-place of the most beloved of the Gods does not appear ; but its reputation for sanctity seems to have been of comparatively modern date. It probably rose into importance as Abydos declined. Herodotus, who is supposed to have gone as far as Elephantine, made minute enquiry concerning the river above that point ; and he relates that the Cataract was in the occupation of "Ethiopian nomads." He, however, makes no mention of Philæ or its Temples. This omission on the part of one who, wherever he went, sought the society of the priests and paid particular attention to the religious observances of the country, shows that either Herodotus never got so far, or that the island had not yet become the home of the Osirian mysteries. Four hundred years later, Diodorus Siculus describes it as the holiest of holy places ; while Strabo, writing about the same time, relates that Abydos had then dwindled to a mere village. It seems possible, therefore, that at some period subsequent to the time of Herodotus and prior to that of Diodorus or Strabo, the priests of Isis may have migrated from Abydos to Philæ ; in which case there would have been a formal transfer not only of the relics of Osiris, but of the sanctity which had attached

---

[1] It has since been pointed out by a writer in *The Saturday Review* that this credence-table was fashioned with part of a shrine destined for one of the captive hawks sacred to Horus. [Note to Second Edition.]

for ages to their original resting-place. Nor is the motive for such an exodus wanting. The ashes of the God were no longer safe at Abydos. Situate in the midst of a rich corn country on the high road to Thebes, no city south of Memphis lay more exposed to the hazards of war. Cambyses had already passed that way. Other invaders might follow. To seek beyond the frontier that security which might no longer be found in Egypt, would seem therefore to be the obvious course of a priestly guild devoted to its trust. This, of course, is mere conjecture, to be taken for what it may be worth. The decadence of Abydos coincides, at all events, with the growth of Philæ ; and it is only by help of some such assumption that one can understand how a new site should have suddenly arisen to such a height of holiness.

The earliest Temple here, of which only a small propylon remains, would seem to have been built by the last of the native Pharaohs (Nectanebo II, B.C. 361) ; but the high and palmy days of Philæ belong to the period of Greek and Roman rule. It was in the time of the Ptolemies that the Holy Island became the seat of a Sacred College and the stronghold of a powerful hierarchy. Visitors from all parts of Egypt, travellers from distant lands, court functionaries from Alexandria charged with royal gifts, came annually in crowds to offer their vows at the tomb of the God. They have cut their names by hundreds all over the principal Temple, just like tourists of to-day. Some of these antique autographs are written upon and across those of preceding visitors ; while others — palimpsests upon stone, so to say — having been scratched on the yet unsculptured surface of doorway and pylon, are seen to be older than the hieroglyphic texts which were afterwards carved over them. These inscriptions cover a period of several centuries, during which time successive Ptolemies and Cæsars continued to endow the island. Rich in lands, in temples, in the localisation of a great national myth, the Sacred College was yet strong enough in A.D. 379 to oppose a practical resistance to the Edict of Theodosius. At a word from Constantinople, the whole land of Egypt was forcibly Christianised. Priests were forbidden under pain of death to perform the sacred rites. Hundreds of temples were plundered. Forty thousand statues of divinities were destroyed at one fell swoop. Meanwhile, the brotherhood of Philæ, entrenched behind the Cataract and the desert, survived the degradation of their order and the ruin of their immemorial faith. It is not known with certainty for how long they continued to transmit their hereditary privileges ; but two of the above-mentioned votive inscriptions show that so late as A.D. 453 the priestly families were still in occupation of the island, and still celebrating the mysteries of Osiris and Isis. There even seems reason for believing that the ancient worship continued to hold its own till the end of the sixth century, at which time, according to an inscription at Kalabsheh, of which I shall have more to say hereafter, Silco, " King of all the Ethiopians," himself apparently a Christian, twice invaded Lower Nubia, where God, he says, gave him the victory, and the vanquished swore to him " *by their idols* " to observe the terms of peace.[1]

There is nothing in this record to show that the invaders went beyond Tafa, the ancient Taphis, which is twenty-seven miles above Philæ ; but it seems reasonable to conclude that so long as the old gods yet reigned in any part of Nubia, the island sacred to Osiris would maintain its traditional sanctity.

At length, however, there must have come a day when for the last time the tomb of the God was crowned with flowers,

---

[1] In the time of Strabo, the island of Philæ, as has been recently shown by Professor Revillout in his *Seconde Mémoire sur les Blemmys*, was the common property of the Egyptians and Nubians, or rather of that obscure nation called the Blemmys, who, with the Nobades and Megabares, were collectively classed at that time as " Ethiopians." The Blemmys (ancestors of the present Barabras) were a stalwart and valiant race, powerful enough to treat on equal terms with the Roman rulers of Egypt. They were devout adorers of Isis, and it is interesting to learn that in the treaty of Maximin with this nation, it is expressly provided that, " according to the old law," the Blemmys were entitled to take the statue of Isis every year from the sanctuary of Philæ to their own country for a visit of a stated period. A graffito at Philæ, published by Letronne, states that the writer was at Philæ when the image of the goddess was brought back from one of these periodical excursions, and that he beheld the arrival of the sacred boats " containing the shrines of the divine statues." From this it would appear that other images than that of Isis had been taken to Ethiopia ; probably those of Osiris and Horus, and possibly also that of Hathor, the divine nurse. [Note to Second Edition.]

and the "Lamentations of Isis" were recited on the threshold of the sanctuary. And there must have come another day when the cross was carried in triumph up those painted colonnades, and the first Christian mass was chanted in the precincts of the heathen. One would like to know how these changes were brought about ; whether the old faith died out for want of worshippers, or was expelled with clamour and violence. But upon this point, history is vague[1] and the graffiti of the time are silent. We only know for certain that the old went out, and the new came in ; and that where the resurrected Osiris was wont to be worshipped according to the most sacred mysteries of the Egyptian ritual, the resurrected Christ was now adored after the simple fashion of the primitive Coptic Church.

And now the Holy Island, near which it was believed no fish had power to swim or bird to fly, and upon whose soil no pilgrim might set foot without permission, became all at once the common property of a populous community. Courts, colonnades, even terraced roofs, were overrun with little crude-brick dwellings. A small basilica was built at the lower end of the island. The portico of the Great Temple was converted into a Chapel, and dedicated to Saint Stephen. "This good work," says a Greek inscription traced there by some monkish hand of the period, "was done by the well-beloved of God, the Abbot-Bishop Theodore." Of this same Theodore, whom another inscription styles "the very holy father," we know nothing but his name.

The walls hereabout are full of these fugitive records. "The cross has conquered, and will ever conquer," writes one anonymous scribe. Others have left simple signatures ; as, for instance—"I, Joseph," in one place, and "I, Theodosius of Nubia," in another. Here and there an added word or two give a more human interest to the autograph. So, in the pathetic scrawl of one who writes himself "Johannes, a slave," we seem to read the story of a life in a single line. These Coptic signatures are all followed by the sign of the cross.

[1] The Emperor Justinian is credited with the mutilation of the sculptures of the large Temple ; but the ancient worship was probably only temporarily suspended in his time.

The foundations of the little basilica, with its apse towards the east and its two doorways to the west, are still traceable. We set a couple of our sailors one day to clear away the rubbish at the lower end of the nave, and found the font— a rough stone basin at the foot of a broken column.

It is not difficult to guess what Philæ must have been like in the days of Abbot Theodore and his flock. The little basilica, we may be sure, had a cluster of mud domes upon the roof ; and I fancy, somehow, that the Abbot and his monks installed themselves in that row of cells on the east side of the great colonnade, where the priests of Isis dwelt before them. As for the village, it must have been just like Luxor —swarming with dusky life ; noisy with the babble of children, the cackling of poultry, and the barking of dogs ; sending up thin pillars of blue smoke at noon ; echoing to the measured chime of the prayer-bell at morn and even ; and sleeping at night as soundly as if no ghost-like, mutilated Gods were looking on mournfully in the moonlight.

The Gods are avenged now. The creed which dethroned them is dethroned. Abbot Theodore and his successors, and the religion they taught, and the simple folk that listened to their teaching, are gone and forgotten. For the Church of Christ, which still languishes in Egypt, is extinct in Nubia. It lingered long ; though doubtless in some such degraded and barbaric form as it wears in Abyssinia to this day. But it was absorbed by Islamism at last ; and only a ruined convent perched here and there upon some solitary height, or a few crosses rudely carved on the walls of a Ptolemaic Temple, remain to show that Christianity once passed that way.

The mediæval history of Philæ is almost a blank. The Arabs, having invaded Egypt towards the middle of the seventh century, were long in the land before they began to cultivate literature ; and for more than three hundred years history is silent. It is not till the tenth century that we once again catch a fleeting glimpse of Philæ. The frontier is now removed to the head of the Cataract. The Holy Island has ceased to be Christian ; ceased to be Nubian ; contains a mosque and garrison, and is the last fortified outpost of the Moslems. It still retains, and apparently continues to retain for some centuries longer, its ancient Egyptian name. That is to say (P being as usual converted into B) the Pilak of the hieroglyphic inscriptions becomes in Arabic Belak;[1] which is much more like the original than the Philæ of the Greeks.

The native Christians, meanwhile, would seem to have relapsed into a state of semi-barbarism. They make perpetual inroads upon the Arab frontier, and suffer perpetual defeat. Battles are fought ; tribute is exacted ; treaties are made and broken. Towards the close of the thirteenth century, their king being slain and their churches plundered, they lose one-fourth of their territory, including all that part which borders upon Assûan. Those who remain Christians are also condemned to pay an annual capitation tax, in addition to the usual tribute of dates, cotton, slaves, and camels. After this we may conclude that they accepted Islamism from the Arabs, as they had accepted Osiris from the Egyptians and Christ from the Romans. As Christians, at all events, we hear of them no more ; for Christianity in Nubia perished root and branch, and not a Copt, it is said, may now be found above the frontier.

Philæ was still inhabited in A.D. 1799, when a detachment of Desaix's army under General Beliard took possession of the island, and left an inscription[2] on the soffit of the doorway of the great pylon to commemorate the passage of the Cataract. Denon, describing the scene with his usual vivacity, relates

---

[1] These and the following particulars about the Christians of Nubia are found in the famous work of Makrizi, an Arab historian of the fifteenth century, who quotes largely from earlier writers. See Burckhardt's *Travels in Nubia*, 4to, 1819, Appendix iii. Although Belak is distinctly described as an island in the neighbourhood of the Cataract, distant four miles from Assûan, Burckhardt persisted in looking for it among the islets below Mahatta, and believed Philæ to be the first Nubian town beyond the frontier. The hieroglyphic alphabet, however, had not then been deciphered. Burckhardt died at Cairo in 1817, and Champollion's discovery was not given to the world till 1822.

[2] This inscription, which M. About considers the most interesting thing in Philæ, runs as follows : " L'An VI de la République, le 15 Messidor, une Armée Française commandée par Bonaparte est descendue a Alexandrie. L'Armée ayant mis, vingt jours après, les Mamelouks en fuite aux Pyramides, Desaix, commandant la première division, les a poursuivis au dela des Cataractes, ou il est arrivé le 18 Ventôse de l'an VII."

how the natives first defied and then fled from the French; flinging themselves into the river, drowning such of their children as were too young to swim, and escaping into the desert. They appear at this time to have been mere savages —the women ugly and sullen ; the men naked, agile, quarrelsome, and armed not only with swords and spears, but with matchlock guns, which they used to keep up "a brisk and well-directed fire."

Their abandonment of the island probably dates from this time ; for when Burckhardt went up in A.D. 1813, he found it, as we found it to this day, deserted and solitary. One poor old man—if indeed he still lives—is now the one inhabitant of Philæ ; and I suspect he only crosses over from Biggeh in the tourist-season. He calls himself, with or without authority, the guardian of the island ; sleeps in a nest of rags and straw in a sheltered corner behind the great Temple ; and is so wonderfully wizened and bent and knotted up, that nothing of him seems quite alive except his eyes. We gave him fifty copper paras [1] for a parting present when on our way back to Egypt ; and he was so oppressed by the consciousness of wealth, that he immediately buried his treasure and implored us to tell no one what we had given him.

With the French siege and the flight of the native population closes the last chapter of the local history of Philæ. The Holy Island has done henceforth with wars of creeds or kings. It disappears from the domain of history, and enters the domain of science. To have contributed to the discovery of the hieroglyphic alphabet is a high distinction ; and in no sketch of Philæ, however slight, should the obelisk [2] that furnished Champollion with the name of Cleopatra be allowed to pass unnoticed. This monument, second only to the Rosetta Stone in point of philological interest, was carried off by Mr. W. Bankes, the discoverer of the first Tablet of Abydos, and is now in Dorsetshire. Its empty socket and its fellow obelisk, mutilated and solitary, remain *in situ* at the southern extremity of the island.

And now—for we have lingered over long in the portico—it is time we glanced at the interior of the Temple. So we

---

[1] About two-and-sixpence English.   [2] See previous note, p. 211.

go in at the central door, beyond which open some nine or ten halls and side-chambers leading, as usual, to the sanctuary. Heré all is dark, earthy, oppressive. In rooms unlighted by the faintest gleam from without, we find smoke-blackened walls covered with elaborate bas-reliefs. Mysterious passages, pitch-dark, thread the thickness of the walls and communicate by means of trap-like openings with vaults below. In the sanctuary lies an overthrown altar ; while in the corner behind it stands the very niche in which Strabo must have seen that poor sacred hawk of Ethiopia which he describes as "sick, and nearly dead."

But in this Temple dedicated not only to Isis, but to the memory of Osiris and the worship of Horus their son, there is one chamber which we may be quite sure was shown neither to Strabo nor Diodorus, nor to any stranger of alien faith, be his repute or station what it might ; a chamber holy above all others ; holier even than the sanctuary ;—the chamber sacred to Osiris. We, however, unrestricted, unforbidden, are free to go where we list ; and our books tell us that this mysterious chamber is somewhere overhead. So, emerging once again into the daylight, we go up a well-worn staircase leading out upon the roof.

This roof is an intricate, up-and-down place ; and the room is not easy to find. It lies at the bottom of a little flight of steps—a small stone cell some twelve feet square, lighted only from the doorway. The walls are covered with sculptures representing the shrines, the mummification, and the resurrection of Osiris.[1] These shrines, containing each some part of his

---

[1] The story of Osiris—the beneficent God, the friend of man, slain and dismembered by Typhon ; buried in a score of graves ; sought by Isis ; recovered limb by limb ; resuscitated in the flesh ; transferred from earth to reign over the dead in the world of Shades—is one of the most complex of Egyptian legends. Osiris under some aspects is the Nile. He personifies Abstract Good, and is entitled Unnefer, or " The Good Being." He appears as a Myth of the Solar Year. He bears a notable likeness to Prometheus, and to the Indian Bacchus.

" Osiris, dit-on, était autrefois descendu sur la terre. Être bon par excellence, il avait adouci les mœurs des hommes par la persuasion et la bienfaisance. Mais il avait succombé sous les embûches de Typhon, son frère, le génie du mal, et pendant que ses deux sœurs, Isis et Nephthys, recueillaient son corps qui avait été jeté dans le fleuve, le dieu ressuscitait

body, are variously fashioned. His head, for instance, rests on a Nilometer; his arm, surmounted by a head, is sculptured on

a stela, in shape resembling a high-shouldered bottle, surmounted by one of the head-dresses peculiar to the God; his legs and

d'entre les morts et apparaissait à son fils Horus, qu'il instituait son vengeur. C'est ce sacrifice qu'il avait autrefois accompli en faveur des hommes qu'Osiris renouvelle ici en faveur de l'âme dégagée de ses liens terrestres. Non seulement il devient son guide, mais il s'identifie à elle; il l'absorbe en son propre sein. C'est lui alors qui, devenu le défunt lui-même, se soumet à toutes les épreuves que celui-ci doit subir avant d'être proclamé juste; c'est lui qui, à chaque âme qu'il doit sauver, fléchit les gardiens des demeures infernales et combat les monstres compagnons de la nuit et de la mort; c'est lui enfin qui, vainqueur des ténèbres, avec l'assistance d'Horus, s'assied au tribunal de la suprême justice et ouvre à l'âme déclarée pure les portes du séjour éternel. L'image de la mort aura été empruntée au soleil qui disparaît à l'horizon du soir : le soleil resplendissant du matin sera la symbole de cette seconde naissance à une vie qui, cette fois, ne connaîtra pas la mort.

"Osiris est donc le principe du bien. . . . Chargé de sauver les âmes de la mort définitive, il est l'intermédiaire entre l'homme et Dieu; il est le type et le sauveur de l'homme." *Notice des Monuments à Boulaq—* AUG. MARIETTE BEY, 1872, pp. 105 *et seq.*

[It has always been taken for granted by Egyptologists that Osiris was originally a local God of Abydos, and that Abydos was the cradle of the

feet lie at full length in a pylon-shaped mausoleum. Upon
another shrine stands the mitre-shaped crown which he wears

as Judge of the Lower World. Isis and Nephthys keep guard
over each shrine. In a lower frieze we see the mummy of the

Osirian Myth. Professor Maspero, however, in some of his recent lectures
at the Collége de France, has shown that the Osirian cult took its rise in
the Delta ; and, in point of fact, Osiris, in certain ancient inscriptions, is
styled the King Osiris "Lord of Tattu" (Busiris), and has his name
enclosed in a royal oval. Up to the time of the Græco-Roman rule, the
only two cities of Egypt in which Osiris reigned as the principal God
were Busiris and Mendes.

"Le centre terrestre du culte d'Osiris, était dans les cantons nord-est
du Delta, situés entre la branche Sébennytique et la branche Pélusiaque,
comme le centre terrestre du culte de Sit, le frère et le meurtrier d'Osiris :
les deux dieux étaient limitrophes l'un de l'autre, et des rivalités de voisinage
expliquent peut-être en partie leurs querelles. . . . Tous les traits de la
tradition Osirienne ne sont pas également anciens : le fond me parait être
d'une antiquité incontestable. Osiris y réunit les caractères des deux
divinités qui se partageaient chaque nome : il est le dieu des vivants et
le dieu des morts en même temps ; le dieu qui nourrit et le dieu qui
détruit. Probablement, les temps où, saisi de pitié pour les mortels, il
leur ouvrit l'accès de son royaume, avaient été précédés d'autres temps où
il était impitoyable et ne songeait qu'à les anéantir. Je crois trouver un
souvenir de ce rôle destructeur d'Osiris dans plusieurs passages des textes
des Pyramides, où l'on promet au mort que Harkhouti viendra vers lui,
' déliant ses liens, brisant ses chaines pour le délivrer de la ruine ; *il ne le
livrera pas à Osiris, si bien qu'il ne mourra pas*, mais il sera glorieux dans
l'horizon, solide comme le Did dans la ville de Didou.' L'Osiris farouche
et cruel fut absorbé promptement par l'Osiris doux et bienveillant.
L'Osiris qui domine toute la religion égyptienne dès le début, c'est l'Osiris
Onnofris, l'Osiris Étre bon, que les Grecs ont connu. Commes ses
parents, Sibou et Nouit, Osiris Onnofris appartient à la classe des dieux
généraux qui ne sont pas confinés en un seul canton, mais qui sont adorés

god laid upon a bier, with the four so-called canopic jars [1] ranged underneath. A little farther on, he lies in state,

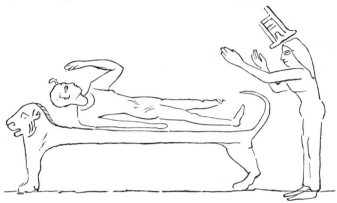

RESURRECTION OF OSIRIS.

surrounded by lotus buds on tall stems, figurative of growth, or returning life.[2] Finally, he is depicted lying on a couch ; his limbs reunited ; his head, left hand, and left foot upraised, as in the act of returning to consciousness. Nephthys, in the guise of a winged genius, fans him with the breath of life.

par un pays entier." See *Les Hypogées Royaux de Thèbes* (Bulletin critique de la religion égyptienne) par Professeur G. Maspero—*Revue de l'histoire des Réligions*, 1888. Note to Second Edition.]

"The astronomical and physical elements are too obvious to be mistaken. Osiris and Isis are the Nile and Egypt. The myth of Osiris typifies the solar year—the power of Osiris is the sun in the lower hemisphere, the winter solstice. The birth of Horus typifies the vernal equinox—the victory of Horus, the summer solstice—the inundation of the Nile. Typhon is the autumnal equinox." *Egypt's Place in Universal History*—BUNSEN, 1st ed. vol. i. p. 437.

"The Egyptians do not all worship the same gods, excepting Isis and Osiris."—HERODOTUS, Book ii.

[1] "These vases, made of alabaster, calcareous stone, porcelain, terra-cotta, and even wood, were destined to hold the soft parts or viscera of the body, embalmed separately and deposited in them. They were four in number, and were made in the shape of the four genii of the Karneter, or Hades, to whom were assigned the four cardinal points of the compass." Birch's *Guide to the First and Second Egyptian Rooms*, 1874, p. 89. See also Birch's *History of Ancient Pottery*, 1873, p. 23 *et seq.*

[2] Thus depicted, he is called "the germinating Osiris." [Note to Second Edition.]

Isis, with outstretched arms, stands at his feet and seems to be calling him back to her embraces. The scene represents, in fact, that supreme moment when Isis pours forth her passionate invocations, and Osiris is resuscitated by virtue of the songs of the divine sisters.[1]

Ill-modelled and ill-cut as they are, there is a clownish naturalness about these little sculptures which lifts them above the conventional dead level of ordinary Ptolemaic work. The figures tell their tale intelligibly. Osiris seems really struggling to rise, and the action of Isis expresses clearly enough the intention of the artist. Although a few heads have been mutilated and the surface of the stone is somewhat degraded, the subjects are by no means in a bad state of preservation. In the accompanying sketches, nothing has been done to improve the defective drawing or repair the broken outlines of the originals. Osiris in one has lost his foot, and in another his face; the hands of Isis are as shapeless as those of a bran doll; and the naïveté of the treatment verges throughout upon caricature. But the interest attaching to them is altogether apart from the way in which they are executed.

And now, returning to the roof, it is pleasant to breathe the fresher air that comes with sunset—to see the island, in shape like an ancient Egyptian shield, lying mapped out beneath one's feet. From here, we look back upon the way we have come, and forward to the way we are going. Northward lies the Cataract—a network of islets with flashes of river between. Southward, the broad current comes on in one smooth, glassy sheet, unbroken by a single rapid. How eagerly we turn our eyes that way; for yonder lie Abou Simbel and all the mysterious lands beyond the Cataracts! But we cannot see far, for the river curves away grandly to the right, and vanishes behind a range of granite hills. A similar chain hems in the opposite bank; while high above the palm-groves fringing the edge of the shore stand two ruined convents on two rocky prominences, like a couple of castles on the Rhine. On the east bank opposite, a few mud houses and a group of superb carob trees mark the site of a village, the

[1] See M. P. J. de Horrack's translation of *The Lamentations of Isis and Nephthys.* RECORDS OF THE PAST, vol. ii. p. 117 *et seq.*

greater part of which lies hidden among palms. Behind this
village opens a vast sand valley, like an arm of the sea from
which the waters have retreated. The old channel along
which we rode the other day went ploughing that way straight
across from Philæ. Last of all, forming the western side of
this fourfold view, we have the island of Biggeh—rugged,
mountainous, and divided from Philæ by so narrow a channel
that every sound from the native village on the opposite steep
is as audible as though it came from the courtyard at our feet.
That village is built in and about the ruins of a tiny Ptolemaic
Temple, of which only a screen and doorway and part of a
small propylon remain. We can see a woman pounding coffee
on the threshold of one of the huts, and some children
scrambling about the rocks in pursuit of a wandering turkey.
Catching sight of us up here on the roof of the Temple, they
come whooping and scampering down to the water-side, and
with shrill cries importune us for backshîsh. Unless the
stream is wider than it looks, one might almost pitch a piastre
into their outstretched hands.

Mr. Hay, it is said, discovered a secret passage of solid
masonry tunnelled under the river from island to island. The
entrance on this side was from a shaft in the Temple of Isis.[1]
We are not told how far Mr. Hay was able to penetrate in the
direction of Biggeh ; but the passage would lead up, most
probably, to the little Temple opposite.

Perhaps the most entirely curious and unaccustomed
features in all this scene are the mountains. They are like
none that any of us have seen in our diverse wanderings.
Other mountains are homogeneous, and thrust themselves up
from below in masses suggestive of primitive disruption and
upheaval. These seem to lie upon the surface foundationless ;
rock loosely piled on rock, boulder on boulder ; like stupendous
cairns, the work of demigods and giants. Here and there, on
shelf or summit, a huge rounded mass, many tons in weight,
hangs poised capriciously. Most of these blocks, I am per-
suaded, would " log," if put to the test.

But for a specimen stone, commend me to yonder amazing

---

[1] *Operations carried on at the Pyramids of Ghizeh*—COL. HOWARD
VYSE, London, 1840, vol. i. p. 63.

monolith down by the water's edge opposite, near the carob
trees and the ferry.　Though but a single block of orange-red
granite, it looks like three ; and the Arabs, seeing in it some
fancied resemblance to an arm-chair, call it Pharaoh's throne.
Rounded and polished by primæval floods, and emblazoned
with royal cartouches of extraordinary size, it seems to have
attracted the attention of pilgrims in all ages.　Kings, conquerors, priests, travellers, have covered it with records of

INSCRIBED MONOLITHIC ROCK, PHILÆ.

victories, of religious festivals, of prayers, and offerings, and
acts of adoration.　Some of these are older by a thousand
years and more than the temples on the island opposite.

Such, roughly summed up, are the fourfold surroundings
of Philæ—the cataract, the river, the desert, the environing
mountains.　The Holy Island—beautiful, lifeless, a thing of
the far past, with all its wealth of sculpture, painting, history,
poetry, tradition—sleeps, or seems to sleep, in the midst.

It is one of the world's famous landscapes, and it deserves
its fame.　Every sketcher sketches it ; every traveller describes

it. Yet it is just one of those places of which the objective and subjective features are so equally balanced that it bears putting neither into words nor colours. The sketcher must perforce leave out the atmosphere of association which informs his subject; and the writer's description is at best no better than a catalogue raisonnée.

CHAPTER XIII.

PHILÆ TO KOROSKO.

SAILING gently southward—the river opening wide before us, Philæ dwindling in the rear—we feel that we are now fairly over the border; and that if Egypt was strange and far from home, Nubia is stranger and farther still. The Nile here flows deep and broad. The rocky heights that hem it in so close on either side are still black on the one hand, golden on the other. The banks are narrower than ever. The space in some places is little wider than a towing-path. In others, there is barely room for a belt of date-palms and a slip of alluvial soil, every foot of which produces its precious growth of durra or barley. The steep verge below is green with lentils to the water's edge. As the river recedes, it leaves each day a margin of fresh, wet soil, in which the careful husbandman hastens to scratch a new furrow and sow another line of seeds. He cannot afford to let so much as an inch of that kindly mud lie idle.

Gliding along with half-filled sail, we observe how entirely the population seems to be regulated by the extent of arable soil. Where the inundation has room to spread, villages come thicker; more dusky figures are seen moving to and fro in the shade of the palms; more children race along the banks, shrieking for backshîsh. When the shelf of soil is narrowed, on the contrary, to a mere fringe of luminous green dividing the rock from the river, there is a startling absence of everything like life. Mile after mile drags its slow length along, uncheered by any sign of human habitation. When now and

then a solitary native, armed with gun or spear, is seen striding
along the edge of the desert, he only seems to make the
general solitude more apparent.

Meanwhile, it is not only men and women whom we miss
—men labouring by the river-side ; women with babies astride
on their shoulders, or water-jars balanced on their heads—
but birds, beasts, boats ; everything that we have been used
to see along the river. The buffaloes dozing at midday in
the shallows, the camels stalking home in single file towards
sunset, the water-fowl haunting the sandbanks, seem suddenly
to have vanished. Even donkeys are now rare ; and as for
horses, I do not remember to have seen one during the seven
weeks we spent in Nubia. All night, too, instead of the usual
chorus of dogs barking furiously from village to village, we
hear only the long-drawn wail of an occasional jackal. It is
not wonderful, however, that animal life should be scarce in a
district where the scant soil yields barely food enough for those
who till it. To realise how very scant it is, one needs only
to remember that about Derr, where it is at its widest, the
annual deposit nowhere exceeds half-a-mile in breadth ; while
for the most part of the way between Philæ and Wady Halfeh
—a distance of 210 miles—it averages from six to sixty
yards.

Here, then, more than ever, one seems to see how entirely
these lands which we call Egypt and Nubia are nothing but
the banks of one solitary river in the midst of a world of
desert. In Egypt, the valley is often so wide that one forgets
the stony waste beyond the corn-lands. But in Nubia, the
desert is ever present. We cannot forget it, if we would.
The barren mountains press upon our path, showering down
avalanches of granite on the one side and torrents of yellow
sand on the other. We know that those stones are always
falling ; that those sands are always drifting ; that the river
has hard work to hold its own ; and that the desert is silently
encroaching day by day.

These golden sand-streams are the newest and most
beautiful feature in the landscape. They pour down from the
high level of the Libyan desert just as the snows of Switzer-
land pour down from the upper plateaux of the Alps. Through

every ravine and gap they find a channel—here trickling in tiny rivulets ; flowing yonder in broad torrents that widen to the river.

Becalmed a few miles above Philæ, we found ourselves at the foot of one of these largest drifts. The M. B.'s challenged us to climb the slope, and see the sunset from the desert. It was about six o'clock, and the thermometer was standing at 80° in the coolest corner of the large saloon. We ventured to suggest that the top was a long way up ; but the M. B.'s would take no refusal. So away we went ; panting, breathless, bewailing our hard fate. L. and the Writer had done some difficult walking in their time, over ice and snow, on lava cold and hot, up cinder-slopes and beds of mountain torrents ; but this innocent-looking sand-drift proved quite as hard to climb as any of them. The sand lies wonderfully loose and light, and is as hot as if it had been baked in an oven. Into this the foot plunges ankle-deep, slipping back at every step, and leaving a huge hole into which the sand pours down again like water. Looking back, you trace your course by a succession of funnel-shaped pits, each larger than a wash-hand basin. Though your slipper be as small as Cinderella's, the next comer shall not be able to tell whether it was a lady who went up last, or a camel. It is toilsome work, too ; for the foot finds neither rest nor resistance, and the strain upon the muscles is unremitting.

But the beauty of the sand more than repays the fatigue of climbing it. Smooth, sheeny, satiny ; fine as diamond-dust ; supple, undulating, luminous, it lies in the most exquisite curves and wreaths, like a snow-drift turned to gold. Re-modelled by every breath that blows, its ever-varying surface presents an endless play of delicate lights and shadows. There lives not the sculptor who could render those curves ; and I doubt whether Turner himself, in his tenderest and subtlest mood, could have done justice to those complex greys and ambers.

Having paused to rest upon an out-cropping ledge of rock about half-way up, we came at length to the top of the last slope and found ourselves on the level of the desert. Here, faithful to the course of the river, the first objects to meet our eyes were the old familiar telegraph-posts and wires. Beyond them, to north and south, a crowd of peaks closed in the view ; but westward, a rolling waste of hillock and hollow opened away to where the sun, a crimson globe, had already half-vanished below the rim of the world.

One could not resist going a few steps farther, just to touch the nearest of those telegraph posts. It was like reaching out a hand towards home.

When the sun dropped, we turned back. The valley below was already steeped in dusk. The Nile, glimmering like a coiled snake in the shade, reflected the evening sky in three separate reaches. On the Arabian side, a far-off mountain-chain stood out, purple and jagged, against the eastern horizon.

To come down was easy. Driving our heels well into the sand, we half ran, half glissaded, and soon reached the bottom. Here we were met by an old Nubian woman, who had trudged up in all haste from the nearest village to question our sailors about one Yûsef, her son, of whom she had heard nothing for nearly a year. She was a very poor old woman—a widow—and this Yûsef was her only son. Hoping to better himself, he had worked his passage to Cairo in a cargo-boat some eighteen months ago. Twice since then he had sent her messages and money ; but now eleven months had gone by in silence, and she feared he must be dead. Meanwhile her date-palm, taxed to the full value of its produce, had this year yielded not a piastre of profit. Her mud-hut had fallen in, and there was no Yûsef to repair it. Old and sick, she now could only beg ; and her neighbours, by whose charity she subsisted, were but a shade less poor than herself.

Our men knew nothing of the missing Yûsef. Reïs Hassan promised when he went back to make inquiries among the boatmen of Boulak : " But then," he added, " there are so many Yûsefs in Cairo ! "

It made one's heart ache to see the tremulous eagerness with which the poor soul put her questions, and the crushed look in her face when she turned away.

And now, being fortunate in respect of the wind, which for the most part blows steadily from the north between sunrise and sunset, we make good progress, and for the next ten days live pretty much on board our dahabeeyah. The main features of the landscape go on repeating themselves with but little variation from day to day. The mountains wear their habitual livery of black and gold. The river, now widening, now narrowing, flows between banks blossoming with lentils and lupins. With these, and yellow acacia-tufts, and blue castor-oil berries, and the weird coloquintida, with its downy leaf and milky juice and puff-bladder fruit, like a green peach tinged with purple, we make our daily bouquet for the dinner-table. All other flowers have vanished, and even these are hard to get in a land where every green blade is precious to the grower.

Now, too, the climate becomes sensibly warmer. The heat of the sun is so great at midday that, even with the north breeze blowing, we can no longer sit on deck between twelve and three. Towards sundown, when the wind drops, it turns so sultry that to take a walk on shore comes to be regarded as a duty rather than as a pleasure. Thanks, however, to that indomitable Painter who is always ready for an afternoon excursion, we do sometimes walk for an hour before dinner ; striking off generally into the desert ; looking for onyxes and carnelians among the pebbles that here and there strew the surface of the sand, and watching in vain for jackals and desert-hares.

Sometimes we follow the banks instead of the desert, coming now and then to a creaking Sakkieh turned by a melancholy buffalo ; or to a native village hidden behind dwarf-palms. Here each hut has its tiny forecourt, in the midst of which stand the mud-oven and mud-cupboard of the family — two dumpy cones of smooth grey clay, like big chimney-pots—the one capped with a lid, the other fitted with a little wooden door and wooden bolt. Some of the houses have a barbaric ornament palmed off, so to say, upon the walls ; the pattern being simply the impression of a human hand dipped in red or yellow ochre, and applied while the surface is moist.

The amount of " bazaar " that takes place whenever we enter one of these villages, is quite alarming. The dogs first give notice of our approach ; and presently we are surrounded by all the women and girls of the place, offering live pigeons, eggs, vegetable marrows, necklaces, nose - rings and silver bracelets for sale. The boys pester us to buy wretched half-dead chameleons. The men stand aloof, and leave the bargaining to the women.

And the women not only know how to bargain, but how to assess the relative value of every coin that passes current on the Nile. Rupees, roubles, reyals, dollars and shillings are as intelligible to them as paras or piastres. Sovereigns are not too heavy nor napoleons too light for them. The times are changed since Belzoni's Nubian, after staring contemptuously at the first piece of money he had ever seen, asked " Who would give anything for that small piece of metal ? "

The necklaces consist of onyx, carnelian, bone, silver, and coloured glass beads, with now and then a stray scarab or amulet in the ancient blue porcelain. The arrangement of colour is often very subtle. The brow - pendants in gold repoussée, and the massive old silver bracelets, rough with knobs and bosses, are most interesting in design, and perpetuate patterns of undoubted antiquity. The M. B.'s picked up one really beautiful collarette of silver and coral, which might have been worn three thousand years ago by Pharaoh's daughter.

When on board, we begin now to keep a sharp look-out for crocodiles. We hear of them constantly—see their tracks upon the sand-banks in the river—go through agonies of expectation over every black speck in the distance ; yet are perpetually disappointed. The farther south we go, the more impatient we become. The E.'s, whose dahabeeyah, homeward-bound, drifts slowly past one calm morning, report "eleven beauties," seen all together yesterday upon a sand island, some ten miles higher up. Mr. C. B.'s boat, garlanded with crocodiles from stem to stern, fills us with envy. We would give our ears (almost) to see one of these engaging reptiles dangling from either our own mainmast, or that of the faithful Bagstones. Alfred, who has set his heart on bagging at least half-a-dozen, says nothing, but grows gloomier day by day. At night, when the moon is up and less misanthropic folk are in bed and asleep, he rambles moodily into the desert, after jackals.

Meanwhile, on we go, starting at sunrise ; mooring at

sunset ; sailing, tracking, punting ; never stopping for an hour
by day, if we can help it ; and pushing straight for Abou
Simbel with as little delay as possible.   Thus we pass the
pylons of Dabôd with their background of desert ; Gertássee,
a miniature Sunium, seen towards evening against the glowing
sunset ; Tafah, rich in palms, with white columns gleaming
through green foliage by the water-side ; the cliffs, islands, and
rapids of Kalabsheh, and the huge Temple which rises like a
fortress in their midst ; Dendûr, a tiny chapel with a single
pylon ; and Gerf Hossayn, which from this distance might be
taken for the mouth of a rock-cut tomb in the face of the
precipice.

About half way between Kalabsheh and Dendûr, we
enter the Tropic of Cancer.   From this day till the day when
we repass that invisible boundary, there is a marked change
in the atmospheric conditions under which we live.   The days
get gradually hotter, especially at noon, when the sun is almost
vertical ; but the freshness of night and the chill of early
morning are no more.   Unless when a strong wind blows from
the north, we no longer know what it is to need a shawl on
deck in the evening, or an extra covering on our beds towards
dawn.   We sleep with our cabin-windows open, and enjoy a
delicious equality of temperature from sundown to sunrise.
The days and nights, too, are of almost equal length.

Now, also, the Southern Cross and a second group of stars,
which we conclude must form part of the Centaur, are visible
between two and four every morning.   They have been creeping up, a star at a time, for the last fortnight ; but are still so
low upon the eastern horizon that we can only see them when
there comes a break in the mountain-chain on that side of the
river.   At the same time, our old familiar friends of the
northern hemisphere, looking strangely distorted and out of
their proper place, are fast disappearing on the opposite side
of the heavens.   Orion seems to be lying on his back, and the
Great Bear to be standing on his tail ; while Cassiopeia and a
number of others have deserted *en masse*.   The zenith, meanwhile, is but thinly furnished ; so that we seem to have
travelled away from the one hemisphere, and not yet to have
reached the other.   As for the Southern Cross, we reserve our

opinion till we get farther south. It would be treason to hint that we are disappointed in so famous a constellation.

After Gerf Hossayn, the next place of importance for which our maps bid us look out is Dakkeh. As we draw near, expecting hourly to see something of the Temple, the Nile increases in breadth and beauty. It is a peaceful, glassy morning. The men have been tracking since dawn, and stop to breakfast at the foot of a sandy bank, wooded with tamarisks and gum-trees. A glistening network of gossamer floats from bough to bough. The sky overhead is of a tender luminous blue, such as we never see in Europe. The air is wonderfully still. The river, which here takes a sudden bend towards the east, looks like a lake, and seems to be barred ahead by the desert. Presently a funeral passes along the opposite bank ; the chief mourner flourishing a long staff, like a drum-major ; the women snatching up handfuls of dust, and scattering it upon their heads. We hear their wild wail long after the procession is out of sight.

TEMPLE OF DAKKEH, NUBIA.

Going on again presently, our whole attention becomes absorbed by the new and singular geological features of the Libyan desert. A vast plain covered with isolated mountains of volcanic structure, it looks like some strange transformation of the Puy de Dôme plateau, with all its wind-swept pastures turned to sand, and its grassy craters stripped to barrenness. The more this plain widens out before our eyes, the more it bristles with peaks. As we round the corner, and Dakkeh, like a smaller Edfû, comes into sight upon the western bank, the whole desert on that side, as far as the eye can see, presents the unmistakable aspect of one vast field of volcanoes. As in Auvergne, these cones are of all sizes and heights ; some low and rounded, like mere bubbles that have cooled without bursting ; others ranging apparently from 1000 to 1500 feet in height. The broken craters of several are plainly distinguishable by the help of a field-glass. One in particular is so like our old friend the Puy de Pariou, that in a mere black-and-white sketch, the one might readily be mistaken for the other.

We were surprised to find no account of the geology of this district in any of our books. Murray and Wilkinson pass it in silence ; and writers of travels—one or two of whom notice only the "pyramidal" shape of the hills—are for the most part content to do likewise. None seem to have observed their obvious volcanic origin.

Thanks to a light breeze that sprang up in the afternoon, we were able to hoist our big sail again, and to relieve the men from tracking. Thus we glided past the ruins of Maharrakeh, which, seen from the river, looked like a Greek portico set in a hollow waste of burning desert. Next came Wady Sabooah, a temple half buried in sand, near which we met a tiny dahabeeyah, manned by two Nubians and flying the star and crescent. A shabby Government Inspector, in European dress and a fez, lay smoking on a mat outside his cabin door ; while from a spar overhead there hung a mighty crocodile. This monster was of a greenish brown colour, and measured at least sixteen feet from head to tail. His jaws yawned ; and one fat and flabby arm and ponderous paw swung with the motion of the boat, looking horribly human.

The Painter, with an eye to foregrounds, made a bid for him on the spot ; but the shabby Inspector was not to be moved by considerations of gain. He preferred his crocodile to infidel gold, and scarcely deigned even to reply to the offer.

Seen in the half-light of a tropical afterglow—the purple mountains coming down in detached masses to the water's edge on the one side ; the desert with its volcanic peaks yet rosy upon the other—we thought the approach to Korosko more picturesque than anything we had yet seen south of the

Cataract. As the dusk deepened, the moon rose ; and the palms that had just room to grow between the mountains and the river turned from bronze to silver. It was half-twilight, half-moonlight, by the time we reached the mooring-place where Talhamy, who had been sent forward in the small boat half an hour ago, jumped on board laden with a packet of letters, and a sheaf of newspapers. For here, where the great caravan-route leads off across the desert to Khartûm, we touched the first Nubian post-office. It was only ten days since we had received our last budget at Assûan ; but it seemed like ten weeks.

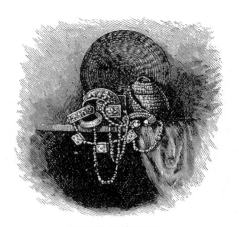

NUBIAN JEWELLERY.

CHAPTER XIV.

KOROSKO TO ABOU SIMBEL.

IT so happened that we arrived at Korosko on the eve of El-'Id el-Kebîr, or the anniversary of the Sacrifice of Abraham; when, according to the Moslem version, Ishmael was the intended victim, and a ram the substituted offering. Now El-'Id el-Kebîr, being one of the great Feasts of the Mohammedan Kalendar, is a day of gifts and good wishes. The rich visit their friends and distribute meat to the poor; and every true believer goes to the mosque to say his prayers in the morning. So, instead of starting as usual at sunrise, we treated our sailors to a sheep, and waited till past noon, that they might make holiday.

They began the day by trooping off to the village mosque in all the glory of new blue blouses, spotless turbans, and scarlet leather slippers; then loitered about till dinner-time, when the said sheep, stewed with lentils and garlic, brought the festivities to an end. It was a thin and ancient beast, and must have been horribly tough; but an epicure might have envied the child-like enjoyment with which our honest fellows squatted, cross-legged and happy, round the smoking cauldron; chattering, laughing, feasting; dipping their fingers in the common mess; washing the whole down with long draughts of Nile water; and finishing off with a hubble-bubble passed from lip to lip, and a mouthful of muddy coffee. By a little after midday they had put off their finery, harnessed themselves to the tow-rope, and set to work to haul us through the rocky shoals which here impede the current.

From Korosko to Derr, the actual distance is about eleven miles and a half ; but what with obstructions in the bed of the river, and what with a wind that would have been favourable but for another great bend which the Nile takes towards the east, those eleven miles and a half cost us the best part of two days' hard tracking.

Landing from time to time when the boat was close in shore, we found the order of planting everywhere the same, lupins and lentils on the slope against the water-line ; an uninterrupted grove of palms on the edge of the bank ; in the space beyond, fields of cotton and young corn ; and then the desert. The arable soil was divided off, as usual, by hundreds of water channels ; and seemed to be excellently farmed as well as abundantly irrigated. Not a weed was to be seen ; not an inch of soil appeared to be wasted. In odd corners where there was room for nothing else, cucumbers and vegetable-marrows flourished and bore fruit. Nowhere had we seen castor-berries so large, cotton-pods so full, or palms so lofty.

Here also, for the first time out of Egypt, we observed among the bushes a few hoopoes and other small birds ; and on a sand-slope down by the river, a group of wild-ducks. We—that is to say, one of the M. B.'s and the Writer—had wandered off that way in search of crocodiles. The two dahabeeyahs, each with its file of trackers, were slowly labouring up against the current about a mile away. All was intensely hot, and intensely silent. We had walked far, and had seen no crocodile. What we should have done if we had met one, I am not prepared to say. Perhaps we should have run away. At all events, we were just about to turn back when we caught sight of the ducks sunning themselves, half-asleep, on the brink of a tiny pool about an eighth of a mile away.

Creeping cautiously under the bank, we contrived to get within a few yards of them. They were four—a drake, a duck, and two young ones—exquisitely feathered, and as small as teal. The parent-birds could scarcely have measured more than eight inches from head to tail. All alike had chestnut coloured heads with a narrow buff stripe down the middle, like a parting ; maroon backs ; wing-feathers maroon and grey ; and tails tipped with buff. They were so pretty, and the little family party was so complete, that the Writer could not help secretly rejoicing that Alfred and his gun were safe on board the Bagstones.

High above the Libyan bank on the sloping verge of the desert, stands, half-drowned in sand, the little Temple of Amada. Seeing it from the opposite side while duck-hunting in the morning, I had taken it for one of the many stone shelters erected by Mohammed Ali for the accommodation of cattle levied annually in the Sûdan. It proved, however, to be a temple, small but massive ; built with squared blocks of sandstone ; and dating back to the very old times of the Usurtesens and Thothmes. It consists of a portico, a transverse atrium, and three small chambers. The pillars of the portico are mere square piers. The rooms are small and low. The roof, constructed of oblong blocks, is flat from end to end. As an architectural structure it is in fact but a few degrees removed from Stonehenge.

A shed without, this little temple is, however, a cameo within. Nowhere, save in the tomb of Ti, had we seen basreliefs so delicately modelled, so rich in colour. Here, as elsewhere, the walls are covered with groups of Kings and Gods and hieroglyphic texts. The figures are slender and animated. The head-dresses, jewellery, and patterned robes are elaborately drawn and painted. Every head looks like a portrait ; every hieroglyphic form is a study in miniature.

Apart from its exquisite finish, the wall-sculpture of Amada has, however, nothing in common with the wall-sculpture of the Ancient Empire. It belongs to the period of Egyptian Renaissance ; and, though inferior in power and naturalness to the work of the elder school, it marks just that moment of special development when the art of modelling in low relief had touched the highest level to which it ever again attained. That highest level belongs to the reigns of Thothmes the Second and Thothmes the Third ; just as the perfect era in architecture belongs to the reigns of Seti the First and Rameses the Second. It is for this reason that Amada is so precious. It registers an epoch in the history of the art, and gives us the best of that epoch in the hour of its zenith. The sculptor is here seen to be working within bounds already prescribed ; yet within those bounds he still enjoys a certain liberty. His art, though largely conventionalised, is not yet stereotyped. His sense of beauty still finds expression. There is, in short, a grace and sweetness about the bas-relief designs of Amada for which one looks in vain to the storied walls of Karnak.

The chambers are half-choked with sand, and we had to crawl into the sanctuary upon our hands and knees. A long inscription at the upper end records how Amenhotep the Second, returning from his first campaign against the Ruten, slew seven kings with his own hand ; six of whom were gibbeted upon the ramparts of Thebes, while the body of the seventh was sent to Ethiopia by water and suspended on the outer wall of the city of Napata,[1] " in order that the negroes might behold the victories of the Pharaoh in all the lands of the world."

In the darkest corner of the atrium we observed a curious tableau representing the King embraced by a Goddess. He holds a short straight sword in his right hand, and the crux ansata in his left. On his head he wears the khepersh, or war-helmet ; a kind of a blue mitre studded with gold stars and ornamented with the royal asp. The Goddess clasps him lovingly about the neck, and bends her lips to his. The artist has given her the yellow complexion conventionally ascribed to women ; but her saucy mouth and nez retroussé are distinctly European. Dressed in the fashion of the nineteenth century, she might have served Leech as a model for his Girl of the Period.

The sand has drifted so high at the back of the Temple, that one steps upon the roof as upon a terrace only just raised above the level of the desert. Soon that level will be equal ; and if nothing is done to rescue it within the next generation or two, the whole building will become engulfed, and its very site be forgotten.

---

[1] A city of Ethiopia, identified with the ruins at Gebel Barkal. The worship of Amen was established at Napata towards the end of the XXth Dynasty, and it was from the priests of Thebes who settled at that time in Napata, that the Ethiopian conquerors of Egypt (XXIIIrd Dynasty) were descended.

The view from the roof, looking back towards Korosko and forward towards Derr, is one of the finest—perhaps quite the finest—in Nubia. The Nile curves grandly through the foreground. The palm-woods of Derr are green in the distance. The mountain region which we have just traversed ranges, a vast crescent of multitudinous peaks, round two-thirds of the horizon. Ridge beyond ridge, chain beyond chain, flushing crimson in light and deepening through every tint of amethyst and purple in shadow, those innumerable summits fade into tenderest blue upon the horizon. As the sun sets, they seem to glow ; to become incandescent ; to be touched with flame— as in the old time when every crater was a fount of fire.

Struggling next morning through a maze of sand-banks, we reached Derr soon after breakfast. This town—the Nubian capital—lies a little lower than the level of the bank, so that only a few mud walls are visible from the river. Having learned by this time that a capital town is but a bigger village, containing perhaps a mosque and a market-place, we were not disappointed by the unimposing aspect of the Nubian metropolis.

Great, however, was our surprise when, instead of the usual clamorous crowd screaming, pushing, scrambling, and bothering for backsheesh, we found the landing-place deserted. Two or three native boats lay up under the bank, empty. There was literally not a soul in sight. L. and the Little Lady, eager to buy some of the basket-work for which the place is famous, looked blank. Talhamy, anxious to lay in a store of fresh eggs and vegetables, looked blanker.

We landed. Before us lay an open space, at the farther end of which, facing the river, stood the Governor's palace ; the said palace being a magnified mud hut, with a frieze of baked bricks round the top, and an imposing stone doorway. In this doorway, according to immemorial usage, the great man gives audience. We saw him—a mere youth, apparently— puffing away at a long chibouque, in the midst of a little group of greybeard elders. They looked at us gravely, immovably ; like smoking automata. One longed to go up and ask them if they were all transformed to black granite from the waists to the feet, and if the inhabitants of Derr had been changed into blue stones.

Still bent on buying baskets, if baskets were to be bought, —bent also on finding out the whereabouts of a certain rock-cut temple which our books told us to look for at the back of the town, we turned aside into a straggling street leading towards the desert. The houses looked better built than usual ; some pains having evidently been bestowed in smoothing the surface of the mud, and ornamenting the doorways with fragments of coloured pottery. A cracked willow-pattern dinner-plate set like a fanlight over one, and a white soup-plate over another, came doubtless from the canteen of some English dahabeeyah, and were the pride of their possessors. Looking from end to end of this street—and it was a tolerably long one, with the Nile at one end, and the desert at the other—we saw no sign or shadow of moving creature. Only one young woman, hearing strange voices talking a strange tongue, peeped out suddenly from a half-opened door as we went by ; then, seeing me look at the baby in her arms (which was hideous and had sore eyes) drew her veil across its face, and darted back again. She thought I coveted her treasure, and she dreaded the Evil Eye.

All at once we heard a sound like the far-off quivering cry of many owls. It shrilled—swelled—wavered—dropped—then died away, like the moaning of the wind at sea. We held our breath and listened. We had never heard anything so wild and plaintive. Then suddenly, through an opening between the houses, we saw a great crowd on a space of rising ground about a quarter of a mile away. This crowd consisted of men only—a close, turbaned mass some three or four hundred in number ; all standing quite still and silent ; all looking in the same direction.

Hurrying on to the desert, we saw the strange sight at which they were looking.

The scene was a barren sandslope hemmed in between the town and the cliffs, and dotted over with graves. The actors were all women. Huddled together under a long wall some few hundred yards away, bareheaded, and exposed to the blaze of the morning sun, they outnumbered the men by a full third. Some were sitting, some standing ; while in their midst, pressing round a young woman who seemed to act as leader, there swayed and circled and shuffled a compact phalanx of dancers. Upon this young woman the eyes of all were turned. A black Cassandra, she rocked her body from side to side, clapped her hands above her head, and poured forth a wild declamatory chant, which the rest echoed. This chant seemed to be divided into strophes, at the end of each of which she paused, beat her breast, and broke into that terrible wail that we had heard just now from a distance.

Her brother, it seemed, had died last night; and we were witnessing his funeral.

The actual interment was over by the time we reached the spot; but four men were still busy filling the grave with sand, which they scraped up, a bowlful at a time, and stamped down with their naked feet.

The deceased being unmarried, his sister led the choir of mourners. She was a tall, gaunt young woman of the plainest Nubian type, with high cheekbones, eyes slanting upwards at the corners, and an enormous mouth full of glittering teeth. On her head she wore a white cloth smeared with dust. Her companions were distinguished by a narrow white fillet, bound about the brow, and tied with two long ends behind. They had hidden their necklaces and bracelets, and wore trailing robes and shawls, and loose trousers of black or blue calico.

We stood for a long time watching their uncouth dance. None of the women seemed to notice us; but the men made way civilly and gravely, letting us pass to the front, that we might get a better view of the ceremony.

By and by an old woman rose slowly from the midst of those who were sitting, and moved with tottering uncertain steps towards a higher point of ground, a little apart from the crowd. There was a movement of compassion among the men; one of whom turned to the Writer and said gently : " His mother."

She was a small, feeble old woman, very poorly clad. Her hands and arms were like the hands and arms of a mummy, and her withered black face looked ghastly under its mask of dust. For a few moments, swaying her body slowly to and fro, she watched the gravediggers stamping down the sand ; then stretched out her arms, and broke into a torrent of lamentations. The dialect of Derr [1] is strange and barbarous ; but we felt as if we understood every word she uttered. Presently the tears began to make channels down her cheeks—her voice became choked with sobs—and falling down in a sort of helpless heap, like a broken-hearted dog, she lay with her face to the ground, and there stayed.

Meanwhile, the sand being now filled in and mounded up, the men betook themselves to a place where the rock had given way, and selected a couple of big stones from the débris. These they placed at the head and foot of the grave ; and all was done.

Instantly—perhaps at an appointed signal, though we saw none given—the wailing ceased ; the women rose ; every tongue was loosened ; and the whole became a moving, animated, noisy throng dispersing in a dozen different directions.

We turned away with the rest, the Writer and the Painter rambling off in search of the temple, while the other three devoted themselves to the pursuit of baskets and native jewellery. When we looked back presently, the crowd was gone ; but the desolate mother still lay motionless in the dust.

It chanced that we witnessed many funerals in Nubia ; so many that one sometimes felt inclined to doubt whether the Governor of Assûan had not reported over-favourably of the health of the province. The ceremonial, with its dancing and chanting, was always much the same ; always barbaric, and in the highest degree artificial. One would like to know how much of it is derived from purely African sources, and how much from ancient Egyptian tradition. The dance is most probably Ethiopian. Lepsius, travelling through the Sûdan in A.D. 1844,[2] saw something of the kind at a funeral in Wed Medineh, about half-way between Sennaar and Khartûm. The white fillet worn by the choir of mourners is, on the other hand, distinctly Egyptian. We afterwards saw it represented in paintings of funeral processions on the walls of several tombs

---

[1] The men hereabout can nearly all speak Arabic ; but the women of Nubia know only the Kensee and Berberee tongues, the first of which is spoken as far as Korosko.

[2] Lepsius's *Letters from Egypt, Ethiopia*, etc., Letter xviii. p. 184. Bohn's ed. A.D. 1853.

at Thebes,[1] where the wailing women are seen to be gathering
up the dust in their hands and casting it upon their heads, just
as they do now.   As for the wail—beginning high, and descending through a scale divided, not by semi-tones, but thirds of
tones, to a final note about an octave and a half lower than
that from which it started—it probably echoes to this day the
very pitch and rhythm of the wail that followed the Pharaohs
to their sepulchres in the Valley of the Tombs of the Kings.
Like the zaghareet, or joy-cry, which every mother teaches to
her little girls, and which, it is said, can only be acquired in
very early youth, it has been handed down from generation to
generation through an untold succession of ages.   The song to
which the Fellâh works his shâdûf, and the monotonous chant
of the sakkieh-driver, have perhaps as remote an origin.   But
of all old, mournful, human sounds, the death-wail that we
heard at Derr is perhaps one of the very oldest—certainly the
most mournful.

The Temple here, dating from the reign of Rameses II, is
of rude design and indifferent execution.   Partly constructed,
partly excavated, it is approached by a forecourt, the roof of
which was supported by eight square columns.   Of these
columns only the bases remain.   Four massive piers against
which once stood four colossi, upheld the roof of the portico
and gave admission by three entrances to the rock-cut chambers
beyond.   That portico is now roofless.   Nothing is left of the
colossi but their feet.   All is ruin ; and ruin without beauty.

Seen from within, however, the place is not without a kind
of gloomy grandeur.   Two rows of square columns, three at each
side, divide the large hall into a nave and two aisles.   This hall
is about forty feet square, and the pillars have been left standing
in the living rock, like those in the early tombs at Siût.   The
daylight, half blocked out by the fallen portico, is pleasantly
subdued, and finds its way dimly to the sanctuary at the farther
end.   The sculptures of the interior, though much damaged,
are less defaced than those of the outer court.   Walls, pillars,
doorways, are covered with bas-reliefs.   The King and Ptah,

---

[1] See the interesting account of funereal rites and ceremonies in Sir
G. Wilkinson's *Ancient Egyptians*, vol. ii. ch. x., Lond. 1871.   Also wood-
cuts Nos. 493 and 494 in the same chapter of the same work.

the King and Ra, the King and Amen, stand face to face,
hand in hand, on each of the four sides of every column.
Scenes of worship, of slaughter, of anointing, cover the walls ;
and the blank spaces are filled in as usual with hieroglyphic
inscriptions. Among these Champollion discovered an imper-
fect list of the sons and daughters of Rameses the Second.

TEMPLE OF DERR, NUBIA.

Four gods once sat enthroned at the upper end of the sanctuary ;
but they have shared the fate of the colossi outside, and only
their feet remain. The wall sculptures of this dark little
chamber are, however, better preserved, and better worth preservation, than those of the hall. A procession of priests,
bearing on their shoulders the bari, or sacred boat, is quite
unharmed ; and even the colour is yet fresh upon a full-length
figure of Hathor close by.

But more interesting than all these—more interesting
because more rare—is a sculptured palm-tree against which the
king leans while making an offering to Amen-Ra. The trunk
is given with elaborate truthfulness ; and the branches, though

formalised, are correct and graceful in curvature.   The tree is but an accessory.   It may have been introduced with reference to the date-harvests which are the wealth of the district ; but it has no kind of sacred significance, and is noticeable only for the naturalness of the treatment.   Such naturalness is unusual in the art of this period, when the conventional persea, and the equally conventional lotus are almost the only vegetable forms which appear on the walls of the Temples.   I can recall, indeed, but one similar instance in the bas-relief sculpture of the New Empire—namely, the bent, broken, and waving bulrushes in the great lion-hunting scene at Medinet Habu, which are admirably free, and studied apparently from nature.

Coming out, we looked in vain along the courtyard walls for the battle-scene in which Champollion was yet able to trace the famous fighting lion of Rameses the Second, with the legend describing him as " the Servant of His Majesty rending his foes in pieces."   But that was forty-five years ago.   Now it·is with difficulty that one detects a few vague outlines of chariot-wheels and horses.

There are some rock-cut tombs in the face of the cliffs close by.   The Painter explored them while the Writer sketched the interior of the Temple ; but he reported of them as mere sepulchres, unpainted and unsculptured.

The rocks, the sands, the sky, were at a white heat when we again turned our faces towards the river.   Where there had so lately been a great multitude there was now not a soul. The palms nodded ; the pigeons dozed ; the mud town slept in the sun.   Even the mother had gone from her place of weeping, and left her dead to the silence of the desert.

We went and looked at his grave.   The fresh-turned sand was only a little darker than the rest, and but for the trampled foot-marks round about, we should scarcely have been able to distinguish the new mound from the old ones.   All were alike nameless.   Some, more cared for than the rest, were bordered with large stones and filled in with variegated pebbles.   One or two were fenced about with a mud wall.   All had a bowl of baked clay at the head.   Wherever we saw a burial-ground in Nubia, we saw these bowls upon the graves.   The mourners, they told us, mourn here for forty days ; during which time they come every Friday and fill the bowl with fresh water, that the birds may drink from it. The bowls on the other graves were dry and full of sand ; but the new bowl was brimming full, and the water in it was hot to the touch.

We found L. and the Happy Couple standing at bay with their backs against a big lebbich tree, surrounded by an immense crowd and far from comfortable. Bent on " bazaaring," they had probably shown themselves too ready to buy ; so bringing the whole population, with all the mats, baskets, nose-rings, finger-rings, necklaces and bracelets in the place, about their ears. Seeing the straits they were in, we ran to the dahabeeyah and despatched three or four sailors to the rescue, who brought them off in triumph.

Even in Egypt, it does not answer, as a rule, to go about on shore without an escort. The people are apt to be importunate, and can with difficulty be kept at a pleasant distance. But in Nubia, where the traveller's life was scarcely safe fifty years ago, unprotected Ingleezeh are pretty certain to be disagreeably mobbed. The natives, in truth, are still mere savages *au fond*—the old war-paint being but half disguised under a thin veneer of Mohammedanism.

Some of the women who followed our friends to the boat, though in complexion as black as the rest, had light blue eyes and frizzy red hair, the effect of which was indescribably frightful. Both here and at Ibrim there are many of these " fair " families, who claim to be descended from Bosnian fathers stationed in Nubia at the time of the conquest of Sultan Selim in A.D. 1517. They are immensely proud of their alien blood, and think themselves quite beautiful.

All hands being safe on board, we pushed off at once, leaving about a couple of hundred disconsolate dealers on the bank. A long-drawn howl of disappointment followed in our wake. Those who had sold, and those who had not sold, were alike wronged, ruined, and betrayed. One woman tore wildly along the bank, shrieking and beating her breast. Foremost among the sellers, she had parted from her gold brow-pendant for a good price ; but was inconsolable now for the loss of it.

It often happened that those who had been most eager to trade, were readiest to repent of their bargains. Even so, however, their cupidity outweighed their love of finery. Moved once or twice by the lamentations of some dark damsel who had sold her necklace at a handsome profit, we offered to annul the purchase. But it invariably proved that, despite her tears, she preferred to keep the money.

The palms of Derr and of the rich district beyond, were the finest we saw throughout the journey. Straight and strong and magnificently plumed, they rose to an average height of seventy or eighty feet. These superb plantations supply all Egypt with saplings, and contribute a heavy tax to the revenue. The fruit, sun-dried and shrivelled, is also sent northwards in large quantities.

The trees are cultivated with strenuous industry by the natives, and owe as much of their perfection to laborious irrigation as to climate. The foot of each separate palm is surrounded by a circular trench into which the water is conducted by a small channel about fourteen inches in width. Every palm-grove stands in a network of these artificial runlets. The reservoir from which they are supplied is filled by means of a Sakkieh, or water-wheel—a primitive and picturesque machine consisting of two wheels, the one set vertically to the river and slung with a chain of pots ; the other a horizontal cog turned sometimes by a camel, but more frequently in Nubia by a buffalo. The pots (which go down empty, dip under the water, and come up full) feed a sloping trough which in some places supplies a reservoir, and in others communicates at once with the irrigating channels. These sakkiehs are kept perpetually going ; and are set so close just above Derr, that the Writer counted a line of fifteen within the space of a single mile. There were probably quite as many on the opposite bank.

The sakkiehs creak atrociously ; and their creaking ranges over an unlimited gamut. From morn till dewy eve, from dewy eve till morn, they squeak, they squeal, they grind, they groan, they croak. Heard after dark, sakkieh answering to sakkieh, their melancholy chorus makes night hideous. To sleep through it is impossible. Being obliged to moor a few miles beyond Derr, and having lain awake half the night, we offered a sakkieh-driver a couple of dollars if he would let his wheel rest till morning. But time and water are more precious

than even dollars at this season ; and the man refused. All
we could do, therefore, was to punt into the middle of the river,
and lie off at a point as nearly as possible equidistant from our
two nearest enemies.

SAKKIEH, OR WATER-WHEEL.

The native dearly loves the tree which costs him so much
labour, and thinks it the chef d'œuvre of creation. When Allah
made the first man, says an Arab legend, he found he had a
little clay to spare ; so with that he made the palm. And to
the poor Nubian, at all events, the gifts of the palm are almost
divine ; supplying food for his children, thatch for his hovel,
timber for his water-wheel, ropes, matting, cups, bowls, and
even the strong drink forbidden by the Prophet. The date-

wine is yellowish-white, like whisky.   It is not a wine, however, but a spirit ; coarse, fiery, and unpalatable.

Certain trees—as for instance the perky little pine of the German wald—are apt to become monotonous ; but one never wearies of the palm.   Whether taken singly or in masses, it is always graceful, always suggestive.   To the sketcher on the Nile, it is simply invaluable.   It breaks the long parallels of river and bank, and composes with the stern lines of Egyptian architecture as no other tree in the world could do.

"Subjects indeed !" said once upon a time an eminent artist to the present Writer ; " fiddlesticks about subjects ! Your true painter can make a picture out of a post and a puddle."

Substitute a palm, however, for a post ; combine it with anything that comes first—a camel, a shadoof, a woman with a water-jar upon her head—and your picture stands before you ready made.

Nothing more surprised me at first than the colour of the palm-frond, which painters of eastern landscape are wont to depict of a hard, bluish tint, like the colour of a yucca leaf. Its true shade is a tender, bloomy, sea-green grey ; difficult enough to match, but in most exquisite harmony with the glow of the sky and the gold of the desert.

The palm-groves kept us company for many a mile, backed on the Arabian side by long level ranges of sandstone cliffs horizontally stratified, like those of the Thebaid.   We now scarcely ever saw a village—only palms, and sakkiehs, and sandbanks in the river.   The villages were there, but invisible ; being built on the verge of the desert.   Arable land is too valuable in Nubia for either the living to dwell upon it or the dead to be buried in it.

At Ibrim—a sort of ruined Ehrenbreitstein on the top of a grand precipice overhanging the river—we touched for only a few minutes, in order to buy a very small shaggy sheep which had been brought down to the landing-place for sale.   But for the breeze that happened just then to be blowing, we should have liked to climb the rock, and see the view and the ruins— which are part modern, part Turkish, part Roman, and little, if at all, Egyptian.

There are also some sculptured and painted grottoes to be seen in the southern face of the mountain. They are, however, too difficult of access to be attempted by ladies. Alfred, who went ashore after quail, was drawn up to them by ropes ; but found them so much defaced as to be scarcely worth the trouble of a visit.

We were now only thirty-four miles from Abou Simbel ; but making slow progress, and impatiently counting every foot of the way. The heat at times was great ; frequent and fitful spells of Khamsîn wind alternating with a hot calm that tried the trackers sorely. Still we pushed forward, a few miles at a time, till by and by the flat-topped cliffs dropped out of sight and were again succeeded by volcanic peaks, some of which looked loftier than any of those about Dakkeh or Korosko.

Then the palms ceased, and the belt of cultivated land narrowed to a thread of green between the rocks and the water's edge ; and at last there came an evening when we only wanted breeze enough to double two or three more bends in the river.

"Is it to be Abou Simbel to-night?" we asked, for the twentieth time before going down to dinner.

To which Reïs Hassan replied, "Aiwah" (certainly).

But the pilot shook his head, and added, "Bûkra" (to-morrow).

When we came up again, the moon had risen, but the breeze had dropped. Still we moved, impelled by a breath so faint that one could scarcely feel it. Presently even this failed. The sail collapsed ; the pilot steered for the bank ; the captain gave the word to go aloft—when a sudden puff from the north changed our fortunes, and sent us out again with a well-filled sail into the middle of the river.

None of us, I think, will be likely to forget the sustained excitement of the next three hours. As the moon climbed higher, a light more mysterious and unreal than the light of day filled and overflowed the wide expanse of river and desert. We could see the mountains of Abou Simbel standing as it seemed across our path, in the far distance—a lower one first ; then a larger ; then a series of receding heights, all close together, yet all distinctly separate.

That large one—the mountain of the Great Temple—held us like a spell. For a long time it looked a mere mountain like the rest. By and by, however, we fancied we detected a something—a shadow—such a shadow as might be cast by a gigantic buttress. Next appeared a black speck no bigger than a porthole. We knew that this black speck must be the doorway. We knew that the great statues were there, though not yet visible; and that we must soon see them.

For our sailors, meanwhile, there was the excitement of a chase. The Bagstones and three other dahabeeyahs were coming up behind us in the path of the moonlight. Their galley fires glowed like beacons on the water; the nearest about a mile away, the last a spark in the distance. We were not in the mood to care much for racing to-night; but we were anxious to keep our lead and be first at the mooring-place.

To run upon a sandbank at such a moment was like being plunged suddenly into cold water. Our sail flapped furiously. The men rushed to the punting poles. Four jumped overboard, and shoved with all the might of their shoulders. By the time we got off, however, the other boats. had crept up half a mile nearer; and we had hard work to keep them from pressing closer on our heels.

At length the last corner was rounded, and the Great Temple stood straight before us. The façade, sunk in the mountain-side like a huge picture in a mighty frame, was now quite plain to see. The black speck was no longer a porthole, but a lofty doorway.

Last of all, though it was night and they were still not much less than a mile away, the four colossi came out, ghost-like, vague, and shadowy, in the enchanted moonlight. Even as we watched them, they seemed to grow—to dilate—to be moving towards us out of the silvery distance.

It was drawing on towards midnight when the Philæ at length ran in close under the Great Temple. Content with what they had seen from the river, the rest of the party then went soberly to bed; but the Painter and the Writer had no patience to wait till morning. Almost before the mooring-rope could be made fast, they had jumped ashore and begun climbing the bank.

They went and stood at the feet of the colossi, and on the threshold of that vast portal beyond which was darkness. The great statues towered above their heads. The river glittered like steel in the far distance. There was a keen silence in the air ; and towards the east the Southern Cross was rising. To the strangers who stood talking there with bated breath, the time, the place, even the sound of their own voices, seemed unreal. They felt as if the whole scene must fade with the moonlight, and vanish before morning.

CHAPTER XV.

RAMESES THE GREAT.

THE central figure of Egyptian history has always been, probably always will be, Rameses the Second. He holds this place partly by right, partly by accident. He was born to greatness ; he achieved greatness ; and he had borrowed greatness thrust upon him. It was his singular destiny not only to be made a posthumous usurper of glory, but to be forgotten by his own name and remembered in a variety of aliases. As Sesoosis, as Osymandias, as Sesostris, he became credited in course of time with all the deeds of all the heroes of the new Empire, beginning with Thothmes III, who preceded him by 300 years, and ending with Sheshonk, the captor of Jerusalem, who lived four centuries after him. Modern science, however, has repaired this injustice ; and, while disclosing the long-lost names of a brilliant succession of sovereigns, has enabled us to ascribe to each the honours which are his due. We know now that some of these were greater conquerors than Rameses II. We suspect that some were better rulers. Yet the popular hero keeps his ground. What he has lost by interpretation on the one hand, he has gained by interpretation on the other ; and the *beau sabreur* of the Third Sallier Papyrus remains to this day the representative Pharaoh of a line of monarchs whose history covers a space of fifty centuries, and whose frontiers reached at one time from Mesopotamia to the ends of the Soudan.

The interest that one takes in Rameses II begins at Memphis, and goes on increasing all the way up the river.

It is a purely living, a purely personal interest ; such as one feels in Athens for Pericles, or in Florence for Lorenzo the Magnificent. Other Pharaohs but languidly affect the imagination. Thothmes and Amenhotep are to us as Darius or Artaxerxes —shadows that come and go in the distance. But with the second Rameses we are on terms of respectful intimacy. We seem to know the man—to feel his presence —to hear his name in the air. His features are as familiar to us as those of Henry the Eighth or Louis the Fourteenth. His cartouches meet us at every turn. Even to those who do not read the hieroglyphic character, those well-known signs convey, by sheer force of association, the name and style[1] of Rameses, beloved of Amen.

CARTOUCHES OF RAMESES THE GREAT.

This being so, the traveller is ill equipped who goes through Egypt without something more than a mere guide-book knowledge of Rameses II. He is, as it were, content to read the Argument and miss the Poem. In the desolation of Memphis, in the shattered splendour of Thebes, he sees only the ordinary pathos of ordinary ruins. As for Abou Simbel, the most stupendous historical record ever transmitted from the past to the present, it tells him a but half-intelligible story. Holding to the merest thread of explanation, he wanders from hall to hall, lacking altogether that potent charm of foregone association which no Murray can furnish. Your average Frenchman straying helplessly through Westminster Abbey under the conduct of the verger has about as vague a conception of the historical import of the things he sees.

[1] Rendered thus into Latin by M. Chabas : *Sol dominus veritatis electus a Sole, Sol genuit eum ; amans Ammonem.* Anglice—Sun Lord of Truth, Chosen of the Sun, Son of the Sun, Ammon-loving. The following is an extract translation of the hieroglyphs :—

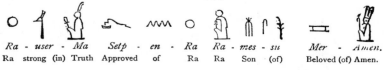

Ra - user - Ma	Setp - en - Ra	Ra - mes - su	Mer - Amen.
Ra strong (in) Truth	Approved of	Ra Ra Son (of)	Beloved (of) Amen.

What is true of the traveller is equally true of those who take their Nile vicariously "in connection with Mudie." If they are to understand any description of Abou Simbel, they must first know something about Rameses II. Let us then, while the Philæ lies moored in the shadow of the rock of Abshek,[1] review, as summarily as may be, the leading facts of this important reign ; such facts, that is to say, as are recorded in inscriptions, papyri, and other contemporary monuments.

Rameses the Second[2] was the son of Seti I, the second Pharaoh of the XIXth Dynasty, and of a certain Princess Tuaa, described on the monuments as "royal wife, royal mother, and heiress and sharer of the throne." She is supposed to have been of the ancient royal line of the preceding dynasty, and so to have had, perhaps, a better right than her husband to the double crown of Egypt. Through her, at all events, Rameses II seems to have been in some sense born a king,[3] equal in rank, if not in power, with his father ; his rights,

---

[1] *Abshek :*—The hieroglyphic name of Abou Simbel. *Gr.* Aboccis.

[2] In the present state of Egyptian chronology, it is hazardous to assign even an approximate date to events which happened before the conquest of Cambyses. The Egyptians, in fact, had no chronology in the strict sense of the word. Being without any fixed point of departure, such as the birth of Christ, they counted the events of each reign from the accession of the sovereign. Under such a system, error and confusion were inevitable. To say when Rameses II was born and when he died is impossible. The very century in which he flourished is uncertain. Mariette, taking the historical lists of Manetho for his basis, supposes the XIXth Dynasty to have occupied the interval comprised within B.C. 1462 and 1288 ; according to which computation (allowing 57 years for the reigns of Rameses I and Seti I) the reign of Rameses II would date from B.C. 1405. Brugsch gives him from B.C. 1407 to B.C. 1341 ; and Lepsius places his reign in the sixty-six years lying between B.C. 1388 and B.C. 1322 ; these calculations being both made before the discovery of the stelâ of Abydos. Bunsen dates his accession from B.C. 1352. Between the highest and the lowest of these calculations there is, as shown by the following table, a difference of 55 years :—

	Rameses II began to reign					B.C.
According to	Brugsch	.	.	.	.	1407
	Mariette	.	.	.	.	1405
	Lepsius	.	.	.	.	1388
	Bunsen	.	.	.	.	1352

[3] See chap. viii. footnote, p. 140.

moreover, were fully recognised by Seti, who accorded him royal and divine honours from the hour of his birth, or, in the language of the Egyptian historians, while he was "yet in the egg." The great dedicatory inscription of the Temple of Osiris at Abydos,[1] relates how his father took the royal child in his arms, when he was yet little more than an infant, showed him to the people as their king, and caused him to be invested by the great officers of the palace with the double crown of the two lands. The same inscription states that he was a general from his birth, and that as a nursling he "commanded the body guard and the brigade of chariot-fighters"; but these titles must of course have been purely honorary. At twelve years of age, he was formally associated with his father upon the throne, and by the gradual retirement of Seti I from the cares of active government, the co-royalty of Rameses became, in the course of the next ten or fifteen years, an undivided responsibility. He was probably about thirty when his father died; and it is from this time that the years of his reign are dated. In other words, Rameses II, in his official records, counts only from the period of his sole reign, and the year of the death of Seti is the "year one" of the monumental inscriptions of his son and successor. In the second, fourth, and fifth years of his monarchy, he personally conducted campaigns in Syria, more than one of the victories then achieved being commemorated on the rock-cut tablets of Nahr-el-Kelb near Beyrût; and that he was by this time recognised as a mighty warrior is shown by the stela of Dakkeh, which dates from the "third year," and celebrates him as terrible in battle—"the bull powerful against Ethiopia, the griffin furious against the negroes, whose grip has put the mountaineers to flight." The events of the campaign of his "fifth year" (undertaken in order to reduce to obedience the revolted tribes of Syria and Mesopotamia) are immortalised in the poem of Pentaur.[2] It was on this occasion that he fought his famous single-handed fight, against overwhelming odds, in the sight of both armies under the walls of Kadesh. Three years

[1] See *Essai sur l'Inscription Dédicatoire du Temple d'Abydos et la Jeunesse de Sesotris.*—G. MASPERO, Paris, 1867.

[2] See chap. viii. p. 139.

later, he carried fire and sword into the land of Canaan, and
in his eleventh year, according to inscriptions yet extant upon
the ruined pylons of the Ramesseum at Thebes, he took,
among other strong places on sea and shore, the fortresses of
Ascalon and Jerusalem.

The next important record transports us to the twenty-first
year of his reign. Ten years have now gone by since the fall
of Jerusalem, during which time a fluctuating frontier warfare
has probably been carried on, to the exhaustion of both armies.
Khetasira, Prince of Kheta,[1] sues for peace. An elaborate treaty
is thereupon framed, whereby the said Prince and "Rameses,
Chief of Rulers, who fixes his frontiers where he pleases," pledge
themselves to a strict offensive and defensive alliance, and to
the maintenance of good-will and brotherhood for ever. This
treaty, we are told, was engraved for the Khetan prince "upon
a tablet of silver adorned with the likeness of the figure of
Sutekh, the Great Ruler of Heaven;" while for Rameses Mer-
Amen it was graven on a wall adjoining the Great Hall at
Karnak,[2] where it remains to this day.

According to the last clause of this curious document, the
contracting parties enter also into an agreement to deliver up
to each other the political fugitives of both countries; providing
at the same time for the personal safety of the offenders.
"Whosoever shall be so delivered up," says the treaty, "himself, his wives, his children, let him not be smitten to death;
moreover, let him not suffer in his eyes, in his mouth, in
his feet; moreover, let not any crime be set up against
him."[3] This is the earliest instance of an extradition treaty

[1] *i.e.* Prince of the Hittites; the Kheta being now identified with that
people.

[2] This invaluable record is sculptured on a piece of wall built out,
apparently for the purpose, at right angles to the south wall of the Hypostyle Hall at Karnak. The treaty faces to the west, and is situate about
half-way between the famous bas-relief of Sheshonk and his captives, and
the Karnak version of the poem of Pentaur. The former lies to the west
of the southern portal; the latter to the east. The wall of the treaty juts
out about sixty feet to the east of the portal. This south wall and its
adjunct, a length of about 200 feet in all, is perhaps the most precious and
interesting piece of sculptured surface in the world.

[3] See *Treaty of Peace between Rameses II and the Hittites*, translated
by C. W. Goodwin, M.A.—RECORDS OF THE PAST, vol. iv. p. 25.

upon record ; and it is chiefly remarkable as an illustration of the clemency with which international law was at that time administered.

Finally, the convention between the sovereigns is placed under the joint protection of the gods of both countries : " Sutekh of Kheta, Amen of Egypt, and all the thousand gods, the gods male and female, the gods of the hills, of the rivers, of the great sea, of the winds and the clouds, of the land of Kheta and of the land of Egypt."

The peace now concluded would seem to have remained unbroken throughout the rest of the long reign of Rameses the Second. We hear, at all events, of no more wars ; and we find the king married presently to a Khetan princess, who in deference to the gods of her adopted country takes the official name of Ma-at-iri-neferu-Ra, or " Contemplating the Beauties of Ra." The names of two other queens—Nefer-t-ari and Ast-nefert—are also found upon the monuments.

These three were probably the only legitimate wives of Rameses II, though he must also have been the lord of an extensive hareem. His family, at all events, as recorded upon the walls of the Temple at Wady Sabooah, amounted to no less than 170 children, of whom 111 were princes. This may have been a small family for a great king three thousand years ago. It was but the other day, comparatively speaking, that Lepsius saw and talked with old Hasan, Kashef of Derr—the same petty ruler who gave so much trouble to Belzoni, Burckhardt, and other early travellers—and he, like a patriarch of old, had in his day been the husband of sixty-four wives, and the father of something like 200 children.

For forty-six years after the making of the Khetan treaty, Rameses the Great lived at peace with his neighbours and tributaries. The evening of his life was long and splendid. It became his passion and his pride to found new cities, to raise dykes, to dig canals, to build fortresses, to multiply statues, obelisks, and inscriptions, and to erect the most gorgeous and costly temples in which man ever worshipped. To the monuments founded by his predecessors he made additions so magnificent that they dwarfed the designs they were intended to complete. He caused artesian wells to be pierced in the stony bed of the desert. He carried on the canal begun by his father, and opened a water-way between the Mediterranean and the Red Sea.[1] No enterprise was too difficult, no project too vast, for his ambition. "As a child," says the stela of Dakkeh, "he superintended the public works, and his hands laid their foundations." As a man, he became the supreme Builder. Of his gigantic structures, only certain colossal fragments have survived the ravages of time ; yet those fragments are the wonder of the world.

To estimate the cost at which these things were done is now impossible. Every temple, every palace, represented a

[1] Since this book was written, a further study of the subject has led me to conjecture that not Seti I, but Queen Hatshepsu (Hatasu) of the XVIIIth Dynasty, was the actual originator of the canal which connected the Nile with the Red Sea. The inscriptions engraved upon the walls of her great Temple at Dayr-el-Baharî expressly state that her squadron sailed from Thebes to the Land of Punt, and returned from Punt to Thebes, laden with the products of that mysterious country which Mariette and Maspero have conclusively shown to have been situate on the Somali coast-line between Bab-el-Mandeb and Cape Guardafui. Unless, therefore, some water-way existed at that time between the Nile and the Red Sea, it follows that Queen Hatshepsu's squadron of discovery must have sailed northward from Thebes, descended the Nile to one of its mouths, traversed the whole length of the Mediterranean Sea, gone out through the Pillars of Hercules, doubled the Cape of Good Hope, and arrived at the Somali coast by way of the Mozambique Channel and the shores of Zanzibar. In other words, the Egyptian galleys would twice have made the almost complete circuit of the African continent. This is obviously an untenable hypothesis ; and there remains no alternative route except that of a canal, or chain of canals, connecting the Nile with the Red Sea. The old Wady Tûmilât canal has hitherto been universally ascribed to Seti I, for no other reason than that a canal leading from the Nile to the ocean is represented on a bas-relief of his reign on the north outer wall of the Great Temple of Karnak ; but this canal may undoubtedly have been made under the preceding dynasty, and it is not only probable, but most likely, that the great woman - Pharaoh, who first conceived the notion of venturing her ships upon an unknown sea, may also have organised the channel of communication by which those ships went forth. According to the second edition of Sir J. W. Dawson's *Egypt and Syria*, the recent surveys conducted by Lieut.-Col. Ardagh, Major Spaight, and Lieut. Burton, all of the Royal Engineers, "render it certain that this valley [*i.e.* the Wady Tûmilât] once carried a branch of the Nile which discharged its waters into the Red Sea" (see chap. iii. p. 55) ; and in such case, if that branch were not already navigable, Queen Hatshepsu would only have needed to canalise it, which is what she probably did. [Note to Second Edition.]

hecatomb of human lives. Slaves from Ethiopia, captives taken in war, Syrian immigrants settled in the Delta, were alike pressed into the service of the State. We know how the Hebrews suffered, and to what an extremity of despair they were reduced by the tasks imposed upon them. Yet even the Hebrews were less cruelly used than some who were kidnapped beyond the frontiers. Torn from their homes without hope of return, driven in herds to the mines, the quarries, and the brick-fields, these hapless victims were so dealt with that not even the chances of desertion were open to them. The negroes from the South were systematically drafted to the North ; the Asiatic captives were transported to Ethiopia. Those who laboured underground were goaded on without rest or respite, till they fell down in the mines and died.

That Rameses II was the Pharaoh of the captivity,[1] and that Meneptah, his son and successor, was the Pharaoh of the Exodus,[2] are now among the accepted presumptions of Egypto-

---

[1] " Les circonstances de l'histoire hébraïque s'appliquent ici d'une manière on ne peut plus satisfaisante. Les Hébreux opprimés batissaient une ville du nom de Ramsès. Ce récit ne peut donc s'appliquer qu'à l'époque où la famille de Ramsès était sur le trône. Moïse, contraint de fuir la colère du roi après le meurtre d'un Egyptien, subit un long exil, parceque le roi ne mourut *qu'après un temps fort long;* Ramsès II regna en effet plus de 67 ans. Aussitôt après le retour de Moïse commença la lutte qui se termina par le célèbre passage de la Mer Rouge. Cet événement eut donc lieu sous le fils de Ramsès II, ou tout au plus tard pendant l'époque de troubles quit suivit son règne. Ajoutons que la rapidité des derniers événements ne permet pas de supposer que le roi eût sa résidence à Thèbes dans cet instant. Or, Merenptah a précisément laissé dans la Basse-Egypte, et spécialement à Tanis, des preuves importantes de son séjour."—De Rougé, *Notice des Monuments Egyptiennes du Rez de Chaussée du Musée du Louvre,* Paris, 1857, p. 22.

" Il est impossible d'attribuer ni à Meneptah I, ni à Seti II, ni à Siptah, ni à Amonmesès, un règne même de vingt années ; à plus forte raison de cinquante ou soixante. Seul, le règne de Ramsès II remplit les conditions indispensables. Lors même que nous ne saurions pas que ce souverain a occupé les Hébreux à la construction de la ville de Ramsès, nous serions dans l'impossibilité de placer Moïse à une autre époque, à moins de faire table rase des renseignements bibliques."—*Recherches pour servir à l'Histoire de la XIX Dynastie:* F. Chabas ; Paris, 1873 ; p. 148.

[2] The Bible narrative, it has often been observed, invariably designates the King by this title, than which none, unfortunately, can be more vague

logical science. The Bible and the monuments confirm each other upon these points, while both are again corroborated by the results of recent geographical and philological research. The "treasure-cities Pithom and Raamses" which the Israelites built for Pharaoh with bricks of their own making, are the Pa-Tum and Pa-Rameses of the inscriptions, and both have recently been identified by M. Naville, in the course of his excavations conducted in 1883 and 1886 for the Egypt Exploration Fund.

The discovery of Pithom, the ancient Biblical "treasure-city" of the first chapter of Exodus, has probably attracted more public attention, and been more widely discussed by European savants, than any archæological event since the discovery of Nineveh. It was in February 1883 that M. Naville opened the well-known mound of Tel-el-Maskhutah, on the south bank of the new sweet-water canal in the Wady Tûmilât, and there discovered the foundations and other remains of a fortified city of the kind known in Egyptian as a *Bekhen*, or store-fort. This *Bekhen*, which was surrounded by a wall 30 feet in thickness, proved to be about 12 acres in extent. In one corner of the enclosure were found the ruins of a temple built by Rameses II. The rest of the area consisted of a labyrinth of subterraneous rectangular cellars, or store-chambers, constructed of sun-dried bricks of large size, and divided by walls varying from 8 to 10 feet in thickness. In

for purposes of identification. "Plus généralement," says Brugsch, writing of the royal titles, "sa personne se cache sous une série d'expressions qui toutes ont le sens de la '*grande maison*' ou du '*grand* palais,' quelquefois au duel, des '*deux grandes maisons*,' par rapport à la division de l'Egypte en deux parties. C'est du titre très frequent ⌐⌐⌐ Per-aā, 'la grande maison,' 'la haute porte,' qu'on a heureusement dérivé le nom biblique *Pharao* donné aux rois d'Egypte."—*Histoire d'Egypte*, BRUGSCH : 2d edition, Part I, p. 35 ; Leipzig, 1875.

This probably is the only title under which it was permissible for the plebeian class to speak or write of the sovereign. It can scarcely have escaped Herr Brugsch's notice that we even find it literally translated in Genesis l. 4, where it is said that "when the days of his mourning were past, Joseph spake *unto the house* of Pharaoh, saying, If now I have found grace in your eyes," etc. etc. If Moses, however, had but once recorded the cartouche name of either of his three Pharaohs, archæologists and commentators would have been spared a great deal of trouble.

the ruins of the temple were discovered several statues more or less broken, a colossal hawk inscribed with the royal ovals of Rameses II, and other works of art dating from the reigns of Osorkon II, Nectanebo, and Ptolemy Philadelphus. The hieroglyphic legends engraved upon the statues established the true value of the discovery by giving both the name of the city and the name of the district in which the city was situate ; the first being Pa-Tum (Pithom), the " Abode of Tum," and the second being Thuku-t (Succoth) ; so identifying " Pa-Tum, in the district of Thuku-t," with Pithom, the treasure-city built by the forced labour of the Hebrews, and Succoth, the region in which they made their first halt on going forth from the land of bondage. Even the bricks with which the great wall and the walls of the store-chambers are built bear eloquent testimony to the toil of the suffering colonists, and confirm in its minutest details the record of their oppression : some being duly kneaded with straw ; others, when the straw was no longer forthcoming, being mixed with the leafage of a reed common to the marshlands of the Delta ; and the remainder, when even this substitute ran short, being literally "bricks without straw," moulded of mere clay crudely dried in the sun. The researches of M. Naville further showed that the Temple to Tum, founded by Rameses II, was restored, or rebuilt, by Osorkon II of the XXIInd Dynasty ; whilst at a still higher level were discovered the remains of a Roman fortress. That Pithom was still an important place in the time of the Ptolemies is proved by a large and historically important tablet found by M. Naville in one of the store-chambers, where it had been thrown in with other sculptures and rubbish of various kinds. This tablet records repairs done to the canal, an expedition to Ethiopia, and the foundation of the city of Arsinoë. Not less important from a geographical point of view was the finding of a Roman milestone which identifies Pithom with Hero (Heroöpolis), where, according to the Septuagint, Joseph went forth to meet Jacob. This milestone gives nine Roman miles as the distance from Heroöpolis to Clysma. A very curious MS. lately discovered by Signore Gamurrini in the library of Arezzo, shows that even so late as the fourth century of the Christian era, this ancient walled enclosure—the camp, or

" Ero Castra," of the Roman period, the " Pithom " of the Bible—was still known to pious pilgrims as " the Pithom built by the Children of Israel " ; that the adjoining town, external to the camp, at that time established within the old Pithom boundaries, was known as " Heroöpolis ; " and that the town of Rameses was distant from Pithom about twenty Roman miles.[1]

As regards Pa-Rameses, the other " treasure-city " of Exodus, it is conjecturally, but not positively, identified by M. Naville with the mound of Saft-el-Henneh, the scene of his explorations in 1886. That Saft-el-Henneh was identical with " Kes," or Goshen, the capital town of the " Land of Goshen," has been unequivocally demonstrated by the discoverer ; and that it was also known, in the time of Rameses II as " Pa-Rameses " is shown to be highly probable.[2] There are remains of a temple built of black basalt, with pillars, fragments of statues, and the like, all inscribed with the cartouches of Rameses II ; and the distance from Pithom is just twenty Roman miles.

It was from Pa-Rameses that Rameses II set out with his army to attack the confederate princes of Asia Minor then lying in ambush near Kadesh ;[3] and it was hither that he

---

[1] This remarkable MS. relates the journey made by a female pilgrim of French birth, *circa* A.D. 370, to Egypt, Mesopotamia, and the Holy Land. The MS. is copied from an older original, and dates from the tenth or eleventh century. Much of the work is lost, but those parts are yet perfect which describe the pilgrim's progress through Goshen to Tanis, and thence to Jerusalem, Edessa, and the Haran. Of Pithom it is said : " Pithona etiam civitas quam œdificaverunt filii Israel ostensa est nobis in ipso itinere ; in eo tamen loco ubi jam fines Egypti intravimus, religentes jam terras Saracenorum. Nam et ipsud nunc Pithona castrum est. Heroun autem civitas quæ fuit illo tempere, id est ubi occurit Joseph patri suo venienti, sicut scriptum est in libro Genesis nunc est comes sed grandis quod nos dicimus vicus . . . nam ipse vicus nunc appellatur Hero." See a letter on " Pithom-Heroopolis " communicated to *The Academy* by M. Naville, March 22, 1884. See also M. Naville's memoir, entitled *The Store-City of Pithom and the Route of the Exodus* (Third Edition) ; published by order of the Committee of the Egypt Exploration Fund, 1888.

[2] See M. Naville's Memoir, entitled *Goshen and the Shrine of Saft-el-Henneh*, published by order of the Committee of the Egypt Exploration Fund, 1887.

[3] Kadesh, otherwise Katesh or Kades. A town on the Orontes. See

returned in triumph after the great victory. A contemporary
letter written by one Panbesa, a scribe, narrates in glowing
terms the beauty and abundance of the royal city, and tells
how the damsels stood at their doors in holiday apparel, with
nosegays in their hands and sweet oil upon their locks, " on
the day of the arrival of the War-God of the world." This
letter is in the British Museum.[1]

Other letters written during the reign of Rameses II have
by some been supposed to make direct mention of the Israelites.

" I have obeyed the orders of my master," writes the scribe
Kauiser to his superior Bak-en-Ptah, " being bidden to serve
out the rations to the soldiers, and also to the Aperiu
[Hebrews?] who quarry stone for the palace of King Rameses
Mer - Amen." A similar document written by a scribe
named Keniamon, and couched in almost the same words,
shows these Aperiu on another occasion to have been quarrying
for a building on the southern side of Memphis ; in which case
Turra would be the scene of their labours.

These invaluable letters, written on papyrus in the hieratic
character, are in good preservation. They were found in the
ruins of Memphis, and now form part of the treasures of the
Museum of Leyden.[2] They bring home to us with startling

a paper entitled, " The Campaign of Rameses the Second, in his V[th] year,
against Kadesh on the Orontes," by the Rev. G. H. Tomkins, in the *Proceedings of the Society of Biblical Archæology*, 1881, 1882 ; also in the
Transactions of the Society, vol. viii.

[1] Anastasi Papyri, No. III, Brit. Mus.

[2] See *Mélanges Egyptologiques*, by F. Chabas, 1 Série, 1862. There
has been much discussion among Egyptologists on the subject of M.
Chabas's identification of the Hebrews. The name by which they are
mentioned in the papyri here quoted, as well as in an inscription in the
quarries of Hamamat, is *Aperi-u*. A learned critic in the *Revue Archéologique* (vol. v. 2d serie, 1862) writes as follows : " La découverte du nom
des Hébreux dans les hiéroglyphes serait un fait de la dernière importance ; mais comme aucun autre point historique n'offre peut-être une pareille
séduction, il faut aussi se méfier des illusions avec un soin méticuleux.
La confusion des sons R et L dans la langue égyptienne, et le voisinage
des articulations B et P nuisent un peu, dans le cas particulier, à la
rigueur des conclusions qu'on peut tirér de la transcription. Néanmoins,
il y a lieu de prendre en considération ce fait que les Aperiu, dans les trois
documents qui nous parlent d'eux, sont montrés employés à des travaux
de même espèce que ceux auxquels, selon l'Ecriture, les Hébreux furent

nearness the events and actors of the Bible narrative. We
see the toilers at their task, and the overseers reporting
them to the directors of public works. They extract from
the quarry those huge blocks which are our wonder to this day.
Harnessed to rude sledges, they drag them to the river-side
and embark them for transport to the opposite bank.[1] Some
are so large and so heavy that it takes a month to get them
down from the mountain to the landing - place.[2] Other
labourers are elsewhere making bricks, digging canals, helping
to build the great wall which reached from Pelusium to
Heliopolis, and strengthening the defences not only of Pithom
and Rameses, but of all the cities and forts between the Red
Sea and the Mediterranean. Their lot is hard ; but not harder
than the lot of other workmen. They are well fed. They
intermarry. They increase and multiply. The season of their
great oppression is not yet come. They make bricks, it is true,
and those who are so employed must supply a certain number
daily ;[3] but the straw is not yet withheld, and the task, though
perhaps excessive, is not impossible. For we are here in the

assujettis par les Egyptiens. La circonstance que les papyrus mentionnant
ce nom ont été trouvés à Memphis, plaide encore en faveur de l'assimilation proposée—découverte importante qu'il est à désirer de voir confirmée
par d'autres monuments." It should be added that the Aperiu also appear
in the Inscription of Thothmes III at Karnak, and were supposed by
Mariette to be the people of Ephon. It is, however, to be noted that the
inscriptions mention two tribes of Aperiu, a greater and a lesser, or an
upper and a lower tribe. This might perhaps consist with the establishment of Hebrew settlers in the Delta, and others in the neighbourhood of
Memphis. The Aperiu, according to other inscriptions, appear to have
been horsemen, or horse-trainers, which certainly tells against the probability of their identity with the Hebrews.

[1] See the famous wall-painting of the Colossus on the Sledge engraved in Sir G. Wilkinson's *Ancient Egyptians;* frontispiece to vol. ii.
ed. 1871.

[2] In a letter written by a priest who lived during this reign (Rameses
II), we find an interesting account of the disadvantages and hardships
attending various trades and pursuits, as opposed to the ease and dignity
of the sacerdotal office. Of the mason he says—" It is the climax of his
misery to have to remove a block of ten cubits by six, a block which it
takes a month to drag by the private ways among the houses."—Sallier
Pap. No. II, Brit. Musæ.

[3] " Ye shall no more give the people straw to make brick, as heretofore:
let them go and gather straw for themselves.

reign of Rameses II, and the time when Meneptah shall succeed
him is yet far distant. It is not till the King dies that the
children of Israel sigh, " by reason of the bondage."

There are in the British Museum, the Louvre, and the
Bibliothèque Nationale, some much older papyri than these
two letters of the Leyden collection—some as old, indeed, as
the time of Joseph — but none, perhaps, of such peculiar
interest. In these, the scribes Kauiser and Keniamon seem
still to live and speak. What would we not give for a few
more of their letters ! These men knew Memphis in its glory,
and had looked upon the face of Rameses the Great. They
might even have seen Moses in his youth, while yet he lived
under the protection of his adopted mother, a prince among
princes.

Kauiser and Keniamon lived, and died, and were mummied
between three and four thousand years ago ; yet these frail
fragments of papyrus have survived the wreck of ages, and the
quaint writing with which they are covered is as intelligible to
ourselves as to the functionaries to whom it was addressed.
The Egyptians were eminently business-like, and kept accurate

" And the tale of the bricks, which they did make heretofore, ye shall
lay upon them : ye shall not diminish ought thereof.—Exodus chap. v. 7, 8.
    M. Chabas says : " Ces détails sont complètement conformes aux
habitudes Egyptiennes.   Le mélange de paille et d'argile dans les briques
antiques a été parfaitement reconnu.   D'un autre côté, le travail à la tâche
est mentionné dans un texte écrit au revers d'un papyrus célébrant la
splendeur de la ville de Ramsès, et datant, selon toute vraisemblance, du
règne de Meneptah I.   En voici la transcription :—' Compte des maçons,
12 ; en outre des hommes à mouler la brique dans leurs villes, amenés
aux travaux de la maison.   Eux à faire leur nombre de briques journelle-
ment ; non ils sont à se relâcher des travaux dans la maison neuve ; c'est
ainsi que j'ai obéi au mandat donné par mon maître.' "   See *Recherches
pour servir à l'Histoire de la XIX Dynastie*, par F. Chabas.   Paris ;
1873, p. 149.
    The curious text thus translated into French by M. Chabas is written
on the back of the papyrus already quoted (*i.e.* Letter of Panbesa, Anastasi
Papyri, No. III), and is preserved in the British Museum.   The wall-
painting in a tomb of the XVIIIth Dynasty at Thebes, which represents
foreign captives mixing clay, moulding, drying, and placing bricks, is well
known from the illustration in Sir G. Wilkinson's *Ancient Egyptians*, ed.
of 1871, vol. ii. p. 196.   Cases 61 and 62 in the First Egyptian Room,
British Museum, contain bricks of mixed clay and straw stamped with the
names of Rameses II.

entries of the keep and labour of their workmen and captives. From the earliest epoch of which the monuments furnish record, we find an elaborate bureaucratic system in full operation throughout the country. Even in the time of the pyramid-builders, there are ministers of public works; inspectors of lands, lakes, and quarries; secretaries, clerks, and overseers innumerable.[1] From all these, we may be sure, were required strict accounts of their expenditure, as well as reports of the work done under their supervision. Specimens of Egyptian bookkeeping are by no means rare. The Louvre is rich in memoranda of the kind; some relating to the date-tax; others to the transport and taxation of corn, the payment of wages, the sale and purchase of land for burial, and the like. If any definite and quite unmistakable news of the Hebrews should ever reach us from Egyptian sources, it will almost certainly be through the medium of documents such as these.

An unusally long reign, the last forty-six years of which would seem to have been spent in peace and outward prosperity, enabled Rameses II to indulge his ruling passion without interruption. To draw up anything like an exhaustive catalogue of his known architectural works would be equivalent to writing an itinerary of Egypt and Ethiopia under the XIXth Dynasty. His designs were as vast as his means appear to have been unlimited. From the Delta to Gebel Barkal, he filled the land with monuments dedicated to his own glory and the worship of the Gods. Upon Thebes, Abydos, and Tanis, he lavished structures of surpassing magnificence. In Nubia, at the places now known as Gerf Hossayn, Wady Sabooah, Derr, and Abou Simbel, he was the author of temples

---

1 "Les affaires de la cour et de l'administration du pays sont expédiées par les 'chefs' ou les 'intendants,' par les 'secretaires' et par la nombreuse classe des scribes. . . . Le trésor rempli d'or et d'argent, et le divan des depenses et des recettes avaient leurs intendants à eux. La chambre des comptes ne manque pas. Les domaines, les propriétés, les palais, et même les lacs du roi sont mis sous la garde d'inspecteurs. Les architectes du pharaon s'occupent de bâtisses d'après l'ordre du pharaon. Les carrières, à partir de celles du Mokattam (le Toora de nos jours) jusqu'à celles d'Assouan, se trouvent exploitées par des chefs qui surveillent le transport des pierres taillées à la place de deur destination. Finalement la corvée est dirigée par les chefs des travaux publics." *Histoire d'Egypte*, Brugsch : 2d edition, 1875 ; chap. v. pp. 34 and 35.

and the founder of cities. These cities, which would probably be better described as provincial towns, have disappeared ; and but for the mention of them in various inscriptions we should not even know that they had existed. Who shall say how many more have vanished, leaving neither trace nor record ? A dozen cities of Rameses [1] may yet lie buried under some of those nameless mounds which follow each other in such quick succession along the banks of the Nile in Middle and Lower Egypt. Only yesterday, as it were, the remains of what would seem to have been a magnificent structure decorated in a style absolutely unique, were accidentally discovered under the mounds of Tel-el-Yahoodeh,[2] about twelve miles to the N.E. of Cairo. There are probably fifty such mounds, none of which have been opened, in the Delta alone ; and it is no exaggeration to say that there must be some hundreds between the Mediterranean and the First Cataract.

An inscription found of late years at Abydos shows that Rameses II reigned over his great kingdom for the space of sixty-seven years. " It is thou," says Rameses IV, addressing himself to Osiris, " it is thou who wilt rejoice me with such length of reign as Rameses II, the great God, in his sixty-

[1] The Pa-Rameses of the Bible narrative was not the only Egyptian city of that name. There was a Pa-Rameses near Memphis, and another Pa-Rameses at Abou Simbel ; and there may probably have been many more.

[2] " The remains were apparently those of a large hall paved with white alabaster slabs. The walls were covered with a variety of bricks and encaustic tiles ; many of the bricks were of most beautiful workmanship, the hieroglyphs in some being inlaid in glass. The capitals of the columns were inlaid with brilliant coloured mosaics, and a pattern in mosaics ran round the cornice. Some of the bricks are inlaid with the oval of Rameses III." See *Murray's Handbook for Egypt*, Route 7, p. 217.
Case D, in the Second Egyptian Room at the British Museum, contains several of these tiles and terra-cottas, some of which are painted with figures of Asiatic and Negro captives, birds, serpents, etc. ; and are extremely beautiful both as regards design and execution. Murray is wrong, however, in attributing the building to Rameses II. The cartouches are those of Rameses III. The discovery was made by some labourers in 1870.
NOTE TO SECOND EDITION.—This mound was excavated last year (1887) by M. Naville, acting as before for the Egypt Exploration Fund. See Supplementary Sheet to *The Illustrated London News*, 17th September 1887, containing a complete account of the excavations at Tel-el-Yahoodeh, etc., with illustrations.

seven years. It is thou who wilt give me the long duration of this great reign."[1]

If only we knew at what age Rameses II succeeded to the throne, we should, by help of this inscription, know also the age at which he died. No such record has, however, transpired, but a careful comparison of the length of time occupied by the various events of his reign, and above all the evidence of age afforded by the mummy of this great Pharaoh, discovered in 1886, show that he must have been very nearly, if not quite, a centenarian.

"Thou madest designs while yet in the age of infancy," says the stela of Dakkeh. "Thou wert a boy wearing the side-lock, and no monument was erected, and no order was given without thee. Thou wert a youth aged ten years, and all the public works were in thy hands, laying their foundations." These lines, translated literally, cannot, however, be said to prove much. They certainly contain nothing to show that this youth of ten was, at the time alluded to, sole king and ruler of Egypt. That he was titular king, in the hereditary sense, from his birth [2] and during the lifetime of his father, is now

---

[1] This tablet is votive, and contains in fact a long Pharisaic prayer offered to Osiris by Rameses IV in the fourth year of his reign. The king enumerates his own virtues and deeds of piety, and implores the God to grant him length of days. See *Sur une Stèle inédite d'Abydos*, par P. Pierret. *Revue Archéologique*, vol. xix. p. 273.

[2] M. Mariette, in his great work on Abydos, has argued that Rameses II was designated during the lifetime of his father by a cartouche signifying only *Ra-User-Ma;* and that he did not take the additional *Setp-en-Ra* till after the death of Seti I. The Louvre, however, contains a fragment of bas-relief representing the infant Rameses with the full title of his later years. This important fragment is thus described by M. Paul Pierret: "Ramsés II enfant, représenté assis sur le signe des montagnes *du:* c'est une assimilation au soleil levant lorsqu'il émerge à l'horizon céleste. Il porte la main gauche à sa bouche, en signe d'enfance. La main droite pend sur les genoux. Il est vétu d'une longue robe. La tresse de l'enfance pend sur son épaule. Un diadème relie ses cheveux, et un uræus se dresse sur son front. Voici la traduction de la courte légende qui accompagne cette représentation. ' Le roi de la Haute et de la Basse Egypte, maître des deux pays, *Ra-User-Ma Setp-en-Ra*, vivificateur, éternel comme le soleil.' " *Catalogue de la Salle Historique.* P. PIERRET. Paris, 1873, p. 8.

M. Maspero is of opinion that this one fragment establishes the disputed fact of his actual sovereignty from early childhood, and so disposes of the entire question. See *L'Inscription dédicatoire du Temple d'Abydos*,

quite certain. That he should, as a boy, have designed public buildings and superintended their construction is extremely probable. The office was one which might well have been discharged by a crown-prince who delighted in architecture, and made it his peculiar study. It was, in fact, a very noble office—an office which from the earliest days of the ancient Empire had constantly been confided to princes of the royal blood ;[1] but it carried with it no evidence of sovereignty. The presumption, therefore, would be that the stela of Dakkeh (dating as it does from the third year of the sole reign of Rameses II) alludes to a time long since past, when the king as a boy held office under his father.

The same inscription, as we have already seen, makes reference to the victorious campaign in the South. Rameses is addressed as " the bull powerful against Ethiopia ; the griffin furious against the negroes ;" and that the events hereby alluded to must have taken place during the first three years of his sole reign is proved by the date of the tablet. The great dedicatory inscription of Abydos shows, in fact, that Rameses II was prosecuting a campaign in Ethiopia at the time when he received intelligence of the death of his father, and that he came down the Nile, northwards, in order, probably, to be crowned at Thebes.[2]

Now the famous sculptures of the commemorative chapel at Bayt-el-Welly relate expressly to the events of this expedition ; and as they are executed in that refined and delicate style which especially characterises the bas-relief work of Gournah, of Abydos, of all those buildings which were either erected by Seti the First, or begun by Seti and finished during the early years of Rameses II, I venture to think we may regard them as contemporary, or very nearly contemporary, with the scenes they represent. In any case, it is reasonable

---

suivi d'un Essai sur la jeunesse de Sesostris. G. MASPERO. 4° Paris, 1867. See also chap. viii. (footnote), p. 140.

[1] " Le métier d'architecte se trouvait confié aux plus hauts dignitaires de la cour pharaonique. Les architectes du roi, les *Murket*, se recrutaient assez souvent parmi le nombre des princes." *Histoire d'Egypte :* BRUGSCH. Second edition, 1875, chap. v. p. 34.

[2] See *L'Inscription dédicatoire du Temple d'Abydos, etc.,* by G. MASPERO.

to conclude that the artists employed on the work would know something about the events and persons delineated, and that they would be guilty of no glaring inaccuracies.

All doubt as to whether the dates refer to the associated reigns of Seti and Rameses, or to the sole reign of the latter, vanish, however, when in these same sculptures [1] we find the conqueror accompanied by his son, Prince Amenherkhopeshef, who is of an age not only to bear his part in the field, but afterwards to conduct an important ceremony of state on the occasion of the submission and tribute-offering of the Ethiopian commander. Such is the unmistakable evidence of the basreliefs at Bayt-el-Welly, as those who cannot go to Bayt-el-Welly may see and judge for themselves by means of the admirable casts of these great tableaux which line the walls of the Second Egyptian Room at the British Museum. To explain away Prince Amenherkhopeshef would be difficult. We are accustomed to a certain amount of courtly exaggeration on the part of those who record with pen or pencil the great deeds of the Pharaohs. We expect to see the king always young, always beautiful, always victorious. It seems only right and natural that he should be never less than twenty, and sometimes more than sixty, feet in height. But that any flatterer should go so far as to credit a lad of thirteen with a son at least as old as himself is surely quite incredible.

Lastly, there is the evidence of the Bible.

Joseph being dead and the Israelites established in Egypt, there comes to the throne a Pharaoh who takes alarm at the increase of this alien race, and who seeks to check their too rapid multiplication. He not only oppresses the foreigners, but ordains that every male infant born to them in their bondage shall be cast into the river. This Pharaoh is now universally believed to be Rameses II. Then comes the old, sweet, familiar Bible story that we know so well. Moses is born, cast adrift in the ark of bulrushes, and rescued by the King's daughter. He becomes to her "as a son." Although no dates are given, it is clear that the new Pharaoh has not been long upon the throne when these events happen. It is equally clear that he

[1] See Rosellini, *Monumenti Storici*, pl. lxxi.

is no mere youth. He is old in the uses of state-craft; and he is the father of a princess of whom it is difficult to suppose that she was herself an infant.

On the whole, then, we can but conclude that Rameses II, though born a King, was not merely grown to manhood, but wedded, and the father of children already past the period of infancy, before he succeeded to the sole exercise of sovereign power. This is, at all events, the view taken by Professor Maspero, who expressly says, in the latest edition of his *Histoire Ancienne,* "that Rameses II, when he received news of the death of his father, was then in the prime of life, and surrounded by a large family, some of whom were of an age to fight under his command." [1]

Brugsch places the birth of Moses in the sixth year of the reign of Rameses II.[2] This may very well be. The fourscore years that elapsed between that time and the time of the Exodus correspond with sufficient exactness to the chronological data furnished by the monuments. Moses would thus see out the sixty-one remaining years of the King's long life, and release the Israelites from bondage towards the close of the reign of Menepthah,[3] who sat for about twenty years on the throne of his fathers. The correspondence of dates this time leaves nothing to be desired.

[1] "A la nouvelle de la mort de son père, Ramsès II désormais seul roi, quitta l'Éthiopie et ceignit la couronne à Thèbes. Il était alors dans la plénitude de ses forces, et avait autour de lui un grand nombre d'enfants, dont quelques-uns étaient assez âgés pour combattre sous ses ordres." *Hist. Ancienne des Peuples de l'Orient,* par G. Maspero. Chap. v. p. 220. 4ᵉᵐᵉ edition, 1886.

[2] "Comme Ramsès II regna 66 ans, le règne de son successeur sous lequel la sortie des Juifs eut lieu, embrassa la durée de 20 ans; et comme Moïse avait l'age de 80 ans au temps de la sortie, il en résulte évidemment que les enfants d'Israël quittèrent l'Egypte une des ces dernières six années du règne de Menepthah; c'est à dire entre 1327 et 1321 avant l'ère chrétienne. Si nous admettons que ce pharaon périt dans la mer, selon le rapport biblique, Moïse sera né 80 ans avant 1321, ou 1401 avant J. Chr., la *sixième* année du règne de Ramsès II."—Chap. viii. p. 157. *Hist. d'Egypte:* BRUGSCH. First edition, Leipzig, 1859.

[3] If the Exodus took place, however, during the opening years of the reign of Menepthah, it becomes necessary either to remove the birth of Moses to a correspondingly earlier date, or to accept the amendment of Bunsen, who says "we can hardly take literally the statement as to the age

The Sesostris of Diodorus Siculus went blind, and died by
his own hand ; which act, says the historian, as it conformed
to the glory of his life, was greatly admired by his people.
We are here evidently in the region of pure fable. Suicide
was by no means an Egyptian, but a classical virtue. Just as
the Greeks hated age, the Egyptians reverenced it ; and it may
be doubted whether a people who seem always to have passion-
ately desired length of days, would have seen anything to admire
in a wilful shortening of that most precious gift of the gods.
With the one exception of Cleopatra—the death of Nitocris
the rosy-cheeked being also of Greek,[1] and therefore question-
able, origin—no Egyptian sovereign is known to have committed
suicide ; and even Cleopatra, who was half Greek by birth,
must have been influenced to the act by Greek and Roman
example. Dismissing, then, altogether this legend of his blindness and self-slaughter, it must be admitted that of the death
of Rameses II we know nothing certain.

Such are, very briefly, the leading facts of the history of
this famous Pharaoh. Exhaustively treated, they would expand
into a volume. Even then, however, one would ask, and ask
in vain, what manner of man he was. Every attempt to evolve
his personal character from these scanty data, is in fact a mere
exercise of fancy.[2] That he was personally valiant may be

of Moses at the Exodus, *twice over* forty years." Forty years is the mode
of expressing a generation, from thirty to thirty-three years. *Egypt's Place
in Universal History :* BUNSEN. Lond. 1859. Vol. iii. p. 184. That
Menepthah did not himself perish with his host, seems certain. The
final oppression of the Hebrews and the miracles of Moses, as narrated in
the Bible, give one the impression of having all happened within a comparatively short space of time ; and cannot have extended over a period of
twenty years. Neither is it stated that Pharaoh perished. The tomb of
Menepthah, in fact, is found in the Valley of the Tombs of the Kings
(Tomb, No. 8).

[1] HERODOTUS, Bk. ii.

[2] Rosellini, for instance, carries hero-worship to its extreme limit when
he not only states that Rameses the Great had, by his conquests, filled
Egypt with luxuries that contributed alike to the graces of every-day life and
the security of the state, but (accepting as sober fact the complimentary
language of a triumphal tablet) adds that " universal peace even secured to
him the love of the vanquished " (l'universal pace assicurata dall' amore dei
vinti stessi pel Faraone).—*Mon. Storici*, vol. iii. part ii. p. 294. Bunsen,
equally prejudiced in the opposite direction, can see no trait of magnanimity

gathered, with due reservation, from the poem of Pentaur ; and that he was not unmerciful is shown in the extradition clause of the Khetan treaty. His pride was evidently boundless. Every temple which he erected was a monument to his own glory ; every colossus was a trophy ; every inscription a pæan of self-praise. At Abou Simbel, at Derr, at Gerf Hossayn, he seated his own image in the sanctuary among the images of the gods.[1] There are even instances in which he is depicted under the twofold aspect of royalty and divinity—Rameses the Pharaoh burning incense before Rameses the Deity.

For the rest, it is safe to conclude that he was neither better nor worse than the general run of Oriental despots—that he was ruthless in war, prodigal in peace, rapacious of booty, and unsparing in the exercise of almost boundless power. Such pride and such despotism were, however, in strict accordance with immemorial precedent, and with the temper of the age in which he lived. The Egyptians would seem, beyond all doubt, to have believed that their King was always, in some sense, divine. They wrote hymns[2] and offered up prayers to him, and regarded him as the living representative of Deity. His princes and ministers habitually addressed him in the language of worship. Even his wives, who ought to have known better, are represented in the performance of acts of religious adoration before him. What wonder, then, if the man so deified believed himself a god ?

or goodness in one whom he loves to depict as " an unbridled despot, who took advantage of a reign of almost unparalleled length, and of the acquisitions of his father and ancestors, in order to torment his own subjects and strangers to the utmost of his power, and to employ them as instruments of his passion for war and building." *Egypt's Place in Universal History :* BUNSEN. Vol. iii. bk. iv. part ii. p. 184.

[1] " Souvent il s'introduit lui-même dans les triades divines auxquelles il dédie les temples. *Le soleil de Ramsès Meïamoun* qu'on aperçoit sur leur murailles, n'est autre chose que le roi lui-même déifié de son vivant." *Notice des Monuments Egyptiennes au Musée du Louvre.* DE ROUGÉ ; Paris, 1875, p. 20.

[2] See *Hymn to Pharaoh* (Menepthah) translated by C. W. Goodwin, M.A. RECORDS OF THE PAST, vol. vi. p. 101.

CHAPTER XVI.

ABOU SIMBEL.

WE came to Abou Simbel on the night of the 31st of January, and we left at sunset on the 18th of February. Of these eighteen clear days, we spent fourteen at the foot of the rock of the Great Temple, called in the old Egyptian tongue the Rock of Abshek. The remaining four (taken at the end of the first week and the beginning of the second) were passed in the excursion to Wady-Halfeh and back. By thus dividing the time, our long sojourn was made less monotonous for those who had no especial work to do.

Meanwhile, it was wonderful to wake every morning close under the steep bank, and, without lifting one's head from the pillow, to see that row of giant faces so close against the sky. They showed unearthly enough by moonlight ; but not half so unearthly as in the grey of dawn. At that hour, the most solemn of the twenty-four, they wore a fixed and fatal look that was little less than appalling. As the sky warmed, this awful look was succeeded by a flush that mounted and deepened like the rising flush of life. For a moment they seemed to glow—to smile—to be transfigured. Then came a flash, as of thought itself. It was the first instantaneous flash of the risen sun. It lasted less than a second. It was gone almost before one could say that it was there. The next moment, mountain, river, and sky, were distinct in the steady light of day ; and the colossi—mere colossi now—sat serene and stony in the open sunshine.

Every morning I waked in time to witness that daily

miracle. Every morning I saw those awful brethren pass from death to life, from life to sculptured stone. I brought myself almost to believe at last that there must sooner or later come some one sunrise when the ancient charm would snap asunder, and the giants must arise and speak.

Stupendous as they are, nothing is more difficult than to see the colossi properly. Standing between the rock and the river, one is too near ; stationed on the island opposite, one is too far off ; while from the sand-slope only a side-view is obtainable. Hence, for want of a fitting standpoint, many travellers have seen nothing but deformity in the most perfect face handed down to us by Egyptian art. One recognises in it the negro, and one the Mongolian type ;[1] while another admires the fidelity with which "the Nubian characteristics" have been seized.

Yet, in truth, the head of the young Augustus is not cast in a loftier mould. These statues are portraits—portraits of the same man four times repeated ; and that man is Rameses the Great.

Now, Rameses the Great, if he was as much like his portraits as his portraits are like each other, must have been

---

[1] The late Vicomte E. de Rougé, in a letter to M. Guigniaut on the discoveries at Tanis, believes that he detects the Semitic type in the portraits of Rameses II and Seti I ; and even conjectures that the Pharaohs of the XIXth Dynasty may have descended from Hyksos ancestors : " L'origine de la famille des Ramsés nous est jusqu' ici complétement inconnue : sa prédilection pour le dieu *Set* ou *Sutech*, qui éclate dès l'abord par le nom de Séti Iere (*Sethos*), ainsi que d'autres indices, pouvaient déjà engager à la reporter vers la Basse Egypte. Nous savions même que Ramsés II avait épousé une fille du prince de Khet, quand le traité de l'an 22 eut ramené la paix entre les deux pays. Le profil très-décidément sémitique de Séti et de Ramsés se distinguait nettement des figures ordinaires de nos Pharaons Thébains." (See *Revue Archéologique*, vol. ix. A.D. 1864.) In the course of the same letter, M. de Rougé adverts to the magnificent restoration of the Temple of Sutech at Tanis (Sān) by Rameses II, and to the curious fact that the God is there represented with the peculiar head-dress worn elsewhere by the Prince of Kheta.

It is to be remembered, however, that the patron deity of Rameses II was Amen-Ra. His homage of Sutech (which might possibly have been a concession to his Khetan wife) seems to have been confined almost exclusively to Tanis, where Ma-at-iri-neferu-Ra may be supposed to have resided.

one of the handsomest men, not only of his own day, but of
all history.   Wheresoever we meet with him, whether in the
fallen colossus at Memphis, or in the syenite torso of the
British Museum, or among the innumerable bas - reliefs of
Thebes, Abydos, Gournah, and Bayt-el-Welly, his features
(though bearing in some instances the impress of youth and
in others of maturity) are always the same.   The face is oval ;
the eyes are long, prominent, and heavy-lidded ; the nose is
slightly aquiline and characteristically depressed at the tip ;
the nostrils are open and sensitive ; the under lip projects ; the
chin is short and square.

Here, for instance, is an outline from a bas-
relief at Bayt-el-Welly.   The subject is commemorative of the king's first campaign.   A
beardless youth fired with the rage of battle, he
clutches a captive by the hair and lifts his mace
to slay.   In this delicate and Dantesque face
which lacks as yet the fulness and repose of the
later portraits, we recognise all the distinctive traits of the
older Rameses.

Here, again, is a sketch from Abydos, in
which the king, although he has not yet ceased
to wear the side-lock of youth, is seen with
a boyish beard, and looks some three or four
years older than in the previous portrait.

It is interesting to compare these heads

with the accompanying profile of one of the caryatid
colossi inside the great Temple of Abou Simbel ;
and all three with one of the giant portraits of the
façade.   This last, whether regarded as a marvel
of size or of portraiture, is the chef-d'œuvre of
Egyptian sculpture.   We here see the great king
in his prime.   His features are identical with those
of the head at Bayt-el-Welly ; but the contours
are more amply filled in, and the expression is
altogether changed.   The man is full fifteen or twenty years
older.   He has outlived that rage of early youth.   He is no
longer impulsive, but implacable.   A godlike serenity, an
almost superhuman pride, an immutable will, breathe from the

sculptured stone. He has learned to believe his prowess irresistible, and himself almost divine. If he now raised his

PROFILE OF RAMESES II.

(From the Southernmost Colossus; Abou Simbel.)

arm to slay, it would be with the stern placidity of a destroying angel.

The annexed woodcut gives the profile of the southern-most colossus, which is the only perfect, or very nearly perfect, one of the four. The original can be correctly seen from but one point of view ; and that point is where the sandslope meets the northern buttress of the façade, at a level just parallel with the beards of the statues. It was thence that the present outline was taken. The sandslope is steep, and loose, and hot to the feet. More disagreeable climbing it would be hard to find, even in Nubia ; but no traveller who refuses to encounter this small hardship need believe that he has seen the faces of the colossi.

Viewed from below, this beautiful portrait is foreshortened out of all proportion. It looks unduly wide from ear to ear, while the lips and the lower part of the nose show relatively larger than the rest of the features. The same may be said of the great cast in the British Museum. Cooped up at the end of a narrow corridor and lifted not more than fifteen feet above the ground, it is carefully placed so as to be wrong from every point of view and shown to the greatest possible disadvantage.

The artists who wrought the original statues were, however, embarrassed by no difficulties of focus, daunted by no difficulties of scale. Giants themselves, they summoned these giants from out the solid rock, and endowed them with superhuman strength and beauty. They sought no quarried blocks of syenite or granite for their work. They fashioned no models of clay. They took a mountain, and fell upon it like Titans, and hollowed and carved it as though it were a cherry-stone, and left it for the feebler men of after-ages to marvel at for ever. One great hall and fifteen spacious chambers they hewed out from the heart of it ; then smoothed the rugged precipice towards the river, and cut four huge statues with their faces to the sunrise, two to the right and two to the left of the doorway, there to keep watch to the end of time.

These tremendous warders sit sixty-six feet high, without the platform under their feet. They measure across the chest 25 feet and 4 inches ; from the shoulder to the elbow, 15 feet and 6 inches ; from the inner side of the elbow joint to the tip of the middle finger, 15 feet ; and so on, in relative proportion. If they stood up, they would tower to a height of at least 83 feet, from the soles of their feet to the tops of their enormous double-crowns.

Nothing in Egyptian sculpture is perhaps quite so wonderful as the way in which these Abou Simbel artists dealt with the thousands of tons of material to which they here gave human form. Consummate masters of effect, they knew precisely what to do, and what to leave undone. These were portrait statues ; therefore they finished the heads up to the highest point consistent with their size. But the trunk and the lower limbs they regarded from a decorative rather than a statuesque point of view. As decoration, it was necessary that they should give size and dignity to the façade. Everything, consequently, was here subordinated to the general effect of breadth, of massiveness, of repose. Considered thus, the colossi are a triumph of treatment. Side by side they sit, placid and majestic, their feet a little apart, their hands resting on their knees. Shapely though they are, those huge legs look scarcely inferior in girth to the great columns of Karnak. The articulations of the knee-joint, the swell of the calf, the outline of the *peroneus longus* are indicated rather than developed. The toe-nails and toe-joints are given in the same bold and general way ; but the fingers, because only the tips of them could be seen from below, are treated *en bloc.*

The faces show the same largeness of style. The little dimple which gives such sweetness to the corners of the mouth, and the tiny depression in the lobe of the ear, are in fact circular cavities as large as saucers.

How far this treatment is consistent with the most perfect delicacy and even finesse of execution, may be gathered from the sketch. The nose there shown in profile is 3 feet and a half in length ; the mouth so delicately curved is about the same in width ; even the sensitive nostril, which looks ready to expand with the breath of life, exceeds 8 inches in length. The ear (which is placed high, and is well detached from the head) measures 3 feet and 5 inches from top to tip.

A recent writer,[1] who brings sound practical knowledge to

[1] " *L'absence de points fouillés*, la simplification voulue, la restriction des

bear upon the subject, is of opinion that the Egyptian sculptors did not even "point" their work beforehand. If so, then the marvel is only so much the greater. The men who, working in so coarse and friable a material, could not only give beauty and finish to heads of this size, but could with barbaric tools hew them out *ab initio* from the natural rock, were the Michael Angelos of their age.

It has already been said that the last Rameses to the southward is the best preserved. His left arm and hand are injured, and the head of the uræus sculptured on the front of the pschent is gone ; but with these exceptions the figure is as whole, as fresh in surface, as sharp in detail, as on the day it was completed. The next is shattered to the waist. His head lies at his feet, half buried in sand. The third is nearly as perfect as the first ; while the fourth has lost not only the whole beard and the greater part of the uræus, but has both arms broken away, and a big, cavernous hole in the front of the body. From the double-crowns of the two last, the top ornament is also missing. It looks a mere knob ; but it measures eight feet in height.

Such an effect does the size of these four figures produce on the mind of the spectator, that he scarcely observes the fractures they have sustained. I do not remember to have even missed the head and body of the shattered one, although nothing is left of it above the knees. Those huge legs and feet covered with ancient inscriptions,[1] some of Greek, some of

détails et des ornements à quelques sillons plus ou moins hardis, l'engorge-ment de toutes les parties délicates, démontrent que les Egyptiens étaient loin d'avoir des procédés et des facilités inconnus."—*La Sculpture Egyptienne*, par EMILE SOLDI, p. 48.

"Un fait qui nous parait avoir dû entraver les progrès de la sculpture, c'est l'habitude probable des sculpteurs ou entrepreneurs égyptiens d'entre-prendre le travail à même sur la pierre, sans avoir préalablement cherché le modèle en terre glaise, comme on le fait de nos jours. Une fois le modèle fini, on le moule et on le reproduit mathematiquement définitive. Ce procédé a toujours été employé dans les grandes époques de l'art ; et il ne nous a pas semblé qu'il ait jamais été en usage en Egypte."—*Ibid.* p. 82.

M. Soldi is also of opinion that the Egyptian sculptors were ignorant of many of the most useful tools known to the Greek, Roman, and modern sculptors, such as the emery-tube, the diamond-point, etc. etc.

[1] On the left leg of this colossus is the famous Greek inscription dis-covered by Messrs. Bankes and Salt. It dates from the reign of Psam-

Phœnician origin, tower so high above the heads of those who look at them from below, that one scarcely thinks of looking higher still.

The figures are naked to the waist, and clothed in the usual striped tunic. On their heads they wear the double-crown, and on their necks rich collars of cabochon drops cut in very low relief. The feet are bare of sandals, and the arms of bracelets ; but in the front of the body, just where the customary belt and buckle would come, are deep holes in the stone, such as might have been made to receive rivets, supposing the belts to have been made of bronze or gold. On the breast, just below the necklace, and on the upper part of each arm, are cut in magnificent ovals, between four and five feet in length, the ordinary cartouches of the king. These were probably tattooed upon his person in the flesh.

Some have supposed that these statues were originally coloured, and that the colour may have been effaced by the ceaseless shifting and blowing of the sand. Yet the drift was probably at its highest when Burckhardt discovered the place in 1813 ; and on the two heads that were still above the surface, he seems to have observed no traces of colour. Neither can the keenest eye detect any vestige of that delicate film of stucco with which the Egyptians invariably prepared their surfaces for painting. Perhaps the architects were for once content with the natural colour of the sandstone, which is here very rich and varied. It happens also that the colossi come in a light-coloured vein of the rock, and so sit relieved against a darker background. Towards noon, when the level of the

metichus I, and purports to have been cut by a certain Damearchon, one of the 240,000 Egyptian troops of whom it is related by Herodotus (Book ii. chaps. 29, 30) that they deserted because they were kept in garrison at Syene for three years without being relieved. The inscription, as translated by Colonel Leake, is thus given in Rawlinson's *Herodotus* (vol. ii. p. 37) : "King Psamatichus having come to Elephantine, those who were with Psamatichus, the son of Theocles wrote this. They sailed, and came to above Kerkis, to where the river rises . . . the Egyptian Amasis. . . . The writer is Damearchon the son of Amœbichus, and Pelephus (Pelekos), the son of Udamus." The king Psamatichus here named has been identified with the Psamtik I of the inscriptions. It was in his reign, and not as it has sometimes been supposed, in the reign of Psammetichus II, that the great military defection took place.

façade has just passed into shade and the sunlight still strikes upon the statues, the effect is quite startling. The whole thing, which is then best seen from the island, looks like a huge onyx-cameo cut in high relief.

A statue of Ra,[1] to whom the temple is dedicated, stands some twenty feet high in a niche over the doorway, and is supported on either side by a bas-relief portrait of the king in an attitude of worship. Next above these comes a superb hieroglyphic inscription reaching across the whole front ; above the inscription, a band of royal cartouches ; above the cartouches, a frieze of sitting apes ; above the apes, last and highest, some fragments of a cornice. The height of the whole may have been somewhat over a hundred feet. Wherever it has been possible to introduce them as decoration, we see the ovals of the king. Under those sculptured on the platforms and over the door, I observed the hieroglyphic character (⟨glyph⟩), which, in conjunction with the sign known as the determinative of metals, signifies gold (Nub) ; but when represented, as here, without the determinative, stands for Nubia, the Land of Gold. This addition, which I do not remember to have seen elsewhere in connection with the cartouches of Rameses II,[2] is here used in an heraldic sense, as signifying the sovereignty of Nubia.

The relative position of the two Temples of Abou Simbel has been already described—how they are excavated in two adjacent mountains and divided by a cataract of sand. The front of the small Temple lies parallel to the course of the Nile, here flowing in a north-easterly direction. The façade

---

[1] *Ra*, the principal solar divinity, generally represented with the head of a hawk, and the sun-disk on his head. " *Ra* veut dire *faire, disposer ;* c'est, en effet, le dieu Ra qui a disposé, organisé le monde, dont la matière lui a été donnée par Ptah."—P. Pierret : *Dictionnaire d'Archéologie Egyptienne.*

"Ra est une autre des intelligences démiurgiques. Ptah avait créé le soleil ; le soleil, a son tour, est *le créateur des êtres, animaux et hommes.* Il est à l'hémisphère supérieure ce qu'Osiris est à l'hémisphère inférieure. Ra s'incarne à Héliopolis."—A. Mariette : *Notice des Monuments à Boulak*, p. 123.

[2] An instance occurs, however, in a small inscription sculptured on the rocks of the Island of Sehayl in the First Cataract, which records the second panegyry of the reign of Rameses II.—See *Récueil des Monuments*, etc. : Brugsch, vol. ii., Planche lxxxii., Inscription No. 6.

of the Great Temple is cut in the flank of the mountain, and faces due east. Thus the colossi, towering above the shoulder of the sand-drift, catch, as it were, a side view of the small Temple and confront vessels coming up the river. As for the sand-drift, it curiously resembles the glacier of the Rhone. In size, in shape, in position, in all but colour and substance, it is the same. Pent in between the rocks at top, it opens out like a fan at bottom. In this its inevitable course, it slants downward across the façade of the Great Temple. For ever descending, drifting, accumulating, it wages the old stealthy war ; and, unhasting, unresting, labours grain by grain to fill the hollowed chambers, and bury the great statues, and wrap the whole Temple in a winding-sheet of golden sand, so that the place thereof shall know it no more.

It had very nearly come to this when Burckhardt went up (A.D. 1813). The top of the doorway was then thirty feet below the surface. Whether the sand will ever reach that height again, must depend on the energy with which it is combated. It can only be cleared as it accumulates. To avert it is impossible. Backed by the illimitable wastes of the Libyan desert, the supply from above is inexhaustible. Come it must ; and come it will, to the end of time.

The drift rose to the lap of the northernmost colossus and half-way up the legs of the next, when the Philæ lay at Abou Simbel. The doorway was clear, however, almost to the threshold, and the sand inside was not more than two feet deep in the first hall. The whole façade, we were told, had been laid bare, and the interior swept and garnished, when the Empress of the French, after opening the Suez Canal in 1869, went up the Nile as far as the Second Cataract. By this time, most likely, that yellow carpet lies thick and soft in every chamber, and is fast silting up the doorway again.

How well I remember the restless excitement of our first day at Abou Simbel! While the morning was yet cool, the Painter and the Writer wandered to and fro, comparing and selecting points of view, and superintending the pitching of their tents. The Painter planted his on the very brink of the bank, face to face with the colossi and the open doorway. The Writer perched some forty feet higher on the pitch of

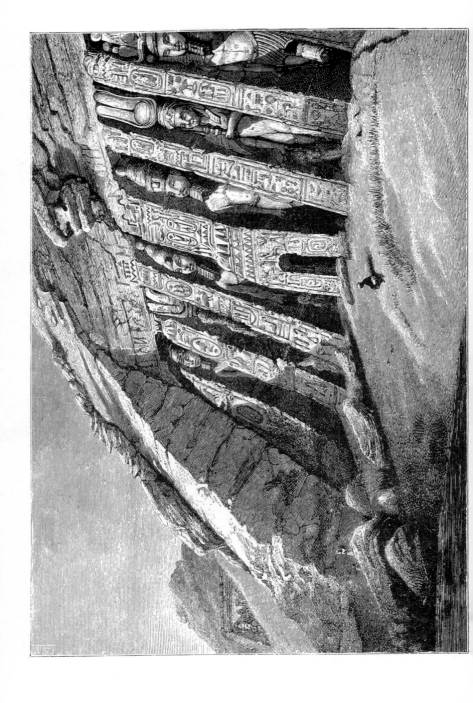

the sandslope ; so getting a side-view of the façade, and a peep of distance looking up the river.[1] To fix the tent up there was no easy matter. It was only by sinking the tent-pole in a hole filled with stones, that it could be trusted to stand against the steady push of the north wind, which at this season is almost always blowing.

Meanwhile the travellers from the other dahabeeyahs were tramping backwards and forwards between the two Temples ; filling the air with laughter, and waking strange echoes in the hollow mountains. As the day wore on, however, they returned to their boats, which one by one spread their sails and bore away for Wady Halfeh.

When they were fairly gone and we had the marvellous place all to ourselves, we went to see the Temples.

The smaller one, though it comes first in order of sailing, is generally seen last ; and seen therefore to disadvantage. To eyes fresh from the " Abode of Ra," the " Abode of Hathor " looks less than its actual size ; which is in fact but little inferior to that of the Temple at Derr. A first hall, measuring some 40 feet in length by 21 in width, leads to a transverse corridor, two side-chambers, and a sanctuary 7 feet square, at the upper end of which are the shattered remains of a cow-headed statue of Hathor. Six square pillars, as at Derr, support what, for want of a better word, one must call the ceiling of the hall ; though the ceiling is in truth the super-incumbent mountain.

In this arrangement, as in the general character of the bas-relief sculptures which cover the walls and pillars, there is much simplicity, much grace, but nothing particularly new. The façade, on the contrary, is a daring innovation. To those who have not seen the place the annexed illustration is worth pages of description ; and to describe it in words only would be difficult. Here the whole front is but a frame for six recesses, from each of which a colossal statue, erect and life-like, seems to be walking straight out from the heart of the mountain. These statues, three to the right and three to the left of the doorway, stand thirty feet high, and represent Rameses II and Nefertari, his queen. Mutilated as they are, the male figures

[1] See the Frontispiece.

are full of spirit, and the female figures full of grace. The Queen wears on her head the plumes and disk of Hathor. The king is crowned with the pschent, and with a fantastic helmet adorned with plumes and horns. They have their children with them; the Queen her daughters, the King his sons—infants of ten feet high, whose heads just reach to the parental knee.

The walls of these six recesses, as they follow the slope of the mountain, form massive buttresses, the effect of which is wonderfully bold in light and shadow. The doorway gives the only instance of a porch that we saw in either Egypt or Nubia. The superb hieroglyphs which cover the faces of these buttresses and the front of this porch are cut half-a-foot deep into the rock, and are so large that they can be read from the island in the middle of the river. The tale they tell—a tale retold, in many varied turns of old Egyptian style upon the architraves within —is singular and interesting.

" Rameses, the Strong in Truth, the Beloved of Amen," says the outer legend, " made this divine Abode [1] for his royal wife, Nefertari, whom he loves."

The legend within, after enumerating the titles of the King, records that " his royal wife who loves him, Nefertari the Beloved of Maut, constructed for him this Abode in the mountain of the Pure Waters."

On every pillar, in every act of worship pictured on the walls, even in the sanctuary, we find the names of Rameses and Nefertari " coupled and inseparable." In this double dedication, and in the unwonted tenderness of the style, one seems to detect traces of some event, perhaps of some anniversary, the particulars of which are lost for ever. It may have

---

[1] Though dedicated by Rameses to Nefertari, and by Nefertari to Rameses, this Temple was placed, primarily, under the patronage of Hathor, the supreme type of divine maternity. She is represented by Queen Nefertari, who appears on the façade as the mother of six children, and adorned with the attributes of the goddess. A Temple to Hathor would also be, from a religious point of view, the fitting pendant to a Temple of Ra. M. Mariette, in his *Notice des Monuments à Boulak*, remarks of Hathor that her functions are still but imperfectly known to us. " Peutêtre était-elle à Ra ce que Maut est à Ammon, le récipient où le dieu s'engendre lui-même pour l'éternité."

been a meeting ; it may have been a parting ; it may have been a prayer answered, or a vow fulfilled. We see, at all events, that Rameses and Nefertari desired to leave behind them an imperishable record of the affection which united them on earth, and which they hoped would reunite them in Amenti. What more do we need to know ? We see that the Queen was fair ; [1] that the King was in his prime. We divine the rest ; and the poetry of the place at all events is ours. Even in these barren solitudes there is wafted to us a breath from the shores of old romance. We feel that Love once passed this way, and that the ground is still hallowed where he trod.

We hurried on to the Great Temple, without waiting to examine the lesser one in detail. A solemn twilight reigned in the first hall, beyond which all was dark. Eight colossi, four to the right and four to the left, stand ranged down the centre, bearing the mountain on their heads. Their height is twenty-five feet. With hands crossed on their breasts, they clasp the flail and crook ; emblems of majesty and dominion. It is the attitude of Osiris, but the face is the face of Rameses II. Seen by this dim light, shadowy, mournful, majestic, they look as if they remembered the past.

Beyond the first hall lies a second hall supported on four

---

[1] It is not often that one can say of a female head in an Egyptian wall-painting that it is beautiful ; but in these portraits of the Queen, many times repeated upon the walls of the first Hall of the Temple of Hathor, there is, if not positive beauty according to our western notions, much sweetness and much grace. The name of Nefertari means Perfect, Good, or Beautiful Companion. That the word " Nefer " should mean both Good and Beautiful—in fact, that Beauty and Goodness should be synonymous terms—is not merely interesting as it indicates a lofty philosophical stand-point, but as it reveals, perhaps, the latent germ of that doctrine which was hereafter to be taught with such brilliant results in the Alexandrian Schools. It is remarkable that the word for Truth and Justice (*Ma*) was also one and the same.

There is often a quaint significance about Egyptian proper names which reminds one of the names that came into favour in England under the Commonwealth. Take for instance *Bak-en-Khonsu*, Servant-of-Khons ; *Pa-ta-amen*, the Gift of Ammon ; *Renpitnefer*, Good-year ; *Nub-en Tekh*, Worth-her-Weight-in-Gold (both women's names) ; and *Hor-mes-out'-a-Shu*, Horus-son-of-the-Eye-of-Shu—which last, as a tolerably long compound, may claim relationship with Praise-God Barebones, Hew-Agag-in Pieces-before-the-Lord, etc. etc.

square pillars; beyond this again, a transverse chamber, the walls of which are covered with coloured bas-reliefs of various Gods; last of all, the sanctuary. Here, side by side, sit four figures larger than life—Ptah, Amen-Ra, Ra, and Rameses deified. Before them stands an altar, in shape a truncated pyramid, cut from the solid rock. Traces of colour yet linger on the garments of the statues; while in the walls on either side are holes and grooves such as might have been made to receive a screen of metal-work.

The air in the sanctuary was heavy with an acrid smoke, as if the priests had been burning some strange incense and were only just gone. For this illusion we were indebted to the visitors who had been there before us. They had lit the place with magnesian wire; the vapour of which lingers long in these unventilated vaults.

To settle down then and there to a steady investigation of the wall-sculptures was impossible. We did not attempt it. Wandering from hall to hall, from chamber to chamber; now trusting to the faint gleams that straggled in from without, now stumbling along by the light of a bunch of candles tied to the end of a stick, we preferred to receive those first impressions of vastness, of mystery, of gloomy magnificence, which are the more profound for being somewhat vague and general.

Scenes of war, of triumph, of worship, passed before our eyes like the incidents of a panorama. Here the King, borne along at full gallop by plumed steeds gorgeously caparisoned, draws his mighty bow and attacks a battlemented fortress. The besieged, some of whom are transfixed by his tremendous arrows, supplicate for mercy. They are a Syrian people, and are by some identified with the Northern Hittites. Their skin is yellow; and they wear the long hair and beard, the fillet, the rich robe, fringed cape, and embroidered baldric with which we are familiar in the Nineveh sculptures.* A man driving off cattle in the foreground looks as if he had stepped out of one of the tablets in the British Museum. Rameses meanwhile towers, swift and godlike, above the crowd. His coursers are of such immortal strain as were the coursers of Achilles. His sons, his whole army, chariot and horse, follow headlong at his heels. All is movement and the splendour of battle.

Farther on, we see the King returning in state, preceded by his prisoners of war. Tied together in gangs, they stagger as they go, with heads thrown back and hands uplifted. These, however, are not Assyrians, but Abyssinians and Nubians, so true to the type, so thick-lipped, flat-nosed, and woolly-headed, that only the pathos of the expression saves them from being ludicrous. It is naturalness pushed to the verge of caricature.

A little farther still, and we find Rameses leading a string of these captives into the presence of Amen-Ra, Maut, and Khons—Amen-Ra weird and unearthly, with his blue complexion and towering plumes ; Maut wearing the crown of Upper Egypt ; Khons by a subtle touch of flattery depicted with the features of the King. Again, to right and left of the entrance, Rameses, thrice the size of life, slays a group of captives of various nations. To the left Amen-Ra, to the right Ra Harmachis,[1] approve and accept the sacrifice. In the second hall we see, as usual, the procession of the sacred bark. Ptah, Khem, and Bast, gorgeous in many-coloured garments, gleam dimly, like figures in faded tapestry, from the walls of the transverse corridor.

But the wonder of Abou Simbel is the huge subject on the north side of the Great Hall. This is a monster battle-piece which covers an area of 57 feet and 7 inches in length, by 25 feet 4 inches in height, and contains over 1100 figures. Even the heraldic cornice of cartouches and asps which runs round the rest of the ceiling is omitted on this side, so that the wall is literally filled with the picture from top to bottom.

Fully to describe this huge design would take many pages. It is a picture-gallery in itself. It represents not a single action but a whole campaign. It sets before us, with Homeric simplicity, the pomp and circumstance of war, the incidents of camp life, and the accidents of the open field. We see the enemy's city with its battlemented towers and triple moat ; the besiegers' camp and the pavilion of the king ; the march of infantry ; the shock of chariots ; the hand-to-hand melée ; the flight of the vanquished ; the triumph of the Pharaoh ; the bringing in of the prisoners ; the counting of the hands of the

---

[1] Ra Harmachis, in Egyptian Har-em-Khou-ti, personifies the sun rising upon the eastern horizon.

slain.   A great river winds through the picture from end to
end, and almost surrounds the invested city.   The king in his
chariot pursues a crowd of fugitives along the bank.   Some
are crushed under his wheels ; some plunge into the water and
are drowned.[1]   Behind him, a moving wall of shields and
spears, advances with rhythmic step the serried phalanx ;
while yonder, where the fight is thickest, we see chariots overturned, men dead and dying, and riderless horses making for
the open.   Meanwhile the besieged send out mounted scouts,
and the country folk drive their cattle to the hills.

A grand frieze of chariots charging at full gallop divides
the subject lengthwise, and separates the Egyptian camp from
the field of battle.   The camp is square, and enclosed, apparently, in a palisade of shields.   It occupies less than one sixth
part of the picture, and contains about a hundred figures.
Within this narrow space the artist has brought together an
astonishing variety of incidents.   The horses feed in rows from
a common manger, or wait their turn and impatiently paw the
ground.   Some are lying down.   One, just unharnessed,
scampers round the enclosure.   Another, making off with the
empty chariot at his heels, is intercepted by a couple of grooms.
Other grooms bring buckets of water slung from the shoulders
on wooden yokes.   A wounded officer sits apart, his head
resting on his hand ; and an orderly comes in haste to bring
him news of the battle.   Another, hurt apparently in the foot,
is having the wound dressed by a surgeon.   Two detachments of
infantry, marching out to reinforce their comrades in action, are
met at the entrance to the camp by the royal chariot returning
from the field.   Rameses drives before him some fugitives, who
are trampled down, seized, and despatched upon the spot.
In one corner stands a row of objects that look like joints of
meat ; and near them are a small altar and a tripod brazier.
Elsewhere, a couple of soldiers, with a big bowl between them,
sit on their heels and dip their fingers in the mess, precisely as
every Fellah does to this day.   Meanwhile it is clear that
Egyptian discipline was strict, and that the soldier who trans-
gressed was as abjectly subject to the rule of stick as his
modern descendant.   In no less than three places do we see

[1] See chap. viii. pp. 139-140 ; also chap. xxi. p. 420.

this time-honoured institution in full operation, the superior officer energetically flourishing his staff; the private taking his punishment with characteristic disrelish. In the middle of the camp, watched over by his keeper, lies Rameses' tame lion; while close against the royal pavilion a hostile spy is surprised and stabbed by the officer on guard. The pavilion itself is very curious. It is evidently not a tent but a building, and was probably an extemporaneous construction of crude brick. It has four arched doorways, and contains in one corner an object like a cabinet, with two sacred hawks for supporters. This object, which is in fact almost identical with the hiero-glyphic emblem used to express a royal panegyry or festival, stands, no doubt, for the private oratory of the King. Five figures kneel before it in adoration.

To enumerate all or half the points of interest in this amazing picture would ask altogether too much space. Even to see it, with time at command and all the help that candles and magnesian torches can give, is far from easy. The relief is unusually low, and the surface, having originally been covered with stucco, is purposely roughened all over with tiny chisel-marks, which painfully confuse the details. Nor is this all. Owing to some kind of saline ooze in that part of the rock, the stucco has not only peeled off, but the actual surface is injured. It seems to have been eaten away, just as iron is eaten by rust. A few patches adhere, however, in places, and retain the original colouring. The river is still covered with blue and white zigzags, to represent water; some of the fighting groups are yet perfect; and two very beautiful royal chariots, one of which is surmounted by a richly ornamented parasol-canopy, are as fresh and brilliant as ever.

The horses throughout are excellent. The chariot frieze is almost Panathenaic in its effect of multitudinous movement; while the horses in the camp of Rameses, for naturalness and variety of treatment, are perhaps the best that Egyptian art has to show. It is worth noting also that a horseman, that *rara avis*, occurs some four or five times in different parts of the picture.

The scene of the campaign is laid in Syria. The river of blue and white zigzags is the Orontes;[1] the city of the besieged

---

[1] In Egyptian, *Aaranatu.*

is Kadesh or Kades ;[1] the enemy are the Kheta. The whole is, in fact, a grand picture-epic of the events immortalised in the poem of Pentaur—that poem which M. de Rougé has described as "a sort of Egyptian Iliad." The comparison would, however, apply to the picture with greater force than it applies to the poem. Pentaur, who was in the first place a courtier and in the second place a poet, has sacrificed everything to the prominence of his central figure. He is intent upon the glorification of the King ; and his poem, which is a mere pæan of praise, begins and ends with the prowess of Rameses Mer-Amen. If, then, it is to be called an Iliad, it is an Iliad from which everything that does not immediately concern Achilles is left out. The picture, on the contrary, though it shows the hero in combat and in triumph, and always of colossal proportions, yet has space for a host of minor characters. The episodes in which these characters appear are essentially Homeric. The spy is surprised and slain, as Dolon was slain by Ulysses. The men feast, and fight, and are wounded, just like the long-haired sons of Achaia ; while their horses, loosed from the yoke, eat white barley and oats

"Hard by their chariots, waiting for the dawn."

Like Homer, too, the artist of the battle-piece is careful to point out the distinguishing traits of the various combatants. The Kheta go three in a chariot ; the Egyptians only two. The Kheta wear a moustache and scalp-lock ; the Egyptians pride themselves on " a clean shave," and cover their bare heads with ponderous wigs. The Sardinian contingent cultivate their own thick hair, whiskers, and mustachios ; and their features are distinctly European. They also wear the curious helmet, surmounted by a ball and two spikes, by which they may always be recognised in the sculptures. These Sardinians appear only in the border-frieze, next the floor. The sand

---

[1] In Egyptian, *Kateshu.* "Aujourdhui encore il existe une ville de Kades près d'une courbe de l'Oronte dans le voisinage de Homs." *Leçons de M. de Rougé, Professées au Collége de France.* See MÉLANGES D'ARCHEOLOGIE, Egyp. and Assyr., vol. ii. p. 269. Also a valuable paper, entitled " The Campaign of Rameses II against Kadesh," by the Rev. G. H. Tomkins, *Trans. of the Soc. of Bib. Arch.* vol. viii. part 3, 1882. The bend of the river is actually given in the bas-reliefs.

had drifted up just at that spot, and only the top of one fantastic helmet was visible above the surface. Not knowing in the least to what this might belong, we set the men to scrape away the sand ; and so, quite by accident, uncovered the most curious and interesting group in the whole picture. The Sardinians [1] (in Egyptian Shardana) seem to have been naturalised prisoners of war drafted into the ranks of the Egyptian army ; and are the first European people whose name appears on the monuments.

There is but one hour in the twenty-four at which it is possible to form any idea of the general effect of this vast subject ; and that is at sunrise. Then only does the pure day stream in through the doorway, and temper the gloom of the side-aisles with light reflected from the sunlit floor. The broad divisions of the picture and the distribution of the masses may then be dimly seen. The details, however, require candle-light, and can only be studied a few inches at a time. Even so, it is difficult to make out the upper groups without the help of a ladder. Salame, mounted on a chair and provided with two long sticks lashed together, could barely hold his little torch high enough to enable the Writer to copy the inscription on the middle tower of the fortress of Kadesh.

It is fine to see the sunrise on the front of the Great Temple ; but something still finer takes place on certain mornings of the year, in the very heart of the mountain. As the sun comes up above the eastern hill-tops, one long, level beam strikes through the doorway, pierces the inner darkness

---

[1] " La légion *S'ardana* de l'armée de Ramses II provenait d'une première descente de ces peuples en Egypte. ' Les *S'ardaina* qui étaient des prisonniers de sa majesté,' dit expressément le texte de Karnak, au commencement du poëme de *Pentaur.* Les archéologues ont remarqué la richesse de leur costume et de leurs armures. Les principales pièces de leur vêtements semblent couvertes de broderies. Leur bouchier est une rondache : ils portent une longue et large épée de forme ordinaire, mais on remarque aussi dans leurs mains une épée d'une longueur démesurée. Le casque des S'ardana est très caracterisque ; sa forme est arrondie, mais il est surmonté d'une tige qui supporte une boule de métal. Cet ornement est accompagné de deux cornes en forme de croissant. . . . Les S'ardana de l'armée Egyptienne ont seulement des favoris et des moustaches coupés très courts."—*Memoire sur les Attaques Dirigées contre l'Egypte,* etc. etc. E. DE ROUGÉ. *Revue Archéologique,* vol. xvi. pp. 90, 91.

like an arrow, penetrates to the sanctuary, and falls like fire
from heaven upon the altar at the feet of the Gods.

No one who has watched for the coming of that shaft of
sunlight can doubt that it was a calculated effect, and that the
excavation was directed at one especial angle in order to produce it. In this way Ra, to whom the temple was dedicated,
may be said to have entered in daily, and by a direct mani-
festation of his presence to have approved the sacrifices of his
worshippers.

I need scarcely say that we did not see half the wall-
sculptures or even half the chambers, that first afternoon at
Abou Simbel. We rambled to and fro, lost in wonder, and
content to wonder, like rustics at a fair. We had, however,
ample time to come again and again, and learn it all by heart.
The Writer went in constantly, and at all hours ; but most
frequently at the end of the day's sketching, when the rest
were walking or boating in the cool of the late afternoon.

It is a wonderful place to be alone in—a place in which
the very darkness and silence are old, and in which Time
himself seems to have fallen asleep. Wandering to and fro
among these sculptured halls, like a shade among shadows,
one seems to have left the world behind ; to have done with
the teachings of the present ; to belong one's self to the past.
The very Gods assert their ancient influence over those who
question them in solitude. Seen in the fast-deepening gloom
of evening, they look instinct with supernatural life. There
were times when I should scarcely have been surprised to hear
them speak—to see them rise from their painted thrones and
come down from the walls. There were times when I felt
I believed in them.

There was something so weird and awful about the place,
and it became so much more weird and awful the farther one
went in, that I rarely ventured beyond the first hall when
quite alone. One afternoon, however, when it was a little
earlier, and therefore a little lighter, than usual, I went to the
very end, and sat at the feet of the Gods in the sanctuary.
All at once (I cannot tell why, for my thoughts just then were
far away) it flashed upon me that a whole mountain hung—
ready, perhaps, to cave in—above my head. Seized by a

sudden panic such as one feels in dreams, I tried to run ; but my feet dragged, and the floor seemed to sink under them. I felt I could not have called for help, though it had been to save my life. It is unnecessary, perhaps, to add that the mountain did not cave in, and that I had my fright for nothing. It would have been a grand way of dying, all the same ; and a still grander way of being buried.

My visits to the Great Temple were not always so dramatic. I sometimes took Salame, who smoked cigarettes when not on active duty, or held a candle while I sketched patterns of cornices, head-dresses of Kings and Gods, designs of necklaces and bracelets, heads of captives, and the like. Sometimes we explored the side-chambers. Of these there are eight ; pitch-dark, and excavated at all kinds of angles. Two or three are surrounded by stone benches cut in the rock ; and in one the hieroglyphic inscriptions are part cut, part sketched in black and left unfinished. As this temple is entirely the work of Rameses II, and betrays no sign of having been added to by any of his successors, these evidences of incompleteness would seem to show that the King died before the work was ended.

I was always under the impression that there were secret places yet undiscovered in these dark chambers, and Salame and I were always looking for them. At Denderah, at Edfû, at Medinet Habu, at Philæ,[1] there have been found crypts in the thickness of the walls and recesses under the pavements, for the safe-keeping of treasure in time of danger. The rock-cut temples must also have had their hiding-places ; and these would doubtless take the form of concealed cells in the walls, or under the floors, of the side-chambers.

To come out from these black holes into the twilight of the Great Hall and see the landscape set, as it were, in the ebon frame of the doorway, was alone worth the journey to Abou Simbel. The sun being at such times in the west, the river, the yellow sand-island, the palms and tamarisks opposite, and the mountains of the eastern desert, were all flooded with a glory of light and colour to which no pen or pencil could

---

[1] A rich treasure of gold and silver rings was found by Ferlini, in 1834, immured in the wall of one of the pyramids of Meröe, in Upper Nubia. See *Lepsius's Letters*, translated by L. and J. HORNER, Bohn, 1853, p. 151.

possibly do justice. Not even the mountains of Moab in Holman Hunt's " Scapegoat " were so warm with rose and gold.

Thus our days passed at Abou Simbel ; the workers working ; the idlers idling ; strangers from the outer world now and then coming and going. The heat on shore was great, especially in the sketching-tents ; but the north breeze blew steadily every day from about an hour after sunrise till an hour before sunset, and on board the dahabeeyah it was always cool.

The Happy Couple took advantage of this good wind to do a good deal of boating, and by judiciously timing their excursions, contrived to use the tail of the day's breeze for their trip out, and the strong arms of four good rowers to bring them back again. In this way they managed to see the little rock-cut Temple of Ferayg, which the rest of us unfortunately missed. On another occasion they paid a visit to a certain Sheyhk who lived at a village about two miles south of Abou Simbel. He was a great man, as Nubian magnates go. His name was Hassan Ebn Rashwan el Kashef, and he was a grandson of that same old Hassan Kashef who was vice-regent of Nubia in the days of Burckhardt and Belzoni. He received our Happy Couple with distinguished hospitality, killed a sheep in their honour, and entertained them for more than three hours. The meal consisted of an endless succession of dishes, all of which, like that bugbear of our childhood, the hated Air with Variations, went on repeating the same theme under a multitude of disguises ; and, whether roast, boiled, stewed or minced, served on skewers, smothered in rice, or drowned in sour milk, were always mutton *au fond.*

We now despaired of ever seeing a crocodile ; and but for a trail that our men discovered on the island opposite, we should almost have ceased to believe that there were crocodiles in Egypt. The marks were quite fresh when we went to look at them. The creature had been basking high and dry in the sun, and this was the point at which he had gone down again to the river. The damp sand at the water's edge had taken the mould of his huge fleshy paws, and even of the jointed armour of his tail, though this last impression was somewhat blurred by the final rush with which he had taken to the water. I doubt if Robinson Crusoe, when he saw the famous footprint on the shore, was more excited than we of the Philæ at sight of this genuine and undeniable trail.

As for the Idle Man, he flew at once to arms and made ready for the fray. He caused a shallow grave to be dug for himself a few yards from the spot ; then went and lay in it for hours together, morning after morning, under the full blaze of the sun,—flat, patient, alert,—with his gun ready cocked, and a Pall Mall Budget up his back. It was not his fault if he narrowly escaped sunstroke, and had his labour for his reward. That crocodile was too clever for him, and took care never to come back.

Our sailors, meanwhile, though well pleased with an occasional holiday, began to find Abou Simbel monotonous. As long as the Bagstones stayed, the two crews met every evening to smoke, and dance, and sing their quaint roundelays together. But when rumours came of wonderful things already done this winter above Wady Halfeh—rumours that represented the Second Cataract as a populous solitude of crocodiles —then our faithful consort slipped away one morning before sunrise, and the Philæ was left companionless.

At this juncture, seeing that the men's time hung heavy on their hands, our Painter conceived the idea of setting them to clean the face of the northernmost Colossus, still disfigured by the plaster left on it when the great cast[1] was taken by Mr.

[1] This cast, the property of the British Museum, is placed over a door leading to the library at the end of the northern Vestibule, opposite the staircase. I was informed by the late Mr. Bonomi that the mould was made by Mr. Hay, who had with him an Italian assistant picked up in Cairo. They took with them some barrels of plaster and a couple of ladders, and contrived, with such spars and poles as belonged to the dahabeeyah, to erect a scaffolding and a matted shelter for the plasterman. The Colossus was at this time buried up to its chin in sand, which made their task so much the easier. When the mould of the head was brought to England, it was sent to Mr. Bonomi's studio, together with a mould of the head of the Colossus at Mitrahenny, a mould of the apex of the fallen obelisk at Karnak, and moulds of the wall-sculptures at Bayt-el-Welly. Mr. Bonomi superintended the casting and placing of all these in the Museum about three years after the moulds were made. This was at the time when Mr. Hawkins held the post of Keeper of Antiquities. I

Hay more than half a century before. This happy thought was promptly carried into effect. A scaffolding of spars and

CLEANING THE COLOSSUS.

oars was at once improvised, and the men, delighted as children at play, were soon swarming all over the huge head, just as the

mention these details, not simply because they have a special interest for all who are acquainted with Abou Simbel, but because a good deal of misapprehension has prevailed on the subject, some travellers attributing the disfigurement of the head to Lepsius, others to the Crystal Palace Company, and so forth. Even so careful a writer as the late Miss Martineau ascribes it, on hearsay, to Champollion.

carvers may have swarmed over it in the days when Rameses was king.

All they had to do was to remove any small lumps that might yet adhere to the surface, and then tint the white patches with coffee. This they did with bits of sponge tied to the ends of sticks ; but Reïs Hassan, as a mark of dignity, had one of the Painter's old brushes, of which he was immensely proud.

It took them three afternoons to complete the job ; and we were all sorry when it came to an end. To see Reïs Hassan artistically touching up a gigantic nose almost as long as himself; Riskalli and the cook-boy staggering to and fro with relays of coffee, brewed " thick and slab " for the purpose ; Salame perched cross-legged, like some complacent imp, on the towering rim of the great pschent overhead ; the rest chattering and skipping about the scaffolding like monkeys, was, I will venture to say, a sight more comic than has ever been seen at Abou Simbel before or since.

Rameses' appetite for coffee was prodigious. He consumed I know not how many gallons a day. Our cook stood aghast at the demand made upon his stores. Never before had he been called upon to provide for a guest whose mouth measured three feet and a half in width.

Still, the result justified the expenditure. The coffee proved a capital match for the sandstone ; and though it was not possible wholly to restore the uniformity of the original surface, we at least succeeded in obliterating those ghastly splotches, which for so many years have marred this beautiful face as with the unsightliness of leprosy.

What with boating, fishing, lying in wait for crocodiles, cleaning the colossus, and filling reams of thin letter paper to friends at home, we got through the first week quickly enough —the Painter and the Writer working hard, meanwhile, in their respective ways; the Painter on his big canvas in front of the Temple ; the Writer shifting her little tent as she listed.

Now, although the most delightful occupation in life is undoubtedly sketching, it must be admitted that the sketcher at Abou Simbel works under difficulties. Foremost among these comes the difficulty of position. The great Temple stands within about twenty-five yards of the brink of the bank, and the lesser Temple within as many feet ; so that to get far enough from one's subject is simply impossible   The present Writer sketched the small Temple from the deck of the dahabeeyah ; there being no point of view obtainable on shore.

Next comes the difficulty of colour.   Everything, except the sky and the river, is yellow——yellow, that is to say, " with a difference ;" yellow ranging through every gradation of orange, maize, apricot, gold, and buff.   The mountains are sandstone ; the Temples are sandstone ; the sandslope is powdered sand-stone from the sandstone desert.   In all these objects, the scale of colour is necessarily the same.   Even the shadows, glowing with reflected light, give back tempered repetitions of the dominant hue.   Hence it follows that he who strives, however humbly, to reproduce the facts of the scene before him, is compelled, *bon gré, mal gré*, to execute what some of our young painters would now-a-days call a Symphony in Yellow.

Lastly, there are the minor inconveniences of sun, sand, wind, and flies.   The whole place radiates heat, and seems almost to radiate light.   The glare from above and the glare from below are alike intolerable.   Dazzled, blinded, unable to even look at his subject without the aid of smoke-coloured glasses, the sketcher whose tent is pitched upon the sandslope over against the great Temple enjoys a foretaste of cremation.

When the wind blows from the north (which at this time of the year is almost always) the heat is perhaps less distress-ing, but the sand is maddening.   It fills your hair, your eyes, your water-bottles ; silts up your colour-box ; dries into your skies ; and reduces your Chinese white to a gritty paste the colour of salad-dressing.   As for the flies, they have a morbid appetite for water-colours.   They follow your wet brush along the paper, leave their legs in the yellow ochre, and plunge with avidity into every little pool of cobalt as it is mixed ready for use.   Nothing disagrees with them ; nothing poisons them—— not even olive-green.

It was a delightful time, however——delightful alike for those who worked and those who rested——and these small troubles counted for nothing in the scale.   Yet it was pleasant, all the same, to break away for a day or two, and be off to Wady Halfeh.

CHAPTER XVII.

THE SECOND CATARACT.

A FRESH breeze, a full sail, and the consciousness of a holiday well earned, carried us gaily along from Abou Simbel to Wady Halfeh. We started late in the afternoon of the first day, made about twelve miles before the wind dropped, and achieved the remaining twenty-eight miles before noon the next day. It was our last trip on the Nile under canvas. At Wady Halfeh the Philæ was doomed to be dismantled. The big sail that had so long been our pride and delight would there be taken down, and our good boat, her grace and swiftness gone at one fell swoop, would become a mere lumbering barge, more suggestive of civic outings on the Thames than of Cleopatra's galley.

For some way beyond Abou Simbel, the western bank is fringed by a long line of volcanic mountains, as much alike in height, size, and shape, as a row of martello towers. They are divided from one another by a series of perfectly uniform sand-drifts; while on the rounded top of each mountain, thick as the currants on the top of a certain cake, known to schoolboys by the endearing name of "black-caps," lies a layer of the oddest black stones in the world. Having more than once been to the top of the rock of Abshek (which is the first large mountain of the chain, and strewn in the same way) we recognised the stones, and knew what they were like. In colour they are purplish black, tinged here and there with dull red. They ring like clinkstone when struck, and in shape are most fantastic. L. picked up some like petrified bunches of grapes. Others are twisted and writhen like the Vesuvian lava of 1871. They lie loose upon the surface, and are of all sizes ; some being as small as currants, and others as large as quartern loaves. Speaking as one having no kind of authority, I should say that these stones are unquestionably of fiery parentage. One seems to see how, boiling and bubbling in a state of fusion, they must have been suddenly checked by contact with some cooler medium.

Where the chain ends, about three or four miles above Abou Simbel, the view widens, and a host of outlying mountains are seen scattered over an immense plain reaching for miles into the western desert. On the eastern bank, Kalat Adda,[1]—

---

[1] "A castle, resembling in size and form that of Ibrim ; it bears the name of Kalat Adda ; it has been abandoned many years, being entirely surrounded by barren rocks. Part of its ancient wall, similar in construction to that of Ibrim, still remains. The habitations are built partly of stone, and partly of bricks. On the most elevated spot in the small town, eight or ten grey granite columns of small dimensions lie on the ground, with a few capitals near them of clumsy Greek architecture."—Burckhardt's *Travels in Nubia*, 1819, p. 38.

In a curious Arabic history of Nubia written in the tenth century A.D. by one Abdallah ben Ahmed ben Solaïm of Assûan, fragments of which are preserved in the great work of Makrizy, quoted by Burckhardt and E. Quatremere (see footnote, p. 224), there occurs the following remarkable passage : " In this province (Nubia) is situated the city of Bedjrasch, capital of Maris, the fortress of Ibrim, and another place called Adwa, which has a port, and is, they say, the birthplace of the sage Lokman and of Dhoul Noun. There is to be seen there a magnificent Birbeh."— (" On y voit un *Berba* magnifique ").—*Mémoires Géographiques sur l'Egypte*, etc. E. QUATREMERE, Paris, 1811 ; vol. ii. p. 8.

If Adwa and Adda are one and the same, it is possible that in this passage we find preserved the only comparatively modern indication of some great rock-cut temple, the entrance to which is now entirely covered by the sand. It is clear that neither Abou Simbel (which is on the opposite bank, and some three or four miles north of Adda) nor Ferayg (which is also some way off, and quite a small place) can here be intended. That another temple exists somewhere between Abou Simbel and Wady Halfeh, and is yet to be discovered, seems absolutely certain from the tenor of a large stela sculptured on the rock a few paces north of the smaller temple at Abou Simbel. This stela, which is one of the most striking and elaborate there, represents an Egyptian gateway surmounted by the winged globe, and shows Rameses II enthroned, and receiving the homage of a certain Prince whose name, as translated by Rosellini, is Rameses-Neniscti-Habai. The inscription, which is in sixteen columns and perfectly preserved, records the titles and praises of the King, and

a huge, rambling Roman citadel, going to solitary ruin on the last water-washed precipice to the left—brings the opposite range to a like end, and abuts on a similar plain, also scattered over with detached peaks. The scene here is desolately magnificent. A large island covered with palms divides the Nile in two branches, each of which looks as wide as the whole river. An unbounded distance opens away to the silvery horizon. On the banks there is no verdure ; neither is there any sign of human toil. Nothing lives, nothing moves, save the wind and the river.

Of all the strange peaks we have yet seen, the mountains hereabout are the strangest. Alone or in groups, they start up here and there from the deserts on both sides, like the pieces on a chess-board. They are for the most part conical ; but they are not extinct craters, such as are the volcanic cones of Korosko and Dakkeh. Seeing how they all rose to about the same height, and were alike capped with that mysterious *couche* of shining black stones, the Writer could not help fancying that, like the isolated Rocher de Corneille and Rocher de St. Michel at Puy, they might be but fragments of a rocky crust, rent and swept away at some infinitely remote period of the world's history, and that the level of their present summits might represent perhaps the ancient level of the plain.

states how "he hath made a monumental abode for Horus, his father, Lord of Ha'm, excavating in the bowels of the rock of Ha'm to make him a habitation of many ages." We know nothing of the Rock of Ha'm (rendered Sciam by Rosellini), but it should no doubt be sought somewhere between Abou Simbel and Wady Halfeh. "Qual sito precisamente dinotisi in questo nome di Sciam, io non saprei nel presente stato delle cose determinare : credo peraltro secondo varie luoghi delle iscrizioni che lo ricordano, che fosse situato sull' una o l'altra sponda del Nilo, nel paese compreso tra Wadi-halfa e Ibsambul, o poco oltre. E qui dovrebbe trovarsi il nominato speco di Horus, fino al presente occulto a noi."— Rosellini, Letterpress to *Monumenti Storici*, vol. iii. part ii. p. 184. It would hence appear that the Rock of Ha'm is mentioned in other inscriptions.

The distance between Abou Simbel and Wady Halfeh is only forty miles, and the likely places along the banks are but few. Would not the discovery of this lost Temple be an enterprise worthier the ambition of tourists, than the extermination of such few crocodiles as yet linger north of the Second Cataract ?

As regards form, they are weird enough for the wildest geological theories. All taper more or less towards the top. One is four-sided, like a pyramid ; another, in shape a truncated cone, looks as if crowned with a pagoda summer-house ; a third seems to be surmounted by a mosque and cupola ; a fourth is scooped out in tiers of arches ; a fifth is crowned, apparently, with a cairn of piled stones ; and so on with variations as endless as they are fantastic. A geologist might perhaps account for these caprices by showing how fire, and earthquake, and deluge, had here succeeded each other ; and how, after being first covered with volcanic stones and then split into chasms, the valleys thus opened had by and by been traversed by torrents which wore away the softer parts of the rock and left the harder standing.

Some way beyond Kalat Adda, when the Abou Simbel range and the palm island have all but vanished in the distance, and the lonely peak, called the Mountain of the Sun (Gebel esh-Shems), has been left far behind, we come upon a new wonder—namely, upon two groups of scattered tumuli, one on the eastern, one on the western bank. Not volcanic forms these ; not even accidental forms, if one may venture to form an opinion from so far off. They are of various sizes ; some little, some big ; all perfectly round and smooth, and covered with a rich greenish-brown alluvial soil. How did they come there ? Who made them ? What did they contain ? The Roman ruin close by—the 240,000[1] deserters who must have passed this way—the Egyptian and Ethiopian armies that certainly poured their thousands along these very banks, and might have fought many a battle on this open plain, suggest all kinds of possibilities, and fill one's head with visions of buried arms, and jewels, and cinerary urns. We are more than half-minded to stop the boat and land that very moment ; but are content on second thoughts with promising ourselves that we will at least excavate one of the smaller hillocks on our way back.

And now, the breeze freshening and the dahabeeyah tearing gallantly along, we leave the tumuli behind and enter upon a still more desolate region, where the mountains recede farther

[1] See footnote, p. 290.

than ever, and the course of the river is interrupted by perpetual sandbanks.

On one of these sandbanks, just a few yards above the edge of the water, lay a log of drift-wood, apparently a battered old palm trunk, with some remnants of broken branches yet clinging to it ; such an object, in short, as my American friends would very properly call a " snag."

Our pilot leaned forward on the tiller, put his finger to his lip, and whispered :—

" Crocodilo ! "

The Painter, the Idle Man, the Writer, were all on deck, and not one believed him. They had seen too many of these snags already, and were not going to let themselves again be excited about nothing.

The pilot pointed to the cabin where L. and the Little Lady were indulging in that minor vice called afternoon tea.

" Sittèh ! " said he, " call Sittèh ! Crocodilo ! "

We examined the object through our glasses. We laughed the pilot to scorn. It was the worst imitation of a crocodile that we had yet seen.

All at once the palm-trunk lifted up its head, cocked its tail, found its legs, set off running, wriggling, undulating down the slope with incredible rapidity, and was gone before we could utter an exclamation.

We three had a bad time when the other two came up and found that we had seen our first crocodile without them.

A sandbank which we passed next morning was scored all over with fresh trails, and looked as if it had been the scene of a crocodile-parliament. There must have been at least twenty or thirty members present at the sitting ; and the freshness of the marks showed that they had only just dispersed.

A keen and cutting wind carried us along the last thirty miles of our journey. We had supposed that the farther south we penetrated, the hotter we should find the climate ; yet now, strange to say, we were shivering in seal-skins, under the most brilliant sky in the world, and in a latitude more southerly than that of Mecca or Calcutta. It was some compensation, however, to run at full speed past the dullest of Nile scenery, seeing only sandbanks in the river ; sand-hills and sand-flats on either

hand ; a disused shadoof or a skeleton boat rotting at the water's
edge ; a wind-tormented Dôm-palm struggling for existence on
the brink of the bank.

At a fatal corner about six miles below Wady Halfeh, we
passed a melancholy flotilla of dismantled dahabeeyahs—the
Fostât, the Zenobia, the Alice, the Mansoorah—all alike weather-
bound and laid up helplessly against the wind.   The Mansoorah,
with Captain and Mrs. E. on board, had been three days doing
these six miles : at which rate of progress they might reasonably hope to reach Cairo in about a year and a month.

WADY HALFEH.

The palms of Wady Halfeh, blue with distance, came into
sight at the next bend ; and by noon the Philæ was once more
moored alongside the Bagstones under a shore crowded with
cangias, covered with bales and packing cases, and, like the
shores of Mahatta and Assûan, populous with temporary huts.
For here it is that traders going by water embark and disembark on their way to and fro between Dongola and the First
Cataract.

There were three temples—or at all events three ancient
Egyptian buildings—once upon a time on the western bank

over against Wady Halfeh.   Now there are a few broken pillars, a solitary fragment of brick pylon, some remains of a flight of stone steps leading down to the river, and a wall of enclosure overgrown with wild pumpkins.   These ruins, together with a rambling native Khan and a noble old sycamore, form a picturesque group backed by amber sand-cliffs, and mark the site of a lost city[1] belonging to the early days of Usurtesen III.

The Second, or Great Cataract, begins a little way above Wady Halfeh and extends over a distance of many miles.   It consists, like the First Cataract, of a succession of rocks and rapids, and is skirted for the first five miles or so by the sand-cliff ridge which, as I have said, forms a background to the ruins just opposite Wady Halfeh.   This ridge terminates abruptly in the famous precipice known as the Rock of Abusîr. Only adventurous travellers bound for Dongola or Khartûm go beyond this point ; and they, for the most part, take the shorter route across the desert from Korosko.   L. and the Writer would fain have hired camels and pushed on as far as Semneh ; which is a matter of only two days' journey from Wady Halfeh, and, for people provided with sketching tents, is one of the easiest of inland excursions.

One may go to the Rock of Abusîr by land or by water. The Happy Couple and the Writer took two native boatmen versed in the intricacies of the Cataract ; and went in the felucca.   L. and the Painter preferred donkeying.   Given a good breeze from the right quarter, there is, as regards time, but little to choose between the two routes.   No one, however, who has approached the Rock of Abusîr by water, and seen it rise like a cathedral front from the midst of that labyrinth of rocky islets—some like clusters of basaltic columns, some crowned with crumbling ruins, some bleak and bare, some green with wild pomegranate trees—can doubt which is the more picturesque.

---

[1] " Un Second Temple, plus grand, mais tout aussi détruit que le précédent, existe un peu plus au sud, c'était le grand temple de la ville Egyptienne de *Béhéni*, qui exista sur cet emplacement, et qui d'après l'étendu des débris de poteries répandus sur la plaine aujourdhui déserte, parait avoir été assez grande."—Champollion, *Lettres écrites d'Egypte*, etc., ed. 1868 ; Letter ix.

Landing among the tamarisks at the foot of the cliff, we come to the spreading skirts of a sand-drift steeper and more fatiguing to climb than the sand-drift at Abou Simbel. We do climb it, however, though somewhat sulkily, and finding the donkey-party perched upon the top, are comforted with draughts of ice-cold lemonade, brought in a kullah from Wady Halfeh.

The summit of the rock is a mere ridge, steep and over-hanging towards east and south, and carved all over with auto-graphs in stone. Some few of these are interesting ; but for the most part they record only the visits of the illustrious-obscure. We found Belzoni's name ; but looked in vain for the signatures of Burckhardt, Champollion, Lepsius, and Ampère.

Owing to the nature of the ground and the singular clear-ness of the atmosphere, the view from this point seemed to me to be the most extensive I had ever looked upon. Yet the height of the rock of Abusîr is comparatively insignificant. It would count but as a mole-hill, if measured against some Alpine summits of my acquaintance. I doubt whether it is as lofty as even the Great Pyramid. It is, however, a giddy place to look down from, and seems higher than it is.

It is hard, now that we are actually here, to realise that this is the end of our journey. The Cataract—an immense multitude of black and shining islets, among which the river, divided into hundreds of separate channels, spreads far and wide for a distance, it is said, of more than sixteen miles,— foams at our feet. Foams, and frets, and falls ; gushing smooth and strong where its course is free ; murmuring hoarsely where it is interrupted ; now hurrying ; now loitering ; here eddying in oily circles ; there lying in still pools unbroken by a ripple ; everywhere full of life, full of voices ; everywhere shining to the sun. Northwards, where it winds away towards Abou Simbel, we see all the fantastic mountains of yesterday on the horizon. To the east, still bounded by out-liers of the same disconnected chain, lies a rolling waste of dark and stony wilderness, trenched with innumerable valleys through which flow streams of sand. On the western side, the continuity of the view is interrupted by the ridge which ends with Abusîr. Southwards, the Libyan desert reaches away in one vast undulating plain ; tawny, arid, monotonous; all sun; all sand; lit here and there with arrowy flashes of the Nile. Farthest of all, pale but distinct, on the outermost rim of the world, rise two mountain summits, one long, one dome-like. Our Nubians tell us that these are the mountains of Dongola. Comparing our position with that of the Third Cataract as it appears upon the map, we come to the conclusion that these ghost-like silhouettes are the summits of Mount Fogo[1] and Mount Arambo—two apparently parallel mountains situate on opposite sides of the river about ten miles below Hannek, and consequently about 145 miles, as the bird flies, from the spot on which we are standing.

In all this extraordinary panorama, so wild, so weird, so desolate, there is nothing really beautiful, except the colour. But the colour is transcendent. Never, even in Egypt, have I seen anything so tender, so transparent, so harmonious. I shut my eyes, and it all comes before me. I see the amber of the sands; the pink and pearly mountains; the Cataract rocks, all black and purple and polished; the dull grey palms that cluster here and there upon the larger islands; the vivid verdure of the tamarisks and pomegranates; the Nile, a greenish brown flecked with yeasty foam; over all, the blue and burning sky, permeated with light, and palpitating with sunshine.

I made no sketch. I felt that it would be ludicrous to attempt it. And I feel now that any endeavour to put the scene into words is a mere presumptuous effort to describe the indescribable. Words are useful instruments; but, like the etching needle and the burin, they stop short at form. They cannot translate colour.

If a traveller pressed for time asked me whether he should or should not go as far as the Second Cataract, I think I should recommend him to turn back from Abou Simbel. The trip must cost four days; and if the wind should happen to be unfavourable either way, it may cost six or seven. The forty miles of river that have to be twice traversed are the dullest on the Nile; the Cataract is but an enlarged and barren edition of the Cataract between Assûan and Philæ; and the great

[1] Mount Fogo, as shown upon Keith Johnston's map of Egypt and Nubia, would seem to be identical with the Ali Bersi of Lepsius.

view, as I have said, has not that kind of beauty which attracts the general tourist.

It has an interest, however, beyond and apart from that of beauty. It rouses one's imagination to a sense of the greatness of the Nile. We look across a world of desert, and see the river still coming from afar. We have reached a point at which all that is habitable and familiar comes abruptly to an end. Not a village, not a bean-field, not a shâdûf, not a sakkieh, is to be seen in the plain below. There is no sail on those dangerous waters. There is no moving creature on those pathless sands. But for the telegraphic wires stalking, ghost-like, across the desert, it would seem as if we had touched the limit of civilisation, and were standing on the threshold of a land unexplored.

Yet for all this, we feel as if we were at only the beginning of the mighty river. We have journeyed well-nigh a thousand miles against the stream ; but what is that to the distance which still lies between us and the Great Lakes ? And how far beyond the Great Lakes must we seek for the Source that is even yet undiscovered ?

We stayed at Wady Halfeh but one night, and paid but one visit to the Cataract. We saw no crocodiles, though they are still plentiful among these rocky islets. The M. B.'s, who had been here a week, were full of crocodile stories, and of Alfred's deeds of arms. He had stalked and shot a monster, two days before our arrival ; but the creature had rushed into the water when hit, waving its tail furiously above its head, and had neither been seen nor heard of since.

Like Achilles, the crocodile has but one vulnerable spot ; and this is a small unarmoured patch behind the forearm. He will take a good deal of killing even there, unless the bullet finds its way to a vital part, or is of the diabolical kind called "explosive." Even when mortally wounded, he seldom drops on the spot. With his last strength, he rushes to the water and dies at the bottom.

After three days the carcase rises and floats, and our friends were now waiting in order that Alfred might bag his big game. Too often, however, the poor brute either crawls into a hole, or, in his agony, becomes entangled among weeds and comes up no more. For one crocodile bagged, a dozen regain the river, and after lingering miserably under water, die out of sight and out of reach of the sportsman.

While we were climbing the Rock of Abusîr, our men were busy taking down the big sail and preparing the Philæ for her long and ignominious journey down stream. We came back to find the mainyard laid along like a roof-tree above our heads ; the sail rolled up in a huge ball and resting on the roof of the kitchen ; the small aftersail and yard hoisted on the mainmast ; the oars lashed six on each side ; and the lower deck a series of yawning chasms, every alternate plank being taken up so as to form seats and standing places for the rowers.

Thus dismantled, the dahabeeyah becomes, in fact, a galley. Her oars are now her chief motive power ; and a crew of steady rowers (having always the current in their favour) can do thirty miles a day. When, however, a good breeze blows from the south, the small sail and the current are enough to carry the boat well along ; and then the men reserve their strength for rowing by night, when the wind has dropped. Sometimes, when it is a dead calm and the rowers need rest, the dahabeeyah is left to her own devices, and floats with the stream—now waltzing ludicrously in the middle of the river ; now drifting sidewise like Mr. Winkle's horse ; now sidling up to the east bank ; now changing her mind and blundering over to the west ; making upon an average about a mile and a half or two miles an hour, and presenting a pitiful spectacle of helpless imbecility. At other times, however, the head wind blows so hard that neither oars nor current avail ; and then there is nothing for it but to lie under the bank and wait for better times.

This was our sad case in going back to Abou Simbel. Having struggled with no little difficulty through the first five-and-twenty miles, we came to a dead lock about half-way between Faras and Gebel-esh-Shems. Carried forward by the stream, driven back by the wind, buffeted by the waves, and bumped incessantly by the rocking to and fro of the felucca, our luckless Philæ, after oscillating for hours within the space of a mile, was run at last into a sheltered nook, and there left in peace till the wind should change or drop.

Imprisoned here for a day and a half, we found ourselves, fortunately, within reach of the tumuli which we had already made up our minds to explore. Making first for those on the east bank, we took with us in the felucca four men to row and dig, a fire-shovel, a small hatchet, an iron bar, and a large wicker basket, which were the only implements we possessed. What we wanted both then and afterwards, and what no dahabeeyah should ever be without, were two or three good spades, a couple of picks, and a crowbar.

Climbing to the top of one of the highest of these hillocks, we began by surveying the ground. The desert here is firm to the tread, flat, compact, and thickly strewn with pebbles. Of the fine yellow sand which characterises the Libyan bank, there is little to be seen, and that little lies like snow in drifts and clefts and hollows, as if carried thither by the wind. The tumuli, however, are mounded of pure alluvial mould, smooth, solid, and symmetrical. We counted thirty-four of all sizes, from five to about five-and-thirty feet in height, and saw at least as many more on the opposite side of the river.

Selecting one of about eight feet high, we then set the sailors to work; and although it was impossible, with so few men and such insufficient tools, to cut straight through the centre of the mound, we at all events succeeded in digging down to a solid substratum of lumps of crude clay, evidently moulded by hand.

Whether these formed only the foundation of the tumulus, or concealed a grave excavated below the level of the desert, we had neither time nor means to ascertain. It was something, at all events, to have convinced ourselves that the mounds were artificial.[1]

As we came away, we met a Nubian peasant trudging northwards. He was leading a sorry camel; had a white

---

[1] On referring to Col. H. Vyse's *Voyage into Upper Egypt*, etc., I see that he also opened one of these tumuli, but "found no indication of an artificial construction." I can only conclude that he did not carry his excavation low enough. As it is difficult to suppose the tumuli made for nothing, I cannot help believing that they would repay a more systematic investigation.

cockerel under his arm ; and was followed by a frightened woman, who drew her shawl over her face and cowered behind him, at sight of the Ingleezeh.

We asked the man what the mounds were, and who made them ; but he shook his head, and said they had been there 'from old time." We then inquired by what name they were known in these parts ; to which, urging his camel forward, he replied hesitatingly that they had a name, but that he had forgotten it.

Having gone a little way, however, he presently turned back, saying that he now remembered all about it, and that they were called " The Horns of Yackma."

More than this we could not get from him. Who Yackma was, or how he came to have horns, or why his horns should take the form of tumuli, was more than he could tell or we could guess.

We gave him a small backshîsh, however, in return for this mysterious piece of information, and went our way with all possible speed ; intending to row across and see the mounds on the opposite bank before sunset. But we had not calculated upon the difficulty of either threading our way among a chain of sandbanks, or going at least two miles farther north, so as to get round into the navigable channel at the other side. We of course tried the shorter way, and after running aground some three or four times, had to give it up, hoist our little sail, and scud homewards as fast as the wind would carry us.

The coming back thus, after an excursion in the felucca, is one of the many pleasant things that one has to remember of the Nile. The sun has set ; the afterglow has faded ; the stars are coming out. Leaning back with a satisfied sense of something seen or done, one listens to the old dreamy chant of the rowers, and to the ripple under the keel. The palms, meanwhile, glide past, and are seen in bronzed relief against the sky. Presently the big boat, all glittering with lights, looms up out of the dusk. A cheery voice hails from the poop. We glide under the bows. Half-a-dozen smiling brown faces bid us welcome, and as many pairs of brown hands are outstretched to help us up the side. A savoury smell is wafted from the kitchen ; a pleasant vision of the dining-saloon, with table ready spread and lamps ready lit, flashes upon us through the open doorway. We are at home once more. Let us eat, drink, rest, and be merry ; for to-morrow the hard work of sight-seeing and sketching begins again.

THE ROCK OF ABUSÎR.

CHAPTER XVIII.

DISCOVERIES AT ABOU SIMBEL.

W E came back to find a fleet of dahabeeyahs ranged along
the shore at Abou Simbel, and no less than three sketching
tents in occupation of the ground. One of these, which
happened to be pitched on the precise spot vacated by our
Painter, was courteously shifted to make way for the original
tenant ; and in the course of a couple of hours, we were all as
much at home as if we had not been away for half-a-day.

Here, meanwhile, was our old acquaintance the Fostât,
with her party of gentlemen ; yonder the Zenobia, all ladies ;
the little Alice, with Sir J. C. and Mr. W. on board ; the
Sirena, flying the stars and stripes ; the Mansoorah, bound
presently for the Fayûm. To these were next day added the
Ebers, with a couple of German savants ; and the Bagstones,
welcome back from Wady Halfeh.

What with arrivals and departures, exchange of visits,
exhibitions of sketches, and sociabilities of various kinds, we
had now quite a gay time. The Philæ gave a dinner-party
and fantasia under the very noses of the colossi, and every
evening there was drumming and howling enough among the
assembled crews to raise the ghosts of Rameses and all his
Queens. This was pleasant enough while it lasted ; but when
the strangers dropped off one by one, and at the end of three
days we were once more alone, I think we were not sorry.
The place was, somehow, too solemn for

"Singing, laughing, ogling, and all that."

It was by comparing our watches with those of the

travellers whom we met at Abou Simbel, that we now found
out how hopelessly our timekeepers and theirs had gone astray.
We had been altering ours continually ever since leaving
Cairo ; but the sun was as continually putting them wrong
again, so that we had lost all count of the true time.   The
first words with which we now greeted a newcomer were—
" Do you know what o'clock it is ? "   To which the stranger as
invariably replied that it was the very question he was himself
about to ask.   The confusion became at last so great that,
finding that we had about eleven hours of day to thirteen
of night, we decided to establish an arbitrary canon ; so we
called it seven when the sun rose, and six when it set, which
answered every purpose.

It was between two and four o'clock, according to this
time of ours, that the Southern Cross was now visible every
morning.   It is undoubtedly best seen at Abou Simbel.   The
river is here very wide, and just where the constellation rises
there is an opening in the mountains on the eastern bank, so
that these four fine stars, though still low in the heavens, are
seen in a free space of sky.   If they make, even so, a less
magnificent appearance than one has been led to expect, it is
probably because we see them from too low a point of view.
To say that a constellation is foreshortened sounds absurd ;
yet that is just what is the matter with the Southern Cross at
Abou Simbel.   Viewed at an angle of about 30°, it necessarily
looks distort and dim.   If seen burning in the zenith, it would
no doubt come up to the level of its reputation.

It was now the fifth day after our return from Wady
Halfeh, when an event occurred that roused us to an unwonted
pitch of excitement, and kept us at high pressure throughout
the rest of our time.

The day was Sunday ; the date February 16th, 1874 ; the
time, according to Philæ reckoning, about eleven A.M., when
the Painter, enjoying his seventh day's holiday after his own
fashion, went strolling about among the rocks.   He happened
to turn his steps southwards, and, passing the front of the
Great Temple, climbed to the top of a little shapeless mound
of fallen cliff, and sand, and crude-brick wall, just against
the corner where the mountain slopes down to the river.

Immediately round this corner, looking almost due south, and approachable by only a narrow ledge of rock, are two votive tablets sculptured and painted, both of the thirty-eighth year of Rameses II. We had seen these from the river as we came back from Wady Halfeh, and had remarked how 'fine the view must be from that point. Beyond the fact that they are coloured, and that the colour upon them is still bright, there is nothing remarkable about these inscriptions. There are many such at Abou Simbel. Our Painter did not, therefore, come here to examine the tablets ; he was attracted solely by the view.

Turning back presently, his attention was arrested by some much mutilated sculptures on the face of the rock, a few yards nearer the south buttress of the Temple. He had seen these sculptures before—so, indeed, had I, when wandering about that first day in search of a point of view—without especially remarking them. The relief was low ; the execution slight ; and the surface so broken away that only a few confused outlines remained.

The thing that now caught the Painter's eye, however, was a long crack running transversely down the face of the rock. It was such a crack as might have been caused, one would say, by blasting.

He stooped—cleared the sand away a little with his hand —observed that the crack widened—poked in the point of his stick ; and found that it penetrated to a depth of two or three feet. Even then, it seemed to him to stop, not because it encountered any obstacle, but because the crack was not wide enough to admit the thick end of the stick.

This surprised him. No mere fault in the natural rock, he thought, would go so deep. He scooped away a little more sand ; and still the cleft widened. He introduced the stick a second time. It was a long palm-stick like an alpenstock, and it measured about five feet in length. When he probed the cleft with it this second time, it went in freely up to where he held it in his hand—that is to say, to a depth of quite four feet.

Convinced now that there was some hidden cavity in the rock, he carefully examined the surface. There were yet visible a few hieroglyphic characters and part of two cartouches, as well as some battered outlines of what had once been figures. The heads of these figures were gone (the face of the rock, with whatever may have been sculptured upon it, having come away bodily at this point), while from the waist downwards they were hidden under the sand. Only some hands and arms, in short, could be made out.

They were the hands and arms, apparently, of four figures ; two in the centre of the composition, and two at the extremities. The two centre ones, which seemed to be back to back, probably represented gods ; the outer ones, worshippers.

All at once, it flashed upon the Painter that he had seen this kind of group many a time before—*and generally over a doorway.*

Feeling sure now that he was on the brink of a discovery, he came back ; fetched away Salame and Mehemet Ali ; and, without saying a syllable to any one, set to work with these two to scrape away the sand at the spot where the crack widened.

Meanwhile, the luncheon bell having rung thrice, we concluded that the Painter had rambled off somewhere into the desert ; and so sat down without him. Towards the close of the meal, however, came a pencilled note, the contents of which ran as follows :—

" Pray come immediately—I have found the entrance to a tomb. Please send some sandwiches—A. M'C."

To follow the messenger at once to the scene of action was the general impulse. In less than ten minutes we were there, asking breathless questions, peeping in through the fast-widening aperture, and helping to clear away the sand.

All that Sunday afternoon, heedless of possible sunstroke, unconscious of fatigue, we toiled upon our hands and knees, as for bare life, under the burning sun. We had all the crew up, working like tigers. Every one helped ; even the dragoman and the two maids. More than once, when we paused for a moment's breathing space, we said to each other : " If those at home could see us, what would they say !"

And now, more than ever, we felt the need of implements. With a spade or two and a wheelbarrow, we could have done wonders ; but with only one small fire-shovel, a birch broom, a couple of charcoal baskets, and about twenty pairs of hands, we were poor indeed. What was wanted in means, however, was made up in method. Some scraped away the sand ; some gathered it into baskets ; some carried the baskets to the edge of the cliff, and emptied them into the river. The Idle Man distinguished himself by scooping out a channel where the slope was steepest ; which greatly facilitated the work. Emptied down this shoot and kept continually going, the sand poured off in a steady stream like water.

Meanwhile the opening grew rapidly larger. When we first came up—that is, when the Painter and the two sailors had been working on it for about an hour—we found a hole scarcely as large as one's hand, through which it was just possible to catch a dim glimpse of painted walls within. By sunset, the top of the doorway was laid bare, and where the crack ended in a large triangular fracture, there was an aperture about a foot and a half square, into which Mehemet Ali was the first to squeeze his way. We passed him in a candle and a box of matches ; but he came out again directly, saying that it was a most beautiful *Birbeh,* and quite light within.

The Writer wriggled in next. She found herself looking down from the top of a sandslope into a small square chamber. This sand-drift, which here rose to within a foot and a half of the top of the doorway, was heaped to the ceiling in the corner behind the door, and thence sloped steeply down, completely covering the floor. There was light enough to see every detail distinctly—the painted frieze running round just under the ceiling ; the bas-relief sculptures on the walls, gorgeous with unfaded colour ; the smooth sand, pitted near the top, where Mehemet Ali had trodden, but undisturbed elsewhere by human foot ; the great gap in the middle of the ceiling, where the rock had given way ; the fallen fragments on the floor, now almost buried in sand.

Satisfied that the place was absolutely fresh and untouched, the Writer crawled out, and the others, one by one, crawled in. When each had seen it in turn, the opening was barricaded for the night ; the sailors being forbidden to enter it, lest they should injure the decorations.

That evening was held a solemn council, whereat it was decided that Talhamy and Reïs Hassan should go to-morrow to the nearest village, there to engage the services of fifty able-bodied natives.   With such help, we calculated that the place might easily be cleared in two days.   If it was a tomb, we hoped to discover the entrance to the mummy pit below ; if but a small chapel, or Speos, like those at Ibrim, we should at least have the satisfaction of seeing all that it contained in the way of sculptures and inscriptions.

This was accordingly done ; but we worked again next morning just the same, till mid-day.   Our native contingent, numbering about forty men, then made their appearance in a rickety old boat, the bottom of which was half full of water.

They had been told to bring implements ; and they did bring such as they had—two broken oars to dig with, some baskets, and a number of little slips of planking which, being tied between two pieces of rope and drawn along the surface, acted as scrapers, and were useful as far as they went.   Squatting in double file from the entrance of the Speos to the edge of the cliff, and to the burden of a rude chant propelling these improvised scrapers, the men began by clearing a path to the doorway.   This gave them work enough for the afternoon. At sunset, when they dispersed, the path was scooped out to a depth of four feet, like a miniature railway cutting between embankments of sand.

Next morning came the Sheykh in person, with his two sons and a following of a hundred men.   This was so many more than we had bargained for, that we at once foresaw a scheme to extort money.   The Sheykh, however, proved to be that same Rashwan Ebn Hassan el Kashef, by whom the Happy Couple had been so hospitably entertained about a fortnight before ; we therefore received him with honour, invited him to luncheon, and, hoping to get the work done quickly, set the men on in gangs under the superintendence of Reïs Hassan and the head sailor.

By noon, the door was cleared down to the threshold, and the whole south and west walls were laid bare to the floor.

We now found that the débris which blocked the north wall and the centre of the floor was not, as we had at first sup-

posed, a pile of fallen fragments, but one solid boulder which
had come down bodily from above. To remove this was impossible. We had no tools to cut or break it, and it was both
wider and higher than the doorway. Even to clear away the
sand which rose behind it to the ceiling would have taken a long
time, and have caused inevitable injury to the paintings around.
Already the brilliancy of the colour was marred where the men
had leaned their backs, all wet with perspiration, against the walls.

ENTRANCE OF SPEOS.

Seeing, therefore, that three-fourths of the decorations were
now uncovered, and that behind the fallen block there appeared
to be no subject of great size or importance, we made up our
minds to carry the work no further.

Meanwhile, we had great fun at luncheon with our Nubian
Sheykh—a tall, well-featured man with much natural dignity
of manner. He was well dressed, too, and wore a white turban
most symmetrically folded ; a white vest buttoned to the throat ;
a long loose robe of black serge ; an outer robe of fine black

cloth with hanging sleeves and a hood ; and on his feet, white
stockings and scarlet morocco shoes.   When brought face to
face with a knife and fork, his embarrassment was great.   He
was, it seemed, too grand a personage to feed himself.   He
must have a " feeder " ; as the great man of the Middle Ages
had a " taster."   Talhamy accordingly, being promoted to this
office, picked out choice bits of mutton and chicken with his
fingers, dipped pieces of bread in gravy, and put every morsel
into our guest's august mouth, as if the said guest were a baby.

The sweets being served, the Little Lady, L., and the
Writer took him in hand, and fed him with all kinds of jams
and preserved fruits.   Enchanted with these attentions, the
poor man ate till he could eat no longer ; then laid his hand
pathetically over the region next his heart, and cried for mercy.
After luncheon, he smoked his chibouque, and coffee was
served.   Our coffee did not please him.   He tasted it, but
immediately returned the cup, telling the waiter with a grimace,
that the berries were burned and the coffee weak.   When,
however, we apologised for it, he protested with Oriental insin-
cerity that it was excellent.

To amuse him was easy, for he was interested in everything ; in L.'s field-glass, in the Painter's accordion, in the
piano, and the lever corkscrew.   With some eau-de-Cologne
he was also greatly charmed, rubbing it on his beard and inhaling it with closed eyes, in a kind of rapture.   To make talk
was, as usual, the great difficulty.   When he had told us that
his eldest son was Governor of Derr ; that his youngest was
five years of age ; that the dates of Derr were better than the
dates of Wady Halfeh ; and that the Nubian people were very
poor, he was at the end of his topics.   Finally, he requested us
to convey a letter from him to Lord D———, who had entertained him on board his dahabeeyah the year before.   Being
asked if he had brought his letter with him, he shook his head,
saying :—" Your dragoman shall write it.'"

So paper and a reed-pen were produced, and Talhamy
wrote to dictation as follows :—

" God have care of you.   I hope you are well.   I am sorry
not to have had a letter from you since you were here.   Your
brother and friend,   RASHWAN EBN HASSAN EL KASHEF."

A model letter this ; brief, and to the point.

Our urbane and gentlemanly Sheykh was, however, not quite so charming when it came to settling time. We had sent at first for fifty men, and the price agreed upon was five piastres, or about a shilling English, for each man per day. In answer to this call, there first came forty men for half a day ; then a hundred men for a whole day, or what was called a whole day ; so making a total of six pounds due for wages. But the descendant of the Kashefs would hear of nothing so commonplace as the simple fulfilment of a straightforward contract. He demanded full pay for a hundred men for two whole days, a gun for himself, and a liberal backshîsh in cash. Finding he had asked more than he had any chance of getting, he conceded the question of wages, but stood out for a game-bag and a pair of pistols. Finally, he was obliged to be content with the six pounds for his men, and for himself two pots of jam, two boxes of sardines, a bottle of eau-de-Cologne, a box of pills, and half-a-sovereign.

By four o'clock he and his followers were gone, and we once more had the place to ourselves. So long as they were there it was impossible to do anything, but now, for the first time, we fairly entered into possession of our newly-found treasure.

All the rest of that day, and all the next day, we spent at work in and about the Speos. L. and the Little Lady took their books and knitting there, and made a little drawing-room of it. The Writer copied paintings and inscriptions. The Idle Man and the Painter took measurements and surveyed the ground round about, especially endeavouring to make out the plan of certain fragments of wall, the foundations of which were yet traceable.

A careful examination of these ruins, and a little clearing of the sand here and there, led to further discoveries. They found that the Speos had been approached by a large outer hall built of sun-dried brick, with one principal entrance facing the Nile, and two side-entrances facing northwards. The floor was buried deep in sand and débris, but enough of the walls remained above the surface to show that the ceiling had been vaulted and the side-entrances arched.

The southern boundary wall of this hall, when the surface sand was removed, appeared to be no less than 20 feet in thickness. This was not in itself so wonderful, there being instances of ancient Egyptian crude-brick walls which measure 80 feet in thickness ;[1] but it was astounding as compared with the north, east, and west walls, which measured only 3 feet. Deeming it impossible that this mass could be solid throughout, the Idle Man set to work with a couple of sailors to probe the centre part of it, and it soon became evident that there was a hollow space about three feet in width running due east and west down not quite exactly the middle of the structure.

All at once the Idle Man thrust his fingers into a skull !

This was such an amazing and unexpected incident, that for the moment he said nothing, but went on quietly displacing the sand and feeling his way under the surface. The next instant his hand came in contact with the edge of a clay bowl, which he carefully withdrew. It measured about four inches in diameter, was hand-moulded, and full of caked sand. He now proclaimed his discoveries, and all ran to help in the work. Soon a second and smaller skull was turned up, then another bowl, and then, just under the place from which the bowls were taken, the bones of two skeletons all detached, perfectly desiccated, and apparently complete. The remains were those of a child and a small grown person—probably a woman. The teeth were sound ; the bones wonderfully delicate and brittle. As for the little skull (which had fallen apart at the sutures), it was pure and fragile in texture as the cup of a water-lily.

We laid the bones aside as we found them, examining every handful of sand, in the hope of discovering something that might throw light upon the burial. But in vain. We found not a shred of clothing, not a bead, not a coin, not the smallest vestige of anything that might help one to judge whether the interment had taken place a hundred years ago or a thousand.

We now called up all the crew, and went on excavating

[1] The enclosure-wall of the Great Temple of Tanis is 80 feet thick. See *Tanis*, Part I, by W. M. F. Petrie ; published by the Committee of the Egypt Exploration Fund, 1885.   [Note to Second Edition.]

downwards into what seemed to be a long and narrow vault measuring some fifteen feet by three.

After-reflection convinced us that we had stumbled upon a chance Nubian grave, and that the bowls (which at first we absurdly dignified with the name of cinerary urns) were but the usual water-bowls placed at the heads of the dead. But we were in no mood for reflection at the time. We made sure that the Speos was a mortuary chapel ; that the vault was a vertical pit leading to a sepulchral chamber ; and that at the bottom of it we should find . . . . who could tell what ? Mummies, perhaps, and sarcophagi, and funerary statuettes, and jewels, and papyri, and wonders without end ! That these uncared-for bones should be laid in the mouth of such a pit, scarcely occurred to us as an incongruity. Supposing them to be Nubian remains, what then ? If a modern Nubian at the top, why not an ancient Egyptian at the bottom ?

As the work of excavation went on, however, the vault was found to be entered by a steep inclined plane. Then the inclined plane turned out to be a flight of much worn and very shallow stairs. These led down to a small square landing, some twelve feet below the surface, from which landing an arched doorway [1] and passage opened into the fore-court of the Speos. Our sailors had great difficulty in excavating this part, in consequence of the weight of superincumbent sand and débris on the side next the Speos. By shoring up the ground, however, they were enabled completely to clear the landing, which was curiously paved with cones of rude pottery like the bottoms of amphoræ. These cones, of which we took out some twenty-eight or thirty, were not in the least like the celebrated funerary cones found so abundantly at Thebes. They bore no stamp, and were much shorter and more lumpy in shape. Finally, the cones being all removed, we came to a compact and solid floor of baked clay.

---

[1] It was long believed that the Egyptians were ignorant of the principle of the arch. This, however, was not the case. There are brick arches of the time of Rameses II behind the Ramesseum at Thebes, and elsewhere. Still, arches are rare in Egypt. We filled in and covered the arch again, and the greater part of the staircase, in order to preserve the former.

The Painter, meanwhile, had also been at work. Having traced the circuit and drawn out a ground-plan, he came to the conclusion that the whole mass adjoining the southern wall of the Speos was in fact composed of the ruins of a pylon, the walls of which were seven feet in thickness, built in regular string-courses of moulded brick, and finished at the angles with the usual *torus*, or round moulding. The superstructure, with its chambers, passages, and top cornice, was gone ; and this part with which we were now concerned was merely the basement, and included the bottom of the staircase.

The Painter's ground-plan demolished all our hopes at one fell swoop. The vault was a vault no longer. The staircase led to no sepulchral chamber. The brick floor hid no secret entrance. Our mummies melted into thin air, and we were left with no excuse for carrying on the excavations. We were mortally disappointed. In vain we told ourselves that the discovery of a large brick pylon, the existence of which had been unsuspected by preceding travellers, was an event of greater importance than the finding of a tomb. We had set our hearts on the tomb ; and I am afraid we cared less than we ought for the pylon.

Having traced thus far the course of the excavations and the way in which one discovery led step by step to another, I must now return to the Speos, and, as accurately as I can, describe it, not only from my notes made on the spot, but by the light of such observations as I afterwards made among structures of the same style and period. I must, however, premise that, not being able to go inside while the excavators were in occupation, and remaining but one whole day at Abou Simbel after the work was ended, I had but short time at my disposal. I would gladly have made coloured copies of all the wall-paintings ; but this was impossible. I therefore was obliged to be content with transcribing the inscriptions and sketching a few of the more important subjects.

The rock-cut chamber which I have hitherto described as a Speos, and which we at first believed to be a tomb, was in fact neither the one nor the other. It was the adytum of a partly-built, partly-excavated monument coeval in date with the Great Temple. In certain points of design this monument resembles the contemporary Speos of Bayt-el-Welly. It is evident, for instance, that the outer halls of both were originally vaulted ; and the much mutilated sculptures over the doorway of the excavated chamber at Abou Simbel are almost identical in subject and treatment with those over the entrance to the excavated parts of Bayt-el-Welly. As regards general conception, the Abou Simbel monument comes under the same head with the contemporary Temples of Derr, Gerf Hossayn, and Wady Sabooah ; being in a mixed style which combines excavation with construction. This style seems to have been peculiarly in favour during the reign of Rameses II.

Situate at the south-eastern angle of the rock, a little way beyond the façade of the Great Temple, this rock-cut adytum and hall of entrance face S.E. by E., and command much the same view that is commanded higher up by the Temple of Hathor. The adytum, or excavated Speos, measures 21 feet $2\frac{1}{2}$ inches in breadth by 14 feet 8 inches in length. The height from floor to ceiling is about 12 feet. The doorway measures 4 feet $3\frac{1}{2}$ inches in width ; and the outer recess for the door-frame, 5 feet. Two large circular holes, one in the threshold and the other in the lintel, mark the place of the pivot on which the door once swung.

It is not very easy to measure the outer hall in its present ruined and encumbered state ; but as nearly as we could judge, its dimensions are as follows :—Length, 25 feet ; width, $22\frac{1}{2}$ feet ; width of principal entrance facing the Nile, 6 feet ; width of two side entrances, 4 feet and 6 feet respectively ; thickness of crude-brick walls, 3 feet. Engaged in the brickwork on either side of the principal entrance to this hall are two stone door-jambs ; and some six or eight feet in front of these, there originally stood two stone hawks on hieroglyphed pedestals. One of these hawks we found *in situ*, the other lay some little distance off, and the Painter (suspecting nothing of these after revelations) had used it as a post to which to tie one of the main ropes of his sketching tent. A large hieroglyphed slab, which I take to have formed part of the door, lay overturned against the side of the pylon some few yards nearer the river.

As far as the adytum and outer hall are concerned, the accompanying ground-plan—which is in part founded on my

own measurements, and in part borrowed from the ground-plan
drawn out by the Painter—may be accepted as tolerably
correct. But with regard to the pylon, I can only say with

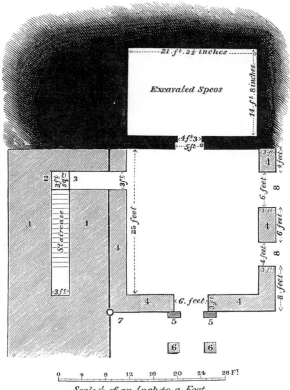

Scale ⅛ of an Inch to a Foot.

1. Wall of pylon.
2. Square landing.
3. Arched doorway and passage leading to vaulted hall.
4. Walls of outer hall or pronaos.
5. Door-jambs.
6. Stone hawks on pedestals.
7. Torus of pylon.
8. Arched entrances in north wall of pronaos.

certainty that the central staircase is three feet in width, and
that the walls on each side of it are seven feet in thickness. So
buried is it in débris and sand, that even to indicate where the
building ends and the rubbish begins at the end next the Nile,

is impossible. This part is therefore left indefinite in the ground-plan.

So far as we could see, there was no stone revêtement upon the inner side of the walls of the pronaos. If anything of the kind ever existed, some remains of it would probably be found by thoroughly clearing the area ; an interesting enterprise for any who may have leisure to undertake it.

I have now to speak of the decorations of the adytum, the walls of which, from immediately under the ceiling to within three feet of the floor, are covered with religious subjects elaborately sculptured in bas-relief, coated as usual with a thin film of stucco, and coloured with a richness for which I know no parallel, except in the tomb of Seti I [1] at Thebes. Above the level of the drifted sand, this colour was as brilliant in tone and as fresh in surface as on the day when it was transferred to those walls from the palette of the painter. All below that level, however, was dimmed and damaged.

PATTERN OF CORNICE.

The ceiling is surrounded by a frieze of cartouches supported by sacred asps ; each cartouche, with its supporters, being divided from the next by a small sitting figure. These figures, in other respects uniform, wear the symbolic heads of various gods—the cow-head of Hathor, the ibis-head of Thoth, the hawk-head of Horus, the jackal-head of Anubis, etc. etc. The cartouches contain the ordinary style and title of Rameses II (Ra-user-ma Sotep-en-Ra Rameses Mer-Amen), and are surmounted by a row of sun-disks. Under each sitting god is depicted the phonetic hieroglyph signifying *Mer*, or Beloved. By means of this device, the whole frieze assumes the character of a connected legend, and describes the king not only as

[1] Commonly known as Belzoni's Tomb.

beloved of Amen, but as Rameses beloved of Hathor, of Thoth, of Horus—in short, of each God depicted in the series.

These Gods excepted, the frieze is almost identical in design with the frieze in the first hall of the great Temple.

West Wall.[1]

The west, or principal wall, facing the entrance, is divided into two large subjects, each containing two figures the size of life. In the division to the right, Rameses II worships Ra ; in the division to the left, he worships Amen-Ra ; thus following the order observed in the other two temples, where the subjects relating to Amen-Ra occupy the left half, and the subjects relating to Ra occupy the right half, of each structure. An upright ensign surmounted by an exquisitely drawn and coloured head of Horus Aroëris separates these two subjects.[2] In the subject to the right, Rameses, wearing the red and white pschent, presents an offering of two small aryballos vases without handles. The vases are painted blue, and are probably intended to represent lapis lazuli ; a substance much prized by the ancient Egyptians, and known

STANDARD OF HORUS AROËRIS.

to them by the name of *khesbet.* The King's necklace, armlets, and bracelets are also blue. Ra sits enthroned, holding in one

hand the " Ankh," or crux ansata, emblem of life, and in the

---

[1] I write of these walls, for convenience, as N., S., E., and W., as one is so accustomed to regard the position of buildings parallel with the river ; but the present monument, as it is turned slightly southward round the angle of the rock, really stands S.E. by E., instead of east and west like the large Temple.

[2] Horus Aroëris.—" Celui-ci, qui semble avoir été frère d'Osiris, porte une tête d'épervier coiffée du pschent. Il est presque complètement identifié avec le soleil dans la plupart des lieux où il était adoré, et il en est de même très souvent pour Horus, fils d'Isis."—*Notice Sommaire des Monuments du Louvre,* 1873. De Rougé. In the present instance, this God seems to have been identified with Ra.

other the greyhound-headed [1] sceptre of the Gods.　He is hawk-headed, and crowned with the sun-disk and asp.　His flesh is painted bright Venetian red.　He wears a pectoral ornament ; a rich necklace of alternate vermilion and black drops ; and a golden-yellow belt studded with red and black stones.　The throne, which stands on a blue platform, is painted in stripes of red, blue, and white.　The platform is decorated with a row of gold-coloured stars and " ankh " emblems picked out with red.　At the foot of this platform, between the God and the King, stands a small altar, on which are placed the usual blue lotus with red stalk, and a spouted libation vessel.

　　To the left of the Horus ensign, seated back-to-back with Ra upon a similar throne, sits Amen-Ra—of all Egyptian Gods the most terrible to look upon—with his blue-black complexion, his corselet of golden chain-armour, and his head-dress of towering plumes.[2]　Here the wonderful preservation of the surface enabled one to see by what means the ancient artists were wont to produce this singular blue-black effect of colour.　It was evident that the flesh of the God had first been laid in with dead black, and then coloured over with a dry,

---

[1] " Le sceptre à tête de lévrier, nommé à tort sceptre à tête de cou-coupha, était porté par les dieux."—*Dic. d'Arch. Egyptienne :* P. PIERRET ; Paris, 1875.

[2] Amen of the blue complexion is the most ancient type of this God. He here represents divine royalty, in which character his title is : " Lord of the Heaven, of the Earth, of the Waters, and of the Mountains." " Dans ce rôle de roi du monde, Amon a les chairs peintes en bleu pour indiquer sa nature céleste ; et lorsqu'il porte le titre de Seigneur des Trônes, il est représenté assis, la couronne en tête : d'ordinaire il est debout."—*Étude des Monuments de Karnak.* DE ROUGÉ. *Mélanges d'Archeologie,* vol. i. 1873.

　　There were almost as many varieties of Amen in Egypt as there are varieties of the Madonna in Italy or Spain.　There was an Amen of Thebes, an Amen of Elephantine, an Amen of Coptos, an Amen of Chemmis (Panopolis), an Amen of the Resurrection, Amen of the Dew, Amen of the Sun (Amen-Ra), Amen Self-created, etc. etc.　Amen and Khem were doubtless identical.　It is an interesting fact that our English words, chemical, chemist, chemistry, etc., which the dictionaries derive from the Arabic *al-kimia,* may be traced back a step farther to the Panopolitan name of this most ancient God of the Egyptians, Khem (Gr. Pan ; Latin, Priapus), the deity of plants and herbs and of the creative principle.　A cultivated Egyptian would, doubtless, have regarded all these Amens as merely local or symbolical types of a single deity.

powdery cobalt-blue, through which the black remained partially visible. He carries in one hand the ankh, and in the other the greyhound-headed sceptre.

RAMESES II OF SPEOS.

To him advances the King, his right hand uplifted, and in his left a small basket containing a votive statuette of Ma, the Goddess of Truth and Justice. Ma is, however, shorn of her distinctive feather, and holds the jackal-headed staff instead of the customary crux ansata.

As portraiture, there is not much to be said for any of these heads of Rameses II; but the features bear a certain resemblance to the well-known profile of the King; the action of the figure is graceful and animated; and the drawing displays in all its purity the firm and flowing line of Egyptian draughtsmanship.

The dress of the King is very rich in colour; the mitre-shaped casque being of a vivid cobalt-blue[1] picked out with gold-colour; the belt, necklace, armlets, and bracelets, of gold, studded apparently with precious stones; the apron, green and gold. Over the King's head hovers the sacred vulture, emblem of Maut, holding in her claws a kind of scutcheon upon which is depicted the crux ansata.

[1] The material of this blue helmet, so frequently depicted on the monuments, *may* have been the Homeric Kuanos, about which so much doubt and conjecture have gathered, and which Mr. Gladstone supposes to have been a metal.—(See *Juventus Mundi*, chap. xv. p. 532.) A paragraph in *The Academy* (June 8, 1876) gives the following particulars of certain perforated lamps of a "blue metallic substance," discovered at Hissarlik by Dr. Schliemann, and there found lying under the copper shields to which they had probably been attached. "An analytical examination by

South Wall.

The subjects represented on this wall are as follows :—

1. Rameses, life-size, presiding over a table of offerings. The king wears upon his head the *klaft*, or head-cloth, striped gold and white, and decorated with the uræus. The table is piled in the usual way with flesh, fowl, and flowers. The surface being here quite perfect, the details of these objects are seen to be rendered with surprising minuteness. Even the tiny black feather-stumps of the plucked geese are given with the fidelity of Chinese art ; while a red gash in the breast of each shows in what way it was slain for the sacrifice. The loaves are shaped precisely like the so-called "cottage-loaves" of to-day, and have the same little depression in the top, made by the baker's finger. Lotus and papyrus blossoms in elaborate bouquet-holders crown the pile.

2. Two tripods of light and elegant design, containing flowers.

3. The Bari, or sacred boat, painted gold-colour, with the usual veil half-drawn across the naos, or shrine ; the prow of the boat being richly carved, decorated with the Uta[1] or symbolic eye, and preceded by a large fan of ostrich feathers.

Landerer (*Berg.* Hüttenm. Zeitung, xxxiv. 430) has shown them to be sulphide of copper. The art of colouring the metal was known to the coppersmiths of Corinth, who plunged the heated copper into the fountain of Peirene. It appears not impossible that this was a sulphur spring, and that the blue colour may have been given to the metal by plunging it in a heated state into the water and converting the surface into copper sulphide."

It is to be observed that the Pharaohs are almost always represented wearing this blue helmet in the battle-pieces, and that it is frequently studded with gold rings. It must therefore have been of metal. If not of sulphuretted copper, it may have been made of steel, which, in the well-known instance of the butcher's sharpener, as well as in representations of certain weapons, is always painted blue upon the monuments.

[1] "This eye, called *uta*, was extensively used by the Egyptians both as an ornament and amulet during life, and as a Sepulchral amulet. They are found in the form of right eyes and left eyes, and they symbolise the eyes of Horus, as he looks to the N. and S. horizons in his passage from E. to W. *i.e.* from sunrise to sunset."

M. Grebaut, in his translation of a hymn to Amen-Ra, observes : "Le soleil marchant d'Orient en Occident éclaire de ses deux yeux les deux régions du Nord et du Midi."—*Révue Arch.* vol. xxv. 1873 ; p. 387.

The boat is peopled with small black figures, one of which kneels at the stern ; while a sphinx couchant, with black body and human head, keeps watch at the prow. The sphinx symbolises the king.[1]

On this wall, in a space between the sacred boat and the figure of Rameses, occurs the following inscription, sculptured in high relief and elaborately coloured :—

NOTE. — This inscription reads according to the numbering of the columns, beginning at 1 and reading to the right ; then resuming at 7 and reading to the left. The spaces lettered A B in the lowest figure of column 5 are filled in with the two cartouches of Rameses II.

TRANSLATION.[2]

Said by Thoth, the Lord of Sesennu,[3] [residing] in Amen-heri,[4]—I give to thee an everlasting sovereignty over the Two

[1] See an accurate facsimile of this Bari, in chromo-lithography, in Mr. Villiers Stuart's "*Nile Gleanings*": Murray, 1879.

[2] This inscription was translated for the first edition of this book by the late Dr. Birch ; for the present translation I am indebted to the courtesy of E. A. Wallis Budge, Esq.

[3] *Sesennu*—Eshmoon or Hermopolis.

[4] *Amenheri*—Gebel Addeh.

Countries, O, Son of [my] body, Beloved, Ra-user-ma Sotep-en-Ra, acting as propitiator of thy *Ka*. I give to thee myriads of festivals of Rameses beloved of Amen, Ra-user-ma Sotep-en-Ra, as prince of every place where the sun-disk revolves. The beautiful living God, maker of beautiful things for [his] father Thoth Lord of Sesennu [residing] in Amenheri. He made mighty and beautiful monuments for ever facing the eastern horizon of heaven.

The meaning of which is that Thoth, addressing Rameses II, then living and reigning, promises him a long life and many anniversaries of his jubilee,[1] in return for the works made in his (Thoth's) honour at Abou Simbel and elsewhere.

NORTH WALL.

At the upper end of this wall is depicted a life-sized female figure wearing an elaborate blue head-dress surmounted by a disk and two ostrich feathers. She holds in her right hand the ankh, and in her left the jackal-headed sceptre. This not being the sceptre of a goddess, and the head-dress resembling that of the Queen as represented on the façade of the Temple of Hathor, I conclude we have here a portrait of Nefertari corresponding to the portrait of Rameses on the opposite wall. Near her stands a table of offerings, on which, among other objects, are placed four vases of a rich blue colour traversed by bands of yellow. They perhaps represent the kind of glass known as the false murrhine.[2] Each of these vases contains an object like a pine, the ground-colour of which is deep yellow, patterned over with scale-like subdivisions in vermilion. We took them to represent grains of maize pyramidally piled.

Lastly, a pendant to that on the opposite wall, comes the

---

[1] These jubilees, or festivals of thirty years, were religious jubilees in celebration of each *thirtieth* anniversary of the accession of the reigning Pharaoh.

[2] There are, in the British Museum, some bottles and vases of this description, dating from the XVIIIth Dynasty; see Case E, *Second Egyptian Room.* They are of dark blue translucent glass, veined with waving lines of opaque white and yellow.

sacred Bari. It is, however, turned the reverse way, with its prow towards the east; and it rests upon an altar, in the centre of which are the cartouches of Rameses II and a small hieroglyphic inscription signifying: " Beloved by Amen-Ra, King of the Gods resident in the Land of Kenus." [1]

Beyond this point, at the end nearest the north-east corner of the chamber, the piled sand conceals whatever else the wall may contain in the way of decoration.

EAST WALL.

If the east wall is decorated like the others (which may be taken for granted), its tableaux and inscriptions are hidden behind the sand which here rises to the ceiling. The doorway also occurs in this wall, occupying a space 4 feet $3\frac{1}{2}$ inches in width on the inner side.

One of the most interesting incidents connected with the excavation of this little adytum remains yet to be told.

I have described the female figure at the upper end of the north wall, and how she holds in her right hand the ankh and in her left the jackal-headed sceptre. The hand that holds the ankh hangs by her side; the hand that holds the sceptre is half raised. Close under this upraised hand, at a height of between three and four feet from the actual level of the floor, there were visible upon the uncoloured surface of the original stucco several lines of free-hand writing. This writing was laid on, apparently, with the brush, and the ink, if ever it had been black, had now become brown. Five long lines and three shorter lines were uninjured. Below these were traces of other fragmentary lines, almost obliterated by the sand.

We knew at once that this quaint faint writing must be in either the hieratic or demotic hand. We could distinguish, or thought we could distinguish, in its vague outlines of forms already familiar to us in the hieroglyphs—abstracts, as it were, of birds and snakes and boats. There could be no doubt, at all events, that the thing was curious; and we set it down in our own minds as the writing of either the architect or decorator of the place.

[1] *Kenus*—Nubia.

Anxious to make, if possible, an exact facsimile of this inscription, the Writer copied it three times. The last and best of these copies is here reproduced in photolithography, with a translation from the pen of the late Dr. Birch. We all know how difficult it is to copy correctly in a language of which one is ignorant ; and the tiniest curve or dot omitted is fatal to the sense of these ancient characters. In the present instance, notwithstanding the care with which the transcript was made, there must still have been errors ; for it has been found undecipherable in places ; and in these places there occur inevitable lacunæ.

Enough, however, remains to show that the lines were written, not as we had supposed by the artist, but by a distinguished visitor, whose name unfortunately is illegible. This visitor was a son of the Prince of Kush, or as it is literally written, the Royal Son of Kush ; that being the official title of the Governor of Ethiopia.[1] As there were certainly eight governors of Ethiopia during the reign of Rameses II (and perhaps more, whose names have not reached us), it is impossible even to hazard a guess at the parentage of our visitor. We gather, however, that he was sent hither to construct a road ; also that he built transport boats ; and that he exercised priestly functions in that part of the Temple which was inaccessible to all but dignitaries of the sacerdotal order.

Site, inscriptions, and decorations taken into account, there yet remains this question to be answered :—

What was the nature and character of the monument just described ?

It adjoined a pylon, and, as we have seen, consisted of a vaulted pronaos in crude brick, and an adytum excavated in the

---

[1] Governors of Ethiopia bore this title, even though they did not themselves belong to the family of the Pharaoh.

It is a curious fact that one of the Governors of Ethiopia during the reign of Rameses II was called Mes, or Messou, signifying son, or child— which is in fact *Moses*. Now the Moses of the Bible was adopted by Pharaoh's daughter, " became to her as a son," was instructed in the wisdom of the Egyptians, and married a Kushite woman, black but comely. It would perhaps be too much to speculate on the possibility of his having held the office of Governor, or Royal Son of Kush.

rock.　On the walls of this adytum are depicted various Gods with their attributes, votive offerings, and portraits of the King performing acts of adoration.　The Bari, or ark, is also represented upon the north and south walls of the adytum.　These are unquestionably the ordinary features of a temple, or chapel.

On the other hand, there must be noted certain objections to these premises.　It seemed to us that the pylon was built first, and that the south boundary wall of the pronaos, being a subsequent erection, was supported against the slope of the pylon as far as where the spring of the vaulting began.　Besides which, the pylon would have been a disproportionately large adjunct to a little monument the entire length of which, from the doorway of the pronaos to the west wall of the adytum, was less than 47 feet.　We therefore concluded that the pylon belonged to the large temple, and was erected at the side, instead of in front of the façade, on account of the very narrow space between the mountain and the river.[1]

The pylon at Kom Ombo is, probably for the same reason, placed at the side of the Temple and on a lower level.　To those who might object that a brick pylon would hardly be attached to a temple of the first class, I would observe that the remains of a similar pylon are still to be seen at the top of what was once the landing-place leading to the Great Temple at Wady Halfeh.　It may, therefore, be assumed that this little monument, although connected with the pylon by means of a doorway and staircase, was an excrescence of later date.

Being an excrescence, however, was it, in the strict sense of the word, a temple ?

Even this seems to be doubtful.　In the adytum there is no trace of any altar—no fragment of stone dais or sculptured image—no granite shrine, as at Philæ—no sacred recess, as at Denderah.　The standard of Horus Aroëris, engraven on page 340, occupies the centre place upon the wall facing the entrance, and occupies it, not as a tutelary divinity, but as a decorative device to separate the two large subjects already described.

[1] At about an equal distance to the north of the Great Temple, on the verge of the bank, is a shapeless block of brick ruin, which might possibly, if investigated, turn out to be the remains of a second pylon corresponding to this which we partially uncovered to the south.

Again, the Gods represented in these subjects are Ra and Amen-Ra, the tutelary Gods of the Great Temple ; but if we turn to the dedicatory inscription on page 344 we find that Thoth, whose image never occurs at all upon the walls [1] (unless as one of the little Gods in the cornice), is really the presiding deity of the place. It is he who welcomes Rameses and his offerings ; who acknowledges the " glory " given to him by his beloved son ; and who, in return for the great and good monuments erected in his honour, promises the king that he shall be given " an everlasting sovereignty over the Two Countries."

Now Thoth was, *par excellence*, the God of Letters. He is styled the Lord of Divine Words ; the Lord of the Sacred Writings ; the Spouse of Truth. He personifies the Divine Intelligence. He is the patron of art and science ; and he is credited with the invention of the alphabet. In one of the most interesting of Champollion's letters from Thebes,[2] he relates how, in the fragmentary ruins of the western extremity of the Ramesseum, he found a doorway adorned with the figures of Thoth and Safek ; Thoth as the God of Literature, and Safek inscribed with the title of Lady President of the Hall of Books. At Denderah, there is a chamber especially set apart for the sacred writings, and its walls are sculptured all over with a catalogue raisonnée of the manuscript treasures of the Temple. At Edfu, a kind of closet built up between two of the pillars of the Hall of Assembly was reserved for the same purpose. Every Temple, in short, had its library ; and as the Egyptian books—being written on papyrus or leather, rolled up, and stored in coffers—occupied but little space, the rooms appropriated to this purpose were generally small.

It was Dr. Birch's opinion that our little monument may have been the library of the Great Temple of Abou Simbel. This being the case, the absence of an altar, and the presence of Ra and Amen-Ra in the two principal tableaux, are sufficiently accounted for. The tutelary deity of the Great Temple and the patron deity of Rameses II would naturally occupy, in this subsidiary structure, the same places that they

---

[1] He may, however, be represented on the north wall, where it is covered by the sand-heap.

[2] Letter XIV. p. 235. *Nouvelle Ed.* Paris, 1868.

occupy in the principal one; while the library, though in one sense the domain of Thoth, is still under the protection of the gods of the Temple to which it is an adjunct.

I do not believe we once asked ourselves how it came to pass that the place had remained hidden all these ages long; yet its very freshness proved how early it must have been abandoned. If it had been open in the time of the successors of Rameses II, they would probably, as elsewhere, have interpolated inscriptions and cartouches, or have substituted their own cartouches for those of the founder. If it had been open in the time of the Ptolemies and Cæsars, travelling Greeks and learned Romans, and strangers from Byzantium and the cities of Asia Minor, would have cut their names on the door-jambs and scribbled ex-votos on the walls. If it had been open in the days of Nubian Christianity, the sculptures would have been coated with mud, and washed with lime, and daubed with pious caricatures of St. George and the Holy Family. But we found it intact—as perfectly preserved as a tomb that had lain hidden under the rocky bed of the desert. For these reasons I am inclined to think that it became inaccessible shortly after it was completed. There can be little doubt that a wave of earthquake passed, during the reign of Rameses II, along the left bank of the Nile, beginning possibly above Wady Halfeh, and extending at least as far north as Gerf Hossayn. Such a shock might have wrecked the Temple at Wady Halfeh, as it dislocated the pylon of Wady Sabooah, and shook the built-out porticoes of Derr and Gerf Hossayn; which last four Temples, as they do not, I believe, show signs of having been added to by later Pharaohs, may be supposed to have been abandoned in consequence of the ruin which had befallen them. Here, at all events, it shook the mountain of the Great Temple, cracked one of the Osiride columns of the First Hall,[1] shattered one of the four great Colossi, more or less injured the other three, flung down the great brick pylon,

---

[1] That this shock of earthquake occurred during the lifetime of Rameses II seems to be proven by the fact that, where the Osiride column is cracked across, a wall has been built up to support the two last pillars to the left at the upper end of the great hall, on which wall is a large stela covered with an elaborate hieroglyphic inscription, dating from

reduced the pronaos of the library to a heap of ruin, and not only brought down part of the ceiling of the excavated adytum, but rent open a vertical fissure in the rock, some 20 or 25 feet in length.

With so much irreparable damage done to the Great Temple, and with so much that was reparable calling for immediate attention, it is no wonder that these brick buildings were left to their fate. The priests would have rescued the sacred books from among the ruins, and then the place would have been abandoned.

So much by way of conjecture. As hypothesis, a sufficient reason is perhaps suggested for the wonderful state of preservation in which the little chamber had been handed down to the present time. A rational explanation is also offered for the absence of later cartouches, of Greek and Latin ex-votos, of Christian emblems, and of subsequent mutilation of every kind. For, save that one contemporary visitor—the son of the Royal Son of Kush—the place contained, when we opened it, no record of any passing traveller, no defacing autograph of tourist, archæologist, or scientific explorer. Neither Belzoni nor Champollion had found it out. Even Lepsius had passed it by.

It happens sometimes that hidden things, which in themselves are easy to find, escape detection because no one thinks of looking for them. But such was not the case in this present instance. Search had been made here again and again ; and even quite recently.

It seems that when the Khedive[1] entertains distinguished guests and sends them in gorgeous dahabeeyahs up the Nile,

the xxxvth year, and the 13th day of the month of Tybi, *of the reign of Rameses II.* The right arm of the external colossus, to the right of the great doorway, has also been supported by the introduction of an arm to his throne, built up of square blocks ; this being the only arm to any of the thrones. Miss Martineau detected a restoration of part of the lower jaw of the northernmost colossus, and also a part of the dress of one of the Osiride statues in the great hall. . I have in my possession a photograph taken at a time when the sand was several feet lower than at present, which shows that the right leg of the northernmost colossus is also a restoration on a gigantic scale, being built up, like the throne-arm, in great blocks, and finished, most probably, afterwards.

[1] This refers to the Ex-Khedive, Ismail Pasha, who ruled Egypt at the time when this book was written and published. [Note to Second Edition.]

he grants them a virgin mound, or so many square feet of a famous necropolis ; lets them dig as deep as they please ; and allows them to keep whatever they may find. Sometimes he sends out scouts to beat the ground ; and then a tomb is found and left unopened, and the illustrious visitor is allowed to discover it. When the scouts are unlucky, it may even sometimes happen that an old tomb is re-stocked ; carefully closed up ; and then, with all the charm of unpremeditation, re-opened a day or two after.

Now Sheykh Rashwan Ebn Hassan el Kashef told us that in 1869, when the Empress of the French was at Abou Simbel, and again when the Prince and Princess of Wales came up in 1872, after the Prince's illness, he received strict orders to find some hitherto undiscovered tomb,[1] in order that the Khedive's guests might have the satisfaction of opening it. But, he added, although he left no likely place untried among the rocks and valleys on both sides of the river, he could find nothing. To have unearthed such a Birbeh as this, would have done him good service with the Government, and have ensured him a splendid backshîsh from Prince or Empress. As it was, he was reprimanded for want of diligence, and he believed himself to have been out of favour ever since.

I may here mention—in order to have done with this subject—that besides being buried outside to a depth of about eight feet, the adytum had been partially filled inside by a gradual infiltration of sand from above. This can only have accumulated at the time when the old sand-drift was at its highest. That drift, sweeping in one unbroken line across the front of the Great Temple, must at one time have risen here to a height of twenty feet above the present level. From thence the sand had found its way down the perpendicular fissure already mentioned. In the corner behind the door, the sand-pile rose to the ceiling, in shape just like the deposit at the bottom of an hour-glass. I am informed by the Painter that when the top of the doorway was found and an opening first effected, the sand poured out *from within*, like water escaping from an opened sluice.

---

[1] There are tombs in some of the ravines behind the Temples, which, however, we did not see.

Here, then, is positive proof (if proof were needed) that we were first to enter the place, at all events since the time when the great sand-drift rose as high as the top of the fissure.

The Painter wrote his name and ours, with the date (February 16th, 1874), on a space of blank wall over the inside of the doorway ; and this was the only occasion upon which any of us left our names upon an Egyptian monument. On arriving at Korosko, where there is a post-office, he also despatched a letter to the " Times," briefly recording the facts here related. That letter, which appeared on the 18th of March following, is reprinted in the Appendix at the end of this book.

I am told that our names are partially effaced, and that the wall-paintings which we had the happiness of admiring in all their beauty and freshness, are already much injured. Such is the fate of every Egyptian monument, great or small. The tourist carves it all over with names and dates, and in some instances with caricatures. The student of Egyptology, by taking wet paper "squeezes," sponges away every vestige of the original colour. The "collector" buys and carries off everything of value that he can get ; and the Arab steals for him. The work of destruction, meanwhile, goes on apace. There is no one to prevent it ; there is no one to discourage it. Every day, more inscriptions are mutilated—more tombs are rifled—more paintings and sculptures are defaced. The Louvre contains a full-length portrait of Seti I, cut out bodily from the walls of his sepulchre in the Valley of the Tombs of the Kings. The Museums of Berlin, of Turin, of Florence, are rich in spoils which tell their own lamentable tale. When science leads the way, is it wonderful that ignorance should follow ?

CHAPTER XIX.

BACK THROUGH NUBIA.

THERE are fourteen Temples between Abou Simbel and
Philæ ; to say nothing of grottoes, tombs, and other ruins.   As
a rule, people begin to get tired of Temples about this time,
and vote them too plentiful.   Meek travellers go through them
as a duty ; but the greater number rebel.   Our Happy Couple,
I grieve to say, went over to the majority.   Dead to shame,
they openly proclaimed themselves bored.   They even skipped
several Temples.

For myself, I was never bored by them.   Though they
had been twice as many, I should not have wished them fewer.
Miss Martineau tells how, in this part of the river, she was
scarcely satisfied to sit down to breakfast without having first
explored a Temple ; but I could have breakfasted, dined,
supped on Temples.   My appetite for them was insatiable, and
grew with what it fed upon.   I went over them all.   I took
notes of them all.   I sketched them every one.

I may as well say at once that I shall reproduce but few
of those notes, and only some of those sketches, in the present
volume.   If, surrounded by their local associations, these ruins
fail to interest many who travel far to see them, it is not to be
supposed that they would interest readers at home.   Here and
there, perhaps, might be one who would care to pore with me
over every broken sculpture ; to spell out every half-legible
cartouche ; to trace through Greek and Roman influences
(which are nowhere more conspicuous than in these Nubian
buildings) the slow deterioration of the Egyptian style.   But

the world for the most part reserves itself, and rightly, for the great epochs and the great names of the past ; and because it has not yet had too much of Karnak, of Abou Simbel, of the Pyramids, it sets slight store by those minor monuments which record the periods of foreign rule and the decline of native art.

For these reasons, therefore, I propose to dismiss very briefly many places upon which I bestowed hours of delightful labour.

We left Abou Simbel just as the moon was rising on the evening of the 18th of February, and dropped down with the current for three or four miles before mooring for the night. At six next morning the men began rowing ; and at half-past eight, the heads of the Colossi were still looking placidly after us across a ridge of intervening hills. They were then more than five miles distant in a direct line ; but every feature was still distinct in the early daylight. One went up again and again, as long as they remained in sight, and bade good-bye to them at last with that same heartache which comes of a farewell view of the Alps.

When I say that we were seventeen days getting from Abou Simbel to Philæ, and that we had the wind against us from sunrise till sunset almost every day, it will be seen that our progress was of the slowest. To those who were tired of Temples, and to the crew who were running short of bread, these long days of lying up under the bank, or of rocking to and fro in the middle of the river, were dreary enough.

Slowly but surely, however, the hard-won miles go by. Sometimes the barren desert hems us in to right and left, with never a blade of green between the rock and the river. Sometimes, as at Tosko,[1] we come upon an open tract, where there are palms, and castor-berry plantations, and corn-fields alive with quail. The Idle Man goes ashore at Tosko with his gun, while the Little Lady and the Writer climb a solitary rock about 200 feet above the river. The bank shelves here, and a crescent-like wave of inundation, about three miles in length, overflows it every season. From this height one sees exactly how far the wave goes, and how it must make a little bay

[1] Tosko is on the eastern bank, and not, as in Keith Johnston's map, on the west.

when it is there.   Now it is a bay of barley, full to the brim,
and rippling with the breeze.   Beyond the green comes the
desert ; the one defined against the other as sharply as water
against land.   The desert looks wonderfully old beside the
young green of the corn, and the Nile flows wide among sandbanks, like a tidal river near the sea.   The village, squared off
in parallelograms, like a cattle-market, lies mapped out below.
A field-glass shows that the houses are simply cloistered courtyards roofed with palm-thatch ; the sheykh's house being
larger than the rest, with the usual open space and spreading
sycamore in front.   There are women moving to and fro in
the courtyards, and husbandmen in the castor-berry patches.
A funeral with a train of wailers goes out presently towards
the burial-ground on the edge of the desert.   The Idle Man, a
slight figure with a veil twisted round his hat, wades, half-hidden,
through the barley, signalling his whereabouts every now and
then by a puff of white smoke.   A cargo-boat, stripped and
shorn, comes floating down the river, making no visible progress.
A native felucca, carrying one tattered brown sail, goes swiftly
up with the wind at a pace that will bring her to Abou Simbel
before nightfall.   Already she is past the village ; and those
black specks yonder, which we had never dreamed were crocodiles, have slipped off into the water at her approach.   And
now she is far in the distance—that glowing, illimitable distance
—traversed by long silvery reaches of river, and ending in a
vast flat, so blue and aerial that, but for some three or four
notches of purple peaks on the horizon, one could scarcely
discern the point at which land and sky melt into each other.

Ibrim comes next ; then Derr ; then Wady Sabooah.   At
Ibrim, as at Derr, there are " fair " families, whose hideous
light hair and blue eyes (grafted on brown-black skins) date
back to Bosnian forefathers of 360 years ago.   These people
give themselves airs, and are the *haute noblesse* of the place.
The men are lazy and quarrelsome.   The women trail longer
robes, wear more beads and rings, and are altogether more
unattractive and castor-oily than any we have seen elsewhere.
They keep slaves, too.   We saw these unfortunates trotting at
the heels of their mistresses, like dogs.   Knowing slavery to be
officially illegal in the dominions of the Khedive, the M. B.'s

applied to a dealer, who offered them an Abyssinian girl for ten pounds. This useful article—warranted a bargain—was to sweep, wash, milk, and churn ; but was not equal to cooking. The M. B.'s, it is needless to add, having verified the facts, retired from the transaction.

At Derr we pay a farewell visit to the Temple ; and at Amada, arriving towards close of day, see the great view for the last time in the glory of sunset.

TEMPLE OF AMADA.

And now, though the north wind blows persistently, it gets hotter every day. The crocodiles like it, and come out to bask in the sunshine. Called up one morning in the middle of breakfast we see two—a little one and a big one—on a sand-bank near by. The men rest upon their oars. The boat goes with the stream. No one speaks ; no one moves. Breathlessly and in dead silence, we drift on till we are close beside them. The big one is rough and black, like the trunk of a London elm, and measures full eighteen feet in length. The little one is pale and greenish, and glistens like glass. All at once, the old one starts, doubles itself up for a spring, and disappears with a tremendous splash. But the little one, apparently unconscious of danger, lifts its tortoise-like head, and eyes us sidewise. Presently some one whispers; and that whisper breaks the spell. Our little crocodile flings up its tail, plunges down the bank, and is gone in a moment.

The crew could not understand how the Idle Man, after lying in wait for crocodiles at Abou Simbel, should let this rare chance pass without a shot. But we had heard since then of so much indiscriminate slaughter at the Second Cataract, that he was resolved to bear no part in the extermination of those old historic reptiles. That a sportsman should wish for a single trophy is not unreasonable; but that scores of crack shots should go up every winter, killing and wounding these wretched brutes at an average rate of from twelve to eighteen per gun, is mere butchery, and cannot be too strongly reprehended. Year by year, the creatures become shyer and fewer; and the day is probably not far distant when a crocodile will be as rarely seen below Semneh as it is now rarely seen below Assûan.

The thermometer stands at 85° in the saloon of the Philæ, when we come one afternoon to Wady Sabooah, where there is a solitary Temple drowned in sand. It was approached once by an avenue of sphinxes and standing colossi, now shattered and buried. The roof of the pronaos, if ever it was roofed, is gone. The inner halls and the sanctuary—all excavated in the rock—are choked and impassable. Only the propylon stands clear of sand; and that, massive as it is, looks as if one touch of a battering-ram would bring it to the ground. Every huge stone in it is loose. Every block in the cornice seems tottering in its place. In all this, we fancy we recognise the work of our Abou Simbel earthquake.[1]

---

[1] This is one of the Temples erected by Rameses the Great, and, I believe, not added to by any of his successors. The colossi, the Osiride columns, the sphinxes (now battered out of all human semblance) were originally made in his image. The cartouches are all his, and in one of the inner chambers there is a list of his little family. All these chambers were accessible till three or four years ago, when a party of German travellers carried off some sculptured tablets of great archæological interest; after which act of spoliation the entrance was sanded up by order of Mariette Bey. See also, with regard to the probable date of the earthquake at this place, chap. xviii. p. 350.

At Wady Sabooah we see a fat native. The fact claims
record, because it is so uncommon. A stalwart middle-aged
man, dressed in a tattered kilt and carrying a palm-staff in his
hand, he stands before us the living double of the famous
wooden statue at Boulak. He is followed by his two wives
and three or four children, all bent upon trade. The women

TEMPLE OF WADY SABOOAH.

have trinkets, the boys a live chameleon and a small stuffed
crocodile for sale. While the Painter is bargaining for the
crocodile and L. for a nose-ring, the Writer makes acquaintance with a pair of self-important hoopoes, who live in the
pylon, and evidently regard it as a big nest of their own building. They sit observing me curiously while I sketch, nodding
their crested polls and chattering disparagingly, like a couple
of critics. By and by comes a small black bird with a white
breast, and sings deliciously. It is like no little bird that I
have ever seen before ; but the song that it pours so lavishly
from its tiny throat is as sweet and brilliant as a canary's.

Powerless against the wind, the dahabeeyah lies idle day
after day in the sun.   Sometimes, when we chance to be near
a village, the natives squat on the bank, and stare at us for
hours together.   The moment any one appears on deck, they
burst into a chorus of "Backshîsh!"   There is but one way to
get rid of them, and that is to sketch them.   The effect is
instantaneous.   With a good sized block and a pencil, a whole
village may be put to flight at a moment's notice.   If on the
other hand one wishes for a model, the difficulty is insuperable.
The Painter tried in vain to get some of the women and girls
(not a few of whom were really pretty) to sit for their portraits.
I well remember one haughty beauty, shaped and draped like
a Juno, who stood on the bank one morning, scornfully watching all that was done on deck.   She carried a flat basket
back-handed ; and her arms were covered with bracelets, and
her fingers with rings.   Her little girl, in a Madame Nubia
fringe, clung to her skirts, half wondering, half frightened.
The Painter sent out an ambassador plenipotentiary to offer
her anything from sixpence to half-a-sovereign, if she would
only stand like that for half an hour.   The manner of her
refusal was grand.   She drew her shawl over her face, took
her child's hand, and stalked away like an offended goddess.
The Writer, meanwhile, hidden behind a curtain, had snatched
a tiny sketch from the cabin-window.

On the western bank, somewhere between Wady Sabooah
and Maharrakeh, in a spot quite bare of vegetation, stand the
ruins of a fortified town which is neither mentioned by Murray
nor entered in the maps.   It is built high on a base of reddish
rock, and commands the river and the desert.   The Painter
and Writer explored it one afternoon, in the course of a long
ramble.   Climbing first a steep slope strewn with masonry,
we came to the remains of a stone gateway.   Finding this
impassable, we made our way through a breach in the battlemented wall, and thence up a narrow road down which had
been poured a cataract of débris.   Skirting a ruined postern
at the top of this road, we found ourselves in a close labyrinth
of vaulted arcades built of crude brick and lit at short intervals
by openings in the roof.   These strange streets—for they were
streets—were lined on either side by small dwellings built of

crude brick on stone foundations. We went into some of the houses—mere ruined courts and roofless chambers, in which were no indications of hearths or staircases. In one lay a fragment of stone column about 14 inches in diameter. The air in these ancient streets was foul and stagnant, and the ground was everywhere heaped with fragments of black, red, and yellowish pottery, like the shards of Elephantine and Philæ. A more desolate place in a more desolate situation I never saw. It looked as if it had been besieged, sacked, and abandoned, a thousand years ago ; which is probably under the mark, for the character of the pottery would seem to point to the period of Roman occupation. Noting how the brick superstructures were reared on apparently earlier masonry, we concluded that the beginnings of this place were probably Egyptian, and the later work Roman. The marvel was that any town should have been built in so barren a spot, there being not so much as an inch-wide border of lentils for a mile or more between the river and the desert.

Having traversed the place from end to end, we came out through another breach on the westward side, and, thinking to find a sketchable point of view inland, struck down towards the plain. In order to reach this, one first must skirt a deep ravine which divides the rock of the citadel from the desert. Following the brink of this ravine to the point at which it falls into the level, we found to our great surprise that we were treading the banks of an extinct river.

It was full of sand now ; but beyond all question it had once been full of water. It came, evidently, from the mountains over towards the north-west. We could trace its windings for a long way across the plain, thence through the ravine, and on southwards in a line parallel with the Nile. Here, beneath our feet, were the water-worn rocks through which it had fretted its way ; and yonder, half-buried in sand, were the boulders it had rounded and polished, and borne along in its course. I doubt, however, if when it was a river of water, this stream was half as beautiful as now, when it is a river of sand. It was turbid then, no doubt, and charged with sediment. Now it is more golden than Pactolus, and covered with ripples more playful and undulating than were ever modelled by Canaletti's pencil.

Supposing yonder town to have been founded in the days when the river was a river, and the plain fertile and well watered, the mystery of its position is explained. It was protected in front by the Nile, and in the rear by the ravine and the river. But how long ago was this? Here apparently was an independent stream, taking its rise among the Libyan mountains. It dated back, consequently, to a time when those barren hills collected·and distributed water—that is to say, to a time when it used to rain in Nubia. And that time must have been before the rocky barrier broke down at Silsilis, in the old days when the land of Kush flowed with milk and honey.[1]

It would rain even now in Nubia, if it could. That same evening when the sun was setting, we saw a fan-like drift of dappled cloud miles high above our heads, melting, as it seemed, in fringes of iridescent vapour. We could distinctly see those fringes forming, wavering, and evaporating; unable to descend as rain, because dispersed at a high altitude by radiated heat from the desert. This, with one exception, was the only occasion on which I saw clouds in Nubia.

Coming back, we met a solitary native, with a string of beads in his hand and a knife up his sleeve. He followed us for a long way, volunteering a but half-intelligible story about some unknown Birbeh[2] in the desert. We asked where it was, and he pointed up the course of our unknown river.

"You have seen it?" said the Painter.

"Marrat ketîr" (many times).

"How far is it?"

"One day's march in the hagar" (desert).

"And have no Ingleezeh ever been to look for it?"

He shook his head at first, not understanding the question; then looked grave and held up one finger.

Our stock of Arabic was so small, and his so interlarded with Kensee, that we had great difficulty in making out what he said next. We gathered, however, that some Howadji, travelling alone and on foot, had once gone in search of this

---

[1] Not only near this nameless town, but in many other parts between Abou Simbel and Philæ, we found the old alluvial soil lying as high as from 20 to 30 feet above the level of the present inundations.

[2] Ar. *Birbeh*, Temple.

Birbeh, and never come back. Was he lost? Was he killed? —Who could say?

"It was a long time ago," said the man with the beads. "It was a long time ago, and he took no guide with him."

We would have given much to trace the river to its source, and search for this unknown temple in the desert. But it is one of the misfortunes of this kind of travelling that one cannot easily turn aside from the beaten track. The hot season is approaching; the river is running low; the daily cost of the dahabeeyah is exorbitant; and in Nubia, where little or nothing can be bought in the way of food, the dilatory traveller risks starvation. It was something, however, to have seen with one's own eyes that the Nile, instead of flowing for a distance of 1200 miles unfed by any affluent, had here received the waters of a tributary.[1]

To those who have a south breeze behind them, the temples must now follow in quick succession. We, however, achieved them by degrees, and rejoiced when our helpless dahabeeyah lay within rowing reach of anything worth seeing. Thus we pull down one day to Maharrakeh—in itself a dull ruin; but picturesquely desolate. Seen as one comes up the bank on landing, two parallel rows of columns stand boldly up against the sky, supporting a ruined entablature. In the foreground, a few stunted Dôm-palms starve in an arid soil. The barren desert closes in the distance.

We are beset here by an insolent crowd of savage-looking men and boys, and impudent girls with long frizzy hair and Nubian fringes, who pester us with beads and pebbles; dance, shout, slap their legs and clap their hands in our faces; and pelt us when we go away. One ragged warrior brandishes an antique brass-mounted firelock full six foot long in the barrel, and some of the others carry slender spears.

The Temple—a late Roman structure—would seem to have

---

[1] "The Nile receives its last tributary, the Atbara, in Lat. 17° 42′ N., at the northern extremity of the peninsular tract anciently called the island of Meröe, and thence flows N. (a single stream without the least accession) through 12 degrees of latitude; or, following its winding course, at least 1200 miles, to the sea."—*Blackie's Imperial Gazetteer*, 1861. A careful survey of the country would probably bring to light the dry beds of many more such tributaries as the one described above.

been wrecked by earthquake before it was completed. The masonry is all in the rough—pillars as they came from the quarry ; capitals blocked out, waiting for the carver. These unfinished ruins—of which every stone looks new, as if the work was still in progress—affect one's imagination strangely. On a fallen wall south of the portico, the Idle Man detected some remains of a Greek inscription ; [1] but for hieroglyphic characters, or cartouches by which to date the building, we looked in vain.[2]

Dakkeh comes next in order ; then Gerf Hossayn, Dendoor, and Kalabsheh. Arriving at Dakkeh soon after sunrise, we find the whole population—screaming, pushing, chattering, laden with eggs, pigeons, and gourds for sale—drawn up to receive us. There is a large sand island in the way here ; so we moor about a mile above the Temple.

We first saw the twin pylons of Dakkeh some weeks ago from the deck of the Philæ, and we then likened them to the majestic towers of Edfu. Approaching them now by land, we are surprised to find them so small. It is a brilliant, hot morning ; and our way lies by the river, between the lentil slope and the castor-berry patches. There are flocks of pigeons

---

[1] Of this wall, Burckhardt notices that " it has fallen down, apparently from some sudden and violent concussion, as the stones are lying on the ground in layers, as when placed in the wall ; a proof that they must have fallen all at once."—*Travels in Nubia:* Ed. 1819, p. 100. But he has not observed the inscription, which is in large characters, and consists of three lines on three separate layers of stones. The Idle Man copied the original upon the spot, which copy has since been identified with an ex-voto of a Roman soldier published in Boeckh's *Corpus Inscr. Græc.*, of which the following is a translation :—

" The vow of Verecundus the soldier, and his most pious parents, and Gaius his little brother, and the rest of his brethren."

[2] A clue, however, might possibly be found to the date. There is a rudely sculptured tableau—the only piece of sculpture in the place—on a detached wall near the standing columns. It represents Isis worshipped by a youth in a short toga. Both figures are lumpish and ill-modelled ; and Isis, seated under a conventional fig-tree, wears her hair erected in stiff rolls over the forehead, like a diadem. It is the face and stiffly-dressed hair of Marciana, the sister of Trajan, as shown upon the well-known coin engraved in Smith's *Dic. of Greek and Roman Biography*, vol. ii. p. 939. Mahar-rakeh is the Hiera Sycaminos, or Place of the Sacred Fig-tree, where ends the Itinerary of Antoninus.

flying low overhead ; barking dogs and crowing cocks in the village close by ; and all over the path, hundreds of beetles—real, live scarabs, black as coal and busy as ants—rolling their clay pellets up from the water's edge to the desert. If we were to examine a score or so of these pellets, we should here and there find one that contained no eggs ; for it is a curious fact that the scarab-beetle makes and rolls her pellets, whether she has an egg to deposit or not. The female beetle, though assisted by the male, is said to do the heavier share of the pellet-rolling ; and if evening comes on before her pellet is safely stowed away, she will sleep holding it with her feet all night, and resume her labour in the morning.[1]

The Temple here—begun by an Ethiopian king named Arkaman (Ergamenes), about whom Diodorus has a long story to tell, and carried on by the Ptolemies and Cæsars—stands in

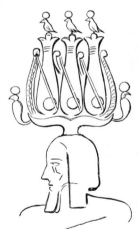

a desolate open space to the north of the village, and is approached by an avenue, the walls of which are constructed with blocks from some earlier building. The whole of this avenue and all the waste ground for three or four hundred yards round about the Temple, is not merely strewn but piled with fragments of pottery, pebbles, and large smooth stones of porphyry, alabaster, basalt, and a kind of marble like verde antico. These stones are puzzling. They look as if they might be fragments of statues that had been rolled and polished by ages of friction in the bed of a torrent. Among the potsherds we find some inscribed fragments, like those of Elephantine.[2] Of the Temple I will only say that, as masonry, it is better put together than

[1] See " *The Scarabæus Sacer* " by C. Woodrooffe, B.A.,—a paper (based on notes by the late Rev. C. Johns) read before the Winchester and Hampshire Scientific and Literary Society, Nov. 8, 1875. *Privately printed.*

[2] See chap. x. p. 181. Dakkeh (the Pselcis of the Greeks and Romans, the Pselk of the Egyptians) was at one time regarded as the confine of Egypt and Ethiopia, and would seem to have been a great military station.

any work of the XVIIIth or XIXth Dynasties with which I am acquainted. The sculptures, however, are atrocious. Such mis-shapen hieroglyphs; such dumpy, smirking goddesses; such clownish kings in such preposterous head-dresses, we have never seen till now. The whole thing, in short, as regards sculpturesque style, is the Ptolemaic out-Ptolemied.

Rowing round presently to Kobban—the river running wide, with the sand island between—we land under the walls of a huge crude-brick structure, black with age, which at first sight looks quite shapeless; but which proves to be an ancient Egyptian fortress, buttressed, towered, loopholed, finished at the angles with the invariable moulded torus, and surrounded by a deep dry moat, which is probably yet filled each summer by the inundation.

Now of all rare things in the valley of the Nile, a purely secular ruin is the rarest; and this, with the exception of some foundations of dwellings here and there, is the first we have seen. It is probably very, very old; as old as the days of Thothmes III, whose name is found on some scattered blocks about a quarter of a mile away, and who built two similar fortresses at Semneh, thirty-five miles above Wady Halfeh. It may even be a thousand years older still, and date from the time of Amenemhat III, whose name is also found on a stela near Kobban.[1]   For here was once an ancient city, when

The inscribed potsherds here are chiefly receipts and accounts of soldiers' pay.   The walls of the Temple outside, and of the chambers within, abound also in free-hand graffiti, most of which are written in red ink.   We observed some that appeared to be trilingual.   The Writer copied the two following from over a doorway.   The first is supposed by Dr. Birch to be in Ethiopian demotic, and is apparently a name.   The characters of the second appear to be quite unknown :—

[1]   "Less than a quarter of a mile to the south are the ruins of a small sandstone Temple with clustered columns; and on the way, near the village, you pass a stone stela of Amenemha III, mentioning his eleventh year."—*Murray's Handbook for Egypt*, p. 481.   M. Maspero, writing of

Pselcis (now Dakkeh) was but a new suburb on the opposite bank. The name of this ancient city is lost, but it is by some supposed to be identical with the Metacompso of Ptolemy.[1] As the suburb grew, the mother town declined, and in time, the suburb became the city, and the city became the suburb. The scattered blocks aforesaid, together with the remains of a small Temple, yet mark the position of the elder city.

The walls of this most curious and interesting fortress have

Thothmes III, says, "Sons fils et successeur, Amenhotep III, fit construire en face de Pselkis une forteresse importante."—*Hist. Ancienne des Peuples de l'Orient.* Chap. iii. p. 113.

At Kobban also was found the famous stela of Rameses II, called the Stela of Dakkeh ; see chap. xv. p. 265. In this inscription, a cast from which is at the Louvre, Rameses II is stated to have caused an artesian well to be made in the desert between this place and Gebel Oellaky, in order to facilitate the working of the gold mines of those parts.

[1] "According to Ptolemy, Metachompso should be opposite Pselcis, where there are extensive brick ruins. If so, Metachompso and Contra Pselcis must be the same town."—*Topography of Thebes*, etc. ; Sir G. Wilkinson. Ed. 1835, p. 488. M. Vivien de St. Martin is, however, of opinion that the island of Derar, near Maharrakeh, is the true Metachompso. See *Le Nord de l'Afrique*, section vi. p. 161. Be this as it may, we at all events know of one great siege that this fortress sustained, and of one great battle fought beneath its walls. "The Ethiopians," says Strabo, "having taken advantage of the withdrawal of part of the Roman forces, surprised and took Syene, Elephantine, and Philæ, enslaved the inhabitants, and threw down the statues of Cæsar. But Petronius, marching with less than 10,000 infantry and 800 horse against an army of 30,000 men, compelled them to retreat to Pselcis. He then sent deputies to demand restitution of what they had taken, and the reasons which had induced them to begin the war. On their alleging that they had been ill treated by the monarchs, he answered that these were not the sovereigns of the country—but Cæsar. When they desired three days for consideration and did nothing which they were bound to do, Petronius attacked and compelled them to fight. They soon fled, being badly commanded and badly armed, for they carried large shields made of raw hides, and hatchets for offensive weapons. Part of the insurgents were driven into the city, others fled into the uninhabited country, and such as ventured upon the passage of the river escaped to a neighbouring island, where there were not many crocodiles, on account of the current. . . . Petronius then attacked Pselcis, and took it."—STRABO'S *Geography*, Bohn's translation, 1857, vol. iii. pp. 267-8. This island to which the insurgents fled may have been the large sand island which here still occupies the middle of the river, and obstructs the approach to Dakkeh. Or they may have fled to the island of Derar, seven miles higher up. Strabo does not give the name of the island.

probably lost much of their original height.   They are in some
parts 30 feet thick, and nowhere less than 20.   Vertical on
the inside, they are built at a buttress-slope outside, with
additional shallow buttresses at regular distances.   These last,
as they can scarcely add to the enormous strength of the
original wall, were probably designed for effect.   There are
two entrances to the fortress ; one in the centre of the north
wall, and one in the south.   We enter the enclosure by the last-
named, and find ourselves in the midst of an immense parallelo-
gram measuring about 450 feet from east to west, and perhaps
300 feet from north to south.

All within these bounds is a wilderness of ruin.   The
space looks large enough for a city, and contains what might
be the débris of a dozen cities.   We climb huge mounds of
rubbish ; skirt cataracts of broken pottery ; and stand on the
brink of excavated pits, honeycombed forty feet below with
brick foundations.   Over these mounds and at the bottom of
these pits, swarm men, women, and children, filling and carrying away basket-loads of rubble.   The dust rises in clouds.
The noise, the heat, the confusion, are indescribable.   One
pauses, bewildered, seeking in vain to discover in this mighty
maze any indication of a plan.   It is only by an effort that one
gradually realises how the place is but a vast shell, and how
all these mounds and pits mark the site of what was once a
huge edifice rising tower above tower to a central keep, such
as we see represented in the battle-subjects of Abou Simbel
and Thebes.

That towered edifice and central keep—quarried, broken
up, carried away piecemeal, reduced to powder, and spread
over the land as manure—has now disappeared almost to its
foundations.   Only the well in the middle of the enclosure,
and the great wall of circuit, remain.   That wall is doomed,
and will by and by share the fate of the rest.   The well, which
must have been very deep, is choked with rubbish to the brim.
Meanwhile, in order to realise what the place in its present condition is like, one need but imagine how the Tower of London
would look if the whole of the inner buildings—White Tower,
Chapel, Armoury, Governor's Quarters and all—were levelled
in shapeless ruin, and only the outer walls and moat were left.

Built up against the inner side of the wall of circuit are the remains of a series of massive towers, the tops of which, as they are, strangely enough, shorter than the external structure, can never have communicated with the battlements, unless by ladders. The finest of these towers, together with a magnificent fragment of wall, faces the eastern desert.

Going out by the north entrance, we find the sides of the gateway, and even the steps leading down into the moat, in perfect preservation ; while at the base of the great wall, on the outer side facing the river, there yet remains a channel or conduit about two feet square, built and roofed with stone, which in Murray is described as a water-gate.

The sun is high, the heat is overwhelming, the felucca waits ; and we turn reluctantly away, knowing that between here and Cairo we shall see no more curious relic of the far-off past than this dismantled stronghold. It is a mere mountain of unburnt brick ; altogether unlovely ; admirable only for the gigantic strength of its proportions ; pathetic only in the abjectness of its ruin. Yet it brings the lost ages home to one's imagination in a way that no Temple could ever bring them. It dispels for a moment the historic glamour of the sculptures, and compels us to remember those nameless and forgotten millions, of whom their rulers fashioned soldiers in time of war and builders in time of peace.

Our adventures by the way are few and far between ; and we now rarely meet a dahabeeyah. Birds are more plentiful than when we were in this part of the river a few weeks ago. We see immense flights of black and white cranes congregated at night on the sandbanks ; and any number of quail may be had for the shooting. It is matter for rejoicing when the Idle Man goes out with his gun and brings home a full bag ; for our last sheep was killed before we started for Wady Halfeh, and our last poultry ceased cackling at Abou Simbel.

One morning early, we see a bride taken across the river in a big boat full of women and girls, who are clapping their hands and shrilling the tremulous zaghareet. The bride—a chocolate beauty with magnificent eyes—wears a gold brow-pendant and nose-ring, and has her hair newly plaited in hundreds of tails, finished off at the ends with mud pellets daubed with yellow ochre. She stands surrounded by her companions, proud of her finery, and pleased to be stared at by the Ingleezeh.

About this time, also, we see one night a wild sort of festival going on for some miles along both sides of the river. Watch-fires break out towards twilight, first on this bank, then on that ; becoming brighter and more numerous as the darkness deepens. By and by, when we are going to bed, we hear sounds of drumming on the eastern bank, and see from afar a torchlight procession and dance. The effect of this dance of torches—for it is only the torches that are visible—is quite diabolic. The lights flit and leap as if they were alive ; circling, clustering, dispersing, bobbing, poussetting, pursuing each other at a gallop, and whirling every now and then through the air, like rockets. Late as it is, we would fain put ashore and see this orgy more nearly ; but Reïs Hassan shakes his head. The natives hereabout are said to be quarrelsome ; and if, as it is probable, they are celebrating the festival of some local saint, we might be treated as intruders.

Coming at early morning to Gerf Hossayn, we make our way up to the Temple, which is excavated in the face of a limestone cliff, a couple of hundred feet, perhaps, above the river. A steep path, glaring hot in the sun, leads to a terrace in the rock ; the Temple being approached through the ruins of a built-out portico and an avenue of battered colossi. It is a gloomy place within—an inferior edition so to say, of the Great Temple of Abou Simbel ; and of the same date. It consists of a first hall supported by Osiride pillars, a second and smaller hall with square columns ; a smoke-blackened sanctuary ; and two side-chambers. The Osiride colossi, which stand 20 feet high without the entablature over their heads or the pedestal under their feet, are thick-set, bow-legged, and mis-shapen. Their faces would seem to have been painted black originally ; while those of the avenue outside have distinctly Ethiopian features. One seems to detect here, as at Derr and Wady Sabooah, the work of provincial sculptors ; just as at Abou Simbel one recognises the master-style of the artists of the Theban Ramesseum.

The side-chambers at Gerf Hossayn are infested with bats.

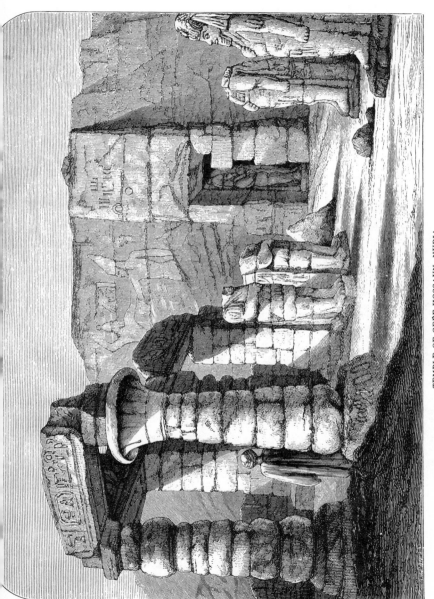

TEMPLE OF GERF HOSSAYN, NUBIA.

These bats are the great sight of the place, and have their appointed showman.   We find him waiting for us with an end of tarred rope, which he flings, blazing, into the pitch-dark door-way.   For a moment we see the whole ceiling hung, as it were, with a close fringe of white, filmy-looking pendants.   But it is only for a moment.   The next instant the creatures are all in motion, dashing out madly in our faces like driven snowflakes. We picked up a dead one afterwards, when the rush was over, and examined it by the outer daylight——a lovely little creature, white and downy, with fine transparent wings, and little pink feet, and the prettiest mousey mouth imaginable.

TEMPLE OF DENDOOR.

Bordered with dwarf palms, acacias, and henna-bushes, the cliffs between Gerf Hossayn and Dendoor stand out in detached masses so like ruins that sometimes we can hardly believe they are rocks.   At Dendoor, when the sun is setting and a delicious gloom is stealing up the valley, we visit a tiny Temple on the western bank.   It stands out above the river surrounded by a wall of enclosure, and consists of a single pylon, a portico, two little chambers, and a sanctuary. The whole thing is like an exquisite toy, so covered with sculptures, so smooth, so new-looking, so admirably built. Seeing them half by sunset, half by dusk, it matters not that these delicately-wrought bas-reliefs are of the Decadence school.[1] The rosy half-light of an Egyptian after-glow covers a multitude of sins, and steeps the whole in an atmosphere of romance.

Wondering what has happened to the climate, we wake shivering next morning an hour or so before break of day, and, for the first time in several weeks, taste the old early chill upon the air. When the sun rises, we find ourselves at Kalabsheh, having passed the limit of the Tropic during the night. Henceforth, no matter how great the heat may be by day, this chill invariably comes with the dark hour before dawn.

The usual yelling crowd, with the usual beads, baskets, eggs, and pigeons, for sale, greets us on the shore at Kalabsheh. One of the men has a fine old two-handed sword in a shabby blue velvet sheath, for which he asks five Napoleons. It looks as if it might have belonged to a crusader. Some of the women bring buffalo-cream in filthy-looking black skins slung round their waists like girdles. The cream is excellent ; but the skins temper one's enjoyment of the unaccustomed dainty.

There is a magnificent Temple here, and close by, excavated in the cliff, a rock-cut Speos, the local name of which is Bayt-el-Weli. The sculptures of this famous Speos have been more frequently described and engraved than almost any sculptures in Egypt. The procession of Ethiopian tribute-bearers, the assault of the Amorite city, the Triumph of Rameses, are familiar not only to every reader of Wilkinson, but to every visitor passing through the Egyptian Rooms of the British Museum. Notwithstanding the casts that have been taken from them, and the ill-treatment to which they have been subjected by natives and visitors, they are still beautiful. The colour of those in the roofless courtyard, though so perfect when

---

[1] " C'est un ouvrage non achevé du temps de l'empereur Auguste. Quoique peu important par son étendue, ce monument m'a beaucoup interessé, puisqu'il est entièrement relatif à l'incarnation d'Osiris sous forme humaine, sur la terre."—*Lettres écrites d'Egypte*, etc. : CHAMPOLLION. Paris, 1868, p. 126.

Bonomi executed his admirable facsimiles, has now almost entirely peeled off; but in the portico and inner chambers it is yet brilliant. An emerald green Osiris, a crimson Anubis, and an Isis of the brightest chrome yellow, are astonishingly pure and forcible in quality. As for the flesh-tones of the Anubis, this was I believe the only instance I observed of a true crimson in Egyptian pigments.

Between the Speos of Bayt-el-Welly and the neighbouring Temple of Kalabsheh there lies about half-a-mile of hilly pathway and a gulf of 1400 years. Rameses ushers us into the presence of Augustus, and we pass, as it were, from an oratory in the Great House of Pharaoh to the presence-chamber of the Cæsars.

But if the decorative work in the presence-chamber of the Cæsars was anything like the decorative work in the Temple of Kalabsheh, then the taste thereof was of the vilest. Such a

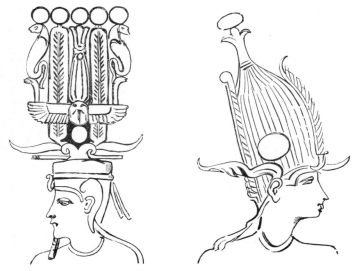

masquerade of deities; such striped and spotted and cross-barred robes; such outrageous head-dresses; such crude and violent colouring,[1] we have never seen the like of. As for the

---

[1] I observed mauve here, for the first and only time; and very brilliant ultramarine. There are also traces of gilding on many of the figures.

TEMPLE OF KALABSHEH, NUBIA.

goddesses, they are gaudier than the dancing damsels of Luxor ; while the kings balance on their heads diadems compounded of horns, moons, birds, balls, beetles, lotus-blossoms, asps, vases, and feathers. The Temple, however, is conceived on a grand scale. It is the Karnak of Nubia. But it is a Karnak that has evidently been visited by a shock of earthquake far more severe than that which shook the mighty pillars of the Hypostyle Hall and flung down the obelisk of Hatasu. From the river, it looks like a huge fortress ; but seen from the threshold of the main gateway, it is a wilderness of ruin. Fallen blocks, pillars, capitals, entablatures, lie so extravagantly piled, that there is not one spot in all those halls and courtyards upon which it is possible to set one's foot on the level of the original pavement. Here, again, the earthquake seems to have come before the work was completed. There are figures outlined on the walls, but never sculptured. Others have been begun, but never finished. You can see where the chisel stopped—you can even detect which was the last mark it made on the surface. One traces here, in fact, the four processes of wall decoration. In some places the space is squared off and ruled by the mechanic ; in others, the subject is ready drawn within those spaces by the artist. Here the sculptor has carried it a stage farther ; yonder the painter has begun to colour it.

More interesting, however, than aught else at Kalabsheh is the Greek inscription of Silco of Ethiopia.[1] This inscription— made famous by the commentaries of Niebuhr and Letronne —was discovered by M. Gau in A.D. 1818. It consists of 21 lines very neatly written in red ink, and it dates from the sixth century of the Christian era. It commences thus :—

I, Silco, puissant king of the Nubians and all the Ethiopians,
I came twice as far as Talmis[2] and Taphis.[3]
I fought against the Blemyes,[4] and God granted me the victory.

---

[1] See chap. xii. p. 221.
[2] TALMIS : (Kalabsheh).   [3] TAPHIS : (Tafah).
[4] Blemyes :—The Blemyes were a nomadic race of Berbers, supposed to be originally of the tribe of Bilmas of Tibbous in the central desert, and settled as early as the time of Eratosthenes in that part of the Valley of the Nile which lies between the First and Second Cataracts. See *Le Nord de l'Afrique*, by M. V. DE ST. MARTIN. Paris, 1863, Section III, p. 73.

I vanquished them a second time ; and the first time
I established myself completely with my troops.
I vanquished them, and they supplicated me.
I made peace with them ; and they swore to me by their idols.
I trusted them ; because they are a people of good faith.
Then I returned to my dominions in the Upper Country.
For I am a king.
Not only am I no follower in the train of other kings,
But I go before them.
As for those who seek strife against me,
I give them no peace in their homes till they entreat my pardon.
For I am a lion on the plains, and a goat upon the mountains.
etc. etc. etc.

The historical value of this inscription is very great. It
shows that in the sixth century, while the native inhabitants of
this part of the Valley of the Nile yet adhered to the ancient
Egyptian faith, the Ethiopians of the south were professedly
Christian.

The descendants of the Blemmys are a fine race ; tall,
strong, and of a rich chocolate complexion. Strolling through
the village at sunset, we see the entire population—old men
sitting at their doors ; young men lounging and smoking ;
children at play. The women, with glittering white teeth and
liquid eyes, and a profusion of gold and silver ornaments on
neck and brow, come out with their little brown babies astride
on hip or shoulder, to stare as we go by. One sick old woman,
lying outside her hut on a palm-wood couch, raises herself for
a moment on her elbow—then sinks back with a weary sigh,
and turns her face to the wall. The mud dwellings here are
built in and out of a maze of massive stone foundations, the
remains of buildings once magnificent. Some of these walls
are built in concave courses ; each course of stones, that is to
say, being depressed in the centre, and raised at the angles ;
which mode of construction was adopted in order to offer less
resistance when shaken by earthquake.[1]

We observe more foundations built thus, at Tafah, where
we arrive next morning. As the masons' work at Tafah is of
late Roman date, it follows that earthquakes were yet frequent
in Nubia at a period long subsequent to the great shock of
B.C. 27, mentioned by Eusebius. Travellers are too ready to

[1] See *The Habitations of Man in all Ages.* V. LE DUC. Chap. ix. p. 93.

ascribe everything in the way of ruin to the fury of Cambyses and the pious rage of the early Christians. Nothing, however, is easier than to distinguish between the damage done to the monuments by the hand of man and the damage caused by subterraneous upheaval. Mutilation is the rule in the one case ; displacement in the other. At Denderah, for example, the injury done is wholly wilful ; at Abou Simbel, it is wholly accidental ; at Karnak, it is both wilful and accidental. As for Kalabsheh, it is clear that no such tremendous havoc could have been effected by human means without the aid of powerful rams, fire, or gunpowder ; any of which must have left unmistakable traces.

RUINED TEMPLE AT TAFAH, NUBIA.

At Tafah there are two little temples ; one in picturesque ruin, one quite perfect, and now used as a stable. There are also a number of stone foundations, separate, quadrangular, subdivided into numerous small chambers, and enclosed in boundary walls, some of which are built in the concave courses just named. These sub - structions, of which the Painter counted eighteen, have long been the puzzle of travellers.[1]

[1] They probably mark the site of a certain Coptic monastery described

Tafah is charmingly placed ; and the seven miles which divide it from Kalabsheh—once, no doubt, the scene of a cataract—are perhaps the most picturesque on this side of Wady Halfeh. Rocky islets in the river ; palm-groves, acacias, carobs, henna and castor-berry bushes, and all kinds of flowering shrubs, along the edges of the banks ; fantastic precipices riven and pinnacled, here rising abruptly from the water's edge, and there from the sandy plain, make lovely sketches whichever way one turns. There are gazelles, it is said, in the ravines behind Tafah ; and one of the natives—a truculent fellow in a ragged shirt and dirty white turban—tells how, at a distance of three hours up a certain glen, there is another Birbeh, larger than either of these in the plain, and a great standing statue taller than three men. Here, then, if the tale be true, is another ready-made discovery for whoever may care to undertake it.

This same native, having sold a necklace to the Idle Man and gone away content with his bargain, comes back by and by with half the village at his heels, requiring double price. This modest demand being refused, he rages up and down like a maniac ; tears off his turban ; goes through a wild manual exercise with his spear ; then sits down in stately silence, with his friends and neighbours drawn up in a semicircle behind him.

This, it seems, is Nubian for a challenge. He has thrown down his gauntlet in form, and demands trial by combat. The noisy crowd, meanwhile, increases every moment. Reïs Hassan looks grave, fearing a possible fracas ; and the Idle Man, who is reading the morning service down below (for it is on a Sunday morning) can scarcely be heard for the clamour outside. In this emergency, it occurs to the Writer to send a message ashore informing these gentlemen that the Howadjis are hold-

in an ancient Arabic MS. quoted by E. Quatremere, which says that " in the town of Tafah there is a fine monastery called the monastery of Ansoun. It is very ancient ; but so solidly built, that after so great a number of years it still stands uninjured. Near this monastery, facing the mountain, are situated fifteen villages." See *Mémoires Hist. et Géographiques sur l'Egypte et le Nubie*, par E. QUATREMERE. Paris, 1811, vol. ii. p. 55.

The monastery and the villages were, doubtless, of Romano-Egyptian construction in the first instance, and may originally have been a sacred College, like the sacred College at Philæ.

ing mosque in the dahabeeyah, and entreating them to be quiet till the hour of prayer is past. The effect of the message, strange to say, is instantaneous. The angry voices are at once hushed. The challenger puts on his turban. The assembled spectators squat in respectful silence on the bank. A whole hour goes by thus, so giving the storm time to blow over ; and when the Idle Man reappears on deck, his would-be adversary comes forward quite pleasantly to discuss the purchase afresh.

It matters little how the affair ended ; but I believe he was offered his necklace back in exchange for the money paid, and preferred to abide by his bargain. It is as evidence of the sincerity of the religious sentiment in the minds of a semi-savage people,[1] that I have thought the incident worth telling.

We are now less than forty miles from Philæ ; but the head wind is always against us, and the men's bread is exhausted, and there is no flour to be bought in these Nubian villages. The poor fellows swept out the last crumbs from the bottom of their bread-chest three or four days ago, and are now living on quarter-rations of lentil soup and a few dried dates bought at Wady Halfeh. Patient and depressed, they crouch silently beside their oars, or forget their hunger in sleep. For ourselves, it is painful to witness their need, and still more painful to be unable to help them. Talhamy, whose own stores are at a low ebb, vows he can do nothing. It would take his few remaining tins of preserved meat to feed fifteen men for two days, and of flour he has barely enough for the Howadjis. Hungry ? well, yes—no doubt they are hungry. But what of that ? They are Arabs ; and Arabs bear hunger as camels bear thirst. It is nothing new to them. They have often been hungry before — they will often be hungry again. Enough ! It is not for the ladies to trouble themselves about such fellows as these !

Excellent advice, no doubt ; but hard to follow. Not to

---

[1] "The peasants of Tafa relate that they are the descendants of the few Christian inhabitants of the city who embraced the Mohammedan faith when the country was conquered by the followers of the Prophet ; the greater part of their brethren having either fled or been put to death on that event taking place. They are still called Oulad el Nusara, or the Christian progeny."—*Travels in Nubia:* BURCKHARDT. London, 1819, p. 121.

be troubled, and not to do what little we can for the poor lads,
is impossible. When that little means laying violent hands on
Talhamy's reserve of eggs and biscuits, and getting up lotteries
for prizes of chocolate and tobacco, that worthy evidently considers that we have taken leave of our wits.

Under a burning sky, we touch for an hour or two at
Gertássee, and then push on for Dabôd. The limestone
quarries at Gertássee are full of votive sculptures and inscriptions ; and the little ruin—a mere cluster of graceful columns
supporting a fragment of cornice—stands high on the brink of
a cliff overhanging the river. Take it as you will, from above
or below, looking north or looking south, it makes a charming
sketch.

TEMPLE OF DABÔD.

If transported to Dabôd on that magic carpet of the fairy-
tale, one would take it for a ruin on the "beached margent"
of some placid lake in dreamland. It lies between two bends
of the river, which here flows wide, showing no outlet and
seeming to be girdled by mountains and palm-groves. The
Temple is small and uninteresting ; begun, like Dakkeh, by an
Ethiopian king, and finished by Ptolemies and Cæsars. The
one curious thing about it is a secret cell, most cunningly

devised. Adjoining the sanctuary is a dark side-chamber; in
the floor of the side-chamber is a pit, once paved over; in one
corner of the pit is a man-hole opening into a narrow passage;
and in the narrow passage are steps leading up to a secret
chamber constructed in the thickness of the wall. We saw
other secret chambers in other Temples;[1] but not one in which
the old approaches were so perfectly preserved.

From Dabôd to Philæ is but ten miles; and we· are bound
for Torrigûr, which is two miles nearer. Now Torrigûr is that
same village at the foot of the beautiful sand-drift, near which
we moored on our way up the river; and here we are to stay
two days, followed by at least a week at Philæ. No sooner,
therefore, have we reached Torrigûr, than Reïs Hassan and
three sailors start for Assûan to buy flour. Old Ali, Riskalli,
and Mûsa, whose homes lie in the villages round about, get
leave of absence for a week; and we find ourselves reduced
all at once to a crew of five, with only Khaleefeh in command.
Five, however, are as good as fifty, when the dahabeeyah lies
moored and there is nothing to do; and our five, having
succeeded in buying some flabby Nubian cakes and green
lentils, are now quite happy. So the Painter pitches his tent
at the top of the sand-drift; and the Writer sketches the
ruined convent opposite; and L. and the Little Lady write
no end of letters; and the Idle Man, with Mehemet Ali for
a retriever, shoots quail; and everybody is satisfied.

Hapless Idle Man!—hapless, but homicidal. If he had
been content to shoot only quail, and had not taken to shooting
babies! What possessed him to do it? Not—not, let us hope
—an ill-directed ambition, foiled of crocodiles! He went serene

---

[1] In these secret chambers (the entrance to which was closed by a
block of masonry so perfectly fitted as to defy detection) were kept the
images of gold and silver and lapis lazuli, the precious vases, the sistrums,
the jewelled collars, and all the portable treasures of the Temples. We
saw a somewhat similar pit and small chamber in a corner of the Temple
of Dakkeh, and some very curious crypts and hiding places under the
floor of the dark chamber to the east of the Sanctuary at Philæ, all of
course long since broken open and rifled. But we had strong reason to
believe that the Painter discovered the whereabouts of a hidden chamber
or passage to the west of the Sanctuary, yet closed, with all its treasures
probably intact. We had, however, no means of opening the wall, which
is of solid masonry.

and smiling, with his gun under his arm, and Mehemet Ali in his
wake. Who so light of heart as that Idle Man? Who so light
of heel as that turbaned retriever? We heard our sportsman
popping away presently in the barley. It was a pleasant sound,
for we knew his aim was true. " Every shot," said we, " means a
bird." We little dreamed that one of those shots meant a baby.

RUINED CONVENT (COPTIC) NEAR PHILÆ.

All at once, a woman screamed. It was a sharp, sudden
scream, following a shot—a scream with a ring of horror in it.
Instantly it was caught up from point to point, growing in
volume and seeming to be echoed from every direction at
once. At the same moment, the bank became alive with
human beings. They seemed to spring from the soil—women
shrieking and waving their arms; men running; all making
for the same goal. The Writer heard the scream, saw the
rush, and knew at once that a gun accident had happened.

A few minutes of painful suspense followed. Then

Mehemet Ali appeared, tearing back at the top of his speed ;
and presently——perhaps five minutes later, though it seemed
like twenty——came the Idle Man ; walking very slowly and
defiantly, with his head up, his arms folded, his gun gone, and
an immense rabble at his heels.

Our scanty crew, armed with sticks, flew at once to the
rescue, and brought him off in safety.   We then learned what
had happened.

A flight of quail had risen ; and as quail fly low, skimming
the surface of the grain and diving down again almost immediately, he had taken a level aim.   At the instant that he
fired, and in the very path of the quail, a woman and child
who had been squatting in the barley, sprang up screaming.
He at once saw the coming danger ; and, with admirable
presence of mind, drew the charge of his second barrel.   He
then hid his cartridge-box and hugged his gun, determined to
hold it as long as possible.   The next moment he was surrounded, overpowered, had the gun wrenched from his grasp,
and received a blow on the back with a stone.   Having
captured the gun, one or two of the men let go.   It was then
that he shook off the rest, and came back to the boat.   Mehemet
Ali at the same time flew to call a rescue.   He, too, came in
for some hard knocks, besides having his shirt rent and his
turban torn off his head.

Here were we, meanwhile, with less than half our crew, a
private war on our hands, no captain, and one of our three
guns in the hands of the enemy.   What a scene it was !   A
whole village, apparently a very considerable village, swarming
on the bank ; all hurrying to and fro ; all raving, shouting,
gesticulating.   If we had been on the verge of a fracas at
Tafah, here we were threatened with a siege.

Drawing in the plank between the boat and the shore, we
held a hasty council of war.

The woman being unhurt, and the child, if hurt at all,
hurt very slightly, we felt justified in assuming an injured tone,
calling the village to account for a case of cowardly assault,
and demanding instant restitution of the gun.   We accordingly
sent Talhamy to parley with the head-man of the place and
peremptorily demand the gun.   We also bade him add——and

this we regarded as a master-stroke of policy—that if due submission was immediately made, the Howadji, one of whom was a Hakeem, would permit the father to bring his child on board to have its hurts attended to.

Outwardly indifferent, inwardly not a little anxious, we waited the event. Talhamy's back being towards the river, we had the whole semicircle of swarthy faces full in view— bent brows, flashing eyes, glittering teeth ; all anger, all scorn, all defiance. Suddenly the expression of the faces changed— the change beginning with those nearest the speaker, and spreading gradually outwards. It was as if a wave had passed over them. We knew then that our *coup* was made. Talhamy returned. The villagers crowded round their leaders, deliberating. Numbers now began to sit down ; and when a Nubian sits down, you may be sure that he is no longer dangerous.

Presently—after perhaps a quarter of an hour—the gun was brought back uninjured, and an elderly man carrying a blue bundle appeared on the bank. The plank was now put across ; the crowd was kept off ; and the man with the bundle, and three or four others, were allowed to pass.

The bundle being undone, a little brown imp of about four years of age, with shaven head and shaggy scalp-lock, was produced. He whimpered at first, seeing the strange white faces ; but when offered a fig, forgot his terrors, and sat munching it like a monkey. As for his wounds, they were literally skin-deep, the shot having but slightly grazed his shoulders in four or five places. The Idle Man, however, solemnly sponged the scratches with warm water, and L. covered them with patches of sticking-plaister. Finally, the father was presented with a Napoleon ; the patient was wrapped in one of his murderer's shirts ; and the first act of the tragedy ended. The second and third acts were to come.

When the Painter and the Idle Man talked the affair over, they agreed that it was expedient, for the protection of future travellers, to lodge a complaint against the village ; and this mainly on account of the treacherous blow dealt from behind, at a time when the Idle Man (who had not once attempted to defend himself) was powerless in the hands of a mob. They therefore went next day to Assûan ; and the governor, charming as ever, promised that justice should be done. Meanwhile we moved the dahabeeyah to Philæ, and there settled down for a week's sketching.

Next evening came a woful deputation from Torrigûr, entreating forgiveness, and stating that fifteen villagers had been swept off to prison.

The Idle Man explained that he no longer had anything to do with it ; that the matter, in short, was in the hands of justice, and would be dealt with according to law. Hereupon the spokesman gathered up a handful of imaginary dust, and made believe to scatter it on his head.

" O dragoman ! " he said, " tell the Howadji that there is no law but his pleasure, and no justice but the will of the Governor ! "

Summoned next morning to give evidence, the Idle Man went betimes to Assûan, where he was received in private by the Governor and Mudîr. Pipes and coffee were handed, and the usual civilities exchanged. The Governor then informed his guest that fifteen men of Torrigûr had been arrested ; and that fourteen of them unanimously identified the fifteenth as the one who struck the blow.

" And now," said the Governor, " before we send for the prisoners, it will be as well to decide on the sentence. What does his Excellency wish done to them ? "

The Idle Man was puzzled. How could he offer an opinion, being ignorant of the Egyptian civil code ? and how could the sentence be decided upon before the trial ?

The Governor smiled serenely.

" But," he said, " this is the trial."

Being an Englishman, it necessarily cost the Idle Man an effort to realise the full force of this explanation—an explanation which, in its sublime simplicity, epitomised the whole system of the judicial administration of Egyptian law. He hastened, however, to explain that he cherished no resentment against the culprit or the villagers, and that his only wish was to frighten them into a due respect for travellers in general.

The Governor hereupon invited the Mudîr to suggest a sentence ; and the Mudîr—taking into consideration, as he said, his Excellency's lenient disposition—proposed to award to the fourteen innocent men one month's imprisonment each ; and to the real offender two months' imprisonment, with a hundred and fifty blows of the bastinado.

Shocked at the mere idea of such a sentence, the Idle Man declared that he must have the innocent set at liberty ; but consented that the culprit, for the sake of example, should be sentenced to the one hundred and fifty blows—the punishment to be remitted after the first few strokes had been dealt. Word was now given for the prisoners to be brought in.

The gaoler marched first, followed by two soldiers. Then came the fifteen prisoners—I am ashamed to write it !—chained neck to neck in single file.

One can imagine how the Idle Man felt at this moment.

Sentence being pronounced, the fourteen looked as if they could hardly believe their ears ; while the fifteenth, though condemned to his one hundred and fifty strokes (" seventy-five to each foot," specified the Governor), was overjoyed to be let off so easily.

He was then flung down ; his feet were fastened soles uppermost ; and two soldiers proceeded to execute the sentence. As each blow fell, he cried : " God save the Governor ! God save the Mudîr ! God save the Howadji ! "

When the sixth stroke had been dealt, the Idle Man turned to the Governor and formally interceded for the remission of the rest of the sentence. The Governor, as formally, granted the request ; and the prisoners, weeping for joy, were set at liberty.

The Governor, the Mudîr, and the Idle Man then parted with a profusion of compliments ; the Governor protesting that his only wish was to be agreeable to the English, and that the whole village should have been bastinadoed, had his Excellency desired it.

We spent eight enchanted days at Philæ ; and it so happened, when the afternoon of the eighth came round, that for

the last few hours the Writer was alone on the island.   Alone,
that is to say, with only a sailor in attendance, which was vir-
tually solitude ; and Philæ is a place to which solitude adds an
inexpressible touch of pathos and remoteness.

PHILÆ FROM THE SOUTH.

It has been a hot day, and there is dead calm on the river.
My last sketch finished, I wander slowly round from spot to
spot, saying farewell to Pharaoh's Bed—to the Painted Columns
—to every terrace, and palm, and shrine, and familiar point of
view.   I peep once again into the mystic chamber of Osiris.
I see the sun set for the last time from the roof of the Temple
of Isis.   Then, when all that wondrous flush of rose and gold
has died away, comes the warm afterglow.   No words can
paint the melancholy beauty of Philæ at this hour.   The surrounding mountains stand out jagged and purple against a pale
amber sky.   The Nile is glassy.   Not a breath, not a bubble,
troubles the inverted landscape.   Every palm is twofold ; every
stone is doubled.   The big boulders in mid-stream are reflected
so perfectly that it is impossible to tell where the rock ends and
the water begins.   The Temples, meanwhile, have turned to a
subdued golden bronze ; and the pylons are peopled with shapes
that glow with fantastic life, and look ready to step down from
their places.

The solitude is perfect, and there is a magical stillness in
the air.   I hear a mother crooning to her baby on the neighbouring island—a sparrow twittering in its little nest in the
capital of a column below my feet—a vulture screaming plain-
tively among the rocks in the far distance.

I look ; I listen ; I promise myself that I will remember it all in years to come—all the solemn hills, these silent colonnades, these deep, quiet spaces of shadow, these sleeping palms. Lingering till it is all but dark, I at last bid them farewell, fearing lest I may behold them no more.

CHAPTER XX.

SILSILIS AND EDFU.

GOING, it cost us four days to struggle up from Assûan to Mahatta ; returning, we slid down—thanks to our old friend the Sheykh of the Cataract—in one short, sensational half hour. He came—flat-faced, fishy-eyed, fatuous as ever—with his head tied up in the same old yellow handkerchief, and with the same chibouque in his mouth. He brought with him a following of fifty stalwart Shellalees ; and under his arm he carried a tattered red flag. This flag, on which were embroidered the crescent and star, he hoisted with much solemnity at the prow.

Consigned thus to the protection of the Prophet ; windows and tambooshy [1] shuttered up ; doors closed ; breakables removed to a place of safety, and everything made snug, as if for a storm at sea, we put off from Mahatta at seven A.M. on a lovely morning in the middle of March. The Philæ, instead of threading her way back through the old channels, strikes across to the Libyan side, making straight for the Big Bab— that formidable rapid which as yet we have not seen. All last night we heard its voice in the distance ; now, at every stroke of the oars, that rushing sound draws nearer.

The Sheykh of the Cataract is our captain, and his men are our sailors to-day ; Reïs Hassan and the crew having only to sit still and look on. The Shellalees, meanwhile, row swiftly and steadily. Already the river seems to be running faster than usual ; already the current feels stronger under our keel. And now, suddenly, there is sparkle and foam on the surface

---

[1] *Ar.* Tambooshy—*i.e.* saloon sky-light.

yonder—there are rocks ahead ; rocks to right and left ; eddies everywhere. The Sheykh lays down his pipe, kicks off his shoes, and goes himself to the prow. His second in command is stationed at the top of the stairs leading to the upper deck. Six men take the tiller. The rowers are reinforced, and sit two to each oar.

In the midst of these preparations, when everybody looks grave, and even the Arabs are silent, we all at once find ourselves at the mouth of a long and narrow strait—a kind of ravine between two walls of rock—through which, at a steep incline, there rushes a roaring mass of waters. The whole Nile, in fact, seems to be thundering in wild waves down that terrible channel.

It seems, at first sight, impossible that any dahabeeyah should venture that way and not be dashed to pieces. Neither does there seem room for boat and oars to pass. The Sheykh, however, gives the word—his second echoes it—the men at the helm obey. They put the dahabeeyah straight at that monster mill-race. For one breathless second we seem to tremble on the edge of the fall. Then the Philæ plunges in headlong !

We see the whole boat slope down bodily under our feet. We feel the leap—the dead fall—the staggering rush forward. Instantly the waves are foaming and boiling up on all sides, flooding the lower deck, and covering the upper deck with spray. The men ship their oars, leaving all to helm and current ; and, despite the hoarse tumult, we distinctly hear those oars scrape the rocks on either side.

Now the Sheykh, looking for the moment quite majestic, stands motionless with uplifted arm ; for at the end of the pass there is a sharp turn to the right—as sharp as a street corner in a narrow London thoroughfare. Can the Philæ, measuring 100 feet from stem to stern, ever round that angle in safety ? Suddenly, the uplifted arm is waved—the Sheykh thunders " Daffet ! " (helm)—the men, steady and prompt, put the helm about—the boat, answering splendidly to the word of command, begins to turn before we are out of the rocks ; then, shooting round the corner at exactly the right moment, comes out safe and sound, with only an oar broken !

Great is the rejoicing. Reïs Hassan, in the joy of his heart, runs to shake hands all round ; the Arabs burst into a chorus of " Taibs " and " Salames " ; and Talhamy, coming up all smiles, is set upon by half-a-dozen playful Shellalees, who snatch his keffîyeh from his head, and carry it off as a trophy. The only one unmoved is the Sheykh of the Cataract. His momentary flash of energy over, he slouches back with the old stolid face ; slips on his shoes ; drops on his heels ; lights his pipe ; and looks more like an owl than ever.

We had fancied till now that the Cataract Arabs for their own profit, and travellers for their own glory, had grossly exaggerated the dangers of the Big Bab. But such is not the case. The Big Bab is in truth a serious undertaking ; so serious that I doubt whether any English boatmen would venture to take such a boat down such a rapid, and between such rocks, as the Shellalee Arabs took the Philæ that day.

All dahabeeyahs, however, are not so lucky. Of thirty-four that shot the fall this season, several had been slightly damaged, and one was so disabled that she had to lie up at Assûan for a fortnight to be mended. Of actual shipwreck, or injury to life and limb, I do not suppose there is any real danger. The Shellalees are wonderfully cool and skilful, and have abundant practice. Our Painter, it is true, preferred rolling up his canvases and carrying them round on dry land by way of the desert ; but this was a precaution that neither he nor any of us would have dreamed of taking on account of our own personal safety. There is, in fact, little, if anything, to fear ; and the traveller who foregoes the descent of the Cataract, foregoes a very curious sight, and a very exciting adventure.

At Assûan we bade farewell to Nubia and the blameless Ethiopians, and found ourselves once more traversing the Nile of Egypt. If instead of five miles of Cataract we had crossed five hundred miles of sea or desert, the change could not have been more complete. We left behind us a dreamy river, a silent shore, an ever-present desert. Returning, we plunged back at once into the midst of a fertile and populous region. All day long, now, we see boats on the river ; villages on the banks ; birds on the wing ; husbandmen on the land ; men and women, horses, camels and asses, passing perpetually to and fro on the towing-path. There is always something moving, something doing. The Nile is running low, and the shâdûfs—three deep, now—are in full swing from morning till night. Again the smoke goes up from clusters of unseen huts at close of day. Again we hear the dogs barking from hamlet to hamlet in the still hours of the night. Again, towards sunset, we see troops of girls coming down to the river-side with their water-jars on their heads. Those Arab maidens, when they stand with garments tightly tucked up and just their feet in the water, dipping the goollah at arm's length in the fresher gush of the current, almost tempt one's pencil into the forbidden paths of caricature.

Kom Ombo is a magnificent torso. It was as large once as Denderah—perhaps larger; for, being on the same grand scale, it was a double Temple and dedicated to two Gods, Horus and Sebek;[1] the Hawk and the Crocodile. Now there remain only a few giant columns buried to within eight or ten feet of their gorgeous capitals; a superb fragment of architrave; one broken wave of sculptured cornice, and some fallen blocks graven with the names of Ptolemies and Cleopatras.

A great double doorway, a hall of columns, and a double sanctuary, are said to be yet perfect, though no longer accessible. The roofing blocks of three halls, one behind the other, and a few capitals, are yet visible behind the portico. What more may lie buried below the surface, none can tell. We only know that an ancient city and a mediæval hamlet have been slowly engulfed; and that an early Temple, contemporary with the Temple of Amada, once stood within the sacred enclosure. The sand here has been accumulating for 2000 years. It lies forty feet deep, and has never been excavated. It will never be excavated now; for the Nile is gradually sapping the bank, and carrying away piecemeal from below what the desert has buried from above. Half of one noble pylon—a cataract of sculptured blocks—strews the steep slope from top to bottom. The other half hangs suspended on the

---

[1] "Sebek est un dieu solaire. Dans un papyrus de Boulak, il est appelé fils d'Isis, et il combat les ennemis d'Osiris; c'est une assimilation complète à Horus, et c'est à ce titre qu'il était adoré à Ombos."—*Dic. Arch.* P. Pierret. Paris, 1875.

brink of the precipice. It cannot hang so much longer. A
day must soon come when it will collapse with a crash, and
thunder down like its fellow.

Between Kom Ombo and Silsilis, we lost our Painter. Not
that he either strayed or was stolen ; but that, having accomplished the main object of his journey, he was glad to seize
the first opportunity of getting back quickly to Cairo. That
opportunity—represented by a noble Duke honeymooning with
a steam-tug—happened half-way between Kom Ombo and
Silsilis. Painter and Duke being acquaintances of old, the
matter was soon settled. In less than a quarter of an hour,
the big picture and all the paraphernalia of the studio were
transported from the stern-cabin of the Philæ to the stern-cabin
of the steam-tug ; and our Painter—fitted out with an ex-
tempore canteen, a cook-boy, a waiter, and his fair share of
the necessaries of life—was soon disappearing gaily in the
distance at the rate of twenty miles an hour. If the Happy
Couple, so weary of head-winds, so satiated with Temples,
followed that vanishing steam-tug with eyes of melancholy
longing, the Writer at least asked nothing better than to drift
on with the Philæ.

Still, the Nile is long, and life is short ; and the tale told
by our logbook was certainly not encouraging. When we
reached Silsilis on the morning of the 17th of March, the north
wind had been blowing with only one day's intermission since
the 1st of February.

At Silsilis, one looks in vain for traces of that great barrier
which once blocked the Nile at this point. The stream is
narrow here, and the sandstone cliffs come down on both sides
to the water's edge. In some places there is space for a
footpath ; in others, none. There are also some sunken rocks
in the bed of the river—upon one of which, by the way, a
Cook's steamer had struck two days before. But of such a
mass as could have dammed the Nile, and, by its disruption
not only have caused the river to desert its bed at Philæ,[1] but
have changed the whole physical and climatic conditions of
Lower Nubia, there is no sign whatever.

The Arabs here show a rock fantastically quarried in the

[1] See chap. xi. p. 203.

shape of a gigantic umbrella, to which they pretend some king of old attached one end of a chain with which he barred the Nile. It may be that in this apocryphal legend there survives some memory of the ancient barrier.

The cliffs of the western bank are rich in memorial niches, votive shrines, tombs, historical stelæ, and inscriptions. These last date from the VIth to the XXIInd Dynasties. Some of the tombs and alcoves are very curious. Ranged side by side in a long row close above the river, and revealing glimpses of seated figures and gaudy decorations within, they look like private boxes with their occupants. In most of these we found mutilated triads of Gods,[1] sculptured and painted ; and in one larger than the rest were three niches, each containing three deities.

The great Speos of Horemheb, the last Pharaoh of the XVIIIth Dynasty, lies farthest north, and the memorial shrines of the Rameses family lie farthest south of the series. The first is a long gallery, like a cloister supported on four square columns ; and is excavated parallel with the river. The walls inside and out are covered with delicately executed sculptures in low relief, some of which yet retain traces of colour. The triumph of Horemheb returning from conquest in the land of Kush, and the famous subject on the south wall described by Mariette [2] as one of the few really lovely things in Egyptian art, have been too often engraved to need description. The votive shrines of the Rameses family are grouped all together in a picturesque nook green with bushes to the water's edge. There are three, the work of Seti I, Rameses II, and Menepthah —lofty alcoves, each like a little proscenium, with painted cornices and side pillars, and groups of Kings and Gods still

---

[1] " Le point de départ de la mythologie egyptienne est une *Triade.*" CHAMPOLLION, *Lettres d'Egypte,* etc., XIᵉ Lettre. Paris, 1868. These Triads are best studied at Gerf Hossayn and Kalabsheh.

[2] " L'un (paroi du sud) représente une déesse nourissant de son lait divin le roi Horus, encore enfant. L'Egypte n'a jamais, comme la Grèce, atteint l'idéal du beau . . . mais en tant qu'art Egyptien, le bas-relief du Spéos de Gebel-Silsileh est une des plus belles œuvres que l'on puisse voir. Nulle part, en effet, la ligne n'est plus pure, et il règne dans ce tableau une certaine douceur tranquille qui charme et étonne à la fois."—*Itinéraire de la Haut Egypte.* A. MARIETTE : 1872, p. 246.

bright with colour. In most of the votive sculptures of Silsilis there figure two deities but rarely seen elsewhere; namely Sebek, the Crocodile God, and Hapi-mu, the lotus-crowned God of the Nile. This last was the tutelary deity of the spot, and was worshipped at Silsilis with special rites. Hymns in his honour are found carved here and there upon the rocks.[1] Most curious of all, however, is a Goddess named Ta-ur-t,[2] represented in one of the side subjects of the shrine of Rameses II. This charming person, who has the body of a hippopotamus and the face of a woman, wears a tie-wig and

TA-UR-T (SILSILIS).   TA-UR-T (PHILÆ).

a robe of state with five capes, and looks like a cross between a Lord Chancellor and a Coachman. Behind her stand Thoth and Nut; all three receiving the homage of Queen Nefertari, who advances with an offering of two sistrums. As a hippopo-

[1] See *Sallier Papyrus No.* 2. HYMN TO THE NILE—translation by C. MASPERO. 4to Paris, 1868.

[2] *Ta-ur-t*, or *Apet the Great.* "Cette Déesse à corps d'hippopotame debout et à mamelles pendantes, paraît être une sorte de déesse nourrice. Elle semble, dans le bas temps, je ne dirai pas se substituer à Maut, mais compléter le rôle de cette déesse. Elle est nommée la grande nourrice; et présidait aux chambres où étaient représentées les naissances des jeunes divinités."—*Dict. Arch.* P. PIERRET. Paris, 1875.

"In the heavens, this Goddess personified the constellation Ursa Major, or the Great Bear."—*Guide to the First and Second Egyptian Rooms.* S. BIRCH. London, 1874.

tamus crowned with the disk and plumes, we had met with this Goddess before. She is not uncommon as an amulet ; and the Writer had already sketched her at Philæ, where she occupies a prominent place in the façade of the Mammisi. But the grotesque elegance of her attire at Silsilis is, I imagine, quite unique.

The interest of the western bank centres in its sculptures and inscriptions ; the interest of the eastern bank, in its quarries. We rowed over to a point nearly opposite the shrines of the Ramessides, and, climbing a steep verge of débris, came to the mouth of a narrow cutting between walls of solid rock, from forty to fifty feet in height. These walls are smooth, clean-cut, and faultlessly perpendicular. The colour of the sandstone is rich amber. The passage is about ten feet in width and perhaps four hundred in length. Seen at a little after mid-day, with one side in shadow, the other in sunlight, and a narrow ribbon of blue sky overhead, it is like nothing else in the world ; unless, perhaps, the entrance to Petra.

Following this passage, we came presently to an immense area, at least as large as Belgrave Square ; beyond which, separated by a thin partition of rock, opened a second and somewhat smaller area. On the walls of these huge amphitheatres, the chisel-marks and wedge-holes were as fresh as if the last blocks had been taken hence but yesterday ; yet it is some 2000 years since the place last rang to the blows of the mallet, and echoed back the voices of the workmen. From the days of the Theban Pharaohs to the days of the Ptolemies and Cæsars, those echoes can never have been silent. The Temples of Karnak and Luxor, of Gournah, of Medinet Habu, of Esneh and Edfu and Hermonthis, all, came from here, and from the quarries on the opposite side of the river.[1]

Returning, we climbed long hills of chips ; looked down into valleys of débris ; and came back at last to the river-side by way of an ancient inclined plane, along which the blocks were slid down to the transport boats below. But the most

[1] For a highly interesting account of the rock-cut inscriptions, graffiti, and quarry-marks at Silsilis, in the desert between Assûan and Philæ, and in the valley called Soba Rigolah, see Mr. W. M. F. Petrie's recent volume entitled *A Season's Work in Egypt*, 1877.

wonderful thing about Silsilis is the way in which the quarrying
has been done. In all these halls and passages and amphitheatres, the sandstone has been sliced out smooth and straight,
like hay from a hayrick. Everywhere the blocks have been
taken out square ; and everywhere the best of the stone has
been extracted, and the worst left. Where it was fine in grain
and even in colour, it has been cut with the nicest economy.
Where it was whitish, or brownish, or traversed by veins of
violet, it has been left standing. Here and there, we saw
places where the lower part had been removed and the upper
part left projecting, like the overhanging storeys of our old
mediæval timber houses. Compared with this puissant and
perfect quarrying, our rough-and-ready blasting looks like the
work of savages.

Struggling hard against the wind, we left Silsilis that same
afternoon. The wrecked steamer was now more than half
under water. She had broken her back and begun filling
immediately, with all Cook's party on board. Being rowed
ashore with what necessaries they could gather together, these
unfortunates had been obliged to encamp in tents borrowed
from the Mudîr of the district. Luckily for them, a couple
of homeward-bound dahabeeyahs came by next morning, and
took off as many as they could accommodate. The Duke's
steam-tug received the rest. The tents were still there, and
a gang of natives, under the superintendence of the Mudîr,
were busy getting off all that could be saved from the wreck.

As evening drew on, our head-wind became a hurricane ;
and that hurricane lasted, day and night, for thirty-six hours.
All this time the Nile was driving up against the current in
great rollers, like rollers on the Cornish coast when tide and
wind set together from the west. To hear them roaring past
in the darkness of the night—to feel the Philæ rocking, shivering, straining at her mooring-ropes, and bumping perpetually
against the bank, was far from pleasant. By day, the scene
was extraordinary. There were no clouds ; but the air was
thick with sand, through which the sun glimmered feebly.
Some palms, looking grey and ghost-like on the bank above,
bent as if they must break before the blast. The Nile was
yeasty, and flecked with brown foam, large lumps of which

came swirling every now and then against our cabin windows. The opposite bank was simply nowhere. Judging only by what was visible from the deck, one would have vowed that the dahabeeyah was moored against an open coast, with an angry sea coming in.

The wind fell about five A.M. the second day ; when the men at once took to their oars, and by breakfast-time brought us to Edfu. Nothing now could be more delicious than the weather. It was a cool, silvery, misty morning—such a morning as one never knows in Nubia, where the sun is no sooner up than one is plunged at once into the full blaze and stress of day. There were donkeys waiting for us on the bank, and our way lay for about a mile through barley flats and cotton plantations. The country looked rich ; the people smiling and well-conditioned. We met a troop of them going down to the dahabeeyah with sheep, pigeons, poultry, and a young ox for sale. Crossing a back-water bridged by a few rickety palm-trunks, we now approached the village, which is perched, as usual, on the mounds of the ancient city. Meanwhile the great pylons—seeming to grow larger every moment—rose, creamy in light, against a soft blue sky.

Riding through lanes of huts, we came presently to an open space and a long flight of roughly-built steps in front of the Temple. At the top of these steps we were standing on the level of the modern village. At the bottom we saw the massive pavement that marked the level of the ancient city. From that level rose the pylons which even from afar off had looked so large. We now found that those stupendous towers not only soared to a height of about seventy-five feet above our heads, but plunged down to a depth of at least forty more beneath our feet.

Ten years ago, nothing was visible of the great Temple of Edfu save the tops of these pylons. The rest of the building was as much lost to sight as if the earth had opened and swallowed it. Its courtyards were choked with foul débris. Its sculptured chambers were buried under forty feet of soil. Its terraced roof was a maze of closely-packed huts, swarming with human beings, poultry, dogs, kine, asses, and vermin. Thanks to the indefatigable energy of Mariette, these Augæan stables were cleansed some thirty years ago. Writing himself of this tremendous task, he says :—" I caused to be demolished the sixty-four houses which encumbered the roof, as well as twenty-eight more which approached too near the outer wall of the Temple. When the whole shall be isolated from its present surroundings by a massive wall, the work of restoration at Edfu will be accomplished."[1]

That wall has not yet been built ; but the encroaching mound has been cut clean away all round the building, now standing free in a deep open space, the sides of which are in some places as perpendicular as the quarried cliffs of Silsilis. In the midst of this pit, like a risen God issuing from the grave, the huge building stands before us in the sunshine, erect and perfect. The effect at first sight is overwhelming.

Through the great doorway, fifty feet in height, we catch glimpses of a grand courtyard, and of a vista of doorways, one behind another. Going slowly down, we see farther into those dark and distant halls at every step. At the same time the pylons, covered with gigantic sculptures, tower higher and higher, and seem to shut out the sky. The custode—a pigmy of six foot two, in semi-European dress—looks up grinning, expectant of backshîsh. For there is actually a custode here, and, which is more to the purpose, a good strong gate, through which neither pilfering visitors nor pilfering Arabs can pass unnoticed.

Who enters that gate crosses the threshold of the past, and leaves two thousand years behind him. In these vast courts and storied halls all is unchanged. Every pavement, every column, every stair, is in its place. The roof, but for a few roofing-stones missing just over the sanctuary, is not only uninjured, but in good repair. The hieroglyphic inscriptions are as sharp and legible as the day they were cut. If here and there a capital, or the face of a human-headed deity, has been mutilated, these are blemishes which at first one scarcely observes, and which in no wise mar the wonderful effect of the whole. We cross that great courtyard in the full blaze of the morning sunlight. In the colonnades on either side there is

[1] Letter of M. Mariette to Vte. E. DE ROUGÉ : *Révue Archéologique*, vol. ii. p. 33, 1860.

shade, and in the pillared portico beyond, a darkness as of night ; save where a patch of deep blue sky burns through a square opening in the roof, and is matched by a corresponding patch of blinding light on the pavement below. Hence we pass on through a hall of columns, two transverse corridors, a side chapel, a series of pitch-dark side chambers, and a sanctuary. Outside all these, surrounding the actual Temple on three sides, runs an external corridor open to the sky, and bounded by a superb wall full forty feet in height. When I have said that the entrance-front, with its twin pylons and central doorway, measures 250 feet in width by 125 feet in height ; that the first courtyard measures more than 160 feet in length by 140 in width ; that the entire length of the building is 450 feet, and that it covers an area of 80,000 square feet, I have stated facts of a kind which convey no more than a general idea of largeness to the ordinary reader. Of the harmony of the proportions, of the amazing size and strength of the individual parts, of the perfect workmanship, of the fine grain and creamy amber of the stone, no description can do more than suggest an indefinite notion.

Edfu and Denderah may almost be called twin Temples. They belong to the same period. They are built very nearly after the same plan.[1] They are even allied in a religious sense; for the myths of Horus[2] and Hathor[3] are interdependent ; the one being the complement of the other. Thus in the inscriptions of Edfu we find perpetual allusion to the cultus of Denderah, and vice versa. Both Edfu and Denderah are rich in inscriptions ; but as the extent of wall-space is greater at

[1] Edfu is the elder Temple ; Denderah the copy. Where the architect of Denderah has departed from his model, it has invariably been for the worse.

[2] *Horus :*—" Dieu adoré dans plusieurs nomes de la basse Egypte. Le personnage d'Horus se rattache sous des noms différents, à deux generations divines. Sous le nom de Haroëris il est né de Seb et Nout, et par consequent frère d'Osiris, dont il est le fils sous un autre nom. . . . Horus, armé d'un dard avec lequel il transperce les ennemis d'Osiris, est appelé Horus le Justicier."—*Dict. Arch.* P. PIERRET, article " *Horus.*"

[3] *Hathor :*—" Elle est, comme Neith, Maut, et Nout, la personnifica- tion de l'espace dans lequel se meut le soleil, dont Horus symbolise le lever : aussi son nom, Hat-hor, signifie-t-il litteralement, *l'habitation d'Horus.*"—*Ibid.* article " *Hathor.*"

Edfu, so is the literary wealth of this Temple greater than the literary wealth of Denderah. It also seemed to me that the surface was more closely filled in at Edfu than at Denderah. Every wall, every ceiling, every pillar, every architrave, every passage and side-chamber however dark, every staircase, every doorway, the outer wall of the Temple, the inner side of the great wall of circuit, the huge pylons from top to bottom, are not only covered, but crowded, with figures and hieroglyphs. Among these we find no enormous battle-subjects as at Abou Simbel—no heroic recitals, like the poem of Pentaur. Those went out with the Pharaohs, and were succeeded by tableaux of religious rites and dialogues of gods and kings. Such are the stock subjects of Ptolemaic edifices. They abound at Denderah and Esneh, as well as at Edfu. But at Edfu there are more inscriptions of a miscellaneous character than in any Temple of Egypt ; and it is precisely this secular information which is so priceless. Here are geographical lists of Nubian and Egyptian nomes, with their principal cities, their products, and their tutelary gods ; lists of tributary provinces and princes ; lists of temples, and of the lands pertaining thereunto ; lists of canals, of ports, of lakes ; kalendars of feasts and fasts ; astronomical tables ; genealogies and chronicles of the gods ; lists of the priests and priestesses of both Edfu and Denderah, with their names ; lists also of singers and assistant functionaries ; lists of offerings, hymns, invocations ; and such a profusion of religious legends as make of the walls of Edfu alone a complete text-book of Egyptian mythology.[1]

No great collection of these inscriptions, like the "Denderah" of Mariette, has yet been published ; but every now and then some enterprising Egyptologist, such as M. Naville or M. Jacques de Rougé, plunges for awhile into the depths of the Edfu mine and brings back as much precious ore as he can carry. Some most singular and interesting details have thus been brought to light. One inscription, for instance, records exactly in what month, and on what day and at what hour, Isis gave birth to Horus. Another tells all about the sacred boats. We know now that Edfu possessed at least two ; and

---

[1] *Rapport sur une Mission en Egypte.* VICOMTE E. DE ROUGÉ. See *Révue Arch. Nouvelle Série*, vol. x. p. 63.

that one was called Hor-Hāt, or The First Horus, and the other Āa-Māfek, or Great of Turquoise. These boats, it would appear, were not merely for carrying in procession, but for actual use upon the water. Another text—one of the most curious—informs us that Hathor of Denderah paid an annual visit to Horus (or Hor-Hāt) of Edfu, and spent some days with him in his Temple. The whole ceremonial of this fantastic trip is given in detail. The Goddess travelled in her boat called Neb-Mer-t, or Lady of the Lake. Horus, like a polite host, went out in his boat Hor-Hāt, to meet her. The two deities with their attendants then formed one procession, and so came to Edfu, where the Goddess was entertained with a succession of festivals.[1]

One would like to know whether Horus duly returned all these visits ; and if the Gods, like modern Emperors, had a gay time among themselves.

Other questions inevitably suggest themselves, sometimes painfully, sometimes ludicrously, as one paces chamber after chamber, corridor after corridor, sculptured all over with strange forms and stranger legends. What about these Gods whose genealogies are so intricate ; whose mutual relations are so complicated ; who wedded and became parents ; who exchanged visits, and who even travelled [2] at times to distant countries ? What about those who served them in the Temples ; who robed and unrobed them ; who celebrated their birthdays, and paraded them in stately processions, and consumed the lives of millions in erecting these mountains of masonry and sculpture to their honour ? We know now with what elaborate rites the Gods were adored ; what jewels they wore ; what hymns were sung in their praise. We know from what a subtle and philosophical core of solar myths their curious personal adventures were evolved. We may also be quite sure that the hidden meaning of these legends was almost wholly lost sight of in the later days of the religion,[3]

[1] *Textes Géographiques du Temple d'Edfou*, by M. J. DE ROUGÉ. *Révue Arch.* vol. xii. p. 209.

[2] See Professor Revillout's *Seconde Mémoire sur les Blemmyes*, 1888, for an account of how the statues of Isis and other deities were taken once a year from the Temples of Philæ for a trip into Ethiopia.

[3] See APPENDIX III, *Religious Belief of the Ancient Egyptians.*

and that the Gods were accepted for what they seemed to be, and not for what they symbolised. What, then, of their worshippers? Did they really believe all these things, or were any among them tormented with doubts of the Gods? Were there sceptics in those days, who wondered how two hierogrammates could look each other in the face without laughing?

The custode told us that there were 242 steps to the top of each tower of the propylon. We counted 224, and dispensed willingly with the remainder. It was a long pull; but had the steps been four times as many, the sight from the top would have been worth the climb. The chambers in the pylons are on a grand scale, with wide bevelled windows like the mouths of monster letter-boxes, placed at regular intervals all the way up. Through these windows the great flagstaffs and pennons were regulated from within. The two pylons communicate by a terrace over the central doorway. The parapet of this terrace and the parapets of the pylons above, are plentifully scrawled with names, many of which were left there by the French soldiers of 1799.

The cornices of these two magnificent towers are unfortunately gone; but the total height without them is 125 feet. From the top, as from the minaret of the great mosque at Damascus, one looks down into the heart of the town. Hundreds of mud-huts thatched with palm-leaves, hundreds of little courtyards, lie mapped out beneath one's feet; and as the Fellâh lives in his yard by day, using his hut merely as a sleeping place at night, one looks down, like the Diable Boiteux, upon the domestic doings of a roofless world. We see people moving to and fro, unconscious of strange eyes watching them from above—men lounging, smoking, sleeping in shady corners—children playing—infants crawling on all fours—women cooking at clay ovens in the open air—cows and sheep feeding—poultry scratching and pecking—dogs basking in the sun. The huts look more like the lairs of prairie-dogs than the dwellings of human beings. The little mosque with its one dome and stunted minaret, so small, so far below, looks like a clay toy. Beyond the village, which reaches far and wide, lie barley fields, and cotton patches, and palm-groves, bounded on one side by the river, and on the other by the desert. A broad road, dotted over with moving specks of men and cattle, cleaves its way straight through the cultivated land and out across the sandy plain beyond. We can trace its course for miles where it is only a trodden track in the desert. It goes, they tell us, direct to Cairo. On the opposite bank glares a hideous white sugar-factory, and, bowered in greenery, a country villa of the Khedive. The broad Nile flows between. The sweet Theban hills gleam through a pearly haze on the horizon.

All at once, a fitful breeze springs up, blowing in little gusts and swirling the dust in circles round our feet. At the same moment, like a beautiful spectre, there rises from the desert close by an undulating semi-transparent stalk of yellow sand, which grows higher every moment, and begins moving northward across the plain. Almost at the same instant, another appears a long way off towards the south, and a third comes gliding mysteriously along the opposite bank. While we are watching the third, the first begins throwing off a wonderful kind of plume, which follows it, waving and melting in the air. And now the stranger from the south comes up at a smooth, tremendous pace, towering at least 500 feet above the desert, till, meeting some cross-current, it is snapped suddenly in twain. The lower half instantly collapses ; the upper, after hanging suspended for a moment, spreads and floats slowly, like a cloud. In the meanwhile, other and smaller columns form here and there—stalk a little way—waver—disperse—form again—and again drop away in dust. Then the breeze falls, and puts an abrupt end to this extraordinary spectacle. In less than two minutes there is not a sand-column left. As they came, they vanish—suddenly.

Such is the landscape that frames the Temple ; and the Temple, after all, is the sight that one comes up here to see. There it lies far below our feet, the courtyard with its almost perfect pavement ; the flat roof compact of gigantic monoliths ; the wall of circuit with its panoramic sculptures ; the portico, with its screen and pillars distinct in brilliant light against inner depths of dark ; each pillar a shaft of ivory, each square of dark a block of ebony. So perfect, so solid, so splendid is the whole structure ; so simple in unity of plan ; so complex in ornament ; so majestic in completeness, that one feels as if it solved the whole problem of religious architecture.

Take it for what it is—a Ptolemaic structure preserved in all its integrity of strength and finish—it is certainly the finest extant Temple in Egypt. It brings before us, with even more completeness than Denderah, the purposes of its various parts, and the kind of ceremonial for which it was designed. Every corridor and chamber tells its own story. Even the names of the different chambers are graven upon them in such wise that nothing[1] would be easier than to reconstruct the ground-plan of the whole building in hieroglyphic nomenclature. That neither the Ptolemaic building nor the Ptolemaic mythus can be accepted as strictly representative of either pure Egyptian art or pure Egyptian thought, must of course be conceded. Both are modified by Greek influences, and have so far departed from the Pharaonic model. But then we have no equally perfect specimen of the Pharaonic model. The Ramesseum is but a grand fragment. Karnak and Medinet Habu are aggregates of many Temples and many styles. Abydos is still half-buried. Amid so much that is fragmentary, amid so much that is ruined, the one absolutely perfect structure —Ptolemaic though it be—is of incalculable interest, and equally incalculable value.

While we are dreaming over these things, trying to fancy how it all looked when the sacred flotilla came sweeping up the river yonder and the procession of Hor-Hāt issued forth to meet the Goddess-guest—while we are half-expecting to see the whole brilliant concourse pour out, priests in their robes of panther-skin, priestesses with the tinkling sistrum, singers and harpists, and bearers of gifts and emblems, and high functionaries rearing aloft the sacred boat of the God—in this moment a turbaned Muëddin comes out upon the rickety wooden gallery of the little minaret below, and intones the call to mid-day prayer. That plaintive cry has hardly died away before we see men here and there among the huts turning

---

[1] Not only the names of the chambers, but their dimensions in cubits and subdivisions of cubits are given. See *Itinéraire de la Haute Egypte.* A. MARIETTE BEY. 1872, p. 241.

towards the east, and assuming the first postures of devotion. The women go on cooking and nursing their babies. I have seen Moslem women at prayer in the mosques of Constantinople, but never in Egypt.

Meanwhile, some children catch sight of us, and, notwithstanding that we are one hundred and twenty-five feet above their heads, burst into a frantic chorus of " Backshîsh ! "

And now, with a last long look at the Temple and the wide landscape beyond, we come down again, and go to see a dismal little Mammesi three-parts buried among a wilderness of mounds close by. These mounds, which consist almost entirely of crude-brick débris with imbedded fragments of stone and pottery, are built up like coral-reefs, and represent the dwellings of some sixty generations. When they are cut straight through, as here round about the Great Temple, the substance of them looks like rich plum-cake.

CHAPTER XXI.

THEBES.

WE had so long been the sport of destiny, that we hardly knew what to make of our good fortune when two days of sweet south wind carried us from Edfu to Luxor. We came back to find the old mooring-place alive with dahabeeyahs, and gay with English and American colours. These two flags well-nigh divide the river. In every twenty-five boats, one may fairly calculate upon an average of twelve English, nine American, two German, one Belgian, and one French. Of all these, our American cousins, ever helpful, ever cordial, are pleasantest to meet. Their flag stands to me for a host of brave and generous and kindly associations. It brings back memories of many lands and many faces. It calls up echoes of friendly voices, some far distant; some, alas! silent. Wherefore—be it on the Nile, or the Thames, or the high seas, or among Syrian camping-grounds, or drooping listlessly from the balconies of gloomy diplomatic haunts in continental cities—my heart warms to the stars and stripes whenever I see them.

Our arrival brought all the dealers of Luxor to the surface. They waylaid and followed us wherever we went; while some of the better sort—grave men in long black robes and ample turbans—installed themselves on our lower deck, and lived there for a fortnight. Go upstairs when one would, whether before breakfast in the morning, or after dinner in the evening, there we always found them, patient, imperturbable, ready to rise up, and salaam, and produce from some hidden pocket a purseful of scarabs or a bundle of funerary statuettes. Some of these gentlemen were Arabs, some Copts—all polite, plausible, and mendacious.

Where Copt and Arab drive the same doubtful trade, it is not easy to define the shades of difference in their dealings. As workmen, the Copts are perhaps the most artistic. As salesmen, the Arabs are perhaps the less dishonest. Both sell more forgeries than genuine antiquities. Be the demand what it may, they are prepared to meet it. Thothmes is not too heavy, nor Cleopatra too light, for them. Their carvings in old sycamore wood, their porcelain statuettes, their hieroglyphed limestone tablets, are executed with a skill that almost defies detection. As for genuine scarabs of the highest antiquity, they are turned out by the gross every season. Engraved, glazed, and administered to the turkeys in the form of boluses, they acquire by the simple process of digestion a degree of venerableness that is really charming.

Side by side with the work of production goes on the work of excavation. The professed diggers colonise the western bank. They live rent-free among the tombs ; drive donkeys or work shâdûfs by day, and spend their nights searching for treasure. Some hundreds of families live in this grim way, spoiling the dead-and-gone Egyptians for a livelihood.

Forgers, diggers, and dealers play, meanwhile, into one another's hands, and drive a roaring trade. Your dahabeeyah, as I have just shown, is beset from the moment you moor till the moment you pole off again from shore. The boy who drives your donkey, the guide who pilots you among the tombs, the half-naked Fellâh who flings down his hoe as you pass, and runs beside you for a mile across the plain, have one and all an " anteekah " to dispose of. The turbaned official who comes, attended by his secretary and pipe-bearer, to pay you a visit of ceremony, warns you against imposition, and hints at genuine treasures to which he alone possesses the key. The gentlemanly native who sits next to you at dinner has a wonderful scarab in his pocket. In short, every man, woman, and child about the place is bent on selling a bargain ; and the bargain, in ninety-nine cases out of a hundred, is valuable in so far as it represents the industry of Luxor—but no farther. A good thing, of course, is to be had occasionally ; but the good thing never comes to the surface as long as a market can be found for the bad one. It is only when the dealer finds he has to do with an experienced customer, that he produces the best he has.

Flourishing as it is, the trade of Luxor labours, however, under some uncomfortable restrictions. Private excavation being prohibited, the digger lives in dread of being found out by the Governor. The forger, who has nothing to fear from the Governor, lives in dread of being found out by the tourist. As for the dealer, whether he sells an antique or an imitation, he is equally liable to punishment. In the one case he commits an offence against the state ; and in the other, he obtains money under false pretences. Meanwhile, the Governor deals out such even-handed justice as he can, and does his best to enforce the law on both sides of the river.

By a curious accident, L. and the Writer once actually penetrated into a forger's workshop. Not knowing that it had been abolished, we went to a certain house in which a certain Consulate had once upon a time been located, and there knocked for admission. An old deaf Fellâha opened the door, and after some hesitation showed us into a large unfurnished room with three windows. In each window there stood a workman's bench strewn with scarabs, amulets, and funerary statuettes in every stage of progress. We examined these specimens with no little curiosity. Some were of wood ; some were of lime-stone ; some were partly coloured. The colours and brushes were there ; to say nothing of files, gravers, and little pointed tools like gimlets. A magnifying glass of the kind used by engravers lay in one of the window-recesses. We also observed a small grindstone screwed to one of the benches and worked by a treadle ; while a massive fragment of mummy-case in a corner behind the door showed whence came the old sycamore wood for the wooden specimens. That three skilled workmen furnished with European tools had been busy in this room shortly before we were shown into it, was perfectly clear. We concluded that they had just gone away to breakfast.

Meanwhile we waited, expecting to be ushered into the

presence of the Consul. In about ten minutes, however, breathless with hurrying, arrived a well-dressed Arab whom we had never seen before. Distracted between his Oriental politeness and his desire to get rid of us, he bowed us out precipitately, explaining that the house had changed owners, and that the Power in question had ceased to be represented at Luxor. We heard him rating the old woman savagely, as soon as the door had closed behind us. I met that well-dressed Arab a day or two after, near the Governor's house ; and he immediately vanished round the nearest corner.

The Boulak authorities keep a small gang of trained excavators always at work in the Necropolis of Thebes. These men are superintended by the Governor, and every mummy-case discovered is forwarded to Boulak unopened. Thanks to the courtesy of the Governor, we had the good fortune to be present one morning at the opening of a tomb. He sent to summon us, just as we were going to breakfast. With what alacrity we manned the felucca, and how we ate our bread and butter half in the boat and half on donkey-back, may easily be imagined. How well I remember that early morning ride across the western plain of Thebes——the young barley rippling for miles in the sun ; the little water-channel running beside the path ; the white butterflies circling in couples ; the wayside grave with its tiny dome and prayer-mat, its well and broken kulleh, inviting the passer-by to drink and pray ; the wild vine that trailed along the wall ; the vivid violet of the vetches that blossomed unbidden in the barley. We had the mounds and pylons of Medinet Habu to the left——the ruins of the Ramesseum to the right——the Colossi of the Plain and the rosy western mountains before us all the way. How the great statues glistened in the morning light ! How they towered up against the soft blue sky ! Battered and featureless, they sat in the old patient attitude, looking as if they mourned the vanished springs.

We found the new tomb a few hundred yards in the rear of the Ramesseum. The diggers were in the pit ; the Governor and a few Arabs were looking on. The vault was lined with brick-work above, and cut square in the living rock below. We were just in time ; for already, through the sand and rubble

DIGGING FOR MUMMIES.

with which the grave had been filled in, there appeared an outline of something buried. The men, throwing spades and picks aside, now began scraping up the dust with their hands, and a mummy-case came gradually to light. It was shaped to represent a body lying at length with the hands crossed upon the breast. Both hands and face were carved in high relief. The ground-colour of the sarcophagus was white ;[1] the surface covered with hieroglyphed legends and somewhat coarsely painted figures of the four lesser Gods of the Dead. The face, like the hands, was coloured a brownish yellow and highly varnished. But for a little dimness of the gaudy hues, and a little flaking off of the surface here and there, the thing was as perfect as when it was placed in the ground. A small wooden box roughly put together lay at the feet of the mummy. This was taken out first, and handed to the Governor, who put it aside without opening it. The mummy-case was then raised upright, hoisted to the brink of the pit, and laid upon the ground.

It gave one a kind of shock to see it first of all lying just as it had been left by the mourners ; then hauled out by rude hands, to be searched, unrolled, perhaps broken up as unworthy to occupy a corner in the Boulak collection. Once they are lodged and catalogued in a museum, one comes to look upon these things as " specimens," and forgets that they once were living beings like ourselves. But this poor mummy looked startlingly human and pathetic lying at the bottom of its grave in the morning sunlight.

After the sarcophagus had been lifted out, a small blue porcelain cup, a ball of the same material, and another little object shaped like a cherry, were found in the débris. The last was hollow, and contained something that rattled when shaken. The mummy, the wooden box, and these porcelain

[1] This was, no doubt, an interment of the period of the XXIIIrd or XXIVth Dynasty, the style of which is thus described by Mariette : " Succèdent les caisses à fond blanc. Autour de celles-çi court une légende en hiéroglyphes de toutes couleurs. Le devant du couvercle est divisé horizontalement en tableaux où alternent les représentations et les textes tracés en hiéroglyphes verdâtres. La momie elle-même est hermétiquement enfermée dans un cartonnage cousu par derrière et peint de couleurs tranchantes."—_Notice des Monuments à Boulak_, p. 46. Paris, 1872.

toys, were then removed to a stable close by ; and the excavators, having laid bare what looked like the mouth of a
bricked-up tunnel in the side of the tomb, fell to work again
immediately.   A second vault—perhaps a chain of vaults—it
was thought would now be discovered.

We went away, meanwhile, for a few hours, and saw some
of the famous painted tombs in that part of the mountain-side
just above, which goes by the name of Sheykh Abd-el-Koorneh.

It was a hot climb ; the sun blazing over-head ; the cliffs
reflecting light and heat ; the white débris glaring under-foot.
Some of the tombs up here are excavated in terraces, and look
from a distance like rows of pigeon holes ; others are pierced
in solitary ledges of rock ; many are difficult of access ; all
are intolerably hot and oppressive.   They were numbered half
a century ago by the late Sir Gardner Wilkinson, and the
numbers are there still.   We went that morning into 14, 16,
17, and 35.

As a child *"The Manners and Customs of the Ancient
Egyptians"* had shared my affections with *"The Arabian
Nights."*   I had read every line of the old six-volume edition
over and over again.   I knew every one of the six hundred
illustrations by heart.   Now I suddenly found myself in the
midst of old and half-forgotten friends.   Every subject on
these wonderful walls was already familiar to me.   Only the
framework, only the colouring, only the sand under-foot, only
the mountain slope outside, were new and strange.   It seemed
to me that I had met all these kindly brown people years and
years ago—perhaps in some previous stage of existence ; that
I had walked with them in their gardens ; listened to the
music of their lutes and tambourines ; pledged them at their
feasts.   Here is the funeral procession that I know so well ;
and the trial scene after death, where the mummy stands
upright in the presence of Osiris, and sees his heart weighed in
the balance.   Here is that well-remembered old fowler crouching in the rushes with his basket of decoys.   One withered
hand is lifted to his mouth ; his lips frame the call ; his thin
hair blows in the breeze.   I see now that he has placed himself
to the leeward of the game ; but that subtlety escaped me in
the reading days of my youth.   Yonder I recognise a sculptor's

studio into which I frequently peeped at that time. His men are at work as actively as ever; but I marvel that they have not yet finished polishing the surface of that red-granite colossus. This patient angler, still waiting for a bite, is another old acquaintance; and yonder, I declare, is that evening party at which I was so often an imaginary guest! Is the feast not yet over? Has that late comer whom we saw hurrying along just now in a neighbouring corridor not yet arrived? Will the musicians never play to the end of their concerto? Are those ladies still so deeply interested in the patterns of one another's ear-rings? It seems to me that the world has been standing still in here for these last five-and-thirty years.

Did I say five-and-thirty? Ah me! I think we must multiply it by ten, and then by ten again, ere we come to the right figure. These people lived in the time of the Thothmes and the Amenhoteps—a time upon which Rameses the Great looked back as we look back to the days of the Tudors and the Stuarts.

From the tombs above, we went back to the excavations below. The bricked-up opening had led, as the diggers expected, into a second vault; and another mummy-case, half-crushed by a fall of débris, had just been taken out. A third was found later in the afternoon. Curiously enough, they were all three mummies of women.

The Governor was taking his luncheon with the first mummy in the recesses of the stable, which had been a fine tomb once, but reeked now with manure. He sat on a rug, cross-legged, with a bowl of sour milk before him and a tray of most uninviting little cakes. He invited me to a seat on his rug, handed me his own spoon, and did the honours of the stable as pleasantly as if it had been a palace.

I asked him why the excavators, instead of working among these second-class graves, were not set to search for the tombs of the Kings of the XVIIIth Dynasty, supposed to be waiting discovery in a certain valley called the Valley of the West. He shook his head. The way to the Valley of the West, he said, was long and difficult. Men working there must encamp upon the spot; and merely to supply them with water would be no easy matter. He was allowed, in fact, only a sum sufficient for the wages of fifty excavators ; and to attack the Valley of the West with less than two hundred would be useless.

We had luncheon that morning, I remember, with the M. B.'s in the second hall of the Ramesseum. It was but one occasion among many ; for the Writer was constantly at work on that side of the river, and we had luncheon in one or other of the western Temples every day. Yet that particular meeting stands out in my memory apart from the rest. I see the joyous party gathered together in the shade of the great columns— the Persian rugs spread on the uneven ground—the dragoman in his picturesque dress going to and fro—the brown and tattered Arabs, squatting a little way off, silent and hungry-eyed, each with his string of forged scarabs, his imitation gods, or his bits of mummy-case and painted cartonnage for sale— the glowing peeps of landscape framed in here and there through vistas of columns—the emblazoned architraves laid along from capital to capital overhead, each block sculptured with enormous cartouches yet brilliant with vermilion and ultramarine—the patient donkeys munching all together at a little heap of vetches in one corner—the intense depths of cloudless blue above. Of all Theban ruins, the Ramesseum is the most cheerful. Drenched in sunshine, the warm limestone of which it is built seems to have mellowed and turned golden with time. No walls enclose it. No towering pylons over-shadow it. It stands high, and the air circulates freely among those simple and beautiful columns. There are not many Egyptian ruins in which one can talk and be merry ; but in the Ramesseum one may thoroughly enjoy the passing hour.

Whether Rameses the Great was ever actually buried in this place is a problem which future discoveries may possibly solve ; but that the Ramesseum and the tomb of Osymandias were one and the same building is a point upon which I never entertained a moment's doubt. Spending day after day among these ruins ; sketching now here, now there ; going over the ground bit by bit, and comparing every detail, I came at last to wonder how an identity so obvious could ever have been doubted. Diodorus was of course inaccurate ; but then one as little looks for accuracy in Diodorus as in Homer. Compared with some of his topographical descriptions, the account he

gives of the Ramesseum is a marvel of exactness. He describes [1]
a building approached by two vast courtyards ; a hall of pillars
opening by way of three entrances from the second courtyard ;
a succession of chambers, including a sacred library ; ceilings
of azure "bespangled with stars" ; walls covered with sculptures
representing the deeds and triumphs of the king whom he calls
Osymandias,[2] amongst which are particularly noticed the assault
of a fortress "environed by a river," a procession of captives
without hands, and a series of all the Gods of Egypt, to whom
the King was represented in the act of making offerings ; finally,
against the entrance to the second courtyard, three statues of
the King, one of which, being of Syenite granite and made "in
a sitting posture," is stated to be not only "the greatest in all
Egypt," but admirable above all others "for its workmanship,
and the excellence of the stone."

Bearing in mind that what is left of the Ramesseum is, as
it were, only the backbone of the entire structure, one can still
walk from end to end of the building, and still recognise every
feature of this description. We turn our backs on the wrecked
towers of the first propylon ; crossing what was once the first
courtyard, we leave to the left the fallen colossus ; we enter the
second courtyard, and see before us the three entrances to the
hall of pillars, and the remains of two other statues ; we walk
up the central avenue of the great hall, and see above our heads
architraves studded with yellow stars upon a ground colour so
luminously blue that it almost matches the sky ; thence, passing
through a chamber lined with sculptures, we come to the library,
upon the door-jambs of which Champollion found the figures of
Thoth and Saf, the Lord of Letters and the Lady of the Sacred
Books ;[3] finally, among such fragments of sculptured decoration

---

[1] Diodorus, *Biblioth. Hist.*, Bk. i. chap. iv. The fault of inaccuracy
ought, however, to be charged to Hecatæus, who was the authority followed
here by Diodorus.

[2] Possibly the Smendes of Manetho, and the Ba-en-Ded whose cartouche is found by Brugsch on a sarcophagus in the museum at Vienna ;
see *Hist. d'Egypte*, chap. x. p. 213, ed. 1859. Another claimant to this
identification is found in a King named Se-Mentu, whose cartouches were
found by Mariette on some small gold tablets at Tanis.

[3] Letter XIV. p. 235, *Lettres d'Egypte;* Paris, 1868. See also chap.
xviii. of the present work ; p. 349.

OSIRIDE COURT AND FALLEN COLOSSUS, RAMESSEUM, THEBES.

as yet remain, we find the King making offerings to a hiero-glyphed list of Gods as well as to his deified ancestors ; we see the train of captives, and the piles of severed hands ; [1] and we discover an immense battle-piece, which is in fact a replica of the famous battle-piece at Abou Simbel. This subject, like its Nubian prototype, yet preserves some of its colour. The enemy are shown to be fair-skinned and light-haired, and wear the same Syrian robes ; and the river, more green than that at Abou Simbel, is painted in zigzags in the same manner. The King, alone in his chariot, sends arrow after arrow against the flying foe. They leap into the river, and swim for their lives. Some are drowned ; some cross in safety, and are helped out by their friends on the opposite bank. A red-haired chief, thus rescued, is suspended head-downwards by his soldiers, in order to let the water that he has swallowed run out of his mouth. The river is once more the Orontes ; the city is once more Kadesh ; the king is once more Rameses II ; and the incidents are again the incidents of the poem of Pentaur.

The one wholly unmistakable point in the narrative is, however, the colossal statue of Syenite, "the largest in Egypt."[2] The siege and the river, the troops of captives are to be found

[1] See Champollion, Letter XIV, footnote, p. 418.

[2] The sitting colossus of the Ramesseum was certainly the largest perfect statue in Egypt when Diodorus visited the Valley of the Nile, for the great standing colossus of Tanis had long before his time been cut up by Sheshonk III for building purposes ; but that the Tanite colossus much exceeded the colossus of the Ramesseum in height and bulk is placed beyond doubt by the scale of the fragments discovered by Mr. Petrie in the course of his excavations in 1884. According to his very cautious calculations, the figure alone of the Tanite colossus was 900 inches, or 75 feet high ; or somewhere between 70 and 80 feet. "To this," says Mr. Petrie, "we must add the height of the crown, which would proportionately be some 14½ feet. To this again must be added the base of the figure, which was thinner than the usual scale, being only 27 inches thick. Thus the whole block appears to have been about 1100 inches, or say 92 feet high. This was, so far as is known, the largest statue ever executed." The weight of the figure is calculated by Mr. Petrie at about 900 tons ; *i.e.* 100 tons more than the colossus of the Ramesseum. That it stood upon a suitable pedestal cannot be doubted ; and with the pedestal, which can scarcely have been less than 18 or 20 feet in height, the statue must have towered some 120 feet above the level of the plain. See *Tanis*, part i. chap. ii. pp. 22, 23. [Note to Second Edition.]

elsewhere ; but nowhere, save here, a colossus which answers
to that description. This statue was larger than even the twin
Colossi of the Plain. They measure eighteen feet and three
inches across the shoulders ; this measures twenty-two feet and
four inches. They sit about fifty feet high, without their
pedestals ; this one must have lifted his head some ten feet
higher still. " The measure of his foot," says Diodorus,
" exceeded seven cubits " ; the Greek cubit being a little over
eighteen inches in length. The foot of the fallen Rameses
measures nearly eleven feet in length by four feet ten inches
in breadth. This, also, is the only very large Theban colossus
sculptured in the red Syenite of Assûan.[1]

Ruined almost beyond recognition as it is, one never
doubts for a moment that this statue was one of the wonders
of Egyptian workmanship. It most probably repeated in
every detail the colossi of Abou Simbel ; but it surpassed
them as much in finish of carving as in perfection of material.
The stone is even more beautiful in colour than that of the
famous obelisks of Karnak ; and is so close and hard in grain,
that the scarab-cutters of Luxor are said to use splinters of it
as our engravers use diamonds, for the points of their graving
tools. The solid contents of the whole, when entire, are
calculated at 887 tons. How this astounding mass was
transported from Assûan, how it was raised, how it was overthrown, are problems upon which a great deal of ingenious
conjecture has been wasted. One traveller affirms that the
wedge-marks of the destroyer are distinctly visible. Another,
having carefully examined the fractured edges, declares that
the keenest eye can detect neither wedge-marks nor any other
evidences of violence. We looked for none of these signs and
tokens. We never asked ourselves how or when the ruin had
been done. It was enough that the mighty had fallen.

Inasmuch as one can clamber upon and measure these
stupendous fragments, the fallen colossus is more astonishing,
perhaps, as a wreck than it would have been as a whole.
Here, snapped across at the waist and flung helplessly back,

[1] The Syenite colossus of which the British Museum possesses the
head, and which is popularly known as the Young Memnon, measured
twenty-four feet in height before it was broken up by the French.

lie a huge head and shoulders, to climb which is like climbing a rock. Yonder, amid piles of unintelligible débris, we see a great foot, and nearer the head, part of an enormous trunk, together with the upper halves of two huge thighs clothed in the usual shenti or striped tunic. The klaft or headdress is also striped, and these stripes, in both instances, retain the delicate yellow colour with which they were originally filled in. To judge from the way in which this colour was applied, one would say that the statue was tinted rather than painted. The surface-work, wherever it remains, is as smooth and highly finished as the cutting of the finest gem. Even the ground of the superb cartouche, on the upper half of the arm, is elaborately polished. Finally, in the pit which it ploughed out in falling, lies the great pedestal, hieroglyphed with the usual pompous titles of Rameses Mer-Amen. Diodorus, knowing nothing of Rameses or his style, interprets the inscription after his own fanciful fashion :—" I am Osymandias, King of Kings. If any would know how great I am, and where I lie, let him excel me in any of my works."

The fragments of wall and shattered pylon that yet remain standing at the Ramesseum face N.W. and S.W. Hence it follows that some of the most interesting of the surface sculpture (being cut in very low relief) is so placed with regard to the light as to be actually invisible after midday. It was not till the occasion of my last visit, when I came early in the morning to make a certain sketch by a certain light, that I succeeded in distinguishing a single figure of that celebrated tableau,[1] on the south wall of the Great Hall, in which the Egyptians are seen to be making use of the testudo and scaling ladder to assault a Syrian fortress. The wall sculptures of the second hall are on a bolder scale, and can be seen at any hour. Here Thoth writes the name of Rameses on the egg-shaped fruit of the persea tree, and processions of shaven priests carry on their shoulders the sacred boats of various Gods. In the centre of each boat is a shrine supported by winged genii, or cherubim. The veils over these shrines, the rings through which the bearing-poles were passed, and all the

[1] See woodcut No. 340 in Sir G. Wilkinson's *Manners and Customs of the Ancient Egyptians*, vol. i. ed. 1871.

appointments and ornaments of the *bari,* are distinctly shown. One seems here, indeed, to be admitted to a glimpse of those original shrines upon which Moses—learned in the sacred lore of the Egyptians—modelled, with but little alteration, his Ark of the Covenant.

Next in importance to Karnak, and second in interest to none of the Theban ruins, is the vast group of buildings known by the collective name of Medinet Habu. To attempt to describe these would be to undertake a task as hopeless as the description of Karnak. Such an attempt lies, at all events, beyond the compass of these pages, so many of which have already been given to similar subjects. For it is of Temples as of mountains—no two are alike, yet all sound so much alike when described that it is scarcely possible to write about them without becoming monotonous. In the present instance, therefore, I will note only a few points of special interest, referring those who wish for fuller particulars to the elaborate account of Medinet Habu in Murray's *Handbook of Egypt.*

In the second name of Medinet Habu—Medinet being the common Arabic for city, and Habu, Aboo, or Taboo being variously spelled—there survives almost beyond doubt the ancient name of that famous city which the Greeks called Thebes. It is a name for which many derivations[1] have been suggested, but upon which the learned are not yet agreed.

The ruins of Medinet Habu consist of a smaller Temple founded by Queen Hatohepsu of the XVIIIth Dynasty, a large and magnificent Temple entirely built by Rameses III of the XXth Dynasty, and an extremely curious and interesting building, part palace, part fortress, which is popularly known as the Pavilion.

The walls of this pavilion, the walls of the great forecourt leading to the smaller Temple, and a corner of the original wall of circuit, are crowned in the Egyptian style with shield-shaped battlements, precisely as the Khetan and Amorite fortresses are battlemented in the sculptured tableaux at Abou

---

[1] Among these are *Abot* or abode ; meaning the abode of Amen ; *Ta-Uaboo,* the mound ; *Ta-Api,* the head or capital, etc. etc. See *Recherches sur le nom Egyptien de Thèbes.* CHABAS: 1863 ; *Textes Géographiques d'Edfoo,* J. DE ROUGÉ: *Revue Arch. Nouvelle Série,* vol. xii. 1865; etc. etc.

Simbel and elsewhere. From whichever side one approaches Medinet Habu, these stone shields strike the eye as a new and interesting feature. They are, moreover, so far as I know, the only specimens of Egyptian battlementing which have survived destruction. Those of the wall of circuit are of the time of Rameses V; those of the pavilion, of the time of Rameses III; and the latest, which are those of the forecourt, are of the period of Roman occupation.

As biographical material, the Temple and Pavilion at Medinet Habu and the great Harris papyrus,[1] are to the life of Rameses III precisely what Abou Simbel, the Ramesseum, and the poem of Pentaur, are to the life of Rameses II. Great wars, great victories, magnificent praises of the prowess of the King, pompous lists of enemies slain and captured, inventories of booty and of precious gifts offered by the victor to the Gods of Egypt, in both instances cover the sculptured walls and fill the written pages. A comparison of the two masses of evidence—due allowance being made both ways for Oriental fervour of diction—shows that in Rameses III we have to

---

[1] The *Great Harris Papyrus* is described by Dr. Birch as "one of the finest, best written, and best preserved, that have been discovered in Egypt. It measures 133 feet long by 16¾ inches broad, and was found with several others in a tomb behind Medinet Habu. Purchased soon after by the late A. C. Harris of Alexandria, it was subsequently unrolled and divided into seventy-nine leaves, and laid down on card-board. With the exception of some small portions which are wanting in the first leaf, the text is complete throughout." The papyrus purports to be a post-mortem address of the King, Rameses III, recounting the benefits he had conferred upon Egypt by his administration, and by his delivery of the country from foreign subjection. It also records the immense gifts which he had conferred on the Temples of Egypt, of Amen at Thebes, Tum at Heliopolis, and Ptah at Memphis, etc. "The last part is addressed to the officers of the army, consisting partly of Sardinian and Libyan mercenaries, and to the people of Egypt, in the thirty-second year of his reign, and is a kind of posthumous panegyrical discourse, or political will, like that of Augustus discovered at Ancyra. The papyrus itself consists of the following divisions, three of which are preceded by large coloured plates or vignettes:—Introduction: donations to the Theban deities; donations to the gods of Heliopolis; donations to the gods of Memphis; donations to the gods of the north and south; summary of donations; historical speech and conclusion. Throughout the monarch speaks in the first person, the list excepted." Introduction to *Annals of Rameses III;* S. BIRCH : *Records of the Past*, vol. vi. p. 21; 1876.

do with a king as brilliant, as valorous, and as successful as Rameses II.[1]

It may be that before the time of this Pharaoh certain Temples were used also as royal residences. It is possible to believe this of Temples such as Gournah and Abydus, the plan of which includes, besides the usual halls, side-chambers, and sanctuary, a number of other apartments, the uses of which are unknown. It may also be that former kings dwelt in houses of brick and carved woodwork, such as we see represented in the wall-paintings of various tombs.

It is at all events a fact that the only building which we can assume to have been a royal palace, and of which any vestiges have come down to the present day, was

---

[1] " Rameses III was one of the most remarkable monarchs in the annals of Egypt. A period of political confusion and foreign conquest of the country preceded his advent to the throne. His father, Setnecht, had indeed succeeded in driving out the foreign invaders, and re-establishing the native dynasty of the Theban kings, the twentieth of the list of Manetho. But Rameses had a great task before him, called to the throne at a youthful age. . . . The first task of Rameses was to restore the civil government and military discipline. In his fifth year, he defeated the Maxyes and Libyans with great slaughter when they invaded Egypt, led by five chiefs ; and in the same year he had also to repulse the Satu, or eastern foreigners, who had attacked Egypt. The maritime nations of the west, it appears, had invaded Palestine and the Syrian coast in his eighth year, and after taking Carchemish, a confederation of the *Pulusata*, supposed by some to be the Pelasgi, *Tekkaru* or Teucri, *Sakaluša* or Siculi, *Tanau* or Daunians, if not Danai, and Uašaša or Osci, marched to the conquest of Egypt. It is possible that they reached the mouth of the eastern branch of the Nile. But Rameses concentrated an army at Taha, in Northern Palestine, and marched back to defend the Nile. Assisted by his mercenary forces, he inflicted a severe defeat on the confederated west, and returned with his prisoners to Thebes. In his eleventh year the Mashuasha or Maxyes, assisted by the Tahennu or Libyans, again invaded Egypt, to suffer a fresh defeat, and the country seems from this period to have remained in a state of tranquillity. . . . The vast Temple at Medinet Habu, his palaces and treasury, still remain to attest his magnificence and grandeur ; and if his domestic life was that of an ordinary Egyptian monarch, he was as distinguished in the battlefield as the palace. Treason, no doubt, disturbed his latter days, and it is not known how he died ; but he expired after a reign of thirty-one years and some months, and left the throne to his son, it is supposed, about B.C. 1200." See *Remarks upon the Cover of the Granite Sarcophagus of Rameses III:* S. BIRCH, LL.D., Cambridge, 1876.

erected by Rameses III, namely, this little pavilion at Medinet Habu.

PALACE ENTRANCE—MEDINET HABU.

It may not have been a palace. It may have been only a fortified gate ; but though the chambers are small, they are well lighted, and the plan of the whole is certainly domestic in character. It consists, as we now see it, of two lodges connected by zigzag wings with a central tower. The lodges and tower stand to each other as the three points of an acute angle. These structures enclose an oblong courtyard leading by a passage under the central tower to the sacred enclosure beyond. So far as its present condition enables us to judge, this building contained only eight rooms ; namely three, one above the other, in each of the lodges, and two over the gateway.[1] These three

---

[1] " There is reason to believe that this is only a fragment of the building,

towers communicate by means of devious passages in the connecting wings. Two of the windows in the wings are adorned
with balconies supported on brackets ; each bracket representing
the head and shoulders of a crouching captive, in the attitude
of a gargoyle. The heads and dresses of these captives—conceived as they are in a vein of Gothic barbarism—are still
bright with colour.

The central, or gateway-tower, is substantially perfect.
The Writer, with help, got as high as the first chamber ; the
ceiling of which is painted in a rich and intricate pattern, as in
imitation of mosaic. The top room is difficult of access ; but
can be reached by a good climber. Our friend F. W. S., who
made his way up there a year or two before, found upon the

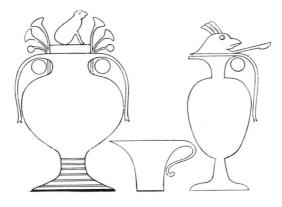

walls some interesting sculptures of cups and vases, apparently
part of an illustrated inventory of domestic utensils. Three
of these (unlike any engraved in the works of Wilkinson or
Rosellini) are here reproduced from his sketch made upon the
spot. The lid of the smaller vase, it will be observed, opens by

and foundations exist which render it probable that the whole was originally
a square of the width of the front, and had other chambers, probably in
wood or brick, besides those we now find. This would hardly detract from
the playful character of the design, and when coloured, as it originally was,
and with its battlements or ornaments complete, it must have formed a
composition as pleasing as it is unlike our usual conceptions of Egyptian
art."—*Hist. of Architecture*, by J. FERGUSSON, Bk. i., ch. iv., p. 118.
Lond. 1865.

means of a lever spooned out for the thumb to rest in, just like the lid of a German beer-mug of the present day.

The external decorations of the two lodges are of especial interest. The lower subjects are historical. Those upon the upper storeys are domestic or symbolical, and are among the most celebrated of Egyptian bas-reliefs. They have long been supposed to represent Rameses III in his hareem, entertained and waited upon by female slaves. In one group the king, distinguished always by his cartouches, sits at ease in a kind of folding chair, his helmet on his head, his sandalled feet upon a footstool, as one returned and resting after battle. In his left hand he holds a round object like a fruit. With the right he chucks under the chin an ear-ringed and necklaced damsel who presents a lotus blossom at his nose. In another much mutilated subject, they are represented playing a game at draughts. This famous subject—which can only be seen when the light strikes sidewise—would scarcely be intelligible save for the help one derives from the cuts in Wilkinson and the plates in Rosellini. It is not that the sculptures are effaced, but that the great blocks which bore them are gone from their places, having probably been hurled down bodily upon the heads of the enemy during a certain siege of which the ruins bear evident traces.[1] Of the lady, there remains little beside one arm and the hand that holds the pawn. The table has disappeared. The king has lost his legs. It happens, however, though the table is missing, that the block next above it contained the pawns, which can still be discerned from below by the help of a glass. Rosellini mentions three or four more subjects of a similar character, including a second group of draught-players, all visible in his time. The Writer, however, looked for them in vain.

---

[1] Medinet Habu continued up to the period of the Arab invasion to be inhabited by the Coptic descendants of its ancient builders. They fled, however, before Amr and his army, since which time the place has been deserted. It is not known whether the siege took place at the time of the Arab invasion, or during the raid of Cambyses ; but whenever it was, the place was evidently forced by the besiegers. The author of Murray's Handbook draws attention to the fact that the granite jambs of the doorway leading to the smaller Temple are cut through exactly at the place where the bar was placed across the door.

These tableaux are supposed to illustrate the home-life of Rameses III, and to confirm the domestic character of the pavilion. Even the scarab-selling Arabs that haunt the ruins, even the donkey-boys of Luxor, call it the Hareem of the Sultan. Modern science, however, threatens to dispel one at least of these pleasant fancies.

The king, it seems, under the name of Rhampsinitus, is the hero of a very ancient legend related by Herodotus. While he yet lived, runs the story, he descended into Hades, and there played a game at draughts with the Goddess Demeter, from whom he won a golden napkin ; in memory of which adventure, and of his return to earth, "the Egyptians," says Herodotus, "instituted a festival which they certainly celebrated in my day."[1] In another version as told by Plutarch, Isis is substituted for Demeter. Viewing these tales by the light of a certain passage of the Ritual, in which the happy dead is promised "power to transform himself at will, to play at draughts, to repose in a pavilion," Dr. Birch has suggested that the whole of this scene may be of a memorial character, and represent an incident in the Land of Shades.[2]

Below these "hareem" groups come colossal bas-reliefs of a religious and military character. The King, as usual, smites his prisoners in presence of the Gods. A slender and spirited figure in act to slay, the fiery hero strides across the wall "like Baal[3] descended from the heights of heaven. His limbs are

---

[1] Herodotus, Bk. ii. chap. 122.

[2] "A Medinet Habou, dans son palais, il s'est fait représenter jouant aux dames avec des femmes qui, d'après certaines copies, semblent porter sur la tête les fleurs symboliques de l'Egypte supérieure et inférieure, comme les deésses du monde supérieur et inférieur, ou du ciel et de la terre. Cette dualité des deésses, qui est indiquée dans les scènes religieuses et les textes sacrés par la réunion de Satis et Anoucis, Pasht et Bast, Isis et Nephthys, etc., me fait penser que les tableaux de Medinet Habou peuvent avoir été considérés dans les légendes populaires comme offrant aux yeux l'allégorie de la scène du jeu de dames entre le roi et la deésse Isis, dont Hérodote a fait la Déméter egyptienne, comme il a fait d'Osiris le Dionysus du même peuple."—*Le Roi Rhampsinite et le Jeu des Dames*, par S. BIRCH. *Revue Arch: Nouvelle Série*, vol. xii., p. 58. Paris : 1865.

[3] BAAL, written sometimes Bar, was, like Sutekh, a God borrowed from the Phœnician mythology. The worship of Baal seems to have been introduced into Egypt during the XIXth Dynasty. The other God here mentioned, Mentu or Month, was a solar deity adored in the Thebaid, and

endued with the force of victory. With his right hand he seizes the multitudes ; his left reaches like an arrow after those who fly before him. His sword is sharp as that of his father Mentu."[1]

Below these great groups run friezes sculptured with kneeling figures of vanquished chiefs, among whom are Libyan, Sicilian, Sardinian, and Etruscan leaders. Every head in these friezes is a portrait. The Libyan is beardless ; his lips are thin ; his nose is hooked ; his forehead retreats ; he wears a close-fitting cap with a pendant hanging in front of the ear. The features of the Sardinian chief[2] are no less Asiatic. He wears the usual Sardinian helmet surmounted by a ball and two spikes. The profile of the Sicilian closely resembles that of the Sardinian. He wears a headdress like the modern Persian cap. As ethnological types, these heads are extremely valuable. Colonists not long since departed from the western coasts of Asia Minor, these early European settlers are seen with the Asiatic stamp of features ; a stamp which has now entirely disappeared.

Other European nations are depicted elsewhere in these Medinet Habu sculptures. Pelasgians from the Greek isles, Oscans perhaps from Pompeii, Daunians from the districts between Tarentum and Brundusium, figure here, each in their national costume. Of these, the Pelasgian alone resembles the modern European. On the left wall of the pavilion gateway, going up towards the Temple, there is a large bas-relief of

especially worshipped at Hermonthis, now Erment ; a modern town of some importance, the name of which is still almost identical with the Per-Mentu of ancient days. Mentu was the Egyptian, and Baal the Phœnician, god of war.

[1] From one of the inscriptions at Medinet Habu, quoted by Chabas. See *Antiquité Historique*, ch. iv. p. 238. Ed. 1873.

[2] It is a noteworthy fact (and one which has not, so far as I know, been previously noticed) that while the Asiatic and African chiefs represented in these friezes are insolently described in the accompanying hieroglyphic inscriptions as " the vile Libyan," " the vile Kushite," " the vile Mashuasha," and so forth, the European leaders, though likewise prostrate and bound, are more respectfully designated as " the Great (◦⊂⊃) of Sardinia," " the Great of Sicily," " the Great of Etruria," etc. etc. May this be taken as an indication that their strength as military powers was already more formidable than that of the Egyptians' nearer neighbours ?

Rameses III leading a string of captives into the presence of Amen-Ra. Among these, the sculptures being in a high state of preservation, there are a number of Pelasgians, some of whom have features of the classical Greek type, and are strikingly handsome. The Pelasgic headdress resembles our old infantry shako ; and some of the men wear disk-shaped amulets pierced with a hole in the centre, through which is passed the chain that suspends it round the neck.

Leaving to the left a fine sitting statue of Khons in green basalt, and to the right his prostrate fellow, we pass under the gateway, cross a space of desolate crude-brick mounds, and see before us the ruins of the first pylon of the Great Temple of Khem. Once past the threshold of this pylon, we enter upon a succession of magnificent courtyards. The hieroglyphs here are on a colossal scale, and are cut deeper than any others in Egypt. They are also coloured with a more subtle eye to effect. Struck by the unusual splendour of some of the blues, and by a peculiar look of scintillation which they assumed in certain lights, I examined them particularly, and found that the effect had been produced by very subtle shades of gradation in what appeared at first sight to be simple flat tints. In some of the reeds (𓏏), for instance, the ground-colour begins at the top of the leaf in pure cobalt, and passes imperceptibly down to a tint that is almost emerald green at the bottom.[1]

The inner walls of this great courtyard, and the outer face of the north-east wall, are covered with sculptures outlined, so to say, in intaglio, and relieved in the hollow, so that the forms, though rounded, remain level with the general surface. In these tableaux the old world lives again. Rameses III, his sons and nobles, his armies, his foes, play once more the brief drama of life and death. Great battles are fought ; great victories are won ; the slain are counted ; the captured drag their chains behind the victor's chariot ; the king triumphs, is

---

[1] The grand blue of the ceiling of the colonnade of the Great Hypæthral Court is also very remarkable for brilliancy and purity of tone ; while to those interested in decoration the capital and abacus of the second column to the right on entering this courtyard, offers an interesting specimen of polychrome ornamentation on a gold-coloured ground.

crowned, and sacrifices to the Gods. Elsewhere more wars ; more slaughter. There is revolt in Libya ; there are raids on the Asiatic border ; there are invaders coming in ships from the islands of the Great Sea. The royal standard is raised ; troops assemble ; arms are distributed. Again the king goes forth in his might, followed by the flower of Egyptian chivalry. " His horsemen are heroes ; his foot soldiers are as lions that roar in the mountains." The king himself flames " like Mentu in his hour of wrath." He falls upon the foe " with the swiftness of a meteor." Here, crowded in rude bullock-trucks, they seek safety in flight. Yonder their galleys are sunk ; their warriors are slain, drowned, captured, scathed, as it were, in a devouring fire. " Never again will they sow seed or reap harvest on the fair face of the earth."

" Behold ! " says the Pharaoh, " Behold, I have taken their frontiers for my frontiers ! I have devastated their towns, burned their crops, trampled their people under foot. Rejoice, O Egypt ! Exalt thy voice to the heavens ; for behold ! I reign over all the lands of the barbarians ! I, King of Upper and Lower Egypt, Rameses III ! " [1]

Such, linked each to each by a running commentary of text, are the illustrations ; the story is written elsewhere. Elaborately hieroglyphed in upwards of seventy closely-packed columns, it covers the whole eastern face of the great north tower of the second propylon. This propylon divides the Osiride and Hypæthral courts, so that the inscription faces those entering the Temple and precedes the tableaux. Not even the poem of Pentaur is more picturesque, not even the Psalms of David are more fervid, than the style of this great Chronicle. [2]

The Writer pitched her tent in the doorway of the first propylon, and thence sketched the north-west corner of the courtyard, including the tower with the inscription and the

---

[1] Inscriptions at Medinet Habu. See Chabas' *Antiquité Historique*, chap. iv. Paris : 1876.

[2] The whole of this chronicle is translated by M. Chabas in *L'Antiquité Historique*, chap. iv. p. 246 *et seq.* It is also engraved in full in Rosellini (*Monumenti Storici*) ; and has been admirably photographed by both M. Hammerschmidt and Signor Beata.

OSIRIDE COURT, MEDINET HABU.

SKELTON.

Osiride colossi. The accompanying illustration faithfully re-produces that sketch. The roof of the colonnade to the right is cumbered with crude-brick ruins of mediæval date. The hieroglyphs, sculptured along the architrave and down the sides of the pillars, are still bright with colour. The colossi are all the worse for 3000 years of ill-usage.. Through the sculptured doorway opposite, one looks across the Hypæthral Court, and catches a glimpse of the ruined Hall of Pillars beyond.

While the Writer was at work in the shade of the first pylon, an Arab story-teller took possession of that opposite doorway, and entertained the donkey-boys and sailors. Well paid with a little tobacco and a few copper piastres, he went on for hours, his shrill chant rising every now and then to a quavering scream. He was a wizened, grizzled old fellow, miserably poor and tattered ; but he had the *Arabian Nights* and hundreds of other tales by heart.

Mariette was of opinion that the Temple of Medinet Habu, erected as it is on the side of the great Theban necropolis, is, like the Ramesseum, a funerary monument erected by Rameses III in his own lifetime to his own memory. These battered colossi represent the king in the character of Osiris, and are in fact on a huge scale precisely what the ordinary funerary statu-ettes are upon a small scale. They would be out of place in any but a monumental edifice ; and they alone suffice to determine the character of the building.

And such, no doubt, was the character of the Amenophium ; of the little Temple called Dayr el Medinet ; of the Temple of Queen Hatshepsu, known as Dayr el Bahari ; of the Temple of Gournah ; of almost every important structure erected upon this side of the river. Of the Amenophium there remain only a few sculptured blocks, a few confused foundations, and—last representatives of an avenue of statues of various sizes—the famous Colossi of the Plain.[1] The Temple of Dayr el Bahari

---

[1] These two statues—the best-known, probably, of all Egyptian monu-ments—have been too often described, painted, engraved, and photographed, to need more than a passing reference. Their featureless faces, their attitude, their surroundings, are familiar as the Pyramids, even to those who know not Egypt. We all know that they represent Amenhotep, or

—built in terraces up the mountain side, and approached once upon a time by a magnificent avenue of sphinxes, the course of which is yet visible—would probably be, if less ruined, the most interesting temple on the western side of the river. The monumental intention of this building is shown by its dedication to Hathor, the Lady of Amenti ; and by the fact that the tomb of Queen Hatshepsu was identified by Rhind some twenty-five years ago as one of the excavated sepulchres in the cliff-side, close to where the temple ends by abutting against the rock.

As for the Temple of Gournah, it is, at least in part, as distinctly a memorial edifice as the Medici Chapel at Florence or the Superga at Turin. It was begun by Seti I in memory of his father Rameses I, the founder of the XIXth Dynasty. Seti, however, died before the work was completed. Hereupon Rameses II, his son and successor, extended the general plan, finished the part dedicated to his grandfather, and added sculptures to the memory of Seti I. Later still, Menepthah, the son and successor of Rameses II, left his cartouches upon one of the doorways. The whole building, in short, is a family monument, and contains a family portrait gallery. Here all the personages whose names figure in the shrines of the

---

Amunoph, III ; and that the northernmost was shattered to the waist by the earthquake of B.C. 27. Being heard to give out a musical sound during the first hour of the day, the statue was supposed by the ancients to be endowed with a miraculous voice. The Greeks, believing it to represent the fabled son of Tithonus and Aurora, gave it the name of Memnon ; notwithstanding that the Egyptians themselves claimed the statues as portraits of Amenhotep III. Prefects, Consuls, Emperors, and Empresses, came "to hear Memnon," as the phrase then ran. Among the famous visitors who travelled thither on this errand, we find Strabo, Germanicus, Hadrian, and the Empress Sabina. Opinion is divided as to the cause of this sound. There is undoubtedly a hollow space inside the throne of this statue, as may be seen by all who examine it from behind ; and Sir G. Wilkinson, in expressing his conviction that the musical sound was a piece of priestly jugglery, represents the opinion of the majority. The author of a carefully considered article in the *Quarterly Review*, No. 276, April 1875, coincides with Sir D. Brewster in attributing the sound to a transmission of rarefied air through the crevices of the stone, caused by the sudden change of temperature consequent on the rising of the sun. The statue, which, like its companion, was originally one solid monolith of gritstone, was repaired with sandstone during the reign of Septimius Severus.

Ramessides at Silsilis are depicted in their proper persons. In one tableau, Rameses I, defunct, deified,[1] swathed, enshrined, and crowned like Osiris, is worshipped by Seti I. Behind Seti stands his Queen Tuaa, the mother of Rameses II. Elsewhere Seti I, being now dead, is deified and worshipped by Rameses II, who pours a libation to his father's statue. Through all these handsome heads there runs a striking family likeness. All more or less partake of that Dantesque type which characterises the portraits of Rameses II in his youth. The features of Rameses I and Seti I are somewhat pinched and stern, like the Dante of elder days. The delicate profile of Queen Tuaa, which is curiously like some portraits of Queen Elizabeth, is perhaps too angular to be altogether pleasing. But in the well-known face of Rameses II these harsher details vanish, and the beauty of the race culminates. The artists of Egyptian Renaissance, always great in profile-portraiture, are nowhere seen to better advantage than in this interesting series.

Adjoining what may be called the monumental part of the building, we find a number of halls and chambers, the uses of which are unknown. Most writers assume that they were the private apartments of the King. Some go so far as to give the name of Temple-Palaces to all these great funerary structures. It is, however, far more probable that these Western Temples were erected in connection, though not in direct communication, with the royal tombs in the adjacent valley of Bab-el-Molûk.

Now every Egyptian tomb of importance has its outer chamber or votive oratory, the walls of which are covered with paintings descriptive, in some instances, of the occupations of

---

[1] This deification of the dead was not deification in the Roman sense; neither was it canonisation in the modern sense. The Egyptians believed the justified dead to be assimilated, or rather identified, in the spirit with Osiris, the beneficent Judge and Deity of the lower world. Thus, in their worship of ancestry, they adored not mortals immortalised, but the dead in Osiris, and Osiris in the dead.

It is worth noting, by the way, that notwithstanding the subsequent deification of Seti I, Rameses I remained, so to say, the tutelary saint of the Temple. He alone is represented with the curious pointed and upturned beard, like a chamois horn reversed, which is the peculiar attribute of deity.

the deceased upon earth, and in others of the adventures of his soul after death. Here at stated seasons the survivors repaired with offerings. No priest, it would seem, of necessity officiated at these little services. A whole family would come, bringing the first fruits of their garden, the best of their poultry, cakes of home-made bread, bouquets of lotus blossoms. With their own hands they piled the altar ; and the eldest son, as representative of the rest, burned the incense and poured the libations. It is a scene constantly reproduced upon monuments [1] of every epoch. These votive oratories, however, are wholly absent in the valley of Bab-el-Molûk. The royal tombs consist of only tunnelled passages and sepulchral vaults, the entrances to which were closed for ever as soon as the sarcophagus was occupied ; hence it may be concluded that each memorial temple played to the tomb of its tutelary saint and sovereign that part which is played by the external oratory attached to the tomb of a private individual. Nor must it be forgotten that as early as the time of the Pyramid Kings, there was a votive chapel attached to every pyramid, the remains of which are traceable in almost every instance, on the east side. There were also priests of the pyramids, as we learn from innumerable funerary inscriptions.

An oratory on so grand a scale would imply an elaborate ceremonial. A dead and deified king would doubtless have his train of priests, his daily liturgies, processions, and sacrifices. All this again implies additional accommodation, and accounts, I venture to think, for any number of extra halls and chambers. Such sculptures as yet remain on the walls of these ruined apartments are, in fact, wholly funereal and sacrificial in character. It is also to be remembered that we have here a

---

[1] There is among the funereal tablets of the Boulak collection a small bas-relief sculpture representing the arrival of a family of mourners at the tomb of a deceased ancestor. The statue of the defunct sits at the upper end. The mourners are laden with offerings. One little child carries a lamb ; another a goose. A scribe stands by, waiting to register the gifts. The tablet commemorates one Psamtik-nefar-Sam, a hierogrammate under some king of the XXVIth Dynasty. The natural grace and simple pathos with which this little frieze is treated lift it far above the level of ordinary Egyptian art, and bear comparison with the class of monuments lately discovered on the Eleusinian road at Athens.

temple dedicated to two kings, and served most likely by a twofold college of priests.[1]

The wall-sculptures at Gournah are extremely beautiful, especially those erected by Seti I. Where it has been accidentally preserved, the surface is as smooth, the execution as brilliant, as the finest mediæval ivory carving. Behind a broken column, for instance, that leans against the south west wall of the sanctuary,[2] one may see, by peeping this way and that, the ram's-head prow of a sacred boat, quite unharmed, and of surpassing delicacy. The modelling of the ram's head is simply faultless. It would indeed be scarcely too much to say that this one fragment, if all the rest had perished, would alone place the decorative sculpture of ancient Egypt in a rank second only to that of Greece.

The Temple of Gournah——northernmost of the Theban group——stands at the mouth of that famous valley called by the Arabs Bab-el-Molûk,[3] and by travellers, the Valley of the Tombs of the Kings. This valley may be described as a bifurcated ravine, ending in two *culs de sacs*, and hemmed in on all sides by limestone precipices. It winds round behind the cliffs which face Luxor and Karnak, and runs almost parallel with the Nile. This range of cliffs is perforated on both sides with tombs. The priests and nobles of many dynasties were buried terrace above terrace on the side next the river. Back to back with them, in the silent and secret valley beyond, slept the kings in their everlasting sepulchres.

Most travellers moor for a day or two at Karnak, and thence make their excursion to Bab-el-Molûk. By so doing they lose one of the most interesting rides in the neighbourhood of Thebes. L. and the Writer started from Luxor one morning about an hour after daybreak, crossing the river at the usual

---

[1] "Une dignité tout à fait particulier est celle que les inscriptions hiéroglyphiques désignent par le titre 'prophète de la pyramide, de tel pharaon.' Il parait qu'après sa mort chaque roi était vénéré par un culte spécial." *Histoire d'Egypte:* BRUGSCH. 2d ed. chap. v. p. 35. Leipzig: 1875.

[2] There is a very curious window at the end of this sanctuary, with grooves for the shutter, and holes in which to slip and drop the bar by which it was fastened.

[3] The Gate of the King.

point and thence riding northwards along the bank, with the Nile on the one hand, and the corn-lands on the other. In the course of· such rides, one discovers the almost incredible fertility of the Thebaid. Every inch of arable ground is turned to account. All that grows, grows lustily. The barley ripples in one uninterrupted sweep from Medinet Habu to a point half-way between the Ramesseum and Gournah. Next come plantations of tobacco, cotton, hemp, linseed, maize and lentils, so closely set, so rich in promise, that the country looks as if it were laid out in allotment grounds for miles together. Where the rice crop has been gathered, clusters of temporary huts have sprung up in the clearings ; for the fellahîn come out from their crowded villages in " the sweet o' the year," and live in the midst of the crops which now they guard, and which presently they will reap. The walls of these summer huts are mere wattled fences of Indian corn straw, with bundles of the same laid lightly across the top by way of roofing. This pastoral world is everywhere up and doing. Here are men plying the shâdûf by the river's brink ; women spinning in the sun ; children playing ; dogs barking ; larks soaring and singing overhead. Against the foot of the cliffs yonder, where the vegetation ends and the tombs begin, there flows a calm river edged with palms. A few months ago, we should have been deceived by that fairy water. We know now that it is the mirage.

Striking off by and by towards the left, we make for a point where the mountains recede and run low, and a wedge-like " spit " of sandy desert encroaches upon the plain. On the verge of this spit stands a clump of sycamores and palms. A row of old yellow columns supporting a sculptured architrave gleams through the boughs ; a little village nestles close by ; and on the desert slope beyond, in the midst of a desolate Arab burial-ground, we see a tiny mosque with one small cupola, dazzling white in the sunshine. This is Gournah. There is a spring here, and some girls are drawing water from the well near the Temple. Our donkeys slake their thirst from the cattle-trough——a broken sarcophagus that may once have held the mummy of a king. A creaking sakkieh is at work yonder, turned by a couple of red cows with mild Hathor-like faces.

The old man who drives them sits in the middle of the cog-wheel, and goes slowly round as if he was being roasted.

We now leave behind us the well, and the trees, and the old Greek-looking Temple, and turn our faces westward, bound for an opening yonder among cliffs pitted with the mouths of empty tombs. It is plain to see that we are now entering upon what was once a torrent-bed. Rushing down from the hills, the pent-up waters have here spread fan-like over the slope of the desert, strewing the ground with boulders, and ploughing it into hundreds of tortuous channels. Up that torrent-bed lies our road to-day.

The weird rocks stand like sentinels to right and left as one enters the mouth of the valley, and take strange shapes as of obelisks and sphinxes. Some, worn at the base, and towering like ruined pyramids above, remind us of tombs on the Appian Way. As the ravine narrows, the limestone walls rise higher. The chalky track glares under-foot. Piles of shivered chips sparkle and scintillate at the foot of the rocks. The cliffs burn at a white heat. The atmosphere palpitates like gaseous vapour. The sun blazes overhead. Not a breath stirs ; neither is there a finger's breadth of shade on either side. It is like riding into the mouth of a furnace. Meanwhile, one looks in vain for any sign of life. No blade of green has grown here since the world began. No breathing creature makes these rocks its home. All is desolation—such desolation as one dreams of in a world scathed by fire from heaven.

When we have gone a long way, always tracking up the bed of the torrent, we come to a place where our donkeys turn off from the main course and make for what is evidently a forced passage cut clean through a wall of solid limestone. The place was once a mere recess in the cliffs; but on the farther side, masked by a natural barrier of rock, there lay another valley leading to a secluded amphitheatre among the mountains. The first Pharaoh who chose his place of burial among those hidden ways, must have been he who cut the pass and levelled the road by which we now travel. This cutting is Bab-el-Molûk —the Gate of the King ; a name which doubtless perpetuates that by which the place was known to the old Egyptians. Once through the Gate, a grand mountain rises into view.

Egypt is the land of strange mountains ; and here is one which reproduces on a giant scale every feature of the pyramid of Ouenephes at Sakkarah. It is square ; it rises stage above stage in ranges of columnar cliffs with slopes of débris between ; and it terminates in a blunt four-sided peak nearly 1800 feet above the level of the plain.

Keeping this mountain always before us, we now follow the windings of the second valley, which is even more narrow, parched, and glaring than the first. Perhaps the intense heat makes the road appear longer than it really is ; but it seems to us like several miles. At length the uniformity of the way is broken. Two small ravines branch off, one to the right, one to the left ; and in both, at the foot of the rocks, there are here and there to be seen square openings, like cellar-doors, half sunk below the surface, and seeming to shoot downwards into the bowels of the earth. In another moment or so, our road ends suddenly in a wild tumbled waste, like an exhausted quarry, shut in all round by impending precipices, at the base of which more rock-cut portals peep out at different points.

From the moment when it first came into sight, I had made certain that in that pyramidal mountain we should find the Tombs of the Kings—so certain, that I can scarcely believe our guide when he assures us that these cellars are the places we have come to see, and that the mountain contains not a single tomb. We alight, however ; climb a steep slope ; and find ourselves on the threshold of No. 17.

" Belzoni-tomb," says our guide ; and Belzoni's tomb, as we know, is the tomb of Seti the First.

I am almost ashamed to remember now that we took our luncheon in the shade of that solemn vestibule, and rested and made merry, before going down into the great gloomy sepulchre whose staircases and corridors plunged away into the darkness below, as if they led straight to the land of Amenti.

The tombs in the Valley of Bab-el-Molûk are as unlike the tombs in the cliffs opposite Luxor as if the Theban kings and the Theban nobles were of different races and creeds. Those sacred scribes and dignitaries, with their wives and families and their numerous friends and dependants, were a joyous set.

They loved the things of this life, and would fain have carried
their pursuits and pleasures with them into the land beyond
the grave.   So they decorated the walls of their tombs with
pictures of the way in which their lives were spent, and hoped
perhaps that the mummy, dreaming away its long term of
solitary waiting, might take comfort in those shadowy reminis-
cences.   The kings, on the contrary, covered every foot of their
last palaces with scenes from the life to come.   The wanderings
of the soul after its separation from the body, the terrors and
dangers that beset it during its journey through Hades, the
demons it must fight, the accusers to whom it must answer, the
transformations it must undergo, afforded subjects for endless
illustration.   Of the fishing and fowling and feasting and
junketing that we saw the other day in those terraces behind
the Ramesseum, we discover no trace in the tombs of Bab-el-
Molûk.   In place of singing and lute-playing, we find here
prayers and invocations ; for the pleasant Nile-boat, and the
water-parties, and the chase of the gazelle and the ibex, we
now have the bark of Charon, and the basin of purgatorial fire,
and the strife with the infernal deities.   The contrast is sharp
and strange.   It is as if an Epicurean aristocracy had been
ruled by a line of Puritan kings.   The tombs of the subjects
are Anacreontics.   The tombs of their sovereigns are peniten-
tial psalms.

To go down into one of these great sepulchres is to descend
one's-self into the Lower World, and to tread the path of the
shades.   Crossing the threshold, we look up—half-expecting
to read those terrible words in which all who enter are warned
to leave hope behind them.   The passage slopes before our
feet ; the daylight fades behind us.   At the end of the passage
comes a flight of steps, and from the bottom of that flight of
steps we see another corridor slanting down into depths of
utter darkness.   The walls on both sides are covered with
close-cut columns of hieroglyphic text, interspersed with ominous
shapes, half-deity, half-demon.   Huge serpents writhe beside
us along the walls.   Guardian spirits of threatening aspect
advance, brandishing swords of flame.   A strange heaven opens
overhead—a heaven where the stars travel in boats across the
seas of space ; and the Sun, escorted by the hours, the months,

and the signs of the zodiac, issues from the East, sets in the West, and traverses the hemisphere of Everlasting Night. We go on, and the last gleam of daylight vanishes in the distance. Another flight of steps leads now to a succession of passages and halls, some smaller, some larger, some vaulted, some supported on pillars. Here yawns a great pit half full of débris. Yonder opens a suite of unfinished chambers abandoned by the workmen. The farther we go, the more weird become our surroundings. The walls swarm with ugly and evil things. Serpents, and bats, and crocodiles, some with human heads and legs, some vomiting fire, some armed with spears and darts, pursue and torture the wicked. These unfortunates have their hearts torn out ; are boiled in cauldrons ; are suspended head downwards over seas of flame ; are speared, decapitated, and driven in headless gangs to scenes of further torment. Beheld by the dim and shifting light of a few candles, these painted horrors assume an aspect of ghastly reality. They start into life as we pass, then drop behind us into darkness. That darkness alone is awful. The atmosphere is suffocating. The place is ghostly and peopled with nightmares.

Elsewhere we come upon scenes less painful. The Sun emerges from the lower hemisphere. The justified dead sow and reap in the Elysian fields, gather celestial fruits, and bathe in the waters of truth. The royal mummy reposes in its shrine. Funerary statues of the king are worshipped with incense, and offerings of meat, and libations of wine.[1] Finally the king arrives, purified and justified, at the last stage of his spiritual

[1] These funerary statues are represented each on a stand or platform, erect, with one foot advanced, as if walking, the right hand holding the ankh, or symbol of life, the left hand grasping a staff. The attitude is that of the wooden statue at Boulak ; and it is worth remark that the figures stand detached, with no support at the back, which was never the case with those carved in stone or granite. There can be no doubt that this curious series of funerary statues represents those which were actually placed in the tomb ; and that the ceremonies here represented were actually peformed before them, previous to closing the mouth of the sepulchre. One of these very wooden statues, from this very tomb, was brought to England by Belzoni, and is now in the British Museum (No. 854, Central Saloon). The wood is much decayed, and the statue ought undoubtedly to be placed under glass. The tableaux representing the above ceremonies are well copied in Rosellini, *Mon. del Culto,* plates 60-63.

journey. He is welcomed by the Gods, ushered into the presence of Osiris, and received into the Abode of the Blest.[1]

Coming out for a moment into blinding daylight, we drink a long draught of pure air, cross a few yards of uneven ground, arrive at the mouth of another excavation, and plunge again into underground darkness. A third and a fourth time we repeat this strange experience. It is like a feverish sleep, troubled by gruesome dreams, and broken by momentary wakings.

These tombs in a general way are very much alike. Some are longer than others ;[2] some loftier. In some the descent is gradual ; in others it is steep and sudden. Certain leading features are common to all. The great serpent,[3] the scarab,[4] the bat,[5] the crocodile,[6] are always conspicuous on the walls. The judgment-scene, and the well-known typical picture of the four races of mankind, are continually reproduced. Some tombs,[7] however, vary both in plan and decoration. That of

[1] A remarkable inscription in this tomb, relating the wrath of Ra and the destruction of mankind, is translated by M. Naville, vol. iv. Pt. i. *Translations of the Biblical Arch. Society.* In this singular myth, which bears a family resemblance to the Chaldæan record of the Flood, the deluge is a deluge of human blood. The inscription covers the walls of a small chamber known as the Chamber of the Cow.

[2] The longest tomb in the valley, which is that of Seti I, measures 470 feet in length to the point where it is closed by the falling in of the rock ; and the total depth of its descent is about 180 feet. The tomb of Rameses III (No. 11) measures in length 405 feet, and descends only 31 feet. The rest average from about 350 to 150 feet in length, and the shortest is excavated to a distance of only 65 feet.

We visited, however, one tomb in the Assaseef, which in extent far exceeds any of the tombs of the kings. This astonishing excavation, which consists of a bewildering labyrinth of halls, passages, staircases, pits, and chambers, is calculated at 23,809 square feet. The name of the occupant was Petamunap, a priest of uncertain date.

[3] *Apophis*, in Egyptian *Apap;* the great serpent of darkness, over whom Ra must triumph after he sets in the west, and before he again rises in the east.

[4] Kheper, the scarab deity. See chap. vi. p. 96.

[5] Symbolical of darkness.

[6] The crocodile represents Sebek. In one of the Boulak papyri, this God is called the son of Isis, and combats the enemies of Osiris. Here he combats Apophis in behalf of Ra.

[7] The tomb numbered 3 in the first small ravine to the left as one rides up the valley, bears the cartouches of Rameses II. The Writer crawled

Rameses III, though not nearly so beautiful as the tomb of Seti I, is perhaps the most curious of all. The paintings here are for the most part designed on an unsculptured surface coated with white stucco. The drawing is often indifferent, and the colouring is uniformly coarse and gaudy. Yellow abounds ; and crude reds and blues remind us of the coloured picture-books of our childhood. It is difficult to understand, indeed, how the builder of Medinet Habu, with the best Egyptian art of the day at his command, should have been content with such wall-paintings as these.

Still Rameses III seems to have had a grand idea of going in state to the next world, with his retainers around him. In a series of small antechambers opening off from the first corridor, we see depicted all the household furniture, all the plate, the weapons, the wealth and treasure of the king. Upon the walls of one the cooks and bakers are seen preparing the royal dinner. In the others are depicted magnificent thrones ; gilded galleys with parti-coloured sails ; gold and silver vases ; rich store of arms and armour ; piles of precious woods, of panther skins, of fruits, and birds, and curious baskets, and all such articles of personal luxury as a palace-building Pharaoh might delight in. Here also are the two famous harpers ; cruelly defaced, but still sweeping the strings with the old powerful touch that erewhile soothed the king in his hours of melancholy. These two spirited figures—which are un-doubtedly portraits [1]—almost redeem the poverty of the rest of the paintings.

In many tombs, the empty sarcophagus yet occupies its ancient place.[2] We saw one in No. 2 (Rameses IV), and another in No. 9 (Rameses VI) ; the first, a grand monolith

in as far as the choked condition of the tomb permitted, but the passage becomes quite impassable after the first thirty or forty yards.

[1] When first seen by Sir G. Wilkinson, these harpers were still in such good preservation, that he reported of one at least, if not both, as obviously blind. The harps are magnificent, richly inlaid and gilded, and adorned with busts of the king. One has eleven strings, the other fourteen.

[2] The sarcophagus of Seti I, which was brought to England by Belzoni, is in Sir J. Soane's Museum. It is carved from a single block of the finest alabaster, and is covered with incised hieroglyphic texts and several hundred figures, descriptive of the passage of the sun through the

of dark granite, overturned and but little injured ; the second, shattered by early treasure-seekers.

Most of the tombs at Bab-el-Molûk were open in Ptolemaic times. Being then, as now, among the stock sights and wonders of Thebes, they were visited by crowds of early travellers, who have as usual left their neatly-scribbled graffiti on the walls. When and by whom the sepulchres were originally violated is of course unknown. Some, doubtless, were sacked by the Persians ; others were plundered by the Egyptians themselves, long enough before Cambyses. Not even in the days of the Ramessides, though a special service of guards was told off for duty in "the Great Valley," were the kings safe in their tombs. During the reign of Rameses IX —whose own tomb is here, and known as No. 6—there seems to have been an organised band, not only of robbers, but of receivers, who lived by depredations of the kind. A contemporary papyrus[1] tells how in one instance the royal mummies

hours of the night. See *Le Sarcophage de Seti I.* P. PIERRET. *Révue Arch.* vol. xxi. p. 285 : 1870.

The sarcophagus of Rameses III is in the Fitz-William Museum, Cambridge, and the lid thereof is in the Egyptian collection of the Louvre. See *Remarks on the Sarcophagus of Rameses III.* S. BIRCH, LL.D. ; Cambridge, 1876. Also *Notice Sommaire des Monuments Egyptiens du Louvre.* E. DE ROUGÉ, p. 51 : Paris, 1873.

[1] Abbot Papyrus, British Museum. This papyrus, which has been translated by M. Chabas (*Mélanges Egyptologiques*, 3d Serie : Paris and Chalon, 1870), gives a list of royal tombs inspected by an Egyptian Commission in the month of Athyr (year unknown), during the reign of Rameses IX. Among the tombs visited on this occasion mention is especially made of "the funeral monument of the king En-Aa, which is at the north of the Amenophium of the terrace. The monument is broken into from the back, at the place where the stela is placed before the monument, and having the statue of the king upon the front of the stela, with his hound, named Bahuka, between his legs. Verified this day, and found intact." Such was the report of the writer of this papyrus of 3000 years ago. And now comes one of the wonders of modern discovery. It was but a few years ago that Mariette, excavating in that part of the Necropolis called the Assaseef, which lies to the north of the ruins of the Amenophium, discovered the remains of the tomb of this very king, and the broken stela bearing upon its face a full-length bas-relief of King En-Aa (or Entef-Aa), with three dogs before him and one between his legs ; the dog Bahuka having his name engraved over his back in hieroglyphic characters.—See *Tablet of Antefaa II.* S. BIRCH, LL.D. *Transactions of the Biblical Arch. Society*, vol. iv. part i. p. 172.

were found lying in the dust, their gold and silver ornaments, and the treasures of their tombs, all stolen. In another instance, a king and his queen were carried away bodily, to be unrolled and rifled at leisure. This curious information is all recorded in the form of a report, drawn up by the Commandant of Western Thebes, who, with certain other officers and magistrates, officially inspected the tombs of the " Royal Ancestors " during the reign of Rameses IX.

No royal tomb has been found absolutely intact in the valley of Bab-el-Molûk. Even that of Seti the First had been secretly entered ages before ever Belzoni discovered it. He found in it statues of wood and porcelain, and the mummy of a bull ; but nothing of value save the sarcophagus, which was empty. There can be no doubt that the priesthood were largely implicated in these contemporary sacrileges. Of thirty-nine persons accused by name in the papyrus just quoted, seven are priests, and eight are sacred scribes.

To rob the dead was always a lucrative trade at Thebes ; and we may be certain that the splendid Pharaohs who slept in the Valley of the Tombs of the Kings,[1] went to their dark

[1] The beautiful jewels found upon the mummy of Queen Aah-Hotep show how richly the royal dead were adorned, and how well worth plundering their sepulchres must have been. These jewels have been so often photographed, engraved, and described, that they are familiar to even those who have not seen them in the Boulak Museum. The circumstances of the discovery were suspicious, the mummy (in its inner mummy-case only) having been found by Mariette's diggers in the loose sand but a few feet below the surface, near the foot of the hillside known as Drah Abu'l Neggah, between Gournah and the opening to the Valley of the Tombs of the Kings. When it is remembered that the great outer sarcophagus of this Queen was found in 1881 in the famous vault at Dayr-el-Bahari, where so many royal personages and relics were discovered " at one fell swoop "; and when to this is added the curious fact that the state axe of Prince Kames, and a variety of beautiful poignards and other miscellaneous objects of value were found laid in the loose folds of this Queen's outer wrappings, it seems to me that the mystery of her unsepulchred burial is susceptible of a very simple explanation. My own conviction is that Queen Aah-Hotep's mummy had simply been brought thither from the depths of the said vault by the Arabs, who had for so many years possessed the secret of that famous hiding-place, and that it was temporarily buried in the sand till a convenient opportunity should occur for transporting to Luxor. Moreover, it is significant that no jewels were found upon the royal mummies in the Dayr-el-Bahari vault, for the

palaces magnificently equipped for the life to come.[1] When, indeed, one thinks of the jewels, furniture, vases, ointments, clothing, arms, and precious documents which were as certainly buried in those tombs as the royal mummies for whom they were excavated, it seems far more wonderful that the parure of one queen should have escaped, rather than that all the rest of these dead and gone royalties should have fallen among thieves.

Of all tombs in the Valley of Bab-el-Molûk, one would rather, I think, have discovered that of Rameses III. As he was one of the richest of the Pharaohs[2] and an undoubted

reason, no doubt, that they had long since been taken out and sold. The jewels found with Aah-Hotep may therefore have represented the final clearance, and have been collected from a variety of other royal mummy-cases. That the state axe of Prince Kames was among them does not, I imagine, prove that Prince Kames was the husband of Queen Aah-Hotep, but only that he himself was also a tenant of that historic vault. The actual proof that he was her husband lies in the fact that the bracelets on her wrists, the diadem on her head, and the pectoral ornament on her breast, were engraved, or inlaid, with the cartouches of that prince. [Note to Second Edition.]

[1] There is in one of the Papyri of the Louvre a very curious illustration, representing—1st, the funeral procession of one Neb-Set, deceased ; 2nd, the interior of the sepulchre, with the mummy, the offerings, and the furniture of the tomb, elaborately drawn and coloured. Among the objects here shown are two torches, three vases, a coffer, a mirror, a Kohl bottle, a pair of sandals, a staff, a vase for ointment, a perfume bottle, and an ablution jar. "These objects, all belonging to the toilette (for the coffer would have contained clothing), were placed in the tomb for that day of waking which the popular belief promised to the dead. The tomb was therefore furnished like the abodes of the living."—Translated from T. Devéria, *Catalogue des Manuscrits Egyptiens du Louvre :* Paris, 1875, p. 80. The plan of the sepulchre of Neb-Set is also drawn upon this papyrus ; and the soul of the deceased, represented as a human-headed bird, is shown flying down towards the mummy. A fine sarcophagus in the Boulak museum (No. 84) is decorated in like manner with a representation of the mummy on its bier being visited, or finally rejoined, by the soul. I have also in my own collection a funeral papyrus vignetted on one side with this same subject ; and bearing on the reverse side an architectural elevation of the monument erected over the sepulchre of the deceased.

[2] "King Rhampsinitus (Rameses III) was possessed, they said, of great riches in silver, indeed, to such an amount that none of the princes, his successors, surpassed or even equalled his wealth."—Herodotus, Book ii. chap. 121.

virtuoso in his tastes, so we may be sure that his tomb was furnished with all kinds of beautiful and precious things. What would we not give now to find some of those elaborate gold and silver vases, those cushioned thrones and sofas, those bows and quivers and shirts of mail so carefully catalogued on the walls of the side-chambers in the first corridor ! I do not doubt that specimens of all these things were buried with the king and left ready for his use. He died, believing that his Ka would enjoy and make use of these treasures, and that his soul would come back after long cycles of probation, and make its home once more in the mummied body. He thought he should rise as from sleep ; cast off his bandages ; eat and be refreshed, and put on sandals and scented vestments, and take his staff in his hand, and go forth again into the light of everlasting day. Poor ghost, wandering bodiless through space ! where now are thy funeral-baked meats, thy changes of raiment, thy perfumes and precious ointments ? Where is that body for which thou wert once so solicitous, and without which resurrection [1] is impossible ? One fancies thee sighing forlorn through these desolate halls when all is silent and the moon shines down the valley.

Life at Thebes is made up of incongruities. A morning among temples is followed by an afternoon of antiquity-hunting ; and a day of meditation among tombs winds up with a dinner-party on board some friend's dahabeeyah, or a fantasia at the British Consulate. L. and the Writer did their fair share of antiquity-hunting both at Luxor and elsewhere ; but chiefly at Luxor. I may say, indeed, that our life here was one long pursuit of the pleasures of the chase. The game, it is true, was prohibited ; but we enjoyed it none

---

[1] Impossible from the Egyptian point of view. "That the body should not waste or decay was an object of anxious solicitude ; and for this purpose various bandlets and amulets, prepared with certain magical preparations, and sanctified with certain spells or prayers, or even offerings and small sacrifices, were distributed over various parts of the mummy. In some mysterious manner the immortality of the body was deemed as important as the passage of the soul ; and at a later period the growth or natural reparation of the body was invoked as earnestly as the life or passage of the soul to the upper regions."—See *Introduction to the Funereal Ritual*, S. BIRCH, LL.D., in vol. v. of BUNSEN'S *Egypt :* Lond. 1867.

the less because it was illegal.   Perhaps we enjoyed it the more.

There were whispers about this time of a tomb that had been discovered on the western side—a wonderful tomb, rich in all kinds of treasures.   No one, of course, had seen these things.   No one knew who had found them.   No one knew where they were hidden.   But there was a solemn secrecy about certain of the Arabs, and a conscious look about some of the visitors, and an air of awakened vigilance about the government officials, which savoured of mystery.   These rumours by and by assumed more definite proportions.   Dark hints were dropped of a possible papyrus ; the M. B.'s babbled of mummies ; and an American dahabeeyah, lying innocently off Karnak, was reported to have a mummy on board.   Now, neither L. nor the Writer desired to become the happy proprietor of an ancient Egyptian ; but the papyrus was a thing to be thought of.   In a fatal hour we expressed a wish to see it.   From that moment every mummy-snatcher in the place regarded us as his lawful prey.   Beguiled into one den after another, we were shown all the stolen goods in Thebes. Some of the things were very curious and interesting.   In one house we were offered two bronze vases, each with a band of delicately-engraved hieroglyphs running round the lip ; also a square stand of basket-work in two colours, precisely like that engraved in Sir G. Wilkinson's first volume,[1] after the original in the Berlin Museum.   Pieces of mummy-case and wall-sculpture and sepulchral tablets abounded ; and on one occasion we were introduced into the presence of—a mummy !

All these houses were tombs, and in this one the mummy was stowed away in a kind of recess at the end of a long rock-cut passage ; probably the very place once occupied by the original tenant.   It was a mummy of the same period as that which we saw disentombed under the auspices of the Governor, and was enclosed in the same kind of cartonnage, patterned in many colours on a white ground.   I shall never forget that curious scene—the dark and dusty vault ; the Arabs with their

[1] *The Ancient Egyptians*, Sir G. Wilkinson ; vol. i. chap. ii. woodcut No. 92.   Lond. 1871.

lanterns ; the mummy in its gaudy cerements lying on an old mat at our feet.

Meanwhile we tried in vain to get sight of the coveted papyrus. A grave Arab dropped in once or twice after night-fall, and talked it over vaguely with the dragoman ; but never came to the point. He offered it first, with a mummy, for £100. Finding, however, that we would neither buy his papyrus unseen nor his mummy at any price, he haggled and hesitated for a day or two, evidently trying to play us off against some rival or rivals unknown, and then finally disappeared. These rivals, we afterwards found, were the M. B.'s. They bought both mummy and papyrus at an enormous price ; and then, unable to endure the perfume of their ancient Egyptian, drowned the dear departed at the end of a week.

Other purchasers are possibly less sensitive. We heard, at all events, of fifteen mummies successfully insinuated through the Alexandrian Custom-house by a single agent that winter. There is, in fact, a growing passion for mummies among Nile travellers. Unfortunately, the prices rise with the demand ; and although the mine is practically inexhaustible, a mummy nowadays becomes not only a prohibited, but a costly luxury.

At Luxor, the British, American, and French Consuls are Arabs. The Prussian Consul is a Copt. The Austrian Consul is, or was, an American. The French Consul showed us over the old tumble-down building called " The French House," [1] which, though but a rude structure of palm-timbers and sun-dried clay, built partly against and partly over the Temple of Luxor, has its place in history. For there, in 1829, Champollion

---

[1] The old French House is now swept away, with the rest of the modern Arab buildings which encumbered the ruins of the Temple of Luxor (see footnote, pp. 143, 144). I sketched it on the spot, and my sketch was reproduced as a whole-page illustration for the first edition of this book. Although the scene is now completely changed, that plate is re-issued with the present edition as a memento of the past, and as a fragment of recent history. With it, and by way of contrast, I am enabled, by the courtesy of the proprietor of the *Illustrated London News*, to give an engraving of part of the colonnade surrounding the sanctuary, over which the old French House was built. These particular columns, if I am not much mistaken, bounded the west side of the courtyard through which one passed to the flight of steps leading up to Lady Duff Gordon's rooms. [Note to Second Edition.]

THE "FRENCH HOUSE," LUXOR.

and Rosellini lived and worked together, during part of their long sojourn at Thebes. Rosellini tells how they used to sit up at night, dividing the fruits of the day's labour ;

COLUMNS OF AMENHOTEP III (LUXOR).

Champollion copying whatever might be useful for his Egyptian grammar, and Rosellini, the new words that furnished material for his dictionary. There, too, lodged the naval officers sent out by the French in 1831 to remove the obelisk which now stands in the Place de la Concorde. And there, writing those charming letters that delight the world, Lady Duff Gordon lingered through the last few winters of her life. The rooms in which she lived first, and the balcony in which she took such pleasure, were no longer accessible, owing to the ruinous state of one of the staircases ; but we saw the rooms she last inhabited. Her couch, her rug, her folding chair were there still. The walls were furnished with a few cheap prints and a pair of tin sconces. All was very bare and comfortless.

We asked if it was just like this when the Sittèh lived here. The Arab Consul replied that she had "a table, and some books." He looked himself in the last stage of consumption, and spoke and moved like one that had done with life.

We were shocked at the dreariness of the place—till we went to the window. That window, which commanded the Nile and the western plain of Thebes, furnished the room and made its poverty splendid.

The sun was near setting. We could distinguish the mounds and pylons of Medinet Habu and the site of the Ramesseum. The terraced cliffs, overtopped by the pyramidal mountain of Bab-el-Molûk, burned crimson against a sky of stainless blue. The footpath leading to the Valley of the Tombs of the Kings showed like a hot white scar winding along the face of the rocks. The river gave back the sapphire tones of the sky. I thought I could be well content to spend many a winter in no matter how comfortless a lodging, if only I had that wonderful view, with its infinite beauty of light and colour and space, and its history, and its mystery, always before my windows.[1]

Another historical house is that built by Sir G. Wilkinson, among the tombs of Sheykh Abd-el-Koorneh. Here he lived while amassing the materials for his *Manners and Customs of the Ancient Egyptians ;* and here Lepsius and his company of artists put up while at work on the western bank. Science

[1] Mehemet Ali gave this house to the French, and to the French it belonged till pulled down three years ago by Professor Maspero. [Note to Second Edition.]

makes little impression on the native mind. No one now remembers Champollion, or Rosellini, or Sir G. Wilkinson ; but every Arab in Luxor cherishes the memory of Lady Duff Gordon in his heart of hearts, and speaks of her with blessings.

The French House was built over the roof of the sanctuary, at the southern end of the Temple. At the northern end, built up between the enormous sandstone columns of the Great Colonnade, was the house of Mustapha Aga, most hospitable and kindly of British Consuls. Mustapha Aga had travelled in Europe, and spoke fluent Italian, English, and French. His eldest son was Governor of Luxor ; his younger—the " little Ahmed " whom Lady Duff Gordon delighted to educate—having spent two years in England as the guest of Lord D., had become an accomplished Englishman.

In the round of gaiety that goes on at Luxor the British Consulate played the leading part. Mustapha Aga entertained all the English dahabeeyahs, and all the English dahabeeyahs entertained Mustapha Aga. We were invited to several fantasias at the Consulate, and dined with Mustapha Aga at his suburban house the evening before we left Luxor.

The appointed hour was 8.30 P.M. We arrived amid much barking of dogs, and were received by our host in a large empty hall surrounded by a divan. Here we remained till dinner was announced. We were next ushered through an anteroom where two turbaned and barefooted servants were in waiting ; the one with a brass basin and ewer, the other with an armful of Turkish towels. We then, each in turn, held our hands over the basin ; had water poured on them ; and received a towel apiece. These towels we were told to keep ; and they served for dinner-napkins. The anteroom opened into a brilliantly-lighted dining-room of moderate size, having in the centre a round brass table with an upright fluted rim, like a big tray. For each person were placed a chair, a huge block of bread, a wooden spoon, two tumblers, and a bouquet. Plates, knives, forks, there were none.

The party consisted of the Happy Couple, the Director of the Luxor Telegraph Office, L., the Writer, Ahmed, and our host.

" To-night we are all Arabs," said Mustapha Aga, as he

showed us where to sit. "We drink Nile water, and we eat with our fingers."

So we drank Nile water ; and for the first time in our lives we ate with our fingers. In fact, we found them exceedingly useful.

The dinner was excellent. Without disrespect to our own accomplished chef, or to the accomplished chefs of our various friends upon the river, I am bound to say that it was the very best dinner I ever ate out of Europe. Everything was hot, quickly served, admirably dressed, and the best of its kind. Here is the *menu :*—

MENU.　MARCH 31, 1874.

———

White soup :—(Turkey).

FISH.
Fried Samak.[1]

ENTRÉES.

Stewed pigeons.　　　　　　　Spinach and rice.

ROAST.
Dall.[2]

ENTRÉES.

Kebobs [3] of mutton.　　　　Kebobs of lambs' kidneys.
Tomatoes with rice.　　　　　Kuftah.[4]

ROAST.
Turkey, with cucumber sauce.

ENTRÉE.
Pilaff [5] of rice.

SECOND COURSE.

Mish-mish.[6]　　　　　　　Rus Blebban.[8]
Kunáfah.[7]　　　　　　　　Totleh.[9]

---

[1] *Samak:* a large flat fish, rather like a brill.
[2] *Dall:* roast shoulder of lamb.
[3] *Kebobs :* small lumps of meat grilled on skewers.
[4] *Kuftah :* broiled mutton.
[5] *Pilaff:* boiled rice, mixed with a little butter, and seasoned with salt and pepper.
[6] *Mish-mish :* apricots (preserved).
[7] *Kunáfah :* a rich pudding made of rice, almonds, cream, cinnamon, etc. etc.
[8] *Rus Blebban :* rice cream.
[9] *Totleh :* sweet jelly, encrusted with blanched almonds.

These dishes were placed one at a time in the middle of the table, and rapidly changed. Each dipped his own spoon in the soup, dived into the stew, and pulled off pieces of fish or lamb with his fingers. Having no plates, we made plates of our bread. Meanwhile Mustapha Aga, like an attentive host, tore off an especially choice morsel now and then, and handed it to one or other of his guests.

To eat gracefully with one's fingers is a fine art ; to carve with them skilfully is a science. None of us, I think, will soon forget the wonderful way in which our host attacked and vanquished the turkey—a solid colossus weighing twenty lbs., and roasted to perfection. Half-rising, he turned back his cuff, poised his wrist, and, driving his forefinger and thumb deep into the breast, brought out a long, stringy, smoking fragment, which he deposited on the plate of the Writer. Thus begun, the turkey went round the table amid peals of laughter, and was punished by each in turn. The pilaff which followed is always the last dish served at an Egyptian or Turkish dinner. After this, our spoons were changed and the sweets were put upon the table. The drinks throughout were plain water, rice-water, and lemonade. Some native musicians played in the anteroom during dinner ; and when we rose from the table, we washed our hands as before.

We now returned to the large hall, and not being accomplished in the art and mystery of sitting cross-legged, curled ourselves up on the divans as best we could. The Writer was conducted by Mustapha Aga to the corner seat at the upper end of the room, where he said the Princess of Wales had sat when their Royal Highnesses dined with him the year before. We were then served with pipes and coffee. The gentlemen smoked chibouques and cigarettes, while for us there were gorgeous rose-water narghilehs with long flexible tubes and amber mouthpieces. L. had the Princess's pipe, and smoked it very cleverly all the evening.

By and by came the Governor, the Kadî of Luxor, the Prussian Consul and his son, and some three or four grave-looking merchants in rich silk robes and ample turbans. Meanwhile the band—two fiddles, a tambourine, and a darabukkeh—played at intervals at the lower end of the hall ; pipes,

coffee, and lemonade went continually round ; and the entertainment wound up, as native entertainments always do wind up at
Luxor, with a performance of Ghawâzi.

We had already seen these dancers at two previous fantasias, and we admired them no more the third time than the
first.   They wore baggy Turkish trowsers, loose gowns of gaudy
pattern, and a profusion of jewellery.   The *première danseuse*
was a fine woman and rather handsome ; but in the "belle" of
the company, a thick-lipped Nubian, we could discover no charm
whatever.   The performances of the Ghawâzi——which are very
ungraceful and almost wholly pantomimic——have been too often
described to need description here.   Only once, indeed, did we
see them perform an actual dance ; and then they swam lightly
to and fro, clattering their castanets, crossing and re-crossing,
and bounding every now and then down the whole length of
the room.   This dance, we were told, was of unknown antiquity.
They sang occasionally ; but their voices were harsh and their
melodies inharmonious.

There was present, however, one native performer whom we
had already heard many times, and of whose skill we never
tired.   This was the leader of the little band——an old man who
played the Kemengeh,[1] or cocoa-nut fiddle.   A more unpromising
instrument than the Kemengeh it would be difficult to conceive ;
yet our old Arab contrived to make it discourse most eloquent
music.   His solos consisted of plaintive airs and extemporised
variations, embroidered with difficult, and sometimes extrava-
gant, cadenzas.   He always began sedately, but warmed to his
work as he went on ; seeming at last to forget everything but
his own delight in his own music.   At such times one could
see that he was weaving some romance in his thoughts, and
translating it into sounds.   As the strings throbbed under his
fingers, the whole man became inspired ; and more than once
when, in shower after shower of keen despairing notes, he had
described the wildest anguish of passion, I have observed his
colour change and his hand tremble.

---

[1] The kemengeh is a kind of small two-stringed fiddle, the body of which
is made of half a cocoa-nut shell.   It has a very long neck, and a long foot
that rests upon the ground, like the foot of a violoncello ; and it is played
with a bow about a yard in length   The strings are of twisted horsehair.

Although we heard him repeatedly, and engaged him more than once when we had friends to dinner, I am sorry to say that I forget the name of this really great artist. He is, however, celebrated throughout the Thebaid, and is constantly summoned to Erment, Esneh, Keneh, Girgeh, and other large towns, to perform at private entertainments.

While at Luxor, we went one Sunday morning to the Coptic church—a large building at the northern extremity of the village. Church, schools, and Bishop's house, are here grouped under one roof and enclosed in a courtyard ; for Luxor is the centre of one of the twelve sees into which Coptic Egypt is divided.

The church, which has been rebuilt of late years, is constructed of sun-dried brick, having a small apse towards the east, and at the lower or western end a screened atrium for the women. The centre aisle is perhaps thirty feet in width ; the side-aisles, if aisles they can be called, being thickly planted with stone pillars supporting round arches. These pillars came from Karnak, and were the gift of the Khedive. They have lotus-bud capitals, and measure about fifteen feet high in the shaft. At the upper end of the nave, some eighteen or twenty feet in advance of the apse, there stands a very beautiful screen inlaid in the old Coptic style with cedar, ebony, rosewood, ivory, and mother-of-pearl. This screen is the pride of the church. Through the opening in the centre, one looks straight into the little waggon-roofed apse, which contains a small table and a suspended lamp, and is as dark as the sanctuary of an Egyptian temple. The reading-desk, like a rickety office stool, faces the congregation ; and just inside the screen stands the Bishop's chair. Upon this plan, which closely resembles the plan of the first cathedral of St. Peter at Rome, most Coptic churches are built. They vary chiefly in the number of apses, some having as many as five. The atrium generally contains a large tank, called the Epiphany tank, into which, in memory of the baptism of our Lord, the men plunge at their festival of El Ghitâs.

Young Todroos, the son of the Prussian Consul, conducted us to the church. We went in at about eleven o'clock and witnessed the end of the service, which had then been going on since daybreak. The atrium was crowded with women and children, and the side-aisles with men of the poorer sort. A few groups of better dressed Copts were gathered near the screen listening to a black-robed deacon, who stood reading at the reading desk with a lighted taper in his left hand. A priest in a white vestment embroidered on the breast and hood with a red Maltese cross, was squatting on his heels at the entrance to the adytum. The Bishop, all in black with a black turban, sat with his back to the congregation.

Every face was turned upon us when we came in. The reader paused. The white-robed priest got up. Even the Bishop looked round. Presently a couple of acolytes, each carrying two cane-bottomed chairs, came bustling down the nave ; and, unceremoniously driving away all who were standing near, placed us in a row across the middle of the church. This interruption over, the reading was resumed.

We now observed with some surprise that every word of the lessons as they were read in Coptic was translated, *viva voce*, into Arabic by a youth in a surplice, who stood against the screen facing the congregation. He had no book, but went on fluently enough, following close upon the voice of the reader. This, we were told, was done only during the reading of the lessons, the Gospel, and the Lord's Prayer. The rest of the service is performed without translation ; and, the Coptic being a dead language, is consequently unintelligible to the people.

When the reading of the Gospel was over, the deacon retired. The priest then came forward and made a sign to the school children, who ran up noisily from all parts of the church, and joined with the choristers in a wild kind of chant. It seemed to us that this chant concluded the first part of the service.

The second part closely resembled the celebration of mass. The priest came to the door of the screen ; looked at the congregation ; folded his hands palm to palm ; went up to the threshold of the apse, and began reciting what sounded like a litany. He then uncovered the sacred vessels, which till now had been concealed under two blue cotton handkerchiefs, and, turning, shook the handkerchiefs towards the people. He then consecrated the wine and wafer ; elevated the host ; and himself partook of the Eucharist in both elements. A little bell was rung during the consecration and again at the elevation. The people, meanwhile, stood very reverently, with their heads bent ; but no one knelt during any part of the service. After this, the officiating priest washed his hands in a brass basin ; and the deacon—who was also the schoolmaster—came round the church holding up his scarf, which was heaped full of little cakes of unleavened bread. These he distributed to all present. An acolyte followed with a plate, and collected the offerings of the congregation.

We now thought the service was over ; but there remained four wee, crumpled, brown mites of babies to be christened. These small Copts were carried up the church by four acolytes, followed by four anxious fathers. The priest then muttered a short prayer ; crossed the babies with water from the basin in which he had washed his hands ; drank the water ; wiped the basin out with a piece of bread ; ate the bread ; and dismissed the little newly-made Christians with a hasty blessing.

Finally, the Bishop—who had taken no part in the service, nor even partaken of the Eucharist—came down from his chair, and stood before the altar to bless the congregation. Hereupon all the men and boys ranged themselves in single file and trooped through between the screen and the apse, crowding in at one side and out at the other ; each being touched by the Bishop on his cheek, as he went by. If they lagged, the Bishop clapped his hands impatiently, and the schoolmaster drove them through faster. When there were no more to come (the women and little girls, be it observed, coming in for no share of this benediction), the priest took off his vestments and laid them in a heap on the altar ; the deacon distributed a basketful of blessed cakes among the poor of the congregation ; and the Bishop walked down the nave, eating a cake and giving a bit here and there to the best dressed Copts as he went along. So ended this interesting and curious service, which I have described thus minutely for the reason that it represents, with probably but little change, the earliest ceremonial of Christian worship in Egypt.[1]

[1] "The Copts are Christians of the sect called Jacobites, Eutychians,

Before leaving, we asked permission to look at the books from which the service had been read. They were all very old and dilapidated. The New Testament, however, was in better condition than the rest, and was beautifully written upon vellum, in red and black ink. The Coptic, of course, looks like Greek to the eyes of the uninitiated ; but some of the illuminated capitals struck us as bearing a marked resemblance to certain of the more familiar hieroglyphic characters.

While we were examining the books, the Bishop sent his servant to invite us to pay him a visit. We accordingly followed the man up an outer flight of wooden steps at one corner of the courtyard, and were shown into a large room built partly over the church. Here we found the Bishop— handsome, plump, dignified, with soft brown eyes, and a slightly grizzled beard—seated cross-legged on a divan, and smoking his chibouque. On a table in the middle of the room stood two or three blue and white bottles of Oriental porcelain. The windows, which were sashless and very large, looked over to Karnak. The sparrows flew in and out as they listed.

The Bishop received us very amiably, and the proceedings opened as usual with pipes and coffee. The conversation which followed consisted chiefly of questions on our part, and of answers on his. We asked the extent of his diocese, and learned that it reached from Assûan on the south to Keneh on the north. The revenue of the see, he said, was wholly derived from endowments in land. He estimated the number of Copts in Luxor at 2000, being two-thirds of the entire population. The church was built and decorated in the time of his pre-decessor. He had himself been Bishop here for rather more than four years. We then spoke of the service we had just witnessed, and of the books we had seen. I showed him my

Monophysites, and Monothelites, whose creed was condemned by the Council of Chalcedon in the reign of the Emperor Marcian. They received the appellation of 'Jacobites,' by which they are generally known, from Jacobus Baradæus, a Syrian, who was a chief propagator of the Eutychian doctrines. . . . The religious orders of the Coptic Church consist of a patriarch, a metropolitan of the Abyssinians, bishops, arch-priests, priests, deacons, and monks. In Abyssinia, Jacobite Christianity is still the prevailing religion." See *The Modern Egyptians;* by E. W. LANE. Supplement 1, p. 531. London : 1860.

prayer-book, which he examined with much curiosity. I explained the differences indicated by the black and the rubricated matter, and pointed out the parts that were sung. He was, however, more interested in the outside than in the contents, and tapped the binding once or twice, to see if it were leather or wood. As for the gilt corners and clasp, he undoubtedly took them for solid gold.

The conversation next turned upon Coptic ; the Idle Man asking him if he believed it to be the tongue actually spoken by the ancient Egyptians.

To this he replied :—

" Yes, undoubtedly. What else should it be ?"

The Idle Man hereupon suggested that it seemed to him, from what he had just seen of the church books, as if it might be a corrupt form of Byzantine Greek.

The Bishop shook his head.

" The Coptic is a distinct language," he said. " Eight Greek letters were added to the Coptic alphabet upon the introduction of Christianity into Egypt ; and since that time many Greek words have been imported into the Coptic vocabulary ; but the main body of the tongue is Coptic, purely ; and it has no radical affinity whatever with the Greek."[1]

---

[1] The Bishop was for the most part right. The Coptic *is* the ancient Egyptian language (that is to say, it is late and somewhat corrupt Egyptian) written in Greek characters instead of in hieroglyphs. For the abolition of the ancient writing was, next to the abolition of the images of the Gods, one of the first great objects of the early Church in Egypt. Unable to uproot and destroy the language of a great nation, the Christian Fathers took care so to reclothe it that every trace of the old symbolism should disappear and be forgotten. Already, in the time of Clement of Alexandria (A.D. 211), the hieroglyphic style had become obsolete. The secret of reading hieroglyphs, however, was not lost till the time of the fall of the Eastern Empire. How the lost key was recovered by Champollion is told in a quotation from Mariette Bey, in the footnote to p. 211, chapter xii. of this book. Of the relation of Coptic to Egyptian, Champollion says : " La langue égyptienne antique ne différait en rien de la langue appelée vulgairement Copte ou Cophte. . . . Les mots égyptiens écrits en caractères hiéroglyphiques sur les monuments les plus anciens de Thèbes, et en caractères Grecs dans les livres Coptes, ne différent en général que par l'absence de certaines voyelles médiales omises, selon la méthode orientale, dans l'orthographe primitive." —*Grammaire Egyptienne*, p. 18.

The Bishop, though perfectly right in stating that Coptic and Egyptian

This was the longest speech we heard him make, and he delivered it with some emphasis.

I then asked him if the Coptic was in all respects a dead language ; to which he replied that many Coptic words, such as the names of the months and of certain festivals, were still in daily use. This, however, was not quite what I meant ; so I put the question in another form, and asked if he thought any fragments of the tongue yet survived among the peasantry.

He pondered a moment before replying.

" That," he said, " is a question to which it is difficult to give a precise answer, but I think you might yet find, in some of the remoter villages, an old man here and there who would understand it a little."

I thought this a very interesting reply to a very interesting question.

After sitting about half an hour we rose and took leave. The Bishop shook hands with us all round, and, but that we protested against it, would have accompanied us to the head of the stairs.

This interview was altogether very pleasant. The Copts are said to be sullen in manner, and so bigoted that even a Moslem is less an object of dislike to them than a Christian of any other denomination. However this may be, we saw nothing of it. We experienced, on the contrary, many acts of civility from the Copts with whom we were brought into communication. No traveller in Egypt should, I think, omit being present at a service in a Coptic church. For a Coptic church is now the only place in which one may hear the last utterances of that far-off race with whose pursuits and pleasures the tomb-paintings make us so familiar. We know that great changes have come over the language since it was spoken by Rameses

were one, and that the Coptic was a distinct language having no affinity with the Greek, was, however, entirely wrong in that part of his explanation which related to the alphabet. So far from eight Greek letters having been added to the Coptic alphabet upon the introduction of Christianity into Egypt, there was no such thing as a Coptic alphabet previous to that time. The Coptic alphabet is the Greek alphabet as imposed upon Egypt by the Fathers of the early Greek Church ; and that alphabet being found insufficient to convey all the sounds of the Egyptian tongue, eight new characters were borrowed from the demotic to supplement the deficiency.

the Great and written by Pentaur. We know that the Coptic of to-day bears to the Egyptian of the Pharaohs some such resemblance, perhaps, as the English of Macaulay bears to the English of Chaucer. Yet it is at bottom the tongue of old Egypt, and it is something to hear the last lingering echoes of that ancient speech read by the undoubted descendants of the Egyptian people. In another fifty years or so, the Coptic will in all probability be superseded by the Arabic in the services of this Church ; and then the very tradition of its pronunciation will be lost. The Copts themselves, it is said, are fast going over to the dominant faith. Perhaps by the time our own descendants are counting the two thousandth anniversary of the Christian era, both Copts and Coptic will be extinct in Egypt.

A day or two after this we dropped down to Karnak, where we remained till the end of the week, and on the following Sunday we resumed our downward voyage.

If the universe of literature was unconditioned, and the present book was independent of time and space, I would write another chapter here about Karnak. But Karnak, to be fairly dealt by, would ask, not a chapter, but a volume. So, having already told something of the impression first made upon us by that wilderness of wonders, I will say no more.

CHAPTER XXII.

ABYDUS AND CAIRO.

OUR last weeks on the Nile went by like one long, lazy, summer's day. Events now were few. We had out-stayed all our fellow-travellers. Even the faithful Bagstones had long since vanished northwards; and the Philæ was the last daha-beeyah of the year. Of the great sights of the river, we had only Abydus and Beni Hassan left to see; while for minor excursions, daily walks, and explorations by the way, we had little energy left. For the thermometer was rising higher and the Nile was falling lower every day; and we should have been more than mortal, if we had not felt the languid influences of the glowing Egyptian Spring.

The natives call it spring; but to our northern fancy it is spring, summer, and autumn in one. Of the splendour of the skies, of the lavish bounty of the soil at this season, only those who have lingered late in the land can form any conception. There is a breadth of repose now about the landscape which it has never worn before. The winter green of the palms is fading fast. The harvests are ripening; the pigeons are pairing; the time of the singing of birds is come. There is just enough south wind most days to keep the boat straight, and the sail from flapping. The heat is great; yet it is a heat which, up to a certain point, one can enjoy. The men ply their oars by night; and sleep under their benches, or croon old songs and tell stories among themselves, by day. But for the thin canopy of smoke that hangs over the villages, one would fancy now that those clusters of mud-huts were all deserted. Not a human being is to be seen on the banks when the sun is high. The buffaloes stand up to their necks in the shallows. The donkeys huddle together wherever there is shade. The very dogs have given up barking, and lie asleep under the walls.

The whole face of the country, and even of the Nile, is wonderfully changed since we first passed this way. The land, then newly squared off like a gigantic chess-board and intersected by thousands of little channels, is now one sea of yellowing grain. The river is become a labyrinth of sandbanks, some large, some small; some just beginning to thrust their heads above water; others so long that they divide the river for a mile or more at a stretch. Reïs Hassan spends half his life at the prow, poling for shallows; and when we thread our way down one of these sandy straits, it is for all the world like a bit of the Suez Canal. The banks, too, are twice as steep as they were when we went up. The lentil patches, which then blossomed on the slope next the water's edge, now lie far back on the top of a steep brown ridge, at the foot of which stretches a moist flat planted with water-melons. Each melon-plant is protected from the sun by a tiny gable-roof of palm-thatch.

Meanwhile, the river being low and the banks high, we unfortunates benefit scarcely at all by the faint breezes that now and then ruffle the barley. Day by day, the thermometer (which hangs in the coolest corner of the saloon) creeps up higher and higher, working its way by degrees to above 99°; but never succeeding in getting up quite to 100°. We, however, living in semi-darkness, with closed jalousies, and wet sails hung round the sides of the dahabeeyah, and wet towels hung up in our cabins, find 99° quite warm enough to be pleasant. The upper deck is of course well deluged several times a day; but even so, it is difficult to keep the timbers from starting. Meanwhile L. and the Idle Man devote their leisure to killing flies, keeping the towels wet, and sprinkling the floors.

Our progress all this time is of the slowest. The men cannot row by day; and at night the sandbanks so hedge us in with dangers, that the only possible way by which we can make a few miles between sunset and sunrise is by sheer hard

punting.   Now and then we come to a clear channel, and
sometimes we get an hour or two of sweet south breeze ; but
these flashes of good luck are few and far between.

In such wise, and in such a temperature, we found ourselves
becalmed one morning within six miles of Denderah.   Not even
L. could be induced to take a six-mile donkey-ride that day
in the sun.   The Writer, however, ordered out her sketching-
tent and paid a last visit to the Temple ; which, seen amid the
ripening splendour of miles of barley, looked gloomier, and
grander, and more solitary than ever.

Two or three days later, we came within reach of Abydus.
Our proper course would have been to push on to Bellianeh,
which is one of the recognised starting-points for Abydus.
But an unlucky sandbank barred the way ; so we moored
instead at Samata, a village about two miles nearer to the
southward.   Here our dragoman requisitioned the inhabitants
for donkeys.   As it happened, the harvest had begun in the
neighbourhood and all the beasts of burden were at work, so
that it was near midday before we succeeded in getting
together the three or four wretched little brutes with which
we finally started.   Not one of these steeds had ever before
carried a rider.   We had a frightful time with them.   My
donkey bolted about every five minutes.   L.'s snarled like a
camel and showed its teeth like a dog.   The Idle Man's, bent
on flattening its rider, lay down and rolled at short intervals.
In this exciting fashion, we somehow or another accomplished
the seven miles that separate Samata from Abydus.

Skirting some palm-groves and crossing the dry bed of a
canal, we came out upon a vast plain, level as a lake, islanded
here and there with villages, and presenting one undulating
surface of bearded corn.   This plain—the plain of ancient
Thinis—runs parallel with the Nile, like the plain of Thebes,
and is bounded to the westward by a range of flat-topped
mountains.   The distance between the river and the mountains
however, is here much greater than at Thebes, being full six
miles ; while to north and south the view ends only with the
horizon.

Our way lies at first by a bridle-track through the thick of
the barley ; then falls into the Bellianeh road—a raised causeway

embanked some twenty feet above the plain.   Along this road, the country folk are coming and going.   In the cleared spaces where the maize has been cut, little encampments of straw huts have sprung up.   Yonder, steering their way by unseen paths, go strings of camels ; their gawky necks and humped backs undulating above the surface of the corn, like galleys with fantastic prows upon a sea of rippling green.   The pigeons fly in great clouds from village to village.   The larks are singing and circling madly in the clear depths overhead.   The bee-eaters flash like live emeralds across our path.   The hoopoes strut by the wayside.   At rather more than half-way across the plain, we come into the midst of the harvest.   Here the brown reapers, barelegged and naked to the waist, are at work with their sickles, just as they are pictured in the tomb of Tih. The women and children follow, gleaning, at the heels of those who bind the sheaves.   The Sheykh in his black robe and scarlet slippers rides to and fro upon his ass, like Boaz among his people.   As the sheaves are bound up, the camels carry them homeward.   A camel-load is fourteen sheaves ; seven to each side of the hump.   A little farther, and the oxen, yoked two and two, are ploughing up the stubble.   In a day or two, the land will be sown with millet, indigo, or cotton, to be gathered in once more before the coming of the inundation.

Meanwhile, as the plain lengthens behind us and the distance grows less between ourselves and the mountains, we see a line of huge irregular mounds reaching for apparently a couple of miles or more along the foot of the cliffs.   From afar off, the mounds look as if crowned by majestic ruins ; but as we draw nearer, these outlines resolve themselves into the village of Arabát-el-Madfûneh, which stands upon part of the mounds of Abydus.   And now we come to the end of the cultivated plain—that strange line of demarcation where the inundation stops and the desert begins.   Of actual desert, however, there is here but a narrow strip, forming a first step, as it were, above the alluvial plain.   Next comes the artificial platform, about a quarter of a mile in depth, on which stands the modern village ; and next again, towering up sheer and steep, the great wall of limestone precipice.   The village is extensive, and the houses, built in a rustic Arabesque, tell of a well-to-do population.   Arched gateways ornamented with black, white, and red bricks, windows of turned lattice-work, and pigeon-towers in courses of pots and bricks, give a singular picturesqueness to the place ; while the slope down to the desert is covered with shrubberies and palms.   Below these hanging gardens, on the edge of the desert, lies the cut corn in piles of sheaves.   Here the camels are lying down to be unladen. Yonder the oxen are already treading out the grain, or chopping the straw by means of a curious sledge-like machine set with revolving rows of circular knives.[1]   Meanwhile, fluttering from heap to heap, settling on the sheaves, feeding unmolested in the very midst of the threshing floors, strutting all over the margin of the desert, trailing their wings, ruffling their plumes, cooing, curtseying, kissing, courting, filling the air with sweet sounds and setting the whole lovely idyll to a pastoral symphony of their own composing, are thousands and tens of thousands of pigeons.[2]

Now our path turns aside and we thread our way among the houses, noticing here a sculptured block built into a mud wall—yonder, beside a dried-up well, a broken alabaster sarcophagus—farther on, a granite column still erect, in the midst of a palm-garden.   And now, the village being left behind, we find ourselves at the foot of a great hill of newly excavated rubbish, from the top of which we presently look down into a kind of crater, and see the Great Temple of Abydus at our feet.

It was now nearly three o'clock ; so, having seen what we could in the time, and having before us a long ride through a strange country, we left again at six.   I will not presume to describe the Temples of Abydus—one of which is so ruined as

---

[1] This machine is called the Nóreg.

[2] The number of pigeons kept by the Egyptian fellahîn is incredible. Mr. Zincke says on this subject that "the number of domestic pigeons in Egypt must be several times as great as the population," and suggests that if the people kept pigs, they would keep less pigeons.   But it is not as food chiefly that the pigeons are encouraged.   They are bred and let live in such ruinous numbers for the sake of the manure they deposit on the land.   M. About has forcibly demonstrated the error of this calculation. He shows that the pigeons do thirty million francs' worth of damage to the crops in excess of any benefit they may confer upon the soil.

to be almost unintelligible, and the other so singularly planned and so obscure in its general purport, as to be a standing puzzle to archæologists—after a short visit of three hours. Enough if I sketch briefly what I saw but cursorily.

Buried as it is, Abydus,[1] even under its mounds, is a place of profound historical interest. At a time so remote that it precedes all written record of Egyptian story, there existed a little way to the northward of this site a city called Teni.[2] We know not to what aboriginal community of prehistoric Egypt this city belonged; but here, presumedly, the men of Kem[3] built their first Temple, evolved their first notions of art, and groped their way to an alphabet which in its origin was probably a mere picture-writing, like the picture-writing of Mexico. Hence, too, came a man named Mena, whose cartouche from immemorial time has stood first in the long list of Egyptian Pharaohs. Of Mena,[4] a shadowy figure hovering on the border-land of history and tradition, we know only that he was the first primitive

---

[1] The Arabic name of the modern village, Arabát-el-Madfûneh, means literally Arabat the Buried.

[2] *Teni*, or more probably Tini, called by the Greeks This or Thinis. It was the capital of the VIIIth Nome. " Quoique nous ayons très-peu de chose à rapporter sur l'histoire de la ville de Teni qui à la basse époque sous la domination romaine, n'était connue que par ses teinturiers en pourpre, elle doit avoir joui d'une très grande renommée chez les anciens Egyptiens. Encore au temps du XIXeme dynastie les plus hauts fonctionnaires de sang royal étaient distingués par le titre de ' Princes de Teni.' " —*Hist. d'Egypte.* BRUGSCH, vol. i. chap. v. p. 29 ; Leipzig, 1874.

NOTE TO SECOND EDITION.—" Des monuments trouvés il y a deux ans, me portent a croire que Thini était située assez loin à l'Est au village actuel de Aoulad-Yahia." Letter of Prof. G. Maspero to the author, April 1878.

[3] The ancient name of Egypt was *Kem, Khem*, or *Kam*, signifying Black, or the Black Land ; in allusion to the colour of the soil.

[4] " Mena, tel que nous le presente la tradition, est le type le plus complet du monarque égyptien. Il est à la fois constructeur et législateur : il fonde le grande temple de Phtah à Memphis et régle le culte des dieux. Il est guerrier, et conduit les expéditions hors de ses frontières."—*Hist. Ancienne des Peuples de l'Orient.* G. MASPERO. Chap. ii. p. 55 : Paris, 1876.

" N'oublions pas qu'avant Ménès l'Egypte était divisée en petits royaumes indépendants que Ménès réunit le premier sous un sceptre unique. Il n'est pas impossible que des monuments de cette antique période de l'histoire Egyptienne subsistent encore."—*Itinéraire de la Haute Egypte.* A. MARIETTE BEY. Avant Propos, p. 40. Alexandrie, 1872.

chieftain who took the title of King of Upper and Lower Egypt, and that he went northward and founded Memphis. Not, however, till after some centuries was the seat of government removed to the new city. Teni—the supposed burial-place of Osiris—then lost its political importance ; but continued to be for long ages the Holy City of Egypt.

In the meanwhile, Abydus had sprung up close to Teni. Abydus, however, though an important city, was never the capital of Egypt. The seat of power shifted strangely with different dynasties, being established now in the Delta, now at Thebes, now at Elephantine ; but having once departed from the site which, by reason of its central position and the unbounded fertility of its neighbourhood, was above all others best fitted to play this great part in the history of the country, it never again returned to the point from which it had started. That point, however, was unquestionably the centre from which the great Egyptian people departed upon its wonderful career. Here was the nursery of its strength. Hence it derived its proud title to an unmixed autochthonous descent. For no greater proof of the native origin of the race can be adduced than the position which their first city occupies upon the map of Egypt. That any tribe of colonists should have made straight for the heart of the country and there have established themselves in the midst of barbarous and probably hostile aborigines, is evidently out of the question. It is, on the other hand, equally clear that if Egypt had been colonised from Asia or Ethiopia, the strangers would on the one hand have founded their earliest settlement in the neighbourhood of the Isthmus ; or on the other, have halted first among the then well-watered plains of Nubia.[1] But the Egyptians started from the fertile heart of their own mother country, and began by being great at home.

Abydus and Teni, planted on the same platform of desert, were probably united at one time by a straggling suburb in-

---

[1] See Opening Address of Professor R. OWEN, C.B., etc. etc., *Report of Proceedings of the Second International Congress of Orientalists, Ethnological Section :* London, 1874. Also a paper on " The Ethnology of Egypt," by the same, published in the *Journal of the Anthropological Institute*, vol. iv. No. 1, p. 246 : Lond. 1874.

habited by the embalmers and other tradesfolk concerned in
the business of death and burial. A chain of mounds, excavated
only where the Temples were situated, now stands to us for
the famous city of Abydus. An ancient crude-brick enclosure
and an artificial tumulus mark the site of Teni. The Temples
and the tumulus, divided by the now exhausted necropolis,
are about as distant from one another as Medinet Habu and
the Ramesseum.

There must have been many older Temples at Abydus
than these which we now see, one of which was built by Seti I,
and the other by Rameses II. Or possibly, as in so many
instances, the more ancient buildings were pulled down and
rebuilt. Be this as it may, the Temple of Seti, as regards its
sculptured decorations, is one of the most beautiful of Egyptian
ruins ; and as regards its plan, is one of the most singular.
A row of square limestone piers, which must once have supported an architrave, are now all that remains of the façade.
Immediately behind these comes a portico of twenty-four
columns leading by seven entrances to a hall of thirty-six
columns. This hall again opens into seven parallel sanctuaries,
behind which lie another hall of columns and a number of
small chambers. So much of the building seems to be homogeneous. Adjoining this block, however, and leading from it
by doorways at the southern end of the great hall, come
several more halls and chambers connected by corridors, and
conducting apparently to more chambers not yet excavated.
All these piers, columns, halls, and passages, and all the seven
sanctuaries,[1] are most delicately sculptured and brilliantly
coloured.

[1] M. Mariette, in his great work on the excavations at Abydus,
observes that these seven vaulted sanctuaries resemble sarcophagi of
the form most commonly in use : namely, oblong boxes with vaulted lids.
Two sarcophagi of this shape are shown in cut 496 of Sir G. Wilkinson's
second volume (see figures 1 and 6), *A Popular Account of the Ancient
Egyptians*, vol. ii. chap. x. ; Lond. 1871. Of the uses and purport of the
temple, he also says—" What do we know of the *idée mère* that presided
at its construction ? What was done in it ? Is it consecrated to a single
divinity, who would be Osiris ; or to seven Gods, who would be the Seven
Gods of the seven vaulted chambers ; or to the nine divinities enumerated
in the lists of deities dispersed in various parts of the temple ? . . . One
leaves the temple in despair, not at being unable to make out its secret

There is so far a family resemblance between Temples of the same style and period, that after a little experience one can generally guess before crossing the threshold of a fresh building, what one is likely to see in the way of sculptures within. But almost every subject in the Temple of Seti at Abydus is new and strange. All the Gods of the Egyptian pantheon seem to have been worshipped here, and to have had each his separate shrine. The walls are covered with paintings of these shrines and their occupants ; while before each the King is represented performing some act of adoration. A huge blue frog, a grey-hound, a double-headed goose, a human-bodied creature with a Nilometer for its head,[1] and many more than I can now remember, are thus depicted. The royal offerings, too, though incense and necklaces and pectoral ornaments abound, are for the most part of a kind that we have not seen before. In one

from the inscriptions, but on finding that its secret has been kept for itself alone, and not trusted to the inscriptions."—*Description des Fouilles d'Abydos.* MARIETTE BEY. Paris, 1869.

" Les sept chambres voûtées du grand temple d'Abydos sont relatifs aux cérémonies que le roi devait y célébrer successivement. Le roi se présentait au côté droit de la porte, parcourait la salle dans tout son pourtour et sortait par le côté gauche. Des statues étaient disposées dans la chambre. Le roi ouvrait la porte ou naos où elles étaient enfermées. Dès que la statue apparaissait à ses yeux il lui offrait l'encens, il enlevait le vêtement qui la couvrait, il lui imposait les mains, il la parfumait, il la recouvrait de son vêtement," etc. etc.—MARIETTE BEY. *Itinéraire de la Haute Egypte :* Avant Propos, p. 62. Alex. 1872.

There is at the upper end of each of these seven sanctuaries a singular kind of false door, or recess, conceived in a style of ornament more Indian than Egyptian, the cutting being curiously square, deep, and massive, the surface of the relief-work flattened, and the whole evidently intended to produce its effect by depths of shadow in the incised portions rather than by sculpturesque relief. These recesses, or imitation doors, may have been designed to serve as backgrounds to statues, but are not deep enough for niches. There is a precisely similar recess sculptured on one of the walls of the westernmost chamber in the Temple of Gournah.

[1] These are all representations of minor Gods commonly figured in the funereal papyri, but very rarely seen in the Temple sculptures. The frog Goddess, for instance, is Hek, and symbolises eternity. She is a very ancient divinity, traces of her being found in monuments of the Vth Dynasty. The goose-headed God is Seb, another very old God. The object called the Nilometer was a religious emblem signifying stability, and probably stands in this connection as only a deified symbol.

place the King presents to Isis a column with four capitals, having on the top capital a globe and two asps surmounted by a pair of ostrich feathers.

The centre sanctuary of the seven appears to be dedicated to Khem, who seems to be here, as in the great Temple of Seti at Karnak, the presiding divinity. In this principal sanctuary, which is resplendent with colour and in marvellous preservation, we especially observed a portrait of Rameses II [1] in the act of opening the door of a shrine by means of a golden key formed like a human hand and arm. The lock seems to consist of a number of bolts of unequal length, each of which is pushed back in turn by means of the forefinger of the little hand. This, doubtless, gives a correct representation of the kind of locks in use at that time.

It was in a corridor opening out from the great hall in this Temple that Mariette discovered that precious sculpture known as the New Tablet of Abydus. In this tableau, Seti I and Rameses II are seen, the one offering incense, the other reciting a hymn of praise, to the manes of seventy-six Pharaohs,[2] beginning with Mena, and ending with Seti himself. To our great disappointment—though one cannot but acquiesce in the necessity for precaution—we found the

---

[1] Rameses II is here shown with the side-lock of youth. This Temple, founded by Seti I, was carried on through the time when Rameses the prince was associated with his father upon the throne, and was completed by Rameses the King, after the death of Seti I. The building is strictly coeval in date and parallel in style with the Temple of Gournah and the Speos of Bayt-el-Welly.

[2] These seventy-six Pharaohs (represented by their cartouches) were probably either princes born of families originally from Abydus, or were sovereigns who had acquired a special title to veneration at this place on account of monuments or pious foundations presented by them to the holy city. A similar tablet, erected apparently on the same principles though not altogether to the same kings, was placed by Thothmes III in a side chamber of the Great Temple at Karnak, and is now in the Louvre. The great value of the present monument consists in its chronological arrangement. It is also of most beautiful execution, and in perfect preservation. " Comme perfection de gravure, comme conservation, comme étendue, il est peu de monuments qui la depassent." See *La Nouvelle Table d'Abydos*, par A. MARIETTE BEY : *Révue Arch.* vol. vii. *Nouvelle Série*, p. 98. This volume of the Review also contains an engraving in outline of the Tablet.

entrance to this corridor closed and mounded up. A ragged old Arab who haunts the Temple in the character of custode, told us that the tablet could now only be seen by special permission.

We seemed to have been here about half an hour when the guide came to warn us of approaching evening. We had yet the site and the great Tumulus of Teni to see; the tumulus being distant about twenty minutes' ride. The guide shook his head; but we insisted on going. The afternoon had darkened over; and for the first time in many months a gathering canopy of cloud shut out the glory of sunset. We, however, mounted our donkeys and rode northwards. With better beasts we might perhaps have gained our end; as it was, seeing that it grew darker every moment, we presently gave in, and instead of trying to push on farther, contented ourselves with climbing a high mound which commanded the view towards Teni.

The clouds by this time were fast closing round, and waves of shadows were creeping over the plain. To our left rose the near mountain-barrier, dusk and lowering; to our right stretched the misty corn-flats; at our feet, all hillocks and open graves, lay the desolate necropolis. Beyond the palms that fringed the edge of the desert—beyond a dark streak that marked the site of Teni—rose, purple in shadow against the twilight, a steep and solitary hill. This hill, called by the natives Kom-es-Sultan, or the Mound of the King, was the tumulus we so desired to see. Viewed from a distance and by so uncertain a light, it looked exactly like a volcanic cone of perhaps a couple of hundred feet in height. It is however wholly artificial, and consists of a mass of graves heaped one above another in historic strata; each layer, as it were, the record of an era; the whole, a kind of human coral reef built up from age to age with the ashes of generations.

For some years past, the Egyptian Government had been gradually excavating this extraordinary mound. The lower it was opened, the more ancient were its contents. So steadily retrogressive, indeed, were the interments, that it seemed as if the spade of the digger might possibly strike tombs of the First Dynasty, and so restore to light relics of men who lived in the age of Mena. "According to Plutarch," wrote Mariette,[1] "wealthy Egyptians came from all parts of Egypt to be buried at Abydus, in order that their bones might rest near Osiris. Very probably the tombs of Kom-es-Sultan belong to those personages mentioned by Plutarch. Nor is this the only interest attaching to the mound of Kom-es-Sultan. The famous tomb of Osiris cannot be far distant ; and certain indications lead us to think that it is excavated in precisely that foundation of rock which serves as the nucleus of this mound. Thus the persons buried in Kom-es-Sultan lay as near as possible to the divine tomb. The works now in progress at this point have therefore a twofold interest. They may yield tombs yet more and more ancient—tombs even of the First Dynasty ; and some day or another they may discover to us the hitherto unknown and hidden entrance to the tomb of the God."[2]

I bitterly regretted at the time that I could not at least ride to the foot of Kom-es-Sultan ; but I think now that I prefer to remember it as I saw it from afar off, clothed with mystery, in the gloom of that dusky evening.

There was a heavy silence in the air, and a melancholy as of the burden of ages. The tumbled hillocks looked like a ghastly sea, and beyond the verge of the desert it was already night. Presently, from among the grave-pits, there crept towards us a slowly-moving cloud. As it drew nearer—soft, filmy, shifting, unreal—it proved to be the dust raised by an immense flock of sheep. On they came, a brown compact mass, their shepherd showing dimly now and then, through openings in the cloud. The last pale gleam from above caught them for a moment ere they melted, ghost-like, into the murky plain. Then we went down ourselves, and threaded the track between the mounds and the valley. Palms and houses loomed vaguely out of the dusk ; and a caravan of camels, stalking by with swift and noiseless footfall, looked like shadows projected

---

[1] See *Itinéraire de la Haute Egypte :* A. MARIETTE BEY : p. 147. Alex. 1872.

[2] *Ibid.* p. 148. The hope here expressed was, however, not fulfilled ; tombs of the IVth or Vth Dynasties being, I believe, the earliest discovered. [Note to Second Edition.]

on a background of mist. As the night deepened the air
became stifling. There were no stars, and we could scarcely
see a yard before us. Crawling slowly along the steep causeway, we felt, but could distinguish nothing of the plain
stretching away on either side. Meanwhile the frogs croaked
furiously, and our donkeys stumbled at every step. When at
length we drew near Samata, it was close upon ten o'clock,
and Reïs Hassan had just started with men and torches to
meet us.

Next morning early we once again passed Girgeh, with its
ruined mosque and still unfallen column ; and about noonday
moored at a place called Ayserat, where we paid a visit to a
native gentleman, one Ahmed Abû Ratab Aga, to whom we
carried letters of introduction. Ratab Aga owns large estates
in this province ; is great in horse-flesh ; and lives in patriarchal
fashion surrounded by a numerous cian of kinsfolk and dependants. His residence at Ayserat consists of a cluster of three or
four large houses, a score or so of pigeon-towers, an extensive
garden, stabling, exercising-ground, and a large courtyard ; the
whole enclosed by a wall of circuit, and entered by a fine
Arabesque gateway. He received us in a loggia of lattice-
work overlooking the courtyard, and had three of his finest
horses—a grey, a bay, and a chestnut—brought out for us to
admire. They were just such horses as Velasquez loved to
paint—thick in the neck, small in the head, solid in the barrel,
with wavy manes, and long silky tails set high and standing off
straight in true Arab fashion. We doubted, however, that they
were altogether *pur sang*. They looked wonderfully picturesque
with their gold - embroidered saddlecloths, peaked saddles
covered with crimson, green, and blue velvet, long shovel-stirrups
and tasselled head-gear. The Aga's brother and nephews put
them through their paces. They knelt to be mounted ; lay
down and died at the word of command ; dashed from perfect
immobility into a furious gallop ; and when at fullest speed,
stopped short, flung themselves back upon their haunches, and
stood like horses of stone. We were told that our host had a
hundred such standing in his stables. Pipes, coffee, and an
endless succession of different kinds of sherbets went round all
the time our visit lasted ; and in the course of conversation, we

learned that not only the wages of agricultural labourers, but even part of the taxes to the Khedive, are here paid in corn.

Before leaving, L., the Little Lady, and the Writer were conducted to the hareem, and introduced to the ladies of the establishment. We found them in a separate building with a separate courtyard, living after the usual dreary way of Eastern women, with apparently no kind of occupation and not even a garden to walk in. The Aga's principal wife (I believe he had but two) was a beautiful woman, with auburn hair, soft brown eyes, and a lovely complexion. She received us on the threshold, led us into a saloon surrounded by a divan, and with some pride showed us her five children. The eldest was a graceful girl of thirteen ; the youngest, a little fellow of four. Mother and daughter were dressed alike in black robes embroidered with silver, pink velvet slippers on bare feet, silver bracelets and anklets, and full pink Turkish trowsers. They wore their hair cut straight across the brow, plaited in long tails behind, and dressed with coins and pendants ; while from the back of the head there hung a veil of thin black gauze, also embroidered with silver. Another lady, whom we took for the second wife, and who was extremely plain, had still richer and more massive ornaments, but seemed to hold an inferior position in the hareem. There were perhaps a dozen women and girls in all, two of whom were black.

One of the little boys had been ill all his short life, and looked as if he could not last many more months. The poor mother implored us to prescribe for him. It was in vain to tell her that we knew nothing of the nature of his disease and had no skill to cure it. She still entreated, and would take no refusal ; so in pity we sent her some harmless medicines.

We had little opportunity of observing domestic life in Egypt. L. visited some of the vice-regal hareems at Cairo, and brought away on each occasion the same impression of dreariness. A little embroidery, a few musical toys of Geneva manufacture, a daily drive on the Shubra road, pipes, cigarettes, sweetmeats, jewellery, and gossip, fill up the aimless days of most Egyptian ladies of rank. There are, however, some who take an active interest in politics ; and in Cairo and Alexandria the opera-boxes of the Khedive and the great Pashas are

nightly occupied by ladies.   But it is not by the daily life of
the wives of princes and nobles, but by the life of the lesser
gentry and upper middle-class, that a domestic system should
be judged.   These ladies of Ayserat had no London-built
brougham, no Shubra road, no opera.   They were absolutely
without mental resources ; and they were even without the
means of taking air and exercise.   One could see that time
hung heavy on their hands, and that they took but a feeble
interest in the things around them.   The hareem stairs were
dirty ; the rooms were untidy ; the general aspect of the place
was slatternly and neglected.   As for the inmates, though all
good-nature and gentleness, their faces bore the expression of
people who are habitually bored.   At Luxor, L. and the Writer
paid a visit to the wife of an intelligent and gentlemanly Arab,
son of the late governor of that place.   This was a middle-class
hareem.   The couple were young, and not rich.   They occupied a small house, which commanded no view and had no
garden.   Their little courtyard was given up to the poultry ;
their tiny terrace above was less than twelve feet square ; and
they were surrounded on all sides by houses.   Yet in this
stifling prison the young wife lived, apparently contented, from
year's end to year's end.   She literally never went out.   As a
child, she had no doubt enjoyed some kind of liberty ; but as
a marriageable girl, and as a bride, she was as much a prisoner
as a bird in a cage.   Born and bred in Luxor, she had never
seen Karnak ; yet Karnak is only two miles distant.   We asked
her if she would like to go there with us ; but she laughed
and shook her head.   She was incapable even of curiosity.

It seemed to us that the wives of the Fellahîn were in
truth the happiest women in Egypt.   They work hard and are
bitterly poor ; but they have the free use of their limbs, and
they at least know the fresh air, the sunshine, and the open
fields.

When we left Ayserat, there still lay 335 miles between us
and Cairo.   From this time, the navigation of the Nile became
every day more difficult.   The dahabeeyah, too, got heated
through and through, so that not even sluicing and swabbing
availed to keep down the temperature.   At night when we
went to our sleeping cabins, the timbers alongside of our berths

were as hot to the hand as a screen in front of a great fire. Our crew, though to the manner born, suffered even more than ourselves ; and L. at this time had generally a case of sunstroke on her hands. One by one, we passed the places we had seen on our way up — Siût, Manfalût, Gebel Abufayda, Roda,

SAKKIEH AT SIÛT.

Minieh. After all, we did not see Beni Hassan. The day we reached that part of the river, a furious sandstorm was raging ; such a storm that even the Writer was daunted. Three days later, we took the rail at Bibbeh and went on tó Cairo, leaving the Philæ to follow as fast as wind and weather might permit.

We were so wedded by this time to dahabeeyah-life, that we felt lost at first in the big rooms at Shepheard's Hotel, and altogether bewildered in the crowded streets. Yet here was Cairo, more picturesque, more beautiful than ever. Here were the same merchants squatting on the same carpets and smoking the same pipes, in the Tunis bazaar ; here was the same old cake-seller still ensconced in the same doorway in the Muski ; here were the same jewellers selling bracelets in the Khan-Khalîli ; the same money-changers sitting behind their little tables at the corners of the streets ; the same veiled ladies riding on donkeys and driving in carriages ; the same hurrying funerals, and noisy weddings ; the same odd cries, and motley costumes, and unaccustomed trades. Nothing was changed. We soon dropped back into the old life of sight-seeing and shopping—buying rugs and silks, and silver ornaments, and old embroideries, and Turkish slippers, and all sorts of antique and pretty trifles ; going from Mohammedan mosques to rare old Coptic churches ; dropping in for an hour or two most afternoons at the Boulak Museum ; and generally ending the day's work with a drive on the Shubra road, or a stroll round the Esbekiyeh Gardens.

" IN THE NAME OF THE PROPHET—CAKES! "

The Môlid-en-Nebi, or Festival of the Birth of the Prophet, was being held at this time in a tract of waste ground on the road to Old Cairo. Here, in some twenty or thirty large open tents ranged in a circle, there were readings of the Koran and meetings of dervishes going on by day and night, without intermission, for nearly a fortnight. After dark, when the tents were all ablaze with lighted chandeliers, and the dervishes were howling and leaping, and fireworks were being let off from an illuminated platform in the middle of the area, the scene was extraordinary. All Cairo used to be there, on foot or in carriages, between eight o'clock and midnight every evening ; the veiled ladies of the Khedive's hareem in their miniature broughams being foremost among the spectators.

The Môlid-en-Nebi ends with the performance of the Dóseh, when the Sheykh of the Saädîyeh Dervishes rides over a road of prostrate fanatics. L. and the Writer witnessed this sight from the tent of the Governor of Cairo. Drunk with opium, fasting, and praying, rolling their heads, and foaming at the mouth, some hundreds of wretched creatures lay down in the road packed as close as paving stones, and were walked and ridden over before our eyes. The standard-bearers came first ; then a priest reading the Koran aloud ; then the Sheykh on his white Arab, supported on either side by barefooted priests. The beautiful horse trod with evident reluctance, and as lightly and swiftly as possible, on the human causeway under his hoofs. The Mohammedans aver that no one is injured, or even bruised,[1] on this holy occasion ; but I saw some men carried away in convulsions, who looked as if they would never walk again.[2]

It is difficult to say but a few inadequate words of a place about which an instructive volume might be written ; yet to pass the Boulak Museum in silence is impossible. This famous collection is due, in the first instance, to the liberality of the late Khedive and the labours of Mariette. With the exception of Mehemet Ali, who excavated the Temple of Denderah, no previous Viceroy of Egypt had ever interested himself in the

---

[1] " It is said that these persons, as well as the Sheykh, make use of certain words (that is, repeat prayers and invocations) on the day preceding this performance, to enable them to endure without injury the tread of the horse ; and that some not thus prepared, having ventured to lie down to be ridden over, have, on more than one occasion, been either killed or severely injured. The performance is considered as a miracle vouchsafed through supernatural power, and which has been granted to every successive Sheykh of the Saädeeyeh." See Lane's *Modern Egyptians,* chap. xxiv. p. 453. Lond. 1860.

[2] This barbarous rite has been abolished by the present Khedive [Note to Second Edition.]

archæology of the country. Those who cared for such rubbish
as encumbered the soil or lay hidden beneath the sands of the
desert, were free to take it ; and no favour was more frequently
asked, or more readily granted, than permission to dig for "anteekahs." Hence the Egyptian wealth of our museums. Hence
the numerous private collections dispersed throughout Europe.
Ismail Pasha, however, put an end to that wholesale pillage; and,
for the first time since ever " mummy was sold for balsam," or
for bric-à-brac, it became illegal to export antiquities. Thus,
for the first time, Egypt began to possess a national collection.

Youngest of great museums, the Boulak collection is the
wealthiest in the world in portrait-statues of private individuals,
in funerary tablets, in amulets, and in personal relics of the
ancient inhabitants of the Nile Valley. It is necessarily less
rich in such colossal statues as fill the great galleries of the
British Museum, the Turin Museum, and the Louvre. These,
being above ground and comparatively few in number, were
for the most part seized upon long since, and transported to
Europe. The Boulak statues are the product of the tombs.
The famous wooden " Sheykh " about which so much has been
written,[1] the magnificent diorite statue of Khafra (Chephren),
the builder of the Second Pyramid, the two marvellous sitting
statues of Prince Ra-hotep and Princess Nefer-t, are all
portraits ; and, like their tombs, were executed during the
lifetime of the persons represented. Crossing the threshold of
the Great Vestibule,[2] one is surrounded by a host of these
extraordinary figures, erect, coloured, clothed, all but in
motion. It is like entering the crowded anteroom of a royal
palace in the time of the Ancient Empire.

The greater number of the Boulak portrait-statues are
sculptured in what is called the hieratic attitude ; that is, with
the left arm down and pressed close to the body, the left hand
holding a roll of papyrus, the right leg advanced, and the right

[1] See *Egypt of the Pharaohs and the Khedive*, J. B. ZINCKE, chap. ix. p.
72. Lond. 1873. Also *La Sculpture Egyptienne*, par E. SOLDI, p. 57.
Paris, 1876. Also *The Ethnology of Egypt*, by PROFESSOR OWEN, C.B.
Journal of Anthropological Institute, vol. iv. 1874, p. 227. The name of
this personage was Ra-em-ka.
[2] It is in the Great Vestibule that we find the statue of Ti. See chap.
iv. p. 59.

hand raised, as grasping the walking staff. It occurred to me
that there might be a deeper significance than at first sight
appears in this conventional attitude, and that it perhaps
suggests the moment of resurrection, when the deceased, holding
fast by his copy of the Book of the Dead, walks forth from his
tomb into the light of life eternal.

Of all the statues here—one may say, indeed, of all known
Egyptian statues—those of Prince Ra-hotep and Princess
Nefer-t are the most wonderful. They are probably the oldest

portrait-statues in the world.[1] They come from a tomb of the
IIIrd Dynasty, and are contemporary with Snefru, a king who
reigned before the time of Khufu and Khafra. That is to say,
these people who sit before us side by side, coloured to the
life, fresh and glowing as the day when they gave the artist
his last sitting, lived at a time when the great pyramids of
Ghîzeh were not yet built, and at a date which is variously
calculated as from about 6300 to 4000 years before the

[1] There is no evidence to show that the statues of Sepa and Nesa in
the Louvre are older than the IVth Dynasty.

present day.   The princess wears her hair precisely as it is still
worn in Nubia, and her necklace of cabochon drops is of a
pattern much favoured by the modern Ghawâzi.   The eyes of
both statues are inserted.   The eyeball, which is set in an
eyelid of bronze, is made of opaque white quartz, with an iris
of rock-crystal enclosing a pupil of some kind of brilliant metal.
This treatment—of which there are one or two other instances
extant—gives to the eyes a look of intelligence that is almost
appalling.   There is a play of light within the orb, and
apparently a living moisture upon the surface, which has never
been approached by the most skilfully made glass eyes of
modern manufacture.[1]

Of the jewels of Queen Aah-hotep, of the superb series of
engraved scarabæi, of the rings, amulets, and toilette ornaments,
of the vases in bronze, silver, alabaster, and porcelain, of the
libation-tables, the woven stuffs, the terra-cottas, the artists'
models, the lamps, the silver boats, the weapons, the papyri,
the thousand-and-one curious personal relics and articles of
domestic use which are brought together within these walls,
I have no space to tell.   Except the collection of Pompeian

[1] " Enfin nous signalerons l'importance des statues de Meydoum au
point de vue ethnographique.   Si la race Egyptienne était à cette époque
celle dont les deux statues nous offrent le type, il faut convenir qu'elle ne
ressemblait en rien à la race qui habitait le nord de l'Egypte quelques
années seulement après Snefrou."—*Cat. du Musée de Boulaq.*   A. MARIETTE
BEY.   P. 277 ; Paris, 1872.

Of the heads of these two statues Professor Owen remarks that " the
brain-case of the male is a full oval, the parietal bosses feebly indicated ;
in vertical contour the fronto-parietal part is little elevated, rather flattened
than convex ; the frontal sinuses are slightly indicated ; the forehead is
fairly developed but not prominent.   The lips are fuller than in the
majority of Europeans ; but the mouth is not prognathic. . . . The
features of the female conform in type to those of the male, but show more
delicacy and finish. . . . The statue of the female is coloured of a lighter
tint than that of the male, indicating the effects of better clothing and
less exposure to the sun.   And here it may be remarked that the racial
character of complexion is significantly manifested by such evidences of
the degree of tint due to individual exposure. . . . The primitive race-tint
of the Egyptians is perhaps more truly indicated by the colour of the
princess in these painted portrait-statues than by that of her more scantily
clad husband or male relative."—*The Ethnology of Egypt*, by SIR RICHARD
OWEN, K.C.B.   *Journal of Anthropological Institute*, vol. iv. Lond. 1874 ;
p. 225 *et seq.*

relics in Naples, there is nothing elsewhere to compare with the collection at Boulak ; and the villas of Pompeii have yielded no such gems and jewels as the tombs of ancient Egypt. It is not too much to say that if these dead and mummied people could come back to earth, the priest would here find all the Gods of his Pantheon ; the king his sceptre ; the queen her crown-jewels ; the scribe his palette ; the soldier his arms ; the workman his tools ; the barber his razors ; the husbandman his hoe ; the housewife her broom ; the child his toys ; the beauty her combs and kohl bottles and mirrors. The furniture of the house is here, as well as the furniture of the tomb. Here, too, is the broken sistrum buried with the dead in token of the grief of the living.

Waiting the construction of a more suitable edifice, the present building gives temporary shelter to the collection. In the meanwhile, if there was nothing else to tempt the traveller to Cairo, the Boulak Museum would alone be worth the journey from Europe.

The first excursion one makes on returning to Cairo, the last one makes before leaving, is to Ghîzeh. It is impossible to get tired of the Pyramids. Here L. and the Writer spent their last day with the Happy Couple.

We left Cairo early, and met all the market-folk coming in from the country—donkeys and carts laden with green stuff, and veiled women with towers of baskets on their heads. The Khedive's new palace was swarming already with masons, and files of camels were bringing limestone blocks for the builders. Next comes the open corn-plain, part yellow, part green— the long straight road bordered with acacias—beyond all, the desert-platform, and the Pyramids, half in light, half in greenish-grey shadow, against the horizon. I never could understand why it is that the Second Pyramid, though it is smaller and farther off, looks from this point of view bigger than the First. Farther on, the brown Fellahîn, knee-deep in purple blossom, are cutting the clover. The camels carry it away. The goats and buffaloes feed in the clearings. Then comes the half-way tomb nestled in greenery, where men and horses stay to drink ; and soon we are skirting a great back-water which reflects the pyramids like a mirror. Villages, shâdûfs, herds and flocks, tracts of palms, corn-flats, and spaces of rich, dark fallow, now succeed each other ; and then once more comes the sandy slope, and the cavernous ridge of ancient yellow rock, and the Great Pyramid with its shadow-side towards us, darkening the light of day.

Neither L. nor the Writer went inside the Great Pyramid. The Idle Man did so this day, and L.'s maid on another occasion ; and both reported of the place as so stifling within, so foul· underfoot, and so fatiguing, that, somehow, we each time put it off, and ended by missing it. The ascent is extremely easy. Rugged and huge as are the blocks, there is scarcely one upon which it is not possible to find a half-way rest for the toe of one's boot, so as to divide the distance. With the help of three Arabs, nothing can well be less fatiguing. As for the men, they are helpful and courteous, and as clever as possible ; and coax one on from block to block in all the languages of Europe.

"Pazienza, Signora ! Allez doucement—all serene ! We half-way now—dem halben-weg, Fräulein. Ne vous pressez-pas, Mademoiselle. Chi va sano, va lontano. Six step more, and ecco la cima !"

"You should add the other half of the proverb, amici," said I. "Chi va forte, va alla morte."

My Arabs had never heard this before, and were delighted with it. They repeated it again and again, and committed it to memory with great satisfaction. I asked them why they did not cut steps in the blocks, so as to make the ascent easier for ladies. The answer was ready and honest.

"No, no, Mademoiselle ! Arab very stupid to do that. If Arab makes good steps, Howadji goes up alone. No more want Arab man to help him up, and Arab man earn no more dollars !"

They offered to sing "Yankee Doodle" when we reached the top ; then, finding we were English, shouted "God save the Queen !" and told us that the Prince of Wales had given £40 to the Pyramid Arabs when he came here with the Princess two years before ; which, however, we took the liberty to doubt.

The space on the top of the Great Pyramid is said to be 30 feet square. It is not, as I had expected, a level platform.

Some blocks of the next tier remain, and two or three of the tier next above that ; so making pleasant seats and shady corners. What struck us most on reaching the top, was the startling nearness, to all appearance, of the Second Pyramid. It seemed to rise up beside us like a mountain ; yet so close, that I fancied I could almost touch it by putting out my hand. Every detail of the surface, every crack and parti-coloured stain in the shining stucco that yet clings about the apex, was distinctly visible.

The view from this place is immense. The country is so flat, the atmosphere so clear, the standpoint so isolated, that one really sees more and sees farther than from many a mountain summit of ten or twelve thousand feet. The ground

SPHINX AND PYRAMIDS.

lies, as it were, immediately under one ; and the great Necropolis is seen as in a ground-plan. The effect must, I imagine, be exactly like the effect of a landscape seen from a balloon. Without ascending the Pyramid, it is certainly not possible to form a clear notion of the way in which this great burial-field is laid out. We see from this point how each royal pyramid is surrounded by its quadrangle of lesser tombs, some in the form of small pyramids, others partly rock-cut, partly built of massive slabs, like the roofing-stones of the Temples.

We see how Khufu and Khafra and Menkara lay, each under his mountain of stone, with his family and his nobles around him. We see the great causeways which moved Herodotus to such wonder, and along which the giant stones were brought. Recognising how clearly the place is a great cemetery, one marvels at the ingenious theories which turn the pyramids into astronomical observatories, and abstruse standards of measurement. They are the grandest graves [1] in all the world—and they are nothing more.

A little way to the southward, from the midst of a sandy hollow, rises the head of the Sphinx. Older than the Pyramids, older than history, the monster lies couchant like a watch-dog, looking ever to the east, as if for some dawn that has not yet risen.[2] A depression in the sand close by marks the site of

[1] The word *pyramid*, for which so many derivations have been suggested, is shown in the Geometrical Papyrus of the British Museum to be distinctly Egyptian, and is written *Per-em-us*.

[2] " On sait par une stèle du musée de Boulaq, que le grand Sphinx est antérieur au Rois Chéops de la IVᵉ Dynastie." *Dic. d'Arch. Egyptienne :* Article *Sphinx.* P. PIERRET. Paris, 1875.

[It was the opinion of Mariette, and is the opinion of Professor Maspero, that the Sphinx dates from the inconceivably remote period of the *Horshesu,* or " followers of Horus "; that is to say, from those prehistoric times when Egypt was ruled by a number of petty chieftains, before Mena welded the ancient principalities into a united kingdom. Those principalities then became the Nomes, or Provinces, of historic times ; and the former local chieftains became semi-independent feudatories, such as we find surviving with undiminished authority and importance during the XIIth Dynasty.— Note to Second Edition.]

A long-disputed question as to the meaning of the Sphinx has of late been finally solved. The Sphinx is shown by M. J. de Rougé, according to an inscription at Edfu, to represent a transformation of Horus, who in order to vanquish Set (Typhon) took the shape of a human-headed lion. It was under this form that Horus was adored in the Nome Leontopolites. In the above-mentioned Stela of Boulak, known as the stone of Cheops, the Great Sphinx is especially designated as the Sphinx of Hor-em-Khou, or Horus-on-the-Horizon. This is evidently in reference to the orientation of the figure. It has often been asked why the Sphinx is turned to the east. I presume the answer would be, Because Horus, avenger of Osiris, looks to the east, awaiting the return of his father from the lower world. As Horus was supposed to have reigned over Egypt, every Pharaoh took the title of Living Horus, Golden Hawk, etc. etc. Hence the features of the reigning King were always given to the Sphinx form when architecturally employed, as at Karnak, Wady Sabooah, Tanis, etc. etc.

that strange monument miscalled the Temple of the Sphinx.[1]
Farther away to the west on the highest slope of this part of
the desert platform, stands the Pyramid of Menkara (Mycerinus).
It has lost but five feet of its original height, and from this
distance it looks quite perfect.

Such—set in a waste of desert—are the main objects, and
the nearest objects, on which our eyes first rest. As a whole,
the view is more long than wide, being bounded to the westward
by the Libyan range, and to the eastward by the Mokattam hills.
At the foot of those yellow hills, divided from us by the cultivated plain across which we have just driven, lies Cairo, all
glittering domes half seen through a sunlit haze. Overlooking
the fairy city stands the Mosque of the Citadel, its mast-like
minarets piercing the clearer atmosphere. Far to the northward, traversing reach after reach of shadowy palm-groves, the
eye loses itself in the dim and fertile distances of the Delta.
To the west and south, all is desert. It begins here at our
feet—a rolling wilderness of valleys and slopes and rivers and
seas of sand, broken here and there by abrupt ridges of rock,
and mounds of ruined masonry, and open graves. A silver
line skirts the edge of this dead world, and vanishes southward
in the sun-mist that shimmers on the farthest horizon. To the
left of that silver line we see the quarried cliffs of Turra,
marble-white ; opposite Turra, the plumy palms of Memphis.
On the desert platform above, clear though faint, the Pyramids
of Abusîr and Sakkârah, and Dahshûr. Every stage of the

---

[1] It is certainly not a Temple. It may be a mastaba, or votive chapel.
It looks most like a tomb. It is entirely built of plain and highly-polished
monoliths of alabaster and red granite, laid square and simply, like a sort
of costly and magnificent Stonehenge ; and it consists of a forecourt, a hall
of pillars, three principal chambers, some smaller chambers, a secret recess,
and a well. The chambers contain horizontal niches which it is difficult
to suppose could have been intended for anything but the reception of
mummies ; and at the bottom of the well were found three statues of King
Khafra (Chephren) ; one of which is the famous diorite portrait-statue of
the Boulak Museum. In an interesting article contributed to the *Révue
Arch.* (vol. xxvi. Paris, 1873), M. du Barry-Merval has shown, as it
seems, quite clearly, that the Temple of the Sphinx is in fact a dependency
of the Second Pyramid. It is possible that the niches may have been
designed for the Queen and family of Khafra, whose own mummy would of
course be buried in his Pyramid.

Pyramid of Ouenephes, banded in light and shade, is plain to
see.   So is the dome-like summit of the great Pyramid of
Dahshûr.   Even the brick ruin beside it which we took for a
black rock as we went up the river, and which looks like a
black rock still, is perfectly visible.   Farthest of them all,
showing pale and sharp amid the palpitating blaze of noon,
stands, like an unfinished tower of Babel, the Pyramid of
Meydûm.   It is in this direction that our eyes turn oftenest—
to the measureless desert in its mystery of light and silence ;
to the Nile where it gleams out again and again, till it melts at
last into that faint far distance beyond which lie Thebes, and
Philæ, and Abou Simbel.

APPENDIX I.

A. M'CALLUM, Esq., to the EDITOR of 'THE TIMES.'[1]

SIR—It may interest your readers to learn that at the south side of the great Temple of Abou Simbel, I found the entrance to a painted chamber rock-cut, and measuring 21 ft. 2½ in., by 14 ft. 8 in., and 12 ft. high to the spring of the arch, elaborately sculptured and painted in the best style of the best period of Egyptian art, bearing the portraits of Rameses the Great and his cartouches, and in a state of the highest preservation. This chamber is preceded by the ruins of a vaulted atrium, in sun-dried brickwork, and adjoins the remains of what would appear to be a massive wall or pylon, which contains a staircase terminating in an arched doorway leading to the vaulted atrium before mentioned.

The doorway of the painted chamber, the staircase, and the arch, were all buried in sand and débris. The chamber appears to have been covered and lost sight of since a very early period, being wholly free from mutilation, and from the scribbling of travellers ancient and modern.

The staircase was not opened until the 18th, and the bones of a woman and child, with two small cinerary urns, were there discovered by a gentleman of our party, buried in the sand. This was doubtless a subsequent interment. Whether this painted chamber is the inner sanctuary of a small Temple, or part of a tomb, or only a speos, like the well-known grottoes at Ibrim, is a question for future excavators to determine.—I have the honour to be, Sir, yours, etc. etc.

ANDREW M'CALLUM.

KOROSKO, NUBIA, *Feb.* 16*th*, 1874.

APPENDIX II.

THE EGYPTIAN PANTHEON.

"THE deities of ancient Egypt consist of celestial, terrestrial, and infernal gods, and of many inferior personages, either representatives of the greater gods or else attendants upon them. Most of the gods were connected with the Sun, and represented that luminary in its passage through the upper hemisphere or Heaven and the lower hemisphere or Hades. To the deities of the Solar cycle belonged the great gods of Thebes and Heliopolis. In the local worship of Egypt the deities were arranged in local triads : thus, at Memphis, Ptah, his wife Merienptah, and their son Nefer Atum, formed a triad, to which was sometimes added the goddess Bast or Bubastis. At Abydus the local triad was Osiris, Isis, and Horus, with Nephthys ; at Thebes,

---

[1] This letter appeared in 'The Times' of March 18th, 1874.

Amen-Ra or Ammon, Mut, and Chons, with Neith ; at Elephantine, Kneph, Anuka, Seti, and Hak. In most instances the names of the gods are Egyptian ; thus, Ptah meant 'the opener' ; Amen, 'the concealed'; Ra, 'the sun' or 'day' ; Athor, 'the house of Horus' ; but some few, especially of later times, were introduced from Semitic sources, as Bal or Baal, Astaruta or Astarte, Khen or Kiun, Respu or Reseph. Besides the principal gods, several inferior or parhedral gods, sometimes personifications of the faculties, senses, and other objects, are introduced into the religious system, and genii, spirits, or personified souls of deities formed part of the same. At a period subsequent to their first introduction the gods were divided into three orders. The first or highest comprised eight deities, who were different in the Memphian and Theban systems. They were supposed to have reigned over Egypt before the time of mortals. The eight gods of the first order at Memphis were— 1. Ptah ; 2 Shu ; 3. Tefnu ; 4. Seb,; 5. Nut ; 6. Osiris ; 7. Isis and Horus ; 8. Athor. Those of Thebes were—1. Amen-Ra ; 2. Mentu ; 3. Atum ; 4. Shu and Tefnu ; 5. Seb ; 6. Osiris ; 7. Set and Nephthys ; 8. Horus and Athor. The gods of the second order were twelve in number, but the name of one only, an Egyptian Hercules, has been preserved. The third order is stated to have comprised Osiris, who, it will be seen, belonged to the first order."—*Guide to the First and Second Egyptian Rooms ; Brit. Musæ.* S. BIRCH, 1874.

The Gods most commonly represented upon the monuments are Phtah, Knum, Ra, Amen-Ra, Khem, Osiris, Nefer Atum or Tum, Thoth, Seb, Set, Khons, Horus, Maut, Neith, Isis, Nut, Hathor, and Bast. They are distinguished by the following attributes :—

Phtah, or *Ptah :*—In form a mummy, holding the emblem called by some the Nilometer, by others the emblem of Stability. Called " the Father of the Beginning, the Creator of the Egg of the Sun and Moon." Chief Deity of Memphis.

Kneph, Knum, or *Knouphis·*—Ram-headed. Called the Maker of Gods and men ; the Soul of the Gods. Chief Deity of Elephantine and the Cataracts.

Ra :—Hawk-headed, and crowned with the sun-disk encircled by an asp. The divine disposer and organiser of the world. Adored throughout Egypt.

Amen-Ra :—Of human form, crowned with a flat-topped cap and two long straight plumes ; clothed in the schenti ; his flesh sometimes painted blue. There are various forms of this god (see footnote, p. 341), but he is most generally described as King of the Gods. Chief Deity of Thebes.

Khem :—Of human form mummified ; wears headdress of Amen-Ra ; his right hand uplifted, holding the flail. The God of productiveness and generation. Chief Deity of Khemmis, or Ekhmeem. Is identified in later times with Amen, and called Amen-Khem.

Osiris :—Of human form, mummified, crowned with a mitre, and holding the flail and crook. Called the Good Being ; the Lord above all ; the One Lord. Was the God of the lower world ; Judge of the dead ; and representative of the Sun below the horizon. Adored throughout Egypt. Local Deity of Abydus.

Nefer Atum :—Human-headed, and crowned with the pschent. This God represented the setting sun, or the sun descending to light the lower world. Local Deity of Heliopolis.

Thoth :—In form a man, ibis-headed, generally depicted with the pen and palette of a scribe. Was the God of the moon, and of letters. Local Deity of Sesoon, or Hermopolis.

Seb :—The " Father of the Gods," and deity of terrestrial vegetation. In form a man with a goose upon his head.

Set :—Represented by a symbolic animal, with a muzzle and ears like a jackal, the body of an ass, and an upright tail, like the tail of a lion. Was originally a warlike God, and became in later times the symbol of evil and the enemy of Osiris.

Khons :—Hawk-headed, crowned with the sun-disk and horns. Is represented sometimes as a youth with the side-lock, standing on a crocodile.

Horus :—Horus appears variously as Horus, Horus Aroëris, and Horus Harpakhrat (Harpocrates), or Horus the child. Is represented under the first two forms as a man, hawk-headed, wearing the double crown of Egypt ; in the latter as a child with the side-lock. Local Deity of Edfu (Apollinopolis Magna).

Maut :—A woman draped, and crowned with the pschent ; generally with a cap below the pschent representing a vulture. Adored at Thebes.

Neith :—A woman draped, holding sometimes a bow and arrows, crowned with with the crown of Lower Egypt. She presided over war, and the loom. Worshipped at Thebes.

Isis :—A woman crowned with the sun-disk surmounted by a throne, and sometimes enclosed between horns. Adored at Abydus and Philæ. Her soul resided in Sothis, or the Dog-star.

Nut :—A woman curved so as to touch the ground with her fingers. She represents the vault of heaven, and is the mother of the Gods.

Hathor :— Cow-headed, and crowned with the disk and plumes. Deity of Amenti, or the Egyptian Hades. Worshipped at Denderah.

Bast and *Sekhet :*—Bast and Sekhet appear to be two forms of the same Goddess. As Sekhet she is represented as a woman, lion-headed, with the disk and urœus ; as Bast, she is cat-headed, and holds a sistrum. Adored at Bubastis.

APPENDIX III.

The Religious Belief of the Egyptians.

Did the Egyptians believe in one Eternal God, whose attributes were merely symbolised by their numerous deities ; or must the whole structure of their faith be resolved into a solar myth, with its various and inevitable ramifications ? This is the great problem of Egyptology, and it is a problem that has not yet been solved. Egyptologists differ so widely on the subject that it is impossible to reconcile their opinions. As not even the description of a temple is complete without some reference to this important question, and as the question itself underlies every notion we may form of ancient Egypt and ancient Egyptians, I have thought it well to group here a few representative extracts from the works of one or two of the greatest authorities upon the subject.

" The religion of the Egyptians consisted of an extended polytheism represented by a series of local groups. The idea of a single deity self-existing or produced was involved in the conception of some of the principal gods, who are said to have given birth to or produced gods, men, all beings and things. Other deities were considered to be self-produced. The Sun was the older object of worship, and in his various forms, as the rising, midday, and setting Sun, was adored under different names, and was often united, especially at Thebes, to the types of other deities, as Amen and Mentu. The oldest of all the local deities, Ptah, who was worshipped at Memphis, was a demiurgos or creator of heaven, earth, gods and men, and not identified with the Sun. Besides the worship of the solar gods, that of Osiris extensively prevailed, and with it the antagonism of Set, the Egyptian devil, the metempsychosis or transmigration of the soul, the future judgment, the purgatory or Hades, the *Karneter*, the *Aahlu* or Elysium, and final union of the soul to the body after the lapse of several centuries. Besides the deities of Heaven, the light, and the lower world, others personified the elements or presided over the operations of nature, the seasons, and events."—*Guide to the First and Second Egyptian Rooms : Brit. Mus.* S. Birch, 1874.

" This religion, obscured as it is by a complex mythology, has lent itself to many interpretations of a contradictory nature, none of which have been unanimously adopted. But that which is beyond doubt, and which shines forth from the texts for the whole world's acceptance, is the belief in one God. The polytheism of the monuments is but an outward show. The innumerable Gods of the Pantheon are but manifestations of the One Being in his various capacities. That taste for allegory which created the hieroglyphic writing, found vent likewise in the expression of the religious idea ; that idea being, as it were, stifled in the later periods by a too-abundant symbolism."—P. PIERRET, *Dictionnaire d'Arch. Egyptienne,* 1875. Translated from article on " *Réligion.*"

" This God of the Egyptians was unique, perfect, endued with knowledge and intelligence, and so far incomprehensible that one can scarcely say in what respects he is incomprehensible. He is the one who exists by essence ; the one sole life of all substance ; the one single generator in heaven and earth who is not himself engendered ; the father of fathers ; the mother of mothers ; always the same ; immutable in immutable perfection ; existing equally in the past, the present, and the future. He fills the universe in such wise that no earthly image can give the feeblest notion of his immensity. He is felt everywhere ; he is tangible nowhere."—G. MASPERO. Translated from *Histoire Ancienne des Peuples de l'Orient.* Paris, 1876, chap. i., p. 26.

" Unfortunately, the more we study the religion of ancient Egypt, the more our doubts accumulate with regard to the character which must finally be attributed to it. The excavations carried on of late at Denderah and Edfu have opened up to us an extraordinary fertile source of material. These Temples are covered with texts, and present precisely the appearance of two books which authoritatively treat not only of the Gods to which these two Temples are dedicated, but of the religion under its more general aspects. But neither in these Temples, nor in those which have been long known to us, appears the One God of Jamblichus. If Ammon is ' The First of the First ' at Thebes, if Phtah is at Memphis ' The Father of all Beings, without Beginning or End,' so also is every other Egyptian God separately endowed with these attributes of the Divine Being. In other words, we everywhere find Gods who are uncreate and immortal ; but nowhere that unique, invisible Deity, without name and without form, who was supposed to hover above the highest summit of the Egyptian pantheon. The Temple of Denderah, now explored to the end of its most hidden inscriptions, of a certainty furnishes no trace of this Deity. The one result which above all others seems to be educed from the study of this Temple, is that (according to the Egyptians) the Universe was God himself, and that Pantheism formed the foundation of their religion."—A. MARIETTE BEY. Translated from *Itinéraire de la Haute Egypte.* Alexandria, 1872, p. 54.

" The Sun is the most ancient object of Egyptian worship found upon the monuments. His birth each day when he springs from the bosom of the nocturnal heaven is the natural emblem of the eternal generation of the divinity. Hence the celestial space became identified with the divine mother. It was particularly the nocturnal heaven which was represented by this personage. The rays of the sun, as they awakened all nature, seemed to give life to animated beings. Hence that which doubtless was originally a symbol, became the foundation of the religion. It is the Sun himself whom we find habitually invoked as the supreme being. The addition of his Egyptian name, Ra, to the names of certain local divinities, would seem to show that this identification constituted a second epoch in the history of the religions of the Valley of the Nile."—VISCOUNT E. DE ROUGÉ. Translated from *Notice Sommaire des Monuments Egyptiens du Louvre.* Paris, 1873, p. 120.

That the religion, whether based on a solar myth or upon a genuine belief in a spiritual God, became grossly material in its later developments, is apparent to every student of the monuments. M. Maspero has the following remarks on the degeneration of the old faith :—

" In the course of ages, the sense of the religion became obscured. In the texts of Greek and Roman date, that lofty conception of the divinity which had been cherished by the early theologians of Egypt still peeps out here and there. Fragmentary phrases and epithets yet prove that the fundamental principles of the religion are not quite forgotten. For the most part, however, we find that we no longer have to do with the infinite and intangible God of ancient days ; but rather with a God of flesh and blood who lives upon earth, and has so abased himself as to be no more than a human king. It is no longer this God of whom no man knew either the form or the substance :—it is Kneph at Esneh ; Hathor at Denderah ; Horus, king of the divine dynasty, at Edfu. This king has a court, ministers, an army, a fleet. His eldest son, Horhat, Prince of Cush and heir-presumptive to the throne, commands the troops. His first minister Thoth, the inventor of letters, has geography and rhetoric at his fingers' ends ; is Historiographer-Royal ; and is entrusted with the duty of recording the victories of the king and of celebrating them in high-sounding phraseology. When this God makes war upon his neighbour Typhon, he makes no use of the divine weapons of which we should take it for granted that he could dispose at will. He calls out his archers and his chariots ; descends the Nile in his galley, as might the last new Pharaoh ; directs marches and counter-marches ; fights planned battles ; carries cities by storm, and brings all Egypt in submission to his feet. We see here that the Egyptians of Ptolemaic times had substituted for the one God of their ancestors a line of God-Kings, and had embroidered these modern legends with a host of fantastic details."—G. MASPERO. Translated from *Histoire Ancienne des Peuples de l'Orient.* Paris, 1876, chap. i. pp. 50-51.

APPENDIX IV.

EGYPTIAN CHRONOLOGY.

" THE chronology of Egypt has been a disputed point for centuries. The Egyptians had no cycle, and only dated in the regnal years of their monarchs. The principal Greek sources have been the canon of Ptolemy, drawn up in the second century A.D., and the lists of the dynasties extracted from the historical work of Manetho, an Egyptian priest, who lived in the time of Ptolemy Philadelphus, B.C. 285-247. The discrepancies between these lists and the monuments have given rise to many schemes and rectifications of the chronology. The principal chronological points of information obtained from the monuments are the conquest of Egypt by Cambyses, B.C. 527, the commencement of the reign of Psammetichus I, B.C. 665, the reign of Tirhaka, about B.C. 693, and that of Bocchoris, about B.C. 720, the synchronism of the reign of Shishak I with the capture of Jerusalem, about B.C. 970. The principal monuments throwing light on other parts of the chronology are the recorded heliacal risings of Sothis, or the Dog-star, in the reigns of Thothmes III and Rameses II, III, VI, IX, the date of 400 years from the time of Rameses II to the Shepherd kings, the dated sepulchral tablets of the bull Apis at the Serapeum, the lists of kings at Sakkarah, Thebes, and Abydus, the chronological canon of the Turin papyrus, and other incidental notices. But of the anterior dynasties no certain chronological dates are afforded by the monuments, those hitherto proposed not having stood the test of historical or philological criticism." — S. BIRCH, LL.D. : *Guide to the First and Second Egyptian Rooms at the Brit. Museum.* 1874, p. 10.

As some indication of the wide divergence of opinion upon this subject, it is enough to point out that the German Egyptologists alone differ as to the date of Menes or Mena (the first authentic king of the ancient empire), to the following extent :—

						B.C.
Boeckh places Mena in	.	*.	.	5702
Unger	,,	,,	.	.	.	5613
Brugsch	,,	,,	.	.	.	4455
Lauth	,,	,,	.	.	.	4157
Lepsius	,,	,,	.	.	.	3892
Bunsen	,,	,,	.	.	.	3623

Mariette, though recognising the need for extreme caution in the acceptance or rejection of any of these calculations, inclined on the whole to abide by the lists of Manetho ; according to which the thirty-four recorded dynasties would stand as follows :—

ANCIENT EMPIRE.

DYNASTIES.	CAPITALS.				B.C.
I. }	This .	.	.	.	5004
II. }					4751
III. }					4449
IV. }	Memphis	.	.	.	4235
V. }					3951
VI.	Elephantine.	.	.	3703
VII. }	Memphis	.	.	.	3500
VIII. }					
IX. }	Heracleopolis	.	.	3358
X. }					3240

MIDDLE EMPIRE.

XI. }	Thebes	.	.	.	3064
XII. }					,,
XIII. }					2851
XIV.	Xoïs .	.	.	.	2398
XV. }	Shepherd Kings .	.	.	2214
XVI. }					
XVII. }					

NEW EMPIRE.

DYNASTIES.	CAPITALS.				B.C.
XVIII. }	Thebes	.	.	.	1703
XIX. }					1462
XX. }					1288
XXI.	Tanis	.	.	.	1110
XXII.	Bubastis .	.	.	980
XXIII.	Tanis	.	.	.	810
XXIV.	Saïs	.	.	.	721
XXV.	(Ethiopians)	.	.	715
XXVI.	Saïs	.	.	.	665
XXVII.	(Persians)	.	.	527
XXVIII.	Saïs .	.	.	405
XXIX.	Mendes .	.	.	399
XXX.	Sebennytis	.	.	378
XXXI.	(Persians)	.	.	340

LOWER EMPIRE.

XXXII.	Macedonians	.	.	332
XXXIII.	(Greeks) .	.	.	305
XXXIV.	(Romans)	.	.	30

To this chronology may be opposed the brief table of dates compiled by M. Chabas. This table represents what may be called the medium school of Egyptian chronology, and is offered by M. Chabas, "not as an attempt to reconcile systems," but as an aid to the classification of certain broadly indicated epochs.

			B.C.
Mena and the commencement of the Ancient Empire	.	.	4000
Construction of the great Pyramids .	.	.	.	3300
VIth Dynasty	.	.	.	.	.	.	2800
XIIth Dynasty	.	.	.	.	.	.	2400 / 2000
Shepherd Invasion .	.	.	.	.	.	?
Expulsion of Shepherds, and commencement of the New Empire	.	1800
Thothmes III	.	.	.	.	.	.	1700
Seti I and Rameses II	.	.	.	.	.	1500 / 1400
Sheshonk (Shishak), the conqueror of Jerusalem	.	.	.	1000
Saïtic Dynasties	.	.	.	.	.	.	700 / 600
Cambyses and the Persians .	.	.	.	.	.	500
Second Persian conquest	.	.	.	.	.	400
Ptolemies	.	.	.	.	.	.	300 / 200 / 100

APPENDIX V.

CONTEMPORARY CHRONOLOGY OF EGYPT, MESOPOTAMIA, AND BABYLON.

A VERY important addition to our chronological information with regard to the synchronous history of Egypt, Palestine, Syria, Mesopotamia, and Babylonia has been brought to light during this present year (1888) by the great discovery of cunei-form tablets at Tel-el-Amarna in Upper Egypt. These tablets consist for the most part of letters and despatches sent to Amenhotep III and Amenhotep IV by the kings of Babylonia and the princes and governors of Palestine, Syria, and Meso-potamia; some being addressed to Amenhotep IV (Khu-en-Aten) by Burna-buryas, King of Babylonia, who lived about B.C. 1430. This gives us the date of the life and reign of Amenhotep IV, and consequently the approximate date of the founda-tion of the city known to us as Tel-el-Amarna, and of the establishment of the new religion of the Disk-worship; and it is the earliest synchronism yet established between the history of ancient Egypt and that of any of her contemporaries.

From these tablets we also learn that the consort of Amenhotep IV was a Syrian princess, and daughter of Duschratta, King of Naharina (called in the tablets "the land of Mitanni") on the upper Euphrates. For a full and learned descrip-tion of some of the most interesting of these newly-discovered documents, see Dr. Erman's paper, entitled *Der Thontafelfund von Tell Amarna*, read before the Berlin Academy on 3d May 1888.